한국의 토익 수험자 여러분께,

토익 시험은 세계적인 직무 영어능력 평가 시험으로, 지난 40여 년간 비즈니스 현장에서 필요한 영어능력 평가의 기준을 제시해 왔습니다. 토익 시험 및 토익스피킹, 토익라이팅 시험은 세계에서 가장 널리 통용되는 영어능력 검증 시험으로, 160여 개국 14,000여 기관이 토익 성적을 의사결정에 활용하고 있습니다.

YBM은 한국의 토익 시험을 주관하는 ETS 독점 계약사입니다.

ETS는 한국 수험자들의 효과적인 토익 학습을 돕고자 YBM을 통하여 'ETS 토익 공식 교재'를 독점 출간하고 있습니다. 또한 'ETS 토익 공식 교재' 시리즈에 기출문항을 제공해 한국의 다른 교재들에 수록된 기출을 복제하거나 변형한 문항으로 인하여 발생할 수 있는 수험자들의 혼동을 방지하고 있습니다.

복제 및 변형 문항들은 토익 시험의 출제의도를 벗어날 수 있기 때문에 기출문항을 수록한 'ETS 토익 공식 교재'만큼 시험에 잘 대비할 수 없습니다.

'ETS 토익 공식 교재'를 통하여 수험자 여러분의 영어 소통을 위한 노력에 큰 성취가 있기를 바랍니다.

감사합니다.

Dear TOEIC Test Takers in Korea,

The TOEIC program is the global leader in English-language assessment for the workplace. It has set the standard for assessing English-language skills needed in the workplace for more than 40 years. The TOEIC tests are the most widely used English language assessments around the world, with 14,000+ organizations across more than 160 countries trusting TOEIC scores to make decisions.

YBM is the ETS Country Master Distributor for the TOEIC program in Korea and so is the exclusive distributor for TOEIC Korea.

To support effective learning for TOEIC test-takers in Korea, ETS has authorized YBM to publish the only Official TOEIC prep books in Korea. These books contain actual TOEIC items to help prevent confusion among Korean test-takers that might be caused by other prep book publishers' use of reproduced or paraphrased items.

Reproduced or paraphrased items may fail to reflect the intent of actual TOEIC items and so will not prepare test-takers as well as the actual items contained in the ETS TOEIC Official prep books published by YBM.

We hope that these ETS TOEIC Official prep books enable you, as test-takers, to achieve great success in your efforts to communicate effectively in English.

Thank you.

KB187816

입문부터 실전까지 수준별 학습을 통해 최단기 목표점수 달성!

ETS TOEIC® 공식수험서
스마트 학습 지원

구글플레이, 앱스토어에서
ETS 토익기출 수험서 다운로드

구글플레이   앱스토어

ETS 토익 모바일 학습 플랫폼!
ETS® 토익기출 수험서 어플

교재 학습 지원
1. 교재 해설 강의
2. LC 음원 MP3
3. 교재/부록 모의고사 채점 및 분석
4. 단어 암기장

부가 서비스
1. 데일리 학습(토익 기출문제 풀이)
2. 토익 최신 경향 무료 특강
3. 토익 타이머

모의고사 결과 분석
1. 파트별/문항별 정답률
2. 파트별/유형별 취약점 리포트
3. 전체 응시자 점수 분포도

ETS TOEIC 공식카페 ▼

etstoeicbook.co.kr

ETS 토익 학습 전용 온라인 커뮤니티!
ETS TOEIC® Book 공식카페

강사진의 학습 지원 토익 대표강사들의 학습 지원과 멘토링

교재 학습관 운영 교재별 학습게시판을 통해 무료 동영상 강의 등 학습 지원

학습 콘텐츠 제공 토익 학습 콘텐츠와 정기시험 예비특강 업데이트

---

www.ybmbooks.com에서도 무료 MP3를 다운로드 받을 수 있습니다.

ETS TOEIC

토익 단기공략

750⁺

LC **RC**

ETS 토익
단기공략 750+

발행인	허문호
발행처	YBM
편집	허유정
디자인	DOTS, 이현숙
마케팅	정연철, 박천산, 고영노, 김동진, 박찬경, 김윤하
초판발행	2020년 8월 25일
15쇄발행	2024년 8월 1일
신고일자	1964년 3월 28일
신고번호	제 1964-000003호
주소	서울시 종로구 종로 104
전화	(02) 2000-0515 [구입문의] / (02) 2000-0429 [내용문의]
팩스	(02) 2285-1523
홈페이지	www.ybmbooks.com
ISBN	978-89-17-23594-4

ETS® TOEIC® 기출문제 한국 독점출간

토익® 단기공략
750⁺

LC RC

PREFACE

Dear test taker,

The purpose of this book is to help you succeed in using English for communication with colleagues and clients in Korea and around the world. Now more than ever, English is a tool that can yield great professional rewards.

This book provides practical steps that you can use right now in a two-week or four-week program of study for the TOEIC test. Use your TOEIC test score as a respected professional credential and a sign that you are ready to take your career to the next level. Your TOEIC score is recognized globally as evidence of your English-language proficiency.

With **<ETS 토익 단기공략 750+>**, you can make sure you have the best and most thorough preparation for the TOEIC test. This book contains key study points that will familiarize you with the test format and content, and you will be able to practice at your own pace. The test questions are created by the same test specialists who develop the TOEIC test itself, and the book contains questions taken from actual TOEIC tests.

Here are some features of **<ETS 토익 단기공략 750+>**.

- This book contains carefully selected questions taken from actual TOEIC tests.
- All TOEIC Listening and Reading test content is included in one book that is suitable for short-term study in two-week or four-week plans.
- You will hear the same ETS voice actors that you will hear in a real ETS test.
- Key study points will help you to achieve your target score with the least amount of time and effort.
- The enhanced analyses and explanations are based on the latest TOEIC test research.

In preparing for the test with **<ETS 토익 단기공략 750+>**, you can be confident that you have a solid resource at hand and are taking the best approach to maximizing your TOEIC test score. Use **<ETS 토익 단기공략 750+>** to become familiar with the test, including actual test tasks, content, and format. You will be well prepared to show the world what you know by taking the test and receiving your score report.

We hope that you will find this high-quality resource to be of the utmost use, and we wish you all the very best success.

●

출제기관이 만든
점수대별
단기 완성 전략서!

• 기출 문항으로 보강된 단기 완성 시리즈

풍부한 기출 문항뿐만 아니라 토익 출제기관인 ETS가 정기시험과 동일한 유형 및 난이도로 개발한 문제들로 구성된 고품질의 전략서이다.

• 단기 목표 달성에 최적화된 구성

LC와 RC를 한권으로 구성하고, 목표 점수 달성에 필요한 핵심 내용만 수록하여 학습 부담을 최소화 하였다.

• 정기시험과 동일한 성우 음원

토익 정기시험 성우가 실제 시험과 동일한 속도와 발음으로 직접 녹음하였으므로 실전에 완벽하게 대비할 수 있다.

• ETS만이 제시할 수 있는 체계적인 공략법

토익 각 파트에 대한 이해를 높이고 원하는 점수를 달성하기 위한 체계적인 공략법을 제시하고 있다.

• 토익 최신 경향을 반영한 명쾌한 분석과 해설

최신 출제 경향을 완벽하게 분석하고 반영하여 고득점을 달성하게 해줄 해법을 낱낱이 제시하고 있다.

CONTENTS

■ LC

■ RC

TOEIC 소개

- **TOEIC** Test of English for international Communication(국제적 의사소통을 위한 영어 시험)의 약자로, 영어가 모국어가 아닌 사람들이 일상생활 또는 비즈니스 현장에서 꼭 필요한 실용적 영어 구사 능력을 갖추었는가를 평가하는 시험이다.

- **시험 구성**

구성	PART		유형	문항 수	시간	배점
Listening	Part 1		사진 묘사	6	45분	495점
	Part 2		질의 응답	25		
	Part 3		짧은 대화	39		
	Part 4		짧은 담화	30		
Reading	Part 5		단문 빈칸 채우기	30	75분	495점
	Part 6		장문 빈칸 채우기	16		
	Part 7	독해	단일 지문	29		
			이중 지문	10		
			삼중 지문	15		
Total	**7 Parts**			**200문항**	**120분**	**990점**

- **평가 항목**

LC	RC
단문을 듣고 이해하는 능력	읽은 글을 통해 추론해 생각할 수 있는 능력
짧은 대화체 문장을 듣고 이해하는 능력	장문에서 특정한 정보를 찾을 수 있는 능력
비교적 긴 대화체에서 주고받은 내용을 파악할 수 있는 능력	글의 목적, 주제, 의도 등을 파악하는 능력
장문에서 핵심이 되는 정보를 파악할 수 있는 능력	뜻이 유사한 단어들의 정확한 용례를 파악하는 능력
구나 문장에서 화자의 목적이나 함축된 의미를 이해하는 능력	문장 구조를 제대로 파악하는지, 문장에서 필요한 품사, 어구 등을 찾는 능력

※ 성적표에는 전체 수험자의 평균과 해당 수험자가 받은 성적이 백분율로 표기되어 있다.

수험 정보

■ **시험 접수 방법**
한국 토익 위원회 사이트(www.toeic.co.kr)에서 시험일 약 2개월 전부터
온라인으로 접수 가능

■ **시험장 준비물**

신분증	규정 신분증만 가능 (주민등록증, 운전면허증, 기간 만료 전의 여권, 공무원증)
필기구	연필, 지우개 (볼펜이나 사인펜은 사용 금지)

■ **시험 진행 시간**

09:20	입실 (9:50 이후 입실 불가)
09:30 ~ 09:45	답안지 작성에 관한 오리엔테이션
09:45 ~ 09:50	휴식
09:50 ~ 10:05	신분증 확인
10:05 ~ 10:10	문제지 배부 및 파본 확인
10:10 ~ 10:55	듣기 평가 (LISTENING TEST)
10:55 ~ 12:10	읽기 평가 (READING TEST)

■ **TOEIC 성적 확인**
시험일로부터 약 10~11일 후 인터넷과 ARS(060-800-0515)로 성적 확인 가능.
성적표는 우편이나 온라인으로 발급 받을 수 있다. 우편으로 발급 받을 경우 성적 발표 후
대략 일주일이 소요되며, 온라인 발급을 선택하면 유효기간 내에 홈페이지에서 본인이
직접 1회에 한해 무료 출력할 수 있다. TOEIC 성적은 시험일로부터 2년간 유효하다.

■ **토익 점수**
TOEIC 점수는 듣기 영역(LC)과 읽기 영역(RC)을 합계한 점수로 5점 단위로 구성되며
총점은 990점이다. TOEIC 성적은 각 문제 유형의 난이도에 따른 점수 환산표에 의해
결정된다.

LC 출제 경향 분석

PART 1

문제 유형 및
출제 비율
(평균 문항 수)

사람을 주어로 하는 사람 묘사
문제가 가장 많은 비중을 차지하며
사람/사물 혼합 문제, 사물/풍경
묘사 문제가 각각 그 다음을 이룬다.

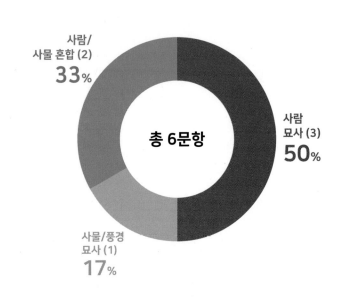

사람/
사물 혼합 (2)
33%

총 6문항

사람
묘사 (3)
50%

사물/풍경
묘사 (1)
17%

PART 2

문제 유형 및
출제 비율
(평균 문항 수)

의문사 의문문이 거의 절반가량을
차지하며 일반 의문문과 평서문이
그 다음을 이룬다. 부가/부정/
선택 의문문은 평균 2문항씩
출제되며 간접 의문문은 간혹
1문제 출제된다.

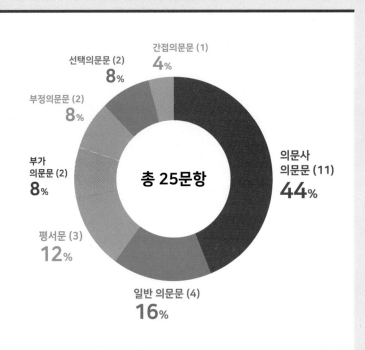

간접의문문 (1)
4%

선택의문문 (2)
8%

부정의문문 (2)
8%

부가
의문문 (2)
8%

총 25문항

의문사
의문문 (11)
44%

평서문 (3)
12%

일반 의문문 (4)
16%

PART 3

문제 유형 및 출제 비율 (평균 문항 수)

세부 사항을 묻는 문제가 가장 많은 비중을 차지하며 주제, 목적, 화자, 장소 문제, 다음에 할 일, 미래 정보 문제가 그 다음을 차지한다. 문제점 및 걱정 거리 문제는 출제 빈도가 다소 낮다. 의도 파악 문제와 시각 정보 문제는 각각 2문항, 3문항 고정 비율로 출제된다.

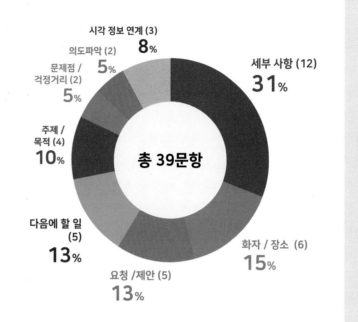

시각 정보 연계 (3) **8**%
의도파악 (2) **5**%
문제점 / 걱정거리 (2) **5**%
주제 / 목적 (4) **10**%
세부 사항 (12) **31**%
총 39문항
화자 / 장소 (6) **15**%
다음에 할 일 (5) **13**%
요청 /제안 (5) **13**%

PART 4

지문 유형 및 출제 비율 (평균 지문 수)

전화 메시지와 공지, 안내, 회의 발췌록이 가장 많이 출제된다. 광고, 방송, 보도가 그 다음을 차지하며 여행, 견학, 관람, 인물, 강연, 설명은 출제 빈도가 다소 낮다.

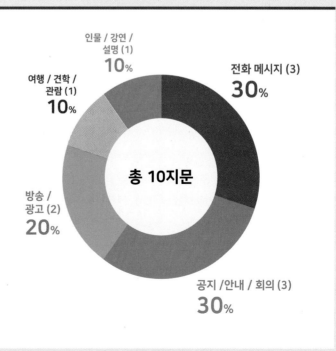

인물 / 강연 / 설명 (1) **10**%
여행 / 견학 / 관람 (1) **10**%
전화 메시지 (3) **30**%
총 10지문
방송 / 광고 (2) **20**%
공지 /안내 / 회의 (3) **30**%

RC 출제 경향 분석

PART 5

문법 문제 유형 및 출제 비율 (평균 문항 수)

전치사와 접속사를 구분하는 문제와 동사 문제, 품사 문제 출제 비중이 가장 높다. 기타 문법에서는 준동사가 1~2문항, 관계사가 매회 거의 1문항씩 출제된다.

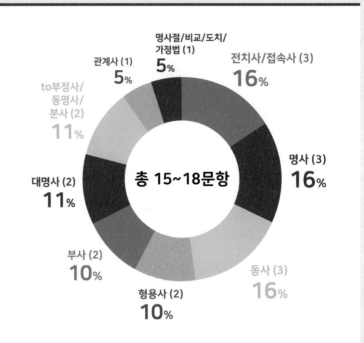

명사절/비교/도치/가정법 (1) 5%
관계사 (1) 5%
전치사/접속사 (3) 16%
to부정사/동명사/분사 (2) 11%
명사 (3) 16%
대명사 (2) 11%
총 15~18문항
동사 (3) 16%
부사 (2) 10%
형용사 (2) 10%

PART 5

어휘 문제 유형 및 출제 비율 (평균 문항 수)

전치사, 명사, 부사 어휘 문제가 가장 많이 출제되며 형용사, 동사 어휘가 그 뒤를 잇는다.

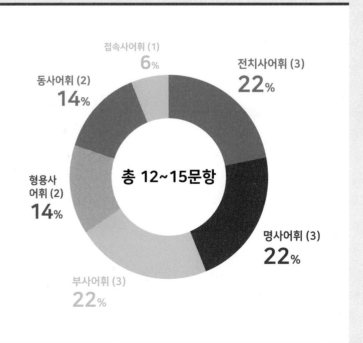

접속사어휘 (1) 6%
동사어휘 (2) 14%
전치사어휘 (3) 22%
형용사어휘 (2) 14%
총 12~15문항
명사어휘 (3) 22%
부사어휘 (3) 22%

PART 6

문제 유형 및
출제 비율
(평균 문항 수)

문법과 어휘 비중이 비슷하게
출제되며 접속부사는 1~2문항
출제된다. 문장 삽입 문제는
4문항 고정 비율로 출제된다.

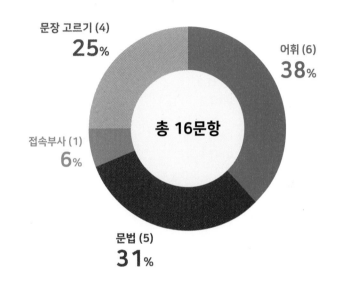

문장 고르기 (4)
25%

어휘 (6)
38%

접속부사 (1)
6%

총 16문항

문법 (5)
31%

PART 7

문제 유형 및
출제 비율
(평균 문항 수)

세부 사항 문제가 가장 높은
비율을 차지하며 추론/암시
문제와 (NOT) mention/true
문제가 그 다음으로 출제율이
높다. 주어진 문장 넣기와 의도
파악 문제는 각각 2문항씩 고정
비율로 출제된다. 이중, 삼중
지문에서는 연계 문제가 8문항
정도 출제된다.

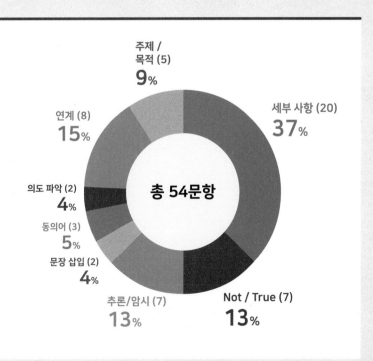

주제 /
목적 (5)
9%

연계 (8)
15%

세부 사항 (20)
37%

의도 파악 (2)
4%

동의어 (3)
5%

문장 삽입 (2)
4%

총 54문항

추론/암시 (7)
13%

Not / True (7)
13%

2주 완성 플랜

초단기에 고득점을 달성하고자 하는 중·고급 수험생을 위한 2주 완성 플랜

	DAY 1	DAY 2	DAY 3	DAY 4	DAY 5
LC	PART 1 UNIT 1&2	PART 1 ETS Actual Test PART 2 UNIT 3	PART 2 UNIT 4&5	PART 2 UNIT 6 ETS Actual Test	PART 3 UNIT 7
RC	PART 5&6 UNIT 1~3	PART 5&6 UNIT 4~6	PART 5&6 UNIT 7~9	PART 5&6 UNIT 10~12	PART 5&6 UNIT 13~15

	DAY 6	DAY 7	DAY 8	DAY 9	DAY 10
LC	PART 3 UNIT 8	PART 3 UNIT 9	PART 3 UNIT 10 ETS Actual Test	PART4 UNIT 11&12	PART 4 UNIT 13&14 ETS Actual Test
RC	PART 5&6 UNIT 16	PART 7 UNIT 17	PART 7 UNIT 18	PART 7 UNIT 19	PART 7 UNIT 20

4주 완성 플랜

짧은 기간 차근차근 고득점을 달성하고자 하는 중·고급 수험생을 위한 4주 완성 플랜

	DAY 1	DAY 2	DAY 3	DAY 4	DAY 5
LC	PART 1 UNIT 1	PART 1 UNIT 2	PART 1 ETS Actual Test	PART 2 UNIT 3	PART 2 UNIT 4
RC	PART 5&6 UNIT 1	PART 5&6 UNIT 2	PART 5&6 UNIT 3	PART 5&6 UNIT 4	PART 5&6 UNIT 5

	DAY 6	DAY 7	DAY 8	DAY 9	DAY 10
LC	PART 2 UNIT 5	PART 2 UNIT 6	PART 2 ETS Actual Test	PART 3 UNIT 7	PART 3 UNIT 8
RC	PART 5&6 UNIT 6	PART 5&6 UNIT 7	PART 5&6 UNIT 8	PART 5&6 UNIT 9	PART 5&6 UNIT 10

	DAY 11	DAY 12	DAY 13	DAY 14	DAY 15
LC	PART 3 UNIT 9	PART 3 UNIT 10	PART 3 ETS Actual Test	PART 4 UNIT 11	PART 4 UNIT 12
RC	PART 5&6 UNIT 11	PART 5&6 UNIT 12	PART 5&6 UNIT 13	PART 5&6 UNIT 14	PART 5&6 UNIT 15

	DAY 16	DAY 17	DAY 18	DAY 19	DAY 20
LC	PART 4 UNIT 13	PART 4 UNIT 14	PART 4 ETS Actual Test	PART 1&2 복습	PART 3&4 복습
RC	PART 5&6 UNIT 16	PART 7 UNIT 17	PART 7 UNIT 18	PART 7 UNIT 19	PART 7 UNIT 20

Part

사진 묘사

주어진 사진을 가장 잘 설명한 보기를 선택하는 유형으로, 사람 및 사물의 동작이나 상태, 배경 등을 묘사하는 문장이 나온다.

■ ETS 예제

문제지

1.

음원

Number 1.
Look at the picture marked number 1 in your test book.

(A) She's mixing a can of paint.
(B) She's painting in a studio.
(C) She's setting paintbrushes on a stool.
(D) She's hanging up a painting.

■ 풀이 전략

1 보기를 듣기 전에 사진을 잘 살핀다.

사진에 등장하는 사람 및 사물의 동작이나 상태, 사물의 위치, 배경 등을 파악하고 표현을 예상한다.

예제 1인 등장 사진

- **여자의 동작 및 자세** painting, drawing, holding, sitting
- **주변 사물** paint, palette, container, paintbrushes
- **배경** studio

2 보기를 들으며 오답을 소거한다.

동작이나 상태를 다르게 묘사하거나, 사진에 등장하지 않는 사물을 언급하거나, 위치를 잘못 묘사한 오답이 자주 등장한다.

(A) She's mixing a can of paint. ☒
　　오답 통에 있는 페인트를 섞고 있는 모습이 아님

(B) She's painting in a studio. ☑
　　정답 작업실에서 그림을 그리고 있는 모습을 적절히 묘사함

(C) She's setting paintbrushes on a stool. ☒
　　오답 등받이가 없는 의자에 붓을 놓고 있는 모습이 아님

(D) She's hanging up a painting. ☒
　　오답 그림을 걸고 있는 모습이 아님

■ 빈출 구문

1 동작이나 상태를 묘사하는 be + -ing

The people are talking on telephones.
사람들이 전화 통화를 하고 있다.

The people are sitting on chairs.
사람들이 의자에 앉아 있다.

2 상태를 묘사하는 be + p.p.와 has / have been + p.p.

Overhead wires are suspended near an unfinished structure.
고가선이 아직 완공되지 않은 건축물 가까이에 늘어져 있다.

Some vehicles have been parked near a construction site.
공사장 옆에 차들이 주차되어 있다.

3 동작의 대상을 묘사하는 be + being + p.p.

Some items are being moved.
물건들이 옮겨지고 있다.

Some materials are being transported on a forklift.
자재들이 지게차로 옮겨지고 있다.

4 위치나 구도를 묘사하는 전치사구와 There is / are

Some people are standing on the bridge.
사람 몇 명이 다리 위에 서 있다.

There is a bridge over the water.
물 위에 다리가 있다.

Unit | 01 인물 등장 사진

■ 1인 등장 사진

한 사람의 주요 동작이나 상태, 동작의 대상 파악

A woman is operating a machine. 여자가 기계를 조작하고 있다.

She is using some office equipment. 여자가 사무실 장비를 사용하고 있다.

She is wearing glasses. 여자가 안경을 쓰고 있다.

[고득점팁] 착용한 상태(wearing)와 착용하는 동작(putting on, trying on)을 구분한다.

■ 2인 이상 등장 사진

사람들의 개별 행동, 공통 행동, 상호 동작 파악

One of the people is using a tool. 사람들 중 한 명이 도구를 사용하고 있다.

Workers are cleaning large window panes. 일꾼들이 큰 창유리를 닦고 있다.

Some cleaning work is being done. 청소 작업이 진행되고 있다.

[고득점팁] 진행 중인 작업이나 업무(construction work, presentation 등)도 주어가 될 수 있다.

■ 사람 · 사물 혼합 사진

눈에 띄는 사람 및 사물의 동작이나 상태 파악

Two people are seated at a table. 두 사람이 탁자에 앉아 있다.

A cabinet door has been left open. 수납장 문이 열린 채로 있다.

A woman is standing in front of a cabinet. 여자가 수납장 앞에 서 있다.

[고득점팁] be sitting과 be seated 모두 앉아 있는 상태를 나타낸다.

1.

(A) He's _____ near a sign.

(B) He's _____ his backpack.

(C) He's _____ a photograph.

(D) He's _____ in the pond.

2.

(A) The women are _____ next to the water.

(B) The women are _____ on their bicycles.

(C) The women are _____ on a bench.

(D) The women are _____ together.

3.

(A) A man is _____ headphones.

(B) A man is _____ a guitar against a couch.

(C) A man is _____ a picture next to a door.

(D) A man is _____ a couch toward a wall.

4.

(A) Cars are _____ on one side of the street.

(B) Lines are _____ on the road.

(C) A man is _____ onto a curb.

(D) A man is _____ into a vehicle.

1.

(A)　　(B)　　(C)　　(D)

2.

(A)　　(B)　　(C)　　(D)

3.

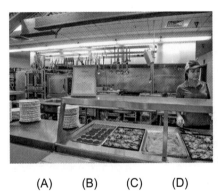

(A)　　(B)　　(C)　　(D)

4.

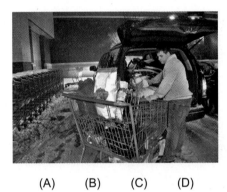

(A)　　(B)　　(C)　　(D)

5.

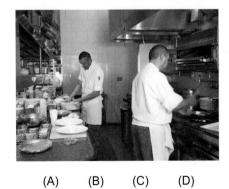

(A)　　(B)　　(C)　　(D)

6.

(A)　　(B)　　(C)　　(D)

7.

(A)   (B)   (C)   (D)

8.

(A)   (B)   (C)   (D)

9.

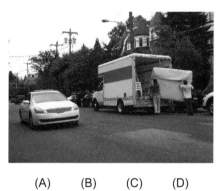

(A)   (B)   (C)   (D)

10.

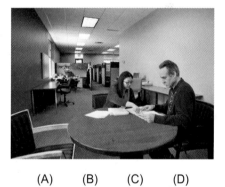

(A)   (B)   (C)   (D)

11.

(A)   (B)   (C)   (D)

12.

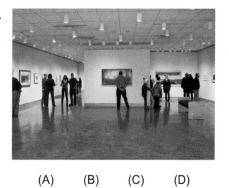

(A)   (B)   (C)   (D)

LC

PART 1

사물 / 풍경 사진

출제 포인트 1 매회 1~2문항 정도 출제되며, 문장이 길고 난이도가 높다.
출제 포인트 2 사물의 상태 및 위치나 풍경의 일부를 묘사하는 문제가 주를 이룬다.
출제 포인트 3 보기에 다양한 주어와 동사 형태가 등장한다.

■ 실내 사물 사진

실내 주요 사물의 상태 및 위치 파악

<u>Some bowls</u> **are displayed** on shelves. 그릇들이 선반 위에 놓여 있다.

<u>Bowls</u> **have been stacked** on shelves. 그릇들이 선반 위에 쌓여 있다.

<u>Merchandise</u> **has been placed** on shelves. 상품이 선반 위에 놓여 있다.

[고득점팁] be being displayed도 진열된 상태를 묘사할 수 있으며, be displayed 및 be on display 와 같은 의미를 나타낸다.

■ 실외 사물 사진

눈에 띄는 사물의 동작 및 상태, 장소 파악

<u>One truck</u> **is transporting** a load of **bricks**. 트럭 한 대가 벽돌을 운반하고 있다.

<u>Vehicles</u> **are parked** in a **construction site**. 차량들이 공사 현장에 주차되어 있다.

<u>A large machine</u> **is digging** the **ground**. 큰 기계가 땅을 파고 있다.

[고득점팁] 사물 / 풍경 사진에서 be being p.p.는 오답 보기로 자주 등장한다. 하지만 사람이 잘 보이지 않아도 관여하는 것이 확실한 동작(예: 중장비 운전 등)은 be being p.p.로 묘사되기도 한다.

■ 풍경 사진

전체적인 풍경 및 눈에 띄는 사물의 구도 파악

<u>Buildings</u> are **overlooking** the **water**. 건물들이 강물을 내려다보고 있다.

There is <u>a bridge</u> over the **river**. 강 위에 다리가 있다.

<u>Trees</u> **have been planted** around the **river**. 나무들이 강 주변에 심어져 있다.

[고득점팁] overlook, face, hang과 같은 동사는 be + -ing 형태로 상태를 나타낼 수 있다.

1.

(A) Bookcases are _____.

(B) A cart is _____ along a hallway.

(C) Packages _____ on the floor.

(D) Boxes _____ on a cart.

2.

(A) Some tents are _____.

(B) The chairs _____ by umbrellas.

(C) Tourists _____ on the beach.

(D) Towels _____ out on the sand.

3.

(A) All of the seats _____.

(B) The railing is _____.

(C) A dining room _____ for a meal.

(D) _____ a large plant _____ two tables.

4.

(A) The fountain _____ water into the air.

(B) People _____ in the pool.

(C) Water _____ down the mountain.

(D) Children _____ from the water fountain.

1.

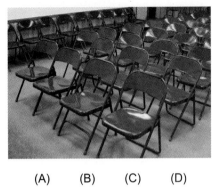

(A)　　(B)　　(C)　　(D)

2.

(A)　　(B)　　(C)　　(D)

3.

(A)　　(B)　　(C)　　(D)

4.

(A)　　(B)　　(C)　　(D)

5.

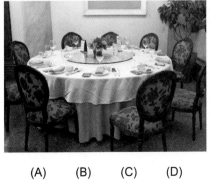

(A)　　(B)　　(C)　　(D)

6.

(A)　　(B)　　(C)　　(D)

7.

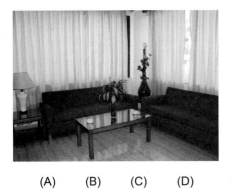

(A)　　　(B)　　　(C)　　　(D)

8.

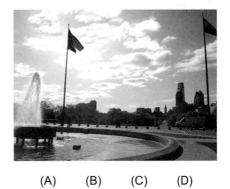

(A)　　　(B)　　　(C)　　　(D)

9.

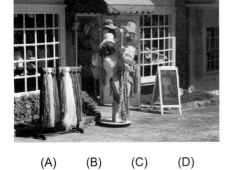

(A)　　　(B)　　　(C)　　　(D)

10.

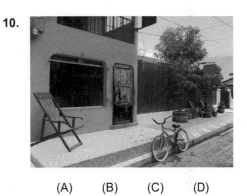

(A)　　　(B)　　　(C)　　　(D)

11.

(A)　　　(B)　　　(C)　　　(D)

12.

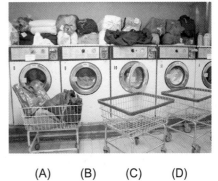

(A)　　　(B)　　　(C)　　　(D)

1.

2.

3.

4.

5.

6.

LC

PART 1

■ 손 동작 묘사

reaching into a drawer 서랍 안으로 손을 뻗고 있다

extending one's arm 팔을 뻗고 있다

loading a cart 카트에 짐을 싣고 있다

unloading some items 물품을 내리고 있다

handing papers 서류를 전달하고 있다

carrying some boxes 상자들을 나르고 있다

folding some clothing 옷을 접고 있다

stapling a document 서류를 철하고 있다

pointing at a screen 스크린을 가리키고 있다

adjusting the glasses 안경을 고쳐 쓰고 있다

hanging a picture on the wall 벽에 사진을 걸고 있다

■ 발 동작 묘사

going up/down some stairs 계단을 올라/내려가고 있다

boarding a train 기차에 승차하고 있다

getting into a boat 보트에 올라타고 있다

stepping down from a bus 버스에서 내리고 있다

strolling on a beach 해변을 거닐고 있다

passing through a doorway 출입문을 통과하고 있다

jogging on a walkway 산책로에서 조깅을 하고 있다

crossing over a stream 개울을 건너고 있다

entering a hallway 현관으로 들어가고 있다

■ 올라타는 동작 vs. 타고 있는 모습

getting on a bicycle 자전거에 올라타고 있다

riding a motorbike 오토바이를 타고 있다

■ 착용하는 동작 vs. 착용 상태

putting[trying] on a jacket 재킷을 입는 중이다 (동작)

removing[taking off] one's hat 모자를 벗고 있다 (동작)

wearing sunglasses 선글라스를 쓰고 있다 (상태)

■ 시선

looking into the refrigerator 냉장고 안을 살펴보고 있다

facing a board 칠판을 향하고 있다

examining a document 서류를 검토하고 있다

reviewing the contents 내용을 살펴보고 있다

inspecting the back of the car
차의 뒷부분을 살피고 있다

studying a drawing 그림을 살펴보고 있다

checking one's phone 자신의 휴대전화를 보고 있다

■ 자세

holding onto a handrail 난간을 잡고 있다

kneeling in the garden 정원에서 무릎을 꿇고 앉아 있다

relaxing in a garden 정원에서 쉬고 있다

resting in a waiting area 대합실에서 쉬고 있다

sitting on a bench 벤치에 앉아 있다

be seated at the table 테이블에 앉아 있다

lying on the grass 잔디 위에 누워 있다

leaning against a wall 벽에 기대어 있다

standing at a counter 카운터에 서 있다

bending over 몸을 구부리고 있다

■ 상태

be lined up at the side of a road
길 측면을 따라 늘어서 있다

be gathered around a table 탁자 주위에 모여 있다

be crowded with pedestrians
보행자들로 가득 차 있다

be filled with people 사람들로 가득 차 있다

be placed on the floor 바닥에 놓여 있다

be cut down 베어져 있다

be covered with leaves 나뭇잎으로 덮여 있다

be on the path 오솔길 위에 있다

■ 사무실

working at a computer 컴퓨터로 작업하고 있다

typing on a keyboard 키보드를 치고 있다

using some office equipment 사무기기를 사용하고 있다

putting paper in a copy machine
복사기에 종이를 넣고 있다

arranging materials on the table
테이블 위 자료를 정리하고 있다

posting a notice on a bulletin board
게시판에 공지를 붙이고 있다

A cord is being plugged in.
코드가 전원에 연결되고 있다.

Some drawers have been left open.
서랍이 몇 개 열려 있다.

Some binders have been stacked on shelves.
바인더들이 선반 위에 쌓여 있다.

Some chairs have been folded up.
의자 몇 개가 접혀 있다.

The books have been arranged in piles.
책들이 수북이 쌓여 있다.

■ 회의실

attending a meeting 회의에 참석하고 있다

greeting each other 서로 인사하고 있다

exchanging business cards 명함을 교환하고 있다

be seated in a circle 둥글게 앉아 있다

facing each other 서로 마주하고 있다

distributing papers 서류를 나눠주고 있다

taking notes 메모하고 있다

writing on a board 칠판에 적고 있다

cleaning[erasing] a whiteboard 화이트보드를 닦고 있다

giving[delivering] a presentation 발표하고 있다

listening to a speaker 발표자의 말을 경청하고 있다

chatting in a conference room
회의실에서 이야기하고 있다

■ 작업실 / 실험실

inspecting some power lines 전선을 점검하고 있다

wiping a counter 작업대를 닦고 있다

unplugging a power cord 전기선을 뽑고 있다

securing a box with tape
테이프로 상자를 단단히 봉하고 있다

operating a machine 기계를 작동하고 있다

packing items into boxes 물품을 상자에 넣고 있다

taking measurements 치수를 재고 있다

pressing a button on a device
장치의 버튼을 누르고 있다

looking into a microscope
현미경을 들여다보고 있다

working with some laboratory equipment
실험 장비를 가지고 일하고 있다

lying on a counter 작업대에 놓여 있다

be spread out on a table 테이블 위에 널려 있다

■ 강의실 / 강당

entering an auditorium 강당에 들어가고 있다

setting up a podium 연단을 설치하고 있다

lining up chairs 의자를 일렬로 배열하고 있다

sitting in rows 여러 줄로 앉아 있다

attending a presentation
프레젠테이션에 참석하고 있다

giving a lecture 강의를 하고 있다

passing around some documents
서류를 나눠주고 있다

addressing an audience 청중에게 연설하고 있다

speaking to a microphone
마이크에 대고 말하고 있다

raising their hands 손을 들고 있다

adjusting a microphone 마이크를 조정하고 있다

Some seats are unoccupied.
좌석 일부가 비어 있다.

■ 실외 작업

be under construction 공사 중이다

be stacked in a pile 무더기로 쌓여 있다

wearing safety helmets 안전모를 쓰고 있다

fastening their helmets 헬멧을 조이고 있다

erecting[setting up] scaffolding 비계를 세우고 있다

drilling a hole 드릴로 구멍을 내고 있다

hammering a nail 못을 박고 있다

standing on a ladder 사다리에 올라 서 있다

pouring cement into a container
시멘트를 용기에 붓고 있다

repairing[fixing] the roof of the house
집의 지붕을 수리하고 있다

replacing some tiles 타일을 교체하고 있다

pushing a wheelbarrow 수레를 밀고 있다

working on the power lines 전선 작업을 하고 있다

adjusting a wire 전선을 조정하고 있다

paving a walkway 보도를 포장하고 있다

painting lines on a road 도로에 선을 그리고 있다

trimming some trees 나무를 다듬고 있다

mowing the lawn 기계로 잔디를 깎고 있다

watering some plants 식물에 물을 주고 있다

using[working with] a shovel 삽으로 작업하고 있다

A ladder is propped against the building.
사다리가 건물에 기대어져 있다.

The signs are being painted.
표지판이 칠해지고 있다.

A construction work is being carried out.
공사 작업이 진행되고 있다.

Fences are being constructed around a building. 건물 둘레에 울타리가 세워지고 있다.

There is heavy machinery in a construction site. 공사장에 중장비가 있다.

■ 교통 / 차량 관련 작업

be stuck in traffic 차가 밀려 갇히다

be stopped at an intersection 교차로에 서 있다

waiting at a traffic light 신호가 바뀌기를 기다리고 있다

driving down the road 도로에서 운전하고 있다

driving across the bridge 다리를 건너고 있다

being towed 견인되고 있다

crossing the road[street] 길을 건너고 있다

traveling in opposite directions
반대 방향으로 이동하고 있다

backing a car into a garage
차고에 차를 후진해서 넣고 있다

crossing at a crosswalk 횡단보도를 건너고 있다

directing traffic 교통정리를 하고 있다

disembarking from a bus 버스에서 내리고 있다

storing luggage above one's seats
좌석 위에 짐을 보관하고 있다

approaching the platform 승강장으로 들어오고 있다

departing from a station 역에서 출발하고 있다

working on a vehicle 차를 수리하고 있다

transporting a load of bricks 벽돌을 한 짐 운반하고 있다

be parked side by side 나란히 주차되어 있다

A bicycle is chained to a pole.
자전거가 기둥에 체인으로 묶여 있다.

There is a railing beside the railroad tracks.
철로 옆에 난간이 있다.

The vehicles are all traveling in the same direction. 차량들이 모두 같은 방향으로 가고 있다.

Traffic lanes are separated by fences.
차선이 펜스로 분리되어 있다.

The truck is parked next to containers.
트럭이 컨테이너 옆에 주차되어 있다.

The vehicle is pulling into a garage.
차가 차고 안으로 들어오고 있다.

■ 상점

stocking shelves 선반에 물건을 채우고 있다

hanging a jacket on a rack 옷걸이에 재킷을 걸고 있다

shopping in an outdoor market
노천 시장에서 장을 보고 있다

examining goods on display 진열된 상품을 살펴보고 있다

browsing in a store 가게 안을 둘러보고 있다

reaching for some merchandise
상품을 집으려고 손을 뻗고 있다

selecting some groceries 식료품을 고르고 있다

showing customers an item
손님들에게 물건을 보여주고 있다

wrapping a product 상품을 포장하고 있다

waiting in line 줄을 서서 기다리고 있다

be stocked with supplies 물품으로 차 있다

be lined up in a display case 진열장 안에 줄지어 놓여 있다

be piled near the entrance 입구 근처에 쌓여 있다

■ 여가 / 취미

walking toward a park 공원을 향해 걷고 있다

rowing a boat 노를 젓고 있다

sailing on the water 항해하고 있다

holding an oar 노를 잡고 있다

running up a ramp 경사로를 뛰어 올라가고 있다

stepping onto a stage 무대에 오르고 있다

playing musical instruments 악기를 연주하고 있다

performing outdoors 야외에서 공연하고 있다

looking at some artwork 미술품을 감상하고 있다

fishing from a dock 부두에서 낚시를 하고 있다

arranging flowers in a vase
꽃병에 꽃꽂이를 하고 있다

drawing on a large canvas
큰 캔버스에 그림을 그리고 있다

taking a photograph 사진을 찍고 있다

be gathered near a fountain 분수대 주위에 모여 있다

■ 식당

having a meal 식사하고 있다

eating[dining] by the water 물가에서 식사를 하고 있다

drinking from a cup 컵에 있는 물을 마시고 있다

reading[studying] the menu 메뉴를 보고 있다

pointing at a menu 메뉴를 손가락으로 가리키고 있다

taking an order 주문을 받고 있다

pouring something into a bowl
무언가를 그릇에 붓고 있다

filling a cup 컵을 채우고 있다

wiping[cleaning] the table 식탁을 닦고 있다

holding a serving tray 쟁반을 들고 있다

be set[prepared] for a meal 식사 준비가 되어있다

■ 사물 / 배경

hanging from the ceiling 천장에 매달려 있다

be hung next to the door 문 옆에 걸려 있다

be decorated with plants 식물로 장식되어 있다

be pulled down 내려져 있다 / 닫혀 있다

be laid out 깔려 있다

be reflected in the water 물에 비치고 있다

be shaded by 그늘이 드리워졌다

casting shadows 그림자를 드리우다

be planted along a path 길을 따라 심어져 있다

be bordered by a fence 가장자리에 담장이 쳐져 있다

overlooking the water 강을 내려다 보고 있다

line the street 거리를 따라 늘어서 있다

LC

질의 응답

Part 2

질문 혹은 서술문과 3개의 보기를 들은 후 가장 적절한 응답을 선택하는 유형으로, 다양한 종류의 의문문과 평서문이 출제된다.

■ ETS 예제

📖 문제지

7. Mark your answer on your answer sheet.

🔊 음원

Number 7.
M Why are you traveling to Denver?
W (A) Only for a few days.
　　(B) To spend time with my relatives.
　　(C) I'm planning to drive there.

■ 풀이 전략

1 질문을 듣고 가능한 답변을 예상한다.
　　의문사 의문문인지 비의문사 의문문인지 재빨리 파악하고 각 질문의 키워드에 집중한다. 질문을 듣고 가능한 답변을 예상하며 보기를 듣는다.

　　예제 **의문사 Why로 시작하는 의문문**
　　· 이유　Because
　　· 목적　To부정사
　　· 기타 가능 응답　Because가 생략/함축된 응답

2 보기를 들으며 오답을 소거한다.
　　정답에 확신이 없을 경우 확실한 오답을 소거한 후 남은 보기를 선택하는 것도 한 방법이다.

　　(A) Only for a few days. ☒
　　　　오답 기간을 묻는 How long 의문문에 적합한 응답
　　(B) To spend time with my relatives. ☑
　　　　정답 덴버에 가는 목적
　　(C) I'm planning to drive there. ☒
　　　　오답 방법을 묻는 How 의문문에 적합한 응답

■ 다양한 응답 방식

질문에 직접적으로 응답하지 않고 우회적으로 답하거나, 답할 수 없음을 나타내는 등 다양한 응답이 정답으로 출제된다. 아래 예시를 보고 응답 패턴을 익혀 두자.

질문	What time does the workshop begin? 워크숍이 몇 시에 시작하죠?
직접 응답	At two o'clock. 2시에요. After the lunch break. 점심 시간 후에요. As soon as the trainer arrives. 교육 강사가 도착하면 바로요.
간접 응답	You should ask Sam. 샘에게 물어보세요. Oh, I thought you were not coming. 아, 안 오시는 줄 알았는데요. Didn't your manager tell you? 매니저가 말해주지 않았나요?

■ 빈출 오답 유형

1 **유사 발음, 반복 어휘, 파생어 활용**

Who's scheduled to clean the break room?

누가 휴게실을 청소하기로 되어있죠?

오답 I could use a break. 좀 쉬었다가 하면 좋겠어요.
정답 Sarah is. 사라요.

---

2 **연상 가능한 어휘 활용**

Have you had your laptop fixed yet?

노트북 수리 받았나요?

오답 Yes, my new computer. 네, 제 새 컴퓨터요.
정답 I'll get a new one. 새로 살 거예요.

---

3 **의문사 의문문에 Yes / No로 답변**

Why did you cancel tomorrow's meeting?

왜 내일 회의를 취소하셨나요?

오답 No, it didn't last long.
아니요, 오래 걸리진 않았어요.
정답 I have an appointment with my client.
고객과 약속이 있어요.

---

4 **다른 의문사에 적합한 답변**

Where will the orientation be held this year?

올해에는 오리엔테이션이 어디서 열리죠?

오답 On September third.
9월 3일이요. (When이면 가능)
정답 In conference room A. A 회의실이요.

Who / When / Where 의문문

① Who 의문문

> 출제 포인트 1 특정 행위를 하는 사람이나 업무 담당자를 묻는 문제가 출제된다.
> 출제 포인트 2 사람 이름, 직위, 직업과 같은 직접적인 대답이 주를 이루지만, 다양한 간접 응답 표현도 등장한다.

■ 빈출 질문 & 응답 패턴

사람 이름	Q	Who will replace Mr. Fernandez when he retires?	페르난데즈 씨가 퇴직하면 누가 그 자리를 대신하나요?
	정답	I heard that **Maria Ortega** will.	마리아 오테가 씨가 대신할 거라고 들었어요.
	오답	No, I'm not tired. → 유사 발음 [retire / tired]	아니요, 전 피곤하지 않아요.

직위/ 직업	Q	Who is the woman in the black suit?	검은색 정장을 입은 여자는 누구인가요?
	정답	She is the new **marketing manager**.	그녀는 새로운 마케팅 매니저입니다.
	오답	Everyone has to be formally dressed. → 연상 작용 [suit / formally dressed]	모두 정장을 입어야 해요.

부정 대명사	Q	Who attended the awards ceremony?	누가 시상식에 참석했죠?
	정답	**No one** in my office.	제 사무실에서는 아무도 안 했어요.
	오답	Attendance is mandatory. → 파생어 [attend / attendance]	의무적으로 참석해야 해요.

여러 사람	Q	Who conducts the quality control test on the brand-new products?	누가 신제품 품질 검사를 하죠?
	정답	**Several people** do.	여러 명이 합니다.
	오답	The testing begins next week.	테스트는 다음 주에 시작해요.

간접 응답	Q	Who do you want to recommend for the job?	그 일에 누구를 추천하고 싶으세요?
	정답	Well, **why don't you ask your supervisor?**	글쎄요, 당신의 상관에게 물어보는 게 어때요?
	오답	The job is still available. → 단어 반복 [job]	그 자리는 여전히 비어 있어요.

ETS 유형 연습 ....

750_P2_01

음원을 듣고 적절한 응답을 고르세요.

정답과 해설 p.011

1 (A)   (B)   (C)   4 (A)   (B)   (C)
2 (A)   (B)   (C)   5 (A)   (B)   (C)
3 (A)   (B)   (C)   6 (A)   (B)   (C)

② When 의문문

■ 빈출 질문 & 응답 패턴

구체적 시점	Q	When is the financial report due?	재무 보고서 제출 기한이 언제죠?
	정답	Not until **next Friday**.	다음 주 금요일이요.
	오답	I'll do it.	제가 그걸 할게요.
	Q	When are we interviewing the next job candidate?	다음 입사 지원자는 언제 면접할 건가요?
	정답	In about **fifteen minutes**.	15분 정도 후에요.
	오답	As part of the hiring process.	채용 과정의 일환으로요.
		→ 연상 작용 [interviewing/hiring process]	

모호한 시점	Q	When can I expect your final decision?	최종 결정이 언제쯤 내려진다고 생각하면 될까요?
	정답	**After** I speak to regional headquarters.	제가 지역 본부에 이야기한 다음에요.
	오답	An increased project budget.	인상된 프로젝트 예산이에요.
	Q	When will the concert start?	음악회는 언제 시작하나요?
	정답	**As soon as** everyone is seated.	사람들이 모두 착석하는 대로요.
	오답	It was first performed ten years ago.	10년 전에 처음 연주되었어요.
		→ 연상 작용 [concert/performed]	

서로 다른 시점	Q	When will the next issue of the magazine be published?	그 잡지의 다음 호는 언제 나오나요?
	정답	Unfortunately, **it's been discontinued**.	유감스럽게도, 그건 폐간되었어요.
	오답	Just on the Internet.	인터넷에서만요.

ETS 유형 연습 ....

750_P2_02 🎧

음원을 듣고 적절한 응답을 고르세요.

정답과 해설 p.012

1	(A)	(B)	(C)		4	(A)	(B)	(C)
2	(A)	(B)	(C)		5	(A)	(B)	(C)
3	(A)	(B)	(C)		6	(A)	(B)	(C)

③ Where 의문문

■ 빈출 질문 & 응답 패턴

장소/위치	Q	Where are you holding the staff meeting?	직원 회의를 어디에서 하나요?
	정답	In the conference room.	회의실에서요.
	오답	Because our deadline's changed.	마감일이 바뀌었기 때문이에요.
	Q	Where did you put your expense report?	당신의 비용 보고서를 어디에 두셨죠?
	정답	I left it in your mailbox.	당신의 우편함에 넣어놨어요.
	오답	It wasn't expensive at all.	그건 전혀 비싸지 않았어요.
		→ 파생어 [expense / expensive]	
담당자	Q	Where should I submit the application form?	지원서를 어디에 제출해야 하죠?
	정답	The personnel manager takes care of it.	인사부장이 그걸 담당해요.
	오답	You should fill it out.	그것을 작성하셔야 합니다.
		→ 연상 작용 [application form / fill out]	
출처	Q	Where can I get a copy of the workshop schedule?	어디에서 워크숍 일정표를 얻을 수 있죠?
	정답	On our Web site.	저희 웹사이트에서요.
	오답	We're right on schedule. → 단어 반복 [schedule]	예정대로 하고 있어요.
간접응답	Q	Where will the first interview take place?	1차 인터뷰를 어디에서 하죠?
	정답	It hasn't been decided.	결정되지 않았습니다.
	오답	Some résumés.	이력서 몇 장요.
	Q	Where can I get a bus to Kingston?	킹스턴행 버스를 어디에서 탈 수 있나요?
	정답	I'll find a transit map.	제가 교통 지도를 찾아볼게요.
	오답	A reduced fare. → 연상 작용 [bus / fare]	할인된 요금이에요.

750_P2_03 🎧

ETS 유형 연습

음원을 듣고 적절한 응답을 고르세요.

정답과 해설 p.013

1 (A)   (B)   (C)   4 (A)   (B)   (C)

2 (A)   (B)   (C)   5 (A)   (B)   (C)

3 (A)   (B)   (C)   6 (A)   (B)   (C)

1. Mark your answer.

(A)   (B)   (C)

_____ sitting next to you at the meeting?

(A) Yes, nice to see you again.

(B) The next _____.

(C) He's the _____.

2. Mark your answer.

(A)   (B)   (C)

_____ your speech?

(A) _____ quickly.

(B) The speakers _____.

(C) At the _____.

3. Mark your answer.

(A)   (B)   (C)

_____ I stay in Shanghai?

(A) I strongly _____.

(B) One hundred _____.

(C) I know a _____.

4. Mark your answer.

(A)   (B)   (C)

_____ while you're away?

(A) This way, please.

(B) _____ the end of the month.

(C) I _____ to do it.

5. Mark your answer.

(A)   (B)   (C)

_____ does the promotional _____?

(A) For _____.

(B) It _____.

(C) She's the _____.

LC

PART 2

1.	Mark your answer.	(A)	(B)	(C)
2.	Mark your answer.	(A)	(B)	(C)
3.	Mark your answer.	(A)	(B)	(C)
4.	Mark your answer.	(A)	(B)	(C)
5.	Mark your answer.	(A)	(B)	(C)
6.	Mark your answer.	(A)	(B)	(C)
7.	Mark your answer.	(A)	(B)	(C)
8.	Mark your answer.	(A)	(B)	(C)
9.	Mark your answer.	(A)	(B)	(C)
10.	Mark your answer.	(A)	(B)	(C)
11.	Mark your answer.	(A)	(B)	(C)
12.	Mark your answer.	(A)	(B)	(C)
13.	Mark your answer.	(A)	(B)	(C)

14. Mark your answer.　　　(A)　　(B)　　(C)

15. Mark your answer.　　　(A)　　(B)　　(C)

16. Mark your answer.　　　(A)　　(B)　　(C)

17. Mark your answer.　　　(A)　　(B)　　(C)

18. Mark your answer.　　　(A)　　(B)　　(C)

19. Mark your answer.　　　(A)　　(B)　　(C)

20. Mark your answer.　　　(A)　　(B)　　(C)

21. Mark your answer.　　　(A)　　(B)　　(C)

22. Mark your answer.　　　(A)　　(B)　　(C)

23. Mark your answer.　　　(A)　　(B)　　(C)

24. Mark your answer.　　　(A)　　(B)　　(C)

25. Mark your answer.　　　(A)　　(B)　　(C)

LC

PART 2

What·Which / Why / How 의문문

① What·Which 의문문

> · 출제 포인트 1 What 의문문은 시간/종류/의견 등 다양한 내용을 묻기 때문에 What 뒤에 오는 부분을 집중해서 들어야 한다.
> · 출제 포인트 2 Which 다음에 오는 명사가 질문의 핵심 포인트가 된다. 이 명사의 하위어나 대명사 one이 들어간 보기가 정답일 가능성이 높다.

■ 빈출 질문 & 응답 패턴

시간	**Q** What time does the presentation begin?	발표가 몇 시에 시작하죠?
	정답 It starts **at 10 o'clock**.	10시에 시작합니다.
	오답 I was present there.	저는 거기 참석했어요.
종류	**Q** **What** would you like for dessert?	디저트로 무엇을 드시겠어요?
	정답 I'll have **ice cream**.	아이스크림으로 할게요.
	오답 Yes, it will arrive soon. → Yes/No 불가 [의문사 의문문]	네, 곧 도착할 겁니다.
의견	**Q** **What do you think** of the new Web site?	새 웹사이트에 대해 어떻게 생각하세요?
	정답 I think **it's well-designed**.	잘 설계된 것 같아요.
	오답 It will be provided on-site.	그건 현장에서 제공될 겁니다.
한 가지 선택	**Q** **Which paint color** did you choose for the kitchen?	주방에 칠할 페인트를 무슨 색으로 선택했나요?
	정답 A bright **shade of pink**.	밝은 분홍색이요.
	오답 On the stove. → 연상 작용 [kitchen/stove]	가스레인지 위에요.
상관 없음	**Q** **Which** restaurant should we eat dinner at?	어느 식당에서 저녁 식사할까요?
	정답 **Either one** is fine.	어느 곳이든 괜찮습니다.
	오답 Dinner is at seven P.M. → 단어 반복 [dinner]	저녁 식사는 오후 7시예요.
아무것도 선택 안 함	**Q** **Which of** these ties will look better with this suit?	이 넥타이들 중 어떤 게 이 정장과 더 잘 어울리나요?
	정답 Actually, **neither**.	사실 다 안 어울려요.
	오답 You should wear them.	그것들을 착용해야 해요.

ETS 유형 연습

750_P2_06 🎧

음원을 듣고 적절한 응답을 고르세요.

정답과 해설 p.019

1 (A) (B) (C)   4 (A) (B) (C)

2 (A) (B) (C)   5 (A) (B) (C)

3 (A) (B) (C)   6 (A) (B) (C)

② Why 의문문

> **출제 포인트 1** 이유/원인/목적을 묻는 Why 의문문 문제에서는 Because나 To부정사로 시작하는 응답이 정답일 확률이 높다. 하지만 이런 표현이 생략된 정답도 자주 나오므로, 질문의 요지가 무엇인지 반드시 파악해야 한다.
>
> **출제 포인트 2** 다른 의문사와 달리 부정 의문문(Why isn't/Why hasn't 등) 형태로도 종종 출제된다.

■ 빈출 질문 & 응답 패턴

이유	**Q** **Why** did you stop using that insurance company?	왜 그 보험회사와 계약을 중단하셨죠?
	정답 **Because** the rates were too high.	왜냐하면 보험료가 너무 비쌌기 때문이에요.
	오답 Yes, I'm sure. → Yes/No 불가 [의문사 의문문]	네, 확신합니다.

목적	**Q** **Why** did you decide to advertise on social media?	왜 소셜 미디어에 광고하기로 결정하신 건가요?
	정답 **To attract** more customers.	더 많은 고객을 유치하기 위해서요.
	오답 At least one post per day.	적어도 하루에 게시물 한 개요.
	→ 연상 작용 [social media/post]	

부정 의문문	**Q** **Why** hasn't the launch date been finalized?	출시 날짜가 왜 확정되지 않았죠?
	정답 **The product is still being tested.**	제품이 여전히 테스트 중입니다.
	오답 They haven't visited before.	그들은 전에 방문한 적이 없어요.

제안	**Q** **Why don't you** join Mary and me for a walk?	나와 메리랑 같이 산책하러 갈래요?
	정답 **Some fresh air would be lovely.**	신선한 공기를 좀 마시는 게 좋겠네요.
	오답 It's a great organization.	그곳은 훌륭한 조직이에요.

간접 응답	**Q** **Why** did they postpone the departmental meeting?	그들이 왜 부서 회의를 연기했죠?
	정답 **I haven't heard anything** about that.	그것에 대해 아무것도 들은 게 없어요.
	오답 There is a post office on the corner.	모퉁이에 우체국이 있어요.
	→ 유사 발음 [postpone/post]	

750_P2_07 🎧

ETS 유형 연습

음원을 듣고 적절한 응답을 고르세요.

정답과 해설 p.020

1	(A)	(B)	(C)		**4**	(A)	(B)	(C)
2	(A)	(B)	(C)		**5**	(A)	(B)	(C)
3	(A)	(B)	(C)		**6**	(A)	(B)	(C)

③ How 의문문

■ 빈출 질문 & 응답 패턴

빈도		
Q	How often do employees at your company have performance reviews?	당신 회사 직원들은 얼마나 자주 업무 평가를 받나요?
정답	We have them **twice a year**.	일 년에 두 번 받아요.
오답	My manager's Ms. Aweel.	제 부서장님은 아웰 씨예요.
	→ 연상 작용 [performance reviews / manager]	

수량		
Q	How many people are coming to the reception?	그 환영회에 사람들이 얼마나 올까요?
정답	There could be **several hundred**.	수백 명은 될 겁니다.
오답	I don't have time tonight. → 단어 반복 [tonight]	저는 오늘 밤에 시간이 없어요.

기간		
Q	How long did you work for your previous employer?	이전 회사에서 얼마나 근무했나요?
정답	**For seven years**.	7년간요.
오답	Yes, I liked my employer.	네, 저는 고용주가 마음에 들었습니다.
	→ Yes / No 불가 [의문사 의문문]	

방법		
Q	How will the new equipment be delivered to the factory?	새 장비는 공장에 어떻게 배달될 건가요?
정답	I think it'll come **by truck**.	아마 트럭으로 올 거예요.
오답	On this delivery form. → 파생어 [deliver / delivery]	이 인수증에요.

의견		
Q	How do you like your new computer?	새 컴퓨터 어때요?
정답	**It's much faster than the old one.**	이전 것보다 훨씬 빨라요.
오답	It's a long way to travel.	이동하기 먼 거리예요.

ETS 유형 연습

750_P2_08

음원을 듣고 적절한 응답을 고르세요.

정답과 해설 p.021

1	(A)	(B)	(C)	**4**	(A)	(B)	(C)
2	(A)	(B)	(C)	**5**	(A)	(B)	(C)
3	(A)	(B)	(C)	**6**	(A)	(B)	(C)

1 Mark your answer.

(A) (B) (C)

_____ about our progress?

(A) She _____ on Wednesday.

(B) Mostly _____.

(C) Yes, she did.

2 Mark your answer.

(A) (B) (C)

_____ to the filing cabinet?

(A) You could _____.

(B) _____ the red tag.

(C) _____ later.

3 Mark your answer.

(A) (B) (C)

Why is a new _____?

(A) _____.

(B) Because it'll _____.

(C) At the _____.

4 Mark your answer.

(A) (B) (C)

_____ can I make _____
with Doctor Feinstein?

(A) She's _____.

(B) Just _____.

(C) It _____.

5 Mark your answer.

(A) (B) (C)

_____ at the workshop this morning?

(A) I'll _____.

(B) It's expected to _____.

(C) _____ for about 25.

LC

PART 2

1. Mark your answer. (A) (B) (C)

2. Mark your answer. (A) (B) (C)

3. Mark your answer. (A) (B) (C)

4. Mark your answer. (A) (B) (C)

5. Mark your answer. (A) (B) (C)

6. Mark your answer. (A) (B) (C)

7. Mark your answer. (A) (B) (C)

8. Mark your answer. (A) (B) (C)

9. Mark your answer. (A) (B) (C)

10. Mark your answer. (A) (B) (C)

11. Mark your answer. (A) (B) (C)

12. Mark your answer. (A) (B) (C)

13. Mark your answer. (A) (B) (C)

14. Mark your answer.   (A)   (B)   (C)

15. Mark your answer.   (A)   (B)   (C)

16. Mark your answer.   (A)   (B)   (C)

17. Mark your answer.   (A)   (B)   (C)

18. Mark your answer.   (A)   (B)   (C)

19. Mark your answer.   (A)   (B)   (C)

20. Mark your answer.   (A)   (B)   (C)

21. Mark your answer.   (A)   (B)   (C)

22. Mark your answer.   (A)   (B)   (C)

23. Mark your answer.   (A)   (B)   (C)

24. Mark your answer.   (A)   (B)   (C)

25. Mark your answer.   (A)   (B)   (C)

LC

PART 2

일반 / 부정 / 부가 의문문

① 일반 의문문

> **출제 포인트 1** Be/Do/Have/조동사로 시작하는 일반 의문문은 사실, 계획, 경험 등을 확인하는 용도로 쓰인다. 따라서 반드시 질문 전체의 요지를 파악해야 한다.
>
> **출제 포인트 2** Yes/No로 응답이 가능하며, Sure/Sorry와 같은 대체 표현이 쓰일 수도 있다. 보기에 Yes와 No가 둘 다 등장할 수 있으므로 뒤따르는 내용을 반드시 들어야 하고, Yes/No가 함축된 응답도 이해할 수 있어야 한다.

■ 빈출 질문 & 응답 패턴

Be동사 (사실 확인)	Q	**Is** this the newest type of battery?	이것이 최신형 배터리인가요?
	정답	I think **it is.**	그런 것 같군요.
	오답	No, I'm not. → 대명사 오류 [Is this/I'm]	아니요, 전 아닙니다.
Do동사 (행위)	Q	**Did** Mark call someone to fix the refrigerator?	마크가 냉장고 수리를 위해 누군가에게 전화를 걸었나요?
	정답	**Yes,** a repair person will be here soon.	네, 수리 기사가 곧 여기 올 거예요.
	오답	To maintain accurate records.	정확한 기록을 유지하려고요.
간접 의문문	Q	**Do you know** where I can check the schedule?	일정표를 어디서 확인할 수 있는지 아세요?
	정답	**Yes,** it's over there on the wall.	네, 저쪽 벽에 붙어 있어요.
	오답	Can I have the check please? → 다의어 [check]	계산서 좀 주시겠어요?
조동사 Will (계획)	Q	**Will** you be attending the trade fair next Monday?	다음 주 월요일에 무역 박람회에 참가하실 건가요?
	정답	**I'm still thinking** about it.	여전히 생각 중이에요.
	오답	I went to Hawaii.	저는 하와이에 갔어요.
Have 동사 (경험, 완료)	Q	**Have** they set up the equipment yet?	그들이 장비를 설치했죠?
	정답	**No,** they'll do it tomorrow.	아니요, 그들은 내일 할 겁니다.
	오답	You can sit over there. → 유사 발음 [set/sit]	저쪽에 앉으셔도 됩니다.

ETS 유형 연습

750_P2_11 🎧

음원을 듣고 적절한 응답을 고르세요.

정답과 해설 p. 027

1	(A)	(B)	(C)	**4**	(A)	(B)	(C)
2	(A)	(B)	(C)	**5**	(A)	(B)	(C)
3	(A)	(B)	(C)	**6**	(A)	(B)	(C)

② 부정 의문문

■ **빈출 질문 & 응답 패턴**

Be동사 부정	Q	**Isn't** the special exhibit at the museum closing soon?	박물관 내 특별 전시전은 곧 끝나지 않나요?
	정답	**Yes**, it's only open for two more weeks.	네, 2주간만 더 공개됩니다.
	오답	It's pretty close to here. → 다의어 [closing / close]	거긴 이곳과 매우 가까워요.
Do동사 부정	Q	**Don't** we have a conference call at ten?	10시에 전화 회의가 있지 않나요?
	정답	**It's been canceled.**	취소되었어요.
	오답	No, only four.	아니요, 네 명뿐이에요.
Have 동사 부정	Q	**Haven't** you filled the secretarial position yet?	이미 비서직 인원을 충원하지 않았나요?
	정답	**We finally hired someone** yesterday.	마침내 어제 사람을 채용했어요.
	오답	I've been a secretary for nine years. → 파생어 [secretarial / secretary]	저는 9년간 비서를 하고 있어요.
조동사 부정	Q	**Shouldn't** we order more paper?	종이를 더 주문해야 하지 않을까요?
	정답	**No**, we have enough for now.	아니요, 지금으로선 충분히 있어요.
	오답	It's written in pencil. → 연상 작용 [paper / pencil]	그건 연필로 쓰였어요.
의문사 부정	Q	**Why didn't** John get the promotion?	존이 왜 승진을 하지 못했죠?
	정답	**He just wasn't qualified.**	그는 자격이 안 됐어요.
	오답	About two weeks ago.	대략 2주 전에요

750_P2_12

ETS 유형 연습

음원을 듣고 적절한 응답을 고르세요.

정답과 해설 p.028

1	(A)	(B)	(C)		4	(A)	(B)	(C)
2	(A)	(B)	(C)		5	(A)	(B)	(C)
3	(A)	(B)	(C)		6	(A)	(B)	(C)

③ 부가 의문문

■ 빈출 질문 & 응답 패턴

Be동사	Q	This package was damaged during delivery, **wasn't it?**	이 소포는 배송 도중에 손상되었죠, 그렇지 않나요?
	정답	Yes, you'll need to fill out a claim form.	네, 배상 청구서를 작성하셔야 할 거예요.
	오답	No, the mail comes in the afternoon.	아니요, 우편물은 오후에 와요.
		→ 연상 작용 [package/mail]	

Do동사	Q	We ordered a cabinet yesterday, **didn't we?**	우리가 어제 수납장 하나를 주문했죠, 그렇지 않나요?
	정답	Yes, it'll be delivered this morning.	네, 그것은 오늘 오전에 배달될 거예요.
	오답	Sorry, they're out of order. → 다의어 [order]	미안하지만, 그것들은 고장이에요.

Have 동사	Q	Ms. Janski's entered the lab results, **hasn't she?**	잰스키 씨가 실험 결과를 입력했죠, 그렇지 않나요?
	정답	No, she's been busy ordering supplies.	아니요, 그녀는 물품을 주문하느라 바빴어요.
	오답	She entered the contest and won.	그녀는 경연대회에 참가해 우승했어요.
		→ 단어 반복 [entered]	

조동사	Q	You'd prefer a seat by the window, **wouldn't you?**	창가 쪽 좌석을 선호하시죠, 그렇지 않나요?
	정답	Yes, I would.	네, 그렇습니다.
	오답	No, I don't see it. → 유사 발음 [seat/see it]	아니요, 안 보입니다.

특수 형태	Q	This train runs every hour, **right?**	이 기차는 매 시간 운행되죠, 그렇죠?
	정답	Here's the schedule.	여기 시간표가 있어요.
	오답	No, we went there by bus.	아니요, 거기에 버스를 타고 갔어요.

ETS 유형 연습

750_P2_13

음원을 듣고 적절한 응답을 고르세요.

정답과 해설 p.029

1	(A)	(B)	(C)		4	(A)	(B)	(C)
2	(A)	(B)	(C)		5	(A)	(B)	(C)
3	(A)	(B)	(C)		6	(A)	(B)	(C)

T **실전 도움닫기** | 음원을 듣고 적절한 응답을 고르세요.
다시 듣고 빈칸을 채우세요.

1 Mark your answer.

(A)　(B)　(C)

Is the _____ on Mondays?

(A) It was an _____.

(B) No, it's _____.

(C) Yes, but _____.

2 Mark your answer.

(A)　(B)　(C)

Do you know why I need to _____?

(A) I don't believe _____.

(B) No, I _____.

(C) Maybe you need to _____.

3 Mark your answer.

(A)　(B)　(C)

Have you finished _____?

(A) Just _____.

(B) He _____ Mr. Garcia.

(C) Yes, the apartment _____.

4 Mark your answer.

(A)　(B)　(C)

_____ in the shipping department?

(A) Please send it _____.

(B) Yes, but he _____.

(C) _____ today.

5 Mark your answer.

(A)　(B)　(C)

We won't be _____, will we?

(A) No, _____.

(B) What date _____ you?

(C) John's _____.

LC

PART 2

1. Mark your answer.   (A)   (B)   (C)

2. Mark your answer.   (A)   (B)   (C)

3. Mark your answer.   (A)   (B)   (C)

4. Mark your answer.   (A)   (B)   (C)

5. Mark your answer.   (A)   (B)   (C)

6. Mark your answer.   (A)   (B)   (C)

7. Mark your answer.   (A)   (B)   (C)

8. Mark your answer.   (A)   (B)   (C)

9. Mark your answer.   (A)   (B)   (C)

10. Mark your answer.   (A)   (B)   (C)

11. Mark your answer.   (A)   (B)   (C)

12. Mark your answer.   (A)   (B)   (C)

13. Mark your answer.   (A)   (B)   (C)

14. Mark your answer.　　　　　(A)　　　(B)　　　(C)

15. Mark your answer.　　　　　(A)　　　(B)　　　(C)

16. Mark your answer.　　　　　(A)　　　(B)　　　(C)

17. Mark your answer.　　　　　(A)　　　(B)　　　(C)

18. Mark your answer.　　　　　(A)　　　(B)　　　(C)

19. Mark your answer.　　　　　(A)　　　(B)　　　(C)

20. Mark your answer.　　　　　(A)　　　(B)　　　(C)

21. Mark your answer.　　　　　(A)　　　(B)　　　(C)

22. Mark your answer.　　　　　(A)　　　(B)　　　(C)

23. Mark your answer.　　　　　(A)　　　(B)　　　(C)

24. Mark your answer.　　　　　(A)　　　(B)　　　(C)

25. Mark your answer.　　　　　(A)　　　(B)　　　(C)

LC

PART 2

선택 / 요청·제안 의문문 / 평서문

① 선택 의문문

> **출제 포인트 1** A or B 구조로 두 가지 선택 사항이 주어지며, A와 B는 구 혹은 문장의 형태를 띤다.
> **출제 포인트 2** 둘 중 하나를 직접적으로 선택하는 응답이나 선택 사항을 우회적으로 드러내는 응답이 보편적이다. 선택을 회피
> 하는 답변이 출제되기도 하며, Either/Neither/Whichever 등의 표현이 있는 보기가 정답일 확률이 높다.

■ 빈출 질문 & 응답 패턴

한 가지 선택	Q	Will the construction be completed **this year or next year?**	공사는 올해 끝나나요, 아니면 내년에 끝나나요?
	정답	It will be done **by the end of the year.**	연말까지는 끝날 거예요.
	오답	I've already read the instructions.	저는 이미 설명서를 읽었어요.

상관 없음	Q	Martin, would you rather **complete the data entry or start the filing project?**	마틴 씨, 데이터 입력을 마무리하실래요, 아니면 서류 정리를 시작하실래요?
	정답	**Either is fine** with me.	어느 것이든 좋아요.
	오답	It is still on file. → 파생어 [filing/file]	아직 보관되어 있어요.

제3의 선택	Q	Can you fix this computer, or should I call the service center?	이 컴퓨터를 고칠 수 있겠어요, 아니면 서비스 센터에 전화할까요?
	정답	I don't think it can be repaired.	그건 수리가 안 될 거 같은데요.
	오답	Usually between ten and six.	대개 10시에서 6시 사이에요.

둘 다 선택 안 함	Q	Are you going to watch **the movie or the game?**	영화를 볼 건가요, 경기를 볼 건가요?
	정답	**Neither;** I'm too tired.	둘 다 안 봐요. 너무 피곤하거든요.
	오답	There was a movie premiere yesterday. → 단어 반복 [movie]	어제 영화 시사회가 있었어요.

Yes/No 응답	Q	Are you hungry after driving for so long, or did you stop and eat?	오래 운전하셔서 배가 고프세요, 아니면 멈춰서 뭘 좀 드셨나요?
	정답	**Yes,** I stopped by a sandwich shop on the way.	네, 오는 길에 샌드위치 가게에 들렀어요.
	※ A와 B가 문장이거나 질문이 or not으로 끝날 경우 가능		

ETS 유형 연습 ⋯⋯⋯⋯⋯⋯⋯⋯⋯⋯⋯⋯⋯⋯⋯⋯⋯⋯⋯⋯⋯⋯⋯⋯⋯⋯⋯⋯ 750_P2_16 🎧

음원을 듣고 적절한 응답을 고르세요.

정답과 해설 p.035

1 (A)   (B)   (C)   4 (A)   (B)   (C)

2 (A)   (B)   (C)   5 (A)   (B)   (C)

3 (A)   (B)   (C)   6 (A)   (B)   (C)

② 요청 · 제안 의문문

■ 빈출 질문 & 응답 패턴

부탁/요청			
	Q	Could you make twenty copies of this report?	이 보고서를 20부 복사해 주시겠어요?
	정답	Sure, I'll do it right now.	네, 지금 당장 할게요.
	오답	Yes, he's a news reporter. → 파생어 [report/reporter]	네, 그는 기자예요.
	Q	Would you mind interviewing a job applicant on Thursday?	목요일에 입사 지원자를 면접하는 게 괜찮으세요?
	정답	Sorry, I'll be away on holiday.	죄송해요, 저는 휴가라 자리를 비울 거예요.
	오답	Three open positions. → 연상 작용 [job applicant/positions]	세 개의 공석이요.

제안/권유			
	Q	Why don't you sign the contract?	그 계약에 서명하는 게 어떠세요?
	정답	I need some more time to review it.	저는 좀 더 검토할 시간이 필요해요.
	오답	You can contact me by phone anytime. → 유사 발음 [contract/contact]	언제든지 제게 전화로 연락하시면 됩니다.
	Q	How about sending Jeremy a thank-you card for his help?	제레미에게 도와줘서 고맙다는 카드를 보내는 게 어떨까요?
	정답	Yes, that's a nice idea.	네, 좋은 생각이에요.
	오답	They came this morning.	그들은 오늘 아침에 왔어요.
	Q	Would you like some help organizing the conference?	회의 준비하는 걸 도와 드릴까요?
	정답	I think I can manage by myself.	저 혼자 할 수 있을 거 같아요.
	오답	To the conference center. → 단어 반복 [conference]	회의장으로요.

ETS 유형 연습

750_P2_17

음원을 듣고 적절한 응답을 고르세요.

정답과 해설 p.037

1	(A)	(B)	(C)		4	(A)	(B)	(C)
2	(A)	(B)	(C)		5	(A)	(B)	(C)
3	(A)	(B)	(C)		6	(A)	(B)	(C)

③ 평서문

■ 빈출 질문 & 응답 패턴

사실/ 정보	Q	They won't bill us for their consulting service.	그들은 우리에게 컨설팅 서비스에 대한 비용을 청구하지 않을 거예요.
	정답	Yes, I saw their advertisement.	네, 저도 광고 봤어요.
	오답	I have change for a 10 dollar bill. → 다의어 [bill]	제게 10달러 지폐를 바꿀 잔돈이 있어요.

의견/ 바람	Q	I hope the articles affect our business positively.	그 기사들이 우리 사업에 긍정적인 영향을 미치면 좋겠어요.
	정답	Our products are already selling well.	우리 상품들은 이미 잘 팔리고 있어요.
	오답	The policy will go into effect next month. → 유사 발음 [affect/effect]	그 정책은 다음 달에 실시될 겁니다.

문제점	Q	The train tickets are all sold out.	기차표가 매진이에요.
	정답	In that case, let's take the bus.	그러면 버스를 탑시다.
	오답	Yes, they are very expensive.	네, 굉장히 비쌉니다.

제안/ 명령	Q	Let's put the new merchandise in the front of the store.	신제품을 상점 전면에 진열합시다.
	정답	That's a good idea.	좋은 생각이에요.
	오답	Yes, everything was half off.	네, 모든 게 반값이었어요.
	Q	Please take a copy of our new catalogue.	새로 나온 카탈로그 한 부 가져가세요.
	정답	I already have one.	전 이미 한 부 있어요.
	오답	I'll take notes. → 단어 반복 [take]	제가 필기를 할게요.

질문하는 응답	Q	I can't make it to the party tonight.	저는 오늘 밤 파티에 못 가요.
	정답	Do you have other plans?	다른 약속이 있나요?
	오답	She will come, too. → 연상 작용 [make it/come]	그녀도 올 겁니다.

750_P2_18

ETS 유형 연습

음원을 듣고 적절한 응답을 고르세요.

정답과 해설 p. 038

1	(A)	(B)	(C)		4	(A)	(B)	(C)
2	(A)	(B)	(C)		5	(A)	(B)	(C)
3	(A)	(B)	(C)		6	(A)	(B)	(C)

1 Mark your answer.

(A)　　(B)　　(C)

Do you need to _____, or can you _____?

(A) _____ are too long.

(B) No thanks, I _____.

(C) _____ go soon.

2 Mark your answer.

(A)　　(B)　　(C)

Could you check these _____ for me?

(A) No, _____.

(B) _____, put them _____.

(C) The quarterly _____.

3 Mark your answer.

(A)　　(B)　　(C)

Please make sure to _____ on this form.

(A) _____ on most days.

(B) Isn't this the _____?

(C) Thanks for _____.

4 Mark your answer.

(A)　　(B)　　(C)

The hotel _____ and they couldn't
_____.

(A) Did he have to _____?

(B) _____ is reserved.

(C) So _____?

5 Mark your answer.

(A)　　(B)　　(C)

_____ that tomorrow when you're not
so tired?

(A) He _____ this time.

(B) Whenever you _____.

(C) That's _____.

LC

PART 2

1. Mark your answer.   (A)   (B)   (C)

2. Mark your answer.   (A)   (B)   (C)

3. Mark your answer.   (A)   (B)   (C)

4. Mark your answer.   (A)   (B)   (C)

5. Mark your answer.   (A)   (B)   (C)

6. Mark your answer.   (A)   (B)   (C)

7. Mark your answer.   (A)   (B)   (C)

8. Mark your answer.   (A)   (B)   (C)

9. Mark your answer.   (A)   (B)   (C)

10. Mark your answer.   (A)   (B)   (C)

11. Mark your answer.   (A)   (B)   (C)

12. Mark your answer.   (A)   (B)   (C)

13. Mark your answer.   (A)   (B)   (C)

14. Mark your answer.　　　(A)　　(B)　　(C)

15. Mark your answer.　　　(A)　　(B)　　(C)

16. Mark your answer.　　　(A)　　(B)　　(C)

17. Mark your answer.　　　(A)　　(B)　　(C)

18. Mark your answer.　　　(A)　　(B)　　(C)

19. Mark your answer.　　　(A)　　(B)　　(C)

20. Mark your answer.　　　(A)　　(B)　　(C)

21. Mark your answer.　　　(A)　　(B)　　(C)

22. Mark your answer.　　　(A)　　(B)　　(C)

23. Mark your answer.　　　(A)　　(B)　　(C)

24. Mark your answer.　　　(A)　　(B)　　(C)

25. Mark your answer.　　　(A)　　(B)　　(C)

LC

PART 2

7. Mark your answer on your answer sheet.

8. Mark your answer on your answer sheet.

9. Mark your answer on your answer sheet.

10. Mark your answer on your answer sheet.

11. Mark your answer on your answer sheet.

12. Mark your answer on your answer sheet.

13. Mark your answer on your answer sheet.

14. Mark your answer on your answer sheet.

15. Mark your answer on your answer sheet.

16. Mark your answer on your answer sheet.

17. Mark your answer on your answer sheet.

18. Mark your answer on your answer sheet.

19. Mark your answer on your answer sheet.

20. Mark your answer on your answer sheet.

21. Mark your answer on your answer sheet.

22. Mark your answer on your answer sheet.

23. Mark your answer on your answer sheet.

24. Mark your answer on your answer sheet.

25. Mark your answer on your answer sheet.

26. Mark your answer on your answer sheet.

27. Mark your answer on your answer sheet.

28. Mark your answer on your answer sheet.

29. Mark your answer on your answer sheet.

30. Mark your answer on your answer sheet.

31. Mark your answer on your answer sheet.

■ 신분 / 직업

assistant 비서, 부하 직원

director 감독, 국장, 이사

board members 임원, 이사진

chairperson 회장 (=president)

vice president 부회장, 부사장

colleague 동료 (=coworker)

supervisor 관리자, 상사

entrepreneur 기업가

proprietor 사업주

tenant 세입자

real estate agent 부동산 중개인

property manager 부동산 관리인

financial consultant 재무 상담가

program coordinator 프로그램 진행자

inspector 검사관, 조사관

contractor 계약자, 도급업자

client 고객, 의뢰인

■ 시간 / 시점

a few months ago 몇 달 전에

since last summer 지난 여름 이후로

the day before yesterday 그저께

at the beginning of August 8월 초에

recently 최근에

any minute now 지금 당장이라도

earlier today 오늘 아까

on October fifteenth 10월 15일에

within the next few days 며칠 이내로

sometime next spring 내년 봄쯤

in about a year or so 대략 1년쯤 후에

at the end of the month 이달 말에

by the end of the day 오늘까지, 오늘 안으로

no later than Thursday 늦어도 목요일까지

not until June 6월 이후에야

by six o'clock at the latest 늦어도 6시까지

at the next staff meeting 다음 직원 회의에서

as soon as it's ready 준비가 되자마자

once the plan is finalized 계획이 확정되면

■ 장소 / 위치

in the front / back row 앞/뒷줄에

in the cabinet 수납장 안에

in the tenth floor meeting room 10층 회의실에서

at the end of the hall 복도 끝에

at the corner of the street 길 모퉁이에

at the customer service desk 고객 서비스 창구에서

on the ceiling 천장에

on the left side 왼쪽에

on the second floor 2층에

on the Web site 웹사이트 상에

on the bottom shelf 맨 아래 선반에

to the address below 아래에 있는 주소로

to the supply room 비품실로

from the printing company 인쇄소로부터

from the city center 시내 중심가에서

next to the movie theater 영화관 옆에

near Fourth Avenue 4번 가 근처에

directly across from the old one 예전 것 바로 맞은편에

down the hall and to the left 복도 끝에서 왼쪽으로

■ 방법 / 수단

in writing 서면으로

in person 직접, 손수 (=personally)

in alphabetical order 알파벳 순으로

by courier 택배로

by credit card 신용 카드로

by bus / plane / subway 버스 / 비행기 / 지하철로

by overnight delivery 익일 배송으로

by searching on the Internet 인터넷 검색으로

through fund-raising events 모금 행사를 통해서

You can register online. 온라인으로 등록할 수 있어요.

You'll need your ID card. 신분증이 필요해요.

Push the button on the side.
측면에 있는 버튼을 누르세요.

■ 기간 / 빈도 / 가격 / 수량

for more than 5 years 5년 이상

every ten minutes 10분마다

every other week / month 격주 / 격월로

on a regular basis 정기적으로 (=regularly)

at least once a month 최소한 한 달에 한번

the rest of the month 이번 달 남은 기간 (동안)

once in a while 가끔

on Saturdays 토요일마다

twenty dollars each 각각 20달러

about a dozen 열두 명[개] 정도

50 euros a month 한 달에 50유로

by 10 percent 10퍼센트

probably around fifty 아마 50 정도

It's almost doubled. 거의 두배입니다.

Your total is 75 dollars. 총 75달러입니다.

■ 이유 / 목적

Because he had an appointment.
그가 약속이 있었기 때문이에요

Because we are understaffed.
왜냐하면 우리가 일손이 부족하기 때문이에요.

probably because of the rain 아마도 비 때문에

due to bad[inclement] weather 악천후 때문에

for personal business 개인적인 용무 때문에

for a dentist appointment 치과 예약 때문에

to shorten the commute 통근 시간을 줄이기 위해서

to accommodate more customers
더 많은 고객을 수용하기 위해

to match the new curtain 새 커튼과 어울리게 하기 위해

to increase efficiency 효율을 높이기 위해

to discuss a new project 새 프로젝트에 관해 논의하기 위해

So that more people can attend.
더 많은 사람들이 참석할 수 있도록요.

■ 상태 / 의견

I enjoyed it. 즐거웠어요.

It couldn't have been better. 정말 최고였어요.

It was helpful. 도움이 되었어요.

It was very informative. 굉장히 유익했어요.

It went very well. 잘 (진행)되었어요.

It has a great view. 전망이 아주 좋아요.

Well, I was disappointed. 음, 실망했어요.

It should be here soon. 그건 곧 올 겁니다.

It's an impressive design. 인상적인 디자인이군요.

It rained all day. 하루 종일 비가 왔어요.

It was too busy[crowded]. 굉장히 붐볐어요.

We may want to consult some experts.
아마 몇몇 전문가들과 상담을 해야 할 겁니다.

■ 잘 모른다 / 듣지 못했다

I wish I knew. 저도 알았으면 좋겠어요.

Nobody knows. 아무도 모르죠.

I have no idea. 몰라요.

We're not sure yet. 아직 잘 모르겠어요.

I don't know anything about it.
그것에 대해선 전혀 몰라요.

I'm not certain. 잘 모르겠어요.

Who knows? 누가 알겠어요?

We won't know until March.
3월이나 되어야 알게 될 거예요.

He hasn't told us yet.
그가 아직 우리에게 말하지 않았어요.

I haven't been told[informed] yet.
아직 듣지(안내받지) 못했어요.

I still haven't heard from them.
그들에게서 아직 소식을 듣지 못했어요.

■ 결정되지 않았다

I'm still considering it. 아직 고려 중이에요.

It's still up in the air. 아직 결정 난 게 아니에요.

I'm still thinking about it.
아직 그것에 대해 생각 중이에요.

They're still deciding. 그들은 아직 결정 중이에요.

The manager is reviewing it. 매니저가 검토 중입니다.

I haven't made up my mind. 아직 결정하지 못했어요.

It hasn't been decided yet. 아직 결정되지 않았어요.

It hasn't been discussed yet. 아직 논의되지 않았어요.

It hasn't been finalized yet. 아직 마무리되지 않았어요.

It depends on the traffic. 교통 상황에 따라 달라요.

It depends on the design. 그건 디자인에 따라 달라요.

It depends on when it is. 그때가 언제인지에 달려 있어요.

■ 확인해 보다 / 문의해 보다

Let me check that for you. 확인해 볼게요.

Let me ask someone. 다른 사람에게 물어볼게요.

Let me call the supplier. 납품업체에 전화해 볼게요.

I'll find out. 제가 알아볼게요.

I'll let you know soon. 곧 알려 드릴게요.

I'll check the schedule. 제가 일정을 확인해 볼게요.

I will take care of it. 제가 처리할게요.

Try asking Mr. Taylor. 테일러 씨에게 문의해 보세요.

Refer to your manual. 설명서를 참고해 주세요.

John knows better than I do. 존이 저보다 더 잘 알아요.

I'll have to ask Chris about that.
크리스에게 물어봐야 해요.

The manager has a floor plan.
매니저가 층 배치도를 가지고 있어요.

Why don't you ask your supervisor?
관리자에게 문의하는 게 어때요?

■ 하나 선택

I prefer green. 초록색이 더 좋아요.

I'll go with the red one. 붉은 것으로 할게요.

I like the grey ones better. 회색인 것이 더 좋아요.

The one with the yellow tag. 노란 꼬리표가 달린 거요.

I'd rather leave early. 저는 빨리 출발하는 게 좋겠어요.

The soup sounds good. 수프가 좋을 것 같아요.

Now would be fine. 지금이 좋겠어요.

Monday is best for me. 월요일이 저한테는 제일 좋아요.

Late afternoon, if possible. 가능하면 늦은 오후로요.

Any time in the morning. 오전이면 언제든요.

Let's try the new restaurant. 새 식당에 가보죠.

Let's order in, since it's raining.
비가 오니 배달시켜 먹어요.

■ 모두 선택 / 반대

I like both. / I like both of them. 둘 다 좋아요.

Both of them would be fine. 둘 다 좋을 것 같아요.

I like all of them. 모두 좋아요.

He did both. 그는 둘 다 했어요.

We can afford to do both. 둘 다 할 수 있어요.

Actually, neither of them. 사실 그 중 아무것도 아니에요.

I prefer neither. 둘 다 별로예요.

I like neither of them. 둘 다 싫어요.

Neither, thanks. 고맙지만 둘 다 됐어요.

■ 제3의 선택

Just some water, please. 그냥 물 좀 부탁할게요.

Can we do it tomorrow instead? 내일 하면 안 될까요?

■ 상관 없다

I don't care. 상관없어요.

Whatever you prefer. 당신이 더 선호하시는 걸로요.

Whichever you like. 좋아하시는 대로요.

Anywhere is fine. 어디라도 좋아요.

Either (one) is fine (with me).
저는 어느 쪽이든 괜찮아요.

Whichever we can get faster.
어떤 것이든 더 빠른 것으로요.

Any day except Monday.
월요일을 제외하고 언제라도요.

It doesn't matter (to me). 저는 상관없어요.

It doesn't make any difference.
(어떤 것이든) 별로 차이가 없어요.

I'll leave it to you. 당신에게 맡길게요.

It's up to you. 당신이 원하는 대로 해요.

I don't have a preference. 선호하는 게 없어요.

■ 수락 / 동의

Suit yourself. 좋을 대로 하세요.

No problem. 문제 없어요.

Not at all. 전혀요.

OK, I'll be sure to do that. 네, 꼭 그렇게 할게요.

You bet. / Certainly. / Absolutely. / Definitely. /
Why not? 물론이죠.

Be my guest. / Go ahead. / By all means.
그렇게 하세요.

I'd love to. / I'd be happy to. 그러고 싶어요.

It certainly was. 정말 그랬어요.

That's a good idea. 좋은 생각이네요.

Yes, that would be great. 네, 그럼 아주 좋겠네요.

If you're not too busy. 당신이 많이 바쁘지 않다면요.

If it's not too much trouble. 그게 너무 수고스럽지 않다면요.

■ 거절 / 부정

I can manage[handle] that, thanks.
내가 혼자 할 수 있어요, 고마워요.

Actually, I already have. 실은 벌써 했습니다.

I'm almost done, thanks. 고맙지만, 거의 다 했어요.

Oh, I can't make it because of a scheduling
conflict. 오, 일정이 겹쳐서 참석을 못 해요.

Thanks, but I have other plans.
고맙지만, 다른 계획이 있어요.

Sorry, I have an appointment then.
미안하지만 그때 약속이 있어요.

I wish I could, but I'm very busy.
그러고 싶지만 너무 바빠요.

I don't have time right now. 지금은 시간이 없어요.

Well, I'm about to leave. 음, 막 퇴근하려던 참이에요.

I have to return to the office right now.
저는 지금 바로 사무실로 돌아가야 해요.

No, it's much too cold. 아니요, 너무 추워요.

LC

짧은 대화

Part 3

Part 3 | 짧은 대화 총 13세트 39문항

대화를 듣고 이와 관련된 세 개의 문제를 푸는 유형으로, 업무와 일상 생활 관련 대화문이 출제된다. 매회 3인 대화가 2개씩 포함되며, 문제 유형은 다음과 같이 크게 두 가지로 나눌 수 있다.

- 전체 내용 관련 문제 주제/목적, 대화가 이루어지는 장소, 화자들의 직업/업종/근무지
- 세부 내용 관련 문제 화자의 요청/제안/추천 사항, 화자의 의도 파악, 다음에 할 일/일어날 일, 이유/원인, 방법, 문제점, 세부 사항, 시각 정보 연계

■ ETS 예제 및 풀이 전략

1 대화를 듣기 전에 문제와 보기를 읽고, 키워드에 표시해 둔다.

2 문제의 키워드가 등장하면 집중해서 듣고, 대화를 듣는 동시에 답을 찾는다.
   각 문제 및 보기의 키워드를 파악한 후, 단서가 나올 부분을 노려 듣는다. 관련 내용을 확인하는 즉시 답을 체크하고 다음 문제로 넘어가야 한다. 문제 순서에 맞춰 단서가 주어지는 경우가 많다.

📑 문제지

32. (Why) is the man (surprised)?
(A) The woman has not finished a report.
(B) The woman knows Sarah.
(C) The woman is still at the office.
(D) The woman lives near him.

33. What is (Sarah's problem)?
(A) Her car is not working.
(B) The store will close soon.
(C) Her home needs some repairs.
(D) She forgot an appointment.

34. What is the woman (planning to do tonight)?
(A) Visit her parents' home
(B) Look for a new house
(C) Work on a report
(D) Go to dinner with Sarah

🔊 음원

Questions 32 through 34 refer to the following conversation.

M ㉜ I didn't expect to see you still here. Are you staying late to work on the Billows report?

W No, actually, ㉝ I'm just waiting for Sarah. Her car broke down; it's in the shop for repairs, so I'm giving her a ride home.

M I didn't know you two lived near each other.

W Oh, we don't—but ㉞ I'm having dinner at my parents' house tonight, and Sarah lives near them.

※ 이후 문제만 읽어주며, 문제 사이에 8초가 주어진다.

---

32. 남자가 놀란 이유: 여자가 아직 사무실에 있어서
33. 사라의 문제: 차 고장
34. 오늘밤 여자의 계획: 부모님 댁에서 저녁 식사

정답 **(C) The woman is still at the office.**
정답 **(A) Her car is not working.**
정답 **(A) Visit her parents' home**

■ 패러프레이징(Paraphrasing)

패러프레이징이란 '다른 말로 바꾸어 표현하는 것'을 뜻한다. 대화 내의 단서가 보기에 그대로 나오는 경우도 있지만, 패러프레이징되어 제시되는 경우가 많으므로 유형을 미리 파악해 두면 실전에 도움이 된다. 자주 나오는 대표적인 표현들을 암기해 두는 것도 좋은 방법이다.

1 동의어, 유의어, 사전적 의미 활용

W I bought this mobile phone yesterday, but it seems to be defective.

여 어제 이 휴대폰을 구매했는데, 결함이 있는 것 같아요

Q What problem does the woman have?

A Her phone is not working properly.

질문 여자가 겪고 있는 문제는?

정답 전화기가 제대로 작동하지 않는다.

→ defective의 사전적 의미에 가까운 'not working properly'로 표현

2 포괄적 개념을 지닌 상위어 활용

M I'm calling to ask you about the upcoming conference.

남 곧 있을 학회와 관련해서 문의하려고 전화했어요.

Q Why is the man calling?

A To inquire about an event

질문 남자가 전화한 이유는?

정답 행사에 관해 문의하려고

→ 'conference'를 더 포괄적인 개념인 'event'로 표현

3 품사 변경

W I'll order a replacement later. Don't worry.

여 제가 이따가 대체품을 주문할게요. 걱정 마세요.

Q What does the woman offer to do?

A Place an order

질문 여자가 하겠다고 제안하는 일은?

정답 주문 넣기

→ 동사 'order'를 명사로 바꾼 뒤 'place'와 함께 사용

4 내용 축약

M I own a small store that sells furniture such as tables and chairs.

남 탁자나 의자 같은 가구를 판매하는 작은 가게를 소유하고 있어요.

Q What kind of business does the man own?

A A furniture store

질문 남자가 소유한 사업체는?

정답 가구점

→ 'a small store that sells furniture such as tables and chairs'를 'furniture store'로 줄여서 표현

LC

PART 3

주제 · 목적 / 화자 · 장소 문제

① 주제 · 목적 문제

> **출제 포인트**　대화 주제나 전화/방문의 목적을 묻는 질문은 주로 첫 번째 문제로 출제된다. 보통 대화 초반에 단서가 등장하지만, 간혹 중반까지 들어야 확인이 가능한 경우도 있다.

주제 질문

What are the speakers **discussing**?
What is the conversation mainly **about**?
What is the (main) **topic** of the conversation?

목적 질문

What is the purpose of the **call/visit**?
Why is the man **calling**?
Why does the woman **call** the business?

750_P3_01 🎧
정답과 해설 **p.049**

■ **공략 포인트** | 대화 초반부에서 주제와 목적을 나타내는 단서를 포착한다.

W I can't believe the trouble we had coming up with **the design for our new logo**. It seems to have taken forever. → 대화 주제 등장

M Yes, but the results are worthwhile, don't you think? **It sums up exactly what our company stands for**: it looks both sporty and dependable.

W Yes, and it comes out well both small on our letterhead and large on our store signs and products.

문제 **What** are the speakers **discussing**?
(A) A new kind of bicycle
(B) A company logo
(C) A letter
(D) A new store

단서 회사를 잘 표현하는 새 로고

정답 **(B) A company logo**

┌─ 정답으로 이어지는 단서 표현 ─

전화나 방문의 목적을 묻는 질문이 있을 경우, 대화 초반에 다음 표현들이 등장할 가능성이 높다. 이 뒤에 이어지는 부분에 집중해야 한다.

I'm here to interview Mr. Park for an article.
기사 작성을 위해 박 씨를 인터뷰 하러 왔습니다.

I need[want, would like] to change my hotel reservation.
제 호텔 예약을 변경해야 합니다[하고 싶습니다].

I'm calling to confirm my attendance at the meeting on Friday.
금요일 회의 참석을 확정하려고 전화했어요.

I'm calling because there seems to be a problem with the heating system.
난방 시스템에 문제가 있는 것 같아서 전화했어요.

1. What are the speakers discussing?
(A) A real estate loan
(B) A ride-sharing initiative
(C) A company budget
(D) A hiring plan

M Thanks for meeting with me to _____
_____, Georgia.

W No problem.

M With the _____ for office space this year, we're definitely _____ right now.

W Yes, we'll have to find areas to _____.

2. Why did the man call?
(A) To speak with a retail clerk
(B) To cancel an appointment
(C) To set up a job interview
(D) To renew a subscription

W _____ Dr. Franklin's office. How may I help you?

M Yes, this is Martin Brown. I need to _____
_____ for an eye exam on Wednesday.

W OK. Would you like to _____? The doctor could see you at two o'clock on Friday.

3. What is the conversation mainly about?
(A) Organizing a meeting
(B) Redecorating an office
(C) Stopping mail delivery
(D) Finding a lost package

W I'm going to be out of town starting Monday, August first, and I'd like to _____
_____, please.

M Certainly. We can _____ at the post office while you're away. Incidentally, did you know that you could _____ to another address instead?

W Well, I'm actually going to be _____, so I don't think that'd be possible.

4. What is the purpose of Martha's call to Jeffrey?
(A) To tell him she is going out of town
(B) To ask him to pay for some additional research
(C) To thank him for meeting with her
(D) To tell him she mailed a report to him

M Hello. Jeffrey Hines speaking.

W This is Martha Benjamin. I'm calling to _____ I've put my _____ in the _____. You should have it this afternoon. I hope you're still _____ for me.

M Of course. I'll be out of town _____ for the next few days, but I'll _____.

② 화자 · 장소 문제

출제 포인트 화자(들)의 신분/직업/업계, 혹은 근무지/대화 장소를 묻는 질문도 첫 번째 문제로 자주 출제된다. 대화 초반부에 특정 직업이나 업체명이 명시되는 경우가 많지만 대화 곳곳에 있는 단서를 조합하여 답을 찾아야 할 수도 있으므로, 직업/업계 관련 표현은 암기해 두는 것이 좋다.

신분/직업/업계 질문

Who (most likely) is the **woman**?

What is the **man's job[occupation, profession]**?

What industry do the speakers most likely **work** in?

근무지/장소 질문

Where does the woman **work**?

Where most likely **are** the speakers?

Where does this conversation most likely **take place**?

750_P3_03 🎧
정답과 해설 p.050

■ **공략 포인트** | 대화 초반부의 직업/업체명, 혹은 대화 곳곳에 있는 관련 표현에 주목한다.

M Hi, I saw on a television commercial that **your art-supply store** offers classes. What kinds of courses do you have? → 여자의 근무지 명시

W Right now we're offering a variety of classes in drawing, painting, and sculpture. Would any of those interest you?

M I'd like to try sculpture. But I've never studied any type of art before, so I'd be looking for an introductory-level class.

문제 **Where** does the **woman work**?

(A) At an art-supply store
(B) At a university
(C) At a photography studio
(D) At a community center

단서 당신(여자)의 미술용품점

정답 **(A) At an art-supply store**

┌─ 정답으로 이어지는 단서 표현 ─

화자/장소 문제의 단서가 제시되는 대표적인 방식을 파악해 둔다.

화자 본인 소개	Hello, **this** is Lewis **calling from** Sunville Marketing. → 마케팅 회사 안녕하세요, 저는 선빌 마케팅의 루이스입니다.
환영 인사	**Welcome to** the Chester Art Museum. → 미술관 체스터 미술관에 오신 걸 환영합니다.
상대방 회사 언급	I heard that you've started **your own** advertising company. → 광고 업계 당신이 직접 광고 회사를 설립했다고 들었어요.
관련 표현 사용	I'm **writing an** article about your company for **our** magazine. → 기자/언론인 저희 잡지에 실을 귀사 관련 기사를 작성 중입니다.

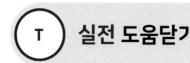
1. Who most likely is the man?
(A) A company owner
(B) A conference employee
(C) A restaurant manager
(D) A travel agent

W Hi, I'm _____. My name's Melissa Han.

M Han ... OK, I have your _____ here. Your _____. Are you staying here or somewhere else?

W I'm staying here, but I _____ _____ late.

2. Where does this conversation most likely take place?
(A) In a theater
(B) At an auto repair shop
(C) In a parking garage
(D) At a car rental agency

W Here are my keys. Can you give me an idea of when I should come back to _____?

M We need to _____, change the oil, and _____, so it'll probably be ready around 5 o'clock.

W I can be back here by five, but I'll need to _____ today.

3. Who most likely are the speakers?
(A) Advertising executives
(B) Apparel salespeople
(C) Fashion designers
(D) Magazine editors

M Lucy, have you _____ any ideas for _____ for The Sawgrass Company's _____?

W Well, from the samples the _____, I think what really stands out is the fabric. The material is _____. Plus, it's washable and wrinkle-resistant.

M Then why don't we _____?

4. Where most likely does the man work?
(A) At a hotel
(B) At a hair salon
(C) At a dry-cleaning business
(D) At a home improvement store

M Hi. Welcome to Jerry's _____. Do you _____ with us?

W No, I don't—I was hoping one of the stylists might be free. I just need to _____.

M Well, let me see… our senior stylist Teresa _____ at eleven thirty, or you could see one of our newer stylists at two.

1. What are the speakers mainly discussing?
   (A) A play
   (B) A sports match
   (C) A movie premiere
   (D) A concert

2. Why was the woman disappointed?
   (A) She could not get a ticket.
   (B) She missed the beginning of the event.
   (C) The sound system was not working well.
   (D) Some people were blocking her view.

3. What does the man think the woman should do?
   (A) Ask for a refund
   (B) Attend a different performance
   (C) Watch a television program
   (D) Write a review

4. Where most likely is the conversation taking place?
   (A) At a job fair
   (B) At a meeting
   (C) In an office kitchen
   (D) In a coffee shop

5. What does Tom suggest about the company?
   (A) It needs to hire more people.
   (B) It treats its employees well.
   (C) It will soon be renovated.
   (D) It is buying some new equipment.

6. What does the woman say about Anil?
   (A) He has recently joined the company.
   (B) He applied for her position.
   (C) He will be reporting to Tom.
   (D) He has just returned from vacation.

7. What is the purpose of the telephone call?
   (A) To confirm a reservation
   (B) To ask about a policy
   (C) To check on the price of a ticket
   (D) To change a departure date

8. Why is the woman disappointed?
   (A) A new fee has been added.
   (B) One of her suitcases has been lost.
   (C) Her seating preference is not available.
   (D) An arrival time has changed.

9. What does the man offer to explain?
   (A) Meal selections
   (B) Visa requirements
   (C) Size limitations
   (D) Payment options

10. Who is the man?
    (A) A real estate agent
    (B) A property owner
    (C) A building inspector
    (D) An interior decorator

11. What does the woman say she likes about the apartment?
    (A) It is located near a park.
    (B) It has an open layout.
    (C) It is reasonably priced.
    (D) It has wooden floors.

12. Where will the speakers go next?
    (A) To the roof garden
    (B) To the laundry facility
    (C) To the storage rooms
    (D) To the parking area

13. What are the speakers discussing?

(A) A home renovation
(B) A landscaping plan
(C) A road repair
(D) A housecleaning service

14. What does the woman say about the work to be done?

(A) It will require special equipment.
(B) It has to begin next week.
(C) It is not a large project.
(D) It may cause inconvenience.

15. What will the man send the woman after they meet?

(A) Design drawings
(B) Product catalogs
(C) A revised contract
(D) A local area map

16. What industry do the speakers most likely work in?

(A) Food production
(B) Machinery sales
(C) Event planning
(D) Textile manufacturing

17. What problem are the speakers discussing?

(A) An employee is not available.
(B) The appliances have not been cleaned.
(C) The quality of a product is poor.
(D) A customer has complained.

18. What does the man suggest?

(A) Alerting the management
(B) Replacing a machine
(C) Lowering a price
(D) Discarding some merchandise

19. Where do the speakers most likely work?

(A) At a park
(B) At a farm
(C) At a garden supply store
(D) At a landscaping company

20. What is the man happy about?

(A) Hiring additional staff
(B) Extending hours of operation
(C) Offering a discount to customers
(D) Changing a brand of fertilizer

21. What will the man do next?

(A) Repair some equipment
(B) Register for a small business license
(C) Order some supplies
(D) Prepare for bad weather

22. Who most likely is the woman?

(A) A building inspector
(B) A management consultant
(C) An architect
(D) A reporter

23. What is the goal of Mr. Howard's firm?

(A) Using recycled materials
(B) Building affordable homes
(C) Preserving historic structures
(D) Increasing energy efficiency

24. What does Mr. Howard plan to do in the future?

(A) Speak at universities
(B) Publish a book
(C) Lead a volunteer project
(D) Open an overseas office

① 세부 사항 문제

> **출제 포인트** What, How, Why 등 다양한 의문사를 사용하여 특정 정보를 묻거나, 화자가 언급한 내용을 묻는 문제가 출제된다. 문제 및 보기의 키워드가 대화에 그대로, 혹은 패러프레이징되어 나타나므로, 문제를 먼저 읽어서 키워드를 파악한 후 해당 부분을 노려 들어야 한다.

특정 정보를 묻는 질문

What is/are ~?

What does[did] the woman ~?

How/Why/When/Where did the man ~?

언급한 내용을 묻는 질문

What does the man **say** ~?

What does the woman **mention about** ~?

According to the man, **what** ~?

750_P3_06 🎧

정답과 해설 p.056

■ **공략 포인트** | 질문의 키워드를 파악한 후 해당 부분을 노려 듣는다.

W Hi, Ken. How are the preparations for the conference going?

M Good. I just finished writing a draft of the **information packet describing the products we'll showcase** at our booth.
   → 키워드 information packet 등장

W That's great. Can you e-mail me a copy? I'd like to proofread it.

문제 **What** is **in the information packet**?
(A) Company descriptions
(B) Booth regulations
(C) Conference schedules
(D) Product details

단서 제품을 설명하는 자료집

정답 **(D) Product details**

┌─ 정답으로 이어지는 단서 표현 ─

정답의 단서는 키워드 뒤에 등장할 수도 있고, 키워드보다 앞서 등장할 수도 있다. 문제를 보고 단서의 대략적인 위치를 예상해 두고, 주요 내용을 간략히 메모하며 듣는 것이 좋다.

How do the speakers hope to **increase sales**? 매출 증대 방식: 키워드가 들리면 집중

We could **increase our sales** by offering a free delivery service. → By offering a new service
무료 배달 서비스를 제공하면 매출을 올릴 수 있을 거예요.   새로운 서비스를 제공함으로써

What does the woman say she **did last week**? 지난주에 한 일: 과거 시제가 들리면 집중

I e-mailed him the contract **last week**, but I haven't heard from him yet. → She sent some document.
지난주에 그에게 이메일로 계약서를 보냈는데, 아직도 소식이 없네요.   서류를 보냈다.

1. Where did Flora stay in Valencia?
(A) In a hotel
(B) At a friend's house
(C) With relatives
(D) At a campsite

M Welcome back, Flora! How was Spain?

W Wonderful, thanks. I went with a few friends—we _____ in Valencia for two weeks.

M Yeah, I really enjoyed Valencia when I _____ _____ there last year.

2. What does the woman say she likes about her job?
(A) Using her creativity
(B) Specializing in one area
(C) Earning bonus pay
(D) Having the chance to travel

M Hi, Barbara. Nice to run into you! We've missed you _____ Allen Real Estate.

W Kevin! Yes, it's been a while. That was a big decision, to change companies. But I _____ a lot.

M That's great. How's _____ what you did with us?

W Well—I only _____ now. But I like being able to _____.

3. How did the woman learn about the man's agency?
(A) From a neighbor
(B) From a magazine
(C) From a coworker
(D) From the Internet

W Hello, my name is Melissa Stein. I'm calling because I'm _____. I was _____ to you _____. You helped her sell her house a while ago, and she was very _____.

M I'd be happy to help you with that, Ms. Stein. Are you ready to _____ immediately?

4. According to the woman, what type of assistance can the staff provide?
(A) Making a payment
(B) Organizing an event
(C) Choosing a product
(D) Unloading some items

M Hello. We're here to set up our booth for the _____. Can you tell us where it's located? We're from Elmheart Electronics.

W Let me see...you're in booth number twelve, right by the service elevators. Do you need _____ _____ anything _____? We have some _____.

M Thanks, that would be great.

LC

PART 3

② 문제점 · 걱정거리 문제

> **출제 포인트**   화자가 언급한 문제점이나 걱정거리를 묻는 질문이 출제되며, 주로 대화의 초·중반에 단서가 제시된다. 부정적인 표현이 등장하면 집중해서 청취해야 한다.

문제점 질문
What is the woman's **problem**?
What problem does the man **mention**?
What problem are the speakers **discussing**?

걱정거리 질문
What is the man **worried about**?
What is the woman **concerned about**?
Why is the man **concerned**?

750_P3_08 🎧
정답과 해설 p. 058

■ **공략 포인트** | 부정적인 표현 뒤에 등장하는 단서를 포착한다.

W Is there any way I can get on the next flight to Los Angeles? **My flight from New York didn't arrive on time so I missed my connection.**
→ 부정어(didn't) 등장

M Let's see, I don't have any direct flights, but if you're willing to connect in San Francisco, there is a flight leaving in twenty minutes.

W As long as it takes me to Los Angeles, I'll take it.

문제 **What** is the woman's **problem**?
(A) She lost her luggage.
(B) She missed a flight.
(C) She forgot her airplane ticket.
(D) She does not know where the gate is.

단서 비행기 연착으로 연결편 놓침

정답 **(B) She missed a flight.**

--- 정답으로 이어지는 단서 표현 ---

문제점/걱정거리 문제의 단서는 아래와 같은 표현과 함께 등장한다.

Not이 포함된 부정어: can't, wasn't, didn't, won't, haven't 등
I **won't** be able to make it to the meeting. 회의에 못 갈 것 같아요.

부정적인 의미를 나타내는 표현: unfortunately, mistake, problem, miss, delay 등
I noticed **a mistake** in one of the presentation slides. 프레젠테이션 슬라이드 중 하나에서 오류를 발견했어요.

대조/반전의 뜻을 지닌 표현: but, however, though, actually 등
I bought this camera yesterday, **but** I think it may be defective. 어제 이 카메라를 샀는데, 결함이 있는 것 같아요.

걱정의 표현: concern, worried, afraid 등
I'm **worried** that we might arrive late. 늦게 도착할까 봐 걱정이 돼요.

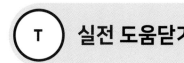
1. What is the man's problem?
   (A) His bill is incorrect.
   (B) His luggage is missing.
   (C) His reservation has been canceled.
   (D) His suit has been damaged.

M Hi, my name's Ron Halberg. I checked in to the hotel earlier today. Do you have any messages for me? My _____, so I've been _____ from Reyes Airlines.

W Ah, Mr. Halberg—I'm sorry, but they _____ _____. Is there any way I can help you?

M Well, I'm _____ this evening, and my only formal clothes are _____. Is there a place nearby where I can _____?

2. What problem are the speakers discussing?
   (A) A piece of art has not arrived.
   (B) A magazine is not available.
   (C) A library card has expired.
   (D) A store is closing.

W I'm looking for the current issue of *Crafts Magazine*. Do you know if the library _____? It wasn't _____ where I usually find it.

M Oh, yes, I'm sorry. The library _____ from last year, so you _____ on the shelves.

3. What is the man concerned about?
   (A) Noise
   (B) Dust
   (C) Expense
   (D) Safety

M Hello. I'm calling about the notice I received today. It said that my apartment's been _____ on Wednesday 21.

W Yes, that's correct. The property managers have _____ new ceramic floor tiles _____ in your building.

M Well, I usually work from home on Wednesdays, so I'm _____ that having my flooring changed while I'm there would _____ for me to _____.

4. What problem does the man mention?
   (A) Some equipment is not working.
   (B) An item is out of stock.
   (C) Prices have recently increased.
   (D) A shop is about to close.

W Excuse me, I _____ here last week, but when I got home, I realized that _____ _____. I'd like to exchange it for another one.

M I'm sorry about that. This jacket has been very _____ and, unfortunately, we're _____ right now.

LC

PART 3

1. What problem does the woman mention?

   (A) Her schedule is very busy.
   (B) A fee has increased.
   (C) A fitness center is closing.
   (D) A building is under construction.

2. What does the man say about the swimming pool?

   (A) It will not be open next month.
   (B) It has swim instructors available.
   (C) Its hours were recently extended.
   (D) It is not used a lot in the morning.

3. How can the woman obtain a discount?

   (A) By presenting a coupon
   (B) By providing a friend's name
   (C) By going to a facility on weekdays only
   (D) By paying for several months in advance

4. What did the woman recently do?

   (A) Enroll in a class
   (B) Start work at a hospital
   (C) Graduate from university
   (D) Send a package

5. Why is the woman concerned?

   (A) She is relocating.
   (B) She starts training soon.
   (C) She has to take final exams.
   (D) She might need a certificate.

6. What does the man suggest the woman do?

   (A) Send a written request
   (B) Talk to a manager
   (C) Pick up a document
   (D) Update a résumé

7. What are the speakers planning to advertise?

   (A) Evening classes
   (B) Job opportunities
   (C) An online store
   (D) A printing demonstration

8. According to the man, what was the problem with last year's pamphlets?

   (A) They were not ready on time.
   (B) They were the wrong size.
   (C) The information was too specific.
   (D) The contact number was missing.

9. What does the man say he will send the woman?

   (A) Free product samples
   (B) A list of participants
   (C) A draft of a document
   (D) A revised schedule

10. What is the company's plan?

    (A) To reduce transportation costs
    (B) To appoint a new board president
    (C) To increase energy efficiency
    (D) To open a branch overseas

11. What is the woman considering?

    (A) Sending an e-mail response
    (B) Conducting a survey
    (C) Applying to relocate
    (D) Joining a committee

12. Why is the man unable to attend the meeting?

    (A) He is giving a presentation.
    (B) He is picking up a colleague.
    (C) He is writing an article.
    (D) He is taking inventory.

13. What is the problem with the current contractor?

(A) Their service is too slow.
(B) Their products are damaged.
(C) Their machines are broken.
(D) Their costs are too high.

14. What does the woman say about Small Plains Contracting?

(A) It is located nearby.
(B) It has a good reputation.
(C) It recently expanded its staff.
(D) It has declined a project.

15. What will Luca most likely do next?

(A) Compile a list
(B) Visit a construction site
(C) Call a pipe company
(D) Review an estimate

---

16. What does the man say he did last month?

(A) He moved to a new town.
(B) He started a new job.
(C) He took a science class.
(D) He visited a park.

17. What task does the woman ask the man to help with?

(A) Leading hikes
(B) Counting birds
(C) Planting trees
(D) Cleaning parks

18. What is the man concerned about?

(A) His busy schedule
(B) His lack of experience
(C) The distance to a work site
(D) The cost to participate

19. According to the woman, what did the company recently do?

(A) Announce a merger
(B) Hire an editor
(C) Launch a Web site
(D) Host a workshop

20. What problem does the man mention?

(A) Content is not displayed correctly.
(B) A deadline was missed.
(C) Sales are lower than expected.
(D) Equipment is outdated.

21. What does the woman say is a growing trend?

(A) Listening to audiobooks
(B) Holding training sessions online
(C) Signing contracts electronically
(D) Reading news on mobile devices

---

22. What problem are the speakers discussing?

(A) A document has not been received.
(B) A client's flight has not arrived.
(C) A colleague has not returned a phone call.
(D) A meeting space has not been reserved.

23. What does the man say he did this morning?

(A) Listened to his voice mail
(B) Checked an online tracking system
(C) Talked to a customer service representative
(D) Prepared a contract

24. Why must the meeting take place tomorrow?

(A) It is the last day of the quarter.
(B) The office is closing early today.
(C) An executive is leaving on a trip.
(D) A press release is scheduled to be distributed.

LC

PART 3

요청·제안 / 다음에 할 일 문제

① 요청·제안 문제

> **출제 포인트** 화자가 요청하거나 제안하는 것이 무엇인지 묻는 질문은 두 번째, 세 번째 문제로 출제되는 경우가 많다. 단서는 주로 대화 중·후반에 등장한다.

요청 사항을 묻는 질문
What does the man **request**?
What does the woman **ask** the man **to do**?

제안 사항을 묻는 질문
What does the man **suggest**?
What does the woman **offer to do**?

750_P3_11 🎧
정답과 해설 p.065

■ **공략 포인트** | 요청/제안의 표현이 등장하면 집중해서 청취한다.

W Jeff, I'm wondering who are these plastic desk covers for?

M They're for us—remember? The contractor starts work on upgrading our office area next Tuesday. There'll be a lot of dust, so…

W Ah, I didn't realize it's starting so soon. Will we need to work elsewhere then?

M We'll stay here. Here's a **timeline** showing which areas the crews will work in each day. Take a look.

W Oh, good. **I can post this on our staff bulletin board**. → 제안의 표현(I can) 등장

문제 **What** does the woman **offer to do**?
(A) Adjust her work hours
(B) Order office supplies
(C) Post a schedule
(D) Expand a training program

단서 일정표를 게시판에 붙이겠다

정답 **(C) Post a schedule**

┌─ 정답으로 이어지는 단서 표현 ─

요청이나 제안할 때 자주 쓰이는 표현은 암기해 두도록 한다.

요청: Can/Could you, Please, I'd like you to, Would you mind, I was wondering if 등
Could you tell me what you think of the video? 그 동영상에 대해 어떻게 생각하는지 말해줄래요?

제안: You could, You might want to, Why don't you, I recommend, I can, Let me 등
You might want to join our membership program. 저희 멤버십 프로그램에 가입하시는 게 좋을 것 같아요.
Let me send you the instructions via e-mail. 설명서를 이메일로 보내드릴게요.

1. What does the woman ask the man to do?
(A) Promote a line of cookware
(B) Participate in some interviews
(C) Submit a magazine article
(D) Give a demonstration

W Mr. Young? I read about your _____ in *Good Food Magazine*, and I was wondering if you'd be interested in _____ in my class.

M I'm definitely interested, but now's not a great time. I'm _____ of my _____, so things have been incredibly busy.

2. What does the man recommend that the woman do?
(A) Come back the following day
(B) Place an order in advance
(C) Park in a nearby garage
(D) Register for a membership card

M Before I start scanning your items, did you _____ _____ for me to put your groceries in?

W Oh, no—I didn't. Was I supposed to _____ _____?

M It is our store policy, but you could _____ one of our _____. You'd receive a reusable bag for free _____, and it only takes _____.

3. What is the man asking the woman to do?
(A) Take charge of a new project
(B) Recruit a consultant
(C) Attend a management meeting
(D) Report on a sales promotion

M Andrea, can I talk to you about a _____ _____? Management would like to see _____ between the sales department and the marketing department. We'd like you to _____.

W That _____, Mark. But, what exactly would this _____?

4. What does the man offer to do?
(A) Cancel an order
(B) Hire a technician
(C) Provide a refund
(D) Arrange a delivery

W I bought a chair from your store, and I was _____ _____ it, but I don't think I have all of the parts I need.

M Oh, I'm sorry to hear that. Do you know _____ _____?

W Well, I have all the long bolts for the legs but none of the other bolts for the seat.

M OK, I have _____ here at the store, and I can have the _____ at your house this afternoon.

② 다음에 할 일 문제

> **출제 포인트**　화자의 할 일이나 미래에 일어날 일을 묻는 질문도 두 번째, 세 번째 문제로 자주 출제되며, 요청/제안 문제와 함께 나오는 경우가 많다. 미래를 나타내는 다양한 시제뿐만 아니라 화자의 의지/결심이 드러나는 표현이나 제안·청유의 표현에도 주목해야 한다.

할 일을 묻는 질문

What will the woman **do next**?
What does the man say he **will do**?

일어날 일을 묻는 질문

What will happen ~?
What will take place ~?

750_P3_13

정답과 해설 p.066

■ **공략 포인트** | 미래를 나타내는 시제와 의지/결심이 드러나는 표현에 주목한다.

M　Hi, Kathy. We talked about going to a movie tonight. Do you still want to go?

W　Oh no, I forgot. I'm sorry, I can't make it to the movies tonight. My cousin Susan is flying in from New York, and we're planning to go out to dinner at Piazza. It's a new restaurant near my house. Why don't you come with us?

M　Dinner sounds great! And I'd love to meet your cousin. **Have you already made a reservation**?

W　You know, **I should do that right now**. It's not an expensive restaurant, but it's very popular.
　　→ 의지/결심이 드러나는 표현(I should) 등장

문제 **What will** Kathy **do next**?
　　(A) Visit Susan
　　(B) Buy some tickets
　　(C) Make a reservation
　　(D) Get some money

단서 당장 (예약을) 해야겠다

정답 **(C) Make a reservation**

정답으로 이어지는 단서 표현

미래를 나타내는 다양한 시제를 알아두고, 해당 표현이 나오면 집중해서 단서를 포착한다.

미래/계획: Will, be going to, be planning to
I'll ask Danna if we can meet next Thursday.　다음주 목요일에 만날 수 있는지 다나에게 물어볼게요.
I'm going to call my supervisor and ask about that.　제 상사에게 전화해서 여쭤볼게요.

예정된 가까운 미래: 단순 현재형, be+ing
I have an appointment with a client **this afternoon**.　오늘 오후에 고객과 약속이 있어요.
I'm meeting with Dr. Ray **tomorrow** to discuss the results of the product testing.
제품 시험 결과를 논의하기 위해 내일 레이 박사와 만날 예정이에요.

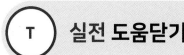
1. What will take place next Wednesday?
(A) A dinner with a client
(B) A farewell party for a coworker
(C) A reception for new employees
(D) A lunch with some friends

M Julie, when are you coming back from London?

W Well, if my meetings go really well, I could be _____ _____, but I may _____ Friday. Why do you ask?

M Stephanie announced that she's _____ Boston _____. So I'm _____ at Vega's Restaurant next Wednesday, and I was hoping you'd be able to come.

2. What does the man say he will do this afternoon?
(A) Place an order
(B) Meet with a supervisor
(C) Update a database
(D) Call a customer

W Amit, a new _____ came in, so I have to put price tags on them, but I don't think we have any more.

M I'm _____ this afternoon so I'll _____ to the list. They should arrive by tomorrow.

3. What will happen in March?
(A) A product will be discounted.
(B) A building will be closed for renovations.
(C) A marketing campaign will launch.
(D) A training course for students will take place.

W Langfield Museum of Art. This is Karima speaking. How can I help you?

M Hi, I heard that the museum will be _____ _____ in March. Will it still be _____ _____?

W The museum _____ for the _____, but the outdoor garden will still be open.

4. What will the speakers most likely do next?
(A) Review a purchase order
(B) Go to a different part of the store
(C) Discuss hiring professional painters
(D) Try out a product

W Excuse me, I'm planning to paint the walls of my kitchen white, but there are so many _____ that I'm not sure which one to buy.

M Well, I'd suggest getting a high gloss paint, since it's going to be in your kitchen and it's _____ _____.

W Great—thanks! I'll need two cans of that, then. Also, can you show me _____?

M Sure—those are in aisle ten. Let me _____.

LC

PART 3

1. What does the man want to know?

   (A) An arrival time
   (B) A boarding location
   (C) An expiration date
   (D) A round-trip price

2. What does the woman recommend that the man do?

   (A) Call an information line
   (B) Speak with a conductor
   (C) Save a ticket receipt
   (D) Check a display monitor

3. What will the man probably do next?

   (A) Buy something to drink
   (B) Use a ticket machine
   (C) Send a text message
   (D) Pick up a schedule

4. Where do the speakers most likely work?

   (A) At a medical-supply store
   (B) At a research institute
   (C) At a security firm
   (D) At a community hospital

5. What will the man ask the security office to give the woman?

   (A) A storage-room key
   (B) A parking permit
   (C) A tour of the building
   (D) A list of safety procedures

6. What does the woman say she will do in the afternoon?

   (A) Make copies of a report
   (B) Conduct an experiment
   (C) Obtain an identification card
   (D) Pick up some work supplies

7. What does the woman mention about the Selwin 6?

   (A) It is easy to use.
   (B) It is an earlier model.
   (C) It is well designed.
   (D) It is very popular.

8. What does the man request?

   (A) A warranty
   (B) A reimbursement
   (C) A replacement part
   (D) An instruction manual

9. What does the woman offer to do?

   (A) Reset a password
   (B) Explain a policy
   (C) Check part of an order
   (D) Send a link to a Web site

10. What product are the speakers discussing?

    (A) A photo printer
    (B) A set of headphones
    (C) Some editing software
    (D) Some ink cartridges

11. What does the man offer to do?

    (A) Process an exchange
    (B) Recommend another store
    (C) Check a supply room
    (D) Call when a shipment arrives

12. What does Irina give the man?

    (A) A business card
    (B) A store coupon
    (C) A shipping address
    (D) Some payment information

13. What are the speakers working on?

  (A) Training a colleague
  (B) Relocating an office
  (C) Planning a budget
  (D) Creating a catalog

14. What are the women waiting for?

  (A) A project proposal
  (B) Some price information
  (C) An official signature
  (D) Some sample products

15. What does the man say he will do?

  (A) Call a department manager
  (B) Hire an assistant
  (C) Make an announcement
  (D) Update a calendar

16. What does the man bring to the woman's attention?

  (A) A product defect
  (B) A safety concern
  (C) Invoice errors
  (D) Customer complaints

17. What change is going to take place next month?

  (A) New equipment will be installed.
  (B) A different supplier will be used.
  (C) Store hours will be extended.
  (D) A new accountant will be hired.

18. What does the man suggest?

  (A) Moving a product display
  (B) Making a staff person available
  (C) Posting a sign at the entrance
  (D) Providing home delivery

19. According to the woman, why are the solar panels popular?

  (A) They are small.
  (B) They are easy to install.
  (C) They are attractive.
  (D) They are inexpensive.

20. What will take place in September?

  (A) A factory tour
  (B) An employee training
  (C) A trade show
  (D) A company merger

21. What will the man most likely do next?

  (A) Make a phone call
  (B) Read a report
  (C) Review a procedure
  (D) Send a payment

22. Where does the man work?

  (A) At a shipping company
  (B) At a travel agency
  (C) At an airline
  (D) At a government agency

23. What does the woman's company make?

  (A) Cargo airplanes
  (B) Ocean ships
  (C) Packaging materials
  (D) Construction machinery

24. What will the speakers probably do next?

  (A) Deliver a machine
  (B) Board an airplane
  (C) Discuss a business contract
  (D) Inspect a building project

LC

PART 3

① 의도 파악 문제

> **출제 포인트** 화자의 의도를 묻는 문제는 매회 2문항씩 출제된다. 앞뒤 문맥을 파악하는 것이 중요하므로 주요 내용은 메모하며 듣고, 제시문 앞뒤 문장이나 상대 화자의 반응에서 단서를 잡아야 한다.

의미/암시하는 바를 묻는 질문
What does the man **mean[imply]** when he says, "~"?

목적을 묻는 질문
Why does the woman **say,** "~"?

750_P3_16
정답과 해설 p.072

■ **공략 포인트** | 제시문 앞뒤 문장이나 상대 화자의 반응에서 단서를 포착한다.

M OK, Ms. Torres, I have your price estimate. To have the whole exterior of your house painted, including the fence, will cost you five thousand dollars.

W **That's quite a bit more than we expected. And actually Colgate Painting said they would do it for four thousand dollars**…
→ 예상보다 큰 금액이라며 타사의 견적가 언급: 협상 시도

M Well, the cost of paint and supplies is included in the price I quoted you, **so we really offer a very good deal.**
→ 저렴하게 해주는 것이라고 강조: 방어

문제 **Why** does the woman **say,** "And actually Colgate Painting said they would do it for four thousand dollars"?
(A) To clarify a request
(B) To negotiate a price
(C) To offer some help
(D) To recommend a service

단서 예상보다 높은 견적가

정답 **(B) To negotiate a price**

┌─ 정답으로 이어지는 단서 표현 ─

제시문 앞에 나온 내용을 놓쳤다면 바로 뒤에 오는 문장이나 상대 화자의 반응에 집중한다.

바로 뒤에 오는 문장: 단서가 될 말을 덧붙이는 경우가 있다.
W Did you contact Norwood? 노우드에 연락했어요?
M **The office closed at four o'clock.** I'll check again tomorrow. 사무실이 4시에 닫아요. 내일 다시 확인할게요.
→ 다시 확인하겠다는 말로 미루어 보아 연락하지 못했음을 알 수 있다.

상대 화자의 반응: 제시문을 어떻게 받아들였는지가 드러난다.
M **Some of us are going to see a movie tonight.** 우리 중 몇 명이서 오늘 밤에 영화를 보러 갈 예정이야.
W That sounds great, but I can't come with you. 재미있을 거 같은데, 나는 같이 갈 수 없어.
→ 제시문을 '초대'로 받아들여 거절했음을 알 수 있다.

1. What does the man mean when he says, "I've been meaning to contact them"?
(A) He is looking forward to discussing a project.
(B) He needs to clarify a statement.
(C) He is aware he needs to do something.
(D) He has forgotten to contact a client.

> W Hi, Girolamo. I just got an e-mail from THY Incorporated. They're _____ we can begin _____. They want a _____.
>
> M I've been meaning to contact them, but I'm _____ from the soil analysis. There's a patch of ground that might be too _____ to build on. Our _____ are doing a few more tests.

2. What does the man imply when he says, "A lot of people have been asking about it"?
(A) Staff are confused about a procedure.
(B) People have heard that a workshop is interesting.
(C) Staff are waiting for a new assignment.
(D) A vacation calendar has not been posted yet.

> M Hi, Gabriella. I wanted to talk to you about using the new _____… A lot of people have been asking about it.
>
> W Yes, well, I've been very busy. But I am _____ for early next week. That should make it quite _____ _____.
>
> M OK.

3. Why does the woman say, "I have three payroll checks left to process"?
(A) To complain about some software
(B) To reject an invitation
(C) To ask for a volunteer
(D) To reassure a colleague

> M Hi, Elaine. It's almost twelve-thirty. I'm _____ _____ with Sam if you'd like to _____.
>
> W I have three payroll checks left to process.
>
> M Oh, OK. I'll see you at the _____ _____.

4. What does the man mean when he says, "Most of the content will be rather technical"?
(A) He wants to revise the content of a workshop.
(B) He is looking forward to attending a workshop.
(C) He thinks presenting a workshop will be challenging.
(D) He thinks a workshop may not benefit all the staff.

> W Fred, the Regional Library Association is _____ _____ in town called Managing Digital Content. It looks useful. I think our _____ _____ should attend, don't you?
>
> M Oh, I've already inquired about that workshop. Uh… Most of the content will be rather technical.
>
> W I see. OK. Then I should have only the _____?
>
> M That sounds like a _____.

LC

PART 3

② 시각 정보 연계 문제

> **출제 포인트** 주어진 시각 정보와 대화 내용을 연계하여 풀어야 하는 문제가 매회 3문항 출제된다. 시각 정보에서 보기와 상응하는 부분, 혹은 질문의 일부가 대화 내 키워드로 등장할 가능성이 높다.

시각 정보 연계: 세부 사항을 묻는 질문
Look at the **graphic**. What/Which/Where ~?

750_P3_18 🎧
정답과 해설 p.074

■ **공략 포인트** | 시각 정보에서 보기와 상응하는 부분을 염두에 두고 청취한다.

M Hi. I'm almost done with the deliveries for today, but I'm having trouble with the one for **Corton Industries. I'm in front of the office building, but it's a busy street**, and I don't see a place to park while I unload.

→ 문제의 보기와 상응하는 정보(고객사) 중 Corton Industries가 키워드로 등장

W Sorry, Corton Industries is a first-time customer, so I should have written the information about parking on the delivery schedule. They have a parking area behind the building.

M OK, I'll go there now.

Today's Deliveries	
Tortalli Bakery	
Customer	**Address**
Martin's Supermarket	1700 Penn St.
Corton Industries	270 Dunbar St.
Fast Shop Convenience Store	43 Forbes St.

문제 Look at the graphic. **What street** is the man on?
(A) Tortalli　　　(B) Penn
(C) Dunbar　　　(D) Forbes

단서 코튼 인터스트리스 건물 앞

정답 **(C) Dunbar**

┌─ 정답으로 이어지는 단서 표현 ─

보기에 상응하는 정보나 질문의 일부가 키워드로 등장하지 않는 경우, 비교급 및 최상급 표현에 귀를 기울인다. 지도나 평면도에서는 위치 관련 표현에 주목한다.

We'd like to limit our cost to **no more than** $400. → 400달러 이하에 해당하는 금액 선택
400달러 이하로 비용을 제한하고 싶습니다.

We've booked tickets for **the second most popular** play instead. → 2위에 해당하는 연극 선택
대신 두 번째로 인기 있는 연극을 예매했어요.

I moved to the office right **next to** the kitchen. → 탕비실 바로 옆 사무실 번호 선택
탕비실 바로 옆에 있는 사무실로 옮겼어요.

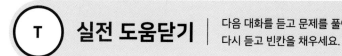

Office Directory

1st FL: HLT Company
2nd FL: Noble Incorporated
3rd FL: Romano Construction
4th FL: Grayton and Sons

1. Look at the graphic. Where is the man currently working?
   (A) On the first floor
   (B) On the second floor
   (C) On the third floor
   (D) On the fourth floor

Prezko
$80

Lunda
$100

Burkel
$150

Stranzoff
$200

2. Look at the graphic. Which model of frames will the man buy?
   (A) Prezko   (B) Lunda
   (C) Burkel   (D) Stranzoff

Options

Seafood platter	$900
Beef platter	$750
Chicken platter	$600
Vegetarian platter	$450

3. Look at the graphic. What option will the man most likely select?
   (A) Seafood platter
   (B) Beef platter
   (C) Chicken platter
   (D) Vegetarian platter

W Hi, Barry. I'm just checking in. How's everything going up here? Are you _____ the Romano Construction offices yet?

M No, it's _____. I vacuumed the carpet, but there are a lot of stains. So I _____ it. But then I _____ and get the steam-cleaning machine and bring it up here.

W Well, before you start shampooing, could you _____? I need some help moving a big table in _____.

W Based on the eye exam I just conducted, your _____ since last time, Mr. Mukherjee. So you can keep using the glasses you have now.

M Great. But... I don't like my old frames anymore, so I was planning to _____.

W OK. You can see our _____ in this catalog.

M Hmm... I like the ones with the _____. _____ isn't too much to spend. I'll get those.

M Hi, I'm calling to _____ about having an event catered at my company.

W Sure. I'll need to know _____ you're expecting and _____ is.

M It's a retirement party for one of our directors. There'll be about thirty people, and we're on a budget of _____.

W We do have a package that _____. On our Web site, if you click on the Options tab, you can see the various menus there.

1. Who most likely is the woman?

(A) A journalist
(B) An advertiser
(C) A publisher
(D) An accountant

2. What does the woman mean when she says, "I just have a few questions"?

(A) She is uncertain about an assignment.
(B) She does not need much time.
(C) She cannot explain a delay.
(D) She thinks some instructions are clear.

3. What does the man suggest the woman do?

(A) Attend a convention
(B) Sign a form
(C) Send another e-mail
(D) Call again later

4. Why does the woman say, "this counter is for domestic services only"?

(A) To criticize a rule
(B) To express confusion
(C) To reject a request
(D) To verify a fact

5. What does the customer decide to do?

(A) Cancel a shipment
(B) Exchange a product
(C) Buy special packaging
(D) Pay for faster delivery

6. What will the customer probably pay an extra fee for?

(A) Damage insurance
(B) Overnight shipping
(C) Delivery confirmation
(D) Oversized parcels

7. What was the woman doing in Vancouver?

(A) Interviewing job candidates
(B) Meeting new clients
(C) Taking a vacation
(D) Teaching a class

8. What does the woman imply when she says, "Is this César Villa's résumé"?

(A) She is surprised to see a document.
(B) She is recommending a candidate.
(C) She is worried about security.
(D) She is unable to read some writing.

9. How does the woman know César Villa?

(A) They used to be neighbors.
(B) They went to the same university.
(C) They organized a conference together.
(D) They worked at the same firm.

10. What has been damaged?

(A) Some furniture
(B) Some appliances
(C) Some flooring
(D) Some windows

11. Why does the woman say, "I have some important clients coming here next week"?

(A) To express concern about a time frame
(B) To refuse an invitation
(C) To suggest choosing a different location
(D) To propose postponing an event

12. What does the woman ask the man for?

(A) A receipt
(B) A business card
(C) A cost estimate
(D) A catalog

Online Registration Form

Name:	Yuri Solokov
Student ID:	867907
Course Number:	145
Start Date:	September 13
E-mail Address:	ys012@pae.net

Nutrition Information

Serving Size: 200 grams

Calories: **150**

	Amount Per Serving
Fat	5 grams
Protein	11 grams
Sugar	32 grams
Sodium	40 milligrams

13. Look at the graphic. According to the woman, what information is incorrect?

(A) The student ID
(B) The course number
(C) The start date
(D) The e-mail address

14. What does the man ask for more information about?

(A) Summer internships
(B) Student loans
(C) Tutoring services
(D) Volunteer opportunities

15. What will the woman do next?

(A) Find a brochure
(B) Print a bill
(C) E-mail an application
(D) Transfer a call

16. Why is the man looking for a certain product?

(A) He wants to eat healthy foods.
(B) He is allergic to a particular ingredient.
(C) He has a coupon for a discount.
(D) He has a favorite brand.

17. Look at the graphic. Which of the ingredients does the man express concern about?

(A) Fat
(B) Protein
(C) Sugar
(D) Sodium

18. What does the woman suggest that the man do?

(A) Try a free sample
(B) Go to a larger branch
(C) Speak with his doctor
(D) Purchase a different item

LC

PART 3

COMMERCIAL PROPERTIES FOR RENT

Address	Property Feature
44 South Street	Parking area
20 Main Street	Storage space
11 Congress Avenue	Price
35 Center Street	Size

19. What type of business does Ms. Wu want to open?

(A) A toy store
(B) An accounting firm
(C) A sandwich shop
(D) A law office

20. Look at the graphic. Which property will be shown to Ms. Wu?

(A) 44 South Street
(B) 20 Main Street
(C) 11 Congress Avenue
(D) 35 Center Street

21. What will the man most likely do next?

(A) Measure a room
(B) Contact a client
(C) Provide driving directions
(D) Supply a cost estimate

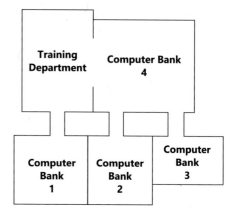

22. What problem does the man mention?

(A) A shipment was delivered to the wrong address.
(B) Some computers are not connected to a network.
(C) Some workers did not receive the correct training.
(D) A computer technician is not available.

23. What does the woman ask for?

(A) Machine instructions
(B) A new computer
(C) Security details
(D) A factory tour

24. Look at the graphic. Where will the woman most likely go?

(A) To Computer Bank 1
(B) To Computer Bank 2
(C) To Computer Bank 3
(D) To Computer Bank 4

32. According to the man, what will happen on Thursday?

(A) A client will visit.
(B) An office will reopen.
(C) A staff member will be interviewed.
(D) A magazine will be published.

33. What does the woman request?

(A) Permission to bring a colleague
(B) Directions to a building
(C) A tour of a facility
(D) A product sample

34. What does the man say he will prepare?

(A) Some forms
(B) Some refreshments
(C) Some badges
(D) Some photographs

35. What problem is the woman calling about?

(A) A pipe is leaking.
(B) A door will not open.
(C) A washing machine is not functioning properly.
(D) A heating unit is broken.

36. Who most likely is the man?

(A) A plumber
(B) A safety inspector
(C) A property manager
(D) A real estate agent

37. What does the man say he will do?

(A) Consult a manual
(B) Contact a repair service
(C) Fill out some paperwork
(D) Find a replacement part

38. Why is the man going to Madrid?

(A) To report on an event
(B) To visit relatives
(C) To buy some artwork
(D) To study at a university

39. What does the man say he wants to do before he travels?

(A) Register for a course
(B) Book a hotel
(C) Research some artists
(D) Purchase a guidebook

40. What does the woman offer to do?

(A) Check her calendar
(B) Find some contact information
(C) Make a telephone call
(D) Consult a price list

41. What event are the speakers discussing?

(A) A press conference
(B) A health fair
(C) A celebration
(D) A workshop

42. What does the woman imply when she says, "Thirty people plan to attend"?

(A) A caterer should be contacted.
(B) A guest list should be updated.
(C) A time frame is too short.
(D) A room is not big enough.

43. What does the woman say she will do this afternoon?

(A) Visit a hotel
(B) Review a budget
(C) Prepare a presentation
(D) Pick up some invitations

LC

PART 3

44. What did the woman like about the event?

    (A) The decorations

    (B) The guest speaker

    (C) The menu options

    (D) The entertainment

45. What does the man ask the woman to do?

    (A) Settle a bill

    (B) Give feedback

    (C) Return some items

    (D) Refer a client

46. What does the man say he will do?

    (A) Check his availability

    (B) Print out an invoice

    (C) Try a new recipe

    (D) Contact his supervisor

47. What are the speakers discussing?

    (A) When to increase warehouse staffing

    (B) Where to open additional stores

    (C) How to reduce transportation costs

    (D) Who to promote to area supervisor

48. What is the man concerned about?

    (A) Finding a reliable supplier

    (B) Having enough storage space

    (C) Delaying a building project

    (D) Securing a bank loan

49. What will Yan most likely do by Friday?

    (A) Organize a training workshop

    (B) Attend a fashion show

    (C) Inspect a warehouse

    (D) Submit a report

50. What position has recently been filled?

    (A) Logistics coordinator

    (B) Customer service representative

    (C) Maintenance technician

    (D) Marketing specialist

51. Where do the speakers most likely work?

    (A) At a travel agency

    (B) At a banquet hall

    (C) At a laundry service

    (D) At a textile factory

52. Why does the woman say, "Today's Thursday"?

    (A) To turn down a request

    (B) To correct a mistake

    (C) To express appreciation

    (D) To propose a deadline

53. What are the speakers discussing?

    (A) A hiring decision

    (B) A budget request

    (C) Some computer software

    (D) Some sales tactics

54. What are some staff now allowed to do?

    (A) Decorate their offices

    (B) Attend a conference

    (C) Work from home

    (D) Wear casual clothes

55. What will the woman do this afternoon?

    (A) Conduct some research

    (B) Meet with a client

    (C) Repair some equipment

    (D) Update a calendar

56. Why is the woman calling?

(A) To discuss a research project
(B) To inquire about a product order
(C) To ask about an employee benefit
(D) To confirm a meeting time

57. What information does the man ask for?

(A) An identification number
(B) An e-mail address
(C) An office location
(D) A telephone number

58. What does the man say the woman needs?

(A) Management approval
(B) Advanced computer skills
(C) A signed application form
(D) An updated agenda

59. What is the conversation mainly about?

(A) Joining a committee
(B) Preparing for a client visit
(C) Attending an event
(D) Changing a safety procedure

60. What does the woman say about the man?

(A) He has good presentation skills.
(B) He knows the production process well.
(C) He has met most of the clients before.
(D) He has worked at the company for a long time.

61. What will the man give the woman?

(A) Credit card receipts
(B) Speaker biographies
(C) Product specifications
(D) Travel expense estimates

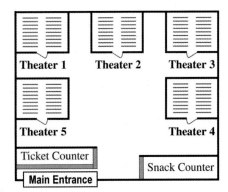

62. What does the man ask the woman about?

(A) Free parking
(B) Seating options
(C) A student discount
(D) A payment method

63. Why does the man decline an offer?

(A) He rarely goes to the theater.
(B) He is meeting a friend.
(C) He buys tickets online.
(D) He just ate a meal.

64. Look at the graphic. Where will the man go next?

(A) To Theater 1
(B) To Theater 2
(C) To Theater 3
(D) To Theater 4

Mon.	3:30–4:30 Meeting w/ Marketing Team
Tues.	11:00–12:00 Meeting w/ Media Team
Wed.	12:00–1:30 Lunch w/ Carol Smith
Thurs.	9:00–10:00 Conference call w/ Balmont Bank 4:00 Doctor's appointment

Collection Location	
Asian Art	North Wing
African Art	East Wing
Latin American Art	South Wing
European Art	West Wing

65. What industry do the speakers most likely work in?

(A) Finance
(B) Clothing
(C) Sports
(D) Film

66. What does the board of directors want to hear about?

(A) The details of a media campaign
(B) The progress of an investment
(C) The plans to increase a budget
(D) The timeline for a project

67. Look at the graphic. On which day will the conference call take place?

(A) Monday
(B) Tuesday
(C) Wednesday
(D) Thursday

68. How did the woman learn about the museum?

(A) From a business client
(B) From a hotel employee
(C) From a television commercial
(D) From a travel magazine

69. Look at the graphic. Which wing will the woman's tour start in?

(A) The North Wing
(B) The East Wing
(C) The South Wing
(D) The West Wing

70. What does the man suggest the woman do later?

(A) Visit a gift shop
(B) Give a donation
(C) Attend an event
(D) Write a review

■ 회의 / 일정

participant 참석자

agenda 안건

top priority 최우선 사항[과제]

sales meeting 영업 회의

videoconferencing 화상 회의

conference call 전화 회의

conference organizer 회의 기획자

handout 유인물, 인쇄물

submit a proposal 제안서를 제출하다

last-minute change 막판 변경

ahead of / behind schedule 일정보다 빠른 / 늦은

a change in policy 정책 변경

come up with (아이디어 등을) 내놓다, 고안하다

interoffice (조직 내에서) 부서간의, 사내의

reschedule 일정을 조정하다

adjust the work schedule 업무 시간을 조정하다

attend the meeting 회의에 참석하다

meet the deadline 마감일을 맞추다

move up the deadline 마감일을 당기다

push back the deadline 마감일을 미루다

expedite the process 과정을 신속하게 처리하다

scheduled 예정된

set up an appointment 약속을 잡다

postpone 미루다, 연기하다

available (만날 수 있는) 시간이 되는

board of directors 이사회

progress report 경과 보고서

■ 출장 / 출근

be out of town (출장 등으로) 도시를 떠나 있다

on a business trip 출장 중인

on assignment 업무 차

report to work 출근하다

security badge 보안 카드

swipe (신용카드 등을) 판독기에 통과시키다

call in sick 아파서 결근하겠다고 전화하다

take a day off 월차 내다, 하루 휴가를 내다

medical leave 병가 (=sick leave)

maternity leave 출산 휴가, 육아 휴직

reimbursement 사용 경비 정산·환급

paid / unpaid leave 유급 / 무급 휴가

■ 인사 / 평가

performance 업무 실적

advancement 승진

benefit (급여 이외의) 혜택, 수당

nomination 지명, 추천

transfer 인사이동하다

understaffed 인원 부족의, 손이 모자라는

personnel department 인사부

performance evaluation / appraisal / review 업무 평가, 인사 고과

hands-on 실제로 참가하는, 실무의

lay off 정리해고하다

get a promotion 승진하다

have a lot of connections 인맥이 넓다

■ 계약

contract 계약(서)

contractor 도급업자[업체], 건축[시공]업체

estimate 견적

expense report 지출 보고서, 경비 내역서

specifications 세부 내역서, 사양

statement 명세서, (사업) 보고서, 계산서

association 협회

manufacture 제조하다

budget 예산

confidentiality 기밀성, 비밀성

reimburse 상환하다, 변제하다

permit 허가하다; 허가서

■ 마케팅

public relations 홍보

findings 조사 결과, 연구 결과

survey results 설문조사 결과

advertising agency 광고 대행사

draft 밑그림, 초안

revision 수정, 개정

expand 확대하다

strategy 전략

demonstration 실물 설명

make revisions 수정하다, 개정하다

marketing strategy 마케팅 전략

place an advertisement 광고를 하다

■ 사무기기 / 시설

office supplies 사무용품

supplier 납품업체

run out of ~이 떨어지다

stockroom 비품 저장실

copy machine 복사기 (=photocopier)

computer components 컴퓨터 부품

installation 설치

malfunctioning 고장 난, 오작동하는

out of service 운행이 중단된

maintenance 유지, 정비

crew 작업자들

floor plan 평면도

■ 사내 행사

upcoming 다가오는, 곧 있을

company retreat 회사 야유회

retirement party 퇴직 송별회

corporate event 기업 행사

awards banquet 시상식 연회

turnout 참가자 수

enroll 등록하다

new employee orientation 신입 직원 오리엔테이션

recruitment fair 채용 박람회

shareholders' meeting 주주총회

company newsletter 사보

attend a training session 교육 과정에 참석하다

■ 교통

driveway 진입로, (사설) 차도

compartment 구획, 칸막이

transportation 운송, 교통편

photo identification 사진이 부착된 신분증

luggage 수하물

return flight 돌아오는 비행편, 귀국 항공편

directions 길 안내

get to ~에 도착하다 (= reach)

congestion 교통 혼잡

make it 제시간에 도착하다, 장소에 나타나다

be scheduled to do ~하기로 예정되다

run late (도착 등이) 늦다

■ 여가

amenities 오락시설, 편의시설

accommodation 숙박 시설

single room 1인실

one-way / round trip 편도 / 왕복 여행

time slot 시간대

exhibition 전시회

performance 공연, 연주

ticket agent 발권 담당 직원

annual fee 연회비

fill out a form 서식을 작성하다, 기입하다

register for ~에 등록하다

hold an event 행사를 열다, 개최하다

■ 쇼핑

representative 담당 직원, 대표

sales associate 영업 사원

flyer 전단, 광고지

instruction manual 사용 설명서

user-friendly 사용하기 쉬운

appliance (가정용) 기구, 전기 제품

subscription 가입, 구독

gift certificate 상품권

store credit 상점 포인트, 적립금

release 출시하다

have ~ in stock ~의 재고가 있다, 물품을 보유하고 있다

total comes to 합이 ~이 되다

■ 식당

vegetarian 채식주의자를 위한

nutritional 영양의

cuisine 요리

culinary 요리의, 음식의

ingredient 요리 재료

seasoning 양념, 조미료

assorted 여러 가지의, 갖은

caterer 출장 연회업체

catering service 출장 연회 서비스

diner 식사하는 사람

gourmet 미식가; (음식이) 고급인

order a meal 음식을 주문하다

■ 부동산

real estate 부동산

property 부동산, 건물

deposit 보증금

renovation 개보수

spacious 널찍한

storage space 수납 공간

residential area 주거지역

relocate to ~로 옮기다

suburb 교외

fully furnished 가구가 모두 갖춰진

have a nice view 전망이 좋다

within walking distance 걸어갈 수 있는 거리 내에

■ 병원

diagnose 진단하다

prescription 처방전

eye exam 눈 검사

sneeze 재채기를 하다

bother 괴롭히다

remedy 치료법

medication 약

get a shot[an injection] 주사 맞다

get some vaccinations 예방 접종하다

take medicine 약을 복용하다

have a high fever 열이 높다

act up (병이) 재발하다

■ 은행

account number 계좌 번호

deposit 예금하다

withdraw 인출하다

deposit/withdrawal slip 입금/출금 전표

transfer 송금하다(remit)

set up a savings account 보통예금 계좌를 개설하다

apply for a loan 대출을 신청하다

endorse (수표에) 이서하다

transaction 거래, 처리

bank statement 은행 입출금 내역서

balance 잔고, 잔액

exchange rate 환율

■ 우체국 및 기타 장소

regular delivery 일반 배송

express mail service 속달 우편 서비스

overnight delivery 익일 배송

by courier 택배로

track (우편물을) 추적하다

pick up a package 소포를 찾아가다

exhibition 전시회

box[ticket] office 매표소

admission fee 입장료

hair salon 미용실

have the hair trimmed 머리를 다듬다

check out (책을) 대출하다, (호텔) 퇴실하다

짧은 담화

Part 4

화자 한 명의 담화를 듣고 이와 관련된 세 개의 문제를 푸는 유형으로, 전화 메시지, 회의 발췌, 안내 방송 등 다양한 담화문이 출제된다. 문제 유형은 다음과 같이 크게 두 가지로 나눌 수 있다.

- 전체 내용 관련 문제　주제/목적, 담화가 나오는 장소, 화자·청자의 직업/업종/근무지
- 세부 내용 관련 문제　화자의 요청/제안/추천 사항, 화자의 의도 파악, 화자·청자가 다음에 할 일, 앞으로 일어날 일, 이유/원인, 방법, 문제점, 세부 사항, 시각 정보 연계

■ ETS 예제 및 풀이 전략

1　담화를 듣기 전에 문제와 보기를 읽고, 키워드에 표시해 둔다.
　　Part 4에서는 화자에 관한 문제인지 청자에 관한 문제인지 정확히 파악해야 한다.

2　단서가 나올 부분을 노려 듣고, 듣는 동시에 답을 선택한다.

📋 문제지

71. What is the (purpose) of the (message)?
(A) To book a business trip
(B) To confirm attendance at a meeting
(C) To cancel a telephone conference
(D) To discuss an e-mail message

72. What did Mr. Patel's (assistant) tell Mr. Walsh?
(A) Mr. Patel's plans are uncertain.
(B) Mr. Patel will attend a meeting.
(C) Mr. Patel is on vacation.
(D) Mr. Patel's e-mail address has changed.

73. What does (Jack Walsh) say he (will do)?
(A) Visit Mr. Patel's office
(B) Inform the board of Mr. Patel's schedule
(C) Send an e-mail message to Mr. Patel
(D) Telephone Mr. Patel again

🔊 음원

Questions 71 through 73 refer to the following telephone message.

Mr. Patel, this is Jack Walsh from the Dublin office. **71** I'm calling to confirm your attendance at the board meeting here in July. The meeting is scheduled for July third. **72** Last week your assistant said you weren't certain if you could attend. Is this still true? If you won't be able to travel here, please let me know whether you could participate in a conference call meeting by phone. **73** I'll send you an e-mail message with possible meeting times for a conference call. I'll also send the meeting agenda in the e-mail. I hope to hear back from you soon.

※ 이후 문제만 읽어주며, 문제 사이에 8초가 주어진다.

---

71. 메시지의 목적: 이사회 참석 여부 확인
72. 파텔 씨의 비서가 한 말: 참석 여부 불확실
73. 잭 월시 씨가 할 일: 이메일 발송

정답 **(B) To confirm attendance at a meeting**
정답 **(A) Mr. Patel's plans are uncertain.**
정답 **(C) Send an e-mail message to Mr. Patel**

■ 담화 유형별 빈출 내용

담화 별로 자주 출제되는 내용을 알아두면, 단서를 노려 듣는 데 도움이 된다.

- **전화 메시지**   정보 전달, 문의, 업무 관련 요청, 예약 확인/변경 등
- **ARS 메시지**   업체/조직 소개, 운영/휴무 시간 안내, 내선 번호 안내 등
- **공지/회의**   고객 대상 안내/당부, 회사 정책 공지, 시스템 도입/변경 공지, 업무 관련 공지 등
- **설명/소개**   행사/견학/오리엔테이션 관련 안내, 회사/제품 소개, 인물과 그의 업적 소개 등
- **광고**   상품/서비스 광고, 개점 광고, 할인/구매 혜택 소개 등
- **방송**   프로그램 내용/인터뷰 소개, 지역/비즈니스 뉴스 보도, 날씨/교통 안내 등

■ 패러프레이징(Paraphrasing)

Part 4는 한 사람이 계속해서 말하기 때문에 상대적으로 긴 문장이 등장하기도 하며, 패러프레이징 방식이 복잡한 양상을 띠는 경우가 있다.

1 한 문장에 두 개가 등장하는 경우

W The new intern hasn't learned how to use the database software yet, so I'd like you to work with him tomorrow.

여 새 인턴이 아직 데이터베이스 소프트웨어 사용법을 배우지 않아서, 내일 당신이 함께 작업해 주었으면 해요.

Q What does the speaker say about the new intern?

A He is not familiar with a procedure.

질문 여자가 새 인턴에 대해 말한 것은?

정답 절차에 익숙하지 않다.

→ 배우지 않았다는 것을 'not familiar with'로, 데이터베이스 소프트웨어 사용법을 'procedure'로 표현

2 두 문장에 있는 단서를 조합해야 하는 경우

M As you all know, we were planning to start work on the camera advertisement this week. But the client called and said the camera won't be ready until the end of this month.

남 모두 아시다시피, 이번 주에 카메라 광고 작업에 착수할 계획이었습니다. 하지만 고객사에서 전화해서 말하길, 카메라가 이번 달 말에나 준비될 겁니다.

Q What is the speaker mainly talking about?

A A delay in the project

질문 화자가 주로 이야기 하는 것은?

정답 프로젝트 지연

→ 광고 작업을 'project'로, 문제가 생겨 이번 달 말이나 되어야 작업이 가능하다는 것을 'delay'로 표현

출제 포인트 발신자가 남기는 음성 메시지, 회사/공공기관 등의 자동 안내/녹음 메시지가 출제된다. 메시지의 주제는 다양하지만, 정보를 전달하거나 문의 및 요청을 하는 내용이 주를 이룬다. 화자의 신분/근무지, 전화의 목적, 화자의 요청/제안 사항을 묻는 문제가 자주 출제된다.

750_P4_01 🎧
정답과 해설 p.090

■ 담화 흐름 파악하기

인사/소개	Hi, this message is for Mr. Walters. My name is Anita Sanchez.
목적/용건	① **I have a small business creating greeting cards, and I'd like to expand my distribution network.**
세부 내용	② **A neighbor of mine told me about your gift store and suggested I contact you.** I think my cards might be a good addition for your store, and I wonder if you'd be willing to display them. ③ **I'd be happy to**
요청/제안	**mail you some samples.**
연락 방법	If you're interested, please give me a call at 555-0112, so we can discuss things further.

① 전화 목적: 소규모 연하장 제작 업체를 운영 중이며 사업 유통망 확장을 희망

② 연락처를 받은 곳: 이웃 중 한 명

③ 제안 사항: 견본을 보내주겠다고 제안

[주제/목적] **1.** **Why** is the speaker **calling**?
초반부 | 전화 목적

정답 **To promote her business**
업체 홍보

- - - - - - - - - -

[세부 사항] **2.** **Where** did the speaker get the listener's **contact information**? 중반부 | 연락처를 받은 곳, 키워드: contact

정답 **From a neighbor**
이웃

- - - - - - - - - -

[제안 사항] **3.** What does the speaker **offer to do**?
후반부 | 화자의 제안 사항

정답 **Send some samples**
샘플 송부

상황별 빈출 표현

수신자 정보	**Hello, this message is for** Lynn Taylor in the maintenance department. 안녕하세요, 이 메시지는 관리부의 린 테일러 씨에게 남기는 것입니다.
발신자 정보	Hi, Mr. Brown. **This is** Stacy Jackson **from** MacDougall's Bookstore. 안녕하세요, 브라운 씨. 맥두걸 서점의 스테이시 잭슨입니다.
전화 목적	**I'm calling to** confirm your appointment for Friday. 귀하의 금요일 예약을 확인하고자 전화 드립니다.
요청 사항/연락 방법	**Please call me back** at your earliest convenience. **My number is** 555-0112. 가능하시다면 빨리 저에게 전화 주십시오. 제 번호는 555-0112입니다.

1. What is the purpose of the voice-mail message?
(A) To request some information
(B) To report an accident

2. What is the caller waiting for?
(A) Insurance papers
(B) X-rays

Hello, this message is for Robert Costa _____
_____. This is Dr. Mina Wilson from
the Rosemont Medical Group. My patient, Sara Santos,
_____ of her foot at your office
last week. It's been six days, and I'm still waiting for the
_____ to me. Could you please give
me a call to let me know _____?
My direct number is 555-3156. Thank you.

3. Where does the speaker most likely work?
(A) At an architecture firm
(B) At an art gallery

4. Why does the speaker say, "I was out of town on business"?
(A) To describe his trip to Taipei
(B) To explain the reason for the delayed call

Hello, Ms. Hu. This is Mr. Hadid from _____.
You sent me your portfolio a couple of weeks ago. I
apologize for _____. I was out of town
on business. I'm very _____ and your
work on the Stacy Building in Taipei, and I'd like to meet
you to _____. If you are still interested,
please contact me at 555-0160 to set up a time.

5. Where is the museum?
(A) In a historic home
(B) On a ship

6. Why will part of the museum be closed temporarily?
(A) To install video cameras
(B) To set up an exhibit

_____ the Monroeville Fishing
Museum. We are _____ in a restored
_____. Our hours of operation
are 10 to 6, Tuesday through Sunday. Unfortunately, part
of the museum _____ this week, as a
_____ is being installed.
We apologize for any inconvenience, and hope to see you
here soon.

LC

PART 4

1. Where does the speaker work?

   (A) At a bank
   (B) At an electronics store
   (C) At a post office
   (D) At a hotel

2. What is the phone call about?

   (A) A defective product
   (B) A forgotten item
   (C) A billing issue
   (D) A shipping delay

3. What information does the speaker need?

   (A) A mailing address
   (B) A credit card number
   (C) A tracking number
   (D) A description of an object

4. Who most likely is the caller?

   (A) A housecleaner
   (B) A carpenter
   (C) A tenant
   (D) A patient

5. What is the purpose of the call?

   (A) To offer advice
   (B) To report a problem
   (C) To settle a bill
   (D) To cancel an appointment

6. What does the caller request?

   (A) A product catalog
   (B) A discount price
   (C) A reference letter
   (D) A return call

7. What did the speaker discuss with Janet Lin?

   (A) A hiring plan
   (B) A product design
   (C) A supply order
   (D) A travel itinerary

8. What does the speaker imply when he says, "she's the head of the department"?

   (A) He wants to introduce a staff member.
   (B) He cannot make the final decision.
   (C) A job title is incorrect.
   (D) A colleague is very successful.

9. What will the speaker most likely do next?

   (A) Set up a meeting
   (B) Check a catalog
   (C) Complete a form
   (D) Call a client

10. Why is the speaker calling?

    (A) To explain an office procedure
    (B) To cancel some travel plans
    (C) To inquire about a meeting place
    (D) To request a schedule

11. What does the speaker suggest?

    (A) Renting a car
    (B) Printing some directions
    (C) Calling a coworker
    (D) Leaving at an earlier time

12. What does the speaker plan to do tomorrow?

    (A) Take some time off
    (B) Participate in a video call
    (C) Register for an event
    (D) Deliver some brochures

13. According to the speaker, what will a conference be about?

(A) Social media marketing
(B) Renewable energy
(C) Earth science
(D) Public libraries

Exclusive Savings
$5 off $25 purchase
$10 off $50 purchase
$15 off $100 purchase
$20 off $150 purchase

14. What does the speaker remind the listener to do?

(A) Pick up a name tag
(B) Send in a photograph
(C) Confirm a registration
(D) Provide a résumé

15. What does the speaker imply when he says, "one of the other presenters is unable to attend"?

(A) Some equipment will be purchased.
(B) Some invitations were received late.
(C) An event schedule may be modified.
(D) A submission deadline has been extended.

16. Where does the speaker most likely work?

(A) At a lawyer's office
(B) At a hardware store
(C) At an electronics store
(D) At a shipping company

17. What does the speaker say about this weekend?

(A) A business will be closed.
(B) An appointment will be required.
(C) A sale will begin.
(D) An order will arrive.

18. According to the speaker, what is the business offering?

(A) A consultation by telephone
(B) A personalized gift
(C) A discount coupon
(D) An extended warranty

19. What does the store sell?

(A) Furniture
(B) Footwear
(C) Building supplies
(D) Landscaping equipment

20. What does the speaker suggest doing?

(A) Writing a product review
(B) Attending a special event
(C) Choosing a different item
(D) Registering for a membership

21. Look at the graphic. How much will the listener most likely save on a purchase?

(A) $5
(B) $10
(C) $15
(D) $20

LC

PART 4

출제 포인트 다수를 대상으로 하는 공지와 회의 발췌도 출제 빈도가 높은 편이다. 고객을 대상으로 안내/당부하는 내용, 회사 정책을 공지하는 내용, 업무 관련 회의 내용이 주를 이룬다. 새로운 시스템 도입과 변경 사항이 언급되는 경우가 많으며, 공지/회의의 주제나 목적, 그리고 청자들(listeners)과 관련된 문제가 자주 출제된다.

750_P4_04

정답과 해설 p.095

■ 담화 흐름 파악하기

인사/소개	Hi, everyone. A quick announcement before we start the day.		
주요 내용	① **While our sales of outerwear here at the store are doing well**, our Web site is having some issues. Namely, ② **the link to view men's jackets isn't working**. IT is looking into this, but we don't know when it will be fixed.	① **근무지 암시**: 매장의 겉옷 판매 실적 우수 ② **문제점 언급**: 웹사이트에 링크 오류	
요청/당부	So, ③ **if any customers come in looking to find the jackets that are online, please send them to our customer service manager.**	③ **요청 사항**: 온라인 제품을 찾는 고객은 고객 서비스 매니저에게 보내라고 당부	
마무리	She'll be able to help them. Thanks!		

근무지 1. **Where** do the **listeners** most likely **work**?
초반부 | 청자들의 근무지

정답 **At a clothing store**
의류 상점

문제점 2. What **problem** does the speaker **mention**?
중반부 | 화자가 언급한 문제점

정답 **A link is not working.**
링크가 작동하지 않는다.

요청 사항 3. What does the speaker **ask the listeners to do**?
후반부 | 청자들에게 요청한 일

정답 **Send some customers to a manager** 고객을 매니저에게 보내기

상황별 빈출 표현

개요/주제	I have one **issue to discuss** at today's meeting. 오늘 회의에서 논의할 한 가지 의제가 있습니다. The last **item on the meeting agenda** is a new system for entering customer orders. 회의의 마지막 안건은 고객 주문을 입력하는 새로운 시스템에 관한 것입니다.
요청/당부	**Please** write your name and e-mail address clearly on the sheet. 종이에 성함과 이메일 주소를 깔끔하게 적어주시기 바랍니다.
주의 환기	**Attention,** passengers flying to London. 런던행 승객 여러분께 알려드립니다.
공지/발표	**I'm happy[pleased] to announce** that we will be opening a new store in July. 7월에 새 지점을 열게 되었다는 것을 알리게 되어 기쁩니다.

1. Where is the announcement being made?
   (A) In a movie theater
   (B) In a library

2. What can listeners do at the service desk?
   (A) Check out materials
   (B) Sign up to use computers

Good evening, _____. We'll be closing in 30 minutes. If you're working on _____, we ask that you shut it down before you leave. If you would like to _____, please _____ near the front entrance. Also, we'd like to remind you that we will be _____ tomorrow evening at six o'clock called *Life in Tuscany*. Please join us for this wonderful film.

Flight	Destination	Boarding Time
542	Auckland	09:20
113	Chicago	09:40
302	Dubai	10:05
737	Shanghai	10:35

3. Look at the graphic. What was the original boarding time of the delayed flight?
   (A) 09:20
   (B) 09:40

4. Why was the flight delayed?
   (A) An airplane had a mechanical problem.
   (B) An incoming flight did not arrive on time

Good morning. This is an announcement for _____ _____ on Soar Wings Air flight _____. There will be a _____. Your new departure time is 10:05. We apologize for this inconvenience due to the _____ from the previous leg of its journey, and we thank you for your patience. Also, this flight _____, so we are offering complimentary meal vouchers for passengers who are willing to be rebooked onto a later flight.

5. What is the purpose of this meeting?
   (A) To announce a policy change
   (B) To introduce new technology

6. What does the speaker ask the staff to do?
   (A) Return telephone calls from customers
   (B) Give each customer a case number

Hello everyone, this will be a quick meeting, and I'll be very brief. I just wanted to let you know of a _____. It used to be that when a customer called to _____ and we couldn't solve the problem during the call, we'd _____. From now on, when you come across that kind of situation, you need to _____ before hanging up. This will help us _____ much more efficiently.

LC

PART 4

1. What is the purpose of the meeting?

   (A) To announce a company merger
   (B) To introduce a new employee
   (C) To provide training for staff members
   (D) To plan for an international conference

2. What were listeners asked to bring to the meeting?

   (A) A laptop computer
   (B) A company ID card
   (C) A current résumé
   (D) A progress report

3. What are listeners asked to do next?

   (A) Move to another meeting room
   (B) Change a password
   (C) Look at an instruction manual
   (D) Provide additional contact information

4. Where is the announcement being made?

   (A) At a museum
   (B) At a university
   (C) At a furniture store
   (D) At a library

5. What are the listeners waiting to attend?

   (A) A lecture
   (B) A film
   (C) An exhibition
   (D) A concert

6. What does the speaker say about the 5 o'clock event?

   (A) It is less expensive.
   (B) It is shorter.
   (C) It will be less crowded.
   (D) It will include refreshments.

7. Where do the listeners most likely work?

   (A) At a seafood restaurant
   (B) At a farm
   (C) At a bakery
   (D) At an ice cream shop

8. What is the speaker happy to announce?

   (A) She can give her employees a pay increase.
   (B) She can put new items on her menu.
   (C) Her company has opened a new location.
   (D) Her company has won a prize.

9. What does the speaker imply when she says, "I've been working late every night"?

   (A) She deserves a promotion.
   (B) She might have made some mistakes.
   (C) She is asking for some volunteers.
   (D) She is working a different shift.

10. Who most likely is the speaker?

    (A) An electrician
    (B) A journalist
    (C) A flight attendant
    (D) A travel agent

11. What complimentary service does the speaker mention?

    (A) Wireless Internet
    (B) Home delivery
    (C) Airport transportation
    (D) Technical support

12. What are the listeners reminded to do?

    (A) Keep a receipt
    (B) Fasten seat belts
    (C) Put on headphones
    (D) Fill out a customer survey

13. What is the talk about?

(A) Building renovations
(B) A computer replacement
(C) An upcoming office move
(D) A company merger

14. What does the speaker remind the listeners to do?

(A) Order supplies by Friday
(B) Label their personal belongings
(C) Turn off all equipment
(D) Keep their offices locked

15. Why should listeners contact Don Brooks?

(A) To get clarification on some instructions
(B) To provide a computer identification number
(C) To volunteer to lead a project
(D) To request new office furniture

---

16. What is the purpose of the announcement?

(A) To review a budget proposal
(B) To discuss an upcoming merger
(C) To explain some survey results
(D) To introduce new staff members

17. What does the woman mean when she says, "And why wouldn't we"?

(A) She supports a decision.
(B) She hopes to relocate.
(C) She wants listeners to share their opinions.
(D) She feels concerned about a shipment.

18. What does the woman ask listeners to do?

(A) Attend a training
(B) Sign some paperwork
(C) Gather a list of questions
(D) Review some information online

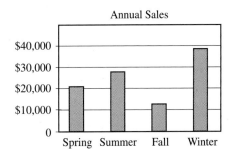

Annual Sales

19. What type of product does the business sell?

(A) Clothing
(B) Footwear
(C) Appliances
(D) Software

20. Look at the graphic. In what season did the business relocate?

(A) Spring
(B) Summer
(C) Fall
(D) Winter

21. What did the business do after it relocated?

(A) It expanded its inventory.
(B) It hired additional staff.
(C) It placed some advertisements.
(D) It organized an inauguration event.

LC

PART 4

> **출제 포인트**   견학, 대회 등 다양한 행사 안내, 업무 개요 설명, 특정 인물 소개, 혹은 제품의 특징을 설명하는 내용의 담화가
> 주를 이룬다. 소개 대상에 관해 묻는 세부 사항 문제와 다음에 할 일 / 일어날 일을 묻는 문제가 자주 출제된다.

750_P4_07 🎧
정답과 해설 p. 101

■ 담화 흐름 파악하기

인사/소개	Welcome, everyone. My name is Isobel, and ① **I'll be your instructor for this evening's cooking class**.	①	**진행 중인 행사**: 요리 교실 강사가 본인 및 수업 소개
행사 개요	Tonight, I'm going to teach you how to bake some artisanal bread.		
진행 상황/ 요청 사항	Now, I've already set the ingredients you'll need on the counter, but ② **could you please come to the front of the room and get one large bowl and a loaf pan**?	②	**요청 사항**: 재료는 조리대에 완비되었으나 도구는 앞에서 가져가라고 요청
할 일/ 일어날 일	Oh, by the way, ③ **in about half an hour, a photographer will be stopping by to take some pictures for our new promotional brochure**. If you'd prefer not to be in the photos, please just let him know.	③	**30분 후에 일어날 일**: 사진 기사가 방문할 예정

세부 사항	**1.** What are listeners **attending**? 초반부	행사 종류	정답 **A cooking class** 요리 교실
요청 사항	**2.** What does the speaker **ask** the **listeners to do**? 중반부	청자들에게 요청한 일	정답 **Gather supplies** 도구 가져가기
일어날 일	**3.** What does the woman say **will happen** in **half an hour**? 후반부	30분 후에 일어날 일, 키워드: half an hour	정답 **Photographs will be taken.** 사진 촬영이 있을 것이다.

┌─ 상황별 빈출 표현 ──────────────────────────

행사 언급   **Thank you for** attending the 5th Creative Art Awards.
제5회 <창의적 예술 시상식>에 참석해 주셔서 감사합니다.

목적   **I am here to** tell you about the features of our new monitor.
저희가 새롭게 출시한 모니터의 특징을 설명드리러 왔습니다.

할 일   **Now, I'm going to show you** how to use the company's accounting software.
이제, 회사의 회계 소프트웨어 사용법을 보여드리겠습니다.

소개   **I'd like to introduce** our keynote speaker, Dr. Cindy Lowe.
기조 연설자인 신디 로우 박사를 소개하겠습니다.

└──

1. Where is the speaker?
(A) At a computer store
(B) At a technology convention

2. What new feature is mentioned by the speaker?
(A) Rooms with Internet access
(B) A special price on software

Welcome to the sixth annual Corzell _____.
I know you're looking forward to a weekend filled with _____, workshops, and some fantastic exhibits of _____. Those of you who participated in previous conventions will notice something new this year—we now have _____ _____. One final note: if you're planning to attend the _____, there's been a change. It will be held in the Hudson Room, not the Bayside Center.

---

3. Why does the speaker say, "make sure you leave some room on those walls"?
(A) To show admiration
(B) To give a warning

4. What will Dr. Trevor do today?
(A) Fly to the Galapagos Islands
(B) Share part of her book

Our next speaker is Dr. Clarissa Trevor, a _____ who has greatly impacted the scientific world. The evidence is on the walls of her office, which are lined with numerous _____. This past year, Dr. Trevor found _____ in the Galapagos Islands. So I think it's safe to tell her—make sure you leave some room on those walls. Her findings are documented in her new book, *The Unknown Turtle*. Today, she will be _____ her amazing discovery. Please join me in welcoming Dr. Clarissa Trevor.

---

5. What is the announcement mainly about?
(A) A new contract
(B) An employee's achievement

6. Who is Juan Mendez?
(A) A client of the company
(B) A graphic designer

I know you've all been waiting to find out who our board of directors selected to receive the Graystone _____ _____. This award recognizes an employee who's really _____ here at LC Sportswear. This year we're proud to _____ to Juan Mendez from _____. He did an outstanding job _____. This image is what consumers see on every one of our athletic products, and Juan's striking design is sure to _____.

1. Who is the speaker addressing?

   (A) Inspectors
   (B) Technicians
   (C) Warehouse workers
   (D) Cleaning staff

2. What does the speaker imply when she says, "I'll be in meetings the rest of the day"?

   (A) She is unhappy with her schedule.
   (B) She can be reached in the meeting room.
   (C) She will not be available to answer questions.
   (D) She will need someone to take over her assignment.

3. What will the listeners do next?

   (A) Gather supplies
   (B) Watch a demonstration
   (C) Put on a uniform
   (D) Fill out a timesheet

4. What is the purpose of the speech?

   (A) To honor a retiring employee
   (B) To explain administrative changes
   (C) To announce a new advertising campaign
   (D) To present an award winner

5. What does the speaker say she appreciates about Nathan Milo?

   (A) His artistic talent
   (B) His financial experience
   (C) His technical skills
   (D) His leadership ability

6. What does the speaker say about the company?

   (A) It is well-known throughout the country.
   (B) It will relocate next year.
   (C) It plans to hire more employees.
   (D) It was featured in a newspaper article.

7. Who is the speaker?

   (A) A travel agent
   (B) An architect
   (C) A museum tour guide
   (D) A librarian

8. What does the speaker say about the building?

   (A) It is located in the center of town.
   (B) It has an advanced security system.
   (C) It was originally a one-story building.
   (D) It has only one entrance.

9. Where are the oldest pieces kept?

   (A) In storage
   (B) On the top floor
   (C) Near the rear entrance
   (D) On the ground floor

10. What is the purpose of the event?

    (A) To honor new graduates
    (B) To dedicate a building
    (C) To celebrate an employee's retirement
    (D) To raise funds for an organization

11. What is the video about?

    (A) A new charity
    (B) A company's development
    (C) A historical landmark
    (D) A training program

12. What will take place after the meal?

    (A) A building tour
    (B) A dance party
    (C) A president's speech
    (D) A group photo

13. What does the speaker say is special about a material?

(A) It is inexpensive to make.
(B) It resembles natural wood.
(C) It is environmentally friendly.
(D) It comes in a variety of colors.

14. Why does the speaker say, "we've already partnered with several other instrument makers"?

(A) To encourage the listeners to do business with them
(B) To provide a reason for a delay
(C) To invite the listeners to an event
(D) To reject a colleague's suggestion

15. What will the speaker do next?

(A) Give a demonstration
(B) Conduct a survey
(C) Describe a process
(D) Distribute some brochures

16. What industry does Mr. Yamada work in?

(A) Finance
(B) Architecture
(C) Health care
(D) Social media

17. What main accomplishment is Mr. Yamada recognized for?

(A) Developing a computer program
(B) Starting a charitable organization
(C) Improving a national curriculum
(D) Publishing survey results

18. According to the speaker, what will Mr. Yamada do next?

(A) Tour a facility
(B) Talk to reporters
(C) Receive an award
(D) Give a demonstration

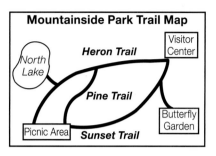

Mountainside Park Trail Map

Visitor Center

Heron Trail

North Lake

Pine Trail

Butterfly Garden

Picnic Area   Sunset Trail

19. Who most likely are the listeners?

(A) Maintenance workers
(B) Bus drivers
(C) Tourists
(D) Park rangers

20. Look at the graphic. Where will the listeners be unable to go today?

(A) The North Lake
(B) The Picnic Area
(C) The Butterfly Garden
(D) The Visitor Center

21. What does the woman encourage the listeners to do?

(A) Bring a map
(B) Check the weather forecast
(C) Store their belongings
(D) Use sun protection

LC

PART 4

광고 / 방송

> **출제 포인트** 상품/서비스/사업체 광고와 라디오 방송 및 뉴스 보도가 자주 출제된다. 광고되는 대상, 방송/뉴스의 주제, 그리고 관련 세부 사항을 묻는 경우가 많다.

750_P4_10 🎧
정답과 해설 p. 107

■ 담화 흐름 파악하기

광고 대상 및 특징 소개	① **City Instruments has opened a new store!** For over ten years, City Instruments has been proud to offer musical instruments at fantastic low prices. Now, in addition to our city-center location, we've opened a new store in the Skylarville Shopping Center.	① 광고 대상: 악기 상점 새 지점 개점 소식 및 상점의 특징 소개
혜택	To welcome our customers to the new location, ② **for a limited time we'll be offering one month of free music lessons for any instrument that you purchase.**	② 특별 혜택: 기간 한정 이벤트로 악기를 구매하면 한 달 무료 수업 제공
추가 정보	③ **And this Saturday only, we'll stay open late for your shopping convenience.**	③ 토요일에 일어날 일: 영업 시간 연장

광고 대상	1. What is **being advertised**? 초반부 | 광고되는 대상	정답 **The opening of a store** 상점 개점
세부 사항	2. What **special offer** is being made? 중반부 | 특별 혜택, 키워드: offer	정답 **Free music instruction** 무료 음악 강좌
일어날 일	3. What will **happen** on **Saturday**? 후반부 | 토요일에 일어날 일, 키워드: Saturday	정답 **Shopping hours will be extended.** 영업 시간이 연장된다.

상황별 빈출 표현

광고 멘트	**Do you want to** stay updated on fashion trends? Subscribe to our magazine, *Fashion Plus*. 최신 패션 트렌드를 계속 확인하고 싶으신가요? 저희 잡지 <패션 플러스>를 구독해 보세요.
특별 혜택	**You'll get[receive]** a 15% discount on the membership fee. 회원비 15% 할인 혜택을 받으실 겁니다.
	For a limited time only, we offer free delivery on any orders over $30. 한시적으로, 30달러 이상 주문 시 무료 배송을 제공합니다.
프로그램 소개	**You're listening to** Breakfast with Tim Smith. **Today, we'll be talking about** your eating habits. <팀 스미스와 함께하는 아침>을 듣고 계십니다. 오늘은 식습관에 대해서 이야기해 보겠습니다.
채널 고정	**Stay tuned** for our traffic report. **We will be back after** a short commercial break. 교통 방송을 들으시려면 채널을 고정해 주세요. 잠시 광고 듣고 오겠습니다.

1. Who is this report for?
   (A) Traffic police
   (B) Car drivers

2. What caused the problem?
   (A) A defective traffic light
   (B) A broken water pipe

This is Ken Harrison with a _____.
If you are driving southbound on Clover Street, you should
be ready for delays. There is a _____
between Morris Boulevard and Ridge Avenue, which has
caused the right lane _____. The police are
now on the scene directing traffic, but things are still moving
quite slowly on Clover. We recommend avoiding Clover
Street altogether and _____. Our next
traffic report will be in fifteen minutes, so keep listening.

3. Why does the speaker say, "She
doesn't usually give radio interviews"?
   (A) To show the value of an opportunity
   (B) To question the certainty of an
      event

4. What will Ms. Vince talk about?
   (A) Weather conditions
   (B) Business advice

Welcome back to Zahara's FM Radio. Before we get to the
weather forecast, I want to _____ that at
ten o'clock Ms. Beatrice Vince _____.
She doesn't usually give radio interviews. Ms. Vince,
famous for building her own shoe company, will be giving
our listeners _____. Don't miss
this talk. OK. And now, _____.

5. What did style experts say about Ella
Bancroft's products?
   (A) They are popular this season.
   (B) They are made from natural
      materials.

6. When will the promotion end?
   (A) On Saturday
   (B) On Sunday

Come to Endwell Shoes this weekend for our annual winter
sale! _____, we're taking twenty percent
off our entire inventory as we _____ our
new styles. The discount even applies to Ella Bancroft
designer boots, _____ on the Forward
Fashion television network say are this season's
_____. You'll be sure to find something
you like—and at a _____. Remember,
_____, so come take advantage of these
great deals while they last!

1. What is the purpose of the broadcast?

   (A) To advertise a store's grand opening
   (B) To announce a business merger
   (C) To discuss a new product
   (D) To report on a change in regulations

2. What type of business is Ashton Holt?

   (A) A construction company
   (B) An interior design firm
   (C) An advertising agency
   (D) A clothing company

3. What does the speaker encourage listeners to do?

   (A) Listen to an interview
   (B) Visit a Web site
   (C) Apply for a job
   (D) Enter a contest

4. What is the advertisement for?

   (A) Some luggage
   (B) An energy drink
   (C) Some clothing
   (D) An electronic device

5. What feature of the product does the speaker emphasize?

   (A) Its material
   (B) Its color
   (C) Its cost
   (D) Its weight

6. According to the speaker, what is offered with a purchase?

   (A) A product sample
   (B) Free gift wrapping
   (C) A coupon
   (D) A magazine subscription

7. What is the main topic of the news report?

   (A) An art contest
   (B) A fund-raising event
   (C) The renovation of a city hall
   (D) The reopening of a museum

8. Who is Soo-Min Lee?

   (A) An artist
   (B) A curator
   (C) A student
   (D) A politician

9. What will the mayor do on Saturday?

   (A) Visit another city
   (B) Participate in a debate
   (C) Give a speech at a ceremony
   (D) Announce the winner of an award

10. What will soon be opening?

    (A) A medical school
    (B) A health center
    (C) A dance studio
    (D) A sporting goods store

11. What will be given away at the event?

    (A) T-shirts
    (B) Memberships
    (C) Fitness evaluations
    (D) Water bottles

12. What can listeners do before May 2?

    (A) Schedule an appointment
    (B) Register for classes
    (C) Order equipment
    (D) Speak with an instructor

13. What does the speaker suggest about today's weather?

(A) It will be unusually warm.
(B) It will rain all day.
(C) It will cause traffic problems.
(D) It will change later today.

14. What will likely happen next week?

(A) Spring will begin.
(B) Temperatures will decrease.
(C) The weather center will close.
(D) The days will be very sunny.

15. When will the next weather report take place?

(A) In twelve minutes
(B) In twenty minutes
(C) In a half hour
(D) In an hour

16. What type of business is being advertised?

(A) A Web-design firm
(B) A hardware store
(C) A real estate agency
(D) A remodeling company

17. What special service does the business offer?

(A) Free installation
(B) A flexible payment plan
(C) A follow-up inspection
(D) Emergency repairs

18. What does the speaker suggest listeners do online?

(A) View work samples
(B) Leave comments
(C) Request a consultation
(D) Find a business location

Radio Schedule

2:00—2:55 P.M.	Keith's Investment Tips
2:55—3:00 P.M.	Commercial Break
3:00—4:30 P.M.	Ask an Expert
4:30—4:35 P.M.	Traffic Update

19. Look at the graphic. What starting time on the schedule is no longer accurate?

(A) 2:00 P.M.
(B) 2:55 P.M.
(C) 3:00 P.M.
(D) 4:30 P.M.

20. What will Cheryl Graves talk about?

(A) Methods of managing money
(B) How to become a banker
(C) Advice for purchasing a home
(D) Workshops for management trainees

21. What does the speaker ask the listeners to do?

(A) Listen to some music
(B) Call with questions
(C) Visit a Web site
(D) Enter a trivia contest

71. Where does the speaker most likely work?

(A) At a bookstore
(B) At a library
(C) At a publishing company
(D) At an advertising firm

72. What problem is the speaker discussing?

(A) A negative press release
(B) Some recent client complaints
(C) An understaffed department
(D) Some missing documents

73. What will employees be required to do in the future?

(A) Receive approval for purchases
(B) Complete a permission form
(C) Request time off in advance
(D) Meet weekly targets

---

74. What is being advertised?

(A) A concert series
(B) A science museum
(C) A pet store
(D) A monthly publication

75. What will new customers receive for a limited time?

(A) Free food samples
(B) Invitations to lectures
(C) Entry tickets to parks
(D) Souvenir T-shirts

76. What are listeners asked to do on a Web site?

(A) Use a promotional code
(B) Look at some photos
(C) Join a mailing list
(D) Enter a contest

---

77. Where does the speaker work?

(A) At an accounting firm
(B) At an Internet service provider
(C) At a real estate agency
(D) At a medical center

78. What does the speaker mean when she says, "he recently moved to New York"?

(A) A hiring decision is surprising.
(B) A location is very popular.
(C) A delay could not be avoided.
(D) A request cannot be accommodated.

79. Why does the speaker recommend visiting a Web site?

(A) To read some profiles
(B) To download some forms
(C) To pay a bill
(D) To find an address

---

80. Where do the listeners work?

(A) At a technology company
(B) At a medical clinic
(C) At an accounting firm
(D) At a manufacturing plant

81. What does the speaker imply when he says, "it's not software you're familiar with"?

(A) A company announcement was incorrect.
(B) A project proposal will not work.
(C) Some software is still being developed.
(D) Some training will be necessary.

82. What will the listeners most likely do next?

(A) Indicate their availability
(B) Call their managers
(C) Analyze some data
(D) Confirm some appointments

83. What is the purpose of the message?

(A) To invite the listener to an event
(B) To follow up on a job application
(C) To discuss an upcoming publication
(D) To advertise a professional organization

84. What is Lisa Cheng's area of expertise?

(A) Social media marketing
(B) Diet and nutrition
(C) Hospital management
(D) Urban planning

85. What does the speaker offer to do?

(A) Share some research data
(B) Create an advertisement
(C) Contact a colleague
(D) Pay for travel costs

86. Who is Erika Bauer?

(A) An author
(B) An actor
(C) A singer
(D) A journalist

87. According to the speaker, what will Erika Bauer do this evening?

(A) Talk about her life
(B) Discuss current events
(C) Review a book
(D) Offer career advice

88. What are listeners invited to do?

(A) Request a song
(B) Submit questions
(C) Enter a contest
(D) Visit the station

89. Where is the speaker?

(A) At a branch opening
(B) At a trade show
(C) At a client dinner
(D) At a shareholder meeting

90. Why does the speaker say, "we just installed new refrigeration units on all our delivery trucks"?

(A) To report on a vehicle inspection
(B) To explain a financial loss
(C) To justify a hiring decision
(D) To question an investment

91. What will the speaker most likely do next?

(A) Introduce a guest speaker
(B) Take inventory
(C) Show a video
(D) Distribute some samples

92. What is the purpose of the talk?

(A) To introduce a guest speaker
(B) To provide a tour schedule
(C) To promote a new exhibit
(D) To explain a museum's history

93. What does the speaker say about the gift shop?

(A) It will be closing for renovations.
(B) It will be selling special merchandise.
(C) It has free maps.
(D) It is offering a discount today.

94. What does the speaker encourage the listeners to do?

(A) Volunteer at the museum
(B) Purchase advance tickets
(C) Register for an annual membership
(D) Meet some visiting artists

LC

PART 4

Pizza Topping	# Votes
Figs	42
Sweep potates	40
Walnuts	33
Eggplant	30

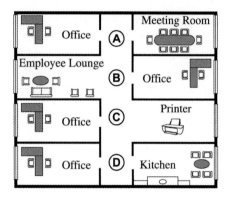

95. Who most likely are the listeners?

(A) Restaurant servers
(B) Cooking instructors
(C) Food journalists
(D) Focus group participants

96. According to the speaker, what took place last week?

(A) A book launch
(B) A kitchen renovation
(C) A tasting event
(D) A training session

97. Look at the graphic. Which topping will be featured on the specials board?

(A) Figs
(B) Sweet potatoes
(C) Walnuts
(D) Eggplant

98. What is the company trying to do?

(A) Encourage recycling
(B) Decrease expenses
(C) Improve workplace safety
(D) Promote employee health

99. Look at the graphic. Where will a new dispenser be located?

(A) At location A
(B) At location B
(C) At location C
(D) At location D

100. What are the listeners asked to do?

(A) Save receipts
(B) Indicate a preference
(C) Read an instruction manual
(D) Report problems immediately

■ 제품 / 서비스 관련 메시지

inquiry about ~에 대한 문의

be calling about the advertisement
광고를 보고 전화한다

replacement 대체품, 교환품

out of stock 재고가 없는

inventory 재고 조사, 재고품, 재고 목록

place an order 주문하다

deliver an item 물품을 배송하다

warranty 품질 보증서

hold until ~까지 보관해 두다

waive a fee 수수료를 면제해 주다

confirm a reservation 예약을 확정하다

compensate 보상하다

■ 업무 관련 메시지

reschedule 일정을 변경하다

appointment 약속, 예약

upcoming 다가오는, 곧 있을

confirm one's attendance 참석 여부를 확인하다

conflicting schedule 겹치는 일정

potential project 향후 있을 프로젝트

discuss the project update
프로젝트 최근 상황을 논의하다

annual report 연례 보고서

out of town on business 업무 차 타 지역에 있는

won't be ready until ~이 되어야 준비될 것이다

at the latest 늦어도

suggestion 제안

■ 기업 / 기관 ARS 메시지

extension 내선, 구내전화

office[business] hours 업무 시간

pound key (전화기) 우물 정자(#)

automated message 자동 응답 메시지

automated information system
자동 정보 안내 시스템

due to national holiday 공휴일로 인해

stay on the line 전화를 끊지 않고 기다리다

You have reached ~로 전화하셨습니다

Our hours of operation are 우리 영업시간은 ~입니다

You will be connected to ~로 연결될 겁니다

Our office is currently closed.
현재는 영업 시간이 아닙니다.

■ 부재중 안내 메시지

relay a message 메시지를 전달하다

return a call 회신 전화를 하다

relocate to ~로 이전하다

while I'm away 내가 자리를 비운 사이 / 멀리 가 있는 동안

I'm currently attending 현재 ~에 참석 중입니다

leave a message 메시지를 남겨 주세요

look forward to -ing ~을 고대하다

in the meantime 그 동안, 그 사이에

after the tone[beep] 삐 소리가 난 후

Please contact ~에게 연락하세요

Please feel free to 편하게 ~하세요

You can reach me at + 전화번호
~로 제게 연락하실 수 있습니다

■ 건물 내 안내 방송

attention 안내 말씀드립니다

patron 고객, 후원자

voucher 상품권, 쿠폰

frequent customer 단골 고객

checkout station 계산대

special offer 특가품, 특별 할인 행사

sign-up sheet 가입 신청서

extend hours of operation 운영 시간을 늘리다

proceed to ~로 가다

bulletin board 게시판

in order to serve you better
여러분들을 더 잘 모시기 위해

Please be advised that ~임을 알려 드립니다

■ 교통 수단 안내 방송

delayed 지연된

departure gate 탑승구

personal belongings 개인 소지품

carry-on baggage 기내 휴대용 수하물

check in 탑승 수속하다

security check point 보안 검색대

have the ticket and identification ready
표와 신분증을 준비하다

connection 연결 항공편

cabin 선실, 기내

inbound/outbound 귀항하는/출항하는

cargo hold 화물 적재실

Welcome aboard ~에 탑승하신 것을 환영합니다

■ 사내 공지사항

identification badge 사원증

efficiency of the work 작업·업무의 효율성

receive a reimbursement 비용을 돌려받다

on[at] short notice 갑작스런 통지에도

be sure to check for updates
추가 공지사항을 꼭 확인하세요

share some good news 몇 가지 좋은 소식을 나누다

Employees are encouraged to
직원 여러분들께 ~하시길 권장합니다

according to the recent market surveys
최근 시장 설문조사에 따르면

This policy will be in effect until
이 방침은 ~까지 유효할 것이다.

adopt a new policy 새로운 정책을 채택하다

how the system works 시스템 작동 방식

■ 회의

call a meeting 회의를 소집하다

shareholder's meeting 주주회의

board meeting 이사회(회의)

meeting agenda 회의 안건

sales fluctuations 매출 변동

potential client 잠재 고객

financially beneficial 재정적으로 이득이 되는

give a quick overview 간략하게 설명하다

make up for the extra cost 추가 비용을 만회하다

familiarize oneself with ~을 숙지하다

meet growing consumer demand
늘어나는 소비자 수요에 부응하다

The other major change regards
~ 다른 주요 변경사항은 ~과 관련된 것입니다

As I mentioned at our last meeting
제가 지난번 회의에서 말씀 드린 대로

■ 발표 / 연설

keynote speaker 기조 연설자

give[make] a presentation on
~에 관해 발표하다

question-and-answer session 질의 응답 시간

journalism conference 언론 회의

conference organizer 회의 주관자

guest lecturer 초청 강사

sound equipment 음향 장비

make an appearance 출연하다

turn off mobile phones 휴대폰을 끄다

secure a budget 예산을 확보하다

on behalf of ~을 대신하여

information session 설명회

■ 인물 소개

award ceremony 시상식

the prestigious award 권위 있는 상

founder 창립자, 설립자

insightful 통찰력 있는

contribute 공헌하다

dedicated to ~에 전념하는, 헌신하는

leading expert on ~분야의 뛰어난 전문가

distinguished work as an economist
경제학자로서의 뛰어난 업적

do an outstanding job 뛰어난 업적을 이루다

begin one's career as ~로서 경력을 쌓기 시작하다

give a round of applause for ~에게 큰 박수를 보내다

as a token of our appreciation 감사의 표시로

■ 관광 / 견학

landmark 주요 지형 지물

observatory 전망대

guided tour 안내원이 딸린 여행[견학]

excursion 소풍, (단체) 여행

featured exhibition 특별 전시회

admission fee 입장료

display area 전시장

plant 공장, 시설 (=factory, facility)

state-of-the-art 최첨단의

refrain from ~을 삼가다

demonstrate 시연하다

safety gear 안전 장비

■ 광고

a large[wide] selection of 많은, 다양한

complimentary 무료로 제공되는

feature ~을 특징으로 하다

authentic 정통의, 진짜의

promotion 홍보, 판촉 행사

guarantee 보장하다 (=warrant)

customized 맞춤식의

trial period 무료 체험 기간

affordable (가격이) 적당한 (=reasonable)

half off 50퍼센트 할인

for a limited time only 제한된 기간에만, 한시적으로

Don't miss out ~을 놓치지 마십시오

■ 라디오 방송

host (TV·라디오 프로그램의) 사회자, 진행자

radio station 라디오 방송국

weekly podcast 주간 팟캐스트

news flash (TV·라디오) 뉴스 속보

commercial break 광고 방송을 위한 프로그램 중단 시간

stay tuned 채널을 고정하다

tune in 주파수를 맞추다

exclusive interview with ~와의 독점 인터뷰

have ~ on the show 프로그램에 ~을 초대하다

come back from the break 광고 듣고 다시 방송을 시작하다

take questions over the phone 전화로 질문을 받다

keep ~ posted ~에게 계속 알려주다

■ 교통 방송

commuter 통근자

renovation 보수 공사

traffic jam[congestion] 교통 체증

be stuck in traffic 교통 체증에 걸리다

time-consuming 시간이 걸리는

expect delays on ~에서의 정체가 예상되다

expressway 고속도로 (=motorway)

transportation network 교통망

bottleneck 좁은 도로, 병목 지역

complimentary shuttle bus 무료 셔틀버스

make[take] a detour 우회하다

take an alternative route 다른 길로 가다, 우회하다

■ 지역 및 비즈니스 뉴스

reveal a plan 계획을 공개하다

go on the market 시판되다

drop in profits 수익 하락

generate a lot of revenue 막대한 수익을 창출하다

latest features 최신 기능

what sets it apart 차별점

flagship store 본점, 주력 상점

merge with ~와 합병하다

merger and acquisition 합병인수

city council 시의회

mayor 시장

election 선거

make headlines 대대적으로 보도되다, 헤드라인을 장식하다

■ 일기 예보

inclement weather 악천후

high pressure 고기압

degree (온도 단위) 도

temperature 온도

precipitation 강수량

average 평균

humid 습기가 많은

heat wave 폭염

snowstorm 눈보라

gusty wind 돌풍

thunderstorm (강풍이 따르는) 뇌우

hail 우박

unseasonably 철에 맞지 않게

MEMO

Part

단문 / 장문 채우기

5&6

Part 5&6 | 기본 다지기

■ 문장 형식

Part 5에서는 기본적인 문장 형식을 알아야 문장 구조를 분석하여 문제를 풀 수 있다. 문장 형식은 Part 5뿐만 아니라 Part 6, 7에서도 필요한 기본 지식이므로 확실히 짚고 넘어가도록 한다.

1형식 **주어+동사**

주어와 동사로만 이루어진 구조이다. 목적어를 취하지 않는 자동사가 쓰인다.

The cost of a room at the River Hotel varies according to size.
　　　　　　　　주어　　　　　　　　　　　　　　　동사

리버 호텔의 객실 요금은 크기에 따라 다르다.

2형식 **주어+동사+주격 보어**

주어와 동사만으로는 의미가 완성되지 않으므로, 주어를 설명해 주는 보어가 필요한 구조이다. 주로 명사와 형용사가 주격 보어 역할을 한다.

The contract will remain valid for 3 months.
　　주어　　　　동사　　주격 보어

계약은 3개월간 유효할 것이다.

3형식 **주어+동사+목적어**

가장 많이 쓰이는 문장 형태로, 목적어를 필요로 하는 타동사가 쓰인다.

Ms. Carson submitted her expense report right after she returned from the trip.
　　주어　　　동사　　　　목적어

카슨 씨는 출장을 다녀온 직후에 지출 품의서를 제출했다.

4형식 **주어+동사+간접 목적어+직접 목적어**

동사 뒤에 간접 목적어(~에게)와 직접 목적어(~을)가 순서대로 오는 구조이다.

Rowell Enterprises offers employees excellent benefits.
　　주어　　　　　동사　　간접 목적어　　직접 목적어

로웰 엔터프라이지즈는 직원들에게 탁월한 복지 혜택을 제공한다.

5형식 **주어+동사+목적어+목적격 보어**

3형식 문장 뒤에 목적어를 보충 설명하는 목적격 보어가 추가된 구조이다. 명사, 형용사, 동사원형, to부정사, 분사가 목적격 보어로 쓰일 수 있으며, 동사에 따라 다른 형태가 온다.

Many readers found Mr. Tsang's article in the second issue very interesting.
　　주어　　　　동사　　　　목적어　　　　　　　　　　　　　　목적격 보어

많은 독자들이 2호에 실린 창 씨의 기사가 굉장히 흥미롭다고 생각했다.

Part 5 | 단문 빈칸 채우기 총 30문항

단문의 빈칸을 채우는 문제로, 총 30문항이 출제된다. 문제 유형은 다음과 같이 크게 두 가지로 나눌 수 있다. 문법 문제의 비중이 약간 더 높으며, 간혹 문법과 어휘가 혼합된 유형이 등장하기도 한다.

- **문법 문제**   명사/동사/형용사/부사/전치사/접속사 자리 문제, 인칭대명사의 격/재귀대명사 문제,
  동사의 태/시제/수 일치 문제, 비교급 및 최상급 문제, 관계대명사 문제 등
- **어휘 문제**   의미상 빈칸에 알맞은 명사/동사/형용사/부사/전치사/접속사 선택 문제

■ ETS 예제 및 풀이 전략

1 문제 유형을 먼저 파악한다.

Part 5는 문제당 권장 풀이 시간이 20~30초로 굉장히 짧으며, 읽는 순간 바로 정답을 선택하고 다음 문제로 넘어가야 한다. 문장 전체를 읽기 전에, 문제의 보기를 보고 유형을 먼저 파악하는 것이 좋다.

문법 문제 **빈칸과 주변의 관계를 살핀다.**

어근이 같지만 품사가 다른 단어들, 혹은 다양한 동사 형태로 보기가 구성되어 있다면, 우선 빈칸과 주변 구성 요소 간의 관계를 살핀 후 정답을 찾아본다. 문장 해석은 필요할 때만 한다.

101. Ms. Seo has ------- experience in community planning and development.
  (A) extent 명사
  (B) extensive 형용사 → 뒤에 오는 명사를 수식하는 형용사 자리
  (C) extensively 부사
  (D) extensiveness 명사   **정답 (B)**

어휘 문제 **문장의 핵심 구성 요소를 중심으로 해석한다.**

어휘 문제라도 기본적으로 문장 구조는 파악해야 한다. 가령 목적어 역할을 하는 명사 어휘를 선택하는 문제라면, 동사와 수식어구를 확인하고 문맥상 가장 어울리는 보기를 선택해야 한다.

102. The marketing team must submit its quarterly progress ------- for analysis by June 1.
  (A) signature 서명
  (B) report 보고서
  (C) payment 지불금 분석(analysis)을 위해 제출(submit)해야 하는 것
  (D) hold 잡기, 지연   **정답 (B)**

2 권장 풀이 시간 내에 정답을 찾을 수 없다면 표시한 후 다음 문제로 넘어간다.

풀리지 않는 문제에 너무 많은 시간을 투자해서는 안 된다. 권장 풀이 시간 내에 문제를 해결하려면, 학습 시 문법 포인트를 정확히 이해하고 Collocation 위주로 어휘를 암기해 두도록 한다.

※ **Collocation이란?** 함께 자주 쓰이는 단어들의 결합 ⓔ **renew** the **contract** 계약을 갱신하다

Part 6 | 장문 빈칸 채우기 총 4지문 16문항

총 4지문이 출제되고 각 지문당 4개의 문제가 있다. 문법/어휘 문제 3문항과 문장 고르기 문제 1문항으로 구성되어 있는데, 문장 고르기 문제를 제외한 3문항의 구성은 지문별로 다르다. 문법과 어휘 문제가 주를 이루며, 앞뒤 문장을 의미상 자연스럽게 연결하는 접속부사를 선택하는 문제도 종종 출제된다.

■ ETS 예제

Questions 131-134 refer to the following e-mail.

To: Douglas Lovato, Floor Manager
From: Jessa Nicols, Production Manager
Subject: Thursday Client Meeting
Date: August 3

Hi Douglas,

Our clients called this morning to inform us that one more person will be joining our meeting at our glass factory this Thursday. This ------- change won't affect us in any major way. The
131.
clients will still arrive at 10 A.M. to discuss technical matters. That afternoon, we will still take them on an ------- and informative tour of the factory. -------, before we start the tour, please
132.   **133.**
have safety equipment ready for four, not three, people. -------.
134.

Call me if you have any questions.

Jessa

어휘 문제
131. (A) doubtful
(B) seasonal
(C) continuous
(D) unforeseen

문법 문제
132. (A) interesting
(B) interestingly
(C) interested
(D) interests

접속부사 문제
133. (A) Instead
(B) However
(C) Besides
(D) Similarly

문장 고르기 문제
134. (A) Now we will look at the tools used to shape that glass.
(B) I hope this time change isn't an inconvenience.
(C) This includes an extra hard hat, earplugs, and boots.
(D) They asked questions about our safety standards during the tour.

■ 풀이 전략

1 지문을 처음부터 읽는다.

Part 6에서는 문맥을 파악해야 풀 수 있는 문제가 대부분이므로, 지문을 처음부터 읽어야 한다. 시간을 절약해 보려고 빈칸이 있는 문장만 읽는 것은 위험하다.

2 순서대로 한 문제씩 해결해 나간다.

문법 문제는 해당 문장만 보고 풀 수 있는 경우가 간혹 있긴 하지만, 시제/지시어/대명사 문제는 앞뒤 문장과 내용의 흐름을 파악하고 풀어야 한다. 따라서 문제 유형에 상관없이, 반드시 순서대로 한 문제씩 해결해 나가도록 한다.

어휘 문제 문장의 핵심 구성 요소를 중심으로 해석한 후, 빈칸 주변 단어를 확인한다.

131. 고객이 아침에 전화해 회의 참석 인원 추가(one more person)
이 변동사항(change)과 가장 어울리는 형용사 선택

정답 **(D) unforeseen(예기치 못한)**

문법 문제 문장의 구조를 분석한다. 시제/지시어/대명사 문제는 앞뒤 문장과 내용의 흐름을 살핀다.

132. 빈칸 앞 | 관사 an
빈칸 뒤 | 등위접속사 and + 형용사 informative + 명사 tour (of the factory)
informative와 함께 tour를 수식할 형용사 선택

정답 **(A) interesting(흥미로운)**

접속부사 문제 빈칸 앞뒤 문장의 내용 관계(대조, 인과, 첨언, 예시, 시간 흐름, 감정 표현)를 파악한다.

133. 빈칸 앞 | 고객들이 여전히(still) 10시에 도착, 오후에 공장 견학 예정 = 일정 변동 X
빈칸 뒤 | 세 명이 아닌 네 명(four, not three)을 위한 안전 장비 준비 = 준비 사항 변동 O
서로 대조적인 내용을 연결해 주는 접속부사 선택

정답 **(B) However(그러나)**

문장 고르기 문제 빈칸 앞뒤 내용을 보고 오답을 소거한 후, 전체 흐름상 가장 적절한 문장을 선택한다.
보기에 지시어, 대명사 등이 있을 경우, 가리키는 대상을 앞 문장에서 찾아야 한다.

134. 빈칸 앞 | 세 명이 아닌 네 명을 위한 안전 장비(safety equipment) 준비 당부
빈칸 뒤 | 질문 있으면 전화 요망

(A) 오답 유리 형태를 잡는 데 쓰는 도구 관찰할 예정 → 견학 중 나올 법한 대사
(B) 오답 해당 시간 변경 양해 → 앞서 일정은 변동이 없다고 고지
(C) 정답 이것은 추가 안전모, 귀마개, 부츠 포함 → this = safety equipment
(D) 오답 견학 동안 안전 기준에 관해 질문 → 견학 후 언급될 만한 내용

Unit | 01 품사와 문장 구조

> **주어와 동사** 모든 문장에는 주어와 동사가 한 쌍씩 있어야 한다. 문장에 동사가 없다면 빈칸은 동사 자리이다.

■ 주어 자리

완전한 문장에는 주어와 동사가 한 쌍씩 포함되어 있다. 주어 자리에는 (대)명사와 명사구, to부정사, 동명사, 명사절 접속사가 이끄는 명사절이 올 수 있다. 주어와 동사는 수가 일치하고 자연스럽게 해석되어야 한다.

명사   Many [investors / investments] have concerns about the recent decline in the stock market.
많은 투자자들이 최근 주식 시장이 하락하는 것을 염려하고 있다.

동명사   [Correcting / Correct] errors in the reports is one of your main responsibilities.
보고서에 있는 오류를 바로잡는 것이 당신의 주요 업무 중 하나이다.
→ 주어 자리에 동명사를 쓸 수 있다. 타동사의 동명사는 목적어(errors)를 동반한다.

명사절   [What / Because] the builder likes about this contract is the early completion bonus.
건축업자가 이 계약에서 마음에 들어한 것은 조기 완공에 대한 보너스다.
→ 명사절을 이끄는 접속사 What이 쓰여야 한다.

■ 동사 자리

완전한 문장에는 반드시 동사가 있어야 한다. 동사 자리에는 to부정사, 분사, 동명사 등의 준동사를 쓸 수 없다. 만약 문장에 접속사가 있으면 주어와 동사를 포함하는 절이 추가된다.

The current board members at Ampifay, Inc., [started / to start] their term two months ago.
엠피화이 주식회사의 현 이사회 위원들은 두 달 전 임기를 시작했다.

[Complete / Completing] the online form if you are interested in the snow sculpture competition.
만약 눈 조각 대회에 관심이 있으시면 온라인 서식을 작성해 주세요.
→ 접속사 if가 이끄는 부사절을 생략하고 나면 문장에 동사가 없다. 주어를 생략하고 동사원형으로 시작하는 문장은 명령문이다.

Once the subscription [begins / to begin], it will continue throughout the year.
일단 구독이 시작되면, 그것은 일 년 동안 지속될 것이다.
→ 접속사(Once)가 두 절을 이어주고 있기 때문에 주어와 동사가 두 개씩 있어야 한다.

ETS 유형 연습

정답과 해설 p. 120

1 Passengers arriving at Gate H had to walk up the stairs to the main terminal because the _____ was temporarily out of order.

(A) escalate
(B) escalator
(C) escalation
(D) escalating

2 Civil engineer Lorenzo Raspallo _____ as the guest speaker at the fifth annual Bridge Conservation Colloquium next month.

(A) to confirm
(B) to be confirmed
(C) has been confirmed
(D) having been confirmed

3 New software that should reduce employee training time _____.

(A) to develop
(B) developing
(C) is being developed
(D) to be developed

<table>
<tr><td>목적어</td><td>동사 뒤에서 동작의 대상을 나타내는 목적어 자리에는 주로 명사가 등장하며 '~을/에게'로 해석한다. 전치사는 뒤
의 명사와 함께 수식어구를 형성하는데, 이때 전치사 뒤에 등장하는 명사를 '전치사의 목적어'라고 부른다.</td></tr>
</table>

■ 동사의 목적어 자리

동사 뒤에는 목적어, 보어, 수식어가 나올 수 있지만, 동사 뒤에 빈칸이 나오면 목적어 자리인지 아닌지 먼저 확인하는 것이 효율적이다. 목적어 자리에는 (대)명사, 명사구, to부정사, 동명사, 명사절이 온다.

명사 Improved working conditions can increase [productivity / productively].
개선된 근무 환경은 생산성을 높일 수 있다.
→ 동사 뒤에 목적어 역할을 하는 명사가 나와서 '~을'이라고 자연스럽게 해석된다.

to부정사 The management team is planning [to transfer / transfers] the plant to South America.
경영진은 공장을 남미로 이전할 계획이다.
→ 목적어 자리에 명사나 to부정사를 쓸 수 있다. 명사 뒤에는 목적어가 올 수 없지만, to부정사 뒤에는 목적어(the plant)가 올 수 있다.

명사절 The survey indicates [that / while] the MCN Hotel provides the highest-quality service in our region. 조사는 MCN 호텔이 우리 지역에서 최고의 서비스를 제공한다는 것을 보여준다.
→ 동사 뒤 목적어 자리이므로 명사절 접속사를 선택한다. that은 명사절 접속사, while은 부사절 접속사이다.

■ 전치사의 목적어 자리

전치사는 전치사 뒤에 등장하는 명사와 결합하여 수식어 덩어리로 사용된다. 전치사의 목적어 자리에는 (대)명사, 명사구, 동명사, 명사절이 온다.

명사 According to the supply contract, the payment should be made upon [delivery / deliver].
납품 계약에 따르면, 배송 즉시 지불이 이루어져야 한다.

동명사 We can improve customer service by [reading / reads] many customer complaint letters.
우리는 많은 고객 항의 서신을 읽음으로써 고객 서비스를 개선할 수 있다.
→ 전치사 바로 뒤에 명사 대신 동명사를 쓸 수 있다. 동사는 올 수 없다.

ETS 유형 연습

정답과 해설 p.120

1 Mr. Yamamoto voiced his _____ for the hard work and dedication of the advertising department during its recent campaign.

(A) appreciate
(B) appreciating
(C) appreciation
(D) appreciated

2 Most government and commercial establishments will be closed on Monday in _____ of Independence Day.

(A) observe
(B) observing
(C) observance
(D) observant

3 Mr. Song's promotion to the position of division _____ was announced at this morning's staff meeting.

(A) manage
(B) manager
(C) managed
(D) manageable

<table>
<tr><td>보어</td><td>보어에는 주어를 보충하는 주격 보어와 목적어를 보충하는 목적격 보어가 있다. 주격 보어와 목적격 보어를 원하는 동사를 기억하자.</td></tr>
</table>

■ 주격 보어 자리

주격 보어 자리에는 주로 형용사나 명사가 온다. 형용사 보어는 주어에 대해 보충 설명을 하고, 명사 보어는 주어와 동격 관계를 이룬다.

형용사 Online shopping has become more [popular / popularly] around the world.
온라인 쇼핑은 세계적으로 더욱 인기를 누리게 되었다. (온라인 쇼핑 → 인기를 누림)

명사 Rural areas with traditional houses have become tourist [attractions / attractive].
전통 가옥들이 있는 시골 지역들이 관광 명소가 되었다. (시골 지역들 = 관광 명소)

┌─ 주격 보어를 원하는 동사 ─

be ~이다   become ~이 되다   remain ~인 채로 (남아) 있다   stay (어떤 상태에) 머무르다   seem / appear ~인 듯하다

look ~처럼 보이다   sound ~하게 들리다   feel 느끼다   turn ~이 되다   taste ~한 맛이 나다

■ 목적격 보어 자리

목적격 보어의 형태는 동사에 따라 다양하므로 각 동사가 이끄는 구조를 기억하도록 한다.

목적격 보어를 원하는 동사	목적어	목적격 보어의 형태
make 만들다, keep 유지하다 find / consider / deem 여기다	the seminar	helpful [형용사]
ask / request / invite 요청하다 encourage 격려하다	more people	to attend [to부정사]
make / have 만들다, let 허락하다	more people	attend [동사원형]
have 만들다, 하게하다	the computer	fixed [과거분사(p.p.)]

Many nutritionists found the results [fascinating / fascinatingly].
많은 영양학자들이 그 결과를 무척 흥미롭다고 생각했다.

┌───
| **고득점 팁** | 보어 자리에는 주로 형용사, 명사를 쓰지만, 다른 품사가 올 수도 있다.

① 주격 보어 자리에 전치사구가 오는 경우
The hospital is [currently / current] under construction.
그 병원은 현재 건설 중이다.   *전치사구 under construction이 보어 역할을 하고 있다.

② 목적격 보어 자리에 동사원형이 오는 경우
The representatives made our partners [feel / feeling] comfortable about the merger.
대표단은 우리 협력업체들이 합병에 대해 편하게 생각하도록 만들었다.
└───

ETS 유형 연습

정답과 해설 p. 120

1 The range of research studies presented on the first day of the conference was very _____.

(A) impressed
(B) impress
(C) impressively
(D) impressive

2 The Ashford Chamber of Commerce invites visitors _____ the restaurants and theaters on the city's waterfront.

(A) patronize
(B) patronized
(C) to patronize
(D) be patronizing

3 Changes to financial markets have made investors even more _____ on quality advice and information.

(A) depends
(B) dependent
(C) to depend
(D) dependency

수식어	수식어는 완전한 문장에 의미를 더하기 위해 쓰는 말로, 다른 요소를 꾸며주는 기능을 한다. 따라서 생략해도 문장 구조에 영향을 미치지 않는다. 수식어 자리에는 부사, 전치사구, 접속사절이 올 수 있다.

■ 부사

부사는 명사를 제외한 모든 품사를 수식할 수 있으며, 문장에서 다양한 위치에 올 수 있다. 수식어인 부사는 생략 가능하며, 생략해도 문장 구조에 영향을 미치지 않는다. 자동사 뒤, 수동태 동사 뒤는 대표적인 부사 자리이다.

All test results should be forwarded [directly / directions] to the university from the testing agency.
모든 시험 결과는 시험 평가 기관에서 그 대학교로 바로 전달되어야 한다.

■ 전치사+명사

전치사는 뒤에 전치사의 목적어 역할을 하는 명사와 결합하여 '전치사+명사'의 전치사구 덩어리를 형성한다. 수식어 역할을 하는 전치사구 역시 생략해도 문장 구조에 영향을 미치지 않는다.

The construction project was completed on time [despite / although] the inclement weather.
건설 프로젝트는 궂은 날씨에도 불구하고 제때 끝났다.
→ although와 despite는 둘 다 양보, 반전의 의미를 지니지만 although는 접속사, despite는 전치사이다.

■ 접속사+주어+동사

접속사는 뒤에 주어와 동사를 포함하는 절을 이끌며, '접속사+주어+동사'의 접속사절 덩어리가 수식어 역할을 하는 경우 생략이 가능하다. 문제의 보기에 접속사가 있으면 빈칸 뒤의 동사의 개수를 먼저 확인해 보고 접속사절인지 아닌지 판단하도록 한다.

[Before / Prior to] we had interviews with qualified applicants, we read their résumés thoroughly.
자격 있는 지원자들과 면접을 하기 전에, 우리는 그들의 이력서를 꼼꼼하게 읽어보았다.

The company needs Middle East specialists [because / due to] it will expand its operations to Egypt.
그 회사는 이집트로 사업을 확장할 것이기 때문에 중동 지역 전문가들이 필요하다.

ETS 유형 연습
정답과 해설 p. 121

1 The keypad should be pressed _____ to ensure that all the digits of the code are transmitted.

(A) firmly
(B) firmness
(C) firm
(D) firmest

2 Plans are under way _____ the extension of the SanPedro Valley water pipeline.

(A) for
(B) next
(C) while
(D) onto

3 _____ money has been budgeted for the staff professional development program, the director is reluctant to proceed.

(A) In spite of
(B) Therefore
(C) Because of
(D) Although

1. The trendy new clothing shop Streetso ------- T-shirts hand painted by well-known graffiti artists.

   (A) having offered   (B) will offer
   (C) to offer   (D) offering

2. After your ------- is finalized, please notify Ms. Tang in human resources of your new home address.

   (A) relocate   (B) relocates
   (C) relocated   (D) relocation

3. At the annual meeting, management will ------- employees who have done outstanding work.

   (A) recognize   (B) recognizing
   (C) recognition   (D) to recognize

4. The financial briefing for our investors will ------- begin at 9:30 A.M. on Thursday.

   (A) precisely   (B) preciseness
   (C) precise   (D) precision

5. The ------- advertised in yesterday's *Shifnal Daily Echo* do not apply to kitchen appliances.

   (A) discounts   (B) discounted
   (C) discounting   (D) discount

6. Some proposed models of the new building will be on display in the lobby for the ------- of the week.

   (A) remainder   (B) remaining
   (C) remained   (D) remain

7. You will find the manual very helpful ------- any problems you encounter when you first use the software.

   (A) must solve   (B) be solved
   (C) will solve   (D) in solving

8. To encourage ------- from respondents, Geojedo Women's Club is offering a 25,000 won gift card to everyone who completes the survey.

   (A) participate   (B) participation
   (C) participatory   (D) participates

9. A recent study has shown that assembly-line workers are likely to be much less ------- during overtime shifts.

   (A) attentively   (B) attention
   (C) attentive   (D) attentiveness

10. Team members are being asked to postpone any vacations ------- the entire project has been completed.

    (A) while   (B) during
    (C) upon   (D) until

11. Sales at Brookes Computer, Inc., are likely to improve this month after a relatively poor ------- in the past few months.

    (A) performing   (B) performance
    (C) performed   (D) perform

12. Fleet Hotel guarantees the lowest rates to guests who book rooms ------- through its Web site.

    (A) directness   (B) directing
    (C) directly   (D) directed

13. If you move, ------- your contact information in the company directory as soon as possible.

(A) updating   (B) updated

(C) updates   (D) update

14. Sonterra Touring Company is the ------- of several deluxe travel excursions to the Amazon jungle.

(A) operations   (B) operational

(C) operator   (D) operating

Questions 15-18 refer to the following e-mail.

From: Australia West Airlines
To: Margaret Burnham
Date: 5 June
Subject: Your flight reservation

Dear Ms. Burnham,

Thank you for choosing Australia West Airlines for your next flight and for using our online reservations and check-in system. ------- . To speed the process of checking baggage and clearing
    15.
the security checkpoints, we suggest that passengers print their boarding passes at home. Doing so will ensure your ------- arrival at the departure gate.
    16.
While at the airport, ------- advantage of the secure wireless network available at our Westward
    17.
Lounge for a small fee of just $10 AUD. You can arrange this ------- through our reservations
    18.
system before your departure date.

Sincerely,
The team at Australia West Airlines

15. (A) Please log on to begin the process.

(B) We fly to six continents.

(C) There is Internet access on the flight.

(D) Your flight is confirmed.

16. (A) timely

(B) quiet

(C) near

(D) together

17. (A) taking

(B) taken

(C) take

(D) took

18. (A) repair

(B) inspection

(C) journey

(D) service

> **명사의 자리** 문장에서 주어와 목적어, 보어 자리에 명사를 쓸 수 있다. 특히 목적어 자리에 명사를 넣는 문제가 자주 출제된다.

■ 주어 자리

문장에서 동사 앞에 등장하는 명사는 주어 역할을 할 수 있다.

[Improvements / ~~Improved~~] in the way we work proved effective in meeting increased demands.
우리 업무 방식의 개선이 늘어난 수요를 충족하는 데 효과가 있는 것으로 드러났다.

→ 동사 proved의 주어 역할을 하는 명사가 필요하다.

■ 목적어 자리

명사는 타동사의 목적어와 전치사의 목적어 역할을 한다. 또한 준동사인 to부정사나 동명사의 목적어 역할도 할 수 있다.

동사의 목적어	If you have [suggestions / ~~suggest~~] for future workshops, please write them down. 앞으로의 워크숍에 대해 제안이 있으면 적어 주세요.
전치사의 목적어	Remember the security code for [entrance / ~~enters~~] into the research facility. 연구 시설로 입장하려면 보안코드를 기억해 주세요.
준동사의 목적어	Some exercise during work helps to increase [productivity / ~~productively~~]. 근무 중에 하는 약간의 운동은 생산성을 높이는 데 도움이 된다.

■ 보어 자리

보어에는 주어를 보충하는 주격 보어, 목적어를 보충하는 목적격 보어가 있다. 형용사 또는 명사가 보어 역할을 하는데, 명사 보어는 주어 또는 목적어와 의미가 100% 일치한다.

주격 보어	Ms. Montgomery is an outstanding [expert / ~~expertise~~] in the foreign exchange market. 몽고메리 씨는 외환 시장의 뛰어난 전문가이다. (Ms. Montgomery = an expert) → be동사 뒤 주격 보어 자리이다. 명사 보어는 주어와 의미상 100% 일치해야 한다.
목적격 보어	Mr. Kim considers himself the most experienced [negotiator / ~~negotiation~~] in his team. 김 씨는 팀에서 가장 능숙한 협상가라고 자처한다. (himself = the negotiator) → consider 동사 뒤 목적격 보어 자리이다. 명사 보어는 목적어와 의미상 100% 일치해야 한다.

ETS 유형 연습 .... 정답과 해설 p.123

1 _____ of homegrown and organic fruits and vegetables, as well as handmade crafts and jewelry, are available for purchase at the Springdale community market.

(A) Varies
(B) Variant
(C) Varieties
(D) Various

2 Naomi Takeda was not able to attend the meeting last Tuesday, but Claire Marsters gave her a _____ of the discussion.

(A) summarily
(B) summarizer
(C) summarized
(D) summary

3 The relationship between Siron Manufacturers and Bonfait Shipping is based on _____ and respect.

(A) cooperate
(B) cooperatively
(C) cooperating
(D) cooperation

명사의 앞뒤	명사 앞에는 관사, 소유격, 형용사 등을 쓸 수 있다. 명사 뒤에는 다양한 품사들이 나올 수 있지만, 단수명사 뒤에 빈 칸이 있다면 복합명사가 될 수 있는지 우선 확인한다.

■ 관사, 소유격, 형용사 뒤 명사 자리

명사는 관사(a, an, the), 소유격(my, your, his, her, its, our, their, Mr. Kim's), 형용사 뒤에 나온다. 관사 'a(n)' 뒤에는 셀 수 있는 명사의 단수형만 쓸 수 있다.

관사 뒤
All workers greeted the [arrival / ~~arrive~~] of the new president with excitement.
모든 직원들이 들뜬 마음으로 신임 사장의 등장을 환영했다.

형용사 뒤
The manual provides comprehensive [instructions / ~~instructed~~] for the maintenance.
설명서는 관리를 위한 포괄적인 설명을 제공한다.

| 고득점 팁 | '관사/소유격＋형용사＋명사' 덩어리를 기억하자. 관사나 소유격 뒤에 명사를 수식하는 형용사가 올 수 있다.
The CEO will announce his [strategic / ~~strategy~~] investment plans soon.
CEO는 곧 그의 전략적인 투자 계획안을 발표할 것이다.

■ 복합명사

두 개의 명사가 결합된 복합명사는 한 단어로 취급된다. 복합명사에서 앞 명사는 주로 뒤 명사의 종류나 목적을 나타내는 수식어 역할을 하고, 뒤의 명사는 복합명사 덩어리의 가산/불가산 또는 단수/복수를 표현한다.

It is common for the application [process / ~~to process~~] of foreign students to take a long time.
외국 학생들의 신청 절차에 시간이 많이 소요되는 것은 흔한 일이다.

┌ 복합명사 적중 리스트 ─

복합명사의 앞 명사는 대부분 단수이지만, 복수형을 쓰는 경우도 있다.

account information 계좌 정보	office supplies 사무용품	building modifications 건축 변경사항
product availability 상품 입수 가능성	workplace safety 작업장 안전	job description 직무 소개
job responsibilities 직무, 책무	staff productivity 직원 생산성	employee performance 직원 성과
awards ceremony 시상식	customs clearance 세관 통관	earnings figures 수익 금액
travel arrangements/expenses 여행 준비/경비	investment decision 투자 (의사) 결정	consumer preference(s) 소비자 기호
safety standards/regulations/guidelines/precautions 안전 기준/규정/지침/예방책		

ETS 유형 연습

정답과 해설 p. 123

1 According to *Star Watch* magazine, singer-songwriter Kylie Norton has announced her upcoming _____ in a charity concert.

(A) participate
(B) participated
(C) participating
(D) participation

2 Leroy-Bontemps researched consumer _____ around the nation as part of the development of its low-calorie beverage products.

(A) preferred
(B) preferable
(C) preferences
(D) preferring

3 Gyeong Designs recently changed its marketing strategy to target hotel and restaurant _____.

(A) to own
(B) owned
(C) owners
(D) own

> **명사의 종류** 명사는 가산명사 단수, 가산명사 복수, 불가산명사로 나뉜다. 명사의 자리를 묻는 문제와 더불어 가산, 불가산명사를 구분하는 문제가 자주 출제된다.

■ 가산명사(셀 수 있는 명사)의 단수형

가산명사는 기본적으로 셀 수 있는 명사를 뜻하지만, 눈에 보이지 않는 개념도 가산명사로 쓸 수 있다. 가산명사의 단수형은 앞에 한정사, 즉 관사, 소유격, 지시/수량형용사 등을 반드시 동반하며, 절대 단독으로 쓰지 않는다.

| 가산명사의 단수형 앞에 쓸 수 있는 한정사 → | ❶ 관사 a(n), the | ❷ 소유격 |
| | ❸ 지시형용사 this, that | ❹ 수량형용사 each, another, every, either |

A more detailed [description / ~~descriptions~~] will be available on the company Web site.
더 상세한 설명은 회사 홈페이지에서 볼 수 있다.

■ 가산명사(셀 수 있는 명사)의 복수형

가산명사의 복수형은 주로 뒤에 -(e)s를 붙인다. 앞에 한정사가 올 수도 있고 단독으로 사용할 수도 있다. '하나의'라는 뜻의 a(n) 뒤에 복수형 명사를 쓸 수 없다.

| 가산명사의 복수형 앞에 쓸 수 있는 한정사 → | ❶ 관사 the | ❷ 소유격 |
| | ❸ 지시형용사 these, those | ❹ 수량형용사 both, (a) few, various, many |

These [surveys / ~~research~~] indicate that approximately 70% of the town residents are dissatisfied with the new government policy. 이 조사는 약 70퍼센트의 지역 주민들이 새로운 정부 정책에 불만족한다는 것을 보여준다.

■ 불가산명사(셀 수 없는 명사)

불가산명사는 앞에 a(n) 또는 뒤에 -(e)s를 붙일 수 없다. 불가산명사는 단수 취급한다.

> **불가산명사 적중 리스트**
>
> | information 정보 | negligence 부주의 | consent 동의, 허락 | advice 조언 | equipment 장비 |
> | machinery 기계류 | access 접근, 이용 | permission 허락 | luggage/baggage 수하물 | clothing 의류 |
> | furniture 가구 | merchandise 상품 | research 연구 | employment 고용 | manufacture 제조, 생산 |
>
> *일부 불가산명사는 의미가 바뀌면서 가산명사가 되기도 하므로 주의한다.
> work 일, 직장 - works 작품 condition 상태 - conditions 조건

Only a few manufacturing plants have [access / ~~accesses~~] to new computer technologies.
단지 몇몇 제조공장들만이 새로운 컴퓨터 기술을 이용할 수 있다.

ETS 유형 연습
정답과 해설 p.123

1 The final day to submit an application for a _____ in the finance department will be next Tuesday.

(A) position
(B) positions
(C) positioning
(D) positioned

2 Mr. Ono asked for _____ of all the documents that were passed out during the presentation.

(A) duplicate
(B) duplicates
(C) duplicated
(D) duplicative

3 Major industries in this district include food processing and aircraft _____.

(A) manufacturer
(B) manufactures
(C) manufactured
(D) manufacture

명사의 형태　품사나 의미, 단복수가 헷갈리는 명사들이 종종 문제로 출제된다. 형태가 특이한 명사는 따로 외워 두도록 한다.

■ 품사가 혼동되는 명사

품사가 혼동되는 명사 적중 리스트 ─

alternative 명 대안 형 대안의	adhesive 명 접착제 형 들러붙는	initiative 명 계획, 주도권	directive 명 지시사항 형 지시하는
perspective 명 관점	objective 명 목적 형 객관적인	original 명 원본 형 원래의	measure 명 수단, 조치 동 측정하다
estimate 명 견적서 동 견적내다	increase 명 증가 동 증가하다	decline 명 감소 동 감소하다	visit 명 방문 동 방문하다
permit 명 허가증 동 허가하다	change 명 변화 동 변화하다	delay 명 지연 동 지연시키다	characteristic 명 특징 형 특유의

■ 주의해야 할 사람명사

사람명사는 가산명사이므로, 단수형일 경우 앞에 한정사 없이 단독으로 쓸 수 없다.

주의해야 할 사람명사 적중 리스트 ─

executive 명 중역 형 경영의	representative 명 대표, 직원 형 대표하는	candidate 명 지원자, 후보자
applicant 명 지원자	delegate 명 대표자 동 파견하다	critic 명 비평가
associate 명 동료 동 연관 짓다	graduate 명 졸업생 동 졸업하다	acquaintance 명 지인
resident 명 주민, 거주자	authority 명 권위, 권위자	attendant 명 참석자, 승무원

I need to have a meeting with account [executives / ~~executive~~] at our advertising agency.
저희 광고 대행사에 있는 광고 기획자들과 회의를 해야 합니다.

■ 동명사와 혼동되는 -ing형 명사

-ing형 명사는 동명사와 형태는 같지만 뒤에 목적어가 올 수 없다. -ing형 명사는 대개 불가산명사이며 앞에 관사나 형용사가 올 수 있다.

-ing형 명사 적중 리스트 ─

seating 명 좌석 배치	ticketing 명 티켓 발급	processing 명 처리	funding 명 재정 지원, 자금
accounting 명 회계	planning 명 계획 수립, 기획	pricing 명 가격 책정	housing 명 주택, 주택 공급

*가산명사로 쓰이는 -ing형 명사도 있다.

openings 명 공석, 개막식	findings 명 발견한 사항	writings 명 저작물, 글

The project was successfully finished thanks to careful [planning / ~~plan~~].
프로젝트는 신중한 기획 덕분에 성공적으로 완료되었다.

ETS 유형 연습 ....

정답과 해설 p. 124

1 Mr. Rouja would like to see all employees take more _____ and develop contacts with potential clients.

(A) initiative
(B) initiated
(C) initiate
(D) initiating

2 Drevno flooring products are designed for _____ in industrial settings.

(A) user
(B) used
(C) useful
(D) use

3 The Manila Wellness Center has part-time and temporary employment _____ for certified nursing attendants in our Makati branch.

(A) opens
(B) openings
(C) openness
(D) opener

1. Recent ------- can learn about employment opportunities in a wide range of industries by attending a career fair.

   (A) graduating   (B) graduated
   (C) graduates   (D) graduation

2. The lightbulbs on the Werriver Building's second ------- are scheduled to be replaced this week.

   (A) floor   (B) floors
   (C) floored   (D) flooring

3. Parnpradub Graphic Design requires that employees possess advanced technical -------, including proficiency in numerous computer programs.

   (A) expert   (B) experts
   (C) expertly   (D) expertise

4. The president announced that a bonus will be awarded to the factory division that has demonstrated the highest ------- over the past year.

   (A) product   (B) productive
   (C) produce   (D) productivity

5. Yalinn Consulting provides interactive online tools that assist clients in making smart investment -------.

   (A) decide   (B) deciding
   (C) decides   (D) decisions

6. ------- from the International Society of Engineers met last week to plan next year's conference.

   (A) Representatives   (B) Representing
   (C) Represented   (D) Represents

7. Access to the database requires completion of an online training module and written ------- from Mr. Cooper.

   (A) to authorize   (B) authorized
   (C) authorizes   (D) authorization

8. As stated in our memo dated March 21, equipment should not be used for non-work related -------.

   (A) purposes   (B) purpose
   (C) purposely   (D) purposeful

9. The engineer approved the building changes because they represented a dramatic ------- in costs.

   (A) reduced   (B) reduction
   (C) reducible   (D) reduces

10. After two years of further -------, Hajalab's improved Dermalos facial cleanser is now on the market.

    (A) developed   (B) development
    (C) develops   (D) developer

11. Ms. Yem has been able to draw statistically valid conclusions from her analysis of the survey -------.

    (A) responses   (B) responded
    (C) respond   (D) responsively

12. We expect that an ------- search for a new human resources director will begin in September.

    (A) actively   (B) active
    (C) activate   (D) activity

13. Ivesci Electronics is taking the necessary ------- to guarantee the superior quality of its products.

    (A) measures   (B) systems

    (C) degrees   (D) activities

14. Staff members must obtain ------- from their managers before removing confidential documents from the building.

    (A) questions   (B) permission

    (C) change   (D) experience

Questions 15-18 refer to the following letter.

September 4

Raquel Taylor
105 Oakland Way
Westfield, MO 63999

Dear Ms. Taylor,

The building permit application you requested is enclosed. ------- beginning construction on a large
15.
patio in the rear of your restaurant, you must make sure that the permit has been approved and is

on file in our office. When you submit your application, please include a building plan that has been

reviewed and certified by a licensed engineer. You should anticipate an approval process taking

------- eight weeks.
16.

Also, please remember that before public ------- , the completed structure will need to be officially
17.

inspected. ------- .
18.

Sincerely,

Henry Bellingsworth, Manager
Office of Building Compliance, Westfield Municipal Center
Enclosure

---

15. (A) Prior to   (B) In addition
    (C) In spite of   (D) As many as

16. (A) approximated   (B) approximately
    (C) approximate   (D) approximation

17. (A) users   (B) useful
    (C) used   (D) use

18. (A) Please notify us when you are ready to schedule this final step.
    (B) Unfortunately, our office is scheduled to be closed tomorrow.
    (C) Please contact me with details of our upcoming meeting.
    (D) After that, a permit for construction will be issued to you.

Unit | 03 대명사

인칭/
소유대명사

인칭대명사의 격을 구별하는 문제는 거의 매달 출제되고 있으며, 인칭대명사가 지칭하는 대상을 확인해야 하는 문제도
간혹 출제된다. 소유대명사는 '소유격+명사' 역할을 하는 말로 '~의 것'이라고 해석한다.

■ 인칭대명사의 종류

수	인칭/성		인칭대명사			소유대명사
			주격(~은)	소유격(~의)	목적격(~을)	주어, 목적어, 보어
			동사 앞 주어 자리	명사 앞 명사 수식	동사 뒤, 전치사 뒤	(~의 것)
단수	1인칭		I	my	me	mine
	2인칭		you	your	you	yours
	3인칭	남성	he	his	him	his
		여성	she	her	her	hers
		사물	it	its	it	-
복수	1인칭		we	our	us	ours
	2인칭		you	your	you	yours
	3인칭(사람/사물)		they	their	them	theirs

The already established companies will be reducing [their / ~~them~~] advertising costs.
이미 기반을 잡은 회사들은 자신들(=회사들)의 광고 비용을 줄일 것이다.

■ 소유대명사

소유격과 달리, 소유대명사는 명사 앞에서 명사를 수식할 수 없다. '~의 것'이라고 해석하며, 주어, 목적어, 보어 자리에 두루 사용된다.

Though the president gathered different opinions, the final choice was [his / ~~him~~].
사장은 다양한 의견을 모았지만, 최종 선택은 그의 몫이었다.
→ be동사 뒤 주격 보어 자리에 소유대명사가 사용되었다.

■ 소유의 의미를 강조하는 one's own

one's own은 형용사와 대명사로 쓰이며 소유를 나타낸다. 소유격 자리에서 소유격을 대신하거나, 전치사 of 또는 on 뒤에 쓰여 '자기
자신(의 것)' 혹은 '스스로'라는 의미를 강조한다.

Ms. Lynne decided to quit the job for reasons of [her own / ~~herself~~].
린 씨는 자신만의 이유로 일을 그만두기로 결정했다.
→ of와 함께 '그녀 자신의 것(이유)'을 강조하는 her own이 쓰여야 한다.

ETS 유형 연습

1 Mr. Kato left the hotel's telephone number with the airport staff so they could notify _____ when the luggage is found.

(A) him
(B) himself
(C) he
(D) his

2 In recognition of Elaine Tang's exceptional service to _____ company, the human resources director will honor her at tonight's employee awards ceremony.

(A) ours
(B) our
(C) us
(D) we

3 The fast-food giant NuTru claims that our logo is a poorly disguised version of _____ own.

(A) them
(B) their
(C) theirs
(D) themselves

재귀대명사	재귀대명사는 '~ 자신, 직접'이라고 해석하며, 문장에서 목적어 자리, 부사 자리에 쓰인다. 목적격 대명사와 재귀대명사를 구분하는 문제가 자주 출제되니 반드시 구별할 수 있도록 하자.

■ 재귀대명사의 종류

재귀대명사는 -self/-selves 형태를 가지며 '(자기) 자신, 직접'을 의미한다. 재귀대명사는 주어 자리에는 쓸 수 없다.

단수					복수		
1인칭	2인칭	3인칭			1인칭	2인칭	3인칭
myself	yourself	himself	herself	itself	ourselves	yourselves	themselves

■ 재귀적 용법: 동사의 목적어 자리

주어와 목적어가 동일할 때 목적어 자리에 재귀대명사를 쓴다. 인칭대명사의 목적격과 재귀대명사를 구별해야 한다.

Painting is an effective way for artists to express [themselves / them].
그림은 예술가들이 자신을 표현할 수 있는 효과적인 방법이다.
→ to express의 의미상 주어 artists와 목적어 themselves의 지칭 대상이 일치한다.

■ 강조적 용법: 부사 자리

재귀대명사는 '직접'이라는 의미로 주어나 목적어를 강조한다. 강조적 용법의 재귀대명사는 부사와 매우 비슷하며 생략 가능하다.

Jason Miller conducted the survey and analyzed the results [himself / themselves].
제이슨 밀러 씨는 직접 설문조사를 시행하고 결과를 분석했다.
→ 단수형 재귀대명사 himself가 주어인 Jason Miller를 강조하고 있다.

■ 관용적 용법: 전치사의 목적어 자리

전치사 뒤 재귀대명사

by oneself 혼자서(= alone)	for oneself 혼자 힘으로	in itself 본래	of itself 저절로
to oneself 혼자서만	in spite of oneself 자신도 모르게	between ourselves (우리끼리) 비밀인데	

Dr. Edwards is unable to conduct his studies by [himself / his own], and he needs some assistance.
에드워드 박사는 혼자 힘으로는 연구할 수 없어서 도움이 필요하다.

ETS 유형 연습 .... 정답과 해설 p.126

1 The laboratory technicians decided to perform the statistical analysis _____ because hiring outside analysts would be too costly.

(A) myself
(B) herself
(C) yourselves
(D) themselves

2 The guests seemed very happy with the meal Chef Mirabel served _____ at the holiday banquet.

(A) they
(B) themselves
(C) their
(D) them

3 Mr. Shin updated the company's Web site by _____ because the other programmer had a problem with her password.

(A) itself
(B) herself
(C) themselves
(D) himself

> | 지시대명사 | 지시대명사에는 this(이것), that(저것), these(이것들), those(저것들)가 있는데, 각 대명사가 지칭하는 대상의 단수/복수를 구별해야 한다. 또한 that, those의 고유한 용법을 기억해야 한다. |

■ those '~하는 사람들'

대명사 those는 '~하는 사람들'이라는 뜻이고, 뒤에 who, -ing, -ed, 전치사구 등 수식어구를 동반한다.

[Those / T̶h̶e̶y̶] who are interested in attending the charity event are welcome to e-mail us.
자선 행사 참석에 관심 있는 분들은 저희에게 이메일을 보내 주세요.

[Those / T̶h̶e̶y̶] remaining in the office are required to leave the building in a few minutes.
사무실에 남아 있는 사람들은 잠시 후 건물을 나가야 한다.

■ 비교 대상을 지칭하는 that / those

두 대상을 비교하는 문장에서 앞에 언급된 명사를 지칭할 때 that / those를 쓴다. that과 those 뒤에는 대체로 수식어가 동반된다.

My relationship with my colleagues is similar to [that / i̶t̶] with my classmates at school.
나와 내 동료들과의 관계는 나와 학교 친구들과의 관계와 비슷하다.
→ 대명사 it은 뒤에 수식어를 동반할 수 없다.

The paintings in the room look much better than [those / t̶h̶a̶t̶] in the lobby.
방에 있는 그림들이 로비에 있는 그림들보다 훨씬 좋아 보인다.
→ 방에 있는 그림들과 로비에 있는 그림들을 비교하는 문장이므로 복수형 those가 쓰였다.

■ 앞서 언급된 내용을 지칭하는 this / these

this와 these는 앞서 언급된 명사를 대신하는 대명사와 형용사로 쓰일 수 있다. this는 단수형, these는 복수형이다.

The seminar includes group discussions and [these / t̶h̶i̶s̶] discussions will be led by the organizer.
세미나는 집단 토론을 포함하며 이 토론들은 주최측에 의해 진행될 것이다.

ETS 유형 연습

정답과 해설 p. 126

1 _____ who have not received the conference housing form should report to the registration desk as soon as possible.

(A) These
(B) This
(C) Those
(D) That

2 Those employees _____ in an assembly area must wear protective gear at all times.

(A) are working
(B) have worked
(C) working
(D) worked

3 This year's revenue figures from major auto rental agencies are remarkably similar to _____ of the preceding four years.

(A) those
(B) that
(C) them
(D) this

부정대명사	'부정'이란 정해지지 않았다는 뜻으로, 부정대명사는 지칭하는 대상을 명확히 밝히지 않을 때 쓰는 대명사이다. 부정대명사는 수량을 표현할 때 숙어처럼 쓰이기도 한다.

■ 부정대명사

부정대명사는 우리말 의미뿐 아니라 품사와 수 일치를 함께 기억해야 한다.

종류	우리말 의미	품사		수 일치	
		대명사	형용사	대명사일 때	형용사일 때
one	(막연한) 하나(의), ~것	O	O	The new one is different. 단수	one reason 단수
another	(막연한) 또 하나(의)	O	O	Another is expensive. 단수	another reason 단수
other	(막연한) 다른	X	O	X	other reasons 복수 other equipment 불가산명사
the other	(특정 범위의) 나머지(의)	O	O	The other looks good. 단수	the other reason(s) 단수/복수 the other equipment 불가산명사
some	(막연한) 몇몇(의)/약간(의)	O	O	Some are from Europe. 복수	some reasons 복수 some equipment 불가산명사
others	(막연한) 다른 것/사람들	O	X	Others are from America. 복수	X
the others	(특정 범위의) 나머지들	O	X	The others are correct. 복수	X
each other one another	서로 서로	O	X	They helped each other. (주어 자리에 못 씀)	X

■ 부분을 나타내는 대명사

부분대명사는 '부정대명사+of+the/소유격+명사' 덩어리를 이루어 숙어처럼 사용된다.

One ~ 중 하나 Either 둘 중 하나	Each 각각 Neither 둘 다 (아니다)		of the candidates 복수명사	is qualified. 3인칭 단수
Several ~ 중 몇몇 A few/Few ~ 중 몇몇/거의 (아니다)	Both 둘 다	Many ~ 중 다수	of the candidates 복수명사	are qualified. 복수
Much ~ 중 많은 부분	A little/Little ~ 중 약간/거의 (아니다)		of the information 불가산명사	is useful. 3인칭 단수
All ~의 전부 Some ~ 중 일부 None ~ 중 아무(것)도 (아니다)	Most ~의 대부분 Any ~ 중 무엇이든지/누구든지	Half ~의 절반	of the candidates 복수명사	are qualified. 복수
			of the information 불가산명사	is useful. 3인칭 단수

ETS 유형 연습

정답과 해설 p.127

1 _____ of the people involved in developing this software imagined it would become so popular.

(A) None
(B) Anybody
(C) Whoever
(D) Something

2 Construction of the carpet showroom will be finished by the end of the week, but operations will not begin for _____ month.

(A) other
(B) another
(C) one another
(D) some other

3 Dr. Hemana and Dr. Wareham, the joint recipients of the Cobalt Research Prize, have known _____ since they were university students in Auckland.

(A) other one
(B) another one
(C) any other
(D) each other

1. At Stanwick and Associates, we pride ourselves on giving ------- of our clients a personalized wealth-management plan.

    (A) each
    (B) whose
    (C) whatever
    (D) every

2. Ms. Prashad is planning a major revision of our hiring procedure after she has had time to study ------- overall effectiveness.

    (A) they
    (B) it
    (C) them
    (D) its

3. Ms. Yan has requested transportation from the office to the new plant site for ------- and three clients this Friday.

    (A) her own
    (B) she
    (C) herself
    (D) hers

4. Please tell Ms. Dupont that there is no way ------- could possibly thank her enough for making the award dinner such a success.

    (A) us
    (B) ourselves
    (C) our
    (D) we

5. Steven Brad, the office manager, requests that all staff communicate directly with ------- about new supply orders.

    (A) he
    (B) his
    (C) him
    (D) his own

6. Although the team worked together to develop the graphics for this report, the text is primarily -------.

    (A) myself
    (B) mine
    (C) me
    (D) my

7. Employees are invited to express ------- opinions about the revised lunch menu by e-mailing Ms. Warren.

    (A) their
    (B) theirs
    (C) they
    (D) them

8. A recent study revealed that people who eat breakfast regularly tend to stay healthier than ------- who skip breakfast.

    (A) those
    (B) such
    (C) this
    (D) someone

9. The home sales and rental markets should strengthen soon, as ------- usually benefit when the local economy improves.

    (A) it
    (B) both
    (C) that
    (D) which

10. Of the three parking garage plans that were submitted, two are unacceptable, while ------- is possible only if an additional $25,000 is budgeted.

    (A) one another
    (B) each other
    (C) the other
    (D) other

11. Although he performed the experiment several times, Professor Katakura's results differed from ------- of his colleagues.

    (A) it
    (B) them
    (C) theirs
    (D) those

12. Staff members should work in pairs during the training workshop to help ------- master the procedure for handling customer service inquiries.

    (A) one such
    (B) each other
    (C) yourself
    (D) everything

13. The last customer survey indicated that ------- were dissatisfied with their hotel dining experience.

(A) much (B) many
(C) somebody (D) anybody

14. Instead of sending the entire staff to an outside course to learn the new software, the director decided to train ------- himself.

(A) ourselves (B) anyone
(C) themselves (D) everyone

Questions 15-18 refer to the following article.

Allure Wear Appoints New CFO

The Milan-based retail company Allure Wear, Inc., has appointed Piper Hsieh as its new chief financial officer (CFO). Hsieh, who most recently served as CFO at Kareena's Sportswear ------- 15. six years, will start her new position on December 1. ------- 16. "We are excited to have Piper join the Allure Wear family," Allure Wear CEO Eugenia Rinaldi said in a statement. "------- 17. strong financial background and retail expertise will undoubtedly help the growth of our company. We look forward to her positive contributions." Hsieh will ------- 18. Segun Simone. Simone, Allure Wear's current CFO, will retire at the end of November.

15. (A) above
(B) from
(C) for
(D) at

17. (A) My
(B) Your
(C) Its
(D) Her

16. (A) In this role, she'll be responsible for finance, accounting, and real estate.
(B) Rinaldi started working at Allure Wear over twenty years ago.
(C) One of these was creating a new line of women's sportswear.
(D) She described her first day on the job as "extremely constructive."

18. (A) find
(B) replace
(C) supervise
(D) assist

형용사

형용사의 자리	형용사는 명사의 앞이나 뒤에서 명사를 수식, 또는 보충하는 말이다. 명사를 수식하는 형용사는 2개 이상 연달아 사용할 수 있다. 형용사를 주격 보어, 목적격 보어로 취하는 동사를 외워두자.

■ 명사의 앞이나 뒤에서 명사를 수식

형용사는 명사의 앞이나 뒤에서 명사를 수식할 수 있다. 형용사는 2개 이상 연달아 사용할 수 있지만, 관사 앞에는 형용사를 쓸 수 없다.

Thanks to the [massive / massively] public campaign, more commuters started to use public transportation.
대대적인 공공 캠페인 덕분에, 보다 많은 통근자들이 대중 교통을 이용하기 시작했다.

➜ 형용사인 massive와 public 둘 다 명사를 수식하고 있다.

Our publication is not [simply / simple] an entertainment magazine, but also a journalistic tool.
우리 출판물은 단순히 연예 잡지만이 아니라 시사 잡지 역할을 하기도 한다.

➜ 관사 앞에는 형용사를 쓸 수 없다.

■ be동사 뒤 주격 보어

be동사 등 2형식 동사 뒤에는 주어를 보충 설명하는 주격 보어가 나온다. 형용사는 주격 보어 역할을 하며 주어의 상태를 설명한다.
* 주격 보어를 원하는 동사 목록은 Unit 01. 품사와 문장 구조 편을 참고한다.

The idea of seeking sponsorship rather than laying off workers seems [persuasive / persuasively].
직원들을 해고하는 대신 후원을 받아보자는 아이디어가 설득력이 있어 보인다.

➜ 형용사 persuasive가 동사 seems의 보어로 오며 부사는 보어로 올 수 없다.

■ 5형식 동사 뒤 목적격 보어

동사 make 등 5형식 동사 뒤에는 목적어를 보충 설명하는 목적격 보어가 나온다. 형용사는 목적격 보어로서 목적어의 상태를 설명할 수 있다.
* 목적격 보어를 원하는 동사 목록은 Unit 01. 품사와 문장 구조 편을 참고한다.

Residents have found the new recycling program [convenient / conveniently].
주민들은 새로운 재활용 프로그램이 편리하다고 생각했다.

➜ 형용사 convenient는 have found의 목적격 보어로서 the new recycling program의 특징을 설명하고 있다.

ETS 유형 연습

정답과 해설 p.129

1 Employees on international assignment with Daniel Windmere Corporation receive _____ financial support when finding a place to live.

(A) extend
(B) extent
(C) extensive
(D) extending

2 The loan application process at Palau Bay Bank is very _____.

(A) efficient
(B) efficiency
(C) efficiently
(D) efficiencies

3 Critics of the recent movie with Michelle Zhao have called the plot too _____.

(A) predicting
(B) predicted
(C) predictable
(D) predictably

수량/ 부정형용사	수와 양을 나타내는 수량형용사, 정해지지 않은 범위를 지칭하는 부정형용사는 수식하는 명사와 수가 일치되어야 한다. 각각의 형용사에 어울리는 명사형을 외워두자.

가산명사의 단수형과 어울리는 형용사

	가산명사의 단수형 (O)	가산명사의 복수형 (X)	불가산명사 (X)
a(n) 하나의, another 또 하나의, each 각각의, every 모든, either 둘 중 하나의	each team	each team~~s~~	each ~~equipment~~
the single/a single 하나의, the entire/the whole 전체의 *뒤에 단수명사, 앞에 관사가 필요한 형용사	the whole team	the whole team~~s~~	the whole ~~equipment~~

*'every+숫자+복수명사'는 '~마다', 'another+숫자+복수명사'는 '추가적인'이라는 뜻이다.
예: every three months 세 달마다, another three months 추가의 세 달

가산명사의 복수형과 어울리는 형용사

	가산명사의 복수형 (O)	가산명사의 단수형 (X)	불가산명사 (X)
many 많은, numerous 많은, several 몇몇의, various 다양한, a few 몇몇의, few 거의 없는, both 둘 다, these 이, those 저, multiple 많은, a couple of 두서넛의, a number of 많은, a series of 일련의, a selection/variety of 다양한	several products	several product	several ~~advice~~

불가산명사와 어울리는 형용사

	불가산명사 (O)	가산명사의 단수형 (X)	가산명사의 복수형 (X)
much 많은, a little 약간의, less 더 적은, little 거의 없는, a great amount/deal of 많은	little information	little ~~question~~	little ~~questions~~

복수명사, 불가산명사와 어울리는 형용사

	불가산명사 (O)	가산명사의 단수형 (X)	가산명사의 복수형 (O)
all 모든, most 대부분의, other 다른, some 몇몇의, more 더 많은, a lot/plenty of 많은	more research	more ~~survey~~	more surveys

ETS 유형 연습

정답과 해설 p.129

1 _____ sample from Ando Biology Labs must be kept at the correct temperature.

(A) All
(B) Most
(C) Other
(D) Every

2 Despite the cost, _____ staff members were in favor of renovating the auditorium.

(A) mass
(B) many
(C) much
(D) plenty

3 Delmoor Corporation is not responsible for damage caused by misuse, improper care, or _____ consumer negligence.

(A) another
(B) the other
(C) others
(D) other

> **형용사의 형태** 같은 어원을 가져 형태는 비슷하지만 의미가 다른 형용사를 정확히 구별하여 외워두자. 그리고 수식하는 명사에 따라 형태가 달라지는 형용사는 '형용사+명사'를 덩어리째로 외워두도록 하자.

■ 끝말의 형태가 특이한 형용사

형용사는 대개 -ous, -ical, -ful, -able, -ish 등과 같은 끝말이 오지만, 이 밖에도 다양한 형태의 형용사들이 있다.

timely 시기적절한	costly 비용이 많이 드는	likely ~할 것 같은	orderly 질서 정연한	wide 넓은
broad 폭넓은	thorough 철저한	diverse 다양한	distinct 뚜렷한	definite 명확한
adequate 충분한	accurate 정확한	complete 완전한	deliberate 의도적인	delicate 섬세한, 민감한

■ 형태는 유사하지만 의미가 다른 형용사

혼동하기 쉬운 형용사 적중 리스트

respectful attitude 존중하는 태도	**informative** presentation 유익한 발표	**competitive** salary 경쟁력 있는 급여
respective rooms 각각의 방들	**informed** decision 정보에 입각한 결정	**competent** person 유능한 사람
successful products 성공적인 제품	**favorite** sport 좋아하는 운동	**reliant** on exports 수출에 의존하는
successive years 계속되는 해	**favorable** response 호의적인 반응	**reliable** source 믿을 만한 소식통
considerate of others 타인을 배려하는	be **confident** of ~을 믿다, 자신하다	**complimentary** mug 무료 머그잔
considerable loss 상당한 손해	**confidential** documents 기밀 문서	**complementary** relations 상호보완적 관계
advisory committee 자문 위원회	**economic** issue 경제 문제	be **responsible** for ~을 책임지다
It is **advisable** to ~하는 것이 바람직하다	**economical** use 경제적인 사용법	be **responsive** to ~에 대응하다

■ -ing / -ed로 끝나는 형용사

동사에 -ing, -ed를 붙인 분사 형태가 형용사로 굳어져 사용되는 경우가 있다. 특히 감정과 관련된 의미의 -ed형용사는 대개 사람명사를 수식한다.

형용사로 굳어버린 -ing / -ed 적중 리스트

lasting 지속되는	remaining 남아 있는	missing 분실된	rewarding 보람 있는
encouraging 고무적인	deteriorating 악화되는	outstanding 뛰어난	fascinating 매력적인
motivated 의욕적인	distinguished 뛰어난, 유명한	impressed 감동받은	satisfied 만족하는
qualified 자격을 갖춘	limited 제한된	unprecedented 유례 없는	repeated 반복적인

ETS 유형 연습

정답과 해설 p. 129

1 The _____ attractions of the Hale Valley continue to delight visitors and residents.

(A) diversification
(B) diversifying
(C) diverse
(D) diversity

2 All passengers should be _____ of others by speaking softly when talking on mobile phones.

(A) considerable
(B) considering
(C) considerate
(D) consideration

3 Enclosed is the latest listing of the _____ companies and institutions that use our firm's specialized consulting services.

(A) distinguishably
(B) distinguishability
(C) distinguished
(D) distinguish

<table>
<tr><td>형용사 어휘</td><td>형용사 어휘 문제는 '형용사＋명사', '주어＋be＋형용사'의 덩어리로 인식하고 해석하면 쉽게 해결된다.
'be＋형용사＋전치사', 'be＋형용사＋to부정사' 관용 표현도 함께 외워두자.</td></tr>
</table>

■ 'be＋형용사＋전치사' 빈출 표현

be responsible for ~할 책임이 있다	be eligible for ~할 자격이 있다 (=be entitled to 명사)	be related to 명사 ~와 관련되다 (=be associated with)
be compliant with ~를 따르다	be accustomed/used to 명사 ~에 익숙하다 (=be familiar with)	be accessible to 명사 ~에 접근 가능하다
be open to 명사 ~에 열려 있다	be comparable to 명사 ~에 필적하다	be compared with ~와 비교되다
be notable for ~로 유명하다 (=be renowned for)	be appreciative of ~을 감사하다	be aware of ~을 알고 있다 (=be conscious of)
be compatible with ~와 호환 가능하다	be indicative of ~을 나타내다	be exempt from ~을 면제받다
be representative of ~을 대표하다	be contingent on ~에 달려 있다	be consistent with ~와 일치하다

■ 'be＋형용사＋to부정사' 빈출 표현

be reluctant to do ~하기를 꺼리다 be hesitant to do ~하기를 주저하다	be eager to do ~하기를 열망하다 be eligible to do ~할 자격이 있다	be pleased to do ~해서 기쁘다 be entitled to do ~할 자격이 있다

We are [pleased / ~~indicative~~] to introduce the new marketing director, who just came back from the headquarters. 우리는 얼마 전 본사에서 돌아온 신임 마케팅 이사를 소개하게 되어 기쁩니다.

■ 기타 주의해야 할 형용사의 용법

형용사	특징	예
possible 가능한	사람을 수식할 수 없다.	a **possible** [merger / ~~supervisor~~]
following 다음의	형용사 following 앞에 반드시 the를 써야 한다.	the **following** year
upcoming 다가오는	명사는 미래에 일어날 일이다.	the **upcoming** election
sincere 진실한	감정과 관련된 명사와 쓴다.	our **sincere** apologies
diverse 다양한	단수명사와 함께 쓸 수 있다.	a **diverse** world

Ron Wiseman was invited to appear as a guest speaker at a conference [next / ~~following~~] Monday.
론 와이즈먼 씨는 다음 월요일 회의에 초청 연사로 나오도록 요청받았다.

ETS 유형 연습

정답과 해설 p.130

1 According to company guidelines, new employees are _____ to receive vacation benefits after three months of full-time employment.

(A) capable
(B) variable
(C) flexible
(D) eligible

2 All passengers are responsible _____ obtaining proper travel documents before departure.

(A) for
(B) to
(C) in
(D) with

3 Please accept our _____ thanks for the fine work you are doing in our sales department.

(A) original
(B) estimated
(C) sincere
(D) completed

1. Ms. Garcia is a devoted and ------- hospital executive who cares about every patient at Millet Medical Center.

   (A) enthusiast
   (B) enthusiastically
   (C) enthusiasm
   (D) enthusiastic

2. Local manufacturers have been ------- to hire additional employees until productivity improves.

   (A) hesitate
   (B) hesitation
   (C) hesitated
   (D) hesitant

3. The candidate for the administrative assistant position must have strong ------- skills.

   (A) organizational
   (B) organizationally
   (C) organizes
   (D) organize

4. Make sure that the door is ------- closed before you leave the building.

   (A) securely
   (B) security
   (C) secure
   (D) securing

5. Consistently ranked among the area's best IT support companies, Extrinet Corporation provides ------- technical assistance.

   (A) dependability
   (B) dependable
   (C) depended
   (D) depending

6. The architects at Brightman Partners, Inc., design buildings that are elegant as well as -------.

   (A) function
   (B) functioned
   (C) functionality
   (D) functional

7. Because there were so ------- people registered for the Business Writing seminar, it was postponed until September.

   (A) few
   (B) barely
   (C) less
   (D) hardly

8. A new version of the program is now readily ------- at the Reyan Software download site.

   (A) accessibility
   (B) accesses
   (C) access
   (D) accessible

9. Several supervisors have complained that the unscheduled maintenance has been ------- to vehicle assembly.

   (A) disruptive
   (B) disruptions
   (C) disrupt
   (D) disrupted

10. In order to keep prices -------, Kim's Bakery will begin making its breads and cakes on the premises.

    (A) reasonable
    (B) reasonably
    (C) reasoning
    (D) reason

11. Third-party inspection of Accuceutical Corporation's clinical laboratory takes place ------- three months.

    (A) enough
    (B) every
    (C) several
    (D) some

12. A number of the world's ancient monuments are in ------- condition and need the help of skilled preservationists.

    (A) deteriorating
    (B) deterioration
    (C) deteriorates
    (D) deteriorate

13. Before the doors open, Graff Center ushers should ensure that they have an ------- number of concert programs on hand.

(A) opposite
(B) adequate
(C) intensive
(D) eligible

14. The projected expansion of the apparel division remains ------- on final approval of the necessary budget allocations.

(A) contingent
(B) eventual
(C) hopeful
(D) speculative

Questions 15-18 refer to the following e-mail.

From: Max Moana <mmoana@egmontflooring.co.nz>
To: Devina Hartono <dhartono@hartonogroup.co.nz>
Subject: New carpet
Date: 3 March

Dear Ms. Hartono:

I am responding to your ------- about our carpet installation service. We are definitely able to work
15.
around your regular business hours to minimize any inconvenience to you. In addition, members of

our staff with expertise in interior decorating ------- you a wide variety of attractive flooring options.
16.

Egmont Flooring offers a huge selection of carpet styles, patterns, and designs that are available

in natural as well as synthetic materials. Our fine carpets transform any workplace, creating a fresh

and ------- atmosphere.
17.

-------. Thank you for contacting us. We look forward to serving you.
18.

Yours truly,

Max Moana
Sales Manager, Egmont Flooring

15. (A) inquiry
(B) article
(C) complaint
(D) evaluation

16. (A) did show
(B) can show
(C) are showing
(D) were showing

17. (A) invite
(B) invitation
(C) inviting
(D) invited

18. (A) I am sorry that we cannot offer you something better at this time.
(B) To get started, visit us at our Midwood Avenue showroom.
(C) My associate, Ms. Fey, will inform you of any updates to the schedule.
(D) Finally, remember to follow the care instructions we provided.

부사의 자리	부사는 동사, 형용사, 부사, 전치사구 등을 수식하는 수식어이며, 없어도 문장 구조가 달라지지 않으므로 생략 가능하다. 부사 자리를 찾는 문제는 출제 빈도가 높고 난이도가 낮은 편이므로 반드시 다 맞힐 수 있도록 하자.

■ 주어와 동사 사이 부사 자리

빈칸 앞이 주어, 뒤가 동사이면 빈칸은 부사 자리이다.

A travel agent [mistakenly / mistakes] cancelled my flight and hotel reservation.
여행사 직원은 나의 항공권 예약과 호텔 예약을 실수로 취소했다.

■ 동사구 사이 부사 자리

동사가 두 단어 이상으로 이루어져 있는 경우, 동사구 사이에 부사를 삽입할 수 있다.

All public facilities must be [fully / full] equipped for convenience of the disabled.
장애인의 편의를 위해 모든 공공 시설이 완벽하게 갖추어져 있어야 한다.

■ 자동사 뒤 부사 자리

부사는 목적어가 필요 없는 자동사 뒤에서 동사를 수식할 수 있다. 'be+p.p.' 형태의 수동태 동사 뒤에서도 부사가 동사를 수식할 수 있다.

Last week's sales figures of the latest computer game rose [significantly / significance] compared to the second quarter. 최근 발매된 컴퓨터 게임의 지난주 매출액이 2/4분기와 비교해 눈에 띄게 증가했다.

■ 형용사, 부사, 전치사, 접속사 앞 부사 자리

부사는 형용사, 부사, 구와 절 앞에서 수식어 역할을 할 수 있다.

The two opposing parties have not found a [mutually / mutual] agreeable solution yet.
반대 의견을 가진 두 당사자들은 상호 간에 동의할 만한 해결책을 아직 찾아내지 못했다.
→ 부사 mutually가 형용사 agreeable 앞에서 형용사를 수식하고 있다.

■ 준동사 앞 부사 자리

부사는 준동사인 to부정사, 동명사, 분사를 수식한다.

Mr. Oman is responsible for [regularly / regular] checking the medical equipment in the clinic.
오만 씨는 병원 내 의료 장비를 정기적으로 점검하는 일을 담당하고 있다.

ETS 유형 연습

정답과 해설 p. 132

1 We may share your mailing address with our subsidiaries for marketing purposes unless you _____ request in writing that we not do so.

(A) specific
(B) specify
(C) specification
(D) specifically

2 Any changes in your tax status should be reported to the payroll division _____ so that corrections can be made in a timely fashion.

(A) prompt
(B) promptly
(C) prompted
(D) prompting

3 A new production device takes manufacturers one step closer to making electronic displays _____ out of plastic.

(A) total
(B) totaling
(C) totally
(D) totaled

부사 어휘 1 | 부사 어휘 문제는 부사의 의미뿐 아니라 동사의 시제 또는 부사의 위치에 따라 정답이 결정되기도 하므로 유의해야 한다. 빈출 부사를 기능에 따라 분류하여 외워두자.

■ 시간부사

시간을 의미하는 부사는 해석하기 전에 동사의 시제가 부사의 시간 표현과 어울리는지 먼저 확인해야 한다.

❶ already 이미 / still 여전히 / yet 아직(안 했다)

already는 주로 현재완료형(have p.p.) 동사와 쓰인다. still은 부정문일 때 'still + not'의 어순으로 사용된다.
yet은 'have not p.p. ~ yet' 또는 'have[be] yet to(아직 ~하지 않았다)' 구문으로 출제된다.

The office furniture arrived this morning, but it has not been assembled [yet / ~~already~~ / ~~still~~].
사무용 가구는 오늘 아침에 도착했지만, 아직 조립되지는 않았다.

The maintenance workers have [already / ~~still~~ / ~~yet~~] inspected the security system throughout the building.
관리 직원들은 건물 곳곳에 있는 보안 시스템을 이미 점검했다.

❷ now / currently / presently 지금, 현재

'현재'를 의미하는 부사는 현재, 현재진행(is / are -ing) 동사와 함께 쓴다.

The analysts are [currently / ~~previously~~] reviewing the data gathered by surveillance cameras.
분석가들은 현재 감시 카메라가 수집한 정보를 검토하고 있다.

❸ ago 전에(과거) / recently(= lately) 최근에(과거, 현재완료)

ago는 과거 동사와 어울리며 '기간 + ago' 형태로 쓰인다. recently는 과거, 현재완료 동사와 모두 어울린다.

Five new interns were hired by the advertising agency some time [ago / ~~recently~~].
얼마 전에 광고회사에 다섯 명의 새 인턴 사원이 채용되었다.

■ 빈도부사

빈도부사는 발생 횟수를 나타내며 be동사나 조동사 뒤, 일반동사 앞에 온다. 이 중 일부는 문장 앞이나 끝에 올 수 있다.

0%	never	hardly / rarely / scarcely / seldom	sometimes	usually / regularly	often	always	100%
	결코 ~ 않다	거의 ~ 않다	가끔	보통	자주	항상	

Visitors [always / ~~even~~] express their amazement at how sophisticated the ancient temple is.
방문객들은 고대 사원이 얼마나 정교한지에 대해 언제나 놀라움을 표현한다.

ETS 유형 연습

정답과 해설 p. 132

1 The central accounting office has _____ not released the annual spending figures for last year.

(A) once
(B) soon
(C) almost
(D) still

2 Due to technical problems, Nelson's Electronic Auctions is _____ not accepting any picture submissions via e-mail.

(A) quickly
(B) currently
(C) precisely
(D) temperately

3 Many investors watch news programs _____ in order to keep up with current events that could impact the financial markets.

(A) shortly
(B) often
(C) soon
(D) hardly

부사 중에는 특정 수식 대상과 함께 쓰는 부사들이 있다. 단어의 우리말 의미뿐 아니라 기능을 같이 기억하도록 하자. 해석할 때는 우선 부사의 의미가 동사와 어울리는지 확인해야 한다.

■ 형태는 비슷하지만 의미는 다른 부사

even 심지어 - evenly 공평하게	hard 열심히 - hardly 거의 ~ 않다
high 높이 - highly 매우	late 늦게 - lately 최근에

Many of the manufacturing staff have worked overtime to meet the demand [lately / ~~late~~].
제조팀의 직원 대부분이 수요를 맞추기 위해 최근 초과 근무를 했다.

■ 명사구를 강조하는 부사

only 오직	simply 단지	just 단지	mainly 주로	formerly 이전에	even 심지어

This building, [formerly / ~~former~~] an elementary school, has been renovated as a children's library.
이 건물은 이전에는 초등학교였으나, 어린이 도서관으로 개조되었다.
→ 형용사는 관사 앞에 쓸 수 없다. 명사구를 강조하는 부사 formerly가 쓰여야 한다.

■ 숫자, 수량을 수식하는 부사

approximately / roughly / around / about / almost / nearly 거의, 대략	over / more than ~이상
barely / only / just / at (the) most / no more than 겨우	at least / at the very least 최소한, 적어도

[About / ~~By~~] 50 percent of the participants gave positive reviews to our product demonstration.
약 50퍼센트의 참가자들이 우리의 제품 시연에 대해 긍정적인 평가를 해주었다.
→ about은 숫자를 수식하는 부사로 쓸 수 있다.

■ 증가, 감소, 변화의 동사를 수식하는 부사

considerably / significantly / substantially 상당히	steadily 꾸준히	gradually 점차적으로
sharply / noticeably / remarkably / dramatically 급격하게, 두드러지게	greatly 크게	slightly 약간

The sales of organic foods increased [remarkably / ~~nearly~~], based on a rising demand for health care.
건강 관리에 대한 관심이 늘면서 유기농 식품 판매량이 눈에 띄게 증가했다.
→ nearly는 '거의'라는 뜻의 부사로 숫자 등의 수식 대상이 뒤에 나온다.

ETS 유형 연습

정답과 해설 p. 132

1 The X200's crisp, film-like images prove that it is the most _____ advanced digital camera on the market.

(A) high
(B) higher
(C) highly
(D) highest

2 Montgomery College has announced that it will make the materials for _____ all of its courses available on the Internet.

(A) nearer
(B) nearly
(C) nearest
(D) nearing

3 If companies standardize their products instead of offering different versions of the same product, they will be able to reduce their expenses _____.

(A) signify
(B) to signify
(C) significantly
(D) significant

> 부사 어휘 3   부사 중에는 특별한 쓰임새가 있는 것들이 있다. 각 부사의 대표적인 용례를 기억하여 어휘 문제에 대비하자.

■ 형용사, 부사를 수식하는 부사

> very / fairly / quite / highly 매우   extremely / excessively / incredibly / overly / exceptionally 극도로
>
> * 형용사, 부사를 수식할 수 있지만 동사를 수식할 수 없다. (예) extremely difficult (o), extremely work (x)

The recent presentation on sales strategies was [quite / ~~well~~] informative.

영업 전략에 대한 최근의 발표는 상당히 유익했다.

> much / still / even / far / a lot 훨씬   * 비교급 표현 앞에서 형용사, 부사를 수식하며 '훨씬'이라고 해석한다.

The fact that the prices are very unstable makes the study much [harder / ~~hard~~].

가격이 매우 불안정하다는 사실은 연구를 훨씬 더 어렵게 만든다.

> | | | |
> |---|---|---|
> | too 너무   enough 충분히 | enough to ~할 만큼 충분히 | such (한정사) 매우 ~한   far / much too 너무, 지나치게 |
> | so 매우   so ~ that ... 너무 ~해서 …하다 | too ~ to ... 너무 ~해서 …할 수 없다 | such (a) 형용사 명사 굉장히 ~한 명사 |

Some models are [so / ~~very~~ / ~~too~~] popular that manufacturers are unable to keep up with the demand.

몇몇 제품은 매우 인기가 있어서 제조업체가 수요를 따라잡지 못하고 있다.

■ 기타 주의해야 할 부사

> | | | |
> |---|---|---|
> | ever (부정문, 조건문, 비교 구문에서) 한 번이라도, 어느 때이든지, 여태까지 | hardly ever 좀처럼 ~ 않다 | ever since ~ 이후로 지금까지 |
> | rarely if ever ~하더라도 극히 드물게 | well (분사 수식) 잘, (전치사구 수식) 훨씬 | well ahead of schedule 일정보다 훨씬 앞서 |

The relations between management and employees are now stronger than [ever / ~~then~~].

경영진과 직원 사이의 관계가 어느 때보다 더 굳건하다.

■ 접속부사

> | | | | | |
> |---|---|---|---|---|
> | however 그러나 | meanwhile 한편, 그 동안에 | besides 게다가 | moreover(=furthermore) 게다가 | also 또한 |
> | therefore 그러므로 | then 그러고 나서 | likewise 마찬가지로 | nevertheless(=nonetheless, even so) 그럼에도 불구하고 | |

The director is eager to expand into China, [but / ~~however~~] he doesn't have any specific plans.

이사는 중국으로 확장하기를 원하지만, 구체적인 계획을 가지고 있지 않다.

→ 접속부사는 문법적으로 부사이기 때문에 뒤에 '주어+동사'를 포함하는 절을 이끌 수 없다.

ETS 유형 연습 ....

정답과 해설 p.133

1 Market research results for Thermabrite's new handheld thermometer prototype were _____ encouraging.

   (A) well
   (B) near
   (C) freely
   (D) very

2 For the period ending June 30, the Horizon Stadium Corporation recorded unprecedented revenues from ticket sales, and _____ more from advertising.

   (A) all
   (B) very
   (C) any
   (D) even

3 Nonaka Consultancy's strength lies in its accomplished team of data analysts, and _____ the company highlights its analytic services when seeking new clients.

   (A) therefore
   (B) now that
   (C) in case
   (D) otherwise

1. Regular mailing-list updates have ------- supported TNI Company's efforts to target the right markets.
   (A) succeed
   (B) succeeded
   (C) successful
   (D) successfully

2. Along with beautiful beaches and delicious food, Santen Island also offers ------- outdoor activities for travelers.
   (A) numerous
   (B) numbering
   (C) numerously
   (D) number

3. The analysis is ------- thorough and will enable readers to understand the recent downturn in Greenview's economy.
   (A) extreme
   (B) extremity
   (C) extremely
   (D) more extreme

4. Sigma Technologies ------- bought new accounting software that better meets the needs of its customers.
   (A) recent
   (B) recently
   (C) more recent
   (D) the most recently

5. ------- after graduating from Pellenem University, classmates Trevor Thorsen and Heidi Smith cofounded a consulting firm.
   (A) As soon as
   (B) Provided that
   (C) Shortly
   (D) Despite

6. Noted author Neha Dehuri will be signing copies of her ------- acclaimed book, *The Forgotten*, on Sunday at the Gloucester University Bookstore.
   (A) critically
   (B) criticism
   (C) critics
   (D) criticize

7. The cost of mahogany furniture rose ------- this year due to a shortage of raw materials.
   (A) considers
   (B) considering
   (C) considered
   (D) considerably

8. Property owners should ------- educate themselves on the value of waterproofing their buildings.
   (A) fill
   (B) fuller
   (C) fully
   (D) filled

9. The Yokohama Orchestra's summer concert will begin at 7:00 P.M. and last ------- two hours.
   (A) approximated
   (B) approximating
   (C) approximation
   (D) approximately

10. To apply for membership, ------- complete the form on the society's Web site.
    (A) simple
    (B) simply
    (C) simplify
    (D) simplicity

11. ------- demonstrating an impressive work ethic, Ms. Hyun often takes on extra projects in addition to her regular workload.
    (A) Consistently
    (B) Consistency
    (C) Consisted
    (D) Consistent

12. Internet shopping allows consumers to have access to products that are not popular ------- to be given space in actual stores.
    (A) well
    (B) enough
    (C) likely
    (D) correctly

13. Visitors have complained that there is ------- any room to park near the entrance to the museum.

(A) closely   (B) normally

(C) hardly   (D) openly

14. New hires are asked to review the employee handbook ------- before contacting human resources with any questions.

(A) thoroughly   (B) incidentally

(C) relatively   (D) previously

Questions 15-18 refer to the following information.

The Fern Lake Community Center is an entirely volunteer-run organization serving the Fern Lake community. ------- known among locals as "the Fern," our center offers high-quality after-school
   15.
care for local children of working parents. We also ------- educational programs for all ages in our
                               16.
buildings on Quentin Street. ------- .
                     17.

In addition, the community center offers several ------- events throughout the year. The largest and
                                        18.
most famous is our annual Fern Fair. All residents are invited to join us on April 12 this year on the Broad Street Pier to enjoy the area's best food, crafts, and musical performances while savoring the cool spring breeze.

For more information, visit www.fernlakecc.com/fair.

15. (A) Cooperatively

(B) Mutually

(C) Popularly

(D) Essentially

16. (A) participate

(B) claim

(C) enroll

(D) host

17. (A) We are not currently looking for volunteers.

(B) Contact our office to rent our main hall.

(C) Most of these programs are no longer available.

(D) These include classes in dancing and painting.

18. (A) outdoor

(B) exclusive

(C) athletic

(D) formal

Unit | 06 — 동사의 형태와 종류

> **동사의 활용** 동사는 문장의 필수 구성 성분일 뿐 아니라 문장 구조를 만드는 데 가장 중요한 역할을 한다. 동사의 형태를 이해하고 나면 시제 일치, 태의 구체적인 어법 사항을 더 쉽게 이해할 수 있다.

■ 동사원형

주어가 3인칭 단수가 아닌 경우, 즉 1, 2인칭 단수와 복수일 때 현재 시제는 동사원형을 쓴다. 이 밖에 동사원형을 쓰는 대표적인 경우는 명령문, 조동사 뒤, 주장/요구/명령/제안의 동사 뒤 that절, 사역동사의 목적격 보어 자리이다.

The wedding and reception will both [take place / ~~taking place~~] in the Grand Hall at Shelton Hotel.
결혼식과 피로연은 모두 셀튼 호텔의 대연회장에서 열릴 것이다.

→ 조동사 will 뒤에 동사원형이 나와야 한다.

The president firmly requested that the authorities [regulate / ~~regulated~~] its copyright laws.
사장은 권한 당국이 저작권 법을 규제해야 한다고 강력하게 요구했다.

→ request나 suggest와 같은 제안, 요청의 동사 뒤에 오는 that절에는 'should + 동사원형'이나 동사원형을 쓴다.

■ 완료형

완료형은 'have + 과거분사(p.p.)' 형태이며 타동사의 완료형은 뒤에 목적어가 필요하다. have동사 뒤에 빈칸을 두고 p.p. 형태를 채우는 문제가 자주 출제된다.

The amazing giant snow sculptures have [attracted / ~~attractions~~] many tourists throughout the winter.
멋진 대형 눈 조각품들이 겨울 내내 많은 관광객들을 끌어모았다.

→ 완료형 동사 have attracted 뒤에 목적어인 many tourists가 왔다. have attractions 뒤에는 목적어가 올 수 없다.

■ 진행형

진행형은 'be + 현재분사(-ing)' 형태이며 타동사의 진행형은 뒤에 목적어가 필요하다.

The director is [producing / ~~productive~~] an independent film about the indigenous African tribes' daily lives.
그 영화 감독은 아프리카 토착 부족의 일상 생활에 관한 독립 영화를 제작 중이다.

→ 진행형 동사 뒤에 an independent film이 있다. is productive 뒤에는 목적어가 올 수 없다.

ETS 유형 연습
정답과 해설 **p. 135**

1 The senior project manager will be on-site next Thursday and has requested that the editors _____ him in his office at 9:30 A.M.

(A) meet
(B) met
(C) have met
(D) will meet

2 Many companies have strongly _____ several provisions in the new government tax plan.

(A) critical
(B) criticism
(C) criticizing
(D) criticized

3 The Desorbo Company will be _____ its new leather boots in the fall catalog.

(A) introduce
(B) introducing
(C) introduces
(D) introduced

<table>
<tr><td>자동사와
타동사</td><td>자동사는 목적어가 필요 없고, 타동사는 목적어가 필요하다. 대표적인 '자동사+전치사', '타동사+목적어' 유형을
암기하자. 결합하는 목적어나 전치사를 이용해서 동사 어휘 문제를 해결할 수 있다.</td></tr>
</table>

■ 자동사 뒤에는 목적어 역할을 하는 명사가 바로 나올 수 없다.

대표 자동사

rise 오르다	appear 나타나다	exist 존재하다	vary 다양하다
expire 만기되다	participate in ~에 참가하다	specialize in ~을 전문으로 하다	apply for ~에 지원하다
commute to ~로 통근하다	subscribe to ~을 정기 구독하다	adhere to ~을 고수하다	depart from ~으로부터 떠나다
benefit from ~로부터 혜택을 얻다	belong to ~에 속하다	make up for ~을 보상하다	refrain from ~을 삼가다
qualify for ~의 자격이 있다	coincide with ~와 동시에 일어나다	comment on ~에 대해 논평하다	focus on ~에 집중하다
comply with ~을 따르다	refer to ~를 참조하다	conform to ~을 따르다	put up with ~을 참다
succeed in ~에서 성공/계승하다	result in/from ~하게 되다/~때문이다	agree with/on ~에 동의하다	cooperate with ~와 협력하다
compete with ~와 경쟁하다	enroll (in)/register for ~에 등록하다	depend/rely on ~에 의존하다	consent to ~에 동의하다

■ 타동사는 뒤에 목적어가 필요하고, 전치사구는 목적어를 대신할 수 없다.

대표 타동사

discuss ~을 토론하다	attend ~에 참석하다	adopt ~을 채택하다	accompany ~와 동반하다
answer ~에 답하다	access ~에 접근하다	exceed ~을 초과하다	comprise ~로 구성되다

Professionals in management, finance and marketing gathered to [**discuss** / ~~talk~~] the main issues related to a new business. 운영, 재정, 마케팅 전문가들은 새로운 사업에 관련된 주요 쟁점을 논의하기 위해 모였다.

➜ 자동사 talk은 뒤에 바로 목적어를 쓸 수 없고 to, with, about 등의 전치사와 함께 쓴다.

혼동하기 쉬운 자동사와 타동사

~을 기다리다 (타) await (자) wait for	~을 매료시키다 (타) attract (자) appeal to	~에 도착하다 (타) reach (자) arrive at/in
~을 야기하다 (타) cause (자) lead to	~에 반대하다 (타) oppose (자) object to	~로 구성되다 (타) comprise (자) consist of
~을 처리하다 (타) handle (자) deal with	~을 방해하다 (타) interrupt (자) interfere with	~을 설명하다 (타) explain (자) account for

Local people adamantly [**object** / ~~oppose~~] to building a shopping center near the national park.
지역 주민들은 국립 공원 근처에 쇼핑 센터를 짓는 것에 단호하게 반대한다.

ETS 유형 연습 ....

정답과 해설 p. 135

1 Preparing a budget encourages an executive to _____ several options before deciding on a course of action.

(A) think
(B) reply
(C) inquire
(D) examine

2 To _____ for the local-shopper discount, customers must show proof of residency.

(A) qualify
(B) award
(C) experience
(D) certify

3 All new employees are required to _____ in the three-day orientation.

(A) attend
(B) take
(C) inquire
(D) participate

> **주의해야 할 타동사** 타동사는 목적어를 필요로 한다. 동사의 종류에 따라 목적어가 두 개 필요하거나, 사람 목적어를 쓰거나, 목적어 뒤 목적격 보어까지 필요한 경우가 있다. 어휘 문제에 대비하여 '동사+목적어' 형태로 덩어리째 외우자.

■ 목적어를 두 개 가지는 4형식 동사

4형식 동사는 대개 '~(해)주다'라는 의미로, 그 뒤에는 간접 목적어와 직접 목적어라는 두 개의 목적어가 필요하다.

> give 주다   offer 제공하다   send 보내주다   bring 가져다주다   award 수여하다   grant 허가하다   show 보여주다   buy 사주다

Mr. Wilson has [offered / ~~provided~~] investors reliable investment advice.
윌슨 씨는 투자자들에게 믿을 만한 투자 조언을 제공해 왔다.

→ 4형식 동사 offered 뒤에 간접 목적어(investors)와 직접 목적어(reliable investment advice)가 왔다. provide는 주로 provide A with B(A에게 B를 제공하다) 형태로 사용된다.

> **사람 목적어를 취하는 동사**
> inform / notify 알려주다   remind 상기시키다   convince 설득하다   assure 확신시키다   brief 간략히 말하다   tell 말해주다   warn 경고하다
> '~해주다'라고 해석되어 사람 목적어를 취하고, 그 뒤에는 전치사구 또는 that절을 주로 동반하는 동사이다.

■ 목적격 보어를 원하는 5형식 동사

대표적인 5형식 동사들은 '…가 ~하도록 시키다'라고 해석되어 목적어 뒤에 목적격 보어로 to부정사를 취할 수 있다.

사람 목적어를 취하는 동사

목적격 보어는 동사와 목적어에 따라 다양한 형태가 있다.

동사	목적어	목적격 보어
keep, find, consider, make	the presentation 명사	impressive 형용사
make, have, let	patients 사람명사	take a short walk 동사원형
get, have, keep, leave	the door 사물명사	locked 과거분사(p.p.)

ETS 유형 연습

정답과 해설 p. 135

1 To avoid leaving anyone behind, the tour operator _____ all the visitors to be in the front lobby by 7 A.M.

(A) recalled
(B) memorized
(C) reminded
(D) identified

2 Mr. Kawano wants the staff to _____ him of any flaws that they see in the store's display furniture.

(A) supply
(B) inform
(C) reply
(D) notice

3 All employees working in the assembly area will be _____ to take a course on machine operation.

(A) recognized
(B) required
(C) given
(D) grown

> **동사 어휘**   명사로도 쓰이는 동사, 감정유발동사와 더불어 '타동사+목적어+전치사' 덩어리를 알아두는 것도 중요하다.

■ 명사로도 쓰이는 동사

review	통 (재)검토하다	review the decision	명 검토, 평가	an annual review
permit	통 허가하다	permit me to continue	명 허가증	a parking permit
access	통 접근하다	access the data	명 (불가산) 접근	access to the Internet
influence	통 영향을 미치다	influence the results	명 영향	have an influence on the results
manufacture	통 제조하다	manufacture products	명 제조(품)	car manufacture

Plastic is widely used in the [manufacture / ~~manufacturer~~] of the kitchen utensils.
플라스틱은 주방 용품의 제조에 폭넓게 사용된다.
→ manufacture가 '제조'라는 의미의 명사로도 쓰일 수 있음을 유념한다. manufacturer는 '제조업체'를 뜻하는 명사이다.

■ 감정유발동사

감정유발동사는 '(감정을 느끼게) 만들다'라고 해석한다. 사물 주어가 감정을 유발하면 능동태, 사람 주어가 감정을 느끼면 수동태로 쓴다.

surprise ~을 놀라게 하다	impress ~을 감동시키다	delight ~을 기쁘게 하다	fascinate ~을 매혹시키다
satisfy ~을 만족시키다	interest ~에게 흥미를 갖게 하다	please ~을 기쁘게 하다	depress ~을 낙담시키다
frustrate ~을 좌절시키다	disappoint ~을 실망시키다	confuse ~을 혼란스럽게 하다	worry ~을 걱정시키다

The sales clerk's attitude [satisfied / ~~was satisfied~~] many of the customers.   그 직원의 태도는 많은 고객들을 만족시켰다.

■ '타동사+목적어+전치사' 관용 표현

clear/deprive A of B A에게서 B를 치우다/빼앗다	inform/notify A of/about B A에게 B에 대해 알려주다	acquaint A with B (be acquainted with) A가 B를 잘 알게 하다 (~에 친숙하다)
prevent/stop/keep A from B A가 B하지 못하게 하다	distinguish/tell A from B A와 B를 구별하다	provide/supply A with B A에게 B를 제공하다
charge A for B B에 대해 A를 부과하다	honor/recognize/blame A for B B에 대해 A를 칭찬하다/인정하다/비난하다	replace A with B A를 B로 교체하다
contribute A to B (contribute to) B에 A를 기여하다 (~에 기여하다)	attribute A to B A를 B 때문이라고 여기다	associate A with B A와 B를 결부하다

ETS 유형 연습

정답과 해설 p.136

1 Please be aware that annual _____ of job performance will take place during the third week of January.

(A) reviews
(B) reviewed
(C) reviewer
(D) reviewers

2 Our chief operating officer was very _____ by the latest sales figures.

(A) impress
(B) impressing
(C) impressed
(D) impressive

3 All commercial catering businesses refrigerate perishable food to _____ it from spoiling.

(A) remove
(B) oppose
(C) prevent
(D) forbid

1. The opening of the new automotive service station on Highway 405 was delayed because the initial fuel shipment did not ------- on time.
   (A) arrive
   (B) arrival
   (C) arrived
   (D) arriving

2. Although we have ------- not to offer you a position at this time, we will keep your résumé on file for future openings.
   (A) decided
   (B) deciding
   (C) decision
   (D) decidedly

3. Mr. Osaki would like the entire staff ------- together and complete the task by the deadline.
   (A) works
   (B) be working
   (C) to work
   (D) will work

4. To celebrate World Health Day, all employees are ------- to replace their sugary snacks with fruits and vegetables.
   (A) encourage
   (B) encouraging
   (C) encouragement
   (D) encouraged

5. Because small businesses can ------- from working with each other, many owners find it helpful to join local business associations.
   (A) benefit
   (B) serve
   (C) assist
   (D) help

6. For a limited time, Becker Street Electronics will ------- shipping costs on all TX266 cameras as part of the July sale.
   (A) proceed
   (B) hesitate
   (C) displace
   (D) waive

7. Textile products shipped overseas must ------- with all international labeling requirements.
   (A) comply
   (B) confront
   (C) update
   (D) assign

8. Employees of Osijek Systems were ------- at the board of directors' decision to make Sasha Vasilev the new vice president.
   (A) surprise
   (B) surprising
   (C) surprised
   (D) surprises

9. Judith Cooke, the manager of the sales department, will inform you ------- the exact shipment date by tomorrow morning.
   (A) of
   (B) along
   (C) over
   (D) through

10. Ms. Rafferty's references noted her strong work ethic, but directors feel she ------- the skills for the position.
    (A) lacks
    (B) pretends
    (C) removes
    (D) vacates

11. Marburg Electro Company is ------- to report a significant increase in profits for the year.
    (A) earned
    (B) outgrown
    (C) expected
    (D) risen

12. Please ------- the doctor's office at least 24 hours in advance if you need to cancel or reschedule your appointment.
    (A) agree
    (B) report
    (C) arrange
    (D) notify

13. When investor Joe Kimura ------- all the assets of Ahearn Manufacturing, he also assumed all the company's debts.

(A) acquired　　　(B) delivered
(C) maintained　　(D) analyzed

14. Although the new design is highly innovative, it would be too costly for us to ------- with development at this time.

(A) examine　　(B) treat
(C) urge　　　 (D) proceed

Questions 15-18 refer to the following e-mail.

To: info@kathyscaterers.com
From: jberthel@bertheltech.com
Date: December 1
Subject: Event catering inquiry

To whom it may concern,

I am currently planning my company's annual holiday party. All of the reviews that I have -------
15.
about your catering company are very positive. However, before I make a final decision, I have a

few ------- .
16.

Are you available to cater for 25 people on Friday, December 16? The event will take place in my

company's building at 138 Larrington Avenue. Would you be able to deliver the refreshments by

2:00 P.M. on that day? I think that your Small Bites menu would work perfectly for the party. ------- .
17.
This would be the easiest way to satisfy everyone's food preferences.

------- , many people are concerned about wasting any leftover food. Can you provide carryout
18.
boxes for people to take any leftovers home with them?

Thank you,

James Berthel, Berthel Technologies

15. (A) seen
　　 (B) saw
　　 (C) sees
　　 (D) seeing

16. (A) numbers
　　 (B) problems
　　 (C) services
　　 (D) questions

17. (A) We use environmentally friendly cups, plates, and utensils.
　　 (B) I like that it offers a variety of delicious options.
　　 (C) Please send only experienced serving staff.
　　 (D) The final cost needs to include beverages.

18. (A) Although
　　 (B) Meanwhile
　　 (C) Finally
　　 (D) Otherwise

수 일치와 태

> **주어와 동사의** 보기에 동사만 있어 동사의 적절한 어형을 골라야 할 때, 우선 주어와 동사의 수 일치를 확인한다.
> **수 일치** 주어가 3인칭 단수일 때 현재동사 뒤에는 -(e)s를 붙여야 한다.

■ be동사의 수 일치

be동사는 주어의 인칭과 단수/복수, 동사의 시제에 따라 다양한 형태가 있다.

The construction project of the public library [was / ~~were~~] approved by the city council.

공공 도서관 건설 프로젝트는 시 의회에 의해 승인되었다.

→ 주어(The construction project)가 3인칭 단수이므로 was를 쓴다.

■ 조동사, 과거동사의 수 일치

조동사와 일반동사의 과거형은 주어의 수에 영향받지 않는다.

The mayor [announced / ~~announce~~] that the hours of subway operation will be extended as of January 3.

시장은 1월 3일부터 지하철 운행 시간이 연장될 것이라고 발표했다.

→ 주어(The mayor)가 3인칭 단수이고 동사가 현재 시제라면 동사 뒤에 -(e)s를 붙여야 한다.

■ 수식어가 붙은 긴 주어

동사 앞부분 전체가 주어이며, 그중 첫 명사가 진짜 주어이다. 주어 뒤에는 전치사구, 관계대명사절, 분사 등의 수식어가 올 수 있다.

The courses the intern will take [focus / ~~focuses~~ / ~~focusing~~] on the basic concepts of security programs.

그 인턴이 받게 될 수업들은 보안 프로그램의 기본 개념에 초점을 맞출 것이다.

→ 문장 중간에 목적격 관계대명사 that이 생략된 관계대명사절(the intern will take)이 삽입된 경우이다. 관계대명사절은 생략해도 문장 구조에 영향을 미치지 않는다. 따라서 주어 (The courses)와 수 일치되어야 한다.

■ There is 명사: 동사와 주어의 수 일치

There are still unfinished business [transactions / ~~transaction~~] involving a huge amount of money.

여전히 큰 액수의 돈이 연관된 미결의 사업 거래들이 있다.

→ There are 뒤에 명사가 나와서 주어 역할을 한다. 이 명사와 be동사의 수가 일치해야 한다.

ETS 유형 연습

정답과 해설 p. 138

1. Although she has been transferred to Mexico City, Ms. Baxter and her former colleagues at the New York branch _____ in contact.

   (A) remain
   (B) remains
   (C) remaining
   (D) has remained

2. Please use the color printer sparingly, since the ink cartridges it requires _____ currently unavailable.

   (A) are
   (B) is
   (C) been
   (D) being

3. The coffee makers we compared _____ in terms of price, size, and durability.

   (A) varies
   (B) vary
   (C) variable
   (D) varying

> 단수주어
> 복수주어
>
> 주어와 동사의 수 일치를 확인할 때, 주어의 단/복수를 구별하기 어려운 경우가 있다. 특히 주어에 수량 표현이 있
> 다면 Unit 03의 부정대명사와 Unit 04의 수량형용사를 기억하여 적용해 보자.

■ 수량 표현이 있는 주어의 수

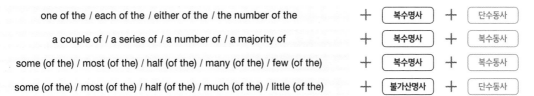

Each of the trainers [has / ~~have~~] a master's degree as well as years of teaching experience.
각 교육관들은 석사 학위뿐 아니라 수년의 교습 경력도 가지고 있다.

A number of large shopping centers positively [affect / ~~affects~~] the local economy.
많은 대형 쇼핑 센터들은 지역 경제에 긍정적으로 영향을 미친다.

■ 주어 자리의 to부정사, 동명사, 명사절은 단수

동명사 주어 [Addressing / ~~Addressed~~] problems with the heating system takes considerable time and effort.
난방 시스템의 문제를 해결하는 것은 상당한 시간과 노력을 필요로 한다.
→ Addressed가 오면 problems가 주어가 되는데 문장의 동사인 takes와 수 일치가 되지 않는다.

명사절 주어 Whether the broken machine will be replaced or repaired [has / ~~have~~] not been decided yet.
고장 난 기계가 교체될지 수리될지 여부는 아직 결정되지 않았다.
→ Whether가 이끄는 명사절이 주어 역할을 하며, 단수 취급을 받는다.

■ 주의해야 할 주어의 수

복합명사 The job opportunities [are / ~~is~~] available for both temporary and permanent employment.
이 취업 기회는 임시직과 상근직 모두에 대해 유효하다.
→ 주어가 복합명사일 때 동사는 뒤의 명사에 따라 수 일치시켜야 한다.

or로 연결된 경우 The sales manager or his team members [are / ~~is~~] invited to deliver several presentations.
영업부장 또는 그의 팀원들은 몇 차례 프레젠테이션을 진행해야 한다.
→ 주어가 or로 연결된 경우 동사는 동사와 가까운 뒤쪽 명사와 수 일치되어야 한다.

ETS 유형 연습

정답과 해설 p. 138

1 While performing my preliminary research, I learned that very _____ has been written about the poetry of Miho Aoki in the past decade.

  (A) some
  (B) few
  (C) other
  (D) little

2 Roughly half of the employees at Century Photo Labs _____ to work by bus.

  (A) commutes
  (B) commute
  (C) is commuting
  (D) has commuted

3 The Stellen Museum's extensive _____ consist of a mix of ancient artifacts and paintings from various cultures.

  (A) holds
  (B) holder
  (C) holding
  (D) holdings

> **동사의 수동태** 수동태는 능동태 문장의 목적어를 주어로 바꾸어 주어가 동작을 당하고 있음을 표현하는 방법이다. 문제에서 동사가 능동태가 되어야 하는지 수동태가 되어야 하는지 판단할 수 있어야 한다.

■ 수동태의 개념

능동태 문장의 목적어가 수동태 문장의 주어가 되어 '~되다, 당하다'라고 해석한다. 수동태 동사는 'be + p.p.' 형태로 사용된다. 대부분의 수동태 동사 뒤에는 목적어가 없고, 전치사 등의 수식어를 동반한다.

능동태 The executives will [discuss / be~discussed] practical ways to promote a higher profit margin.
간부들은 수익을 높이기 위한 현실적인 방법을 논의할 것이다.

수동태 Practical ways to promote a higher profit margin will [be discussed / discuss] by the executives.
수익을 높이기 위한 현실적인 방법이 간부들에 의해 논의될 것이다.
→ 수동태 동사 'be + p.p.' 뒤에는 목적어가 없고, 주로 전치사구가 등장한다.

■ 수동태로 바뀔 수 없는 자동사

목적어를 취하지 않는 자동사는 수동태(be + p.p.)가 될 수 없다.

Car accidents [occur / are~occurred] more often because of careless driving rather than bad weather.
자동차 사고는 나쁜 날씨보다는 부주의한 운전 때문에 더 자주 일어난다.

■ 목적어가 2개인 동사의 수동태

'~(해)주다'로 해석되는 4형식 동사는 목적어가 두 개이므로, 간접목적어가 주어로 바뀌어도 동사 뒤에 여전히 목적어가 남는다. 'be given + 명사(~을 받다)' 형식으로 익혀 두도록 한다.

> be offered + 명사 ~을 제공받다   be granted + 명사 ~을 받다   be awarded + 명사 ~을 수여받다   be charged + 명사 ~을 청구받다

Only those with a visitor pass [are given / give] access to the university's museums and collections.
방문증을 가진 사람만 그 대학의 박물관과 전시관에 입장할 수 있다.

■ 5형식 동사의 수동태

5형식 동사는 목적어와 목적격 보어를 가지며, 목적격 보어 자리에는 명사, 형용사, to부정사 등 다양한 형태가 올 수 있다.
따라서 5형식 문장의 수동태는 동사 뒤에 다양한 형태가 올 수 있다.

The movie [is considered / consider] one of the 100 most influential films of the century.
그 영화는 세기의 가장 영향력 있는 영화 100선 중 하나로 여겨진다.

ETS 유형 연습
정답과 해설 p. 139

1 Due to new restrictions on international travelers, certain types of plants cannot _____ into most countries without a permit.

(A) bring
(B) be brought
(C) brought
(D) bringing

2 Library patrons who fail to return an item by the due date _____ a fee.

(A) charge
(B) will be charged
(C) have charged
(D) are charging

3 The delegation will depart from the embassy at 9 A.M. and _____ to the airport by the Minister of Sports.

(A) will accompany
(B) accompanied
(C) will be accompanied
(D) being accompanied

여러 가지 수동태 | 특정 전치사와 결합하는 수동태 동사들이 있다. 행위 주체를 표현할 때에는 주로 by를 쓰지만, 동사의 의미에 따라 다양한 전치사가 나올 수 있다.

■ be p.p. + 전치사

with	be concerned with ~와 관련이 있다 (*cf.* be concerned about ~에 대해 걱정하다) be acquainted with ~을 알고 있다 be equipped with ~을 갖추고 있다 be associated with ~와 연관되어 있다 be disappointed with ~에 실망하다 be provided with ~을 제공받다 be satisfied with ~에 만족하다 be faced with ~에 직면하다
to	be accustomed/used to ~에 익숙하다 be limited to ~에게만 하도록 제한되다 be related to ~와 관련이 있다 be exposed to ~에 노출되다 be attributed/ascribed to ~ 때문이다 be committed to ~에 헌신하다 be dedicated to ~에 헌신하다 be devoted to ~에 헌신하다 be assigned to ~에 배정되다
in	be interested in ~에 관심을 갖다 be engaged in ~에 종사하다 be involved in ~에 연관되어 있다
for	be known for ~로 알려져 있다 (업적) be honored for ~로 표창을 받다 be blamed for ~로 비난받다
기타	be based on ~에 기초해 있다 be accused of ~에 대해 비난받다 be divided into ~으로 나누어지다

■ '자동사 + 전치사'의 수동태

'자동사 + 전치사'가 결합하여 마치 타동사처럼 수동태로 바꿀 수 있다. 이때 수동태 동사 뒤에는 여전히 전치사가 결합되어 있다.

account for ~을 설명하다 ↳ be accounted for 설명되다	deal with ~을 다루다 ↳ be dealt with 다루어지다	take care of ~을 처리하다 ↳ be taken care of 처리되다
refer to ~을 언급하다 ↳ be referred to 언급되다	carry out ~을 수행하다 ↳ be carried out 수행되다	dispose of ~을 처분하다 ↳ be disposed of 처분되다

Safety issues should be [dealt / ~~dealing~~] with immediately.
안전 문제는 즉시 처리되어야 한다.

→ deal with는 하나의 동사 덩어리이다. 뒤에 목적어가 없고 수식어인 부사가 있으므로 수동태 동사를 써야 한다.

ETS 유형 연습

정답과 해설 p.139

1 Each month, we will select five outstanding employees to be honored _____ their exceptional contributions to the company's performance.

(A) for
(B) at
(C) across
(D) over

2 Sleeping-car passengers will be provided _____ the bedding they need for the journey.

(A) with
(B) for
(C) to
(D) of

3 The apartments on the lower floors cost less because they are more exposed _____ dust and the noise of traffic.

(A) to
(B) without
(C) from
(D) against

1. The new menu for the Watchill Bistro ------- almond-crusted salmon, beef tenderloin, and mushroom risotto.

   (A) includes
   (B) include
   (C) including
   (D) inclusion

2. The retail division is facing a deadline, so department sales ------- are required by the end of the week.

   (A) report
   (B) reports
   (C) reported
   (D) reporting

3. The number of customers requesting refunds ------- over the last few years due to the improved quality.

   (A) declined
   (B) has declined
   (C) decline
   (D) have declined

4. Employees who would like to contribute to the company charity drive ------- to place their donations in the box in Jack Elliott's office.

   (A) will invite
   (B) are inviting
   (C) can invite
   (D) are invited

5. Comco, Inc., became the leading supplier of computer parts last year, less than ten years after it -------.

   (A) was founded
   (B) founds
   (C) have founded
   (D) founded

6. ------- hundreds of technical specialists at the convention in Zurich last month.

   (A) Several
   (B) Many of the
   (C) Having had
   (D) There were

7. Jalesen Office Tower's heating system ------- by the city's building-safety department.

   (A) inspection
   (B) is being inspected
   (C) were inspecting
   (D) inspector

8. Full-time ------- of Hauto Production Plant are entitled to take a fifteen-minute break for each four-hour shift.

   (A) employment
   (B) employees
   (C) employs
   (D) employ

9. The airport shuttle ------- every hour from the hotel's front entrance.

   (A) depart
   (B) was departed
   (C) are departing
   (D) departs

10. Inclement weather and a reduced workforce ------- the greatest challenges to the renovation of the Kern Science Center.

    (A) have posed
    (B) is posing
    (C) does pose
    (D) will have been posed

11. The fabric used in Alpinta nursing uniforms ------- to withstand the wear and tear of daily use.

    (A) is confirming
    (B) has been confirmed
    (C) will confirm
    (D) confirm

12. Starting next Monday, Ironcastle Hardware ------- its store hours until 9:00 P.M. daily.

    (A) had extended
    (B) was extending
    (C) will be extended
    (D) will be extending

13. The new Vitrolux X500 camera comes ------- with an integrated flash and a simple control panel.

(A) equipped   (B) advanced

(C) captured   (D) pointed

14. Mayor Williams proudly described the city as a place where the citizens are ------- for their hospitality.

(A) returned   (B) known

(C) taken   (D) held

Questions 15-18 refer to the following e-mail.

To: All Staff <staff@bensonwellslegal.com>
From: Abdullah Alharbi <a.alharbi@bensonwellslegal.com>
Date: September 10
Subject: Mandatory training

To All Staff:

Regular advances in technology ------- constant challenges in managing our company's information.
    15.
At Benson Wells Legal Solutions, we always work to keep ------- our company's data and our clients'
    16.
data safe. This is why we have partnered with Consider the Click, one of the leading data safety

firms in North America. It will be providing this ------- training, and all employees have already been
    17.
enrolled. The more we know, the safer and, ultimately, more successful we will be.

Please reserve at least 45 minutes for the training, which is to be completed by December 1. ------- .
    18.

Sincerely,
Abdullah Alharbi
Director of Information Technology

15. (A) present   (B) to present

    (C) are presented   (D) presenting

16. (A) either   (B) both

    (C) not only   (D) as though

17. (A) financial   (B) fitness

    (C) security   (D) electrical

18. (A) This program is completely optional for each employee.

(B) With your help, our Web site can present a more welcoming image.

(C) You will receive an e-mail shortly, containing a link to start the training.

(D) We can prosper only by making full use of the information we collect.

Unit | o8 시제

<table>
<tr><td>단순 시제</td><td>시제 문제는 빈칸 주변의 시간 표현을 먼저 단서로 활용하고, 별다른 단서가 없는 경우 해석으로 풀어야 한다. 시간 표현에는 부사, 전치사구, 부사절(접속사＋주어＋동사), 주변 동사의 시제가 있다.</td></tr>
</table>

■ 현재 시제

현재 시제는 주로 현재의 상황, 반복적인 일, 기정사실 등을 표현한다.

┌─ 현재 시제와 잘 어울리는 시간 표현 ─────────────────────────

| every week 매주 | usually 보통 | regularly 정기적으로 | routinely 일상적으로 |
| always 항상 | generally 일반적으로 | often 자주 | frequently 자주 |

Online shopping malls [offer / ~~are offering~~] special discounts and promotions usually on weekends.
온라인 쇼핑몰은 보통 주말에 특별 할인 및 판촉 행사를 제공한다.

■ 과거 시제

과거 시제는 과거의 상태 또는 과거 시점에 발생한 일을 나타낸다. 빈도부사와 함께 쓰여 과거의 습관을 표현하기도 한다.

┌─ 과거 시제와 잘 어울리는 시간 표현 ─────────────────────────

| yesterday 어제 | two days ago 이틀 전에 | last Friday 지난주 금요일에 | in 2010 2010년에 |
| recently / lately 최근에 | when＋주어＋과거동사 ~했을 때 | the other day 요전에 | once 한때 |

Colin Phillips [was / ~~has been~~] awarded the World's Best Architect Award four years ago.
콜린 필립스 씨는 4년 전 세계 최고의 건축가 상을 받았다.

■ 미래 시제

미래 시제는 미래 시점에 발생할 일을 나타낸다. 미래를 나타내는 동사는 'will＋동사원형', 'is / are -ing' 등으로 다양하다.

┌─ 미래 시제와 잘 어울리는 시간 표현 ─────────────────────────

| tomorrow 내일 | next week 다음 주 | this coming Sunday 다가오는 일요일에 | soon / shortly 곧 |
| as of / effective / starting May 10 5월 10일부로 | | anticipate / predict that ~일 것으로 예상하다 | |

Registration for the public relations conference [will open / ~~has opened~~] shortly.
홍보 콘퍼런스의 등록이 곧 시작될 것이다.

ETS 유형 연습

정답과 해설 p. 141

1 Seating in the Bogor Stadium completely _____ the field so that all visitors are afforded excellent views of events.

(A) surround
(B) surrounds
(C) surrounded
(D) surrounding

2 The engineers had only begun analyzing the problem when a new discovery _____ their working model obsolete.

(A) rendering
(B) rendered
(C) renders
(D) will render

3 After the current model year, the automobile manufacturer CFG _____ three older models and introduce two new ones.

(A) to discontinue
(B) will discontinue
(C) discontinued
(D) have discontinued

> 진행 시제 진행 시제는 be동사 뒤에 -ing를 붙여 특정 시점에 일어나고 있는 동작을 표현한다. 현재진행 시제와 단순 현재 시제를 잘 구별하도록 하자.

■ 현재진행 (is / are -ing)

❶ 현재진행은 현재의 한 시점에 진행되고 있는 일을 나타내며 '~하는 중이다'라고 해석한다.

┌─ 현재진행 시제와 잘 어울리는 시간 표현 ───────────────────────────

  now 지금   currently 현재   presently 현재   at the moment 지금

The product development team [is discussing / ~~discusses~~] the feasibility of new ideas at the moment.
제품 개발팀은 현재 새로운 아이디어들의 실현 가능성에 대해 논의하고 있다.

❷ 현재진행 시제는 가까운 미래를 나타낼 수 있다.

Train EXP101 is arriving in approximately 20 minutes. EXP101 열차는 약 20분 후에 도착할 것이다.

■ 과거진행 (was / were -ing)

과거진행 시제는 과거의 한 시점에 진행되었던 일을 표현한다.

Craig Martin gained valuable experience while he [was working / ~~works~~] on a team a few years ago.
크레이그 마틴 씨는 몇 년 전에 팀으로 일하면서 소중한 경험을 얻었다.

■ 미래진행 (will be -ing)

미래진행 시제는 미래의 한 시점에 진행될 일을 표현한다.

The vice president [will be delivering / ~~was delivered~~] a speech at the annual meeting next Monday.
다음 주 월요일에 열릴 연례 회의에서 부사장님이 연설하고 있을 것이다.

ETS 유형 연습
정답과 해설 p. 142

1 LTD Enterprises is currently _____ an accomplished individual to replace the current director, who will be retiring at the end of the month.

 (A) seeking
 (B) seeks
 (C) being sought
 (D) having sought

2 Ms. Yoon _____ from jet lag when she returned on Thursday, so the meeting has been postponed until next week.

 (A) will suffer
 (B) suffers
 (C) will have suffered
 (D) was suffering

3 While Ms. Atitam is on vacation next June, Mr. Al-Jamri _____ over the contract negotiations with our Mumbai vendor.

 (A) takes
 (B) have taken
 (C) had taken
 (D) will be taking

■ 현재완료(have / has p.p.)

현재완료 시제는 과거의 불특정 시점에 일어난 사건이 현재까지 지속되거나 영향을 미치고 있음을 나타낸다. 따라서 특정 과거 시점을 나타내는 부사와 함께 쓸 수 없다.

┌─ 현재완료 시제와 잘 어울리는 시간 표현 ──────────────────────────────────────┐
│ since 2010 2010년 이후   since+주어+과거동사 ~한 이후로   already 이미   (not) yet 아직 (~ 안 했다) │
│ for the last decade 지난 10년 동안   over the past few years 지난 몇 년에 걸쳐서   │
└───┘

Since the bridge [was built / ~~has built~~] in 2005, it [has become / ~~became~~] a popular attraction in the city.
다리가 2005년에 세워진 이후로, 그것은 도시에서 인기 있는 명소가 되었다.

■ 과거완료(had p.p.)

과거완료 시제는 주로 '~했었다'라고 해석하며, 특정 과거 시점보다 이전에 일어난 일을 표현한다.

┌─ 과거완료 시제와 잘 어울리는 시간 표현 ──────────────────────────────────────┐
│ before+주어+과거동사 ~하기 전에   by the time+주어+과거동사 ~했을 즈음에   │
└───┘

Ms. Han [had conducted / ~~conducts~~] extensive research before she finally came to a conclusion.
한 씨는 광범위한 연구 끝에 결론에 이르렀다.

By the time the documents arrived, the planning team [had / ~~will have~~] already concluded its meeting.
서류가 도착했을 무렵 기획팀은 이미 회의를 마쳤다.

■ 미래완료(will have p.p.)

미래완료 시제는 주로 '~했을 것이다'라고 해석한다. 미래의 어느 시점까지 계속되거나 미래를 기준으로 완료될 일을 나타낸다.

┌─ 미래완료 시제와 잘 어울리는 시간 표현 ──────────────────────────────────────┐
│ by the time+주어+현재동사 ~할 즈음에   by next year 내년 즈음에   │
└───┘

By the time Ms. Anderson is promoted to the vice president, she [will have worked / ~~will work~~] for 10 years at our company.
앤더슨 씨가 부사장으로 승진될 즈음이면, 그녀는 우리 회사에서 10년 동안 일한 것이 될 것이다.

ETS 유형 연습 ··· 정답과 해설 p.142

1 For the last fifteen years, Matlock, Inc., has consistently _____ among the nation's ten leading toy manufacturers.

(A) rank
(B) ranked
(C) ranking
(D) ranks

2 The hiring committee _____ the possibility of interviewing the candidates in person but decided on telephone interviews instead.

(A) discuss
(B) had discussed
(C) will be discussed
(D) discussing

3 By the time Clear Blaze Technology's word processing program goes on the market, software engineers _____ its remaining flaws.

(A) will have corrected
(B) had been correcting
(C) are correcting
(D) will correct

> **시제 일치의 예외** 시간과 조건의 부사절, 그리고 주장/요구/제안의 동사 뒤 that절은 일반적인 시제의 규칙을 따르지 않는다.
> when, if, request that 등이 보이면 시제 문제일 가능성이 높다는 것을 기억하자.

■ 시간, 조건의 부사절에서는 현재(완료) 시제가 미래(완료) 시제를 대신한다.

시간, 조건의 부사절에서는 미래의 일을 이야기하더라도 현재 시제를 쓴다. 그러나 주절의 동사는 미래 시제로 미래의 일임을 표현한다.

┌─ 시간과 조건의 부사절을 이끄는 접속사 ─────────────────────────────

| when ~할 때 | until ~할 때까지 | before ~하기 전에 | after ~한 후에 | while ~하는 동안 |
| as soon as ~하자마자 | if ~라면 | unless ~하지 않는다면 | once 일단 ~하면 | |

The hotel [**will be** / ~~is~~] able to accommodate guests after the plumbers [**repair** / ~~will repair~~] the pipes tomorrow. 배관공들이 내일 수도관을 수리하고 나면, 호텔은 손님들을 받을 수 있을 것이다.

If you [**sign** / ~~will sign~~] up for a membership, you will get additional 10% discount for any purchases.
만약 당신이 회원권을 신청하시면 어떤 구매에 대해서든 10퍼센트의 추가 할인을 받을 수 있습니다.

> | 고득점 팁 | if로 시작하는 명사절에서는 미래 시제를 쓸 수 있다.
>
> Many customers have asked us if their orders [**will be** / ~~are~~] delivered soon.
> 많은 고객들이 그들의 주문품이 곧 배달될 것인지 아닌지 우리에게 물었다.

■ 주장, 요구, 제안의 동사 / 형용사 / 명사 뒤 that절에 동사원형을 쓴다.

'주장한다' 다음에는 '~해야 한다'라는 의미의 조동사 should가 나오는 것이 자연스럽다. 하지만 should가 생략되는 경우가 많아 that 다음에는 '주어+동사원형'이 나오게 된다.

주장하다	insist / urge
요구하다	require / request / ask
명령하다	order
제안하다	suggest / recommend
중요한	important / essential / imperative
요청, 제안	request / suggestion / recommendation

+ [that] + [주어] + [동사원형]

During the meeting, Mr. James insisted that the new security policy [**be implemented** / ~~was implemented~~] without delay.
회의 중 제임스 씨는 새로운 보안 정책이 신속히 시행되어야 한다고 주장했다.

ETS 유형 연습
정답과 해설 p. 142

1 When you _____ to access your account, please type your password in the appropriate field.

(A) wanted
(B) want
(C) will want
(D) wanting

2 As soon as the warehouse _____ examined for fire hazards, you may resume your normal business operations.

(A) has been
(B) was
(C) had been
(D) will be

3 Executive Director Rajiv Kutty has complied with shareholders' requests that he _____ quality control procedures at Srinivisan Foods facilities.

(A) review
(B) was reviewing
(C) be reviewed
(D) reviewed

1. Every summer, Brighton store owners ------- unique window displays in an effort to attract more tourists.

(A) create
(B) creating
(C) creates
(D) were created

2. Magnum Plus cameras ------- very popular right now because they are so easy to use.

(A) became
(B) are becoming
(C) to become
(D) becomes

3. Because the boardroom is being painted, the meeting this afternoon will ------- in the conference room on the fourth floor.

(A) have held
(B) be holding
(C) hold
(D) be held

4. After Mr. Li ------- some adjustments, the engine worked more smoothly than it had before.

(A) to make
(B) made
(C) is making
(D) having made

5. Larper Painting ------- a special sale next month to celebrate its new store on Abagael Avenue.

(A) has run
(B) will be running
(C) will be run
(D) ran

6. Ever since Mr. Derrick joined the staff, Mr. Zapata and Ms. Coleman have ------- the marketing team for its excellent results.

(A) to be praised
(B) praise
(C) been praising
(D) been praised

7. Ritoc Engineering ------- checked all of the electrical wiring of the building by the time new tenants move in.

(A) will
(B) have
(C) having
(D) will have

8. To validate today's results, Dr. Lum is requesting that the experiment ------- tomorrow by a second research group.

(A) be repeated
(B) is repeating
(C) will have repeated
(D) had been repeating

9. If the plumbing problem -------, we recommend that you contact the product manufacturer.

(A) to persist
(B) was persisting
(C) persists
(D) persistence

10. Until Ms. Yang returns from the international travel conference in Taipei, Mr. Woo ------- all hotel reservations.

(A) handled
(B) had been handling
(C) will be handled
(D) will handle

11. The customer service department ------- a dramatic decrease in the number of complaints over the past year.

(A) see
(B) was seen
(C) seeing
(D) has seen

12. By the time Ms. Okada ------- in Incheon for the sales meeting, she had already completed preliminary negotiations by telephone.

(A) arrives
(B) arrived
(C) has arrived
(D) will arrive

13. Sylvia Cho ------- her training at Frio County Animal Hospital last week and will begin working as a veterinary technician.

(A) will conclude

(B) to conclude

(C) concludes

(D) concluded

14. It is ------- that the documents be meticulously examined before they are sent out to clients.

(A) immediate

(B) imperative

(C) ultimate

(D) conclusive

Questions 15-18 refer to the following e-mail.

From: Retina, Sonia
Sent: Monday, June 18, 9:28 A.M.
To: Company Staff
Subject: Reimbursement requests and credit card receipts

Good morning, everyone.

Please remember that when you submit a request for travel reimbursement, it must include detailed receipts of your purchases. This policy ------- to expenses for meals, hotel, flights, ground

15.

transportation, and others. Credit card receipts alone do not provide full ------- of the actual goods

16.

or services you purchased. We have received several reimbursement requests recently from

------- who used their personal credit cards while traveling. ------- . We cannot issue reimbursement

17. **18.**

checks unless we have itemized receipts for these purchases. Please keep this in mind.

Sonia Retina, Director of Accounting

15. (A) applies

(B) apply

(C) is applying

(D) had applied

16. (A) document

(B) documented

(C) documenting

(D) documentation

17. (A) visitors

(B) suppliers

(C) customers

(D) employees

18. (A) However, the company does not reimburse entertainment expenses.

(B) Unfortunately, they have only submitted credit card receipts.

(C) Most of the expenses pertained to office supplies.

(D) Employees commonly use personal credit cards while traveling.

to부정사와 동명사

> **to부정사의 용법** to부정사는 'to+동사원형'의 형태로 명사, 형용사, 부사 역할을 할 수 있지만 동사로는 쓸 수 없는 준동사이다.
> to부정사 자리 문제에 대비하여 to부정사를 동반하는 동사와 명사, to부정사의 숙어 표현을 외워두어야 한다.

■ 명사적 용법(~하는 것): 주어, 목적어, 보어

주어 It is necessary [to make / for making] a reservation at least a week in advance to receive a discount.
할인을 받기 위해서는 최소 일주일 전에 예약하는 것이 필요하다.

→ It이 가주어, 뒤에 오는 to부정사가 진주어 역할을 하는 가주어-진주어 구문이다.

목적어 Ms. Paik plans [to convert / converted] an empty office space into a meeting room.
백 씨는 비어 있는 사무실 공간을 회의실로 바꿀 계획이다.

보어 Those with good communication skills seem [to perform / performing] well in their workplace.
의사소통을 잘하는 사람들이 직장에서 일을 잘하는 것 같다.

→ to부정사 주격 보어를 동반하는 동사에는 remain (to be), seem (to be), appear (to be) 등이 있다.

┌─ 동사 + to부정사 적중 리스트 ──────

want to do ~하는 것을 원하다	would like to do ~하고 싶다	hesitate to do ~하기를 주저하다
expect to do ~할 것을 기대하다	plan to do ~하는 것을 계획하다	tend to do ~하는 경향이 있다
manage to do 가까스로 ~하다	afford to do ~할 여유가 있다	fail to do ~하지 않다/못하다

■ 형용사적 용법(~할, ~하기 위한): 명사 뒤에서 명사 수식

┌─ 명사 + to부정사 적중 리스트 ──────

ability to do ~할 수 있는 능력	right to do ~할 권리	way to do ~할 방법
authority to do ~할 수 있는 권한	opportunity to do ~할 기회	attempt to do ~하기 위한 시도
effort to do ~하기 위한 노력	decision to do ~하겠다는 결정	plan to do ~할 계획

■ 부사적 용법(~하기 위해서, ~해서): 수식어 역할

목적 The editor insisted that publication be suspended in order to [reflect / reflecting] last-minute changes. 편집자는 막판 변경사항을 반영하기 위해 출간을 잠시 중단해야 한다고 주장했다.

→ '~하기 위해서'는 to 동사원형, in order to 동사원형, so as to 동사원형으로 표현할 수 있다.

ETS 유형 연습

정답과 해설 p.144

1 The purpose of this government program is _____ schools with better access to new learning technologies.

(A) to provide
(B) provides
(C) provided
(D) to providing

2 Today Tenopy Tech announced its plans _____ with Shaffly Energy Systems to manufacture solar panels in Quito and Caracas.

(A) to partner
(B) be partnering
(C) is partnered
(D) will partner

3 In order to _____ overseas clients, the Majeski Group will open offices in both Europe and Asia.

(A) accommodation
(B) accommodates
(C) accommodate
(D) accommodating

> **to부정사의 활용**   to부정사는 '~하다'라는 뜻이 아니므로 동사는 아니지만, 동사와 마찬가지로 뒤에 목적어, 보어, 수식어가 올 수 있다. to부정사를 목적격 보어로 취하는 동사 관련 문제도 자주 출제되므로 빈출 표현을 외워두자.

■ to부정사의 동사적 특징

to부정사는 동사의 성격이 남아 있어 뒤에 목적어를 취하거나 부사의 수식을 받을 수 있다.

The conference organizers need [to produce / ~~production~~] a large number of copies of the materials for all attendees. 회의 기획자들은 모든 참석자들에게 줄 많은 부수의 자료들을 제작해야 한다.

■ 목적격 보어 자리에 쓰이는 to부정사

┌─ 동사 + 목적어 + to부정사 적중 리스트 ─

ask 명사 to do ~하라고 요구[요청]하다	require 명사 to do ~하라고 요구하다	allow 명사 to do ~할 수 있게 하다
invite 명사 to do ~하도록 요청하다	instruct 명사 to do ~하라고 지시하다	encourage 명사 to do ~하도록 독려하다

The mass storage devices allow users [to process / ~~processing~~] much information at a time.
대용량 저장 장치는 사용자들이 많은 정보를 한 번에 처리할 수 있도록 해준다.

┌─ 자주 출제되는 5형식 동사의 수동태형 ─

be required to do ~하도록 요청받다	be invited to do ~하도록 요청받다	be encouraged to do ~하도록 독려받다
be reminded to do ~할 것을 주의받다	be forced to do ~하도록 강요받다	be advised to do ~하도록 조언받다

The mayor [was invited / ~~invited~~] to appear as a special guest speaker at the conference.
시장은 회의에 특별 초청 연사로 참석해 달라는 요청을 받았다.

■ 원형부정사

사역동사 have는 목적어와 목적격 보어가 능동이면 원형부정사를, 수동이면 과거분사를 쓴다. 준사역동사 help 뒤에는 원형부정사 또는 to부정사를 쓸 수 있다.

사역동사   Please make sure to have all your mail [forwarded / ~~forward~~] to your new address.
반드시 모든 우편물이 새 주소로 전달되도록 하세요.

준사역동사   The investment guideline will help potential buyers [make / ~~making~~] an informed decision.
투자 지침서는 잠재적 구매자들이 현명한 결정을 내리도록 도와줄 것이다.

ETS 유형 연습 ....   정답과 해설 p.145

1 Anisk Pharmaceuticals makes every effort _____ the confidentiality of all participants in the clinical study.

(A) to maintain
(B) maintains
(C) will maintain
(D) is maintaining

2 _____ the processing of your claim, include your customer identification number on all correspondence.

(A) To be expedited
(B) Will expedite
(C) Expedited
(D) To expedite

3 The director strongly believes that professional development seminars can help _____ the knowledge and expertise of employees in many areas.

(A) broaden
(B) broader
(C) broadly
(D) broad

■ 동명사의 자리

동명사는 주어나 보어, 그리고 동사 및 전치사의 목적어로 쓰인다.

주어   [Advertising / ~~Advertise~~] on social media is the most effective way to attract customers.
소셜 미디어에 광고하는 것이 고객을 유치하는 가장 효과적인 방법이다.

보어   Our first priority is [making / ~~made~~] sure that the project is completed on time.
우리의 최우선 과제는 그 프로젝트가 제 시간에 완료되도록 하는 것이다.

동사의 목적어   We decided to discontinue [selling / ~~to sell~~] shoes and focus on clothes.
우리는 신발 판매를 중단하고 옷에 집중하기로 결정했다.

전치사의 목적어   Mr. Bradley is responsible for [developing / ~~develop~~] the company's Web site.
브래들리 씨는 회사에서 웹사이트 개발을 담당하고 있다.

동사 + 동명사(-ing) 적중 리스트

consider -ing ~을 고려하다	suggest -ing ~을 제안하다	recommend -ing ~을 추천하다	avoid -ing ~을 피하다
admit -ing ~을 인정하다	deny -ing ~을 부인하다	discontinue -ing ~을 중단하다	quit -ing ~을 중단하다
keep -ing ~을 계속하다	include -ing ~을 포함하다	mind -ing ~을 꺼리다	give up -ing ~을 포기하다

■ 동명사 vs 명사

동명사 뒤에는 목적어가 올 수 있지만 명사 뒤에는 목적어가 올 수 없다. 또한 부정관사(a/an) 뒤에는 동명사가 올 수 없다.

We should discuss how to solve the problem after [analyzing / ~~analysis~~] the data.
우리는 데이터 분석 후 문제를 해결할 방법에 대해 논의해야 한다.

→ 명사 analysis는 목적어를 취할 수 없다.

■ 동명사 관용 표현

동명사 관용 표현 적중 리스트

before -ing ~하기 전에	after -ing ~한 후에	on -ing ~하자마자	in -ing ~하는 데 있어서
by -ing ~함으로써	feel like -ing ~하고 싶다	spend 시간/돈 -ing ~하는 데 (시간/돈)을 쓰다	
be capable of -ing ~할 수 있다	cannot help -ing ~하지 않을 수 없다	have difficulty -ing ~하는 데 어려움을 겪다	

ETS 유형 연습

정답과 해설 p.145

1 For many years the local government has considered _____ Red Valley as a wilderness park.

(A) designate
(B) designates
(C) designating
(D) designation

2 To avoid _____ your audience during your presentation, please do not use complex layouts.

(A) distraction
(B) distracts
(C) distracted
(D) distracting

3 Ms. Baxter would like to meet with all members of the hiring committee again after _____ candidates.

(A) interview
(B) interviews
(C) interviewing
(D) interviewed

> | to부정사/ | 'to+동사원형'의 to와 전치사 to를 잘 구별하자. 전치사 to 뒤에는 명사, 동명사가 오고 동사원형은 쓸 수 없다. |
> | 전치사 to | to부정사는 '~하는 것, ~해야 할' 등으로 해석되고, 전치사 to는 '~에게, ~로'라는 의미로 방향성을 나타낸다. |

■ to부정사 관련 표현

┌─ be동사 + 형용사 + to부정사 적중 리스트 ─────────────────────────────

be able to do ~할 수 있다   be pleased to do ~하게 되어 기쁘다   be available to do ~할 시간이 있다

be anxious to do ~하기를 간절히 바라다   be eager to do ~하기를 갈망하다   be willing to do 기꺼이 ~할 것이다

be likely to do ~할 것 같다   be liable to do ~할 것 같다   be apt to do ~하기 쉽다

be about to do 막 ~하려고 하다   be eligible to do ~할 자격이 있다   be prone to do ~하기 쉽다

be supposed to do ~하기로 되어 있다   be scheduled to do ~할 예정이다   be designed to do ~하도록 고안되다

be hesitant to do ~하기를 망설이다   be reluctant to do ~하기를 꺼리다   be ready to do ~할 준비가 되어 있다

└───

Mr. Smith will be [able / ~~capable~~] to manage hundreds of accounts by himself.

스미스 씨는 혼자서 수백 개의 거래를 관리할 수 있을 것이다.

→ capable은 뒤에 전치사 of를 붙여 'be capable of+(동)명사(~할 수 있다)' 덩어리로 사용된다.

The planning department is supposed to [arrange / ~~arranging~~] next week's company meeting.

기획부에서 다음 주 회사 회의를 준비하기로 되어 있다.

■ 전치사 to 관련 표현

전치사 to는 뒤에 명사 또는 동명사와 결합하여 주로 '~에'라고 해석한다.

┌─ 동사 + 전치사 to + 명사/동명사 적중 리스트 ─────────────────────────

be subject to ~에 달려 있다, ~될 수 있다   be accustomed to ~에 익숙하다   be committed/dedicated/devoted to ~에 헌신하다

contribute to ~에 기여[기부]하다   look forward to ~을 기대하다   object to ~에 반대하다 (= be opposed to)

come close to 거의 ~할 뻔하다   be resistant to ~에 저항하다, 강하다   be vulnerable to ~에 취약하다

└───

This guidebook is sure to contribute to [improving / ~~improve~~] the experience of travelers.

이 안내서는 분명 여행자들이 더 좋은 경험을 하게 해 줄 것이다.

The new agricultural method made crops more [resistant / ~~reluctant~~] to specific pests.

새로운 농사법은 작물들이 특정 해충에 더욱 강해지도록 만들었다.

→ reluctant는 to부정사와 쓰인다.

Many civil groups [objected / ~~opposed~~] to the legislation on a new free trade agreement.

많은 시민 단체가 새 자유무역협정 입법에 반대했다.

ETS 유형 연습 정답과 해설 p. 145

1 Sweetness Chocolate is pleased _____ that it will be listed on the Public Stock Exchange as of August 1.

(A) to announce
(B) announcement
(C) announced
(D) be announcing

2 The newspaper's circulation department is committed to _____ excellent service.

(A) provision
(B) provided
(C) providing
(D) provides

3 A few of the Fairmont Finance employees object to _____ for parking on the company premises.

(A) charge
(B) have charged
(C) be charged
(D) being charged

1. Editor-in-chief Kyra Daley confirmed plans to expand the distribution area of the *Harnett Times* ------- Wilston County.

   (A) inclusive
   (B) to include
   (C) inclusion
   (D) will include

2. Please note that all outdoor programs are subject to ------- without prior notice.

   (A) cancellation
   (B) canceling
   (C) canceled
   (D) cancel

3. To handle the increase in sales, the human resources department intends ------- a number of new employees.

   (A) recruited
   (B) recruitment
   (C) recruiting
   (D) to recruit

4. ------- an international conference for over 1,000 participants was the most challenging assignment for the team.

   (A) Preparation
   (B) Preparing
   (C) Prepared
   (D) Being prepared

5. The management of Eurosan Enterprises is in the process of ------- a new set of guidelines for customer service.

   (A) establish
   (B) establishes
   (C) established
   (D) establishing

6. Artour Cycling executives cited slow sales as the reason for the decision ------- the Nordique bicycle line.

   (A) have discontinued
   (B) was discontinuing
   (C) will discontinue
   (D) to discontinue

7. At the end of November, author Eunice Kim is scheduled ------- her fifth lecture in Turnham.

   (A) to give
   (B) will be giving
   (C) giving
   (D) may have given

8. The consulting firm is responsible for ------- customized marketing solutions to small businesses.

   (A) offer
   (B) offered
   (C) offering
   (D) offers

9. It is usually most effective ------- a meeting agenda to the attendees in advance.

   (A) to circulate
   (B) circulating
   (C) circulated
   (D) circulation

10. The sales manager spends considerable time ------- his team members and new employees.

    (A) training
    (B) trains
    (C) trained
    (D) trainer

11. The CEO of Vento Cosmetics did not let the recent problems with foreign sales ------- the company's long-term export plans.

    (A) have affected
    (B) to affect
    (C) affect
    (D) affecting

12. The corporate charter requires its executives ------- in the best interest of the company.

    (A) acting
    (B) to act
    (C) are acting
    (D) acted

13. All dancers should have at least two years of prior experience ------- be considered for the City Ballet.

    (A) likewise   (B) in order to
    (C) currently   (D) only if

14. The carpentry firm of Marcello & Buhl is seeking a summer apprentice with a strong interest in ------- the craft.

    (A) to learn   (B) will learn
    (C) learning   (D) learns

Questions 15-18 refer to the following advertisement.

As a business owner, you probably have comprehensive insurance coverage for your commercial property and inventory. But when you or your employees have to travel for business purposes, you will also need commercial auto insurance. At Miranda Brothers' Auto Insurance, we pride ourselves on our ability ------- an insurance plan that best meets the needs of your company. By insuring your
15.

------- , you are guaranteed that they will be repaired or replaced in case of an accident.
16.

------- . Coverage plans vary depending on whether employees use company cars or their own cars
17.
for work purposes. We also offer plans for companies that allow for ------- options.
18.

15. (A) to design
    (B) designing
    (C) but design
    (D) designed for

16. (A) antiques
    (B) computers
    (C) boats
    (D) vehicles

17. (A) The Miranda brothers founded the company twenty years ago.
    (B) Businesses of all sizes save money on auto coverage with us.
    (C) We won an award for excellence ten years ago.
    (D) We recently hired a new Vice President of Marketing.

18. (A) good
    (B) both
    (C) same
    (D) limited

Unit | 10 분사와 분사구문

> **분사의 자리** 분사는 동사에 -ing, -ed가 붙어 형용사 역할을 하는 준동사이다. 문제를 풀 때는 먼저 빈칸이 형용사 자리인지 확인하고, 수식 및 보충하는 명사와 능동 관계인지 수동 관계인지 확인해야 한다.

■ 명사 앞에서 수식

분사는 형용사처럼 명사 앞에서 명사를 수식할 수 있다.

The National Savings Bank will offer small business loans at [reduced / reduces] interest rates as of next Monday. 국영 저축 은행은 다음 주 월요일부터 할인된 이자율로 중소기업 대출을 제공할 것이다.

■ 명사 뒤에서 수식

명사 뒤에 온 '주격 관계대명사+be동사'를 생략하면 분사가 명사 뒤에서 명사를 수식하게 된다.

명사 뒤에서 수식할 때	분사 뒤에 목적어가 있으면 주로 능동 (-ing)	the paper [detailing / detailed] the requirements 요구사항을 상세히 설명하는 서류
	분사 뒤에 전치사가 있으면 주로 수동 (p.p.)	the report [written / writing] by a new assistant 새 조수에 의해 쓰인 보고서

Invitations were e-mailed for a banquet (which is) [celebrating / celebrated] the company's 60th anniversary. 회사 창립 60주년을 기념하는 연회를 위해 이메일로 초대장이 보내졌다.

■ 주격 보어

be동사와 같은 2형식 동사 뒤 주격 보어 자리에 분사를 쓸 수 있다. 주어와 보어의 능동/수동 관계에 주목한다.

The results of inspections on the food safety and quality in some restaurants were [disappointing / disappointed]. 몇몇 식당의 식품 안전성과 품질에 관한 조사 결과는 실망스러웠다.

■ 목적격 보어

keep, find, consider 동사와 같은 5형식 동사의 목적어 뒤 목적격 보어 자리에 분사를 쓸 수 있다. 목적어와 목적격 보어의 능동/수동 관계에 주목해야 한다.

Novice readers might not **find some of the award-winning books** [appealing / appealed].
초보 독자들은 수상작들 중 일부가 흥미롭다고 생각하지 않을 수도 있다.

ETS 유형 연습

정답과 해설 p.148

1 Abraham Consulting Corporation specializes in offering _____ staffing solutions for small and midsize businesses.

(A) customize
(B) customizes
(C) customizing
(D) customized

2 Our office secretary had made a backup of the computer files, so the information was _____ successfully after the power failure.

(A) recovered
(B) recover
(C) recovering
(D) recovery

3 A thunderstorm _____ by gusty winds is expected to arrive in the northeast region by late afternoon.

(A) will accompany
(B) accompanying
(C) to accompany
(D) accompanied

분사의 종류	분사는 현재분사일 때 능동, 과거분사일 때 수동의 의미가 된다. 분사와 수식/보충하는 명사의 관계가 '주어-동사' 관계이면 능동(-ing), '목적어-동사' 관계이면 수동(p.p.)을 선택한다. 자주 출제되는 분사와 명사를 숙어처럼 암기하자.

■ 현재분사

현재분사는 수식 또는 보충하는 명사와 '주어-동사'의 능동 관계이다.

Some consumers have complained that **the labels** on appliances are [confusing / confused].
일부 소비자들은 가전제품에 있는 표시들이 혼란스럽다고 불평했다.
→ 빈칸은 주격 보어 자리이다. 주어인 the labels와 보어인 confusing(혼란을 주는)은 능동 관계이다.

■ 과거분사

과거분사는 수식 또는 보충하는 명사와 '목적어-동사'의 수동 관계이다. 완료의 의미를 나타내기도 한다.

The president has finally approved the [revised / revising] **proposals** after several months of consideration. 사장은 수개월간의 고민 끝에 결국 수정된 제안을 승인했다.
→ 수식하는 명사 proposals는 revise(수정하다)와 수동 관계이다.

현재분사, 과거분사 빈출 표현

challenging assignment 힘든 (도전을 주는) 과제
opposing opinions 반대 의견
overwhelming demand 압도적인 수요

closing ceremony 폐회식
outstanding debts 미불 채무
preceding years 지난 몇 년

distinguished economist 뛰어난 경제학자
dedicated staff 헌신적인 직원
designated area 지정된 장소

confirmed reservation 확인된 예약
sophisticated system 정교한 시스템
written consent 서면 동의

■ 감정동사의 분사

-ed형(감정을 느끼는)은 주로 사람명사와, -ing형(감정을 유발시키는)은 주로 사물명사와 어울린다.

사람명사와 어울리는 과거분사(p.p.)

pleased 기쁜 | excited 신난 | satisfied 만족하는 | amused 즐거운 | impressed 감동받은
fascinated 매혹된 | overwhelmed 압도된 | confused 혼란스러운 | frustrated 좌절한 | concerned 걱정하는

ETS 유형 연습 .... 정답과 해설 p.148

1 Based on the _____ number of advance ticket sales, we expect to see record attendance levels at this year's festival in Donegal.
(A) overwhelm
(B) overwhelms
(C) overwhelming
(D) overwhelmingly

2 The phone lines at Simon's House of Fine Furniture are staffed by _____ representatives with a thorough knowledge of the company's products.
(A) dedicate
(B) dedication
(C) dedicated
(D) dedicating

3 Mr. and Ms. Cooper decided to build their house outside the city limits when the city's rigid building codes became too _____ to accommodate.
(A) frustrated
(B) frustration
(C) frustrate
(D) frustrating

> **분사의 활용** 분사 자리 찾기 유형 문제는 다른 품사 문제들에 비해 적용 능력, 해석 능력을 많이 요구한다. 분사와 형용사, 동명사, 동사를 구별하는 방법, 분사와 자주 결합하는 단어들을 익히도록 한다.

■ 분사 구별하기

현재분사는 동명사와 형태가 같고, 과거분사는 과거 시제 동사와 형태가 같은 경우가 많다.

[Satisfying / Satisfied] regular customers with the best service possible is our priority.
가능한 최고의 서비스로 단골 고객을 만족시키는 것이 우리의 우선순위이다.

→ Satisfying은 동명사(주어) 역할을 하고 있다. Satisfied를 선택하면 주어(regular customers)와 동사(is)의 수가 불일치한다.

The paper **[included / including]** more details of the contracts with our suppliers.
그 서류에는 우리 공급업체와의 계약에 대한 상세 내용이 들어 있었다.

→ 문장에 동사가 없으므로 빈칸에 과거동사인 included가 필요하다.

The cost of leasing office equipment would be **[comparable / comparing]** to buying.
사무용 기기 임대 비용은 구매 비용과 맞먹을 수 있다.

→ 형용사와 분사를 구별할 때는 먼저 해석으로 구별하고, 해석상 차이가 없다면 형용사를 정답으로 선택한다.

■ 자동사의 분사

자동사는 목적어가 필요 없는 동사이므로, 수동의 의미를 가지는 과거분사(p.p.) 형태로 쓰지 않는다.

┌─ **오직 -ing 형태로만 쓰는 분사** ─────────────────────────────
│ existing facilities 기존의 시설   emerging market 신흥 시장   rising costs 증가하는 비용
│ lasting impression 지속되는 인상   missing luggage 분실 수하물   remaining work 남은 업무
└──

Few in the IT industry have reported **[rising / risen]** profits in the past few years.
지난 몇 년간 수익 증가를 보고한 IT 업계 회사들은 거의 없었다.

■ as p.p. / than p.p. 구문

as 바로 뒤에 p.p.를 동반하여 '~했듯이, ~했던 대로'라고 해석한다. than 뒤에 p.p.를 쓰면 '~했던 것보다'라고 해석한다.

┌──
│ **as expected** 예상했던 대로   **as requested** 요청했던 대로   **than anticipated** 예상했던 것보다
└──

As **[discussed / discusses]** before, special group rates will be applied.
전에 논의했던 대로 특별 단체 요금이 적용될 것이다.

ETS 유형 연습

정답과 해설 p. 148

1 Adequate storage space is very important to companies _____ large quantities of materials.

(A) produced
(B) produces
(C) produce
(D) producing

2 Mr. Matthews, a reporter for the *International Daily* newspaper, will be on _____ assignment until further notice.

(A) special
(B) specialize
(C) specially
(D) specializing

3 As _____ in our telephone conversation this morning, Mr. Fox will arrive at your factory at 2 P.M. on Wednesday, March 14.

(A) discuss
(B) discussion
(C) discussing
(D) discussed

> **분사구문**   분사구문은 수식어 역할을 하는 부사절이 변형된 것으로, 분사 자리의 능동과 수동을 구별하는 문제가 가장 많이 출제된다.

■ 분사구문 만들기

'접속사+주어+동사'의 부사절에서 접속사와 주어를 생략하면 분사구문을 만들 수 있다.

Once it hires a famous chef, the restaurant will make more profits.

→ **Hiring** a famous chef, the restaurant will make more profits.
  유명한 주방장을 고용하면, 그 식당은 더 많은 수익을 낼 것이다.

❶ 접속사 생략 가능
❷ 주어(가 주절의 주어와 같으면) 생략
❸ 동사를 '동사원형+-ing' 형태로 바꾸기

■ 분사구문의 특징

분사구문은 주로 콤마를 동반하며, 분사 자리에 동사나 명사는 쓸 수 없다. 생략된 주어를 찾아 주어와 동사의 능동/수동 관계를 파악해야 하는데, 타동사인 경우 목적어가 있으면 현재분사(능동), 없으면 과거분사(수동)를 쓰면 된다. 분사구문에서 -ing는 '~하면서, ~하기 때문에' 등으로 다양하게 해석할 수 있다.

[**Posting** / ~~Posted~~] a comment on the product review page, you will not be able to edit or delete it later.
제품 평가 페이지에 의견을 남기시면, 이후에 그것을 편집 또는 삭제하실 수 없습니다.

→ 빈칸 앞에 생략된 주어와 분사의 관계가 능동 관계이며, 분사 뒤에 목적어가 있으므로 현재분사를 쓴다.

■ 수동 분사구문

분사구문에서 be동사는 being으로 바뀌는데, being 또는 having been을 생략하면 과거분사로 시작하는 수동 분사구문이 될 수 있다. 과거분사는 주로 뒤에 전치사가 온다.

[**Faced** / ~~Facing~~] with problems with some machines, the management decided to extend the deadline for production. 몇몇 기계들에 발생한 문제에 직면하자, 경영진은 생산 마감일을 연장하기로 결정했다.

■ 완료 분사구문

분사구문의 시제가 주절의 시제보다 앞설 때 쓴다.

[**Having traveled** / ~~Traveled~~] all around the globe, the photographer is having her photo exhibition at London Museum. 세계를 여행한 뒤, 그 사진작가는 런던 박물관에서 사진전을 열고 있다.

ETS 유형 연습 ....

정답과 해설 p.149

1 The city has experienced an unusually large amount of rainfall this year, _____ it difficult for road projects to be completed on time.

   (A) made
   (B) make
   (C) makes
   (D) making

2 _____ by the product demonstration last week, the operations manager has decided to order several of Handimaid's appliances.

   (A) Impressed
   (B) Impressive
   (C) Impressing
   (D) Impression

3 _____ a degree in accounting, Ms. Sakai is considered one of the top candidates for the management position.

   (A) Having earned
   (B) Earned
   (C) Being earned
   (D) Earn

1. In accordance with Chandu Museum policy, any personal items left in the building that are not ------- within one week will be discarded.

(A) claim
(B) claims
(C) claimed
(D) claiming

2. New employees should report to their ------- training locations at 8 A.M. with all necessary paperwork.

(A) assigned
(B) assign
(C) assigns
(D) assigning

3. Ms. Harrison is a long-time human resources professional ------- in the field for her outstanding achievements.

(A) recognized
(B) recognizes
(C) recognizing
(D) recognize

4. Most of our clients are ------- about the prospect of our showroom moving to a larger space.

(A) exciting
(B) to excite
(C) excites
(D) excited

5. Next week, the candidates in the local city council election will be on television ------- their ideas.

(A) introduction
(B) introducing
(C) introduce
(D) introductory

6. Lavelle Hospital's policy states that patients' personal information may not be released without ------- consent.

(A) writing
(B) written
(C) write
(D) wrote

7. Ever since the management of Glover Company was restructured, the quality of the company's products has been much -------.

(A) improved
(B) improving
(C) improvement
(D) improvable

8. Citing a survey ------- by an independent polling firm, *The Town Voice* reported that 70 percent of residents were in favor of constructing a new stadium.

(A) conduct
(B) conductor
(C) conducted
(D) conducting

9. When ------- your Galaxy glass dishware in boxes, first wrap it in soft tissue paper to protect against scratches.

(A) stores
(B) storing
(C) store
(D) stored

10. Alinton Hardware's policy is that customers may return any item within 30 days if they are not ------- with their purchase.

(A) satisfactory
(B) satisfaction
(C) satisfied
(D) satisfy

11. The accommodations and services at the Gwanghwamun Inn were stellar, ------- the organizers of the annual conference.

(A) delight
(B) delights
(C) delighting
(D) delighted

12. Due to the late arrival of his flight, Mr. Medina was unable to speak with reporters as -------.

(A) scheduled
(B) scheduling
(C) schedule
(D) schedules

13. There are many ------- signs that high-quality job-training programs in the Winton Area are expanding the pool of qualified workers for companies in the area.

(A) encourage   (B) encouraged
(C) encouraging   (D) encouragement

14. ------- that her order would not arrive on time, Ms. Chang requested the express delivery option.

(A) Concern   (B) Concerning
(C) Concerns   (D) Concerned

Questions 15-18 refer to the following notice.

NOTICE OF PROPOSED DEVELOPMENT

The City of Shelton has received a building permit application from Mitchell Brothers Builders to erect an apartment building on the site ------- at 6410 North Columbia Boulevard. The building plan
                                       15.
includes a utility line connection that overlaps with a protected environmental zone. The purpose of this notice is to inform residents of the Cully neighborhood and other interested persons of the proposed action.

Please note that all ------- within environmental zones in the City of Shelton will adhere to the
                      16.
environmental development standards found in chapter 33.430 of the zoning code. All comments and questions from the public should be submitted to Zara Wong, City Planner, Shelton City Hall, 62 Haye Street, Shelton, TN 37201. ------- the public may contact Ms. Wong's office at 615-555-
                                                17.
0163. -------.
      18.

---

15. (A) located
    (B) locating
    (C) a location
    (D) that locates

16. (A) purchases
    (B) discussion
    (C) advertising
    (D) construction

17. (A) Instead
    (B) As a result
    (C) In any event
    (D) Alternatively

18. (A) The site has been vacant since June.
    (B) Plans must be submitted to the City of Shelton in writing.
    (C) All public comments on the proposal are due by October 31.
    (D) Mitchell Brothers opened for business six years ago.

전치사 어휘 1	전치사 어휘 문제는 매회 3문제 내외로 출제된다. 전치사의 기본 의미 두세 개 정도는 정확하게 외워 두어야 한다. '전치사 + 명사' 또는 '동사 + 전치사' 덩어리를 먼저 해석하면 문제풀이 시간을 단축할 수 있다.

■ at, on, in, by, until

at + 시점, 지점, 금액, 회사명	~에(서)	at 9:00, at night, at the station, at a low price, at YBM
on + 날짜, 요일, 주제, 인터넷	~에 (대한)	on March 6, on Saturday, a book on education, on the Web site
in + 월, 계절, 연도, 아침/오후, 기간, 큰/독립된 공간, 분야	~후에, ~만에, ~(안)에	in March, in summer, in 2016, in the morning, in a week in the last ten years, in New York, in a conference room an increase in profits, advances in science
by + 시점 행위자(수동태 뒤)	~까지, ~전에 ~에 의해	should arrive by this Friday suggested by customers
until + 시점	~까지	not arrive until this weekend

*this / last / next Friday 앞에는 전치사 at, on, in을 쓸 수 없다.

*by, until은 시점 명사와 함께 쓰여 모두 '~까지'라고 해석되지만, 함께 쓰이는 동사 짝이 다르다. 완료를 나타내는 by는 1회성 동사(arrive, submit, complete 등), until은 지속성 동사(postpone, stay 등) 또는 동사의 부정형(not arrive)과 함께 쓴다.

■ for, during, throughout, within

for + 기간(주로 숫자) 이유, 목적, 교환	~ 동안 ~ 때문에, ~ 대신에	for an hour, for the next five years blame A for B B 때문에 A를 비난하다 substitute A for B B를 A로 대체하다
during + 기간(주로 명사)	~ 동안	during the presentation
throughout + 기간, 장소	~ 동안, 내내, ~ 도처에	throughout winter, throughout the building
within + 기간, 범위	~ 이내에	within a week, within 10 kilometers, within the budget

■ around, beside, to, through

around + 장소	~근처에	around the office
beside + 장소	~옆에	beside(= next to) the escalator
to + 지점, 도착점	~에게	send packages to customers, given to the sales team
through + 장소, 추상 수단, 과정	~를 통하여, 내내	through the tunnel, through the Internet, through the process

ETS 유형 연습

정답과 해설 p. 151

1 Club members are allowed to attend the Healthy Living seminar _____ no cost.

(A) at
(B) by
(C) over
(D) from

2 Daniel will be checking the report _____ mistakes before it is submitted to the group manager.

(A) in
(B) for
(C) over
(D) from

3 Maria Gomez submitted her plan for the new transit system _____ the city's board of directors for review.

(A) to
(B) by
(C) along
(D) on

<table>
<tr><td>전치사 어휘 2</td><td colspan="2">전치사 중에는 두세 단어로 이루어진 구 전치사와 주로 동명사와 함께 쓰이는 전치사가 있다. 전치사의 기본 의미
와 더불어 빈출 용례를 함께 기억하자.</td></tr>
</table>

■ 다양한 빈출 전치사

of+소유, 소속 동격, 관련	~의	a film of the famous director, president of the medical clinic the fact of being late, a story of success
with+동반, 소유	~와 함께, ~을 가지고	bring the notepad with you, with care(=carefully)
without	~ 없이	without previous experiences, without getting enough funds
behind	~ 뒤에, ~에 뒤처져	behind the building, behind schedule
unlike	~와 달리	unlike most other companies
except	~을 제외하고	every day except (on) Sunday
under+진행, 영향	~ 중인, ~ 아래	under consideration, under control, under the direction of
against	~에 반대하는	compete against, vote against
for	~에 찬성하는	vote for, advocate for
*between	~ 사이에	between A and B, between the (two) options
*among	~ 중에	Among the candidates, Dan is the most qualified.
across	~을 가로질러, ~ 전체에 걸쳐	across the river, all across Canada

*between(둘 사이에)과 among(셋 이상 사이에) 뒤에는 복수명사가 온다.

■ 구 전치사와 -ing 전치사

prior to ~ 이전에	ahead of ~보다 앞서	regardless of ~와 상관없이	apart from ~ 이외에
because of / due to / owing to ~ 때문에	with regard to ~에 관하여	as to ~에 관하여	in addition to ~뿐만 아니라
on account of ~ 때문에	by means of ~을 이용하여	on behalf of ~을 대신하여	in spite of ~에도 불구하고
regarding / concerning ~에 관하여	notwithstanding ~에도 불구하고	including ~을 포함하여	following ~ 이후에

| 고득점 팁 | '전치사+-ing' 관용 표현
전치사 뒤 명사 자리에 동명사를 주로 쓰는 전치사를 외워두도록 한다.
by -ing ~함으로써   in -ing ~하는 데 있어서   on -ing ~하자마자   instead of -ing ~하는 것 대신에

ETS 유형 연습

정답과 해설 p.151

1 The Grovesburg Historical Society leads tours of local historical sites every day _____ Sunday.

(A) other
(B) except
(C) than
(D) some

2 _____ Ms. Wattanasin, everyone on the team needed additional time to complete the Web design tutorial.

(A) Even
(B) Rather than
(C) Apart from
(D) If not for

3 Please contact Ms. Blackwell in the personnel office if you have not received information _____ company reimbursement procedures.

(A) regard
(B) regards
(C) regarding
(D) regarded

> | 전치사와 | 연결어 문제는 어휘 해석 능력을 묻는 것 같지만 먼저 품사를 구분하는 것이 중요하다. Part 5에서는 접속사와 전치사 |
> |---|---|
> | 접속사 | 중 적절한 품사를 선택하는 문제가 특히 자주 출제되고, Part 6에서는 접속부사를 이용한 어휘 문제가 자주 출제된다. |

■ 접속사와 전치사

접속사는 대개 절과 절을 연결하는 역할을 하며, '접속사+주어+동사'의 덩어리를 만든다. 전치사는 '전치사+명사(구)'의 수식어 덩어리를 만들며, 뒤에 '주어+동사'가 올 수 없다.

의미가 비슷한 접속사와 전치사

	접속사+주어+동사	전치사+명사
시간	when ~할 때 while ~하는 동안 as soon as ~하자마자	during ~동안 following ~ 이후에 prior to ~ 전에
조건	if ~라면 unless ~ 않는다면 as long as ~하는 한	in case of ~의 경우에 without ~가 없다면
이유	because ~하기 때문에	because of/due to/owing to ~ 때문에
양보	though/although/even though/even if 비록 ~일지라도	despite/in spite of ~에도 불구하고

Every visitor should not take a photo [while / ~~during~~] they take a tour of the facility.
모든 방문객은 시설을 둘러보는 동안 사진을 찍으면 안 된다.

→ during은 전치사이고 while은 접속사이다. 접속사 뒤에는 주어와 동사가 뒤따른다.

No matter how attractive, any proposal will not be accepted [without / ~~unless~~] the cost projections.
얼마나 매력적인지에 상관없이, 어떤 제안도 비용 계획이 없다면 받아들여지지 않을 것이다.

→ unless는 접속사이고 without은 전치사이다. 전치사는 뒤에 명사(구)와 결합한다.

두 가지 이상의 품사를 가지는 연결어

	접속사 (뒤에 절 추가)	전치사 (뒤에 명사 결합)	부사 (생략 가능)
as	~할 때, ~하듯이, ~ 때문에	~로서, ~만큼	-
besides	-	~ 이외에도	게다가
once	일단 ~하면	-	한때, 한 번
since	~ 이후로, ~ 때문에	~ 이후로	그 이후로
however	얼마나 ~든지, 어떻게 ~든지	-	하지만

ETS 유형 연습

정답과 해설 p. 152

1 Employees may not request a repayment of business travel expenses _____ a detailed itinerary is submitted with the claim.

(A) without
(B) unless
(C) as a result of
(D) while

2 Despite _____ declines in revenue over the past six months, the Mori & McGee firm intends to hire three new patent lawyers next year.

(A) will experience
(B) having experienced
(C) has experienced
(D) have been experiencing

3 _____ the probationary three months are completed, employees will be eligible for full company benefits.

(A) Soon
(B) Then
(C) Later
(D) Once

> **등위/상관 접속사** 접속사의 종류에는 종속절을 이끌어 명사절, 부사절 등을 형성하는 종속접속사 외에 앞과 뒤의 단어, 구, 절 등을 연결하는 등위접속사, 두 단어가 짝을 이루어 부분 또는 전체를 나타내는 상관접속사가 있다.

■ 등위접속사의 종류와 병렬 구조

등위접속사는 대등한 단어, 구, 절을 연결한다. 단, so와 for는 절과 절만 연결할 수 있다. 등위접속사는 앞뒤에 있는 동일한 품사를 연결한다.

and 그리고	but/yet 그러나	or 혹은, 그렇지 않으면	so 그래서	for 왜냐하면

The budget for the new project has been approved, [so / therefore] renowned architects and designers will be hired. 새 프로젝트를 위한 예산이 승인되었고, 따라서 유명한 건축가들과 디자이너들이 고용될 것이다.
→ 등위접속사 so가 문장과 문장을 연결하고 있다. therefore는 부사이기 때문에 뒤에 절(문장)을 추가할 수 없다.

The weekly talk show was very informative [but / and] too long.
주간 토크쇼는 매우 유익했지만 너무 길었다.

The promotional materials should be concise and easily [understandable / understands].
홍보 자료는 간결하고 이해하기 쉬워야 한다.

■ 상관접속사의 종류와 수 일치

상관접속사는 두 단어가 짝을 이루어 단어와 단어, 구와 구, 절과 절을 연결한다. 상관접속사가 주어 자리에 사용된 경우 주어와 동사의 수 일치에 유의한다.

both A and B A와 B 둘 다		복수동사
either A or B A와 B 둘 중 하나	neither A nor B A와 B 둘 다 아닌	B에 수 일치
not only A but (also) B/B as well as A A뿐 아니라 B도	not A but B/B but not A A가 아니라 B	

Both the main entrance [and / also] the elevators [are / is] not available today for the regular inspection.
정기점검으로 인해 오늘 정문과 엘리베이터 둘 다 이용이 불가하다.

Ms. Patel **not only** graduated from university, majoring in economics, [but / and] had abundant experience.
퍼텔 씨는 경제학 전공으로 대학교를 졸업했을 뿐 아니라 풍부한 경험도 가지고 있었다.

Neither the plot **nor** characters in the play [were / was] very attractive to the kids.
연극의 줄거리나 등장인물 모두 아이들에게 그다지 매력적이지 않았다.

ETS 유형 연습 ....

정답과 해설 p. 152

1 The international catalog is comprehensive, _____ certain items may not be available in every country.

(A) but
(B) whereas
(C) how
(D) whenever

2 Conference participants can get to the Wyatt Hotel _____ by train or by bus.

(A) unless
(B) both
(C) either
(D) without

3 After discussing the terms of the new health-benefits contract, _____ management and employees were satisfied.

(A) both
(B) also
(C) either
(D) too

ETS 실전문제

1. ------- the renovation project, employees in Building A will be relocated to the third floor of Building B.
(A) Instead
(B) During
(C) Although
(D) While

2. Margaret Nelson was hired to lead the company ------- the complicated process of organizational restructuring.
(A) behind
(B) above
(C) except
(D) through

3. Customers who wish to provide us with feedback or suggestions may do so ------- filling out the enclosed form.
(A) into
(B) over
(C) by
(D) from

4. Buyers must pay inspection fees ------- other expenses related to completing a property transaction.
(A) although
(B) as well as
(C) according to
(D) that is

5. ------- the three charity programs share much in common, unmistakable differences exist in their funding methods.
(A) Although
(B) Despite
(C) In spite
(D) Already

6. Most of the maps in the Brigg County Historical Collection can be photocopied ------- permission from the publisher.
(A) except
(B) besides
(C) without
(D) around

7. ------- your event, one of our associates will contact you to confirm menu choices and the guest count.
(A) When
(B) As long as
(C) Prior to
(D) Together with

8. The report suggests that neither insufficient advertising ------- a lack of effort were factors in the decreasing sales.
(A) but
(B) nor
(C) so
(D) yet

9. ------- the equipment did not function according to specifications, it was shipped back to the engineering department.
(A) In order that
(B) While
(C) Because
(D) Due to

10. Customers who do not wish to receive information ------- sales and promotions from Harmony Home Goods can change their account settings.
(A) regard
(B) regards
(C) regarded
(D) regarding

11. The office manager at Mellington Associates decided to purchase the photocopier ------- leasing it.
(A) with regard to
(B) instead of
(C) according to
(D) on behalf of

12. The town of Monkark in the central part of the province has ------- natural beauty and attractive architecture.
(A) neither
(B) both
(C) either
(D) not

13. ------- offering lightweight clothing, Hurvitz Travel Wear also sells stylish luggage and accessories.

(A) Except   (B) Besides
(C) However   (D) Unless

14. The contractor's crew was able to complete work on the Coastland Parkway ------- the shortage of construction equipment.

(A) despite   (B) although
(C) regarding   (D) about

Questions 15-18 refer to the following information.

Volunteers Needed

Public Health Services (PHS) is seeking twelve employees wishing to volunteer at our information booth ------- Grayerson University's Career Fair Weekend. The event will be held on April 13 and
    15.

14 from 10:00 A.M. to 6:00 P.M. Volunteers will work in four-hour shifts and inform ------- about
    16.

job opportunities, educational requirements, and possibilities for advancement. They will also be expected to discuss PHS's activities and describe a typical day in ------- job. ------- . A one-hour
    17.   **18.**

coaching session will be held in advance of the event. Interested employees can fill out a form, available at https://phs.employees.site.com/grayerson_cfw.

---

15. (A) onto
(B) around
(C) during
(D) towards

16. (A) workers
(B) students
(C) agents
(D) contestants

17. (A) them
(B) her
(C) his
(D) their

18. (A) Volunteers will offer suggestions following the presentation.
(B) Volunteers must indicate that they have read the policy.
(C) Volunteers will receive a complimentary lunch.
(D) Volunteers must re-register online each calendar year.

부사절 접속사

시간, 조건의 부사절	시간, 조건의 부사절은 '부사절 접속사 + 주어 + 동사' 덩어리가 문장에서 부사 역할을 하는 것으로, 수식어이기 때문에 생략해도 전체 문장에 영향을 주지 않는다. 부사절 접속사 뒤에는 보통 주어와 동사를 갖춘 절이 나온다.

■ 시간을 나타내는 부사절 접속사

when/as ~할 때	before ~전에	after ~후에	while ~하는 동안
until ~까지	since ~이후로	once ~하자마자	as soon as ~하자마자

[As / ~~During~~] actors appeared on the stage, the audience applauded enthusiastically.
배우들이 무대에 등장했을 때, 관중들은 열광적으로 박수갈채를 보냈다.

→ 시간의 접속사 as 뒤에 완전한 절이 뒤따르며, 전치사 during 뒤에는 절이 올 수 없다.

The travel guide book has been translated into multiple languages [since / ~~when~~] it was published in 2005.
여행 안내서는 2005년에 출간된 이후로 다양한 언어로 번역되어 왔다.

→ 부사절 접속사 since가 '~ 이후로'라고 해석되는 경우, 부사절의 동사는 과거 시제, 주절의 동사는 현재완료 시제를 쓴다.

■ 조건을 나타내는 부사절 접속사

if 만약 ~라면	unless (if not) 만약 ~이 아니라면	once 일단 ~하면	as long as ~하는 한
as far as ~하는 한	considering that ~을 고려하면	provided that ~라면	in case ~의 경우에, ~의 경우에 대비하여

The new business plan will be implemented soon [unless / ~~if~~] there is something seriously wrong with it.
심각하게 잘못된 것이 있는 게 아니라면, 새로운 사업 계획은 곧 시행될 것이다.

The client may make suggestions to the design [as long as / ~~in case of~~] they are made before work begins.
작업이 시작되기 전에 한다는 전제 하에, 고객은 디자인에 대해 제안을 할 수 있다.

→ as long as는 부사절 접속사로서 뒤에 완전한 절을 이끌고, in case of는 전치사로서 뒤에 절이 올 수 없다.

| 고득점 팁 | 시간과 조건의 부사절에서는 현재 시제로 미래의 일을 나타낸다.

Once the crops have been harvested, they [will be / ~~have been~~] neatly packaged and arranged.
일단 농작물이 수확되고 나면, 그것들은 깔끔하게 포장되고 정리될 것이다.

Please be reminded that the class will be cancelled if there [are / ~~will be~~] less than 4 students.
만약 학생이 네 명 미만일 경우 수업이 취소될 것임을 잊지 마세요.

ETS 유형 연습

정답과 해설 p. 154

1 Insurance specialists at Datweiler & Associates receive three months of intensive training _____ they begin working with clients.

(A) rather
(B) whereas
(C) before
(D) nearly

2 _____ the training period continues, new employees will receive sixty percent of their starting salary.

(A) As long as
(B) At times
(C) In time for
(D) By

3 _____ something is done, traffic congestion on the Winfield Parkway will continue to worsen.

(A) Unless
(B) Also
(C) Except
(D) Therefore

> 양보, 이유, 부사절 접속사 문제는 전치사나 명사절 접속사와 구별하는 문제, 해석상 적절한 부사절 접속사를 선택하는 문제, 능동
> 목적의 부사절 태/수동태 문장이 축약됐을 때 접속사 뒤 동사의 -ing / p.p. 형태를 고르는 문제 등이 나온다.

■ 양보를 나타내는 부사절 접속사

> though/although/even though/even if 비록 ~일지라도   while/whereas ~인 반면에

[Although / ~~Despite~~] there is a parking lot behind the west wing, it is not large enough for all employees.
서쪽 별관 뒤에 주차장이 있지만, 그것은 모든 직원을 수용할 만큼 크지 않다.

→ although는 부사절 접속사로서 절을 이끌고, despite는 전치사이므로 명사(구)가 온다.

■ 이유 / 목적을 나타내는 부사절 접속사

> because/since/as ~ 때문에   now that 이제 ~하니까   in that ~라는 점에서, ~ 때문에
> so that ~하기 위해서, ~할 수 있도록   in order that ~하기 위해서

[Now that / ~~Even if~~] you have renewed your rental agreement, you can continue to use the office space for a year. 당신이 임대 계약을 갱신했기 때문에, 사무실 공간을 일 년 더 사용할 수 있다.

■ 부사절 접속사의 축약

❶ 능동태 문장의 축약: 접속사+-ing+목적어

부사절에서 주어는 생략하고 동사를 -ing형으로 바꿀 수 있다.

Mr. Pearson found out that some parts were missing [while / ~~during~~] assembling the shelves.
피어슨 씨는 선반을 조립하다가 몇몇 부품이 빠진 것을 발견했다.

→ while he was assembling the shelves ~에서 주어와 be동사를 생략한 구문이 사용되었다. during 다음에는 명사가 와야 한다.

❷ 수동태 문장의 축약: 접속사+p.p.(+부사(구))

부사절에서 주어와 be동사를 함께 생략한다.

As [stated / ~~states~~] in the supply contract, customized items cannot be returned without any defects.
공급 계약서에 명시된 대로, 맞춤 제작 제품들은 결함이 없다면 반품될 수 없다.

→ 주어 it과 be동사가 생략된 'as+p.p.' 관용 표현에는 as stated, as requested, as discussed, as mentioned 등이 있다.

ETS 유형 연습

정답과 해설 p. 154

1 _____ the Kendal Company has been in business for only nine months, it has very quickly become profitable.

(A) Although
(B) Unless
(C) Before
(D) During

2 _____ the band has finally confirmed its availability, the outdoor concert will be scheduled for Sunday, June 11.

(A) In order for
(B) Now that
(C) So that
(D) Regarding

3 In his five years with Techniflex, Inc., Mr. Park has demonstrated repeatedly that he excels when _____ with a challenge.

(A) faces
(B) face
(C) facing
(D) faced

1. Caldwell Computers accepts returns ------- products have not been removed from the packaging.

   (A) in order that
   (B) such as
   (C) in case
   (D) as long as

2. Please notify Ms. Chen that the meeting has been rescheduled ------- that tomorrow's visitors from the overseas office can attend.

   (A) so
   (B) concerning
   (C) over
   (D) since

3. This afternoon's flights to Barcelona, London, and Rome have all been delayed ------- inclement weather in the destination cities.

   (A) as for
   (B) due to
   (C) now that
   (D) only if

4. ------- First Regional Bank has done so well in Juniper, it will be opening branches in Pinewood and North Haven.

   (A) Unless
   (B) Since
   (C) Rather
   (D) Therefore

5. ------- receiving notice that the director of the Deerfield Orchestra will retire, the board of directors has been searching for a replacement.

   (A) Since
   (B) While
   (C) Once
   (D) Because

6. Mr. Winthrop is a dynamic, determined, and articulate person who will succeed in sales ------- he has limited experience in this area of the business.

   (A) already
   (B) perhaps
   (C) as far as
   (D) even though

7. Employees currently working in Ridge Manufacturing's branch offices will move into the new headquarters ------- the building is finished.

   (A) once
   (B) even
   (C) besides
   (D) moreover

8. This month's newsletter will be delayed ------- staff members are still learning to use the new publishing software.

   (A) whether
   (B) because
   (C) in case of
   (D) so that

9. The deadline to submit vacation requests is January 15, ------- your vacation time is predetermined based on your job classification.

   (A) thus
   (B) unless
   (C) besides
   (D) despite

10. ------- the company faced hardships initially, it has now found success as the country's biggest manufacturer of plant-based cosmetics.

    (A) Instead
    (B) Unless
    (C) Whatever
    (D) Although

11. Although initially ------- to be too heavy, the truck's load was well within state guidelines.

    (A) believed
    (B) believing
    (C) was believed
    (D) had been believed

12. Because our company receives a high volume of customer inquiries, it may be two or three days ------- we can respond to yours.

    (A) if
    (B) before
    (C) while
    (D) but

13. Passengers must present photo identification ------- boarding trains that cross international borders.

(A) because   (B) when

(C) and   (D) whether

14. Please note that products ordered from Herb Emporium Online will not be shipped ------- full payment is received.

(A) within   (B) until

(C) during   (D) inside

Questions 15-18 refer to the following instructions.

Your CM200 microwave oven can be placed easily in your kitchen, family room, or office. Set the oven on a flat surface such as a kitchen countertop or a sturdy table. It is important to allow air to flow ------- around the oven. Allow at least 10 centimeters of space around the sides, top, and back
    15.
of the microwave oven. Do not ------- the oven in an enclosed space. Do not place it above a gas or
        16.
electric range. ------- . The reason for this is that blocked air exits will cause the oven to shut down
      17.
automatically ------- it is turned on.
    18.

15. (A) freedom
    (B) freer
    (C) freely
    (D) freeing

16. (A) remove
    (B) install
    (C) choose
    (D) purchase

17. (A) Keep all vents clear during cooking.
    (B) Follow all directions when preparing packaged meals.
    (C) Do not use the oven to boil any liquids.
    (D) Do not microwave more than two plates at a time.

18. (A) from
    (B) next
    (C) like
    (D) after

> **관계대명사의 종류** 관계대명사는 '접속사+대명사' 역할을 한다. 관계대명사 자리를 확인하는 문제, 관계대명사의 종류를 묻는 문제가 출제된다.

■ 관계대명사의 이해

관계대명사는 두 문장을 하나로 이어주는 접속사 역할을 하는 동시에, 관계사절에서 주어, 한정사, 또는 목적어 역할을 한다. 관계사절은 선행사를 수식하거나, 앞서 언급한 것에 대한 부연 설명을 한다.

We have already received feedback from the employees. + The employees attended yesterday's workshop.

We have already received feedback from the employees [who / those] attended yesterday's workshop.
우리는 이미 어제 워크숍에 참석했던 직원들로부터 피드백을 받았다.

→ 관계대명사 who가 관계사절에서 동사 attended의 주어 역할을 한다.

■ 관계대명사의 종류

관계대명사의 형태는 첫째, 선행사가 사람인지 아닌지, 둘째, 관계대명사절에서 관계대명사의 격이 무엇인지에 따라 결정된다.

선행사(앞 명사) / 격	주격 (바로 뒤 동사)	소유격 (바로 뒤 명사 수식)	목적격 (뒤에 목적어가 없는 문장)
사람	who, that	whose	whom, that
사물	which, that	whose	which, that
선행사를 포함한 관계대명사	what	-	what

*what은 선행사를 포함한 관계대명사로서 앞 명사를 수식할 수 없다.

❶ **주격 관계대명사:** 바로 뒤에 동사가 나온다.

The novel is based on **the documentary** [which / whom] **was produced** in the 1990s.
그 소설은 1990년대에 제작된 다큐멘터리에 기초하고 있다.

❷ **소유격 관계대명사:** 바로 뒤의 명사를 수식한다.

The crowds gathered to see **the prime minister** [whose / who] **visit** hit the headlines in local papers.
군중들은 총리를 보려고 모여들었고, 그의 방문은 지역 신문에 대서특필되었다.

❸ **목적격 관계대명사:** 뒤에 주어와 동사가 나오며, 관계사절에서 목적어 역할을 하므로 뒤에 따로 목적어가 없다.

The discount coupon [that / whose] **purchasers receive** with their first order is valid for a month.
구매자들이 첫 주문과 함께 받게 되는 할인 쿠폰은 한 달 동안 유효하다.

ETS 유형 연습
정답과 해설 p.156

1 Supervisors _____ have questions about the new expense report process should contact the budget office for assistance.

(A) what
(B) whose
(C) which
(D) who

2 Fong & Haas, Inc., has automated its toothpaste mixing processes, _____ used to take up more than half of the production time.

(A) and
(B) which
(C) though
(D) when

3 Metropolitan Artworks is an organization _____ mission is to support public art projects in the Twin Rivers area.

(A) that
(B) what
(C) which
(D) whose

> 관계대명사의 목적격 관계대명사나 '주격 관계대명사+be동사'가 생략된 경우의 문제도 자주 출제된다. 이때 능동, 수동 관계를
> 생략   구분해야 한다.

■ 목적격 관계대명사의 생략

목적격 관계대명사는 생략 가능하다.

The architect showed officials a floor plan of the airport he [designed / ~~was designed~~].
= **that** he designed

건축가는 관계자들에게 자신이 설계한 공항의 평면도를 보여주었다.

■ '주격 관계대명사+be동사'의 생략

주격 관계대명사 자체만은 생략할 수 없지만, '주격 관계대명사+be동사'는 생략 가능하다. 이 경우 선행사 뒤에 바로 현재분사 또는
과거분사가 와서 능동태와 수동태의 축약 구조를 이룬다. 뒤에 목적어가 있으면 능동태형인 -ing, 뒤에 목적어가 없으면 수동태형인
p.p.가 온다.

Dr. Gilbert [leading / ~~lead~~] the motivation workshop has recently been awarded a prize from the mayor.
= **(who is) leading** the motivation workshop

동기부여 워크숍을 이끌고 있는 길버트 박사는 최근 시장으로부터 상을 받았다.

It will take at least 4 years to restore the historic palace [damaged / ~~was damaged~~] by a big fire.
= **that was** damaged by a big fire

큰 화재로 손상된 유서 깊은 궁전을 복구하는 데 최소 4년이 걸릴 것이다.

➜ 뒤에 목적어가 없으므로 수동태의 축약으로 p.p.가 왔다.

| 고득점 팁 | **that의 용법**

관계대명사 that은 선행사가 사람일 때와 사물일 때 모두 수식할 수 있으며 뒤에 불완전한 절을 이끈다. 하지만 콤마 뒤, 전치사 뒤에는 관계대명사
that을 쓸 수 없다.

The office is near the subway station, [which / ~~that~~] makes daily commutes easy.
사무실이 지하철역 근처에 있는데, 이 점이 매일 통근을 쉽게 만들어준다.
*여기서 which는 앞 문장 전체를 가리킨다. (= and this)

There was a retirement celebration of John Weinstein for [whom / ~~that~~] employees have great respect.
직원들이 대단히 존경하는 존 와인스타인 씨의 은퇴 기념식이 있었다.
*관계대명사 that은 전치사 for의 목적어 역할을 할 수 없다.

ETS 유형 연습
정답과 해설 p.157

1 Province Bank customers are requested to update annually the passwords _____ use for online banking.
(A) they
(B) them
(C) their
(D) themselves

2 Of all the business plans _____ by the marketing manager, Mr. Martin's idea is the most impressive.
(A) review
(B) reviewed
(C) are reviewed
(D) which reviewed

3 The Springden government has published regulations _____ owners of rental property to provide recycling services for tenants.
(A) required
(B) will require
(C) requiring
(D) are required

┌───┐
│ 관계대명사의   '전치사+관계대명사' 구조도 시험에 자주 출제된다. 선행사가 사람인지 사물인지 구분하여 적절한 목적격 관계대 │
│   활용   명사를 선택하거나, 선행사와 어울리는 전치사를 선택할 수 있어야 한다. │
└───┘

■ 전치사 + 관계대명사

선행사가 관계대명사절에서 전치사의 목적어로 쓰인 경우 '전치사+관계대명사' 덩어리를 만든다.

The weather is scorching this week. + Citizens are encouraged not to go outside **during this week**.

The weather is scorching this week **during [which / ~~when~~]** citizens are encouraged not to go outside.

이번 주 날씨가 타는 듯이 더우니 (이번 주 동안) 시민 여러분은 밖으로 나가지 않는 것이 좋겠습니다.

Ms. Peng, the former HR director, was respected by the people with [whom / ~~which~~] she worked.

전 인사부장이었던 펑 씨는 함께 일했던 사람들의 존경을 받았다.

➜ 선행사가 사람이므로 whom이 쓰여야 한다.

■ 수량 표현 + of + 관계대명사

수량 표현 뒤에 'of+관계대명사' 형태로 one of whom/which, some of whom/which, all of whom/which, none of whom/which 등이 쓰인다. '수량 표현+of+관계대명사' 뒤에는 불완전한 절이 온다.

The reporter interviewed 10 entrepreneurs, **most of [whom / ~~them~~] didn't have** enough money in their early stages. 기자는 10명의 사업가들을 인터뷰했는데, 그들 중 다수가 초기에 충분한 자본이 없었다.

➜ 두 문장을 연결하는 접속사가 없으므로 them은 쓸 수 없으며, 접속사 역할을 하는 동시에 전치사 of의 목적어 역할을 하는 목적격 관계대명사 whom을 써야 한다.

Students are asked to read reference books, **all of which [are / ~~is~~]** written in English.

학생들은 참고도서를 읽어야 하는데, 그것들은 모두 영어로 쓰여 있다.

➜ which가 가리키는 대상이 reference books이므로 all of reference books와 어울리는 복수형 동사를 써야 한다.

The new staff lounge, **half of which [has / ~~have~~]** been painted, is still under construction.

새 직원 휴게실은 절반만 페인트칠이 되었고 여전히 공사 중이다.

➜ which가 가리키는 대상이 The new staff lounge이므로 단수형 동사를 써야 한다.

ETS 유형 연습

정답과 해설 p. 157

1 The names of the department heads to _____ the monthly reports should be sent are located on the last page of the manual.

(A) whoever
(B) whom
(C) what
(D) where

2 Candidates are asked to indicate their research interests by checking the boxes next to the projects on _____ they prefer to work.

(A) that
(B) whom
(C) which
(D) where

3 VECTO Design Co. has 12 graphic artists, all of _____ are skilled designers with at least 3 years of experience.

(A) what
(B) them
(C) they
(D) whom

관계부사	관계부사는 '접속사 + 부사' 역할을 한다. 관계부사의 종류를 선택하는 문제, 관계대명사와 관계부사를 구별하는 문제가 출제된다.

■ 관계부사의 종류

관계부사는 '접속사 + 부사' 역할을 한다. 관계부사절은 선행사를 수식하지만, 관계부사의 선행사는 생략되기도 한다.
관계부사는 '전치사 + 관계대명사'로 대체할 수 있다.

선행사	관계부사	전치사 + 관계대명사
시간을 나타내는 명사 (time)	when	in which / on which / at which
장소를 나타내는 명사 (place)	where	in which / on which / at which
이유를 나타내는 명사 (reason)	why	for which
방법을 나타내는 명사 (way)	how	in which

* 관계부사 how는 선행사와 함께 쓸 수 없다. 선행사 또는 관계부사 중 하나만 사용해야 한다.

┌ Welmart will install **self-checkout counters**. + Customers can process their own purchases **at the counters**.
└→ Welmart will install self-checkout counters **at** [which / ~~where~~] customers can process their own purchases.

Welmart will install self-checkout counters [where / ~~which~~] customers can process their own purchases.
웰마트는 고객들이 직접 자신의 구매품을 계산할 수 있는 셀프계산대를 설치할 예정이다.

We aim to reply to all emails within 24 hours, but there may be times [when / ~~which~~] we are slow to respond.
모든 이메일에 24시간 이내로 답변하려고 하지만, 대응이 늦어질 때가 있을 수도 있습니다.

■ 관계부사 vs 관계대명사

관계부사와 관계대명사는 뒤 문장의 구조를 통해 구별할 수 있다. 소유격을 제외한 주격, 목적격 관계대명사 뒤에는 불완전한 절이 오고, '전치사 + 관계대명사' 또는 관계부사 뒤에는 완전한 절이 온다.

The strong demand for commercial buildings is one of the reasons [why / ~~which~~] the overall price of properties has increased. 상가 건물에 대한 높은 수요는 전반적인 부동산 가격이 증가하는 원인 중 하나이다.
➜ 관계부사 why 뒤에 '주어 + 자동사'의 완전한 절이 왔다.

We should update the directory [that / ~~where~~] includes the details about hotel amenities.
우리는 호텔 시설에 대한 세부 사항을 포함하는 안내책자를 갱신해야 한다.
➜ 관계대명사 that 뒤에 주어가 없는 불완전한 절이 나왔다. 관계부사 where 뒤에는 완전한 절이 나와야 한다.

ETS 유형 연습

정답과 해설 p. 157

1 All shipments arrive at the receiving dock, _____ a warehouse worker checks their tracking labels.

(A) who
(B) which
(C) for which
(D) where

2 The facility manager has the key to the storage room _____ the office supplies are kept.

(A) where
(B) how
(C) when
(D) why

3 Dr. Kim's acceptance speech is expected to last about ten minutes, after _____ dessert will be served.

(A) that
(B) whose
(C) whom
(D) which

1. The carpet in the lobby of the Chiang Mai Opera House will be replaced with material ------- is easier to maintain.

   (A) what
   (B) where
   (C) that
   (D) this

2. The furniture store is owned by a talented carpenter ------- sells handmade as well as factory-made products.

   (A) who
   (B) whom
   (C) whose
   (D) which

3. Dr. Thomsen, a leading biologist ------- work has been published in numerous journals, will be the featured speaker at next week's conference.

   (A) whose
   (B) which
   (C) that
   (D) their

4. Dr. Johnson is offering a three-hour workshop during ------- she will share some perspectives on effective time management.

   (A) whose
   (B) while
   (C) whatever
   (D) which

5. The jacket you ordered is currently unavailable in the color you -------, but we will send the rest of your order promptly.

   (A) requests
   (B) requested
   (C) are requested
   (D) requesting

6. Content strategist Lorna Poggioli is an expert on the trends ------- the business world.

   (A) shape
   (B) shaped
   (C) shaping
   (D) shaper

7. Ella Portofino, ------- is known for her motivational speeches, will be the guest speaker at ORIL Leadership Conference in June.

   (A) each
   (B) which
   (C) who
   (D) this

8. All motorists are required to avoid the areas of Fifth Street ------- traffic lanes are being repainted.

   (A) which
   (B) whom
   (C) where
   (D) why

9. When the foreign delegates visited La Fleur Restaurant, ------- were served a special mushroom appetizer.

   (A) who
   (B) theirs
   (C) whom
   (D) they

10. *Red Sand Garden*, ------- was released by Dream Town Studios last week, has been popular with those in their 30s.

    (A) when
    (B) which
    (C) who
    (D) whose

11. Factory personnel ------- job is to operate industrial machinery must attend a safety course once a year.

    (A) whose
    (B) they
    (C) that
    (D) these

12. To improve efficiency, Boisclair Robotics designed a machine ------- can monitor the entire assembly line in the factory.

    (A) that
    (B) like
    (C) near
    (D) so

13. Managers often have to decide between several courses of action, none of ------- is completely right or wrong.

(A) that   (B) which

(C) when   (D) where

14. ------- for server positions who have not received a response within two weeks should send a follow-up e-mail.

(A) Applications   (B) Applies

(C) Applicants   (D) Applying

Questions 15-18 refer to the following e-mail.

To: Melissa Hart <melissahart@hmail.com>
From: Myles Winters <mwinters@fivestarsrestaurantonline.com>
Re: Assistant Chef position
Date: November 2

Dear Ms. Hart,

Thank you for applying to and interviewing for the position of Assistant Chef at the Five Stars Restaurant. We unexpectedly received a large number of applications. -------, we decided
  15.
to interview a total of seven potential job candidates. In the end, we hired an exceptionally experienced chef ------- a number of prestigious culinary awards.
  16.

------- . We would like to speak with you again regarding a different position in our kitchen. If you
  17.
are ------- , please call me at 518-555-2213, or you can just reply to this e-mail.
  18.

Thank you.

Myles Winters

---

15. (A) Instead
(B) As a result
(C) On the contrary
(D) In the meantime

16. (A) that is receiving
(B) the reception of
(C) who has received
(D) whose reception is

17. (A) However, we were also very impressed with your credentials.
(B) Our kitchen staff was looking forward to meeting you.
(C) In addition, we are planning renovations to our dining area.
(D) We will soon be expanding our menu options.

18. (A) worried
(B) occupied
(C) interested
(D) determined

Unit | 14 명사절 접속사

> **명사절 접속사의 이해** 명사절 접속사는 문장의 주어나 목적어 역할을 하는 명사절을 이끌며, 관계대명사나 부사절/등위 접속사와 구별하는 문제가 자주 출제된다. that, whether가 특히 자주 출제되며, 다른 명사절 접속사들의 비중도 높아지고 있다.

■ 명사절 접속사의 역할

'접속사+(주어)+동사'로 이루어진 덩어리가 문장에서 주어나 목적어, 또는 보어의 역할을 할 때 명사절이라고 부른다. 명사절 접속사는 다음과 같으며, 명사절 접속사 자리에 although, because, while 등과 같은 부사절 접속사를 쓸 수 없다.

that ~라는 것	whether/if ~인지 아닌지	who 누가	whose 누구의	whom 누구를
what 무슨, 무엇	which 어느, 어느 것	when 언제	where 어디에	how 어떻게, 얼마나 why 왜

주어   [Whether / ~~While~~] **we can secure the research funding or not** is still uncertain.
우리가 연구 자금을 확보할 수 있을지는 아직 미지수다.

동사의 목적어   The clinic decided [that / ~~because~~] **it will terminate the contract with the current supplier.** 병원은 현재 납품 업체와의 계약을 해지하기로 결정했다.

■ 명사절 접속사와 관계대명사의 구별

that절이 주어, 목적어, 또는 보어 역할을 하면 명사절이고, 앞 명사를 수식하면 관계사절이다.

| 명사절 접속사 that ~라는 것 | → | 앞 명사 없음 | + | that | + | 완전한 절 |
| 관계대명사 that ~하는 | → | 앞 명사 수식 | + | that | + | 불완전한 절 |

명사절 접속사   The director asked [that / ~~whereas~~] researchers meet her in person .
                          동사   완전한 절(주어+동사+목적어)
이사는 연구원들이 자신을 직접 만나야 한다고 요청했다.
→ that 명사절이 asked의 목적어 역할을 하고 있다. whereas는 '~인 반면에'라는 의미의 부사절 접속사이다.

관계대명사   The lecturer will answer inquiries [that / ~~whether~~] you might have .
                                        불완전한 절(주어+동사+목적어)
강연자는 당신이 할 수 있는 질문들에 대답해줄 것이다.
→ that 관계대명사절이 앞 명사(선행사 inquiries)를 수식하고 있다. whether 명사절은 앞 명사를 수식할 수 없다.

ETS 유형 연습

정답과 해설 p.160

1 Hua Husing's achievements in biochemistry were remarkable, especially considering _____ he was only twenty-six at the time.
(A) that
(B) what
(C) since
(D) whether

2 It is widely expected _____ Ms. Asano will be nominated for another five-year term.
(A) that
(B) when
(C) before
(D) then

3 The policy clearly states _____ food and beverages are not allowed in the museum.
(A) that
(B) what
(C) unless
(D) then

> 명사절 접속사 명사절 접속사 that은 뒤에 '주어+동사'와 결합하여 '~라는 것'이라고 해석하며, 문장에서 주어, 목적어, 보어 역할을
> that/what 한다. that의 다양한 쓰임을 이해하고 that과 자주 쓰이는 명사 및 동사를 외워 두면 문제를 보다 빠르게 풀 수 있다.

■ 주어 역할을 하는 that

that이 이끄는 명사절은 It~that 구문의 진주어 역할을 한다.

It is obvious [that / since] the domestic demand has risen for six months.
국내 수요가 지난 6개월 동안 증가하고 있다는 것은 명백하다.

■ 목적어 역할을 하는 that

that 명사절을 직접목적어로 취하는 동사를 기억해야 한다.

> assure 사람 that ~에게 …라는 것을 장담하다 inform/notify 사람 that ~에게 …라는 것을 알려주다 remind 사람 that ~에게 …라는 것을 상기시키다

We **assure** you [that / before] business will continue as usual. 우리는 업무가 평상시와 같이 지속될 것임을 당신에게 장담한다.

■ that절 관용표현

형용사 뒤에 오는 that절 관용표현	be aware that ~라는 것을 알고 있다		be certain/sure/confident that ~을 확신하고 있다
	be hopeful/optimistic that ~라는 것을 희망/낙관하다		be afraid that ~할 것을 걱정하다
명사 뒤에 오는 that절 (동격절) 관용표현	the fact that ~라는 사실	the news that ~라는 소식	the rumor that ~라는 소문
	the evidence that ~라는 증거	the idea that ~라는 생각[발상]	the opinion that ~라는 의견

■ 명사절 접속사 that과 what의 구별

명사절 접속사 that 뒤에는 완전한 절이, what 뒤에는 불완전한 절이 온다.

The book **talks about** [what / that] is most important for success. 그 책은 성공을 위해 가장 중요한 것에 대해 이야기한다.
불완전한 절(주어+be동사+보어)

ETS 유형 연습

정답과 해설 p.160

1 When you subscribe to *News Update*, you can be confident _____ you will receive a reliable analysis of the latest political and economic trends.

(A) that
(B) whether
(C) which
(D) whoever

2 The administration of Holya Office Park has assured us _____ work will be only minimally impacted while construction continues.

(A) whoever
(B) they
(C) that
(D) because

3 _____ pleased the clients most was the effective customer service provided by Moradon Bank.

(A) Who
(B) That
(C) What
(D) This

> **명사절 접속사 whether/if** whether는 문장의 주어, 목적어, 보어 자리에 쓰여 '~인지 아닌지'라고 해석한다. 다른 접속사와 whether를 구별하는 문제가 자주 출제된다. 접속사 해석 능력과 더불어 whether와 자주 쓰이는 단어를 기억해야 한다.

■ 명사절 접속사 whether / if

명사절 접속사 whether는 '~인지 아닌지'라고 해석하며 미정의 사실을 나타내므로 or를 자주 동반한다. if는 동사의 목적어 자리에서만 whether를 대신할 수 있고, 주어나 보어 자리에 쓸 수 없다.

주어　　[Whether / ~~If~~] the gallery will rearrange its displays **has not been approved**.
　　　　미술관이 전시품을 재배치할 것인지는 승인되지 않았다.

　　　　→ whether절은 not approved와 같이 불확실성을 나타내는 표현과 함께 쓰인다. 주어 자리에 if절은 쓸 수 없다.

동사의 목적어　I **wondered** [if / ~~about~~] the university was first founded in Sydney **or** in Melbourne.
　　　　나는 그 대학교가 처음에 시드니에서 지어졌는지 멜버른에서 지어졌는지 궁금했다.

　　　　→ about은 전치사이므로 바로 뒤에 '주어+동사'가 올 수 없다.

■ whether + to부정사

접속사 whether 뒤에 이어지는 주어가 주절의 주어와 같을 경우, 주어를 생략하고 동사를 to부정사로 바꾸어 쓸 수 있다. that과 if를 제외한 모든 명사절 접속사는 '접속사 + to부정사' 형태로 쓸 수 있다.

The manager hasn't yet decided [whether / ~~while~~] **to attend** the weeklong seminar series.
부장은 일주일 동안 진행하는 세미나 시리즈에 참석할지 여부를 아직 결정하지 않았다.

→ 부사절 접속사인 while은 뒤에 주어를 생략할 경우 분사(-ing, -ed)가 온다.

Ms. Jackson is unsure as to **whether** [to buy / ~~buy~~] **or rent** a car.　잭슨 씨는 차를 살지 빌릴지 확신이 없다.

(= Ms. Jackson is unsure as to whether she should buy or rent a car.)

│고득점 팁│ that과 whether 구별하기		
접속사 that ~라는 것	확정 사실을 나타내는 동사	뒤에 완전한 문장
접속사 whether ~인지 아닌지	미정 사실을 암시하는 동사	뒤에 완전한 문장

One of the largest computer companies concluded [that / ~~whether~~] it will acquire the software developing company.
가장 큰 컴퓨터 회사 중 하나가 소프트웨어 개발사를 인수하기로 결정했다.

Our team is wondering [whether / ~~that~~] we will win the contract.
우리 팀은 우리가 계약을 따낼지 아닐지 궁금해하고 있다.

ETS 유형 연습
정답과 해설 p. 160

1 The fax machine is out of service, and an experienced technician has been called in to see _____ it can be repaired.

(A) if
(B) that
(C) what
(D) though

2 Eun Sung Han, president of Westhaven Glassworks, is considering _____ to renew the contract with Pineford Trucking.

(A) whether
(B) if
(C) what
(D) so

3 Harmony Design consultants can help clients decide whether to use curtains _____ blinds when decorating their windows.

(A) so
(B) but
(C) nor
(D) or

> **의문사와 복합** 의문사에는 의문대명사, 의문형용사, 의문부사가 있다. 각각의 의문사가 가지는 우리말 의미뿐 아니라 뒤에
> **관계대명사** 이어지는 문장 구조를 파악해야 한다.

■ 의문대명사

의문대명사는 명사절을 이끌며, 명사절에서 주어/목적어 역할을 한다. 뒤에 주어나 목적어가 없는 불완전한 절이 온다.

> who 누가 ~인지   whom 누구를 ~인지   what 무엇을 ~인지   which 어느 것[사람]을 ~인지

The newsletter provides a comprehensive explanation about [what / ~~where~~] employees **need to know**.
회사 소식지는 직원들이 알아야 하는 것에 대해 종합적 설명을 제공한다.

■ 의문형용사

의문형용사는 명사절을 이끄는 접속사이면서, 명사절에서는 바로 뒤 명사를 수식하는 한정사 역할을 한다.

> which 어느 ~인지   what 무슨 ~인지   whose 누구의 ~인지

The survey asked [which / ~~where~~] **design** for the new product is the best. 설문조사는 어떤 신제품 디자인이 가장 좋은지 물었다.

■ 의문부사

의문부사는 명사절을 이끌며 명사절에서 부사 역할을 한다. 뒤에 완전한 절이 온다.

> when 언제 ~인지   where 어디에서 ~인지   how 어떻게/얼마나 ~인지   why 왜 ~인지

The restaurant should be able to explain [how / ~~which~~] long it has had each ingredient on shelf.
식당은 각 재료를 얼마나 오랫동안 선반에 놔두었는지를 설명할 수 있어야 한다.

■ 복합관계대명사

명사절을 이끌어 주어/목적어 역할을 하거나, 부사절을 이끌어 수식어 역할을 한다. 뒤에 불완전한 절이 온다.

복합관계대명사	명사절	부사절
who(m)ever	anyone who ~하는 사람은(을) 누구든지	no matter who 누가 ~하든 상관없이
whatever	anything that ~하는 것은(을) 무엇이든지	no matter what 무엇이 ~하든 상관없이
whichever	anything that ~하는 것은(을) 어떤 것이든지	no matter which 어느 것이 ~하든 상관없이

*whatever, whichever는 한정사 역할을 할 수도 있다.

[Whoever / ~~Who~~] wants to take a paid vacation of more than a week should tell their supervisor.
(= Anyone who) 일주일 이상의 유급 휴가를 받기 원하는 사람은 누구든지 자신의 팀장에게 말해야 한다.

ETS 유형 연습

정답과 해설 p. 161

1 A good résumé tells employers _____ a candidate's qualifications match the job responsibilities.

(A) how
(B) what
(C) which
(D) whose

2 Members of the Foster City Historical Society are petitioning to have _____ remains of the courthouse's original architectural elements preserved.

(A) which
(B) that
(C) what
(D) it

3 _____ acquires the Grotten painting will probably have purchased the most expensive piece of artwork at the auction.

(A) Who
(B) Whom
(C) Whose
(D) Whoever

1. One frequent complaint air travelers make
   is ------- the overhead compartments are too
   small.
   (A) then (B) to
   (C) whether (D) that

2. Miyo Technologies encourages managers
   to take responsibility for ------- their teams
   produce.
   (A) them (B) that
   (C) what (D) whose

3. ------- should impress passengers most is
   the comfort of the reupholstered seating at
   Liverpool Regional Airport.
   (A) Who (B) What
   (C) When (D) Where

4. Mr. Song has not yet decided ------- of the
   three candidates is right for the position of
   lead product developer.
   (A) which (B) what
   (C) whom (D) whoever

5. The manufacturer guarantees that its cosmetic
   products are good for three years or until
   the expiration date on the package, ------- is
   sooner.
   (A) what (B) when
   (C) that (D) whichever

6. When asked ------- she will retire soon, Ms.
   Johannsen said that she will never stop
   working.
   (A) while (B) whereas
   (C) whenever (D) whether

7. One recent study published in *Working Trends
   Today* magazine suggests ------- people who
   are left-handed are more likely to succeed in
   business.
   (A) that (B) which
   (C) when (D) as to

8. The market-research department conducted
   a survey on ------- often people listen to the
   radio while driving their cars.
   (A) who (B) how
   (C) that (D) which

9. The executive team of Trannelin Industries is
   determining ------- divisions will transfer to the
   West Coast next year.
   (A) any (B) none
   (C) each (D) which

10. Today, ------- is known that even moderate
    exercise is beneficial to the heart.
    (A) which (B) that
    (C) what (D) it

11. ------- needs assistance is welcome to come
    to the personnel office for a job application or
    information on application procedures.
    (A) Whoever (B) What
    (C) If (D) Since

12. Many readers state that the editorial page of
    the daily newspaper is more enlightening but
    admit that ------- they read first is the sports
    page.
    (A) what (B) these
    (C) if (D) because

13. Although multiple studies were conducted by market research groups, it is still uncertain ------- customers are ready to purchase their groceries on the Internet.

(A) who
(B) so as to
(C) whether
(D) whichever

14. Spring Flower Gifts trains every manager in its retail stores in ------- they should deal with customer inquiries.

(A) which
(B) who
(C) what
(D) how

Questions 15-18 refer to the following notice.

POSTED MARCH 3

The Phnom Penh School of Foreign Languages is seeking an experienced French language instructor to ------- our French department. -------. The successful candidate will assume a
15.   16.
managerial role as the head of this small team and be expected to train new instructors. -------
17.
an applicant has a degree in education is not as important as his or her work history. An ideal applicant will have a minimum of five years of teaching experience. Interested parties ------- a
18.
résumé and letter of introduction to Ruben Chastain at chastain@ppsfl.ca.ed. A list of references is not needed at this stage of recruitment.

15. (A) close
(B) lead
(C) assess
(D) meet

16. (A) Our students come from diverse backgrounds.
(B) French is an increasingly important global language.
(C) We congratulate Inez Robert on her new position.
(D) The department currently has three full-time teachers.

17. (A) Who
(B) Whereas
(C) Whether
(D) Which

18. (A) sent
(B) have sent
(C) are sending
(D) should send

Unit | 15 비교 / 도치 구문

원급 비교   원급 비교 구문은 두 대상이 서로 동등할 때 쓴다. 시험에는 'as+형용사/부사+as', 'the same+(명사)+as' 구문의 짝 찾기나 원급 비교에서 형용사, 부사의 품사를 판단하는 문제가 자주 출제된다.

■ 'as+형용사/부사의 원급+as' ~만큼 …한/하게

The incoming coach will be faced with [as / ~~enough~~] many problems **as** other managers have.

새로 취임한 코치는 다른 관리자들이 가지고 있는 것만큼 많은 문제들에 직면할 것이다.

➔ 주어진 문장에서 as를 보고 as ~ as 구문을 파악할 수 있다.

The outdoor jacket is made of a new material which is **as** [light / ~~lighter~~] **as** a feather.

야외용 재킷은 깃털처럼 가벼운 신소재로 만들어진다.

■ 'the same+(명사)+as' ~와 똑같은

The title of the film is actually **the same** [as / ~~than~~] the main character's name.

영화의 제목은 사실 주인공의 이름과 똑같다.

The newest computer model has **the same** features [as / ~~than~~] the one released three years ago.

최신형 컴퓨터 모델은 3년 전에 출시된 것과 똑같은 특징을 가지고 있다.

■ 원급 강조

as ~ as 앞에 just(꼭, 똑같이), almost/nearly(거의), twice(두 배로) 등을 써서 원급의 의미를 강조한다.

Investment has risen [twice / ~~second~~] as fast as consumption for the last decade.

지난 10년 간 투자는 소비의 두 배만큼 증가했다.

■ 원급의 품사 판단

원급의 품사를 판단하려면 as ~ as를 빼고 문장 구조를 살펴야 한다.

Houses in New York City are almost as [expensive / ~~expensively~~] as those in Seoul.

뉴욕 시의 주택들은 거의 서울만큼 비싸다.

➔ almost as ~ as those in Seoul을 빼고 문장 구조를 살피면 are 뒤에 보어가 없으므로 형용사 expensive가 와야 한다.

In the case of an emergency, please **leave** the building as [rapidly / ~~rapid~~] as possible.

응급 상황이 발생할 경우에, 가능한 한 빨리 건물을 떠나십시오.

➔ as ~ as possible을 빼고 문장 구조를 살피면 문장 끝에서 동사 leave를 수식하는 부사 rapidly가 와야 한다.

ETS 유형 연습

정답과 해설 p.163

1 The new FRI-25 digital camera model has the same high-tech features _____ many standard models in the market.

(A) as
(B) than
(C) most
(D) more

2 A consumer report has revealed that less expensive laundry detergents can be _____ as effective as the more expensive products.

(A) soon
(B) just
(C) very
(D) so

3 After the disk driver is installed, the protective cover should be replaced as _____ as possible to prevent the accumulation of dust.

(A) quick
(B) quicker
(C) quickest
(D) quickly

비교급

비교급 구문은 두 대상 중에서 하나가 우월하거나 열등할 때 쓴다. 시험에는 '비교급+than' 구문에서의 짝 찾기 문제뿐 아니라 비교급 강조 부사 또는 관용 표현과 관련된 문제도 자주 출제된다.

■ **'형용사 / 부사의 비교급+than'** ~보다 더 ···한 / 하게

비교급은 형용사/부사 뒤에 -er 또는 앞에 more를 붙이고, 주로 than과 함께 쓴다.

Due to rising demand, it is necessary to process orders [faster / ~~fast~~] **than** before.
증가하는 수요 때문에, 주문을 전보다 빠르게 처리하는 것이 필요하다.

The new version of the inventory program is [more / ~~much~~] **difficult than** the old version.
새로운 버전의 재고 관리 프로그램은 구 버전보다 더 복잡하다.

Our mobile phones are guaranteed to require [fewer / ~~less~~] **repairs than** other competitors' goods.
우리 휴대전화는 다른 경쟁사들 제품보다 수리가 덜 필요할 것임을 보장한다.

➔ 'fewer+복수명사'는 '더 적은 수의 ~'를 뜻하며, less 뒤에는 불가산명사가 나와야 한다.

■ **비교급 강조: 'much / even / still / far / a lot+비교급'** 훨씬 더 / 덜 ~한

Most drinks on the market were found to contain [much / ~~very~~] more sugar than the stated.
시중에 나와 있는 대부분의 음료들이 명시된 것보다 훨씬 더 많은 설탕을 함유하고 있는 것으로 밝혀졌다.

■ **비교급의 품사 판단**

Dr. Watson's latest forecast on the economy **is** more [optimistic / ~~optimistically~~] than his previous one.
왓슨 박사의 최신 경제 전망은 그의 이전 전망보다 더 낙관적이다.

➔ is 뒤 보어 자리이므로, 형용사 optimistic이 와야 한다.

■ **비교급 관련 표현**

more than ~ 이상	less than ~ 이하, ~ 미만	no sooner than ~ 이후에
no later than 늦어도 ~까지	no/not any longer 더 이상 ~ 않다	other than ~ 이외에
rather than ~보다는	the 비교급 of the two 둘 중에서 더 ~한	the 비교급 ~, the 비교급 ··· ~하면 할수록 점점 더 ···하다

The more employees satisfy the customers, **the** [more / ~~most~~] the company will generate profits.
직원들이 고객을 더욱 만족시킬수록, 회사는 더 많은 이윤을 창출할 것이다.

ETS 유형 연습

정답과 해설 p.163

1 In a survey of Office Supply Warehouse's customers, the majority reported that they could order _____ from the Web site than over the phone.

(A) efficient
(B) most efficient
(C) more efficiently
(D) efficiently

2 In order for Mr. Song's group to complete the data collection project on time, we will need _____ more administrative support.

(A) so
(B) even
(C) too
(D) very

3 The advertising campaign for the new Cool Fizz soft drink will feature flavor _____ price.

(A) rather than
(B) in the event of
(C) except for
(D) as for

최상급	최상급 구문은 셋 이상의 대상 중에서 하나가 가장 우월하거나 열등하다는 것을 표현할 때 쓴다. 최상급 앞에 주로 the가 오기 때문에 문제를 풀 때 the 뒤에 빈칸이 있으면 형용사/부사의 최상급이 올 수 있다는 것을 기억해야 한다.

■ 최상급의 의미와 형태

최상급은 형용사/부사 뒤에 -est 또는 앞에 most를 써서 '가장 ~한/하게'라고 해석하며, 앞에 주로 the가 온다. 최상급 뒤에는 'of+복수명사/시간명사', 'in+장소명사', 'that 주어 have/has ever p.p.' 등 범위를 나타내는 표현이 자주 붙는다.

What we used for this furniture is the [most durable / durability] of all materials available.
우리가 이 가구에 사용한 것은 이용할 수 있는 모든 소재 중에서 가장 견고한 것이다.

The program is the [most reliable / more reliable] way to manage network systems in the industry.
그 프로그램은 업계 내에서 네트워크 시스템을 관리하기 위한 가장 믿을 만한 방법이다.

The musical performance last night was [the most / more] impressive (that) I have ever seen.
어젯밤에 본 뮤지컬 공연은 내가 여태껏 본 것 중 가장 인상적인 공연이었다.
→ impressive 다음에 one(= musical performance)이 생략된 것으로 볼 수 있다.

■ 최상급 관련 표현

the+서수+최상급	The taste is the second [most / more] important factor in restaurants after the hygiene. 맛은 식당에서 위생 다음으로 두 번째로 가장 중요한 요소이다.
one of the+최상급+복수명사	Plastic is one of the most widely used [materials / material] in daily goods. 플라스틱은 일상 용품에 가장 널리 사용되는 소재 중 하나이다.

■ 최상급의 품사 판단

Price competition may make it hard to supply the [highest / most highly] quality products.
가격 경쟁은 최고 품질의 제품을 공급하는 것을 어렵게 할 수 있다.
→ 명사 quality를 수식해 주는 형용사의 최상급이 와야 한다.

■ 최상급 강조: 'much/easily/by far/quite+최상급' 단연코 가장 ~한

This year's performance is being considered [by far / extremely] the most successful.
올해의 공연은 단연 가장 성공적인 공연으로 여겨지고 있다.

ETS 유형 연습

정답과 해설 p.163

1 Of the subway lines that stop in the central business district, the green line is the _____ to walk to from the Franklin Building.

(A) more easily
(B) easiest
(C) most easily
(D) easy

2 From among the five applicants for the job, naturally we will hire the _____ candidate to fill the position.

(A) qualified
(B) most qualified
(C) qualifying
(D) most qualifying

3 The funds allocated to new product development in this year's budget are expected to be _____ amount in recent history.

(A) generously
(B) more generous
(C) more generously
(D) the most generous

<table>
<tr><td>도치 구문</td><td>강조하려는 말을 앞으로 보냈을 때 주어와 동사의 어순이 바뀌는 경우들이 있다. be동사나 조동사인 경우 주어와 동사의 순서가 바뀌고, 일반동사인 경우 'do / does / did + 주어 + 동사원형'의 순서로 쓰인다.</td></tr>
</table>

■ 보어가 문두에 올 때: 보어 + 동사 + 주어

보어가 문두에 오는 경우, 보어 자리를 주어 자리로 착각하기 쉽다. enclosed, attached와 같이 문두에 자주 나오는 보어를 기억하도록 한다.

[Enclosed / ~~Enclosure~~] **is a copy** of our product catalog, along with descriptions of the promotional events.

저희 제품 카탈로그 한 부가 판촉 행사에 대한 설명과 함께 동봉되어 있습니다.

➜ 만약 주어 자리로 착각해서 Enclosure를 쓰면 a copy가 보어가 되는데, 주어 Enclosure와 명사 보어 a copy는 동격이 아니므로 잘못된 문장이 된다.

Attached [are / ~~is~~] **the minutes** of the all weekly management meetings for the last six months.

지난 6개월 간의 주간 경영진 회의 회의록 전부가 첨부되어 있다.

➜ 보어 Attached가 문두에 나와 '주어-동사'가 도치되었으므로, 동사는 뒤에 있는 주어 the minutes의 수에 일치시킨다.

■ 부정어가 문두에 올 때: 부정어 + 동사 + 주어

never / not / hardly / seldom / rarely / little / nothing / nor + 조동사 + 주어 + 동사원형

[Never / ~~Always~~] **do we start** selling our products without thoroughly inspecting the quality of products.

우리는 제품의 품질을 철저하게 검사하지 않고서 판매를 시작한 적이 결코 없다.

➜ 여기서 do는 일반동사가 아닌 조동사의 역할을 한다.

■ only가 이끄는 구나 절이 문두에 올 때: only 구 / 절 + 동사 + 주어

only가 바로 뒤의 부사, 전치사구, 접속사절과 결합하여 문두로 나오는 경우, 문장의 주어와 동사가 도치된다.

부사   Only recently [has / ~~have~~] **the whole marketing team been** able to concentrate fully on the new marketing strategy. 최근에야 비로소 마케팅 팀 전체가 새로운 마케팅 전략에 온전히 집중할 수 있게 되었다.

접속사절   [Only / ~~Soon~~] after the regular inspection is completed **should the plant begin** operations.

정기점검이 끝나고 나서야 비로소 공장이 운영을 시작할 것이다.

■ so, neither가 문두에 올 때: so / neither + 동사 + 주어

'so + 동사 + 주어'는 '~도 …하다', 'neither + 동사 + 주어'는 '~도 …하지 않다'라고 해석한다.

Ms. Langton didn't like the new shift schedule, and [neither / ~~so~~] **did her associates.**

랭튼 씨는 새로운 근무 일정표를 좋아하지 않았고, 그녀의 동료들도 마찬가지였다.

➜ so / neither는 뒤에 '주어-동사'가 도치된다. 'so + 동사 + 주어'는 긍정문 뒤에, 'neither + 동사 + 주어'는 부정문 뒤에 쓰인다.

ETS 유형 연습
정답과 해설 p. 164

1 Ms. Park will not be able to attend the sales presentation, and _____ will Mr. Jefferson.

(A) also
(B) however
(C) now
(D) neither

2 _____ have market conditions been more ideal for buying a new house.

(A) Seldom
(B) Ever
(C) Appropriately
(D) Moreover

3 As the number of local residents' visits to public swimming facilities climbs, _____ the demand for lifeguards to supervise them.

(A) as long as
(B) whereas
(C) so does
(D) as to

1. Rising costs have made it ------- than ever for small companies to remain profitable in the current competitive market conditions.

   (A) hard   (B) harden
   (C) harder   (D) hardly

2. Auron Energy, one of the nation's ------- energy suppliers, delivers electricity to nearly twenty million customers.

   (A) largest   (B) more largely
   (C) largely   (D) enlarge

3. Candidates for positions at Pereira Consulting should answer the questions on the application form as ------- as possible.

   (A) accurate   (B) accuracy
   (C) accuracies   (D) accurately

4. Tough stains can be removed more ------- with Pearl Glow's extra-strength laundry detergent.

   (A) ease   (B) easier
   (C) easiest   (D) easily

5. Among the available transportation options, taking the subway is the ------- way to get to the airport from the West Afterton Convention Center.

   (A) more quickly (B) quickly
   (C) quickest   (D) quick

6. Our shop carries as ------- household appliances as our main competitors.

   (A) many   (B) much
   (C) such   (D) same

7. Trentelle Business Consulting Ltd. stresses that retaining loyal customers is ------- important than attracting new ones.

   (A) most   (B) more
   (C) very   (D) much

8. Passwords utilizing a combination of letters, numbers, and symbols create the ------- security.

   (A) strength   (B) strongly
   (C) strengthen   (D) strongest

9. The merger of Darco Motors and Kessler Automotive has resulted in more production problems ------- analysts predicted.

   (A) while   (B) whether
   (C) than   (D) or

10. The engineering department has announced that only at the end of the month ------- a progress report of the project be published.

    (A) is   (B) has
    (C) will   (D) does

11. In order for you to receive the early registration rate, your application form must be postmarked ------- Friday, October 28.

    (A) in advance   (B) beforehand
    (C) previously   (D) no later than

12. The delivery of flowers for the Hwang wedding reception will be completed by Friday, May 12, -------.

    (A) as late   (B) later than
    (C) at the latest (D) the later

13. Ms. Vialobos has reported that the new mobile telephones are the lightest ------- to be purchased by the department.

(A) ever

(B) before

(C) quite

(D) well

14. Our marketing manager, Hawa Abdella, is away from the office and will not return ------- than January 12.

(A) earlier

(B) more recently

(C) longer

(D) more frequently

Questions 15-18 refer to the following e-mail.

From: deaneckhart@gbhosp.org
To: amanpour@sevcon.org
Subject: Chief of Surgery position
Date: December 10

Dear Mr. Amanpour,

I received your curriculum vitae from a mutual ------- of ours, Gloria Manning. -------. I am curious if
                                                                15.   **16.**
you are aware of the open position at Grace Beth Hospital for Chief of Surgery. We are seeking a

talented surgeon like you to fill the position. Because of its size, Grace Beth is an excellent place

to enhance your healthcare management career. Actually, Grace Beth Hospital is the ------- of the
                                                                                                                            17.
region's four hospitals. I believe you would find the position to be a very close match to your -------
                                                                                                                                      18.
clinical background. Please review the open position at gbhosp.org/openpositions.htm and contact

me if you would like to learn more.

Regards,

Dean Eckhart
Recruitment Manager Grace Beth Hospital

15. (A) acquaint

(B) acquainted

(C) acquainting

(D) acquaintance

16. (A) I was impressed with your extensive experience.

(B) Dr. Manning is currently our Chief of Surgery.

(C) I hope you will carefully consider her application.

(D) We also require letters of recommendation from our applicants.

17. (A) large

(B) larger

(C) largely

(D) largest

18. (A) opaque

(B) particular

(C) forthright

(D) generic

기출 어휘 – 동사

accommodate
(사람을) 수용하다, (의견 등을) 수용하다

표현 accommodate a large tour group
단체 관광객을 수용하다
accommodate your request
당신의 요청 사항을 수용하다

address
연설하다, (일·문제 등을) 처리하다

표현 address the audience
청중에게 연설하다
address customers' complaints
고객들의 불만사항을 처리하다

allocate
할당하다, 배정하다

동 assign 할당하다

표현 allocate a team to the project
프로젝트에 팀을 배정하다
allocated budget 할당된 예산

assume
추정하다, 떠맡다, ~인 체하다

파 assumption 가정 assumably 추측컨대

표현 assume that traffic is light
교통량이 적으리라 추정하다
assume the responsibility 책임을 맡다

attribute
~ 탓으로 돌리다, ~ 덕분으로 여기다; 속성, 특질

동 credit A with B(B to A)
B를 A의 공으로 돌리다

표현 attribute his success to his hard
work 성공을 열심히 일한 덕분이라고 여기다

certify
인증하다, 확신시키다

파 certificate 인증서 certified 인증된

표현 certify the building as eco-friendly
환경친화적인 건물로 인증하다
a certified agent 공인 중개업자

comply
(법규 등을) 따르다, 지키다

파 compliance 준수
compliant 준수하는

표현 comply with the legal requirements
법적 요구 조건을 따르다

conduct
(업무 등을) 행하다; 처신, 행위

파 conductor 지휘자
동 carry out 수행하다

표현 conduct market research
시장 조사를 하다
conduct a job interview
채용 면접을 실시하다

consult
상의하다, 참고하다

파 consultant 컨설턴트
consultation 상의
동 refer to ~을 참조하다

표현 consult an expert 전문가와 상의하다
consult the manual 설명서를 참고하다

designate
지정하다, 임명하다

파 designation 지정 designated 지정된
동 appoint 임명하다

표현 designated parking areas
지정된 주차 구역

determine
결심하다, 밝히다

파 determined 결심이 확고한
동 decide 결정하다

표현 determine the cause of the delay
지연 이유를 밝히다

direct
지시하다, (길을) 안내하다; 직접적인

파 director 이사, 감독관 direction 지시, 방향
directly 바로, 직접

표현 be directed toward the project
프로젝트에 투입되다

distinguish
구별하다

파 distinguished 저명한, 뛰어난
distinguishable 구별할 수 있는
동 differentiate A from B, tell A from B
A와 B를 구별하다

endorse
지지하다, (광고 등에서 상품을) 보증하다,
이서하다

파 endorsement 지지, 이서

표현 endorse the new makeup line
신상 화장품 라인을 광고에서 홍보하다
endorse a check 수표에 이서하다

enforce
집행하다, 실시하다

파 enforcement 집행, 시행
동 carry out 수행하다

표현 enforce new safety regulations
새 안전 규정을 실시하다

engage
~에 관여하다, 종사시키다

파 engagement 관여; 약혼 engaged 관여된

표현 be engaged in online sales
온라인 판매에 종사하다
engage in volunteer work
자원봉사 업무에 관여하다

exceed
초과하다

파 excess 초과
excessive 과도한, 지나친
동 surpass 초과하다

표현 exceed the speed limit
제한 속도를 초과하다

expire
기한이 되다, 만료하다

파 expiration 만기
expired 기한이 지난
동 run out 만기가 되다

표현 food that will expire soon
유통 기한이 곧 만료될 음식

extend
연장하다

파 extension 연장; 내선번호
extensive 광범위한
동 prolong 연장하다

표현 extend its business hours
영업시간을 연장하다

feature
~을 특징으로 하다, 크게 다루다; 특징, 기능

파 featured 특집의, 주연의

표현 feature a stylish design
세련된 디자인을 특징으로 하다

implement
시행하다, 이행하다; 도구

파 implementation 시행, 이행

표현 implement the latest data-analysis
methods 최신 데이터 분석 기법을 시행하다

institute
(규칙·제도 등을) 마련하다, 실시하다; 협회

- 파 institution 기관, 제도
- 표현 institute a new dress code
  새로운 복장 규정을 마련하다

interrupt
가로막다, 방해하다

- 파 interruption 중단, 방해
- 동 hinder 방해가 되다
- 표현 The bus service was interrupted.
  버스 운행이 중단되었다.

issue
발급하다, 발행하다, 발표하다;
출판물, 쟁점, 발행

- 표현 issue a ticket 표를 발권하다
  will issue a statement officially
  공식적으로 성명서를 발표할 것이다
  the May issue 5월호

lead
이끌다, ~에 이르다

- 파 leading 선도적인
- 표현 lead the training session
  교육 훈련을 이끌다
  lead to greater opportunities
  더 좋은 기회로 이어지다

locate
위치시키다, ~의 위치를 알아내다

- 파 location 위치, 지점
  located 위치한
- 표현 The office is located in the city.
  사무실은 도시에 위치하고 있다.

mark
표시하다, 나타내다, 기념하다; 점수

- 동 indicate 표시하다
- 표현 This event marks our 10th
  anniversary.
  이 행사는 10주년을 기념하는 것이다.

notify
통보하다, 통지하다

- 파 notification 통지
- 동 inform 알리다
- 표현 notify Ms. Suh of her promotion
  서 씨에게 승진을 통보하다

offset
상쇄하다, 만회하다

- 동 set off 상쇄하다
- 표현 Losses were offset by gains.
  손해가 이익으로 상쇄되었다.

outfit
~을 채비시키다, 착용케 하다; 장비(일체)

- 동 equip 장비를 갖추게 하다
- 표현 should be outfitted with this device
  이 장비를 착용해야 한다

outline
간추려 말하다; 개요

- 동 brief, summarize 간략히 설명하다
- 표현 outline the year's budget
  그해 예산을 간략히 설명하다
  the outline of the contract 계약의 개요

prohibit
~하지 못하게 하다, 금지하다

- 파 prohibition 금지
- 표현 prohibit visitors from entering
  방문객들의 입장을 금지하다

recognize
인정하다, 인식하다

- 파 recognition 인식, 인지
- 표현 recognize Ms. Dale's efforts
  데일 씨의 노고를 인정하다

refer
~을 참조하다, 언급하다, 소개하다, 보내다

- 파 reference 추천(서); 참고 referral 소개, 추천
- 표현 refer to the manual first
  먼저 설명서를 참고하다
  referred me to a specialist
  나를 전문의에게 보냈다

reflect
반사하다, 반영하다

- 파 reflection 반사
  reflective 반사하는
- 표현 reflect the current trend
  현재 경향을 반영하다

remind
~하도록 상기시키다

- 파 reminder 상기시키는 것
- 표현 Please be reminded that
  ~라는 점을 명심하세요

replace
교체하다, 대신하다

- 파 replacement 대체물, 후임자
- 표현 replace a defective item
  불량품을 교체하다

retain
유지하다, 보유하다

- 파 retention 보유
  retained 보유한
- 동 hold, keep 유지하다
- 표현 retain loyal customers
  단골 고객을 유지하다

secure
확보하다, ~을 고정시키다; 안전한

- 파 security 안전, 보안 securely 확실하게
- 표현 secure a parking space
  주차할 곳을 확보하다
  secure the lock on the door
  문의 잠금 장치를 고정시키다

specify
상세히 말하다, 구체화하다

- 파 specification 세부 사항
  specific 특정한, 구체적인
- 표현 specify the date
  날짜를 명확히 하다

streamline
간소화하다, 능률적으로 하다

- 파 streamlined 유선형의, 간결한
- 동 simplify 단순화하다
- 표현 streamline the production process
  생산 과정을 능률적으로 하다

sustain
지탱하다, 지속하다

- 파 sustainability 지속 가능성
  sustainable 유지할 수 있는
- 표현 sustain strong profits
  큰 수익을 유지하다

기출 어휘 – 명사

access
접근, 이용(권한); 접근하다
- 파 accessible 접근 가능한
- 동 approach 접근
- 표현 to get access to the data
  자료 이용 권한을 받으려면

advance
발전, 진보; 나아가다; 사전의
- 파 advanced 최신의, 진보된
- 표현 a seminar about advances in mobile phone technology
  휴대전화 기술 발전에 관한 세미나
  advance notice 사전 통지

affiliation
제휴, 소속기관
- 파 affiliate 제휴하다; 계열사
- 동 partnership 협력, 제휴
- 표현 have an affiliation with foreign banks 외국계 은행과 제휴하다

agreement
동의, 계약
- 반 disagreement 불일치
- 표현 reach an agreement
  합의에 다다르다, 계약을 체결하다

alternative
대안; 대안의
- 파 alternation 교대, 교체
  alternate 번갈아 하다; 번갈아 하는, 대안의
- 표현 seek an alternative 대안을 찾다

appraisal
평가
- 파 appraise 평가하다
- 동 evaluation, assessment 평가
- 표현 performance appraisal 업무 평가

concentration
집중, 밀집, 농도
- 파 concentrate on ~에 집중하다
  concentrated 밀집된, 농축된
- 표현 a concentration of population
  인구의 집중

concern
걱정, 근심, 관심(사)
- 파 concerned 염려하는
- 표현 a matter of little concern
  별로 중요하지 않은 문제
  have concerns about[over]
  ~에 대해 걱정하다

confidence
확신, 자신, 신뢰
- 파 confident 확신하는, 자신 있는
  confidential 비밀의
- 표현 restore confidence in their products
  제품에 대한 신뢰를 회복하다

consent
동의; 동의하다
- 표현 without written consent 서면 동의 없이
  mutual consent 상호 합의
  give one's consent to ~에 동의하다

contribution
공헌, 기부(금)
- 파 contributor 공헌자, 기고가
  contribute 기여하다, 기부하다
- 표현 contribution to the company
  회사에 대한 기여

defect
결함, 하자
- 파 defective 결함이 있는
- 동 flaw 결점
- 표현 find defects in the product
  제품의 하자를 발견하다

distraction
주의 산만, 방해물
- 파 distract 혼란시키다
  distracting 주의를 산만하게 하는
- 표현 distractions due to noise
  소음으로 인한 주의 산만

emphasis
강조
- 파 emphasize 강조하다
- 동 stress, highlight 강조
- 표현 put[place] an emphasis on quality
  품질을 강조하다

estimate
견적(서); 견적을 내다
- 파 estimation 추정, 판단
  estimated 추정되는
- 동 quotation 견적
- 표현 get a cost estimate 비용 견적을 받다

exception
예외, 제외
- 파 except ~을 제외하고
- 표현 with the exception of personal matters 개인적인 문제들은 제외하고

expense
지출, 경비
- 파 expenditure 소비, 지출
  expend 소비하다
- 표현 by lowering business expenses
  사업비를 낮춤으로써

fluctuation
변동, 불안정
- 파 fluctuate 변동하다
- 반 stability 안정
- 표현 fluctuation in exchange rates
  환율의 변동

fraction
일부, 작은 부분
- 동 part, portion 일부
- 표현 pay off a fraction of the debts
  빚의 일부를 갚다

funding
재원, 자금 제공
- 파 fund 자금(을 대다)
  fund-raiser 모금 행사
- 동 financing 자금 조달
- 표현 increase funding for cultural events
  문화 행사를 위한 자금을 증원하다

implication
암시, 함축, 영향
- 파 implicate 연루시키다, 암시하다
- 표현 have serious implications for
  ~에 심각한 영향을 끼치다

ingredient
재료, 구성 요소

동 part 부품 component 구성 요소

표현 use fresh ingredients
신선한 재료를 사용하다

initiative
새로운 계획, 주도권; 처음의

파 initiation 가입, 개시 initiate 시작하다
동 plan 계획

표현 take the initiative
솔선수범하다, 주도권을 쥐다

inspection
검사, 점검, 검열

파 inspect 점검하다
동 investigation 조사

표현 pass a safety inspection
안전 검사를 통과하다

malfunction
오작동; 오작동하다

동 failure 고장
반 function 기능; 행사; 기능하다

표현 a malfunction of the software
소프트웨어의 오작동

means
수단, 방법

동 way, method 방법

표현 various means of payment
다양한 지불 수단

measure
수단, 조치; 재다

파 measurement 측정, 치수

표현 implement cost-cutting measures
비용 삭감 조치를 취하다

authorization
허가, 승인, 권한 부여

파 authority 권한, 관계자
authorize 허가하다
동 approval 승인

표현 without authorization 허가 없이

benefit
이익, 혜택; ~에게 도움이 되다

파 beneficial 도움이 되는, 혜택이 되는
beneficiary 수혜자

표현 take advantage of membership
benefits 회원 혜택을 이용하다

capacity
용량, 능력

파 capacious 용량이 큰, 널찍한

표현 a seating capacity 좌석 수

possession
소유물, 소유

파 possess 소유하다
possessive 소유의
동 belongings 소지품

표현 pack one's possessions
소지품을 챙기다

potential
잠재력, 가능성; 잠재력이 있는

파 potentially 잠재적으로, 어쩌면

표현 employees with great potential
굉장한 잠재력이 있는 직원들

practice
관행, 실행, 연습; 실행하다

파 practical 실제의, 실용적인
동 convention 관습
training 연습

표현 common practice 일반적 관행

preference
선호, 우선권

파 prefer 선호하다
preferred 선호되는, 우선시되는

표현 preference will be given to
~에게 우선권이 주어질 것이다
food preference 음식 선호도

promotion
승진, 홍보, 촉진

파 promote 승진시키다, 홍보하다
promotional 홍보용의

표현 be eligible for the promotion
승진할 자격이 있다

reputation
평판, 명성

파 reputable 평판이 좋은

표현 maintain a good reputation
좋은 명성[평판]을 유지하다

requirement
필요(한 것), 필요 조건

파 require 요구하다
required 필수적인
동 demand, needs 요구

표현 meet the job requirements
직무 필요 조건에 부합하다

resource
자원, 재산, 능력

파 resourceful 자원이 풍부한

표현 natural resources 천연 자원
human resources 인력 자원, 인사부

schedule
일정; 일정을 정하다

파 scheduled 예정된

표현 behind schedule 일정에 뒤처진
on schedule 일정대로
ahead of schedule 일정보다 앞선

transaction
거래, 처리

파 transact 거래하다
transactional 거래의, 업무의

표현 online transactions 온라인 거래
each business transaction 각 사업 거래

transfer
이체, 양도; 옮기다

파 transferable 양도 가능한
동 move, relocation 이전, 이주

표현 electronic transfer 온라인 이체

variety
다양성

파 various 다양한 varied 다양한
동 diversity 다양성

표현 a (wide) variety of dishes
각양각색의 요리들

기출 어휘 - 형용사

abundant
충분한, 넘치는
- 명 abundance 풍부함
- 동 ample, sufficient 충분한
- 표현 abundant rainfall 풍부한 강수량
  be abundant in ~가 풍부하다

accomplished
뛰어난, 통달한
- 명 accomplishment 달성, 성취
  accomplish 달성하다, 성취하다
- 동 distinguished 뛰어난
- 표현 an accomplished artist 뛰어난 화가

accustomed
익숙해진, 습관의
- 동 accustom ~을 익숙하게 하다
- 동 used 익숙한
- 표현 get accustomed to a new
  environment 새로운 환경에 익숙해지다

adaptable
적응할 수 있는
- 명 adaptation 적응, 각색
  adapt to ~에 적응하다
- 표현 a recipe adaptable to different
  styles of cooking
  다양한 요리 방식에 맞출 수 있는 조리법

additional
추가적인
- 명 addition 추가
- 동 extra 여분의 further 더 많은
- 표현 additional workers 추가 직원들
  for additional information
  추가 정보를 위해서는

affordable
알맞은, 적정한 가격의
- 명 affordability
  적당한 가격으로 구입할 수 있는 것
  afford ~할 여유가 있다
- 동 reasonable 가격이 적정한
- 표현 at an affordable price[rate]
  적정한 가격[요금]에

appropriate
적절한
- 동 suitable 적절한
- 반 inappropriate 부적절한
- 표현 appropriate strategies 적절한 전략들

aware
알고 있는
- 명 awareness 인식, 앎
- 동 conscious, cognizant 인식하고 있는
- 표현 be fully aware of sudden weather
  changes 갑작스러운 날씨 변화를 잘 알다

brief
간략한; 간략히 보고하다
- 명 briefly 간략하게
- 동 concise 간결한
- 표현 hold a brief meeting 간략한 회의를 하다

capable
할 수 있는
- 명 capability 능력, 수용력
- 반 incapable ~할 수 없는
- 표현 mobile phones capable of browsing
  the Internet 인터넷 검색을 할 수 있는 휴대폰

central
중심의, 중추적인, 주된
- 명 centralize 중심에 모으다
- 표현 Online advertising is central to the
  marketing strategy.
  온라인 광고가 마케팅 전략의 중심이다.

compatible
호환이 되는, 화합할 수 있는
- 명 compatibility 호환성
- 표현 software compatible with other
  systems
  다른 시스템과 호환 가능한 소프트웨어

competitive
경쟁의, 경쟁심이 강한, 경쟁력이 있는
- 명 competition 경쟁 compete 경쟁하다
- 표현 competitive salary 경쟁력 있는 월급
  gain a competitive edge from this
  seminar 세미나를 통해 경쟁력을 얻다

complimentary
무료의, 칭찬의
- 명 compliment 칭찬; 칭찬하다
- 표현 a complimentary dinner coupon
  무료 저녁 식사 쿠폰

dedicated
헌신적인, 전념하는
- 명 dedication 헌신
- 표현 The Green Parks Club is dedicated
  to protecting the environment.
  그린 파크 클럽은 환경보호에 헌신적이다.

deliberate
고의의, 신중한; 숙고하다
- 명 deliberation 심사숙고
  deliberately 고의로, 신중히
- 동 prudent 신중한
- 표현 in a deliberate way 신중하게

demanding
지나치게 요구하는, 까다로운
- 명 demand 수요; 요구하다
- 동 tricky 까다로운
- 표현 have a demanding job
  힘든 직업을 갖고 있다

due
지불해야 하는, 만기인, 적당한
- 반 overdue (지불) 기한이 지난
- 표현 The report is due next Monday.
  보고서는 다음 주 월요일까지 제출해야 한다.

eligible
적격의, 적임의, 자격이 있는
- 명 eligibility 적임, 적격
- 동 entitled, qualified 적격의
- 표현 be eligible to apply for the manager
  position 부장직에 지원할 자격이 있다

enclosed
동봉된, 둘러싸인
- 명 enclosure 동봉, 둘러쌈
  enclose 동봉하다, 둘러싸다
- 동 attached 첨부된
- 표현 the enclosed document 동봉된 서류

exempt
면제되는; 면제하다
- 명 exemption 면제
- 표현 be exempt from taxes 세금이 면제되다

experienced
경험이 많은, 능숙한
- 🅟 experience 경험; 경험하다
- 🅢 seasoned, skilled 경험 많은, 숙련된
- 표현 experienced job candidates
  경험이 많은 채용 후보자들

familiar
익숙한, 잘 알고 있는, 친한
- 🅟 familiarize oneself with ~을 숙지하다
- 🅐 unfamiliar 익숙하지 않은
- 표현 be familiar with the rules
  그 규칙들에 익숙하다

impending
임박한, 곧 일어날
- 🅟 impend 임박하다
- 🅢 imminent 임박한 upcoming 곧 있을
- 표현 impending issues 임박한 문제들
  an impending conference 임박한 회의

outstanding
뛰어난, 훌륭한, 미납의
- 🅢 distinguished 뛰어난 unpaid 미납의
- 표현 outstanding service 훌륭한 서비스
  outstanding debt 미변제 채무

preliminary
예비의; 예비 단계
- 🅢 preparatory 예비의
- 표현 preliminary tests 예비 검사
  do preliminary market research
  사전 시장 조사를 하다

prior
~ 전의, 앞선
- 🅟 priority 우선순위 prior to ~ 전에
- 🅐 following 그 다음의
- 표현 prior approval 사전 승인

promising
전도유망한, 장래가 밝은
- 🅟 promised 약속된
  promise 약속, 가망; 약속하다
- 표현 among promising candidates
  전도유망한 후보자들 중에서

receptive
수용하는, 받아들이는
- 🅟 reception 연회 receive 받아들이다
- 🅢 open-minded 마음이 열린
- 표현 be receptive to new ideas
  새로운 아이디어들에 수용적이다

reliable
믿을 만한, 신뢰할 만한
- 🅟 reliability 믿을 만함
  rely on[upon] ~에 의존하다
  reliant 의존하는
- 표현 reliable service 믿을 만한 서비스

remote
거리가 떨어진, 희박한
- 🅢 distant 멀리 떨어진
- 🅐 close, nearby 가까운
- 표현 at a remote distance 멀리 떨어져서

responsible
책임이 있는, 관할하는
- 🅟 responsibility 책임
- 🅢 in charge 담당하는
- 표현 be responsible for supervising
  assemblers
  조립자들을 감독하는 책임을 지고 있다

restricted
제한된, 한정된
- 🅟 restriction 규제, 제약, 규정
  restrict 제한하다
- 🅢 limited 제한된
- 표현 be restricted to the first 50
  customers 최초 50명의 고객들로 제한되다

rewarding
가치가 있는, 보람 있는
- 🅟 reward 보상; 보상하다
- 🅢 worthy 가치 있는
- 표현 a rewarding discussion
  가치 있는 토론회

rigorous
엄격한, 가혹한
- 🅢 rigid, thorough 엄격한
- 🅐 flexible 유연성 있는
- 표현 be subjected to a rigorous test
  엄격한 테스트를 거치다

sensitive
민감한, 섬세한
- 🅟 sensitivity 민감함
- 🅢 delicate 섬세한
- 표현 be sensitive to loud noise
  큰 소음에 매우 민감하다

significant
상당한, 중요한
- 🅟 significance 중요성 significantly 상당히
- 🅢 considerable, substantial 상당한
- 표현 a significant number of visitors
  상당수의 방문객들

similar
유사한, 비슷한
- 🅟 similarity 유사성
- 🅐 various, different 다양한
- 표현 be similar to other artists' works
  다른 화가들의 작품과 유사하다

subject
될 수 있는; 주제, 과목; 복종시키다
- 표현 The schedule is subject to change
  without prior notice.
  일정은 사전 통보 없이 변경될 수 있습니다.

thorough
철저한, 빈틈없는
- 🅢 rigorous, stringent 엄격한
- 표현 undergo a thorough inspection
  철저한 검사를 받다

temporary
임시의, 일시적인
- 🅟 temporarily 임시로
- 🅢 provisional 임시 변통의
- 🅐 permanent 영구적인
- 표현 a temporary employee 임시 직원

valid
유효한, 타당한
- 🅟 validity 유효성
- 🅢 good, effective 유효한
- 🅐 invalid 유효하지 않은
- 표현 valid identification card 유효한 신분증

기출 어휘 - 부사

accordingly
그에 맞게, 따라서
- 파 accord 일치; 부합하다 (with)
  according to ~에 따라
- 표현 Mr. Kim is a manager, so he should be treated accordingly. 김 씨는 매니저이니까, 그에 따라 대접받아야 한다.

adversely
불리하게, 나쁘게
- 파 adversity 역경, 불운
  adverse 반대의, 불리한
- 동 unfavorably 불리하게
- 표현 adversely affect 부정적인 영향을 끼치다

alike
마찬가지로, 똑같은, 비슷한
- 파 alikeness 유사함
- 표현 the performers and the audience alike 연주자들과 청중 모두

altogether
아주, 완전히, 전부 합하여
- 동 completely 완전히
- 반 partially 부분적으로
- 표현 grossed over 1 million dollars altogether
  합계 1백만 달러 이상의 수익을 올렸다

approximately
대략, 거의
- 파 approximate 대략의
- 동 about, around 거의
- 표현 approximately twice a month
  대략 한 달에 두 번

closely
면밀히, 주의 깊게
- 파 closure 폐쇄 close 가까운; 닫다
- 동 thoroughly 면밀히, 철저히
- 표현 closely examine the records
  기록을 면밀히 조사하다

collaboratively
합작으로
- 파 collaborate 협력하다, 공동 작업하다
  collaboration 협력
- 표현 work collaboratively to develop a better product
  더 좋은 제품 개발을 위해 협업하다

completely
완전히
- 파 complete 완전한; 완료하다
- 표현 completely free of charge
  완전히 무료로

concisely
간결하게
- 파 conciseness 간결함
  concise 간결한
- 반 lengthily 장황하게
- 표현 speak clearly and concisely
  명료하고 간결하게 말하다

consecutively
연속하여
- 파 consecutive 연속적인
- 동 successively 연속하여
- 표현 The two holidays occur consecutively. 휴일이 이틀 연속으로 있다.

consistently
지속적으로, 일관되게
- 파 consist 구성되다 (of)
  consistent 지속적인, 일관적인, 일치하는
- 동 constantly 끊임없이
- 표현 consistently happening 꾸준히 발생하는

correctly
올바르게, 정확하게
- 파 correction 수정 correct 올바른; 수정하다
- 동 accurately 정확하게
- 표현 correctly understand the contract's conditions
  계약 조건들을 정확히 이해하고 있다

definitely
분명히, 반드시, 명확하게
- 파 definite 명확한, 확정된
- 반 indefinitely 무기한으로, 불분명하게
- 표현 should definitely apply for the internship 인턴십에 반드시 신청해야 한다

discreetly
신중하게, 조심스레
- 파 discreet 신중한, 조심스러운
- 동 deliberately 신중하게
- 표현 deal with private customer information discreetly
  사적인 고객 정보를 신중히 다루다

dramatically
극적으로
- 파 dramatic 극적인
- 표현 dramatically increase[decrease]
  극적으로 증가[감소]하다

efficiently
효율적으로
- 파 efficiency 효율성 efficient 효율적인
- 동 effectively 효과적으로
- 표현 process orders efficiently
  주문을 효율적으로 처리하다

exclusively
독점적으로, 전적으로
- 파 exclude 제외하다
  excluding ~을 제외하고
- 표현 exclusively available
  독점적으로 이용 가능한

extremely
몹시, 극도로
- 동 highly, very 매우, 몹시
- 반 moderately 알맞게
- 표현 extremely successful 매우 성공적인
  extremely hot weather 극도로 더운 날씨

generously
관대히, 후하게
- 파 generous 관대한
- 동 leniently 관대하게
- 표현 donate generously to several charities 몇몇 자선 단체에 후하게 기부하다

gradually
점차로, 서서히
- 동 progressively 점진적으로
  steadily 꾸준하게
- 반 abruptly, suddenly 갑자기
- 표현 gradually become popular
  점차 인기가 높아지다

inadvertently
무심코, 부주의하게
- 파 inadvertent 부주의한
- 동 negligently 태만하게
- 표현 inadvertently made a mistake
  무심코 실수를 저질렀다

independently
독립적으로, 따로

- ■ independence 독립
  independent 독립적인
- ■ separately 떨어져서
- 표현 handle the project independently
  독립적으로 프로젝트를 다루다

individually
개별적으로, 개인적으로

- ■ individual 개별적인; 개인
- ■ personally 개인적으로
- 표현 be individually interviewed
  개별 면접을 보다

meticulously
꼼꼼하게, 세심하게

- ■ meticulous 꼼꼼한
- ■ carelessly 부주의하게
- 표현 a meticulously researched book
  꼼꼼하게 연구된 책

mutually
서로, 상호간에

- ■ mutual 상호적인, 서로 관계가 있는
- 표현 be mutually beneficial
  상호 이득이 되다

nearly
거의

- ■ near 가까운, 가까이에; 다가가다
- ■ almost, around, about, approximately, roughly 대략
- 표현 nearly 500 participants
  거의 500명의 참석자들

necessarily
반드시, 어쩔 수 없이

- ■ necessity 필요성, 생필품
  necessary 필요한
- 표현 Money does not necessarily bring happiness. 돈이 반드시 행복을 가져다 주는 것은 아니다.

notably
주목할 만하게, 두드러지게

- ■ note 주목하다, 언급하다
  notable 주목할 만한, 현저한
- ■ markedly, noticeably 두드러지게
- 표현 most notably 가장 주목할 만하게, 특히

originally
원래, 독창적으로

- ■ origin 기원, 시작
  original 원래의, 최초의, 독창적인
- 표현 was higher than we originally predicted
  우리가 원래 예상했던 것보다 높았다

otherwise
다르게, 그렇지 않으면

- 표현 a device otherwise known as "an e-reader" '이리더'로도 알려진 기기
  unless otherwise indicated
  별도의 표시가 없다면

overwhelmingly
압도적으로

- ■ overwhelm 압도하다
  overwhelming 압도적인
- ■ intensely 격렬히 powerfully 강력하게
- 표현 overwhelmingly defeat competitors
  경쟁자들을 압도적으로 이기다

periodically
주기적으로, 정기적으로

- ■ periodical 정기 간행물; 주기적인
  periodic 주기적인
- ■ regularly, routinely 정기적으로
- 표현 a meeting held periodically
  정기적으로 열리는 회의

primarily
주로, 무엇보다도 먼저

- ■ primary 주요한
- ■ mainly 주로
- 표현 primarily due to its low cost
  무엇보다 저렴한 가격 때문에

promptly
즉각, 신속히

- ■ prompt 신속한; 촉발하다
- ■ immediately, instantly 즉각
- 표현 promptly report it to the supervisor
  그것을 즉시 상관에게 보고하다

properly
적절하게, 알맞게

- ■ proper 적절한
- ■ adequately, appropriately 적절하게
- ■ improperly 부적절하게
- 표현 be properly installed
  올바르게 설치되어 있다

reasonably
합리적으로, 적당하게

- ■ reason 이유, 이성; 판단을 내리다
  reasonable 합리적인, (가격이) 알맞은
- 표현 a reasonably-priced compact car
  합리적인 가격의 소형차

recently
최근에

- ■ recent 최근의
- ■ lately 최근에
- 표현 a recently upgraded building
  최근에 개보수된 건물

relatively
상대적으로, 비교적

- ■ relate 관련시키다 relative 상대적인; 친척
- ■ comparatively 비교적, 어느 정도
- 표현 at a relatively low price
  상대적으로 낮은 가격에

shortly
곧, 즉시

- ■ shorten 줄이다
- ■ soon 곧
- 표현 will answer your questions shortly
  질문에 곧 답해 줄 것이다

slightly
약간, 조금

- ■ slight 조금의
- ■ marginally 아주 조금
- ■ considerably 상당히
- 표현 be slightly modified 약간 수정되다

solely
혼자서, 유일하게, 오직

- ■ sole 독점적인, 유일한
- ■ only 오직
- 표현 The manager is solely responsible for the manufacturing line.
  매니저가 제조 라인에 대해 전적으로 책임진다.

unanimously
만장일치로

- ■ unanimous 만장일치의
- 표현 voted unanimously to change the company logo
  만장일치로 회사 로고 변경에 투표했다

1. Fordham Stationers recently decided to switch suppliers because Valley Paper has been ------- late in shipping their orders.

   (A) steadily
   (B) sensibly
   (C) exactly
   (D) consistently

2. After reviewing our corporate policies, please sign the ------- contract and return it before July 1.

   (A) surrounding
   (B) enclosed
   (C) concerned
   (D) accepting

3. The Produce Growers Association has distributed a pamphlet to area supermarkets that lists fruits and vegetables with the highest ------- of vitamins.

   (A) attractions
   (B) concentrations
   (C) beneficiaries
   (D) commands

4. Governor Jayson won the election because she ------- to reduce taxes and allocate more funding to schools.

   (A) followed
   (B) predicted
   (C) invented
   (D) promised

5. Because of the large number of tourists in summer months, travelers should plan ------- and make their reservations early.

   (A) accordingly
   (B) subsequently
   (C) conversely
   (D) assuredly

6. Engineers in the Welber Machine Factory in Cologne work to correct minor flaws in the designs of ------- drilling systems.

   (A) confused
   (B) complex
   (C) informative
   (D) cautious

7. Salesman Carlos Diaz displayed ------- by actively engaging potential customers as they entered the Valley Stream Furniture showroom.

   (A) amount
   (B) objective
   (C) reliance
   (D) initiative

8. Initial projections of quarterly earnings have already been ------- with a month still remaining.

   (A) exceeded
   (B) outdated
   (C) overdrawn
   (D) impressed

9. Sports fans around the world ------- await the results of the annual tennis championship.

   (A) perfectly
   (B) evenly
   (C) rapidly
   (D) eagerly

10. Peerplane, Inc., stated yesterday that its new prototype airplane has passed all ------- testing.

    (A) undeveloped
    (B) foregone
    (C) subordinate
    (D) preliminary

11. Hiring a logistics consultant has resulted in faster ------- of goods to our stores.

    (A) founding
    (B) distribution
    (C) treatment
    (D) revision

12. Swabian Motors will ------- its current name even after it merges with a rival company.

    (A) receive
    (B) inquire
    (C) grant
    (D) retain

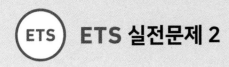

1. The terms and conditions outlined in this document are ------- to change without notice.

   (A) dependent
   (B) subject
   (C) immediate
   (D) final

2. The new plant director, Ha-Jae Cheon, will be ------- for reducing the maintenance costs at the Tamarindo facility.

   (A) fortunate
   (B) possible
   (C) senseless
   (D) responsible

3. The latest microwave oven from Dabato Industries ------- a stainless steel interior and ten different heat settings.

   (A) features
   (B) produces
   (C) implies
   (D) appoints

4. Sign up now for deals available ------- to Platinum members of the Bordner Gym Club.

   (A) exclusively
   (B) financially
   (C) relatively
   (D) productively

5. The XT1000 is one of the most ------- home-kitchen scales on the market, providing accurate measurement to the milligram.

   (A) tentative
   (B) deliberate
   (C) investigative
   (D) sensitive

6. You will receive a ------- e-mail from the Nicoya Hotel verifying your travel plans within two hours of making your reservation.

   (A) sponsor
   (B) confirmation
   (C) margin
   (D) permit

7. A new lighting system has been installed in the administrative offices, ------- the older, less efficient one.

   (A) replacing
   (B) comparing
   (C) brightening
   (D) repairing

8. Dale Department Store will have a special sale on jewelry ------- before the holidays.

   (A) sensitively
   (B) extremely
   (C) immediately
   (D) figuratively

9. Last night Channel Five News aired an exclusive interview with the ------- actor Sandy Sawyer.

   (A) accomplish
   (B) accomplishment
   (C) accomplished
   (D) accomplishing

10. The Wellborn Science Museum's new astronomy theater has a seating ------- of 250.

    (A) aptitude
    (B) capacity
    (C) demonstration
    (D) compliance

11. To be more environmentally responsible, IKM, Inc., has ------- a paperless expense reimbursement system.

    (A) confided
    (B) resolved
    (C) surrounded
    (D) initiated

12. The impressive floral display at the building entrance is ------- made up of blue flowers, with a few red ones artfully placed throughout.

    (A) enough
    (B) exclusively
    (C) primarily
    (D) everywhere

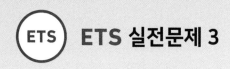
1. The buildings in the Jamison Complex are open until 7:00 P.M. on workdays, but staff with proper ------- may enter at any time.

   (A) reinforcement (B) participation
   (C) competency   (D) authorization

2. Wyncote Airlines has announced that it will ------- the £15 baggage fee for members of its Sky Flyer Club.

   (A) prove (B) cost
   (C) waive (D) align

3. If you no longer wish to receive promotional offers, Heugland's Market will delete your name from the mailing list -------.

   (A) previously (B) overall
   (C) neither   (D) promptly

4. There will be a ------- fifteen-minute intermission between the two performances.

   (A) narrow (B) deep
   (C) brief   (D) sharp

5. The Janug Corporation's newer-model refrigerators use only a ------- of the energy that its older models use.

   (A) relation (B) moderation
   (C) fraction (D) correction

6. The accounting department has ------- a new policy in order to decrease paper usage.

   (A) preoccupied   (B) represented
   (C) characterized (D) implemented

7. Guest rooms must be cleaned ------- within two hours after hotel patrons have checked out.

   (A) widely   (B) highly
   (C) sturdily (D) thoroughly

8. The Global Marketing Manager is required to travel extensively and so must be ------- to unfamiliar situations.

   (A) opposed   (B) versatile
   (C) relative (D) adaptable

9. Employees who cannot attend the training session on March 12 will be scheduled for an ------- date.

   (A) unoccupied   (B) increased
   (C) irreplaceable (D) alternative

10. Fales Bookstores reported a 20 percent decrease in net profit this year, which the company ------- to fierce competition from Yule Booksellers, Inc.

    (A) accused   (B) presented
    (C) disapproved (D) attributed

11. The prevention of environmental pollution has become an important consideration for small and large businesses -------.

    (A) forth (B) even
    (C) alike (D) beyond

12. Please be ------- that the terms and conditions of the Meyer Company contract are subject to change annually.

    (A) proposed (B) known
    (C) aware   (D) noticed

234

ETS ETS 실전문제 4

정답과 해설 p.169

RC

PART 5&6

1. With the new Web site enhancements, Hill Street Design customers will be able to view a ------- of recent purchases.
(A) voucher
(B) coupon
(C) summary
(D) payment

2. In my opinion, the company's stock price is ------- low compared to its annual earnings.
(A) audibly
(B) relatively
(C) plentifully
(D) anonymously

3. The work shifts at Stella's Confectionary are eight hours long and ------- a 30-minute break for lunch.
(A) prepare
(B) release
(C) assemble
(D) include

4. After reviewing the training program for new sales staff, Mr. Vance concluded that more ------- should be placed on networking skills.
(A) appeal
(B) analysis
(C) distinction
(D) emphasis

5. The Fitzton Gallery has been the ------- promoter of the arts in Worthington, sponsoring numerous public events.
(A) precise
(B) separate
(C) certain
(D) primary

6. Photos and related documents were supplied by the author, unless ------- noted.
(A) else
(B) otherwise
(C) instead
(D) rather

7. To best serve its clients, Noguchi Investments regularly conducts ------- analyses of current business trends.
(A) spacious
(B) eventual
(C) thorough
(D) probable

8. Although our employees did not write the correct address on the shipping form, the machine parts arrived at the dairy farm on -------.
(A) schedule
(B) appointment
(C) authority
(D) condition

9. Mehri Translations Ltd. suggests that, when ------- with a business associate through an interpreter, you politely focus your attention on the associate.
(A) regulating
(B) acquainting
(C) communicating
(D) contemplating

10. According to the city planning director, Adelaide's old civic center must be ------- demolished before construction on a new center can begin.
(A) completely
(B) defectively
(C) plentifully
(D) richly

11. The Plimpton Report, a television news program, is known for its ------- coverage of world events.
(A) reliable
(B) reliably
(C) relying
(D) reliance

12. The Sanulife Web site brings you news of all the latest ------- in medical research.
(A) novelties
(B) advances
(C) elevations
(D) formations

Unit 16 어휘 235

1. The employee handbook clearly ------- the procedure for filing expense reports.

   (A) purchases
   (B) outlines
   (C) rations
   (D) invests

2. When answering calls, telephone representatives are to do what they can, within -------, to address customer concerns.

   (A) return
   (B) reason
   (C) role
   (D) rest

3. Rain fell ------- throughout the night, providing a welcome relief from the recent dry spell.

   (A) continuously
   (B) mutually
   (C) needlessly
   (D) optimistically

4. Employees are ------- to take family and medical leave if they have been employed for at least twelve months.

   (A) eligible
   (B) desirable
   (C) preferred
   (D) suitable

5. Ms. Nunokawa's keynote speech will be ------- by a reception in the main lobby of the convention center.

   (A) continued
   (B) acquired
   (C) detailed
   (D) followed

6. Quivtech Design has recently improved its process for measuring the ------- of job applicants.

   (A) feature
   (B) fact
   (C) resource
   (D) suitability

7. The new quality assurance policy requires that all machines be inspected if more than five ------- items are found in a single day.

   (A) collective
   (B) efficient
   (C) immediate
   (D) defective

8. Advertisements placed by merchants in *The Weekly Roundup* do not ------- imply endorsement by the management of the newspaper.

   (A) barely
   (B) highly
   (C) gradually
   (D) necessarily

9. This Saturday, Rose's Fashion Boutique will be ------- a 20 percent discount to all shoppers.

   (A) notifying
   (B) offering
   (C) performing
   (D) joining

10. Department managers must send ------- employee evaluations to Mr. Gang.

    (A) steady
    (B) skillful
    (C) turned
    (D) completed

11. Use of this Web site implies ------- with our terms and conditions.

    (A) contentment
    (B) agreement
    (C) placement
    (D) development

12. When not on display, the rare manuscripts are stored in conditions that are ------- for their preservation.

    (A) attentive
    (B) credible
    (C) optimal
    (D) competent

1. Ms. Pattison received an award for ------- missing a deadline in her three years of work at the company.

   (A) even   (B) quite

   (C) still   (D) never

2. The city council's proposal to attract more businesses to the Wharton Avenue area will be ------- later this month.

   (A) reminded   (B) reduced

   (C) finalized   (D) confused

3. Mild weather is ------- to continue throughout the week, with a chance of light rain on Thursday.

   (A) probable   (B) frequent

   (C) considerable   (D) likely

4. Lab tests show that a precise combination of the various ------- is necessary for the cleaning compound to be effective.

   (A) divisions   (B) prospects

   (C) ingredients   (D) compartments

5. The demand for decorative plant varieties is expected to rise -------, so gardeners are encouraged to stock up.

   (A) mainly   (B) soon

   (C) eagerly   (D) ever

6. We prefer to ------- our ingredients from local, environmentally friendly companies like Sunrise Farms.

   (A) comprise   (B) produce

   (C) obtain   (D) achieve

7. Mello Advertising is known for its brightly colored and eye-catching logos, flyers, and other ------- material.

   (A) conditional   (B) promotional

   (C) natural   (D) historical

8. Cross Cove is home to several New Zealand artists, most ------- Francis Seward and Kyle McIntyre.

   (A) easily   (B) notably

   (C) separately   (D) commonly

9. Heston Property Management apologizes for any ------- that the current renovation work may cause to our tenants.

   (A) resolution   (B) inconvenience

   (C) improvement   (D) distinction

10. If there is time at the end of tomorrow's meeting, Cilla Sampson will speak ------- about the Toronto Arts Festival.

    (A) rarely   (B) slightly

    (C) recently   (D) briefly

11. Located far from the stresses of the city, the Cozcal Hotel prides itself on offering guests a ------- vacation experience.

    (A) reclining   (B) restored

    (C) relaxing   (D) retired

12. Ms. Atembe of Hartwick Trucking will conduct a workshop on the best ways to ------- customers' concerns about freight delivery.

    (A) inform   (B) address

    (C) supervise   (D) promise

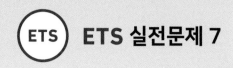
1. ------- regarding employment at Craddock Surgical Products should be directed to the human resources department.

   (A) Inquiries
   (B) Influences
   (C) Occasions
   (D) Qualifications

2. Business analysts expect the ------- merger decision to be made soon by Jemquist Ltd.

   (A) sparse
   (B) related
   (C) pending
   (D) attentive

3. Customers ------- return to Performance Wireless because of its low fees and excellent customer service.

   (A) greatly
   (B) moderately
   (C) mutually
   (D) frequently

4. Linella Media Group has indicated that growth in its new media revenues last year helped ------- a decrease in television advertising.

   (A) offset
   (B) outplay
   (C) input
   (D) overact

5. The complicated new time-reporting guidelines at Prindell Communications have caused ------- for employees.

   (A) confusion
   (B) attention
   (C) information
   (D) impression

6. Dr. Xiu Ying Zhang was awarded the ------- Loland Medal for her significant contributions to the field of molecular biology.

   (A) successful
   (B) dominant
   (C) cooperative
   (D) prestigious

7. On August 6, the Oakman Corporation ------- the appointment of its new president.

   (A) informed
   (B) created
   (C) announced
   (D) earned

8. The Wiltshire Orchestra's concert was ------- three hours long, ending just after 11 P.M.

   (A) attentively
   (B) approximately
   (C) endlessly
   (D) comparatively

9. Fischer's Cafeteria is looking for a full-time assistant manager to oversee the evening ------- on weekdays from 3:00 to 10:00 P.M.

   (A) chance
   (B) shift
   (C) practice
   (D) effect

10. Frequent, positive interactions between coworkers have been associated with ------- productivity throughout the year.

    (A) licensed
    (B) gathered
    (C) increased
    (D) presented

11. Because Oswalt International has completed over 200 development projects -------, its services are now in high demand.

    (A) successfully
    (B) instantly
    (C) financially
    (D) hugely

12. It will be difficult to ------- the safety regulations without effective monitoring.

    (A) entrust
    (B) enforce
    (C) imply
    (D) implore

1. Personnel who are ------- to attend Thursday's meeting should inform Everett Watson.

   (A) busy
   (B) easy
   (C) unable
   (D) unpleasant

2. Blinds made by Halligan Window Dressing ------- in a variety of colors and can be customized to fit most windows.

   (A) offer
   (B) buy
   (C) come
   (D) get

3. Construction of the new swimming pool is currently in ------- and is expected to be completed by May 1.

   (A) progress
   (B) place
   (C) use
   (D) demand

4. Danner Corporation met its recruitment goals for the third ------- year.

   (A) following
   (B) consecutive
   (C) approximate
   (D) absolute

5. While some of the trees in Cresson Park were planted ------- by landscaping professionals, most of them have developed naturally from seeds.

   (A) intentionally
   (B) highly
   (C) profoundly
   (D) indefinitely

6. Sondergard heating units are highly -------, resulting in lower heating costs for homeowners.

   (A) produced
   (B) reasonable
   (C) efficient
   (D) preferred

7. Unless customers opt for expedited service, orders ------- take three days to process.

   (A) substantially
   (B) perpetually
   (C) familiarly
   (D) typically

8. When he served as president of Delvan Manufacturing, Pierre Dunn ------- several policies that transformed the company.

   (A) instituted
   (B) relieved
   (C) interviewed
   (D) fabricated

9. The purpose of the WHJ research study was to determine the ------- of adding bicycle lanes throughout the Wilmingdale business district.

   (A) feasibility
   (B) dependency
   (C) intensity
   (D) accuracy

10. Researchers from Wynne University have spent several months ------- the plant species in the Mojowarno Nature Preserve.

    (A) experimenting
    (B) documenting
    (C) commenting
    (D) accomplishing

11. Although Ms. Gu's manuscript is not due for six months, she has ------- completed her first draft.

    (A) daily
    (B) nearly
    (C) locally
    (D) rarely

12. By ------- the furniture shipping process, we can lower expenses and cut the delivery time in half.

    (A) outpacing
    (B) streamlining
    (C) persevering
    (D) forestalling

Part

독해

지문을 읽고 이와 관련된 문제를 풀어야 하는 파트로, 단일 지문 10개에 29문항, 이중 지문 2세트에 10문항, 삼중 지문 3세트에 15문항으로 구성되어 있다. 이메일, 기사, 회람 등이 주로 나오며, 일정표, 후기, 송장 등 기타 양식도 등장한다. 주제·목적이나 세부 사항을 묻는 문제, Not/True(사실 확인) 문제, 문장 삽입 문제, 추론/암시 문제, 동의어 문제, 의도 파악 문제가 출제된다.

■ ETS 예제

Questions 147-148 refer to the following **notice.** •----------

147 Attention Waylon Concert Hall Guests • ----------------| ① 지문 종류와 제목 읽기

- 147 Ticket holders arriving late will not be admitted to the auditorium until a suitable break during the performance and must be shown to their seats by an usher.

- 147 Mobile telephones must be turned off during all performances. ----------| ③ 147번 관련 내용 확인

- 148 Cameras and video or audio recorders of any kind are prohibited unless specifically authorized by the **promoter**. •------------| ③ 148번 관련 내용 확인 Those found during the performance will be held at the box office until the end of the show.

- Standing in the aisles during performances is forbidden by the fire regulations.

- Smoking is prohibited throughout the building.

- Food or beverages may not be brought into the auditorium at any time.

Please be courteous to those around you while you enjoy the show.

---

147. (What) does the notice (mainly discuss)?
    (A) Rules for concertgoers
    (B) Equipment used by concert-hall staff
    (C) Safety procedures •----------| ② 문제 유형 및 키워드 파악
    (D) Performance schedules

148. According to the notice, (what) might a (promoter do)?
    (A) Distribute concert programs
    (B) Escort guests who arrive late to their seats
    (C) Approve the use of audio devices
    (D) Collect mobile phones

■ 풀이 전략

1 지문의 종류와 제목을 읽고 내용을 예상한다.

지문 유형마다 자주 다뤄지는 내용이 있다. 지문 유형에 따른 내용 전개 방식을 예상하는 것이 좋다.

Questions 147-148 **refer to the following** notice.
공지: 정책/변경 사항 안내, 당부 사항, 주의 사항 등의 내용 예상

Attention Waylon Concert Hall Guests
웨일런 콘서트 홀 관람객을 대상으로 하는 공지: 홀 이용 관련 안내 사항 열거

2 질문을 읽고 문제 유형과 키워드를 파악한다.

147. What **does the notice** mainly discuss?
주제/목적 | 제목과 초반부에 초점

148. According to the notice, what might a promoter do?
세부 사항+추론 | 키워드 'promoter'가 있는 부분에 초점

3 지문을 읽으며 주요 내용을 파악하고, 문제와 관련된 내용이 나오면 집중해서 읽는다.

147. 공지에서 주로 다루는 내용은?

Ticket holders arriving late will not be admitted to the auditorium until a suitable break
첫 번째 안내 사항: 늦게 도착하는 사람은 휴식시간 전에는 입장 불가

Mobile telephones must be turned off during all performances
두 번째 안내 사항: 공연 중 휴대전화 전원 OFF

정답 (A) Rules for concertgoers 콘서트 관람객이 지켜야 하는 규정

148. 기획자가 할 것 같은 업무는?

Cameras and ~ audio recorders of any kind are prohibited unless specifically authorized by the promoter.
기획자가 승인하지 않은 카메라나 녹음 장치는 사용 금지 = 기획자가 기기 사용 승인

정답 (C) Approve the use of audio devices 오디오 기기 사용 승인

■ 지문 구성과 독해 전략

정답과 해설 p. 175

수신인	To: Rachel Morse <rmorse@mailnet.com>
발신인	From: Frank's Auto Repair <cs@franksautorepair.com>
제목	Subject: Vehicle service
날짜	Date: July 1

1 수신인, 발신인 관계 파악
수신인: 레이첼 모스
발신인: 자동차 수리점

Dear **Ms. Morse**,

주제/목적 **Q1** Based on our records, your vehicle is due for a service appointment. Schedule your appointment in the next 30 days to **Q2** receive a 20% discount on the following inspections.

2 제목에서 내용 예상
자동차 서비스 관련

3 메일을 보낸 목적 파악
점검 서비스 시기 안내, 30일 이내 예약시 일부 점검 20% 할인 혜택

세부 사항
- Engine
- Fluid Levels
- Tires
- Battery

4 세부 내용 요지 파악
링크 클릭, 쿠폰 출력 후 결제 시 제출

Just click on the following link, print out the coupon, and when you come in for your appointment, submit it with your payment: www.franksautorepair.com/inspectioncoupon.

추가 안내 Call (206) 555-0117 to schedule an appointment. We look forward to seeing you!

5 추가 안내 사항 확인
특정 번호로 전화 예약

발신인 정보	Customer Care Department
	Frank's Auto Repair

Q1 What is the **purpose** of the e-mail?

(A) To confirm that a refund has been issued

(B) To request that a customer make a payment

(C) To remind a customer to make an appointment

(D) To confirm that an appointment has been scheduled

주제/목적 문제 | 초반부 확인하기
점검 시기 안내, 서비스 예약 권장
정답 (C) 예약할 것을 상기시키기 위해
※ 주제/목적이 지문 전체에 걸쳐 나타나는 경우 다른 문제를 먼저 해결한다.

Q2 What is **indicated** about **Ms. Morse**?

(A) She recently purchased a new vehicle.

(B) Her vehicle is currently being repaired.

(C) Her driver's license is expired.

(D) She is eligible for a discount.

Not/True 문제 | 명확한 근거 찾기
수신자인 모스 씨에 관한 사실:
점검 예약시 일부 항목 할인
정답 (D) 할인을 받을 자격이 있다.
※ 'NOT'이 포함된 질문은 오답을 소거해가며 정답을 찾는다.

Letter

Dear Ms. Kovin,

Our records show that the June issue of *Today's Trends* will be your last and that you have not yet renewed your subscription. To encourage you to renew, we would like to offer you *Today's Trends* at a reduced price. You are currently paying $3.00 per issue. We will offer you the magazine for six months at only $2.25 per monthly issue. That means that you will save a total of $4.50 from July to December if you renew your subscription.

Please contact our business office at 888-555-3214 Monday through Friday from 9 A.M. to 5 P.M. or on Saturday from 10 A.M. to 3 P.M. The business office is closed on Sundays. We look forward to continuing to serve you in the future.

Sincerely,
Marsha Clemmins
Marsha Clemmins
Director of Sales

1. When will Ms. Kovin's current subscription end?

   (A) In June
   (B) In December

2. What is Ms. Kovin currently paying for her subscription per month?

   (A) $2.25
   (B) $3.00

E-mail

From: mburnes@worldstore.com
To: wpitts@pma.net

Dear Mr. Pitts:

Severe weather conditions have caused substantial disruptions to air traffic in and out of many airports in the Midwest, where the World StoreTM sorting facilities are located. As a result, many deliveries will be delayed by approximately 24 to 48 hours.
World StoreTM is committed to providing the highest level of service possible. For the latest package status information, please go to "My Account" on Worldstore.com, where you will be able to track your package.
Thank you for your patience and understanding as we work through this situation.

Yours,

Michael Burnes
President
Worldstore.com

3. What is the purpose of the e-mail?

   (A) To postpone travel plans
   (B) To give information about shipping delays

4. What does Mr. Burnes suggest Mr. Pitts do?

   (A) Contact the carrier service immediately
   (B) Visit a Web site for more information

RC

PART 7

Questions 1-2 refer to the following e-mail.

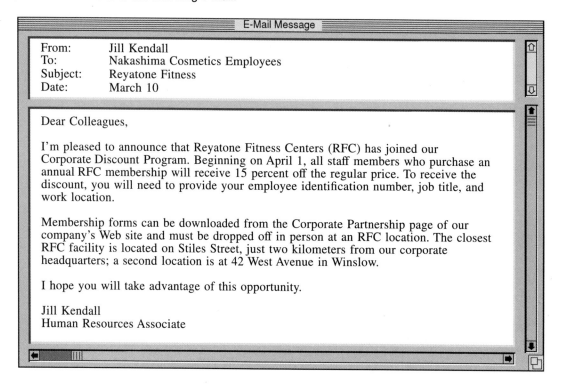

E-Mail Message

From: Jill Kendall
To: Nakashima Cosmetics Employees
Subject: Reyatone Fitness
Date: March 10

Dear Colleagues,

I'm pleased to announce that Reyatone Fitness Centers (RFC) has joined our Corporate Discount Program. Beginning on April 1, all staff members who purchase an annual RFC membership will receive 15 percent off the regular price. To receive the discount, you will need to provide your employee identification number, job title, and work location.

Membership forms can be downloaded from the Corporate Partnership page of our company's Web site and must be dropped off in person at an RFC location. The closest RFC facility is located on Stiles Street, just two kilometers from our corporate headquarters; a second location is at 42 West Avenue in Winslow.

I hope you will take advantage of this opportunity.

Jill Kendall
Human Resources Associate

1. Why was the e-mail written?

(A) To sell discounted exercise equipment

(B) To announce the opening of a new fitness club

(C) To introduce a company regulation

(D) To describe an employee benefit

2. What is mentioned about Reyatone Fitness?

(A) It is next to Nakashima Cosmetics.

(B) Its fees have recently increased.

(C) It has more than one location.

(D) It will be hiring additional staff.

Questions 3-4 refer to the following letter.

1 March

Ms. Juliet Skeffery
129 Acres Road
Linstead, St. Catherine

Dear Ms. Skeffery,

You are cordially invited to the 33rd annual shareholders meeting of Montego Bay Investment Ltd. (MBI) on Wednesday, 20 March, at 6:00 P.M. Please see the enclosed agenda and the annual report. Because of ongoing construction at our corporate headquarters, this year's gathering will not be held there as is customary but at the Wind Chime Inn, 135 Taino Drive.

Given the success of our most recent fiscal year, the board of directors will be proposing a dividend payment of $1.00 per share. Moreover, as board members are confident about the current fiscal year, the creation of a low-cost investment fund, called Xchange 21, is being proposed. It will provide an investment option for young people just entering the labor force. Both of these matters will be put to a vote at the meeting.

Should you decide to attend, please reserve your seat at www.mbi.com.jm/asm/rsvp.

Sincerely,

Emerson Mottley
Emerson Mottley
Chair, Board of Directors

Enclosure

3. What is NOT indicated about the meeting?

(A) It generally takes place at MBI's main office.

(B) It has been held annually for over 30 years.

(C) It requires advance registration.

(D) It typically is well attended.

4. According to the letter, what will happen on March 20 ?

(A) Construction of a new headquarters will be approved.

(B) Certain proposals will be considered.

(C) Changes within the labor force will be reviewed.

(D) A new board of directors will be elected.

RC

PART 7

To:	Mei Ying <mying@brightstar.com>
From:	Pedro Alvarez <palvarez@tbkfoods.com>
Subject:	Tasty Foods
Date:	November 4

Dear Ms. Ying:

We appreciate the feedback we received from you when you took our recent breakfast foods survey; your feedback was important to us in developing our new Tasty Breakfast Foods line of products. As a token of our appreciation, we are sending you some free samples of Tasty Breakfast Foods products. They should arrive within two weeks.

In about three months, you may be asked to participate in another telephone consumer survey for Tasty Breakfast Foods. If you would prefer not to be contacted about participating, please send an e-mail to me, or telephone me at 232-555-0151.

Be sure to check the Tasty Breakfast Foods Web site, www.tastybreakfastfoods.com, for information about where you can purchase our new products. You will also find nutrition information about the complete line of Tasty Breakfast Foods products as well as discount coupons.

Sincerely,

Pedro Alvarez
Product Manager

5. Why was the e-mail sent to Ms. Ying?

(A) To invite her to a meeting
(B) To answer a question she asked about a product
(C) To thank her for her help
(D) To explain why a shipment was delayed

6. What is being sent to Ms. Ying?

(A) A survey
(B) Nutrition information
(C) Consumer reports
(D) Some product samples

7. What is mentioned as a feature of the Tasty Breakfast Foods Web site?

(A) A collection of recipes using the products
(B) Consumers' opinions about the quality of the products
(C) A list of prices for the products
(D) A list of stores where the products are available

Questions 8-10 refer to the following letter.

Eagle Rock Cable Company
1 Eagle Rock Way, Jersey City, NJ 07306

Current Resident
3382 Avalon Court
Hoboken, NJ 07030

Are you tired of paying for cable television packages that include many channels that you do not watch? If so, we have a deal you will like. Eagle Rock Cable is now offering an Internet and television contract for the low monthly price of $49.99. We call it Customer's Choice. — [1] —. Unlike the plans offered by other providers, Customer's Choice from Eagle Rock Cable allows you to choose the channels in your subscription. Select up to twelve channels representing a wide assortment of news, sports, movies, education, comedy, and more. — [2] —. And you can include additional channels for an extra $2.99 per month each.

Better yet, with Customer's Choice you are not tied to an annual contract. — [3] —. To take advantage of this offer, simply call us at 1-201-555-0142. — [4] —. Friendly Eagle Rock Cable representatives are waiting to speak with you.

Yours truly,

Loren Cramer
Loren Cramer, Customer Service Representative

8. For whom is the letter most likely intended?

   (A) Owners of local businesses
   (B) Customers with standard cable contracts
   (C) People who have recently bought televisions
   (D) Viewers who would rather watch sports than movies

9. What is NOT mentioned as a feature of Customer's Choice?

   (A) Customers may select from many TV channels.
   (B) Customers can pay more to add extra TV channels.
   (C) Phone service can be added to the plan.
   (D) Internet service is included in the plan.

10. In which of the positions marked [1], [2], [3], and [4] does the following sentence best belong?

    "You can cancel the service at any time."

    (A) [1]
    (B) [2]
    (C) [3]
    (D) [4]

Questions 11-14 refer to the following e-mail.

```
*E-mail*

From:      office@chibagrandhotel.com
To:        erik.carlsen@gowmail.com
Subject:   Your recent stay at the Chiba Grand
Date:      April 18
```

Dear Mr. Carlsen,

At the request of the hotel management, I am writing to ask if you would take a few minutes to share feedback with us regarding your April 8-12 stay at the Chiba Grand Hotel. I would like to know your impressions of our hotel. How happy were you with the amenities? Did you find your stay here enjoyable? Was there anything that was not up to your expectations? If there is room for improvement, let us know. We are one hundred percent committed to total satisfaction for our guests!

Please share your opinions with us directly by going to www.chibagrand.com/yourstay and completing our Total Satisfaction Survey. We ask that you provide responses in all of the listed fields so that we will have a summary of your overall experience. Also, if you provide your feedback by April 30, you will be entered into the $500 Reward Chiba Grand Sweepstakes. Thank you.

Best regards,

Kana Hirota
Chiba Grand Hotel

---

11. Why was the e-mail written?

(A) To apologize for bad service
(B) To deliver a payment summary
(C) To inform a guest about a change
(D) To inquire about customer satisfaction

12. When did Mr. Carlsen arrive at the hotel?

(A) On April 8
(B) On April 12
(C) On April 18
(D) On April 30

13. According to the e-mail, what can be found at the online address?

(A) A questionnaire form
(B) Directions to the hotel
(C) A detailed list of expenses
(D) A description of hotel facilities

14. What does Ms. Hirota offer to Mr. Carlsen?

(A) A full refund
(B) A guided tour
(C) A discount on a future visit
(D) An opportunity to win a prize

Meadlin Books

147 Woodland Ave.
Roanoke, VA 24016
Phone: (540) 555-0128 • Fax: (540) 555-0139
www.meadlinbooks.com

Hyun Sil Kim
451 Aspen Drive
Richmond, VA 23219
July 15

Dear Ms. Kim:

Thank you for becoming a preferred member of Meadlin Books. Your preferred member number is H2389X, and your membership is valid for one year.

Our records indicate that the e-mail address associated with your account is hskim@redkin.net. As you have requested, all correspondence will be sent to you by both postal mail and e-mail. If you wish to change your contact details, please call us at (540) 555-0128 between the hours of 9:00 A.M. and 6:00 P.M., Monday through Friday, or visit us online at www.meadlinbooks.com.

You may continue to purchase books from us online, or you may use your membership card at our store in Roanoke. As a member, you will save 15% on all new books, and you can preregister online for book signings, question-and-answer sessions with notable authors, and other popular in-store events.

Your business is important to us, and we hope you enjoy your membership. For your convenience, your Meadlin Books membership card is enclosed so that you can take advantage of your savings immediately.

Sincerely,

John Hewitt

John Hewitt
Member Services
Meadlin Books
Enclosure

15. What is the purpose of the letter?

(A) To confirm a deadline

(B) To ask for a donation

(C) To renew an account

(D) To provide membership details

16. What is suggested about Ms. Kim?

(A) She has organized a book fair.

(B) She has designed a Web site.

(C) She buys books on the Internet.

(D) She manages a bookstore.

17. What is indicated about Meadlin Books?

(A) It holds promotional events in the store.

(B) It offers discounts on magazines.

(C) It contains a large selection of travel books.

(D) It advertises in area newspapers.

18. What did Mr. Hewitt send with the letter?

(A) A receipt

(B) A card

(C) An order form

(D) A catalog

O'Dwyer Lumber

12 May

Monica Forde
Office Manager, Whelan Quality Remodeling
146 Glenrea Road
Dangan, Galway NW1

Dear Ms. Forde,

We are writing to let you know that O'Dwyer Lumber is moving! Effective Monday, 26 May, we will no longer be operating from our Dangan location. On Monday, 2 June, we will be opening in our new location at 54 Rathmoy Street in Spiddal. Our new facility is much larger, allowing us to stock a wider variety of building materials and tools.

Please note that O'Dwyer Lumber will be closed from 26 May until 1 June while we carry out our relocation. On reopening day, 2 June, we will be hosting a grand opening celebration from 10 A.M. to 2 P.M. during which we will demonstrate some of our new products and hold drawings for valuable prizes. We'll also have an exciting tool-trivia competition, with everyone invited to play. Please join us if you are in the area on that day.

Since we have made significant investments in our new facility, it is necessary for us to implement modest price increases on some of our products; the same policy will apply to delivery charges. Companies like yours that have been doing business with us for five years or more will be excluded from any price increases on products or delivery for one year. Additionally, we offer you a 20% discount on orders placed during the month of June.

Feel free to contact us if you have any questions or concerns about our relocation. As of 26 May, our telephone number will be 020 918 0245. We look forward to continuing to do business with Whelan Quality Remodeling.

Sincerely,

Jenna Granger

Jenna Granger
Marketing Director, O'Dwyer Lumber

19. What is suggested about O'Dwyer Lumber?

    (A) It will soon have two locations.

    (B) It has hired several new delivery drivers.

    (C) It has merged with another company.

    (D) It will expand its inventory.

20. The phrase "carry out" in paragraph 2, line 2, is closest in meaning to

    (A) remove

    (B) accomplish

    (C) reconsider

    (D) lift

21. What can an O'Dwyer Lumber customer do on June 2?

    (A) Enter a contest

    (B) Visit a warehouse in Dangan

    (C) Sign up for discounts

    (D) Vote on the best new products

22. What is NOT indicated about Whelan Quality Remodeling?

    (A) It has been in business for at least five years.

    (B) It is located in Dangan.

    (C) It plans to increase its orders from O'Dwyer Lumber.

    (D) It will pay less for purchases made next month at O'Dwyer Lumber.

RC

PART 7

출제 포인트 1 회람/공지는 초반에 주제/목적이 드러나며, 요청, 혹은 당부 사항으로 마무리되는 경우가 많다.

출제 포인트 2 광고는 제품/서비스/업체 소개 → 특징/장점 → 혜택, 구인 광고는 직책 및 업무 개요 → 자격 요건과 복리후생 → 지원 방법 순으로 구성된다.

출제 포인트 3 기사에서는 지역 소식부터 인물/사업체 소개, 기업 합병 소식에 이르기까지 다양한 주제가 다뤄진다. 세부 내용이 나온 후 인터뷰 내용이나 향후 전망으로 마무리된다.

■ 지문 구성과 독해 전략

정답과 해설 p. 181

기사 주제

TURNER BAY (July 11)— The Riverrun Complex has received this year's Ribbon of Excellence. **Q1** The Ribbon is awarded each year by **Evertrail**, a Web site that showcases local firms. —[1]—.

> **1** 기사 제목이나 초반에서 주제 확인
> 리버런 콤플렉스의 수상

세부 내용

To qualify for the award, an enterprise must receive an average of 3.5 stars on a 4-star **Q1, Q2** rating scale. —[2]—. Past and present winners include hotels, attractions, and restaurants throughout the Turner Bay area. This marks the third consecutive year that Riverrun has won the award. —[3]—.

> **2** 세부 내용 요지 파악
> 수상 조건: 별 3.5/4개
> 수상 대상: 호텔, 명소, 식당 등
> 리버런 3년 연속 수상

인터뷰 내용

"We at Riverrun are thrilled by this honor," said spokesperson Lucia Berrios. "Since we opened six years ago, we have worked hard to provide families with exciting rides and healthy foods. We are especially proud of our Pavilion of the Sciences, which provides games and interactive experiences that educate and delight patrons of all ages." —[4]—.

> **3** 인터뷰 내용 파악
> 리버런 대변인의 수상 소감 및 서비스
> (놀이기구, 건강에 좋은 음식, 과학
> 전시장 등) 소개

Q1 According to the article, what does the **Evertrail** Web site do?

(A) It offers discounts on hotel reservations.
(B) It describes scenic train rides.
(C) It sells products made in Turner Bay.
(D) It evaluates local companies.

> **세부 사항 문제 | 키워드에 주목하기**
> 에버트레일 웹사이트가 하는 일: 지역
> 사업체 장점 소개, 별점 평가, 시상
> 정답 (D) 지역 기업들을 평가한다.
> ※ 세부 사항 문제에서도 약간의 추론이 필요
> 할 수 있다.

Q2 In which of the positions marked [1], [2], [3], and [4] does the following sentence best belong?

"**The ratings** indicate a business's degree of dedication to quality and customer service."

(A) [1] **(B) [2]** (C) [3] (D) [4]

> **문장 삽입 문제 | 삽입문 분석하기**
> ratings 앞에 정관사 the가 쓰였으므로
> 삽입문 앞에 평가 점수와 관련된
> 내용이 나와야 한다. [2] 앞에서 rating
> scale(평가 척도)이 언급되었다.
> 정답 (B)
> ※ 관사, 지시 형용사/대명사, 접속부사, 시간
> 표현 등이 결정적 단서가 된다.

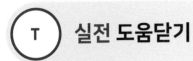
Advertisement

Summer in Sinchon

One-bedroom lodging located in Sinchon, one of the trendiest neighborhoods in Seoul!
- Newly renovated and fully furnished, including modern appliances
- Only steps away from art galleries, restaurants, tearooms, and shopping malls
- Three-minute walk from Sinchon Station, Subway Line 2
- Available August 1-31 only—perfect for a summer vacation in Korea
- Monthly rent ₩900,000, plus ₩900,000 refundable security deposit

Contact Chan Joon Gil at cjgil293@maponet.co.kr to schedule an apartment viewing.

1. What is being advertised?

   (A) A short-term rental offer

   (B) Recently renovated houses for sale

2. According to the advertisement, how should someone arrange to look at the property?

   (A) By placing a phone call

   (B) By sending an e-mail

Article

Johannesburg (7 July) — Jaquin Publishers announced on Friday that Aurelia Martino's new book, *Stars in the Sky*, will be released on 8 September. This is Ms. Martino's second book, and early reviews say that readers are in for a treat. Ms. Martino, an acclaimed actress from Johannesburg, decided to give up acting and begin writing books when she had her first child, Matilda, two years ago. She is perhaps best known for her ten-year role as the mother on the popular South African television series *Living with the Monroes.*

3. What is the purpose of the article?

   (A) To announce a book release date

   (B) To offer an opinion about a book

4. What is suggested about Ms. Martino?

   (A) She has been an author for over ten years.

   (B) She changed careers.

RC

PART 7

Questions 1-2 refer to the following advertisement.

Ground Design

43 Elston Street
Brisbane, Queensland 400
3229 2626
www.grounddesign.com.au

We have over 24 years of experience in residential outdoor construction and landscaping in the Brisbane area.

We specialize in building:
- Natural stone and block walls
- Patios
- Driveways and walkways

We enhance these with garden designs, lighting, and trees to complete your look. We are a fully licensed business and can provide a complete colour portfolio of work we have done for previous clients. Please contact us Monday-Friday to schedule a complimentary consultation.

---

1. What is NOT a service that Ground Design advertises?

   (A) Planting trees
   (B) Building walls
   (C) Installing lights
   (D) Designing fountains

2. What does Ground Design offer potential clients?

   (A) A discount on large projects
   (B) Images of past jobs
   (C) Rapid completion of work
   (D) Complimentary painting supplies

Questions 3-5 refer to the following notice.

Walking Tour of Bridgeton
Saturday, October 26, at 10:30 A.M.

Did you know that the current Bridgeton Town Hall building was originally the Bridgeton National Bank, built in 1890? Are you aware that the Finesco Hardware Store, located on the corner of Broad and Main Streets, opened fifty years ago and once was the site of the first public library? Join us for an informative Saturday morning stroll and learn about historic Bridgeton.

Librarian Vera Rosenski will lead the tour with facts and stories about Bridgeton's early years. The tour will begin at the library's main entrance and conclude in front of the Northside Coffeehouse around noon.

Local artist Bill Takata will hold a creative drawing class for children ages 5 to 12 while adults participate in the tour. Class size is limited, so please sign up at the library before Saturday!

---

3. What is the purpose of the notice?

   (A) To invite people to a community event
   (B) To attract support for a new service
   (C) To show off a renovated town hall
   (D) To celebrate a town's anniversary

4. What used to be located at Broad and Main Streets in Bridgeton's early years?

   (A) A coffeehouse
   (B) A library
   (C) A bank
   (D) An art studio

5. What is suggested about the activity led by Ms. Rosenski?

   (A) It is not intended for young children.
   (B) It includes a free lunch.
   (C) It is promoting a recent book.
   (D) It will be canceled in case of rain.

Positive Change for Mechelen

Wind Dynamics, the leading producer of wind turbines and wind energy technology across Europe, has announced plans to open a production plant in Mechelen, Belgium. — [1] —. The Dutch company is spending more than €15 million to purchase, renovate, and equip the abandoned Cantek Telephone factory. The venture is expected to create about two hundred new production jobs and fifty new office jobs over the next two years. This is good news for Mechelen, an industrial area that has been hit hard by factory closures and job loss in recent years. — [2] —. Battel Builders has already been contracted to undertake the plant's transformations. — [3] —.

The plant will primarily be used for the assembly and testing of gear drives to be incorporated in the company's wind turbines. — [4] —. Wind Dynamics, in cooperation with the Mechelen Business Development Association (MBDA), will provide development grants to train its incoming workforce in green technology. Jane Arens, MBDA president, says "Mechelen is proud to be part of something that contributes to energy conservation and to the economic growth of our region."

6. What does the article mainly discuss?

    (A) The appointment of a new company CEO
    (B) The merger of two companies
    (C) The process of producing wind turbines
    (D) The opening of a facility

7. What will happen to the Cantek Telephone factory?

    (A) It will be restored as a historic site.
    (B) It will be used by a different industry.
    (C) It will be moved to a new location.
    (D) It will be demolished to create an open space.

8. Who is Ms. Arens?

    (A) A Wind Dynamics employee
    (B) A newspaper journalist
    (C) The president of an association
    (D) The mayor of a town in Belgium

9. In which of the positions marked [1], [2], [3], and [4] does the following sentence best belong?

    "It also anticipates hiring additional workers to complete the construction project."
    (A) [1]
    (B) [2]
    (C) [3]
    (D) [4]

MEMORANDUM

DATE: January 28
TO: Building M community
FROM: Janis Ting, Director of the Office Space Committee
SUBJECT: Jay Voon Auditorium Renovation

We wanted to alert you to the fact that the renovation of the Jay Voon Auditorium, the first Phase of a two-phase project, will begin in mid-February. The second phase, reconstruction of the first-floor offices adjacent to the auditorium, could begin as early as August, with an intended completion date of late November.

A project of this scope, in such a central location, will necessarily cause a certain degree of disruption to our community, and every effort will be made to minimize this disruption. Plans have already been made to provide alternative venues during renovation; for those of you who anticipate needing to schedule events for these alternative venues, inform Lidia Ibrahim(ext. 3372, librahim@m.galleries.com) as soon as possible.

Should these time lines change in any way as this work progresses, we will keep the community informed.

We greatly appreciate your patience as we continue to enhance our facilities.

RC

PART 7

10. Why was the memo written?

(A) To announce alternative venues
(B) To warn about possible disruptions
(C) To revise the schedule for a project
(D) To inform employees about new staff

11. What does the second phase of the renovation involve?

(A) Adding another floor
(B) Reconstructing office space
(C) Centralizing event facilities
(D) Upgrading an adjacent building

12. When is the project expected to be completed?

(A) In January
(B) In February
(C) In August
(D) In November

13. What should people who want to reserve a large space do?

(A) E-mail Janis Ting
(B) Contact Lidia Ibrahim
(C) Complete the new forms
(D) Fill out an online application

Questions 14-17 refer to the following job advertisement.

REGIONAL APPLIANCES, INCORPORATED

Regional Appliances, Inc., (RAI) is a privately owned manufacturing company. We manufacture and warehouse air-conditioning units for domestic and international distribution. With fresh projects under way, the company is seeking talented professionals for the following positions:

HUMAN RESOURCES MANAGER–Toronto (#4699)
This exciting role focuses on staff recruitment and retention within the organization. The human resources manager will ensure sufficient labor availability to meet operational requirements. Proven negotiation skills are essential.

PROJECT MANAGER–Toronto (#4654)
The project management team organizes and reports on RAI's mechanical projects while maintaining quality standards and client relations. This role requires a minimum of five years' project management experience.

SENIOR QUANTITY SURVEYOR–Calgary (#4827)
This position covers project administration with regard to finance and budgeting, providing project managers and accountants with timely financial reports. The senior quantity surveyor will oversee a team of junior quantity surveyors and provide annual performance evaluations.

ACCOUNTANT–Calgary and Toronto (#4222)
This is a senior-level position requiring extensive accounting experience. The ideal candidate will be a licensed accountant and have a proven track record of accurate bookkeeping for a fast-growing company.

To apply for one of these positions, e-mail your résumé to elevine@raijobs.com, quoting the four-digit position code in the subject line.

14. What is suggested about Regional Appliances, Inc.?

(A) Its products are sold in multiple countries.
(B) Its main factory is in Calgary.
(C) It is relocating its warehouse.
(D) It has recently hired several mechanical engineers.

15. According to the advertisement, who would be responsible for supervising a group of employees?

(A) The human resources manager
(B) The project manager
(C) The senior quantity surveyor
(D) The accountant

16. What is indicated about project managers?

(A) They must interact with clients.
(B) They must sign a five-year contract.
(C) They often travel between Calgary and Toronto.
(D) They often negotiate project costs.

17. What are applicants asked to provide along with a résumé?

(A) Salary requirements
(B) A list of references
(C) A job number
(D) Proof of professional licensure

Boulland to Penalize Wholesalers

(Oct. 5)—Laboratory equipment retailer Boulland reported today that, as part of a push for greater inventory control, it will begin charging its wholesale suppliers penalties if they do not meet agreed-upon delivery windows at least 90 percent of the time.

"There is a significant financial cost when we do not maintain an optimal amount of stock on our shelves," says Joca Galvan, Boulland's chief receiving officer. "So it is critical that our suppliers deliver their goods as soon as our stores need them. We have had them sign updated service agreements with these new terms clearly stated."

While suppliers understand Boulland's goal of timely delivery, some say imposing charges will not solve the problem unless challenges faced by suppliers are also taken into account.

"There are situations when on-time delivery is out of our control," says Enrique Zapata, a shipping supervisor at one of Boulland's suppliers. "My company often struggles to fulfill orders on time when retailers fail to notify us before their inventories fall to critically low levels. Last-minute adjustments to orders are a significant cause of delayed delivery."

Mr. Zapata insists that if Boulland were to adopt better communication strategies, the issue could be readily resolved. Boulland, however, intends to move forward with its plan and reassess it next year.

---

18. According to the article, what action by a supplier could result in a penalty?

(A) Missing delivery deadlines
(B) Packaging items improperly
(C) Mislabeling product shipments
(D) Failing to report inventory updates

19. The word "terms" in paragraph 2, line 8, is closest in meaning to

(A) conditions
(B) periods
(C) reports
(D) figures

20. What is suggested about Boulland's plan?

(A) The company's leadership must approve the details.
(B) The publicity will be good for business.
(C) Suppliers are eager to put it into action.
(D) Further actions may be necessary.

21. Why does Mr. Zapata mention communication strategies?

(A) To question a marketing decision
(B) To propose a new marketing idea
(C) To offer advice about improving job satisfaction
(D) To suggest a solution to supply problems

기타 양식

■ 지문 구성과 독해 전략

정답과 해설 p. 186

| 연락 이유/
용건 | **Anna Ricci**   **[9:02 A.M.]** | 1 연락 이유/용건 확인 |
| | **Q1** Where did you get your car fixed last month? | 그린 씨에게 자동차 수리 업체 정보 문의 |

Bonnie Green   **[9:05 A.M.]**
Mark's Automotive on Linden Avenue. Are you having vehicle trouble?

| 세부 내용 | **Anna Ricci**   **[9:06 A.M.]** | 2 세부 내용 요지 파악 |
| | No. I'm at the coffee shop chatting with Kevein Peters from work. **Q1** His car needs to be repaired. | 수리 대상: 리치 씨의 동료인 피터스 씨의 자동차 |

Bonnie Green   **[9:08 A.M.]**
Q1, Q2 Tell him Mark's was great. They found good prices on parts and charged a reasonable amount for labor.

그린 씨의 업체 추천: 합리적인 비용 언급

| 끝인사 | **Anna Ricci**   **[9:09 A.M.]** | 3 대화의 마무리 확인 |
| | **Q2** Thanks. **I'll pass it on.** | 감사 인사 후 해당 업체 정보를 피터스 씨에게 전달하겠다고 함 |

Q1 Why **most likely** does Ms. Ricci contact Ms. Green?
(A) She wants a recommendation.
(B) She needs directions to a location.
(C) She wants a cup of coffee.
(D) She needs her car fixed.

추론 문제 | 근거를 바탕으로 추론하기
그린 씨가 자동차를 맡겼던 업체 문의 →
동료가 자동차를 수리해야 한다고 첨언
→ 업체를 추천받기 위해 연락
정답 (A) 추천을 원한다.
※ 근거 없는 추측은 지양해야 한다.

Q2 At 9:09 A.M., what does Ms. Ricci most likely **mean** when she writes, "**I'll pass it on**"?
(A) She will pick up Ms. Green on the way to work.
(B) She will search for a different repair shop.
(C) She will share information with Mr. Peters.
(D) She will bring money to Mr. Peters.

의도 파악 문제 | 앞뒤 문맥 살피기
리치 씨는 그린 씨가 추천한 자동차
수리 업체 정보를 피터스 씨에게
전달하겠다고 한 것이다.
정답 (C) 피터스 씨와 정보를 공유할
것이다.
※ 대화의 주요 흐름을 파악한 후 앞뒤 문장에서 근거를 찾는다.

Postcard

May 4

Dr. Charles Somerville
1785 Taylor Street
Allentown, PA 18102

This is a friendly reminder that your next dental cleaning is scheduled for Friday, May 11, at 8:30 A.M. If you are unable to keep your appointment, please call us by 3:00 P.M. on Wednesday, May 9, during regular office hours. We can be reached from 8:00 A.M. to 5:00 P.M., Monday through Saturday, at 555-0119.

Please note, we will be closed on Monday, May 28 for the holiday.

To. Mr. Steven Hines
15 Greenwood Way
Bethlehem, PA 18018

1. When does Mr. Hines have an appointment?

(A) On May 9
(B) On May 11

2. According to the postcard, why would Mr. Hines call the dental office?

(A) To confirm an appointment
(B) To cancel an appointment

Guest pass

Present this pass to receive one complimentary visit to

Blue River Fitness Center

- Valid for first-time visitors only.
- Guests must be at least 18 years of age or accompanied by an adult.
- Guests must attend an information session with a staff member to receive a tour of the facility and learn about membership options.
- Valid during limited hours only:
  Tuesday to Thursday 10:00 A.M. – 5:00 P.M., Saturday 10:00 A.M. – 3:00 P.M.

Blue River has long been Detroit's premier fitness center, helping members of all ages and interests to improve their health. Whether you are a novice looking to begin a fitness routine or a fitness expert seeking new challenges, Blue River will help you attain your goals.

3. What must a visitor do in order to use the guest pass?

(A) Present identification
(B) Meet with a representative

4. When can the pass be used?

(A) On Wednesday
(B) On Friday

Questions 1-2 refer to the following text-message chain.

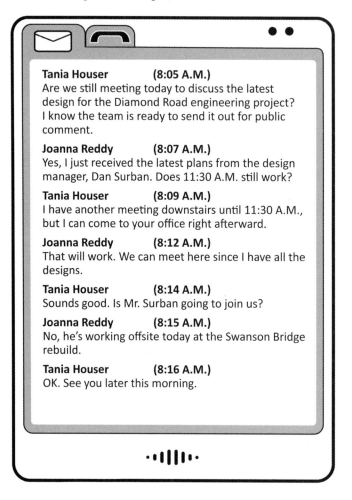

Tania Houser (8:05 A.M.)
Are we still meeting today to discuss the latest design for the Diamond Road engineering project? I know the team is ready to send it out for public comment.

Joanna Reddy (8:07 A.M.)
Yes, I just received the latest plans from the design manager, Dan Surban. Does 11:30 A.M. still work?

Tania Houser (8:09 A.M.)
I have another meeting downstairs until 11:30 A.M., but I can come to your office right afterward.

Joanna Reddy (8:12 A.M.)
That will work. We can meet here since I have all the designs.

Tania Houser (8:14 A.M.)
Sounds good. Is Mr. Surban going to join us?

Joanna Reddy (8:15 A.M.)
No, he's working offsite today at the Swanson Bridge rebuild.

Tania Houser (8:16 A.M.)
OK. See you later this morning.

1. What is suggested about Mr. Surban?

   (A) He is unable to attend a meeting today.
   (B) He does not like the new design plans.
   (C) He is waiting to receive the designs.
   (D) He has an appointment at 11:30 A.M.

2. At 8:14 A.M., what does Ms. Houser mean when she writes "Sounds good"?

   (A) She is ready to send the design for public comment.
   (B) She will contact Mr. Surban about the plans.
   (C) She will look at the designs in Ms. Reddy's office.
   (D) She is planning to meet at the Swanson Bridge.

Questions 3-4 refer to the following order form.

Brixton and Cray
13 Hansdale Road
Ottawa, Ontario K1V 7W1
(613) 555-0409

Order Form

Date: March 6

Customer Name: Jenny Nguyen
                            Balkin Graphic Design

Customer Address: 185 Morris Dr., Ottawa, Ontario, K1A OH2
Payment Information: Billed to Account #281907
Delivery Information: Customer requests delivery no later than
                       5:00 P.M. on March 8.

Item #	Item Description	Quantity	Unit Price	Total
1886	Stapler	8	$9.45	$75.60
1742	Yellow file folders, box of 50	3	$11.20	$33.60
2480	Black ballpoint pens, box of 12	2	$14.00	$28.00
2333	Printer paper, size A4, 500 sheets per package	10	$13.25	$132.50
			Total	$269.70

Order filled by: <u>Chun Liu</u>

---

3. What type of business is Brixton and Cray most likely?

(A) An office-supply store
(B) A design company
(C) A book publisher
(D) An electronics store

4. What is indicated about the order?

(A) It will be shipped to Chun Liu.
(B) It must be paid for in cash.
(C) It should be delivered by March 8.
(D) It includes pens in many different colors.

Questions 5-7 refer to the following schedule.

Bay City **19th Annual Community Festival** **Sunday, August 11**	
9:00 A.M.–5:00 P.M.	*Art Display and Sale* Local artists will be displaying their work in booths along the north side of Elmwood Park, across the street from the community center.
11:00 A.M.–11:30 A.M.	*Family Puppet Show* Popular children's stories will be performed by the Bay City Community Theater Players at the Elmwood Park Outdoor Stage.
11:45 A.M.–2:00 P.M.	*Barbecue Food Tasting* Bay City's own Mesquite Grill will be giving away samples of some of its most popular dishes on the lawn directly behind the Outdoor Stage; stop by and try some!
1:30 P.M.–2:30 P.M.	*Bluegrass Concert* The O'Reilly Quartet will perform classic songs and old-time favorites at the Outdoor Stage.
2:30 P.M.–3:30 P.M.	*Table Tennis Tournament* Individual and team tournaments will be held on Elmwood Park's main lawn. There is no charge to enter the competition, but participants must complete a registration form at the Festival Information Booth.
For more information, visit the Festival Information Booth, located at the Elmwood Park entrance on Cypress Street.	

5. According to the schedule, what will be available for purchase?

   (A) Work by local artists
   (B) Books for children
   (C) Some special foods
   (D) Musical recordings

6. When will a musical event start?

   (A) At 9:00 A.M.
   (B) At 11:00 A.M.
   (C) At 1:30 P.M.
   (D) At 2:30 P.M.

7. Where can registration forms for a sports competition be obtained?

   (A) At the community center
   (B) On the main lawn
   (C) At the park entrance
   (D) On the outdoor stage

Dear Guest:

Your opinions and ideas matter to us. Please take a few minutes to complete this survey form. Thank you!

The Management

For each of the following, please check (V) the category that best describes your experience with us.

	Excellent	*Good*	*Average*	*Fair*	*Poor*
Ease of checking in and out		✓			
Condition of the room		✓			
Overall quality of service	✓				
Housekeeping services			✓		
Overall cleanliness		✓			
Quality of food and beverages				✓	
Price			✓		

Additional Comments

Initially, my husband and I thought that coming here was a mistake. We were upset when, at check-in, we learned that there was no record of our reservation, even though we had booked months in advance and had a confirmation number. However, the clerk at the reception desk resolved the matter satisfactorily by offering us a room that was more comfortable and spacious than the one we had originally reserved. Overall, we were pleased with the professional attitude of your personnel, including the housekeeping staff, the waiters at the restaurant, and the driver of the hotel shuttle bus. We are looking forward to visiting again.

Lisa Browning

8. What is the purpose of this form?

   (A) To ask for opinions about a hotel
   (B) To book a room at a hotel
   (C) To express interest in employment at a hotel
   (D) To indicate methods of payment at a hotel

9. To whom is Ms. Browning addressing her comments?

   (A) The driver of the hotel shuttle bus
   (B) The waiters at the hotel restaurant
   (C) The management of the hotel
   (D) The staff at the hotel reception desk

10. Why was Ms. Browning initially upset?

    (A) The hotel rate was higher than expected.
    (B) The hotel had no record of her reservation.
    (C) Her husband had forgotten to book a room.
    (D) She had lost her confirmation number.

11. What did Ms. Browning like the least about the hotel?

    (A) The attitude of the personnel
    (B) The checkout procedures
    (C) The quality of the meals
    (D) The condition the rooms were in

Questions 12-15 refer to the following online chat discussion.

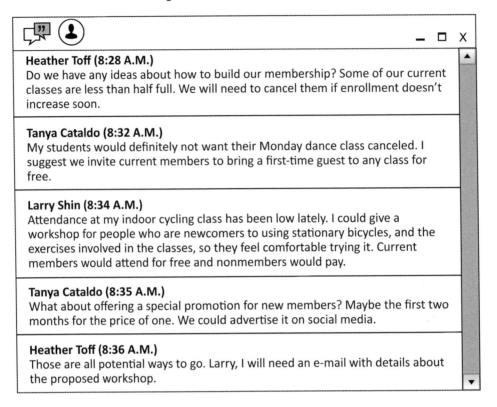

Heather Toff (8:28 A.M.)
Do we have any ideas about how to build our membership? Some of our current classes are less than half full. We will need to cancel them if enrollment doesn't increase soon.

Tanya Cataldo (8:32 A.M.)
My students would definitely not want their Monday dance class canceled. I suggest we invite current members to bring a first-time guest to any class for free.

Larry Shin (8:34 A.M.)
Attendance at my indoor cycling class has been low lately. I could give a workshop for people who are newcomers to using stationary bicycles, and the exercises involved in the classes, so they feel comfortable trying it. Current members would attend for free and nonmembers would pay.

Tanya Cataldo (8:35 A.M.)
What about offering a special promotion for new members? Maybe the first two months for the price of one. We could advertise it on social media.

Heather Toff (8:36 A.M.)
Those are all potential ways to go. Larry, I will need an e-mail with details about the proposed workshop.

12. What are the writers discussing?

(A) How to attract more members
(B) When to schedule new classes
(C) Where to find good locations for workshops
(D) Which membership fees to raise

13. What is indicated about the dance class?

(A) Ms. Toff has canceled it.
(B) Ms. Cataldo teaches it.
(C) It is offered daily.
(D) It has run for two months.

14. At 8:36 A.M., what does Ms. Toff most likely mean when she writes, "Those are all potential ways to go"?

(A) She thinks the ideas are worth considering.
(B) She will consider hiring recent applicants.
(C) She thinks both employees deserve promotions.
(D) She enjoys taking indoor cycling classes.

15. What will Mr. Shin most likely do next?

(A) Invite a guest to his class
(B) Buy advertising on social media
(C) Send a workshop description
(D) Attend a professional development seminar

Harper Fields Business News Online

Search

Home	About Us	Free Materials	Blogs	Contact	My Account

For 25 years, *Harper Fields Business News* (HFBN) has been a major resource for business professionals. In print and online, we offer professional coverage of business news, background analyses, and commentaries on the world of finance. Our Web site offers additional features that are available only to online subscribers. These include staff picks, press releases issued by major players in the business world, and various software applications that allow users to create sophisticated data charts.

To those considering a subscription to our online service, we offer a 30-day free trial. You must be at least 18 years old and provide a valid credit card to subscribe. No money will be charged to your credit card during your trial period. Your card will only be used to automatically upgrade you to paid online subscriber status at the end of the trial period, at which time you will be charged an annual subscription fee of $45.

If you do not wish to become a paid online subscriber, you must cancel the service before the trial period expires. To do so, go to the My Account page on our Web site and select Do Not Upgrade. This action will prevent your credit card from being charged. You will, however, continue to enjoy our service for the remainder of the trial period.

(Get started now!)

16. What is being described on the Web page?

(A) A software program
(B) A trial subscription
(C) A subscription renewal
(D) An advanced business course

17. What are readers asked to provide?

(A) Their credit card details
(B) Their membership number
(C) Their subscription expiration date
(D) Their professional qualifications

18. What is NOT indicated about HFBN?

(A) It offers online software tools.
(B) It covers topics related to finance.
(C) It has been in business for 25 years.
(D) It has stopped publishing in a print format.

■ 연계 문제 풀이 전략

정답과 해설 p.191

Important Notice:

Carter's Farm-Fresh has announced that several cases of their canned vegetables (420g/14.5 oz. size) were shipped to area stores last week with incorrect labels. The mislabeled cans are stamped with product codes G7780 or G7781.

To receive a refund, return the product on or before September 12 to the store at which the purchase was made. Per manufacturer policy, the original **receipt** must be submitted along with the returned product.

Dear Mr. Delgado,

We have received the shipment of canned corn from your store. In two weeks you should receive a check by mail in the amount of $67.50. This should cover the money refunded to your customers when they returned the mislabeled cans. As we discussed, this includes the $7.50 that you refunded a customer who did not have a **receipt**.

We apologize for the inconvenience this has caused you and your patrons.

Sincerely,

Karen Woo

Customer Service Director, Carter's Farm-Fresh

지문 1 공지
1 공지 주요 내용 파악 라벨이 잘못 부착된 제품 반품 및 환불 안내
2 반품 및 환불 정책 확인 9월 12일까지 반품 신청 제조사 Carter's Farm-Fresh의 규정: 반품 시 영수증 지참

지문 2 이메일
1 이메일 주요 내용 파악 제조사 Carter's Farm-Fresh의 직원인 우 씨가 델가도 씨의 가게에서 반품된 제품을 수령한 후 환불 안내
2 특이 사항에 주목 델가도 씨가 반품 영수증이 없는 고객에게 환불한 금액까지 환불 수표에 포함

Q   What is **suggested** about **Ms. Woo**?
(A) She expects to receive additional canned goods.
(B) She will send a check later than she originally promised.
(C) She made an exception to a policy.
(D) She will meet with Mr. Delgado.

연계 문제 | 지문 간 연결 고리 찾기
우 씨는 델가도 씨가 영수증이 없는
고객에게 환불한 금액까지 포함해
수표를 발행했는데, 이는 공지에 명시된
규정과 다르다.
정답 (C) 정책에 예외를 뒀다.
※ 주요 내용만 파악하면서 속독한 후, 질문의
키워드가 있는 지문과 다른 지문 사이의 연
결 고리를 찾는다.

Advertisement + E-mail

Drive Right Rent-A-Car

Special Prices for Spring Getaways–Valid March 30–June 15

Vehicle Class	Features	Base Price
Economy	2 doors Air-conditioning AM/FM stereo Room for four passengers	Now only $39/day!
Intermediate	2 doors Air-conditioning AM/FM stereo with CD player Room for four passengers	Now only $45/day!
Standard	4 doors Air-conditioning AM/FM stereo with CD player Room for five passengers	Now only $50/day!
Premium	4 doors Air-conditioning AM/FM stereo with CD player Room for seven passengers	Now only $68/day!

Limited-time offer. Rental car must be returned by June 15 in order to qualify for base price listed. Base prices do not include surcharges assessed for cars rented at any of our airport locations. We regret that your desired vehicle class may not be available at all Drive Right locations.

E-Mail Message

To:	amanda.j.mitchell@raewyncorp.com
From:	ting.c.hwang@raewyncorp.com
Date:	June 3
Subject:	New reservation

Hi Amanda,

I need to ask for your help again with my upcoming trip to the Kelleysville office. Mr. Jordan has just asked me and our team from the Kelleysville office to go together to a meeting in Riccardi City. For this reason, please change the car rental reservation you made for me earlier. I will pick up the car from the Kelleysville airport on June 13 as originally planned, but then I'll keep it longer than planned; I will drive the group from the Kelleysville office to Riccardi City for the meeting there on June 15. To accommodate the group, I'll need a car that seats six people. I will now be returning the car to the Kelleysville airport on June 17. Finally, if you could change my flight reservation so that I'll return from Kelleysville on the evening of June 17, I would appreciate it.

Ting-Chun

---

1. What class of car will most likely be reserved for Ting-Chun Hwang?

(A) Standard

(B) Premium

2. What is suggested about the base price that Ting-Chun Hwang will pay to rent a car?

(A) It will be different from the base price listed in the advertisement.

(B) It will be lower because he has rented the car from an airport location.

Questions 1-5 refer to the following form and e-mail.

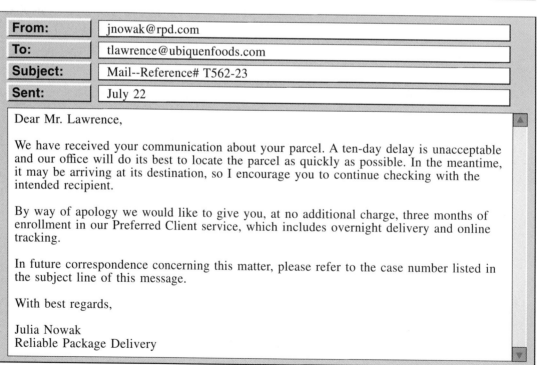

Reliable Package Delivery
Customer Inquiry

Check the box that best describes your inquiry:

_X_ Mail not received	_____ Contents damaged during handling
_____ Mail received after unreasonable delay	_____ Parcel arrived with missing contents

Sender information: **Addressee information:**

Trent Lawrence   Leila Adams
Affiliation: Ubiquen Foods   101 Wilson Court
      230 Aspen Road   Salford 954-372
      Jamestown 733-700

Type of mail: A small parcel

Date mailed: July 12

Description of problem:
The contents include perishable food products with a shelf life of about four weeks.
I would appreciate prompt attention to this inquiry.

Name: Trent Lawrence   **Signature:** _Trent Lawrence_

From:	jnowak@rpd.com
To:	tlawrence@ubiquenfoods.com
Subject:	Mail--Reference# T562-23
Sent:	July 22

Dear Mr. Lawrence,

We have received your communication about your parcel. A ten-day delay is unacceptable and our office will do its best to locate the parcel as quickly as possible. In the meantime, it may be arriving at its destination, so I encourage you to continue checking with the intended recipient.

By way of apology we would like to give you, at no additional charge, three months of enrollment in our Preferred Client service, which includes overnight delivery and online tracking.

In future correspondence concerning this matter, please refer to the case number listed in the subject line of this message.

With best regards,

Julia Nowak
Reliable Package Delivery

1. According to Mr. Lawrence, what is the status of the parcel?

   (A) It was shipped with incorrect contents.
   (B) It has not reached its destination.
   (C) It arrived damaged.
   (D) It arrived with some contents missing.

2. What action does Ms. Nowak recommend taking?

   (A) Visiting the Salford post office
   (B) Calling the Jamestown post office
   (C) Contacting Ms. Adams
   (D) Writing to Ubiquen Foods

3. What is Mr. Lawrence offered?

   (A) Shipping supplies
   (B) Compensation for the value of the package
   (C) A premium service plan
   (D) A free e-mail account

4. In the e-mail, the word "matter" in paragraph 3, line 1, is closest in meaning to

   (A) situation
   (B) reason
   (C) material
   (D) element

5. What is Mr. Lawrence asked to do in future communications?

   (A) Include an identification number
   (B) Contact Ms. Nowak's assistant
   (C) Limit e-mails to one recipient
   (D) Update contact information

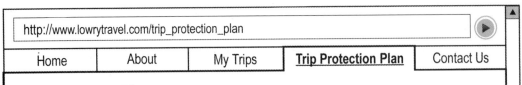

http://www.lowrytravel.com/trip_protection_plan

| Home | About | My Trips | **Trip Protection Plan** | Contact Us |

Trip Protection Plan

You have booked your tour and are eagerly looking forward to it. But unforeseen circumstances sometimes arise. To protect your investment, Lowry Travel offers a reasonably priced Trip Protection Plan.

Our plan offers a full refund if you must cancel your trip because of a documented illness of, or injury to, you or your traveling companion, or a weather emergency, such as a major storm. If you need to cancel for any other reason, you will receive a credit that can be applied to a future trip booked within 18 months of the cancellation. Unlike other plans, ours covers the cost of your airfare as well as lodging costs, even if you did not book your air travel through Lowry Travel.

The Trip Protection Plan must be purchased within five days of your final trip payment and can be canceled within ten days of purchase. To purchase the plan or to cancel a tour, call us at 800-555-0132 or e-mail us at customerservice@lowrytravel.com.

E-mail

To:	customerservice@lowrytravel.com
From:	kay.chung@cmail.com
Date:	July 5
Subject:	Trip cancellation

Dear Customer Service Representative:

My husband and I are currently booked on the Highlights of Europe tour that begins on July 9. However, my employer just suffered a data breach, and all employees are required to report to work next week to attend to the matter. Therefore, with regret, we must cancel. My Trip Protection Plan policy number is HE4587.

Do you have space on the same tour that leaves on August 25? Alternatively, we would also be interested in going on the Italian Cities and Countryside tour that leaves on September 7. Please let me know about the availability as soon as possible so that I can rebook my flights.

Sincerely,

Kay Chung

6. For whom is the Web page likely intended?

(A) Tour guides

(B) Insurance agents

(C) Clients of Lowry Travel

(D) Employees of Lowry Travel

7. What information about the Trip Protection Plan is NOT mentioned?

(A) The cost of the plan

(B) The deadline for canceling

(C) The terms for receiving credit

(D) The details of the plan's coverage

8. What is Ms. Chung entitled to receive?

(A) A full refund

(B) Free lodging

(C) Discounted airfare

(D) Credit toward a future trip

9. What does Ms. Chung suggest in the e-mail?

(A) She works for an airline.

(B) She just started a new job.

(C) She is willing to book a different tour.

(D) She is visiting Europe for the first time.

10. What does Ms. Chung ask Lowry Travel to do?

(A) Rebook her flights

(B) Send her a detailed itinerary

(C) Cancel her Trip Protection Plan

(D) Inform her about space availability

The Camarillo University Medical Center Wednesday Lecture Series Presents

Hospital Management in Urban Areas
Stephen S. Sebastian, Pottstown University
Wednesday, November 12, at 4 P.M.
Medical Center Lecture Hall A
Introduced by Dr. Jann Ericson, Dean of Medicine

Dr. Sebastian is an internationally renowned expert in hospital management and healthcare in urban environments. His latest book on the topic, *Urban Hospitals: New Management Challenges*, has just been published. He teaches hospital administration and public health at the Pottstown University School of Medicine.

His lecture will focus on the challenges presented by urban environments to hospital management and administration, with an emphasis on community relations. He will discuss strategies for leadership and organization in urban communities aimed at helping to build better relationships between hospital administrators and local politicians and community leaders.

The Camarillo University Medical Center Wednesday Lecture Series is funded by a generous gift from the Rosemary Fernandez Memorial Trust. Please contact Dana Goode, assistant to the dean of medicine, by e-mail at dgoode@camarillo.edu if you have any questions about the lecture series.

E-Mail Message	
To:	sssebastian@pottstown.edu
From:	jzericson@camarillo.edu
Date:	October 23
Subject:	final details

Dear Stephen,

I'm so pleased that you'll be coming to speak at our next Wednesday lecture series. I just finished reading your latest book, as have several of my colleagues, and we are eager to hear more about the ideas you present in it.

I want to confirm that, as I mentioned when we spoke on the phone recently, my assistant will be meeting you at the train station to take you to the medical center. Also, Dr. Ahmad al-Janabi, our new dean of students here at Camarillo, has asked if you might be available when the lecture ends around 5:30 P.M. to speak for fifteen minutes or so with some of our students who are considering pursuing careers in public health.

Finally, are you still interested in staying to have dinner with some of the faculty here after the lecture? I have made a reservation for dinner at 6:30 P.M. at the Camarillo Inn—you may remember it from your own student days here. One of us will be happy to drive you back to the train station in order for you to get the 8:45 P.M. train back to Pottstown.

Best regards,

Jann

11. Who is the lecturer?

(A) A hospital administrator
(B) A public health official
(C) A medical school professor
(D) A local politician

12. What will probably be discussed during the lecture?

(A) Communication among hospital managers and community leaders
(B) The latest trends in hospital construction
(C) Ways to obtain funding for lectures at medical centers
(D) Strategies for attracting more doctors to work in urban areas

13. Who will take Dr. Sebastian to the medical center?

(A) Jann Ericson
(B) Rosemary Fernandez
(C) Dana Goode
(D) Ahmad al-Janabi

14. What will most likely happen at 6:30 P.M. on November 12?

(A) Dr. Sebastian's lecture will end.
(B) Some faculty members will have dinner together.
(C) Some students interested in public health careers will meet Dr. Sebastian.
(D) Dr. Sebastian will take a train back to Pottstown.

15. What is implied about Dr. Sebastian?

(A) He applied for the dean of students position at Camarillo University.
(B) He will stay overnight at the Camarillo Inn.
(C) He used to be a student at Camarillo University.
(D) He will present copies of his latest book to faculty members at Camarillo University.

RC

PART 7

MEMO

To: All staff
From: Donna Rutherford, Personnel Director
Date: 2 May
Subject: Guyana Financial Services Communication Guidelines

1. Attendance at departmental and all-staff meetings is expected. You must obtain prior approval from your manager to be excused.

2. Whenever you are out of the office for one or more days, please indicate the dates of your absence on your online calendar and set up an out-of-office notification with those dates for your incoming e-mails and calls. It may be appropriate, although it is not mandatory, to include the name of a colleague who can be contacted in case of urgent matters.

3. In an out-of-office notification, you may also include a brief message to promote a product or service currently being offered by your department. This message type is optional.

Thank you for your attention to these company guidelines.

GUYANA FINANCIAL SERVICES (GFS)
May Calendar of Indira Sharma

Monday	Tuesday	Wednesday	Thursday	Friday
1 May Day Holiday: Office closed	2 Last day to register for CABE conference	3	4 Complete my presentation outline for CABE	5 Begin work on project proposal
8 Lunch out with department trainees	9	10 Work on project proposal	11 Update team by e-mail: project proposal	12 GFS company anniversary dinner 6:00 P.M.
15 Loan inquiry: Mr. and Ms. Hill	16 Retail banking department meeting	17 Work on Hill family mortgage contract	18 Travel to CABE Conference in Suriname	19 CABE
22 CABE	23 Last day-CABE conference	24		

```
┌─────────────────────────────────────────────────────────────────────┐
│ ≡≡≡≡≡≡≡≡≡≡≡≡≡≡≡≡≡≡≡≡≡≡≡≡≡ *E-mail* ≡≡≡≡≡≡≡≡≡≡≡≡≡≡≡≡≡≡≡≡≡≡≡≡≡    ⊏⊐  │
├─────────────────────────────────────────────────────────────────────┤
│  To:       hillfamily@viczonicmail.com.gy                             │
│                                                                       │
│  From:     isharma@gfs.com.gy                                         │
│                                                                       │
│  Date:     22 May                                                     │
│                                                                       │
│  Subject:  Automatic reply-mortgage request update                    │
├─────────────────────────────────────────────────────────────────────┤
│  Thank you for your message. I am out of the office from Thursday,    │
│  18 May, through Tuesday, 23 May, attending the annual conference     │
│  of the Caribbean Association of Bank Employees (CABE). If you        │
│  require an immediate response regarding a residential or             │
│  commercial property loan, please contact Mr. Nathan Westford at      │
│  592-555-0122, or send a message to nwestford@gfs.com.gy.             │
│  Otherwise, I will be happy to respond to you upon my return to       │
│  the office on 24 May.                                                │
│                                                                       │
│  Please note: for first-time buyers, Guyana Financial Services        │
│  offers a series of home-buyer education workshops free of charge.    │
│  Contact us to learn more!                                            │
│                                                                       │
│  Indira Sharma, Senior Loan Officer                                   │
│  Retail Banking                                                       │
└─────────────────────────────────────────────────────────────────────┘
```

16. What is the purpose of the memo?

(A) To announce upcoming events

(B) To call attention to company policies

(C) To make corrections to a calendar

(D) To ask employees to promote new services

17. For what date would Ms. Sharma need her manager's approval to be absent from work?

(A) May 1

(B) May 12

(C) May 16

(D) May 17

18. What is suggested about Ms. Sharma?

(A) She is purchasing a new home.

(B) She will give a speech at a company dinner.

(C) She will be a presenter at a professional conference.

(D) She will be organizing an event on May 9.

19. What detail included in the e-mail is required by the communication guidelines?

(A) The period of May 18 through May 23

(B) The conference name Caribbean Association of Bank Employees

(C) The telephone number of a colleague

(D) The workshops on home-buyer education

20. According to Ms. Sharma, who might want to contact Mr. Westford?

(A) Department trainees

(B) Workshop speakers

(C) CABE members

(D) Loan applicants

Metro Area Business Watch - October

The grand opening of the Ocean Crest Mall in Marlow Bay is scheduled for next spring, and available spaces are filling rapidly. Once the mall opens, business is expected to take off just as quickly. While the Ocean Crest Mall is not the only such establishment in Marlow Bay, it will be the first to open directly onto the boardwalk. The mall will include boutiques, specialty stores, and a variety of food vendors. The mall management is hoping to attract business owners from outside Marlow Bay. According to rental manager Barbara Lancer, a number of the businesses that have rented space are new to the area. "This was by design," she explained. "The Marlow Bay City Council offered the mall owners a tax incentive if we are able to bring new businesses to Marlow Bay. We're still a little short of our goal to have 75% of our spaces rented to nonlocal businesses. We are offering reduced rental prices on new leases for out-of-town businesses."

Applications from business owners looking to lease retail and restaurant space will be accepted until the December 15 deadline. Interested business owners are encouraged to contact Lancer by e-mail at blancer@oceancrestmall.com.

From:	Tracy Fernandez <tfernandez@kmail.com>
To:	Barbara Lancer <blancer@oceancrestmall.com>
Date:	October 9
Subject:	Available space

Dear Ms. Lancer,

I am a friend of Eric Raye, owner of The Shoe Horn, and he suggested that I contact you about a rental space in the Ocean Crest Mall. He told me about a great benefit that he received that is available to business owners like me. I own Edge Fashion and sell contemporary women's apparel. I have two retail locations in the nearby city of Hazelton, and I am considering expanding to Marlow Bay. If possible, I would like to be near my friend's store, but I do not want a space that is beside a restaurant or food service. A space on the boardwalk side that overlooks the beach would be ideal.

Could you please send me a map of the mall showing any available spaces that might meet my needs? Also, could you provide information about the size of each space and rental fees?

Thank you in advance,

Tracy Fernandez

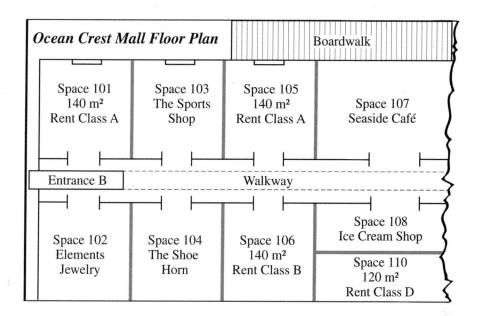

Ocean Crest Mall Floor Plan

Boardwalk

| Space 101 140 m² Rent Class A | Space 103 The Sports Shop | Space 105 140 m² Rent Class A | Space 107 Seaside Café |

Entrance B — Walkway

| Space 102 Elements Jewelry | Space 104 The Shoe Horn | Space 106 140 m² Rent Class B | Space 108 Ice Cream Shop |
| | | | Space 110 120 m² Rent Class D |

21. What is the purpose of the article?

(A) To explain why the opening of a new mall has been postponed

(B) To announce plans to build a new mall

(C) To review the stores and restaurants in a new mall

(D) To encourage business owners to rent space in a new mall

22. In the article, the phrase "take off" in paragraph 1, line 4, is closest in meaning to

(A) remove

(B) discount

(C) increase quickly

(D) leave suddenly

23. What is stated about the Ocean Crest Mall?

(A) It will be the only mall in Marlow Bay.

(B) It will have direct access to the boardwalk.

(C) It will include 75 retail spaces to rent.

(D) It will open for business on December 15.

24. What is indicated about Mr. Raye?

(A) He is a friend of Ms. Lancer.

(B) His business was the first to open.

(C) He is paying a reduced rental rate.

(D) His store opens onto the beach.

25. What space will Ms. Fernandez most likely be interested in renting?

(A) Space 101

(B) Space 105

(C) Space 106

(D) Space 110

Skin Product Shows Promise

12 October—Ricoeur Pharmaceuticals, a multinational corporation with offices in Canada, France, and South Korea, said today that its experimental cream for excessively dry skin, Dermava, has proved highly effective in a recent research study. Ricoeur highlighted the encouraging results indicating the cream's long-lasting effectiveness. This bodes well for Ricoeur, as the cream, if released, could compensate for the limited growth that Ricoeur has experienced over the past five years.

Dr. Laura Scheffner, an expert consultant, noted, "I was pleasantly surprised by the immediate benefits of the cream. Participants felt relief after a single application." Dr. Heung Soo Choi, a senior researcher for Ricoeur, added that the safety of the medication was also confirmed during the study.

A spokesperson for Ricoeur announced that, while initial results are promising, a follow-up study with very young and elderly participants must be pursued. Only then can the cream be approved by the International Medication Association (IMA) and become available on the market. The IMA is expected to begin its review at the end of the year.

Positions Available at Ricoeur Pharmaceuticals, Ottawa, Canada

Ricoeur Pharmaceuticals has immediate openings for nearly 100 administrative, customer service, and warehouse jobs supporting the launch of Dermava, a new medical treatment for dry skin. Positions do not require previous experience, are part time, and end in December, though exceptional workers may be offered extended assignments. Those applying for customer service positions should be fully bilingual in French and English. Those applying for warehouse positions must be able to work nights and weekends. Candidates can submit their applications at this time by visiting www.ricoeurpharma.ca. Interested parties can also attend group interviews on 11 March at 9:00 A.M. at our production facility, 72B Industrial Way, Ottawa, K2A 3P1. Be sure to bring your résumé and reference list.

RICOEUR PHARMACEUTICALS

To:	Ahmed Abedi
From:	Simona Jordan
Subject:	Ricoeur Reference
Date:	11 March, 1:43 P.M.

Dr. Abedi,

I wanted to thank you for providing a reference for me. I was one of about twenty applicants who was hired today at Ricoeur Pharmaceuticals. My first day will be this coming Monday, and I'll be working directly after your evening class. I may have to leave class a few minutes early to catch the 7:15 P.M. bus into town. I hope that won't be a problem.

Thanks again.

Best,
Simona Jordan

26. What does Dr. Scheffner mention about Dermava?

(A) It works very quickly.

(B) It should be used twice a day.

(C) It is surprisingly inexpensive.

(D) It can be used for up to three days.

27. According to the article, what does Ricoeur Pharmaceuticals plan to do?

(A) Develop safer creams

(B) Conduct additional research

(C) Compensate the study participants

(D) Review the production schedule

28. What is implied about Ricoeur Pharmaceuticals?

(A) Its production facility is located in France.

(B) Its laboratories will be inspected in October.

(C) Its latest medication has been approved by the IMA.

(D) Its products have gained in popularity during the past five years.

29. What is indicated by the advertisement?

(A) Applicants should have previous work experience.

(B) Group interviews will be held over several days.

(C) The application process is very time-consuming.

(D) The available positions are temporary.

30. For what job was Ms. Jordan most likely hired?

(A) An administrative job

(B) A customer service job

(C) A research job

(D) A warehouse job

■ 감사

as a token of appreciation
감사의 표시로

be grateful for ~에 감사하다

compensate 보상하다

complimentary 무료의

courteous 공손한, 정중한

delighted 기쁜

on behalf of ~을 대표하여, 대신하여

patronage 애용

recognize 인정하다, 치하하다

■ 초대

banquet 연회

broadcast 방송하다

charity 자선 (단체)

compassionate 인정 많은, 동정적인

cordially 진심으로, 다정하게

credit 칭찬, 인정

decent 괜찮은, 품위 있는

devote 바치다, 헌신하다

donor 기증자

fundraiser 모금행사

■ 사업

acquire 획득하다, 인수하다

approve 승인하다

asset 재산

bid 입찰에 응하다

endorse 보증하다, 지지하다

establishment 설립, 기관

generate 산출하다, 만들어 내다

patent 특허

profitable 수익성 좋은 (=lucrative)

prototype 원형, 시제품

■ 구매 / 할인

affordable 가격이 적당한

at no cost 무료로 (=free of charge)

extend 늘이다, 연장하다

voucher 상품권, 쿠폰

giveaway 증정품, 경품

installment 할부

inventory 재고, 재고 목록

markdown 가격 인하

range 범위(가 ~에 이르다)

redeem 현금이나 상품으로 바꾸다

■ 추천

certificate 증명서

considerate 신중한, 사려 깊은

cooperation 협동, 협력

enthusiastic 열성적인

expertise 전문 지식

potential 잠재력 있는

promote 승진시키다, 홍보하다

prospective 장래성 있는, 유망한

qualification 자격 요건

reference 추천서, 추천인

■ 자금

contribution 기부, 공헌

deposit 보증금; 입금하다

exceed 초과하다

financial 금융의, 재무의

generous 후한, 너그러운

monetary donation 금전적 기부

possess 소유하다

property 재산, 부동산

reimburse 상환하다, 변제하다

withdraw 인출하다

■ 축하 / 기념

anniversary 기념일

cater 음식을 공급하다

celebrate 축하하다

eligible 자격이 있는 (=entitled)

honor 명예; 기리다

in advance 사전에, 미리

plaque 명판, 상패

refreshments 다과

retirement 은퇴

venue 장소

■ 문제 / 사과

apology 사과

concern 관심사, 우려

defective 결함 있는

delay 지연시키다 (=postpone)

disruption 중단

dissatisfied 불만족스러운

insufficient 불충분한

patience 참을성

regretful 유감스러운

struggle 고군분투하다

■ 경제 / 경영

aid 원조, 지원; 돕다

aspiring 장차 ~이 되려는

boost 북돋우다

competitor 경쟁업체

enormous 거대한

entrepreneur 기업가

executive 임원; 행정의

expansion 확장

investment 투자

prosperous 번영하는, 번창하는

■ 부동산

district 구역

floor plan 평면도

fully-furnished 내부가 완비된

lease 임대하다

real estate agent 부동산 중개인

rent 임대료; 임대하다

residential 주거용의

separate 분리된

tenant 세입자

utilities 공공요금

■ 서비스 1

around the clock 24시간 내내

atmosphere 분위기

exemplary 본보기가 되는

expire 만료되다

hospitality 서비스업, 환대

subscribe 구독하다

substitute 대체하다; 대체품

meet demands 수요를 충족시키다

termination 종결

under the terms of 조항에 따라

■ 전자제품 / 가구

appliance 전자제품

cutting-edge 최신식의
(= state-of-the-art)

furnishing 가구

light fixture 조명

instructions 설명서

vacuum cleaner 진공 청소기

valid 유효한

vendor 상인

warehouse 창고

warranty 품질보증(서)

■ 커뮤니티

grant 승인하다; 보조금

make arrangement 준비하다

make an effort 노력하다 (= endeavor)

mayor 시장

much-anticipated 매우 기대되는

municipal 시의, 지방 자치의

prestigious 명망 있는

proceeds 수익

publicize 홍보하다

town hall 시청

■ 서비스 2

accommodate 수용하다

customized 맞춤식의

exclusively 독점적으로

practical 실용적인

promotional material 홍보 자료

reasonable price 적당한 가격

reliable 믿을 만한

renew 갱신하다

specialize in ~을 전문으로 하다

testimonial 추천의 글

■ 주문

account 계정, 계좌

charge 요금(을 부과하다)

confirm 확인하다, 확정하다

due 회비; 지불 기일이 된

estimate 견적 (= quote)

in stock 재고가 있는

in transit 수송 중인

outstanding balance 미지불 잔액

standing order 고정[계속] 주문

statements 명세서

■ 식당

appetite 식욕

entrée 주요리

assortment 모둠

cuisine 요리(법)

culinary 요리의, 주방의

dip (소스 등에) 담그다

family-owned 가족 소유의

ingredient 재료, 성분

platter 여러 음식을 차려 놓은 요리

signature dish 대표 요리

■ 상품

apparel 옷

artifact 공예품, 인공물

bulk order 대량 주문

compact 소형의

craft 공예

durable 내구성이 좋은

exquisite 정교한, 매우 아름다운

portable 휴대용의

versatile 다재다능한, 다용도의

well-suited 적절한, 잘 어울리는

■ 청구 / 결제

amount 액수, 금액

billing address 청구 주소

deduct 빼다, 공제하다

expedite 신속히 처리하다

incur 초래하다, 발생시키다

measurement 치수, 측정

partial payment 부분 지불

quantity 수량

reduction 할인, 축소

status 상태

■ 구인 1

applicant 지원자

benefits 복지 혜택

candidate 후보자

certified 공인된

cover letter 자기소개서

degree 학위

fluent 능숙한

human resources 인사부

multi-lingual 여러 언어를 구사하는

negotiation 협상

■ 구인 2

preference 우대사항

primary duty 주요 업무

proficiency 능숙함

promising 전도유망한

qualified 자격을 갖춘

relevant experience 관련 경력

required 필수적인

responsibilities 책무

salary requirement 희망 연봉

temporary 임시의, 임시직의

■ 회사 생활

absence 부재, 결석

achieve 달성하다

attendance record 출근 기록

division 부서

duplicate 복사하다

extension 내선번호

job descriptions 직무 기술서

labor 근로, 노동

on duty 근무 중인

performance evaluation 업무 평가

■ 회의

address 다루다, 취급하다

the board of directors 이사회

committee 위원회

make a decision 결정을 내리다

minutes 회의록 (= proceedings)

nomination 지명, 임명

nominee 후보

outline 약술하다

shareholder 주주 (= stockholder)

unanimous 만장일치의

■ 정책 변경

activate 작동시키다, 활성화시키다

alternative entrance 대체 출입구

appraisal 평가

compensation 보상

expenditure 지출

immediate supervisor 직속 상관

install 설치하다

mandatory 의무적인, 필수적인

tutorial 교육 자료

violation 위반

■ 행사

awards ceremony 시상식

drawing 추첨, 제비뽑기

entry 입장, 출품(작)

flat rate 고정 요금

foster 촉진하다, 조성하다

function 대규모 행사[파티]

mark 기념하다 (= celebrate)

recognized 인정받은

spectator 관중

tentative 잠정적인

■ 대회

be suitable for ~에 적합하다

competition 경쟁, 대회

content 내용

depict 묘사하다

electronically 컴퓨터로, 온라인으로

foremost 가장 중요한, 맨 앞의

judge 심사위원

on a first-come, first-served basis 선착순으로

participate in ~에 참가하다

precede ~에 앞서다

■ 건강 / 의료

antibiotic 항생제, 항생물질의

contagious 전염성의

diagnosis (병원) 진단, 진찰

immune 면역성이 있는

infect 감염시키다

over the counter 처방전 없이 살 수 있는

pharmaceutical 제약(의)

prescription 처방(전)

symptom 증상

vaccinate 예방 접종하다

■ 환경

climate change 기후 변화

conservation 보존, 보호

contamination 오염

dispose of ~을 버리다, 처분하다

endangered 멸종 위기에 처한

environmentally friendly 친환경적인

extinction 멸종, 소멸

pollutant 오염 물질

solar power 태양열

species 종

■ 관광

accommodations 숙소

attraction 명소

excursion 여행

landscape 풍경

lodge 산장

picturesque 그림 같은

scenic 경치가 좋은

spectacular 장관인

stunning 놀랄 만큼 멋진, 훌륭한

vacancy 빈방, 빈 자리

■ 여행 1

amenities 생활 편의 시설

botanic garden 식물원

budget 예산; 저렴한

courtesy bus 무료 버스

customs 세관

departure 출발

dining establishment 식당

exotic 이국적인

expedition 탐험

fatigue 피로, 피곤

■ 여행 2

house 수용하다

immigration 출입국 관리소

itinerary 여행 일정표

outskirts 변두리, 교외

off season 비수기

ruins 폐허, 유적

rural 시골풍의 (=rustic)

stopover 경유, 단기간 체류

vessel 선박, 배

voyage 항해(하다)

■ 공사

aim 목표; 겨냥하다

annex 부속 건물

interrupt 방해하다, 중단시키다

plumbing 배관 (작업)

procedure 절차

put into actions 조치를 취하다

repave 도로를 재포장하다 (=resurface)

resume 재개하다

under construction 공사 중인

upon completion 완공 시에

■ 도로 / 교통

be advised ~을 권고받다

boulevard 대로

duration 기간

encounter 직면하다, 맞닥뜨리다

fine 벌금, 과태료

intersection 교차로

lane 길, 차선

motorist 운전자

pedestrian 보행자

speed limit 속도 제한

■ 건물 / 건설

adjacent 인접한

architect 건축가

capacity 수용력, 능력

convert 전환하다

deterioration 악화, 하락

excavation 발굴

insulation 단열

proximity 인접, 근접

refurbish 재단장하다

restoration 복구, 복원

■ 문화 / 예술

acclaimed 호평 받는

admission 입장

author 작가

award-winning 수상 경력이 있는

critic 비평가

extend an invitation 초대장을 보내다

feature 특집; 포함하다

inspiration 영감

statue 조각상

take place 열리다, 일어나다

■ 전시

artifact 공예품

artwork 작품

collection 소장품

commemorate 기념하다

contemporary art 현대 예술

exhibition 전시회

existing 현존하는

gathering 모임

host 주최하다

material 재료, 자료

■ 공연

choir 합창단

intermission 중간 휴식 시간

masterpiece 명작, 걸작

overwhelming 압도적인

poet 시인

premiere 개봉, 초연

prohibit 금지하다

remarkable 주목할 만한

star 주연(을 맡다)

usher (극장 등의) 안내인

ETS TOEIC

기출문제 한국 독점출간

토익® 단기공략
750+

정답과 해설

LC RC

정답과 해설

PART 1 LC

Unit 01 인물 등장 사진

● 실전 **도움닫기** 본책 p. 021

1 (A) **2** (C) **3** (A) **4** (A)

1

(A) He's <u>standing</u> near a sign.
(B) He's <u>opening</u> his backpack.
(C) He's <u>taking</u> a photograph.
(D) He's <u>fishing</u> in the pond.

(A) 남자가 표지판 근처에 서 있다.
(B) 남자가 배낭을 열고 있다.
(C) 남자가 사진을 찍고 있다.
(D) 남자가 연못에서 낚시를 하고 있다.

해설 | 1인 등장 사진 - 호숫가
(A) **정답**: 남자가 표지판(sign) 근처에 서 있는(is standing) 모습을 잘 묘사했으므로 정답이다.
(B) **동작 묘사 오답**: 남자가 배낭을 열고 있는(is opening) 모습이 아니다.
(C) **동작 묘사 오답**: 남자가 사진을 찍고 있는(is taking a photograph) 모습이 아니다.
(D) **동작 묘사 오답**: 남자가 낚시를 하고 있는(is fishing) 모습이 아니다.

2

(A) The women are <u>standing</u> next to the water.
(B) The women are <u>getting</u> on their bicycles.
(C) The women are <u>resting</u> on a bench.
(D) The women are <u>walking</u> together.

(A) 여자들이 물가에 서 있다.
(B) 여자들이 자전거에 올라 타고 있다.
(C) 여자들이 벤치에서 쉬고 있다.
(D) 여자들이 함께 걷고 있다.

해설 | 2인 이상 등장 사진 - 공원
(A) **동작 묘사 오답**: 여자들이 물가에 서 있는(are standing) 모습이 아니다.
(B) **동작 묘사 오답**: 여자들이 자전거에 올라타고 있는(are getting on) 모습이 아니다.
(C) **정답**: 여자들이 벤치에 앉아 쉬고 있는(are resting) 모습을 잘 묘사했으므로 정답이다.

(D) **동작 묘사 오답**: 여자들이 걷고 있는(are walking) 모습이 아니다.

3

(A) A man is <u>wearing</u> headphones.
(B) A man is <u>propping</u> a guitar against a couch.
(C) A man is <u>hanging</u> a picture next to a door.
(D) A man is <u>moving</u> a couch toward a wall.

(A) 남자가 헤드폰을 끼고 있다.
(B) 남자가 기타를 소파에 받쳐 놓고 있다.
(C) 남자가 문 옆에 그림을 걸고 있다.
(D) 남자가 소파를 벽 쪽으로 옮기고 있다.

해설 | 1인 등장 사진 - 거실
(A) **정답**: 남자가 헤드폰을 착용하고 있는(is wearing) 상태를 잘 묘사했으므로 정답이다.
(B) **동작 묘사 오답**: 남자가 기타를 소파에 받쳐 놓고 있는(is propping) 모습이 아니다.
(C) **동작 묘사 오답**: 그림은 문 옆에 걸려 있는 상태이며, 남자가 걸고 있는(is hanging) 모습이 아니다.
(D) **동작 묘사 오답**: 남자가 소파를 벽 쪽으로 옮기고 있는(is moving) 모습이 아니다.

어휘 | prop A against B A를 B에 받쳐 놓다[세우다]

4

(A) Cars are <u>parked</u> on one side of the street.
(B) Lines are <u>being painted</u> on the road.
(C) A man is <u>stepping</u> onto a curb.
(D) A man is <u>getting</u> into a vehicle.

(A) 차들이 거리 한쪽에 주차되어 있다.
(B) 도로에 선들이 그려지고 있다.
(C) 남자가 도로 경계석에 올라서고 있다.
(D) 남자가 차량에 탑승하고 있다.

해설 | 사람·사물 혼합 사진 - 거리
(A) **정답**: 차들이 거리 한쪽(one side of the street)에 주차되어 있는(are parked) 상태를 잘 묘사했으므로 정답이다.
(B) **진행 상황 묘사 오답**: 도로에 선들이 그려지고 있는(are being painted) 상황이 아니다.
(C) **동작 묘사 오답**: 남자가 도로 경계석(curb)에 올라서고 있는(is stepping onto) 모습이 아니다.
(D) **동작 묘사 오답**: 남자가 차량에 탑승하고 있는(is getting into) 모습이 아니다.

어휘 | step onto ~에 올라서다 curb 도로 경계석 vehicle 차량

● ETS 실전문제

1 (A)	**2** (A)	**3** (B)	**4** (B)	**5** (B)	**6** (A)
7 (B)	**8** (B)	**9** (C)	**10** (D)	**11** (D)	**12** (D)

1

(A) The man is cleaning a vehicle.
(B) The man is getting out of a car.
(C) The man is putting on a hat.
(D) The man is changing a tire.

(A) 남자가 세차를 하고 있다.
(B) 남자가 차에서 내리고 있다.
(C) 남자가 모자를 착용해보고 있다.
(D) 남자가 타이어를 갈고 있다.

해설 | 1인 등장 사진 - 세차장
(A) **정답:** 남자가 세차하고 있는(is cleaning) 모습을 잘
묘사했으므로 정답이다.
(B) **동작 묘사 오답:** 남자가 차에서 내리고 있는(is getting out of)
모습이 아니다.
(C) **동작 묘사 오답:** 남자가 이미 모자를 쓴 상태로, 착용해보고
있는(is putting on) 모습이 아니다.
(D) **동작 묘사 오답:** 남자가 타이어를 교체하고 있는(is changing)
모습이 아니다.

2

(A) Some people are stocking shelves.
(B) Some people are paying for groceries.
(C) A man is taping up a box of merchandise.
(D) A woman is stacking shopping baskets.

(A) 사람들이 선반에 물건을 채우고 있다.
(B) 사람들이 식료품 값을 지불하고 있다.
(C) 남자가 물품 상자를 테이프로 붙이고 있다.
(D) 여자가 장바구니들을 쌓고 있다.

해설 | 2인 이상 등장 사진 - 상점
(A) **정답:** 사람들이 선반에 물건을 채우고 있는(are stocking)
모습을 잘 묘사했으므로 정답이다.
(B) **사진에 없는 명사 언급·동작 묘사 오답:** 사진 속에
식료품(groceries)이 보이지 않으며, 사람들이 값을 지불하고
있는(are paying for) 모습도 아니다.
(C) **동작 묘사 오답:** 남자가 물품 상자를 테이프로 붙이고 있는(is
taping up) 모습이 아니다.
(D) **사진에 없는 명사 언급·동작 묘사 오답:** 사진 속에
장바구니들(shopping baskets)이 보이지 않으며, 여자가
뭔가를 쌓아 올리고 있는(is stacking) 모습도 아니다.

어휘 | stock (식품, 책 등으로) 채우다 **grocery** 식료품
merchandise 물품, 상품 **stack** 쌓다, 포개다

3

(A) Plates are being put in the dishwasher.
(B) Serving trays have been filled with food.
(C) A woman is handing out some menus.
(D) A woman is wiping off the counter.

(A) 접시들이 식기세척기 안에 놓이고 있다.
(B) 쟁반들이 음식으로 채워졌다.
(C) 여자가 메뉴를 나눠주고 있다.
(D) 여자가 조리대를 닦아내고 있다.

해설 | 사람·사물 혼합 사진 - 식당
(A) **사진에 없는 명사 언급 오답:** 사진 속에
식기세척기(dishwasher)가 보이지 않는다.
(B) **정답:** 쟁반들이 음식으로 채워져 있는(have been filled with)
상태를 잘 묘사했으므로 정답이다.
(C) **사진에 없는 명사 언급 오답:** 사진 속에 메뉴(menus)가 보이지
않는다.
(D) **동작 묘사 오답:** 여자가 앞에 있는 조리대를 닦고 있는(is
wiping off) 모습이 아니다.

어휘 | dishwasher 식기세척기 **be filled with** ~로 채워지다 **hand
out** 나눠주다 **wipe off** 닦아내다 **counter** 조리대, 계산대

4

(A) He's placing groceries on a shelf.
(B) He's unloading a shopping cart.
(C) He's purchasing food at a counter.
(D) He's shutting the door of a van.

(A) 남자가 선반에 식료품을 놓고 있다.
(B) 남자가 쇼핑 카트에서 짐을 내리고 있다.
(C) 남자가 계산대에서 음식을 사고 있다.
(D) 남자가 승합차의 문을 닫고 있다.

해설 | 1인 등장 사진 - 주차장
(A) **사진에 없는 명사 언급 오답:** 식료품을 놓고 있는 곳은
선반(shelf)이 아니라 차량이다.
(B) **정답:** 남자가 쇼핑 카트에서 짐을 내리고 있는(is unloading)
모습을 잘 묘사했으므로 정답이다.
(C) **사진에 없는 명사 언급 오답:** 사진 속에 계산대(counter)가
보이지 않는다.
(D) **동작 묘사 오답:** 남자가 승합차의 문을 닫고 있는(is shutting)
모습이 아니다.

어휘 | place 놓다, 두다 **unload** ~에서 짐을 내리다 **purchase**
구입하다

LC

PART 1

5

(A) Some aprons are hanging from a hook.
(B) Some cooks are working in a kitchen.
(C) Some dishes are being washed in a sink.
(D) Some food is being put into an oven.

(A) 앞치마들이 옷걸이에 걸려 있다.
(B) 요리사들이 주방에서 일하고 있다.
(C) 접시들이 개수대에서 씻기고 있다.
(D) 음식이 오븐에 넣어지고 있다.

해설 | **사람·사물 혼합 사진 - 주방**
(A) **상태 묘사 오답:** 앞치마들이 옷걸이에 걸려 있는(are hanging) 상태가 아니다.
(B) **정답:** 주방에서 일하고 있는(are working) 요리사들의 모습을 잘 묘사했으므로 정답이다.
(C) **진행 상황 묘사 오답:** 접시들이 씻기고 있는(are being washed) 상황이 아니다.
(D) **진행 상황 묘사 오답:** 음식이 오븐에 넣어지고 있는(is being put) 상황이 아니다.

어휘 | apron 앞치마 hook 걸이, 고리

6

(A) A presentation is being shown on a screen.
(B) Equipment is being stored in a closet.
(C) A clock is being removed from a wall.
(D) Participants are being given some documents.

(A) 화면에 프레젠테이션이 보여지고 있다.
(B) 장비가 벽장에 보관되어 있다.
(C) 시계가 벽에서 떼어지고 있다.
(D) 참가자들에게 서류가 주어지고 있다.

해설 | **사람·사물 혼합 사진 - 강당**
(A) **정답:** 화면에 프레젠테이션이 보여지고 있는(is being shown) 상황을 잘 묘사했으므로 정답이다.
(B) **상태 묘사 오답:** 장비가 벽장(closet)에 보관되어(is being stored) 있는지 사진상으로 확인할 수 없다. 참고로, be being stored는 물건이 보관되어 있는 상태를 묘사한다.
(C) **진행 상황 묘사 오답:** 시계가 벽에서 떼어지고 있는(is being removed) 상황이 아니다.
(D) **진행 상황 묘사 오답:** 참가자들에게 서류가 주어지고 있는(are being given) 상황이 아니다.

어휘 | presentation 발표, 프레젠테이션 equipment 장비 store 보관하다, 저장하다 participant 참가자

7

(A) She's filling some water bottles.
(B) She's writing in a notebook.
(C) She's talking on the phone.
(D) She's holding a coffee cup.

(A) 여자가 물병들을 채우고 있다.
(B) 여자가 공책에 글씨를 쓰고 있다.
(C) 여자가 전화로 이야기하고 있다.
(D) 여자가 커피잔을 들고 있다.

해설 | **1인 등장 사진 - 식당**
(A) **사진에 없는 명사 언급·동작 묘사 오답:** 사진 속에 물병들(water bottles)이 보이지 않으며, 여자가 뭔가를 채우고 있는(is filling) 모습도 아니다.
(B) **정답:** 여자가 공책에 글씨를 쓰고 있는(is writing) 모습을 잘 묘사했으므로 정답이다.
(C) **동작 묘사 오답:** 여자가 통화하고 있는(is talking on the phone) 모습이 아니다.
(D) **동작 묘사 오답:** 여자가 커피잔을 들고 있는(is holding) 모습이 아니다.

8

(A) The man is seated in a waiting area.
(B) The woman is handing over a clipboard.
(C) The man is reaching for an item on a shelf.
(D) The woman is looking through a file cabinet.

(A) 남자가 대기실에 앉아 있다.
(B) 여자가 클립보드를 건네고 있다.
(C) 남자가 선반의 물건을 잡으려고 손을 뻗고 있다.
(D) 여자가 문서 보관함을 훑어보고 있다.

해설 | **2인 이상 등장 사진 - 병원**
(A) **동작 묘사 오답:** 남자가 대기실에 앉아 있는(is seated) 모습이 아니다.
(B) **정답:** 여자가 남자에게 클립보드를 건네고 있는(is handing over) 모습을 잘 묘사했으므로 정답이다.
(C) **동작 묘사 오답:** 남자가 선반의 물건을 잡으려고 손을 뻗고 있는(is reaching for) 모습이 아니다.
(D) **동작 묘사 오답:** 여자가 문서 보관함을 훑어보고 있는(is looking through) 모습이 아니다.

어휘 | hand over 건네다, 인도하다 reach for ~를 잡으려고 손을 뻗다 look through 살펴보다, 훑어보다 file cabinet 문서 보관함

9

(A) Workers are climbing up some steps.
(B) Some groceries are being loaded into a car.
(C) The back door of a truck has been opened.
(D) A car is turning at a stoplight.

(A) 인부들이 계단을 오르고 있다.
(B) 식료품들이 차에 실리고 있다.
(C) 트럭의 뒷문이 열려 있다.
(D) 자동차 한 대가 신호등에서 방향을 바꾸고 있다.

해설 | 사람·사물 혼합 사진 - 도로

(A) 동작 묘사 오답: 인부들이 건물의 계단을 올라가고 있는(are climbing up) 모습이 아니다.
(B) 사진에 없는 명사 언급 오답: 차에 실리고 있는 것은 식료품(groceries)이 아니다.
(C) 정답: 트럭의 뒷문이 열려 있는(has been opened) 상태를 잘 묘사했으므로 정답이다.
(D) 사진에 없는 명사 언급·동작 묘사 오답: 사진 속에 신호등(stoplight)이 보이지 않으며, 자동차가 방향을 바꾸고 있는(is turning) 모습도 아니다.

어휘 | climb 오르다 stoplight 신호등, 정지 신호

10

(A) A man is distributing some handouts.
(B) A woman is pointing at a computer screen.
(C) Some people are getting up from a table.
(D) Some people are reviewing documents.

(A) 남자가 인쇄물을 나눠주고 있다.
(B) 여자가 컴퓨터 화면을 가리키고 있다.
(C) 사람들이 탁자에서 일어서고 있다.
(D) 사람들이 서류를 검토하고 있다.

해설 | 2인 이상 등장 사진 - 사무실

(A) 동작 묘사 오답: 남자가 인쇄물을 나눠주고 있는(is distributing) 모습이 아니다.
(B) 동작 묘사 오답: 여자가 뒤에 있는 컴퓨터 화면을 가리키고 있는(is pointing at) 모습이 아니다.
(C) 동작 묘사 오답: 사람들이 탁자에서 일어나고 있는(are getting up) 모습이 아니다.
(D) 정답: 사람들이 서류를 검토하고 있는(are reviewing) 모습을 잘 묘사했으므로 정답이다.

어휘 | distribute 나누어 주다 handout 인쇄물, 유인물 review 검토하다

11

(A) A man is paying for a meal.
(B) A man is washing dishes.
(C) A man is reaching for a coat on a hook.
(D) A man is selecting some food from a buffet.

(A) 남자가 식사비를 지불하고 있다.
(B) 남자가 설거지를 하고 있다.
(C) 남자가 옷걸이에 걸린 코트를 집으려고 손을 뻗고 있다.
(D) 남자가 뷔페에서 음식을 고르고 있다.

해설 | 1인 등장 사진 - 식당

(A) 동작 묘사 오답: 남자가 식사비를 지불하는(is paying for) 모습이 아니다.
(B) 동작 묘사 오답: 남자가 들고 있는 그릇을 설거지하는(is washing) 모습이 아니다.
(C) 사진에 없는 명사 언급·동작 묘사 오답: 사진 속에 옷걸이(hook)가 보이지 않으며, 남자가 코트를 집으려고 손을 뻗고 있는(is reaching for) 모습이 아니다.
(D) 정답: 남자가 뷔페에서 음식을 고르고 있는(is selecting) 모습을 잘 묘사했으므로 정답이다.

12

(A) Some people are resting on a bench.
(B) Some people are waiting in line.
(C) Some lights are being installed.
(D) Some people are looking at artwork.

(A) 사람들이 벤치에서 쉬고 있다.
(B) 사람들이 줄을 서서 기다리고 있다.
(C) 조명들이 설치되고 있다.
(D) 사람들이 미술품을 감상하고 있다.

해설 | 사람·사물 혼합 사진 - 전시실

(A) 동작 묘사 오답: 사진 속에 벤치가 있지만, 사람들이 벤치에서 쉬고 있는(are resting) 모습은 아니다.
(B) 동작 묘사 오답: 사람들이 줄을 서서 기다리고 있는(are waiting in line) 모습이 아니다.
(C) 진행 상황 묘사 오답: 조명들이 설치되고 있는(are being installed) 상황이 아니다.
(D) 정답: 사람들이 미술품을 감상하고 있는(are looking at) 모습을 잘 묘사했으므로 정답이다.

어휘 | wait in line 줄 서서 기다리다 install 설치하다

Unit 02 사물/풍경 사진

● 실전 도움닫기

본책 p.025

1 (D) **2** (B) **3** (D) **4** (A)

1

(A) Bookcases are being assembled.
(B) A cart is being pushed along a hallway.
(C) Packages have been placed on the floor.
(D) Boxes are stacked on a cart.

(A) 책장들이 조립되고 있다.
(B) 수레가 복도를 따라 밀리고 있다.
(C) 소포들이 바닥에 놓여 있다.
(D) 상자들이 수레 위에 쌓여 있다.

해설 | **사물 사진 - 실내**
(A) **진행 상황 묘사 오답:** 책장들이 조립되고 있는(are being assembled) 상황이 아니다.
(B) **진행 상황 묘사 오답:** 수레가 복도를 따라 밀리고 있는(is being pushed) 상황이 아니다.
(C) **위치 묘사 오답:** 소포들이 수레 위에 놓여 있지만 바닥에는(on the floor) 놓여 있지 않다.
(D) **정답:** 상자들이 수레 위에 쌓여 있는(are stacked) 상태를 잘 묘사했으므로 정답이다.

어휘 | assemble 조립하다 hallway 복도 stack 쌓다, 포개다

2

(A) Some tents are being assembled.
(B) The chairs are shaded by umbrellas.
(C) Tourists are relaxing on the beach.
(D) Towels have been spread out on the sand.

(A) 텐트들이 조립되고 있다.
(B) 의자들에 파라솔 그늘이 드리워져 있다.
(B) 관광객들이 해변에서 휴식을 취하고 있다.
(C) 수건들이 모래사장에 펼쳐져 있다.

해설 | **사물·풍경 사진 - 해변가**
(A) **사진에 없는 명사 언급 오답:** 사진 속에 텐트(tents)가 보이지 않는다.
(B) **정답:** 의자에 파라솔의 그늘이 드리워진(are shaded) 상태를 잘 묘사했으므로 정답이다.
(C) **사진에 없는 명사 언급 오답:** 사진에 관광객(Tourists)이 없다.
(D) **사진에 없는 명사 언급 오답:** 사진에 수건(Towels)이 보이지 않는다.

어휘 | shade 그늘지게 하다 spread out 펼치다

3

(A) All of the seats are occupied.
(B) The railing is being repaired.
(C) A dining room has been prepared for a meal.
(D) There's a large plant between two tables.

(A) 좌석이 모두 차 있다.
(B) 난간이 수리되고 있다.
(C) 식당에 식사가 준비되어 있다.
(D) 탁자 두 개 사이에 큰 식물이 있다.

해설 | **사물 사진 - 실내**
(A) **상태 묘사 오답:** 모든 좌석이 비어 있는 상태이다.
(B) **진행 상황 묘사 오답:** 난간이 수리되고 있는(is being repaired) 상황이 아니다.
(C) **상태 묘사 오답:** 식당에 식사가 준비되어 있는(has been prepared) 상태가 아니다.
(D) **정답:** 탁자 두 개 사이에 있는 큰 식물(a large plant)의 위치를 잘 묘사했으므로 정답이다.

어휘 | occupy 차지하다 repair 수리하다

4

(A) The fountain is spraying water into the air.
(B) People are swimming in the pool.
(C) Water is flowing down the mountain.
(D) Children are drinking from the water fountain.

(A) 분수에서 물이 공중으로 뿜어져 나오고 있다.
(B) 사람들이 수영장에서 수영을 하고 있다.
(C) 물이 산에서 흘러내리고 있다.
(D) 아이들이 분수식 음수대에서 물을 마시고 있다.

해설 | **사물·풍경 사진 - 분수**
(A) **정답:** 분수에서 물이 공중으로 뿜어져 나오고 있는(is spraying water) 모습을 잘 묘사했으므로 정답이다.
(B) **사진에 없는 명사 언급 오답:** 사진에 사람들(People)과 수영장(pool) 모두 보이지 않는다.
(C) **사진에 없는 명사 언급 오답:** 사진에 산(mountain)이 보이지 않는다.
(D) **사진에 없는 명사 언급 오답:** 사진에 아이들(Children)과 분수식 음수대(water fountain) 모두 보이지 않는다.

어휘 | spray 분사하다, 뿜어내다 into the air 공중으로 flow 흐르다 water fountain 분수식 음수대

본책 p.026

| **1** (C) | **2** (B) | **3** (B) | **4** (A) | **5** (B) | **6** (C) |
| **7** (C) | **8** (A) | **9** (B) | **10** (C) | **11** (A) | **12** (A) |

1

(A) The chairs are folded against the wall.
(B) The audience is sitting down.
(C) The chairs have been arranged in rows.
(D) The presentation has begun.

(A) 의자들이 접힌 채로 벽에 세워져 있다.
(B) 청중들이 앉고 있다.
(C) 의자들이 여러 줄로 놓여 있다.
(D) 발표가 시작되었다.

해설 | **사물 사진 - 강당**
(A) **상태 묘사 오답**: 벽에 기대어 있는 의자들도 보이지만 접혀 있는(are folded) 것이 아니라 펼쳐져 있다.
(B) **사진에 없는 명사 언급 오답**: 청중(The audience)은 사진에 등장하지 않는다.
(C) **정답**: 의자들이 줄지어 놓여 있는 모습(have been arranged in rows)을 잘 묘사했으므로 정답이다.
(D) **사진에 없는 명사 언급 오답**: 발표(The presentation)를 하는 사람이 보이지 않는다.

어휘 | fold 접다 audience 청중 arrange 배열하다, 정돈하다 in rows 줄지어, 여러 줄로 늘어서

2

(A) A towel is hanging on a fence.
(B) Some plants have been placed in pots.
(C) Some chairs have been set around a table.
(D) The door to a house has been left open.

(A) 수건이 울타리에 걸려 있다.
(B) 몇몇 식물들이 화분에 심어져 있다.
(C) 의자 몇 개가 탁자 주변에 배치되어 있다.
(D) 집 대문이 열려 있다.

해설 | **사물 사진 - 실외**
(A) **사진에 없는 명사 언급 오답**: 사진에 울타리에 걸린 수건(A towel)이 보이지 않는다.
(B) **정답**: 식물이 화분에 심어져 있는(have been placed in pots) 상태를 잘 묘사했으므로 정답이다.
(C) **사진에 없는 명사 언급 오답**: 사진에 탁자(table)가 보이지 않는다.
(D) **상태 묘사 오답**: 문이 열려 있는(has been left open) 상태가 아니다.

어휘 | be left open 열려 있다

3

(A) People are stepping onto a boat from a pier.
(B) There's a parking area near the beach.
(C) Ships are passing under a bridge.
(D) Trees are being planted along the shore.

(A) 사람들이 부두에서 배에 올라타고 있다.
(B) 해변 근처에 주차 공간이 있다.
(C) 배들이 다리 밑을 지나고 있다.
(D) 나무들이 해변을 따라 심어지고 있다.

해설 | **사물·풍경 사진 - 해변**
(A) **사진에 없는 명사 언급·동작 묘사 오답**: 사진 속에 배(boat)가 보이지 않으며, 사람들이 올라타고 있는(are stepping onto) 모습도 확인되지 않는다.
(B) **정답**: 해변 근처에 있는 주차 공간(parking area)의 위치를 잘 묘사했으므로 정답이다.
(C) **사진에 없는 명사 언급 오답**: 사진 속에 다리 밑을 지나고 있는 배들(Ships)이 보이지 않는다.
(D) **진행 상황 묘사 오답**: 나무들이 해변을 따라 심어지고 있는(are being planted) 상황이 아니다.

어휘 | pier 부두 plant 심다

4

(A) There are some mountains in the distance.
(B) There's a restaurant on the roof of the building.
(C) Fences are being constructed around a building.
(D) The residents are leaning out their windows.

(A) 저 멀리 산들이 있다.
(B) 건물 옥상에 식당이 있다.
(C) 울타리들이 건물 주변에 세워지고 있다.
(D) 주민들이 창문 밖으로 몸을 내밀고 있다.

해설 | **사물·풍경 사진 - 건물**
(A) **정답**: 멀리(in the distance) 보이는 산의 모습을 잘 묘사한 정답으로, There are mountains in the background라고 표현할 수도 있다.
(B) **위치 묘사 오답**: 식당으로 보이는 야외 카페는 건물 옥상(roof)이 아닌 지상에 있다.
(C) **진행 상황 묘사 오답**: 울타리가 설치되고 있는(being constructed) 상황이 아니다.
(D) **사진에 없는 명사 언급 오답**: 창 밖으로 몸을 내민(are leaning out) 주민들(residents)이 보이지 않는다.

어휘 | in the distance 저 멀리, 먼 곳에 roof 지붕, 옥상 fence 울타리 construct 건설하다, 만들다 resident 주민 lean out ~밖으로 몸을 내밀다

LC

PART 1

5

(A) The chairs are stacked by the wall.
(B) The table has been set for a meal.
(C) Menus have been placed on some chairs.
(D) Some glasses are drying on a rack.

(A) 벽 옆에 의자들이 쌓여 있다.
(B) 탁자에 식사 준비가 되어 있다.
(C) 의자 몇 개에 메뉴가 놓여 있다.
(D) 선반 위에 유리잔 몇 개가 건조되고 있다.

해설 | 사물 사진 - 식당
(A) 상태 묘사 오답: 의자들이 벽 옆에 쌓여 있는(are stacked) 상태가 아니다.
(B) 정답: 탁자에 식사 준비가 되어 있는(has been set for a meal) 상태를 잘 묘사했으므로 정답이다.
(C) 위치 묘사 오답: 메뉴가 탁자 위에는 있지만, 의자 위에는(on some chairs) 놓여 있지 않다.
(D) 사진에 없는 명사 언급 오답: 사진 속에 선반(rack)은 보이지 않는다.

어휘 | stack 쌓다, 포개다 set for ~할 준비가 된 rack 선반

6

(A) Some umbrellas are set up on the beach.
(B) Some trees have been cut down.
(C) Some chairs are lined up outside.
(D) Some boats are in the water.

(A) 해변에 파라솔들이 설치되어 있다.
(B) 나무들이 베어져 있다.
(C) 의자들이 바깥에 줄지어 있다.
(D) 배들이 물 위에 있다.

해설 | 사물·풍경 사진 - 해변
(A) 사진에 없는 명사 언급 오답: 사진 속에 파라솔(umbrellas)이 보이지 않는다.
(B) 상태 묘사 오답: 나무들이 베어져 있는(have been cut down) 상태가 아니다.
(C) 정답: 의자들이 바깥에 줄지어 있는(are lined up) 모습을 잘 묘사했으므로 정답이다.
(D) 위치 묘사 오답: 배들이 해변에 있지만 물 위에(in the water) 떠있지는 않다.

어휘 | set up 설치하다 cut down (밑부분을 잘라) 넘어뜨리다 line up 줄을 서다

7

(A) There's a lamp between the plants.
(B) The curtains have been pulled back.
(C) There are two sofas in the corner of the room.
(D) The tables are stacked on top of each other.

(A) 식물들 사이에 램프가 있다.
(B) 커튼들이 걷어져 있다.
(C) 방의 구석에 소파 두 개가 있다.
(D) 탁자들이 겹겹이 쌓여 있다.

해설 | 사물 사진 - 거실
(A) 위치 묘사 오답: 램프는 소파 옆(by a sofa)이나 탁자 위에(on a table) 있다고 해야 적절하다.
(B) 상태 묘사 오답: 커튼이 열려 있는 상태(have been pulled back[open])가 아니라 닫혀 있는(have been pulled closed[shut]) 상태이다.
(C) 정답: 구석에 있는(in the corner) 소파의 위치를 잘 묘사했으므로 정답이다.
(D) 상태 묘사 오답: 탁자들이 겹겹이 쌓여 있는(stacked on top of each other) 모습이 아니다.

어휘 | pull back (커튼 등을) 걷다 in the corner of ~의 구석에 on top of each other 겹겹이, 차곡차곡

8

(A) Some flags are waving in the wind.
(B) A plaza is bordered by a fence.
(C) A van is entering a tunnel.
(D) Fountains are on both sides of a park entrance.

(A) 깃발 몇 개가 바람에 나부끼고 있다.
(B) 광장의 가장자리에 담장이 있다.
(C) 승합차가 터널로 진입하고 있다.
(D) 공원 입구 양쪽에 분수대가 있다.

해설 | 사물·풍경 사진 - 광장 분수대
(A) 정답: 사진에 깃발들이 바람에 나부끼고(are waving) 있는 모습을 잘 묘사했으므로 정답이다.
(B) 사진에 없는 명사 언급 오답: 사진에는 담장(fence)이 보이지 않는다.
(C) 사진에 없는 명사 언급 오답: 사진에는 터널(tunnel)이 보이지 않는다.
(D) 위치·수량 묘사 오답: 분수대는 한 개이며, 공원 입구 양쪽(both sides of a park entrance)에 있지 않다.

어휘 | wave 흔들리다, 나부끼다 border 가장자리를 이루다 fence 담장 fountain 분수(대) entrance 입구

9

(A) Some scarves have been arranged on a table.
(B) Some merchandise is on display outside a store.
(C) Leaves have covered a walkway.
(D) A sign is hanging from an awning.

(A) 스카프들이 탁자에 배열되어 있다.
(B) 상품들이 가게 바깥에 진열되어 있다.
(C) 나뭇잎들이 보도를 덮었다.
(D) 간판이 차양에 매달려 있다.

해설 | **사물·풍경 사진 - 상점 앞 보도**
(A) **사진에 없는 명사 언급 오답**: 사진 속에 스카프들이 배열되어 있는 탁자(table)가 보이지 않는다.
(B) **정답**: 상품이 가게 바깥에(outside a store) 상품들이 진열되어 있는(is on display) 상태를 잘 묘사했으므로 정답이다.
(C) **상태 묘사 오답**: 나뭇잎들이 보도를 덮은(have covered) 상태가 아니다.
(D) **위치·상태 묘사 오답**: 간판이 차양(awning)에 매달려 있는(is hanging) 상태가 아니라 바닥에 놓여 있다.

어휘 | arrange 배열하다, 정돈하다 merchandise 상품 be on display 진열 중이다 walkway 보도 awning 차양

10

(A) A shop door has been left open.
(B) Some plants have been arranged in a window.
(C) A bicycle has been propped up against a curb.
(D) A chair has been folded up next to a wall.

(A) 상점 문이 열려 있다.
(B) 창문에 식물들이 놓여져 있다.·
(C) 자전거가 도로 경계석에 기대어 세워져 있다.
(D) 의자가 벽 옆에 접혀 있다.

해설 | **사물·풍경 사진 - 건물 앞**
(A) **상태 묘사 오답**: 상점 문이 열려 있는(has been left open) 상태가 아니다.
(B) **위치 묘사 오답**: 식물들이 울타리 앞에는 있지만 창문에는(in a window) 없다.
(C) **정답**: 자전거가 도로 경계석에 기대어 세워져 있는(has been propped up) 상태를 잘 묘사했으므로 정답이다.
(D) **상태 묘사 오답**: 의자가 접혀 있는(has been folded up) 상태가 아니다.

어휘 | prop A against B A를 B에 받쳐 놓다[세우다]

11

(A) Some books have been placed on a cart.
(B) A librarian is posting a sign near an entrance.
(C) Some bookshelves are being installed.
(D) The doors to a hallway have been propped open.

(A) 책들이 수레에 놓여 있다.
(B) 사서가 입구 근처에 게시물을 붙이고 있다.
(C) 책장들이 설치되고 있다.
(D) 복도로 통하는 문이 괴어져 열려 있다.

해설 | **사물 사진 - 도서관**
(A) **정답**: 일부 책들이 수레에 놓여져 있는(have been placed) 상태를 잘 묘사했으므로 정답이다.
(B) **사진에 없는 명사 언급 오답**: 사진 속에 게시물을 붙이고 있는 사서(librarian)가 보이지 않는다.
(C) **진행 상황 묘사 오답**: 책장들이 설치되고 있는(are being installed) 상황이 아니다.
(D) **상태 묘사 오답**: 문이 무언가에 받쳐 열려 있는(have been propped open) 상태가 아니다.

어휘 | librarian 사서 post a sign 게시물을 붙이다 entrance 입구 install 설치하다

12

(A) Some carts have been left unattended.
(B) Customers are sorting clothing into piles.
(C) Some appliances are stacked on top of each other.
(D) Laundry detergent is being poured into a machine.

(A) 카트 몇 개가 방치되어 있다.
(B) 손님들이 옷을 분류해 쌓고 있다.
(C) 가전 제품들이 차곡차곡 쌓여 있다.
(D) 세탁용 세제가 기계 안에 부어지고 있다.

해설 | **사물 사진 - 세탁실**
(A) **정답**: 카트 몇 개가 방치되어 있는(have been left unattended) 상태를 잘 묘사했으므로 정답이다.
(B) **사진에 없는 명사 언급 오답**: 사진 속에 옷을 분류해 쌓고 있는 손님들(Customers)이 보이지 않는다.
(C) **상태 묘사 오답**: 가전 제품들이 차곡차곡 쌓여 있는(are stacked on top of each other) 상태가 아니다.
(D) **진행 상황 묘사 오답**: 세탁용 세제가 기계 안에 부어지고 있는(is being poured) 상황이 아니다.

어휘 | unattended 방치되어 있는 sort 분류하다 appliance 가전제품 laundry detergent 세탁용 세제 pour 쏟다, 붓다

1 (C)　**2** (A)　**3** (C)　**4** (C)　**5** (D)　**6** (C)

1

(A) A woman is organizing some flyers.
(B) A woman is filing some folders.
(C) A woman is operating some office equipment.
(D) A woman is answering a phone.

(A) 여자가 전단지들을 정리하고 있다.
(B) 여자가 폴더들을 철하고 있다.
(C) 여자가 사무용 기기를 작동하고 있다.
(D) 여자가 전화를 받고 있다.

해설 | 1인 등장 사진 - 사무실
(A) **동작 묘사 오답**: 여자가 전단지들을 정리하고 있는(is organizing) 모습이 아니다.
(B) **동작 묘사 오답**: 여자가 폴더들을 철하고 있는(is filing) 모습이 아니다.
(C) **정답**: 여자가 사무용 기기를 작동하고 있는(is operating) 모습을 잘 묘사했으므로 정답이다.
(D) **동작 묘사 오답**: 여자가 전화를 받고 있는(is answering a phone) 모습이 아니다.

어휘 | organize 정리하다　flyer (광고용) 전단지　file 철하다, 보관하다　operate 가동하다, 작동시키다　equipment 장비

2

(A) Some garments have been hung outside a storefront.
(B) Some patterned scarves are being folded.
(C) A woman is getting on her motorbike.
(D) A woman is trying on a straw hat.

(A) 옷들이 가게 밖에 걸려 있다.
(B) 무늬가 있는 스카프들이 개어지고 있다.
(C) 여자가 자신의 오토바이에 올라타고 있다.
(D) 여자가 밀짚모자를 착용해보고 있다.

해설 | 사람·사물 혼합 사진 - 상점 앞
(A) **정답**: 옷들이 가게 밖에(outside a storefront) 걸려 있는(have been hung) 상태를 잘 묘사했으므로 정답이다.
(B) **진행 상황 묘사 오답**: 스카프들이 개어지고 있는(are being folded) 상황이 아니다.
(C) **동작 묘사 오답**: 여자가 오토바이에 올라타고 있는(is getting on) 모습이 아니다.
(D) **동작 묘사 오답**: 여자가 밀짚모자를 착용해보고 있는(is trying on) 모습이 아니다.

어휘 | garment 의복, 옷　storefront 가게 앞, 상점　patterned 무늬가 있는　fold 접다　try on ~를 착용해 보다

3

(A) Some customers are picking out shirts.
(B) Some shoes are being displayed on tables.
(C) One of the men is trying on shoes.
(D) One of the men is putting on a hat.

(A) 손님들이 셔츠들을 고르고 있다.
(B) 신발들이 탁자에 진열되어 있다.
(C) 남자들 중 한 명이 신발을 신어보고 있다.
(D) 남자들 중 한 명이 모자를 착용해보고 있다.

해설 | 사람·사물 혼합 사진 - 상점
(A) **동작 묘사 오답**: 손님들이 셔츠들을 고르고 있는(are picking out) 모습이 아니다.
(B) **사진에 없는 명사 언급 오답**: 사진 속에 신발이 진열되어 있는 탁자(tables)가 보이지 않는다.
(C) **정답**: 남자들 중 한 명이 신발을 신어보고 있는(is trying on) 모습을 잘 묘사했으므로 정답이다.
(D) **동작 묘사 오답**: 남자들 중 한 명이 이미 모자를 쓰고 있는(is wearing) 상태로, 착용해보고 있는(is putting on) 모습이 아니다.

어휘 | pick out 선택하다　display 진열하다

4

(A) A man is riding a bicycle along a street.
(B) A man is leaning against a tree.
(C) A building is reflected in a pool.
(D) Leaves are being swept off a walkway.

(A) 남자가 거리에서 자전거를 타고 있다.
(B) 남자가 나무에 기대고 있다.
(C) 건물이 연못에 비치고 있다.
(D) 보도에서 나뭇잎들이 쓸려나가고 있다.

해설 | 사람·사물 혼합 사진 - 연못가
(A) **동작 묘사 오답**: 남자가 자전거를 타고 있는(is riding) 모습이 아니다.
(B) **동작 묘사 오답**: 남자가 나무에 기대고 있는(is leaning against) 모습이 아니다.
(C) **정답**: 건물이 연못에 반사되어 비치고 있는(is reflected) 상태를 잘 묘사했으므로 정답이다.
(D) **진행 상황 묘사 오답**: 나뭇잎들이 보도에서 쓸려나가고 있는(are being swept off) 상황이 아니다.

어휘 | lean against ~에 기대다　reflect 비추다, 반사하다　sweep off 쓸어내다

5

(A) The woman is removing her apron.
(B) The woman is eating in a restaurant.
(C) The man is handing a cup to the woman.
(D) The man is pouring a mixture into a pot.

(A) 여자가 앞치마를 벗고 있다.
(B) 여자가 음식점에서 식사하고 있다.
(C) 남자가 여자에게 컵을 건네고 있다.
(D) 남자가 반죽을 냄비에 붓고 있다.

해설 | **2인 이상 등장 사진 - 주방**
(A) **동작 묘사 오답:** 여자가 앞치마를 벗고 있는(is removing) 모습이 아니다.
(B) **동작·장소 묘사 오답:** 여자가 음식점에서 식사하고 있는(is eating) 모습이 아니다.
(C) **사진에 없는 명사 언급·동작 묘사 오답:** 사진 속에 컵(cup)이 보이지 않으며, 남자가 여자에게 뭔가를 건네고 있는(is handing) 모습도 아니다.
(D) **정답:** 남자가 반죽을 냄비에 붓고 있는(is pouring a mixture) 모습을 잘 묘사했으므로 정답이다.

어휘 | remove 벗다, 치우다 hand 건네다 pour 붓다, 따르다 mixture 반죽, 혼합 재료

6

(A) Some books are stacked on the floor.
(B) Some curtains are being taken down.
(C) One of the walls is lined with shelves.
(D) Chairs have been pushed into a corner.

(A) 책들이 바닥에 쌓여 있다.
(B) 커튼이 떼어 내지고 있다.
(C) 한쪽 벽면에 책장들이 늘어서 있다.
(D) 의자들이 한쪽 구석에 몰려 있다.

해설 | **사물 사진 - 실내**
(A) **위치 묘사 오답:** 책들이 선반에는 있지만 바닥에(on the floor) 쌓여 있지는 않다.
(B) **진행 상황 묘사 오답:** 커튼이 떼어 내지고 있는(is being taken down) 상황이 아니다.
(C) **정답:** 한쪽 벽면(One of the walls)에 위치한 책장(shelves)의 모습을 잘 묘사했으므로 정답이다.
(D) **위치·상태 묘사 오답:** 의자들이 한쪽 구석(a corner)에 몰려 있는(have been pushed) 상태가 아니다.

어휘 | be lined with 줄지어 있다, 늘어서 있다

PART 2

Unit 03 Who / When / Where 의문문

① Who 의문문

ETS 유형 연습 본책 p.038

1 (B)	**2** (C)	**3** (B)	**4** (C)	**5** (B)	**6** (A)

1 Who's going to take the director to the airport?
(A) Tomorrow morning.
(B) Her secretary will.
(C) Follow the map.

누가 이사님을 공항까지 모셔드릴 건가요?
(A) 내일 아침에요.
(B) 그녀의 비서가요.
(C) 지도를 따라가세요.

해설 | **담당자를 묻는 Who 의문문**
(A) **관련 없는 오답:** When 의문문에 가능한 답변이다.
(B) **정답:** 구체적인 직책(secretary)을 언급했으므로 정답이다.
(C) **연상 작용 오답:** 질문의 director를 direct(안내하다)로 잘못 들었을 경우 연상 가능한 map을 이용한 오답이다.

어휘 | director 이사 secretary 비서

2 Who's coordinating the corporate retreat?
(A) No, at a seminar.
(B) OK, good idea.
(C) Stanley's doing that.

누가 사내 수련회를 준비하고 있나요?
(A) 아니요, 세미나에서요.
(B) 네, 좋은 생각이에요.
(C) 스탠리가 하고 있어요.

해설 | **담당자를 묻는 Who 의문문**
(A) **Yes / No 대답 불가 오답:** Who 의문문에는 Yes / No로 대답할 수 없다.
(B) **관련 없는 오답:** 제안하는 의문문에 적합한 대답이다.
(C) **정답:** 사내 수련회를 준비하고 있는 담당자를 묻는 질문에 구체적인 이름(Stanley)을 제시했으므로 정답이다.

어휘 | coordinate 준비하다, 조직화하다 corporate retreat 사내 수련[수양]회

3 Who ordered the fish?
(A) It was delivered today.
(B) The customer at table two.
(C) Can we have the bill?

누가 생선을 주문했죠?
(A) 오늘 배달됐어요.
(B) 2번 테이블 손님요.
(C) 계산서 좀 갖다 주시겠어요?

해설 | **주문자를 묻는 Who 의문문**
(A) **관련 없는 오답:** 배달 시점을 묻는 When 의문문에 적합한 대답이다.

(B) **정답:** 생선을 주문한 사람을 묻는 질문에 구체적인 인물(The customer at table two)을 제시했으므로 정답이다.

(C) **연상 작용 오답:** 질문의 ordered에서 연상 가능한 bill을 이용한 오답이다.

어휘 | order 주문하다 deliver 배송하다 bill 계산서

4 Who booked the airline tickets?
  (A) Laura returned the book.
  (B) Flights leave every hour.
  (C) Someone in the Paris office.

항공권은 누가 예약했나요?
(A) 로라가 책을 반납했어요.
(B) 비행기는 매시간 있어요.
(C) 파리 지점 소속 누군가요.

해설 | 담당자를 묻는 Who 의문문
(A) **다의어 오답:** 질문의 booked(예약하다)와 품사와 뜻이 다른 명사 book(책)을 이용한 오답이다.
(B) **연상 작용 오답:** 질문의 airline tickets에서 연상 가능한 Flights를 이용한 오답이다.
(C) **정답:** 누가 예약했는지를 묻는 질문에, 파리 지점 소속 누군가라고 특정 소속을 언급하고 있으므로 정답이다.

어휘 | return 반환하다, 반납하다

5 Who put the ladder in the hallway?
  (A) The letter was mailed.
  (B) It was probably the painters.
  (C) On the way down.

누가 복도에 사다리를 뒀나요?
(A) 편지가 발송되었습니다.
(B) 아마도 페인트칠하는 사람들일 거예요.
(C) 내려가는 길에요.

해설 | 행위자를 묻는 Who 의문문
(A) **유사 발음 오답:** 질문의 ladder와 발음이 유사한 letter를 이용한 오답이다.
(B) **정답:** 누가 복도에 사다리를 두었는지 묻는 질문에 페인트를 칠하고 있는 사람들(the painters)일 것이라고 적절히 대답하고 있다.
(C) **유사 발음 오답:** 질문의 hallway와 부분적으로 발음이 동일한 way를 이용한 오답이다.

어휘 | ladder 사다리

6 Who's writing the article about the new art museum?
  (A) It hasn't been decided yet.
  (B) Yes, I'm a writer.
  (C) The museum's closed.

새 미술관에 대한 기사는 누가 쓰고 있나요?
(A) 아직 결정이 안 됐어요.
(B) 네. 저는 작가입니다.
(C) 그 미술관은 문을 닫았어요.

해설 | 담당자를 묻는 Who 의문문
(A) **정답:** 기사를 쓰고 있는 담당자를 묻는 질문에 아직 결정되지 않았다(It hasn't been decided yet)며 관련된 상황을 언급하고 있으므로 가장 적절한 응답이다.
(B) **Yes/No 대답 불가 오답:** Who 의문문에는 Yes/No로 대답할 수 없다.

(C) **단어 반복 오답:** 질문의 museum을 반복 이용한 오답이다.

어휘 | article 기사 art museum 미술관 decide 결정하다

② When 의문문

ETS 유형 연습

본책 p.039

| **1** (B) | **2** (C) | **3** (A) | **4** (B) | **5** (B) | **6** (B) |

1 When should I renew my membership?
  (A) I joined a gym recently, too.
  (B) You can do it now if you'd like.
  (C) I met her last year.

회원 자격을 언제 갱신해야 하나요?
(A) 저도 최근에 체육관에 등록했어요.
(B) 원하시면 지금 가능해요.
(C) 그녀를 작년에 만났어요.

해설 | 갱신 시기를 묻는 When 의문문
(A) **연상 작용 오답:** 질문의 membership에서 연상 가능한 gym을 이용한 오답이다.
(B) **정답:** 회원 자격의 갱신 시기를 묻는 질문에 지금도 가능하다(You can do it now)며 지금이 갱신 기간임을 알려 주었으므로 정답이다.
(C) **인칭 오류 오답:** 대명사 her가 가리키는 대상이 질문에 없다.

어휘 | renew 갱신하다, 연장하다 recently 최근

2 When did Ralph leave for the airport?
  (A) From the office.
  (B) Flight 63.
  (C) About two hours ago.

랄프 씨는 언제 공항으로 출발했나요?
(A) 사무실에서요.
(B) 63편 항공기요.
(C) 약 두 시간 전에요.

해설 | 출발 시점을 묻는 When 의문문
(A) **관련 없는 오답:** Where 의문문에 어울리는 응답이다.
(B) **연상 작용 오답:** 질문의 airport에서 연상 가능한 Flight를 사용한 오답이다.
(C) **정답:** 출발 시점을 two hours ago라고 구체적으로 언급한 정답이다.

어휘 | leave for ~로 떠나다 flight 항공편, 항공기

3 When are the conference proposals due?
  (A) On January twenty-seventh.
  (B) For three days.
  (C) He'll do it.

회의 제안서 마감일이 언제예요?
(A) 1월 27일이요.
(B) 3일 동안이요.
(C) 그가 그것을 할 거예요.

해설 | 마감 시점을 묻는 When 의문문
(A) **정답:** 회의 제안서 마감일을 묻는 질문에 구체적인 날짜를 제시했으므로 정답이다.
(B) **연상 작용 오답:** conference의 기간 측면에서 연상 가능한 three days를 사용한 오답이다.
(C) **유사 발음 오답:** 질문의 due와 발음이 유사한 do를 사용한 오답이다.

어휘 | conference 회의 proposal 제안(서) due 제출 기한이 된

4 When was the new laboratory equipment delivered?
  (A) A pharmaceutical company.
  (B) Earlier today.
  (C) That's a big shipment.

새 실험실 장비들이 언제 배송되었나요?
(A) 제약 회사요.
(B) 오늘 아까요.
(C) 수송량이 많네요.

해설 | 배달 시점을 묻는 When 의문문
(A) 연상 작용 오답: 질문의 laboratory equipment에서 연상 가능한 pharmaceutical company를 이용한 오답이다.
(B) 정답: 장비 배송 시점을 묻는 질문에 '오늘 아까'라고 답하고 있으므로 정답이다.
(C) 연상 작용 오답: 질문의 deliver에서 연상 가능한 shipment를 이용한 오답이다.

어휘 | laboratory 실험실 equipment 장비 deliver 배달[배송]하다

5 When will the next phase of construction begin?
  (A) A major improvement.
  (B) Once the blueprints are finalized.
  (C) In a three-story apartment building.

공사 다음 단계는 언제 시작될 예정인가요?
(A) 주요한 개선이죠.
(B) 설계도가 완성되면요.
(C) 3층짜리 아파트 건물에서요.

해설 | 시작 시점을 묻는 When 의문문
(A) 연상 작용 오답: 질문의 construction(공사)에서 연상 가능한 improvement(개선)를 이용한 오답이다.
(B) 정답: 공사 다음 단계의 시작 시점을 묻는 질문에 '설계도가 완성되면요(Once the blueprints are finalized)'라며 우회적으로 시작 시점을 언급하고 있으므로 정답이다.
(C) 관련 없는 오답: 공사 장소를 묻는 Where 의문문에 적합한 대답이다.

어휘 | phase 단계 construction 공사 improvement 개선 blueprint 청사진, 설계도 finalize 완결하다

6 When are they announcing the winner of the competition?
  (A) At the radio station.
  (B) By the end of the week.
  (C) A gift certificate.

대회 우승자를 언제쯤 발표할까요?
(A) 라디오 방송국에서요.
(B) 이번 주 말 즈음에요.
(C) 상품권이요.

해설 | 발표 시기를 묻는 When 의문문
(A) 관련 없는 오답: 발표 장소를 묻는 Where 의문문에 적합한 대답이다.
(B) 정답: 발표 시기를 묻는 질문에 By the end of the week라는 구체적인 시점을 언급하고 있으므로 정답이다.
(C) 연상 작용 오답: 질문의 the winner에서 연상 가능한 gift certificate를 이용한 오답이다.

어휘 | announce 발표하다 competition 대회, 경쟁 gift certificate 상품권

③ **Where 의문문**

ETS 유형 연습
본책 p.040

1 (B)	**2** (A)	**3** (B)	**4** (C)	**5** (C)	**6** (B)

1 Where's the registration sheet?
  (A) The printer was fixed.
  (B) It's on the front desk.
  (C) She's new here.

등록 용지는 어디에 있나요?
(A) 프린터가 수리됐어요.
(B) 안내 데스크에 있습니다.
(C) 그녀는 여기가 처음이에요.

해설 | 보관 장소를 묻는 Where 의문문
(A) 연상 작용 오답: 질문의 sheet에서 연상 가능한 printer를 이용한 오답이다.
(B) 정답: 등록 용지가 있는 장소를 묻는 질문에 구체적인 장소로 대답하고 있다.
(C) 인칭 오류 오답: 질문의 주어와 맞지 않는다.

2 Where's the international arrival gate?
  (A) Follow the yellow signs.
  (B) At five o'clock.
  (C) Close it behind you.

국제선 도착 게이트가 어디죠?
(A) 노란 표지판을 따라가세요.
(B) 5시에요.
(C) 들어간 후에 닫으세요.

해설 | 위치를 묻는 Where 의문문
(A) 정답: 국제선 도착 게이트의 위치를 묻는 질문에 노란 표지판을 따라가라(Follow the yellow signs)며 우회적으로 게이트가 있는 곳을 제시하고 있으므로 정답이다.
(B) 관련 없는 오답: 도착 시점을 묻는 When 의문문에 적합한 대답이다.
(C) 연상 작용 오답: 질문의 gate에서 연상 가능한 문을 닫는 상황(Close it behind you)을 이용한 오답이다.

어휘 | international 국제적인 arrival 도착

3 Where do you store the batteries?
  (A) The room looks bare.
  (B) In the top drawer.
  (C) From 9 A.M. to 5 P.M.

건전지를 어디에 보관하시나요?
(A) 방이 텅 빈 것 같아요.
(B) 맨 위 서랍에요.
(C) 오전 9시부터 오후 5시까지요.

해설 | 보관 장소를 묻는 Where 의문문
(A) 유사 발음 오답: batteries와 부분적으로 발음이 유사한 bare를 사용한 오답이다.
(B) 정답: 건전지 보관하는 곳에 대한 질문에 top drawer라는 구체적인 장소를 언급한 정답이다.

(C) 연상 작용 오답: store를 상점으로 잘못 이해했을 때 연상 가능한 영업 시간 관련 응답이다.

어휘 | store 보관하다 battery 건전지 bare (방이) 텅 빈 drawer 서랍

4 Where can I read about the organization's history?
(A) Whenever you have time.
(B) He seems very organized.
(C) On the company Web site.

그 조직의 역사는 어디에서 읽어볼 수 있나요?
(A) 시간 되실 때 아무 때나요.
(B) 그는 매우 체계적으로 보여요.
(C) 회사 웹사이트에서요.

해설 | **확인처를 묻는 Where 의문문**
(A) 관련 없는 오답: 시점을 묻는 When 의문문에 적합한 대답이다.
(B) 파생어 오답: 질문의 organization과 파생 관계인 organized를 이용한 오답이다.
(C) 정답: 조직의 역사를 읽어볼 수 있는 곳을 묻는 질문에 구체적인 확인처(On the company Web site)를 알려 주었으므로 정답이다.

어휘 | organization 조직, 단체 organized 정돈된, 체계적인

5 Where is the temperature control for this room?
(A) Nearly four-thirty.
(B) Some cold water.
(C) Next to the door.

이 방의 온도 조절기는 어디에 있죠?
(A) 대략 4시 30분입니다.
(B) 냉수요.
(C) 문 옆에요.

해설 | **위치를 묻는 Where 의문문**
(A) 연상 작용 오답: 질문의 temperature에서 연상 가능한 숫자(four-thirty)를 이용한 오답이다.
(B) 연상 작용 오답: 질문의 temperature에서 연상 가능한 cold를 이용한 오답이다.
(C) 정답: 온도 조절기의 위치를 묻는 질문에 문 옆(Next to the door)이라는 구체적인 위치로 대답했으므로 정답이다.

어휘 | temperature control 온도 조절기 nearly 대략, 거의

6 Where did you make the dinner reservation?
(A) Tomorrow at twelve-thirty.
(B) Didn't you make it?
(C) For fourteen people.

저녁 식사 어디로 예약했어요?
(A) 내일 12시 30분에요.
(B) 당신이 한 거 아니에요?
(C) 14명이요.

해설 | **예약 장소를 묻는 Where 의문문**
(A) 관련 없는 오답: 예약 시간을 묻는 When 의문문에 적합한 대답이다.
(B) 정답: 어디로 예약했는지를 묻는 질문에, 상대방이 예약한 것이 아닌지(Didn't you make it?) 되묻고 있으므로 가장 적절한 응답이다.

(C) 관련 없는 오답: 예약 인원을 묻는 How many 의문문에 적합한 대답이다.

어휘 | make a reservation 예약하다

● 실전 **도움닫기**   본책 p.041

1 (C) **2** (C) **3** (C) **4** (C) **5** (B)

1. Who was the man sitting next to you at the meeting?
(A) Yes, nice to see you again.
(B) The next team meeting.
(C) He's the plant manager.

회의 때 당신 옆에 앉아 있던 남자는 누군가요?
(A) 네, 다시 뵙게 되어 반갑습니다.
(B) 다음 팀 회의요.
(C) 그는 공장 관리자예요.

해설 | **특정 인물을 묻는 Who 의문문**
(A) Yes/No 대답 불가 오답: Who 의문문에 Yes/No로 대답할 수 없다.
(B) 단어 반복 오답: 질문의 meeting을 반복 이용한 오답이다.
(C) 정답: 남자의 신분을 묻는 질문에 plant manager라는 구체적인 직책으로 답변했으므로 정답이다.

어휘 | plant 공장

2. When are you delivering your speech?
(A) It got there quickly.
(B) The speakers weren't working.
(C) At the conference in May.

언제 연설하나요?
(A) 그것이 그곳에 빨리 도착했어요.
(B) 스피커들이 작동하지 않았어요.
(C) 5월 회의에서요.

해설 | **연설 시점을 묻는 When 의문문**
(A) 연상 작용 오답: deliver에서 연상 가능한 got there를 사용한 오답이다.
(B) 연상 작용 오답: speech에서 연상 가능한 speakers를 언급한 오답이다.
(C) 정답: 연설 시점을 구체적으로 in May라고 밝혔으므로 정답이다. 장소 표현 at the conference 때문에 오답으로 생각하지 않도록 주의한다.

어휘 | deliver a speech 연설하다 work 작동하다 conference 회의

3. Where do you recommend I stay in Shanghai?
(A) I strongly recommend it.
(B) One hundred pounds a night.
(C) I know a great place downtown.

상하이에서 머물 곳으로 어디를 추천하십니까?
(A) 저는 그것을 강력히 추천해요.
(B) 하루에 100파운드입니다.
(C) 시내에 아주 좋은 곳을 알고 있어요.

해설 | **장소를 묻는 Where 의문문**
(A) **단어 반복 오답**: 질문에 쓰인 recommend를 반복 사용한 오답이다.
(B) **연상 작용 오답**: stay에서 연상 가능한 one hundred pounds와 a night를 사용한 오답이다.
(C) **정답**: 숙박 장소를 추천해달라는 질문에 좋은 곳을 알고 있다는 간접 응답을 했으므로 정답이다.

어휘 | recommend 추천하다 strongly 강력하게 downtown 시내에

4. Who's watering your plants while you're away?
(A) This way, please.
(B) Not until the end of the month.
(C) I asked my neighbor to do it.

당신이 없는 동안 누가 당신 화초에 물을 줄 건가요?
(A) 이쪽으로 오시죠.
(B) 월말이나 되어서요.
(C) 제 이웃에게 해달라고 부탁했어요.

해설 | **담당자를 묻는 Who 의문문**
(A) **유사 발음 오답**: 유사 발음 away/way를 이용한 오답이다.
(B) **관련 없는 오답**: When 의문문에 어울리는 답변이다.
(C) **정답**: 화초에 물을 줄 사람에 대한 질문에 구체적으로 my neighbor로 답했으므로 정답이다.

어휘 | water 물을 주다 away 자리를 비운 neighbor 이웃

5. When does the promotional offer begin?
(A) For large orders.
(B) It starts next week.
(C) She's the assistant editor.

판촉 할인이 언제 시작되나요?
(A) 대량 주문이에요.
(B) 다음 주에 시작됩니다.
(C) 그녀는 보조 편집자예요.

해설 | **시작 시점을 묻는 When 의문문**
(A) **관련 없는 오답**: 어떤 종류의 주문에 할인을 제공하는지 묻는 질문에 적절한 대답이다.
(B) **정답**: 판촉 행사가 언제 시작되는지 묻는 질문에 구체적인 시점으로 대답했으므로 정답이다.
(C) **관련 없는 오답**: Who 의문문에 가능한 대답이다.

어휘 | promotional 판촉의, 홍보의 offer 할인 assistant 보조(의)

● ETS 실전문제
본책 p.042

1 (B)	2 (A)	3 (C)	4 (B)	5 (A)
6 (A)	7 (C)	8 (C)	9 (C)	10 (A)
11 (A)	12 (A)	13 (C)	14 (C)	15 (C)
16 (A)	17 (A)	18 (B)	19 (B)	20 (C)
21 (B)	22 (A)	23 (A)	24 (A)	25 (C)

1 Who explained this report to you?
(A) Sure, let's meet this afternoon.
(B) Mr. Novak did, yesterday.
(C) The plane leaves at two.

누가 이 보고서를 당신에게 설명해 주었나요?
(A) 좋아요, 오늘 오후에 만납시다.
(B) 어제 노박 씨가 해줬어요.
(C) 비행기는 2시에 떠나요.

해설 | **특정 인물을 묻는 Who 의문문**
(A) **Yes/No 대답 불가 오답**: Who 의문문에 Yes의 대체 표현인 Sure로 대답할 수 없다.
(B) **정답**: 보고서를 설명한 사람으로 구체적인 이름을 제시했다.
(C) **유사 발음 오답**: 질문의 explained와 부분적으로 발음이 비슷한 plane을 이용한 오답이다.

어휘 | explain A to B A를 B에게 설명하다

2 When will I need to check out of my hotel room?
(A) By 11 A.M., please.
(B) You'll need a light jacket.
(C) Sorry, checks aren't accepted.

호텔 객실에서 언제 체크아웃해야 하죠?
(A) 오전 11시까지 해 주세요.
(B) 가벼운 겉옷이 필요할 거예요.
(C) 죄송하지만 수표는 안 됩니다.

해설 | **시점을 묻는 When 의문문**
(A) **정답**: 체크아웃해야 할 시점을 묻는 질문에 오전 11시까지(By 11 A.M.)라는 구체적인 시점을 알려 주었으므로 정답이다.
(B) **단어 반복 오답**: 질문의 need를 반복 이용한 오답이다.
(C) **다의어 오답**: 질문의 check는 out과 함께 '체크아웃하다, 나가다'라는 뜻을 나타내는 동사이고, 보기의 checks는 '수표'라는 뜻의 명사이다.

어휘 | check out of ~에서 비용을 지불하고 나가다, 체크아웃하다 accept 받아들이다, 수락하다

3 Where did you say the research lab is?
(A) At six o'clock in the evening.
(B) They needed more space.
(C) It's behind the library.

연구소가 어디라고 하셨죠?
(A) 저녁 6시예요.
(B) 그들은 공간이 더 필요해요.
(C) 도서관 뒤편요.

해설 | **위치를 묻는 Where 의문문**
(A) **관련 없는 오답**: 시점을 묻는 When 의문문에 적합한 대답이다.
(B) **연상 작용 오답**: research lab에서 연상할 수 있는 space를 이용한 오답이다.
(C) **정답**: 연구소의 위치를 묻는 질문에 구체적인 위치(behind the library)를 알려 주었으므로 정답이다.

어휘 | research lab 연구소 space 공간 behind ~의 뒤에

4 Who needs to sign off on the final budget proposal?
(A) You can pay later.
(B) Ms. Perez has the list of names.
(C) On the bottom of the last page, please.

최종 예산 제안서에 누가 승인 서명을 해야 하나요?
(A) 나중에 계산하시면 됩니다.
(B) 페레즈 씨가 명단을 갖고 있어요.
(C) 마지막 페이지 하단에 해 주세요.

해설 | 담당자를 묻는 Who 의문문
(A) **연상 작용 오답**: 질문의 final에서 연상 가능한 later를 이용한 오답이다.
(B) **정답**: 최종 예산 제안서에 승인 서명을 해야 하는 사람을 묻는 질문에 해당 정보를 제공할 수 있는 특정 인물(Ms. Perez)을 언급하고 있으므로 가장 적절한 응답이다.
(C) **연상 작용 오답**: 질문의 sign에서 연상 가능한 서명 위치(On the bottom of the last page)를 언급한 오답이다.

어휘 | sign off (~에 서명하여) 승인하다 budget 예산 proposal 제안 bottom 맨 아래

5 When do you expect the remodeling to be finished?
(A) Not until next week.
(B) He is a role model for all of us.
(C) I'm expecting one.

개조 공사가 언제 끝날 것으로 예상하나요?
(A) **다음 주나 되어야 해요.**
(B) 그는 저희 모두에게 모범이 되는 분이세요.
(C) 한 명이 올 거예요.

해설 | 예상 시점을 묻는 When 의문문
(A) **정답**: 공사 종료 예상 시점을 묻는 질문에 Not until next week라는 구체적인 시점을 언급한 정답이다.
(B) **유사 발음 오답**: remodeling과 발음이 유사한 role model로 혼동을 준 오답이다.
(C) **단어 반복 오답**: 질문의 expect를 반복 이용한 오답이다.

어휘 | expect 예상하다 remodeling 개보수, 리모델링 not until ~가 되어서야 비로소 role model 역할 모델

6 Where did you put the documents?
(A) They're in the file cabinet.
(B) With a new camera.
(C) Twenty pages.

서류를 어디에 두었죠?
(A) **문서 보관함에 있어요.**
(B) 새 카메라로요.
(C) 20쪽요.

해설 | 장소를 묻는 Where 의문문
(A) **정답**: 서류를 둔 장소를 묻는 질문에 서류가 있는 곳(in the file cabinet)을 알려 주었으므로 정답이다.
(B) **관련 없는 오답**: 서류를 둔 장소를 묻는 질문에 '새 카메라로(With a new camera)'라고 하는 것은 상황에 맞지 않는 대답이다.
(C) **연상 작용 오답**: 질문의 documents에서 연상 가능한 Twenty pages를 이용한 오답이다.

어휘 | file cabinet 문서 보관함

7 Who should I call about replacing the printer ink cartridge?
(A) On Monday mornings.
(B) Yes, they were delivered yesterday.
(C) Mr. Bauer usually takes care of that.

프린터 잉크 카트리지 교체 건에 대해 누구에게 전화해야 해요?
(A) 월요일 아침마다요.
(B) 네, 어제 배송됐어요.
(C) **보통 바우어 씨가 맡아서 해요.**

해설 | 담당자를 묻는 Who 의문문
(A) **관련 없는 오답**: 시점을 묻는 When 의문문에 적합한 대답이다.
(B) **Yes/No 대답 불가 오답**: Who 의문문에는 Yes/No로 대답할 수 없다.
(C) **정답**: 교체 건에 대해 전화해야 할 대상을 묻는 질문에 보통 바우어 씨가 맡아서 한다(Mr. Bauer usually takes care of that)며 연락할 대상을 특정했으므로 정답이다.

어휘 | replace 교체하다 deliver 배송하다

8 When are we meeting to discuss the project update?
(A) On the second floor.
(B) Yes, I updated my e-mail address.
(C) Do you have time on Monday?

프로젝트 최근 상황을 논의하기 위해 언제 회의하나요?
(A) 2층에서요.
(B) 네, 저는 이메일 주소를 변경했어요.
(C) **월요일에 시간 되세요?**

해설 | 시점을 묻는 When 의문문
(A) **관련 없는 오답**: 회의 장소를 묻는 Where 의문문에 적합한 대답이다.
(B) **Yes/No 대답 불가 오답**: When 의문문에는 Yes/No로 대답할 수 없다.
(C) **정답**: 언제 회의할지 묻는 질문에 월요일에 시간이 되는지(Do you have time on Monday?) 되묻고 있으므로 가장 적절한 응답이다.

어휘 | discuss 논의하다

9 Where is the human resources department located?
(A) Mr. Wong does.
(B) Monday through Friday.
(C) On the second floor.

인사부는 어디에 있나요?
(A) 웡 씨가 합니다.
(B) 월요일부터 금요일까지요.
(C) **2층에요.**

해설 | 위치를 묻는 Where 의문문
(A) **관련 없는 오답**: 담당자를 묻는 Who 의문문에 적합한 대답이다.
(B) **관련 없는 오답**: 시점을 묻는 When 의문문에 적합한 대답이다.
(C) **정답**: 인사부의 위치를 묻는 질문에 구체적인 위치(On the second floor)를 알려 주었으므로 정답이다.

어휘 | human resources 인사부 department 부서 be located 위치해 있다

10 Who owns the blue car parked out front?
(A) That sounds like it could be Mr. Hardin's.
(B) It looks much higher.
(C) The park has beautiful trees.

입구 쪽에 주차된 파란색 자동차의 주인이 누구죠?
(A) **그건 하딘 씨의 차 같은데요.**
(B) 훨씬 더 높아 보여요.
(C) 그 공원에는 아름다운 나무들이 있어요.

해설 | **자동차 소유주를 묻는 Who 의문문**

(A) **정답**: 자동차의 소유주로 Mr. Hardin이라는 구체적인 이름을 언급한 정답이다.
(B) **관련 없는 오답**: 질문의 내용과 관련 없는 답변이다.
(C) **다의어 오답**: 질문의 parked(주차된)와 형태는 비슷하지만 뜻은 다른 park(공원)를 이용한 오답이다.

어휘 | own 소유하다 out front 입구 쪽에

11 When can I expect to hear from you about the interview?
(A) Within the next few days.
(B) At the end of the street.
(C) I found it right here.

면접에 대해 언제 소식을 들을 수 있을까요?
(A) 며칠 내로요.
(B) 거리 끝에요.
(C) 바로 여기서 발견했어요.

해설 | **예상 시점을 묻는 When 의문문**

(A) **정답**: 소식을 들을 수 있는 시점을 묻는 질문에 며칠 내(Within the next few days)라며 대략적인 시점을 언급하고 있으므로 정답이다.
(B) **관련 없는 오답**: 위치를 묻는 Where 의문문에 적합한 대답이다.
(C) **유사 발음 오답**: 질문의 hear와 발음이 동일한 here를 이용한 오답이다.

어휘 | expect 기대하다, 예상하다

12 Where do I register for the training course?
(A) You can sign up right here.
(B) Yes, of course I have.
(C) A thirty-dollar registration fee.

교육 과정은 어디에서 등록하나요?
(A) 여기서 신청하시면 됩니다.
(B) 네, 물론 그랬죠.
(C) 등록비 30달러요.

해설 | **장소를 묻는 Where 의문문**

(A) **정답**: 교육 과정의 등록 장소를 묻는 질문에 여기서 신청하면 된다(You can sign up right here)고 답하고 있으므로 정답이다.
(B) **Yes/No 대답 불가 오답**: Where 의문문에는 Yes/No로 대답할 수 없다.
(C) **파생어 오답**: 질문의 register와 파생어 관계인 registration을 이용한 오답이다.

어휘 | register for ~에 등록하다 sign up 등록하다, 신청하다 registration fee 등록비

13 Who's picking Mr. Lim up from the airport?
(A) It's not mine.
(B) Thanks, I dropped it.
(C) I'm going to.

누가 공항에서 임 씨를 픽업할 건가요?
(A) 제 것이 아닙니다.
(B) 고맙습니다. 제가 떨어뜨렸어요.
(C) 제가요.

해설 | **담당자를 묻는 Who 의문문**

(A) **관련 없는 오답**: 픽업할 담당자를 묻는 질문에 내 것이 아니다(It's not mine)라고 하는 것은 상황에 맞지 않는 대답이다.

(B) **연상 작용 오답**: 질문의 pick up을 '집어 들다, 들어 올리다'라는 뜻으로 잘못 이해했을 경우 연상 가능한 dropped를 이용한 오답이다.
(C) **정답**: 픽업할 담당자를 묻는 질문에 자신(I'm going to)이라고 답하고 있으므로 정답이다.

어휘 | pick A up A를 차에 태우러 가다 drop 떨어뜨리다

14 When can the building inspector approve the electrical work?
(A) Yes, they do good work.
(B) The building's on Marigold Avenue.
(C) Next week at the earliest.

건물 검사관이 언제 전기 공사를 승인할 수 있을까요?
(A) 네, 그들은 일을 잘해요.
(B) 그 건물은 메리골드 애비뉴에 있어요.
(C) 빨라도 다음 주요.

해설 | **승인 시점을 묻는 When 의문문**

(A) **Yes/No 대답 불가 오답**: When 의문문에는 Yes/No로 대답할 수 없다.
(B) **단어 반복 오답**: 질문의 building을 반복 이용한 오답이다.
(C) **정답**: 전기 공사의 승인 시점을 묻는 질문에 빨라도 다음 주(Next week at the earliest)라며 가능한 예상 시점을 언급하고 있으므로 정답이다.

어휘 | inspector 조사관, 검사관 approve 승인하다 electrical 전기의 at the earliest 빨라도, 일러도

15 Where are the copies of today's schedule?
(A) Just a small cup.
(B) Every Monday and Wednesday.
(C) The printer is still broken.

오늘 일정표 인쇄본은 어디에 있나요?
(A) 그냥 작은 컵이요.
(B) 매주 월요일과 수요일에요.
(C) 프린터가 아직도 고장 난 상태에요.

해설 | **위치를 묻는 Where 의문문**

(A) **연상 작용 오답**: 질문의 copies를 coffees로 잘못 들었을 경우 연상 가능한 cup을 이용한 오답이다.
(B) **연상 작용 오답**: 질문의 schedule에서 연상 가능한 Every Monday and Wednesday를 이용한 오답이다.
(C) **정답**: 인쇄본의 위치를 묻는 질문에 프린터가 고장(The printer is still broken)이라 아직 인쇄가 되지 않았음을 우회적으로 나타냈으므로 가장 적절한 응답이다.

어휘 | copy 인쇄본, 복사본

16 Who owns the bakery in Merrittville?
(A) George's family just bought it.
(B) Across from Forrest Avenue.
(C) Because it's near my office.

메릿빌에 있는 제과점은 누구 건가요?
(A) 조지네 가족이 막 사들였어요.
(B) 포레스트 애비뉴 맞은편요.
(C) 제 사무실과 가깝거든요.

해설 | **소유자를 묻는 Who 의문문**

(A) **정답**: 제과점의 소유자를 묻는 질문에 조지네 가족이 막 사들였다(George's family just bought it)며 우회적으로 소유주를 특정했으므로 정답이다.

(B) **관련 없는 오답**: 위치를 묻는 Where 의문문에 적합한 대답이다.
(C) **관련 없는 오답**: 이유를 묻는 Why 의문문에 적합한 대답이다.

어휘 | own 소유하다 across from ~의 맞은편에 있는

17 When will we add another science writer to our department?
(A) As soon as we find someone who's qualified.
(B) A three-page article with photographs.
(C) Several years of writing experience.

우리 부서에 과학 부문 저술가를 언제 충원할 예정인가요?
(A) 자격을 갖춘 사람을 찾는 대로요.
(B) 사진이 들어간 3쪽짜리 기사요.
(C) 수년간의 집필 경력요.

해설 | 충원 예정 시점을 묻는 When 의문문
(A) **정답**: 과학 부문 저술가의 충원 예정 시점을 묻는 질문에 '자격을 갖춘 사람을 찾는 대로(As soon as we find someone who's qualified)'라고 답했으므로 가장 적절한 응답이다.
(B) **연상 작용 오답**: 질문의 writer에서 연상 가능한 article을 이용한 오답이다.
(C) **파생어 오답**: 질문의 writer와 파생어 관계인 writing을 이용한 오답이다.

어휘 | department 부서 as soon as ~하자마자 qualified 자격을 갖춘 article 기사 experience 경험, 경력

18 Where is the next convention going to be held?
(A) It was too crowded as usual.
(B) I'll find out.
(C) Sooner than we expect.

다음 총회는 어디에서 열리죠?
(A) 평소처럼 매우 붐볐어요.
(B) 알아볼게요.
(C) 예상보다 더 일찍이요.

해설 | 총회 장소를 묻는 Where 의문문
(A) **연상 작용 오답**: 의미상 연결이 가능한 두 단어(convention 총회 / crowded 붐비는)를 이용한 오답이다.
(B) **정답**: 총회 장소를 묻는 Where 의문문에 간접 응답 '내가 알아보겠다'로 잘 답변한 정답이다.
(C) **관련 없는 오답**: 시점을 묻는 When 의문문에 대한 답변이다.

어휘 | convention 대회, 총회 crowded 붐비는 as usual 평소대로, 여느 때처럼 expect 예상하다

19 Who was hired to replace Mr. Tang?
(A) Yes, I like this place, too.
(B) They haven't made a decision yet.
(C) The price is higher.

탱 씨의 후임으로 누가 채용되었나요?
(A) 네, 저도 이곳이 마음에 들어요.
(B) 그들이 아직 결정하지 않았어요.
(C) 가격이 더 높아요.

해설 | 특정 대상을 묻는 Who 의문문
(A) **Yes/No 대답 불가 오답**: Who 의문문에는 Yes/No로 대답할 수 없다.
(B) **정답**: 탱 씨의 후임자를 묻는 질문에 그들(= 결정권자, 회사)이 아직 결정하지 않았다(They haven't made a decision yet)며 관련된 상황을 언급하고 있으므로 가장 적절한 응답이다. They가 가리키는 대상이 질문에는 없지만, 문맥상 채용

결정권자들을 의미하는 것으로 파악할 수 있다.
(C) **유사 발음 오답**: 질문의 hired와 발음이 유사한 higher를 이용한 오답이다.

어휘 | replace 대체[대신]하다 decision 결정

20 When is the Morrison Bridge going to be repaired?
(A) A pair of them.
(B) He was stuck in traffic.
(C) Sometime next spring.

모리슨 다리가 언제 수리되나요?
(A) 한 쌍이요.
(B) 그가 교통 체증에 꼼짝 못했어요.
(C) 다음 봄쯤이에요.

해설 | 시점을 묻는 When 의문문
(A) **유사 발음 오답**: 질문의 repair와 부분적으로 발음이 유사한 pair를 이용한 오답이다.
(B) **연상 작용 오답**: 질문의 Bridge에서 연상 가능한 stuck in traffic을 이용한 오답이다.
(C) **정답**: 다리가 수리되는 시점을 묻는 When 의문문에 대략적인 시점(Sometime next spring)으로 답하므로 정답이다.

어휘 | repair 수리하다 a pair of 한 쌍의 be stuck in traffic 교통 체증에 걸려 꼼짝 못하다

21 Where can I find an extra box of staples?
(A) 500 to a box.
(B) In the supply closet.
(C) For the report.

여러분의 스테이플러 침 상자를 어디에서 찾을 수 있나요?
(A) 한 상자에 500개요.
(B) 비품 수납장 안에요.
(C) 보고서를 위해서요.

해설 | 보관 장소를 묻는 Where 의문문
(A) **관련 없는 오답**: 수량을 묻는 How many 의문문에 대한 답변이다.
(B) **정답**: 스테이플러 침 상자가 있는 곳을 묻는 질문에 구체적인 위치(In the supply closet)를 알려주었으므로 정답이다.
(C) **관련 없는 오답**: 이유나 목적을 묻는 Why 의문문에 가능한 답변이다.

어휘 | extra 여분의, 추가의 staple (스테이플러에 넣는) 철사 침 to a box 한 상자에 supply closet 비품 수납장

22 Who's organizing the fund-raiser?
(A) Suki volunteered to do it.
(B) Please rearrange the files.
(C) It's on Friday.

모금 행사는 누가 준비하나요?
(A) 수키가 하겠다고 자원했어요.
(B) 파일들을 재배치해 주세요.
(C) 금요일이에요.

해설 | 담당자를 묻는 Who 의문문
(A) **정답**: 모금 행사의 준비 담당자를 묻는 질문에 수키가 하겠다고 자원했다(Suki volunteered to do it)며 우회적으로 담당자를 특정했으므로 정답이다.
(B) **연상 작용 오답**: 질문의 organizing을 '정리하다'라는 뜻으로 잘못 이해했을 경우 연상 가능한 rearrange를 이용한

오답이다.

(C) **관련 없는 오답:** 시점을 묻는 When 의문문에 적합한 대답이다.

어휘 | organize 준비하다, 조직하다 fund-raiser 모금 행사 volunteer 자원하다 rearrange 재배열하다, 재배치하다

23 When will the sales report be ready to distribute?
(A) It's almost finished.
(B) There's a special discount today.
(C) To the distribution center.

영업보고서 배포 준비가 언제쯤 될까요?
(A) 거의 완성됐어요.
(B) 오늘 특별 할인이 있어요.
(C) 유통센터로요.

해설 | **배포 시점을 묻는 When 의문문**
(A) **정답:** 영업보고서의 배포 시점을 묻는 질문에 거의 완성됐다(It's almost finished)며 곧 배포될 것임을 우회적으로 드러내고 있으므로 정답이다.
(B) **연상 작용 오답:** 질문의 sales에서 연상 가능한 discount를 이용한 오답이다.
(C) **파생어 오답:** 질문의 distribute와 파생어 관계인 distribution을 이용한 오답이다.

어휘 | sales report 영업보고서 distribute 분배하다, 배포하다, 나눠주다 discount 할인 distribution 유통, 배포

24 Where do you usually take your dry cleaning?
(A) To Pierre's Cleaners.
(B) It's not dry yet.
(C) All the time.

드라이클리닝 할 세탁물을 주로 어디로 가져가나요?
(A) 피에르 세탁소로요.
(B) 그것은 아직 마르지 않았어요.
(C) 언제나요.

해설 | **장소를 묻는 Where 의문문**
(A) **정답:** 세탁물을 맡기는 장소를 묻는 질문에 업체명을 알려주었으므로 정답이다.
(B) **단어 반복 오답:** 질문에 사용된 dry를 반복 이용한 오답이다.
(C) **관련 없는 오답:** 시점을 묻는 When 의문문에 대한 답변이다.

어휘 | dry cleaning 드라이클리닝(할 세탁물) cleaner 세탁소 all the time 언제나, 줄곧

25 Who's speaking at the next conference session?
(A) No, it's later on.
(B) I liked the lesson.
(C) The vice president.

다음 회의 시간에 누가 이야기할 건가요?
(A) 아니요. 그건 나중이에요.
(B) 그 수업 좋았어요.
(C) 부회장님요.

해설 | **담당자를 묻는 Who 의문문**
(A) **Yes/No 대답 불가 오답:** Who 의문문에는 Yes/No로 대답할 수 없다.
(B) **연상 작용 오답:** 질문의 conference session에서 연상 가능한 lesson을 이용한 오답이다.
(C) **정답:** 다음 회의의 발표 담당자를 묻는 질문에 구체적인 인물(The vice president)을 제시했으므로 정답이다.

어휘 | conference 회의 session 시간 later on 나중에 vice president 부회장

Unit 04 What · Which / Why / How 의문문

① What · Which 의문문

ETS 유형 연습

본책 p.044

1 (B) **2** (C) **3** (A) **4** (B) **5** (B) **6** (B)

1 What time are you serving lunch?
(A) Down at the harbor.
(B) From 11 A.M. to 2 P.M.
(C) Yes, I have time.

몇 시에 점심 식사가 가능한가요?
(A) 항구 아래쪽에서요.
(B) 오전 11시부터 오후 2시까지요.
(C) 네, 저는 시간 있어요.

해설 | **식사 가능 시간을 묻는 What 의문문**
(A) **관련 없는 오답:** Where 의문문에 어울리는 장소 표현이다.
(B) **정답:** 식사 가능 시간을 묻는 질문에 구체적인 시간대로 답변했으므로 정답이다.
(C) **Yes/No 대답 불가 오답:** What 의문문에 Yes/No로 대답할 수 없다.

어휘 | serve (음식을) 제공하다 harbor 항구

2 What is the purpose of your visit to Singapore, sir?
(A) Yes, five or six times.
(B) At a hotel downtown.
(C) I'm here for a convention.

싱가포르를 방문하신 목적이 무엇입니까?
(A) 네, 대여섯 번이요.
(B) 시내 호텔에서요.
(C) 컨벤션에 참석하려고 왔어요.

해설 | **방문 목적을 묻는 What 의문문**
(A) **Yes/No 대답 불가 오답:** What 의문문에 Yes/No로 답변할 수 없다.
(B) **관련 없는 오답:** Where 의문문에 어울리는 답변이다.
(C) **정답:** 컨벤션에 참가하기 위해서라고 방문 목적을 밝혔으므로 정답이다.

어휘 | downtown 시내에 convention 대회, 컨벤션

3 What kind of tea would you like?
(A) I'll have some green tea.
(B) Yes, I'd like to.
(C) After I finish eating.

어떤 차를 드실래요?
(A) 녹차 마실게요.
(B) 네, 그러겠습니다.
(C) 다 먹고 나서요.

해설 | **차의 종류를 묻는 What 의문문**
(A) **정답:** 마시고 싶은 차의 종류를 묻는 질문에 구체적으로 녹차 (some green tea)라고 알려 주었으므로 정답이다.

(B) **Yes/No 대답 불가 오답**: 종류를 묻는 What kind 질문에는 Yes/No로 대답할 수 없다.

(C) **관련 없는 오답**: 차를 마실 시점을 묻는 When 의문문에 적합한 대답이다.

4 Which travel case did you buy for your laptop?
(A) For my trip to Malaysia.
(B) The brown leather one.
(C) I bought it yesterday.

노트북용으로 어떤 여행 가방을 샀어요?
(A) 말레이시아 여행을 위해서요.
(B) **갈색 가죽 가방요.**
(C) 어제 그걸 샀어요.

해설 | 구매한 여행 가방을 묻는 Which 의문문
(A) **관련 없는 오답**: 구매한 여행 가방의 용도를 묻는 질문에 적합한 대답이다.
(B) **정답**: 구매한 여행 가방을 묻는 질문에 대명사 one(=travel case)를 사용하여 갈색 가죽 가방(The brown leather one)이라고 답하고 있으므로 정답이다.
(C) **관련 없는 오답**: 구매 시점을 묻는 When 의문문에 적합한 대답이다.

어휘 | laptop 노트북 컴퓨터 **leather** 가죽

5 Which stores are open late tonight?
(A) They were delayed by the storm.
(B) None of them except the supermarket.
(C) We store them in plastic containers.

어느 상점들이 오늘 밤 늦게까지 문을 여나요?
(A) 그것들은 폭풍 때문에 지연되었어요.
(B) **그 슈퍼마켓 말고는 없어요.**
(C) 저희는 플라스틱 용기에 그것들을 저장해요.

해설 | 늦게까지 운영하는 상점을 묻는 Which 의문문
(A) **연상 작용 오답**: 의미상 연결이 가능한 두 단어(late 늦게/delayed 지연된)를 이용한 오답이다.
(B) **정답**: 어느 상점들이 늦게까지 문을 여는지 묻는 질문에, 한 곳을 제외하고는 없다고 알려주었으므로 정답이다.
(C) **다의어 오답**: 질문의 store는 '상점'을, 보기의 store는 '저장하다'를 의미한다.

어휘 | store 상점; 저장하다 **delay** 지연시키다 **except** ~을 제외하고 **container** 그릇, 용기

6 Which route do you usually take to work?
(A) I didn't bring it with me.
(B) I go down Elm Street.
(C) Not until Wednesday.

보통 출근할 때 어떤 길로 가세요?
(A) 안 가져왔어요.
(B) **엘름 가를 따라가요.**
(C) 수요일이나 되어서요.

해설 | 출근 경로를 묻는 Which 의문문
(A) **연상 작용 오답**: 질문의 take를 '가지고 가다'라는 뜻으로 잘못 이해했을 경우 연상 가능한 bring을 이용한 오답이다.
(B) **정답**: 출근 경로를 묻는 질문에 구체적인 거리명(Elm Street)을 언급했으므로 정답이다.
(C) **관련 없는 오답**: 기한을 묻는 When 의문문에 적합한 대답이다.

어휘 | route 길, 노선 **usually** 대개, 보통 **bring** 가져오다 **not until** ~이후에야 비로소

② Why 의문문

ETS 유형 연습

본책 p.045

1 (A)	**2** (C)	**3** (B)	**4** (B)	**5** (C)	**6** (C)

1 Why is the office supply store closed today?
(A) It's a holiday.
(B) Yes, it's close to our office.
(C) In the supply closet.

오늘 사무용품점이 왜 문을 닫았죠?
(A) **오늘은 공휴일이에요.**
(B) 네, 우리 사무실과 가까워요.
(C) 비품 창고예요.

해설 | 문을 닫은 이유를 묻는 Why 의문문
(A) **정답**: 사무용품점이 문을 닫은 이유를 묻는 질문에 공휴일(a holiday)이기 때문이라는 구체적인 이유를 제시했으므로 정답이다.
(B) **Yes/No 대답 불가·다의어 오답**: 이유를 묻는 Why 의문문에는 Yes/No로 대답할 수 없으며, 질문의 closed는 '닫혀진'이라는 뜻의 과거분사이고, 보기의 close는 '가까운'이라는 뜻의 형용사이다.
(C) **단어 반복 오답**: 질문의 supply를 반복 이용한 오답이다.

어휘 | office supply 사무용품 **holiday** 공휴일, 휴일 **supply closet** 비품 창고

2 Why has the workshop been canceled?
(A) About twenty minutes ago.
(B) In room fourteen.
(C) Because many people couldn't attend.

워크숍은 왜 취소됐나요?
(A) 대략 20분 전에요.
(B) 14번 방에서요.
(C) **사람들이 많이 참석할 수 없었기 때문에요.**

해설 | 행사 취소 이유를 묻는 Why 의문문
(A) **관련 없는 오답**: 취소 시점을 묻는 When 의문문에 대한 응답이다.
(B) **관련 없는 오답**: 행사 장소를 묻는 Where 의문문에 대한 응답이다.
(C) **정답**: 사람들이 많이 참석할 수 없었기 때문(Because many people couldn't attend)이라는 구체적인 이유를 제시했으므로 정답이다.

어휘 | cancel 취소하다 **attend** 참석하다

3 Why isn't Doctor Gutierrez working here anymore?
(A) An appointment tomorrow.
(B) He retired at the end of last year.
(C) Please fill out a patient form.

구티에레즈 의사 선생님은 왜 여기서 더 이상 일하지 않는 거죠?
(A) 내일 약속요.
(B) **작년 말에 은퇴하셨어요.**
(C) 진료 신청서를 작성하세요.

해설 | **일하지 않는 이유를 묻는 Why 의문문**
(A) **연상 작용 오답**: 질문의 Doctor에서 연상 가능한 appointment를 이용한 오답이다.
(B) **정답**: 의사가 일하지 않는 이유를 묻는 질문에 작년 말에 은퇴했다(He retired at the end of last year)는 구체적인 이유를 제시했으므로 정답이다.
(C) **연상 작용 오답**: 질문의 Doctor에서 연상 가능한 patient를 이용한 오답이다.

어휘 | appointment 약속, 예약 retire 은퇴하다, 퇴직하다 fill out 작성하다, 기입하다 patient (registration) form 진료 신청서

4 Why do you have to get certified again?
(A) Please register online.
(B) It's required every five years.
(C) A teaching certificate.
왜 다시 자격증을 취득해야 하죠?
(A) 온라인으로 등록해 주세요.
(B) 5년마다 요구되거든요.
(C) 교사 자격증이요.

해설 | **자격증 재취득 이유를 묻는 Why 의문문**
(A) **연상 작용 오답**: 의미상 연결이 가능한 두 단어(certify 자격증을 주다/register 등록하다)를 이용한 오답이다.
(B) **정답**: Because를 생략하고, '5년마다 필수'라고 자격증 재취득이 필요한 이유를 제시했으므로 정답이다.
(C) **파생어 오답**: 질문에 나오는 certified와 파생어 관계인 certificate를 이용한 오답이다.

어휘 | get certified 자격증을 취득하다 register 등록하다 require 필요로 하다 certificate 증명서, 자격증

5 Why did Ms. Khan bring an assistant to the trade fair?
(A) I traded it in.
(B) No, not this time.
(C) To help with a demonstration.
칸 씨는 왜 무역박람회에 비서를 데리고 왔나요?
(A) 제가 거래했어요.
(B) 아니요. 이번엔 아닙니다.
(C) 시연을 돕게 하려고요.

해설 | **비서를 동반한 이유를 묻는 Why 의문문**
(A) **다의어 오답**: 질문의 trade는 '무역'이라는 뜻의 명사이고, 보기의 traded는 '거래하다'라는 뜻의 동사이다.
(B) **Yes/No 대답 불가 오답**: 이유를 묻는 Why 의문문에는 Yes/No로 대답할 수 없다.
(C) **정답**: 무역박람회에 비서를 동반한 이유를 묻는 질문에 시연을 돕게 하기 위해(To help with a demonstration)라며 구체적인 목적을 밝혔으므로 정답이다.

어휘 | trade fair 무역박람회 trade in ~을 거래하다, 사고 팔다 demonstration 설명, 시연

6 Why has the book's release date been delayed?
(A) I approved the payment.
(B) It was about a month.
(C) The editor requested additional changes.
책 출간일이 왜 연기되었죠?
(A) 제가 지급을 승인했어요.
(B) 한 달 정도였어요.
(C) 편집자가 추가 수정을 요청했어요.

해설 | **출간 연기 이유를 묻는 Why 의문문**
(A) **관련 없는 오답**: 질문의 내용과 관련 없는 답변이다.
(B) **연상 작용 오답**: delayed에서 연상 가능한 about a month를 이용한 오답이다.
(C) **정답**: 출간일 지연 사유로 편집자의 추가 수정 요구를 제시하므로 정답이다.

어휘 | release date 출간일 delay 연기하다 approve 승인하다 payment 지불, 대금 editor 편집자 additional 추가적인

③ How 의문문

ETS 유형 연습   본책 p.046

1 (B)	2 (B)	3 (C)	4 (A)	5 (B)	6 (C)

1 How much is your gym membership fee?
(A) That's good to know.
(B) It's 65 dollars a month.
(C) I've never met them before.
당신의 헬스클럽 회원권은 얼마인가요?
(A) 알게 되어 다행이네요.
(B) 한 달에 65 달러예요.
(C) 전에 그들을 만나본 적이 없어요.

해설 | **가격을 묻는 How 의문문**
(A) **관련 없는 오답**: 소식을 알려주는 평서문에 어울리는 응답이다.
(B) **정답**: 회원권의 가격을 묻는 질문에 구체적인 금액(65 dollars a month)을 알려 주었으므로 정답이다.
(C) **연상 작용 오답**: 질문의 membership을 members로 잘못 들었을 경우 연상 가능한 상황(I've never met them before)을 이용한 오답이다.

2 How many copies of the document do you need?
(A) That really wasn't necessary.
(B) Twelve should be enough.
(C) No coffee for me, thanks.
그 서류가 몇 부나 필요하나요?
(A) 그건 정말 필요 없었어요.
(B) 12부면 충분하겠어요.
(C) 저는 커피 안 주셔도 됩니다, 고마워요.

해설 | **수량을 묻는 How 의문문**
(A) **연상 작용 오답**: 질문의 need에서 연상 가능한 necessary를 이용한 오답이다.
(B) **정답**: 서류가 몇 부나 필요한지 묻는 질문에 Twelve라는 구체적인 숫자를 제시하고 있으므로 정답이다.
(C) **유사 발음 오답**: 질문의 copies와 발음이 비슷한 coffee를 이용한 오답이다.

어휘 | copy (책·신문 등) 한 부 document 서류 necessary 필요한

3 How was the opening ceremony?
(A) The Stockton Stadium.
(B) Yesterday at 10.
(C) It was very exciting.
개막식은 어땠나요?
(A) 스톡턴 경기장요.
(B) 어제 10시요.
(C) 굉장히 흥미진진했어요.

LC

PART 2

해설 | **의견을 묻는 How 의문문**
(A) 관련 없는 오답: 개막식 장소를 묻는 Where 의문문에 적합한
대답이다.
(B) 관련 없는 오답: 개막식 시간을 묻는 When 의문문에 적합한
대답이다.
(C) 정답: 개막식에 대한 의견을 묻는 질문에 굉장히 흥미진진했다(It
was very exciting)며 구체적으로 답했으므로 정답이다.

어휘 | opening ceremony 개막식, 개업식

4 How will you get to the hotel from here?
(A) I'll take a taxi.
(B) In the lobby.
(C) She left yesterday.
여기서 호텔까지 어떻게 갈 겁니까?
(A) 택시를 탈 겁니다.
(B) 로비에서요.
(C) 그녀는 어제 떠났어요.

해설 | **수단·방법을 묻는 How 의문문**
(A) 정답: 호텔에 어떻게 갈지 묻는 질문에 택시라는 교통 수단을
언급하고 있으므로 적절한 대답이다.
(B) 연상 작용 오답: 질문의 hotel에서 연상 가능한 lobby를 사용한
오답이다.
(C) 관련 없는 오답: When 의문문에 가능한 대답이다.

5 How often do you fly for business?
(A) Half an hour ago.
(B) Usually twice a year.
(C) I'd prefer an aisle seat.
얼마나 자주 비행기로 출장을 가세요?
(A) 30분 전에요.
(B) 보통 1년에 두 번.
(C) 저는 통로 쪽 좌석이 좋습니다.

해설 | **빈도를 묻는 How 의문문**
(A) 관련 없는 오답: 시점을 묻는 When 의문문에 적합한 대답이다.
(B) 정답: 비행기로 출장 가는 빈도를 묻는 질문에 구체적인
횟수(Usually twice a year)를 알려 주었으므로 정답이다.
(C) 연상 작용 오답: 질문의 fly에서 연상 가능한 aisle seat를
이용한 오답이다.

어휘 | for business 업무상 usually 대개, 보통 prefer 좋아하다,
선호하다 aisle 통로

6 How can we reduce our energy costs?
(A) Only twenty percent.
(B) On the hard drive.
(C) By installing better windows.
어떻게 하면 연료비를 줄일 수 있을까요?
(A) 20퍼센트만요.
(B) 하드 드라이브에요.
(C) 더 좋은 창문을 설치해서요.

해설 | **연료비 절감 방법을 묻는 How 의문문**
(A) 관련 없는 오답: 정도를 묻는 How much 의문문에 어울리는
대답이다.
(B) 관련 없는 오답: 보관 장소를 묻는 Where 의문문에 적합한
대답이다.
(C) 정답: 연료비를 줄이는 방법을 묻는 질문에 더 좋은 창문을
설치해서(By installing better windows)라는 구체적인
방안을 제시했으므로 정답이다.

어휘 | reduce 줄이다, 감소시키다 energy cost 에너지 비용, 연료비
install 설치하다

● 실전 **도움닫기** 본책 p.047

1 (B) **2** (B) **3** (B) **4** (A) **5** (A)

1. What did Ms. Newton have to say about our
progress?
(A) She stayed on Wednesday.
(B) Mostly positive things.
(C) Yes, she did.
뉴턴 씨는 우리의 진척 상황에 대해 어떤 말씀을 하셨나요?
(A) 그녀는 수요일에 머물렀어요.
(B) 대체로 긍정적인 것들이었어요.
(C) 네, 그녀가 했어요.

해설 | **의견을 묻는 What 의문문**
(A) 유사 발음 오답: 질문의 say와 발음이 비슷한 stay를 이용한
오답이다.
(B) 정답: 뉴턴 씨의 의견이 대체로 긍정적인 것들이었다고
답변했으므로 정답이다.
(C) Yes / No 대답 불가 오답: What 의문문에 Yes / No로 대답할
수 없다.

어휘 | progress 진척 (상황), 진전 positive 긍정적인

2. Which is the key to the filing cabinet?
(A) You could file a complaint.
(B) The one with the red tag.
(C) Fill it in later.
서류 보관함 열쇠는 어떤 거예요?
(A) 당신은 불만을 제기할 수도 있어요.
(B) 빨간 꼬리표가 달린 거요.
(C) 나중에 그것을 채워 넣으세요.

해설 | **보관함 열쇠를 묻는 Which 의문문**
(A) 파생어 오답: 질문에 나오는 filing과 파생어 관계인 file을
사용한 오답이다.
(B) 정답: 보관함 열쇠가 어느 것인지 묻는 질문에, 빨간 꼬리표가
달린 것이라고 구체적으로 답했으므로 정답이다.
(C) 연상 작용 오답: 질문의 filing cabinet에서 수납 공간을 연상할
때 가능한 응답을 이용하였다.

어휘 | filing cabinet 서류 보관함 file a complaint 불만을
제기하다, 고소하다 tag 꼬리표 fill in ~을 기입하다, 채우다

3. Why is a new telephone system being installed?
(A) In about a month.
(B) Because it'll save us money.
(C) At the security desk.
왜 새로운 전화 시스템이 설치되고 있나요?
(A) 약 한 달 후에요.
(B) 돈을 절약할 수 있기 때문이에요.
(C) 보안 창구에서요.

해설 | **설치 이유를 묻는 Why 의문문**
(A) 관련 없는 오답: 미래의 시점을 묻는 When 의문문에 적절한
응답이다.

(B) **정답**: 전화 시스템이 새로 설치되는 이유를 Because를 사용해 구체적으로 답변했으므로 정답이다.

(C) **관련 없는 오답**: 위치나 장소를 묻는 Where 의문문에 대한 답변이다.

어휘 | install 설치하다 save (경비·시간 등을) 절약하다 security 보안, 경비

4. How soon can I make an appointment with Doctor Feinstein?

(A) She's available on Thursday.

(B) Just the first part.

(C) It was at 9:30.

파인스타인 박사님과의 예약을 빠르면 언제로 잡을 수 있나요?

(A) 그녀는 목요일에 시간이 됩니다.

(B) 첫 부분만요.

(C) 그것은 9시 30분이었어요.

해설 | **가능한 시간을 묻는 How 의문문**

(A) **정답**: 빠르면 언제 예약을 잡을 수 있는지 묻는 질문에 구체적인 시점(on Thursday)으로 답변했으므로 정답이다.

(B) **관련 없는 오답**: What이나 Which 의문문에 적절한 답변이다.

(C) **시제 오류 오답**: 미래에 가능한 시간을 묻는 질문에 과거로 답하는 것은 어색하다.

어휘 | appointment (진료 등의) 예약, 약속 available 시간이 되는

5. What was covered at the workshop this morning?

(A) I'll lend you my notes.

(B) It's expected to finish early.

(C) There's seating for about 25.

오늘 오전 워크숍에서 어떤 것이 다루어졌나요?

(A) 제가 필기한 것을 빌려드릴게요.

(B) 일찍 끝날 것으로 예상돼요.

(C) 약 25명 분의 좌석이 있어요.

해설 | **워크숍의 주제를 묻는 What 의문문**

(A) **정답**: 워크숍의 주제를 묻는 질문에 자신이 필기한 것(notes)을 빌려주겠다고 했으므로 가장 적절한 응답이다.

(B) **관련 없는 오답**: 시점을 묻는 When 질문에 적절한 답변이다.

(C) **연상 작용 오답**: 질문의 workshop에서 연상 가능한 seating을 이용한 오답이다.

어휘 | cover 다루다, 포함시키다 lend 빌려주다 notes 필기, 기록 expect 기대하다, 예상하다 seating 좌석, 자리

● **ETS 실전문제**   본책 p.048

- -

1 (C)	2 (A)	3 (C)	4 (A)	5 (A)
6 (A)	7 (C)	8 (A)	9 (B)	10 (B)
11 (A)	12 (B)	13 (C)	14 (C)	15 (C)
16 (B)	17 (A)	18 (A)	19 (C)	20 (A)
21 (C)	22 (C)	23 (C)	24 (A)	25 (B)

1 What kind of company does Mr. Perez manage?

(A) For twenty years.

(B) I can manage that.

(C) An advertising agency.

페레즈 씨는 어떤 종류의 회사를 경영하나요?

(A) 20년 동안이요.

(B) 제가 할 수 있어요.

(C) 광고 대행사요.

해설 | **회사의 종류를 묻는 What 의문문**

(A) **관련 없는 오답**: For twenty years는 How long으로 묻는 의문문에 가능한 대답이다.

(B) **단어 반복 오답**: 질문의 manage를 반복 이용한 오답이다.

(C) **정답**: 페레즈 씨가 어떤 회사를 운영하고 있는지 묻는 질문에 구체적인 회사의 종류(advertising agency)를 언급하고 있으므로 정답이다.

어휘 | manage 관리하다, 경영하다 advertising agency 광고 대행사

2 Which projects are you involved in these days?

(A) I'm on several design teams.

(B) Mondays and Fridays.

(C) At the laboratory.

요즘에는 어떤 프로젝트에 참여하고 있나요?

(A) 저는 여러 디자인 팀들에 속해 있어요.

(B) 월요일과 금요일마다요.

(C) 연구실에서요.

해설 | **소속 프로젝트를 묻는 Which 의문문**

(A) **정답**: 어느 프로젝트와 관련된 일을 하는지 묻는 질문에 자신의 소속(여러 디자인 팀)을 밝혔으므로 정답이다.

(B) **유사 발음 오답**: 질문의 days와 일부 발음이 동일한 Mondays, Fridays를 이용한 오답으로, When 의문문에 대한 답변으로 어울린다.

(C) **관련 없는 오답**: 장소를 묻는 Where의문문에 대한 답변으로 어울린다.

어휘 | be involved in ~에 관계되다 these days 요즘에는 on (소속) ~의 일원인, ~에서 일하여 laboratory 연구실

3 Why did Mr. Feng postpone the staff meeting?

(A) Yes, he did.

(B) For a minimum of five days.

(C) Because he's going on vacation.

펭 씨는 왜 직원 회의를 미뤘나요?

(A) 네, 그가 그랬어요.

(B) 적어도 5일간요.

(C) 휴가를 갈 예정이라서요.

해설 | **연기 이유를 묻는 Why 의문문**

(A) **Yes/No 대답 불가 오답**: 이유를 묻는 Why 의문문에는 Yes/No로 대답할 수 없다.

(B) **관련 없는 오답**: 기간을 묻는 How long 의문문에 어울리는 대답이다.

(C) **정답**: 펭 씨가 직원 회의를 연기한 이유를 묻는 질문에 휴가를 갈 예정이기 때문(Because he's going on vacation)이라는 구체적인 이유를 제시했으므로 정답이다.

어휘 | postpone 미루다, 연기하다 staff meeting 직원 회의 minimum 최소 go on vacation 휴가 가다

4 How much do these sweaters cost?

(A) They're thirty euros each.

(B) A variety of styles.

(C) Not too much longer.

이 스웨터들은 가격이 얼마인가요?
(A) 그것들은 각각 30유로입니다.
(B) 다양한 스타일들이요.
(C) 그렇게 오래 걸리지는 않아요.

해설 | **가격을 묻는 How 의문문**
(A) 정답: 가격을 묻는 질문에, 화폐 단위인 euro를 사용해서 금액을
    알려주었으므로 정답이다.
(B) 연상 작용 오답: 의미상 연결이 가능한 두 단어(sweater
    스웨터/style 스타일)를 이용한 오답이다.
(C) 단어 반복 오답: 질문에 사용된 much를 반복 이용한 오답이다.

어휘 | a variety of 다양한

5 What answer did you get from the technology
    department?
   (A) Nothing so far.
   (B) Did you buy a computer?
   (C) Sometimes it does.

기술부서에서 어떤 답을 들었나요?
(A) 아직까지는 답이 없네요.
(B) 컴퓨터 사셨어요?
(C) 가끔 그래요.

해설 | **대답의 내용을 묻는 What 의문문**
(A) 정답: 기술부서에서 들은 대답의 내용을 묻는 질문에 아직까지
    답이 없다(Nothing so far)며 알려 줄 내용이 없음을
    우회적으로 드러내고 있으므로 정답이다.
(B) 연상 작용 오답: 질문의 technology department에서 연상
    가능한 computer를 이용한 오답이다.
(C) 관련 없는 오답: 기술부서에서 들은 대답의 내용을 묻는 질문에
    가끔 그렇다고 응답하는 것은 적절하지 않다.

어휘 | technology 기술 department 부서 so far 지금까지

6 Which packages need to be sent?
   (A) All of them.
   (B) Yes, especially the packages.
   (C) Express delivery, please.

어느 소포들이 발송되어야 하나요?
(A) 그것들 모두요.
(B) 네, 특히 그 소포들이요.
(C) 빠른 우편으로 해주세요.

해설 | **발송 물품을 묻는 Which 의문문**
(A) 정답: 발송되어야 할 소포를 묻는 질문에, all을 사용해 모두라고
    답했으므로 정답이다.
(B) Yes/No 대답 불가 오답: 의문사 의문문에 Yes/No로 답변할
    수 없다.
(C) 연상 작용 오답: 질문의 package에서 연상 가능한 express
    delivery를 이용한 오답이다.

어휘 | package 소포, (포장용) 봉지 especially 특히 express
delivery 속달

7 Why are you still using the old version of the
    software?
   (A) Every once in a while.
   (B) From the technical support staff.
   (C) It's too expensive to upgrade.

왜 아직도 소프트웨어의 오래된 버전을 쓰고 있나요?
(A) 가끔요.
(B) 기술 지원부서 직원인데요.
(C) 너무 비싸서 업그레이드할 수가 없어요.

해설 | **사용 이유를 묻는 Why 의문문**
(A) 관련 없는 오답: 사용 빈도를 묻는 How often 의문문에
    어울리는 대답이다.
(B) 연상 작용 오답: 질문의 software에서 연상 가능한 technical
    support staff를 이용한 오답이다.
(C) 정답: 소프트웨어의 오래된 버전을 사용하는 이유를 묻는 질문에
    너무 비싸서 업그레이드할 수가 없다(It's too expensive to
    upgrade)는 구체적인 이유를 제시했으므로 정답이다.

어휘 | still 아직도, 여전히 every once in a while 이따금, 가끔
expensive 비싼

8 How do you like the new conference room
    furniture?
   (A) It's exactly what we needed.
   (B) The conference was very interesting.
   (C) Did you try the other one?

새로운 회의실 가구 어때요?
(A) 딱 필요했던 거예요.
(B) 회의는 매우 흥미로웠어요.
(C) 다른 것 해보셨어요?

해설 | **의견을 묻는 How 의문문**
(A) 정답: 새로운 회의실 가구에 대한 의견을 묻는 질문에 딱
    필요했던 것(It's exactly what we needed)이라며
    우회적으로 긍정적인 의견을 표현하고 있으므로 정답이다.
(B) 단어 반복 오답: 질문의 conference를 반복 이용한 오답으로,
    회의(conference)에 대한 의견을 묻는 질문에 적합한
    대답이다.
(C) 관련 없는 오답: 새로운 회의실 가구에 대한 의견을 묻는 질문에
    다른 것을 시도해 봤는지(Did you try the other one?)
    되묻는 것은 상황에 어울리지 않는다.

어휘 | conference room 회의실 furniture 가구 exactly 정확히

9 What are the dimensions of the apartment on
    Maple Road?
   (A) It's rather far from the city center.
   (B) I don't remember the exact measurements.
   (C) The real estate agent showed it to us.

메이플 가에 있는 아파트 면적이 어떻게 되나요?
(A) 시내 중심가에서 다소 멀어요.
(B) 정확한 크기는 기억이 안 나네요.
(C) 부동산 중개인이 우리에게 보여 줬어요.

해설 | **아파트 면적을 묻는 What 의문문**
(A) 관련 없는 오답: Where 의문문에 가능한 답변이다.
(B) 정답: 아파트 면적이 어떻게 되느냐는 질문에 정확한 크기가 잘
    기억나지 않는다고 했으므로 정답이다.
(C) 연상 작용 오답: 질문의 apartment에서 연상 가능한 real
    estate agent를 사용한 오답이다.

어휘 | dimensions 넓이, 면적 measurements 크기, 면적 real
estate agent 부동산 중개업자

10 Which building is the city going to renovate?
(A) Starting next year.
(B) The old courthouse.
(C) I don't have any plans.

시에서 어떤 건물을 개조할 건가요?
(A) 내년부터요.
(B) 예전 법원 청사요.
(C) 저는 아무 계획도 없어요.

해설 | **개조 대상 건물을 묻는 Which 의문문**
(A) **관련 없는 오답:** 시작 시점을 묻는 When 의문문에 적합한 대답이다.
(B) **정답:** 개조하려는 건물을 묻는 질문에 구체적인 대상(The old courthouse)을 알려 주었으므로 정답이다.
(C) **관련 없는 오답:** 개조 대상인 건물을 묻는 질문에 자신의 계획 유무(I don't have any plans)를 언급하는 것은 상황에 어울리지 않는다.

어휘 | renovate 개조하다, 보수하다 courthouse 법원 청사

11 Why are they raising the toll prices on the Hampton Highway?
(A) To pay for road construction costs.
(B) It's near exit ten.
(C) Up to 75 kilometers an hour.

그들은 왜 햄튼 하이웨이 통행료를 올리는 거죠?
(A) 도로 공사 비용을 지불하려고요.
(B) 10번 출구 근처요.
(C) 시속 75km까지요.

해설 | **통행료 인상 이유를 묻는 Why 의문문**
(A) **정답:** 통행료를 올리는 이유를 묻는 질문에 도로 공사 비용을 지불하기 위해서(To pay for road construction costs)라는 구체적인 목적을 제시했으므로 정답이다.
(B) **연상 작용 오답:** 질문의 the Hampton Highway에서 연상 가능한 exit를 이용한 오답이다.
(C) **연상 작용 오답:** 질문의 the Hampton Highway에서 연상 가능한 제한 속도(Up to 75 kilometers an hour)를 언급한 오답이다.

어휘 | raise 올리다 toll 요금, 통행료 construction 공사 cost 비용 up to ~까지

12 How many workstations have lost Internet access?
(A) What's your password?
(B) Seven of them.
(C) In a few minutes.

몇 대의 컴퓨터에서 인터넷 연결이 끊겼나요?
(A) 패스워드가 뭔가요?
(B) 7개요.
(C) 몇 분 후에요.

해설 | **수량을 묻는 How 의문문**
(A) **연상 작용 오답:** 질문의 Internet access에서 연상 가능한 password를 이용한 오답이다.
(B) **정답:** 인터넷 연결이 끊긴 컴퓨터의 수를 묻는 질문에 구체적인 수량(Seven of them)을 알려 주었으므로 정답이다.
(C) **관련 없는 오답:** 시점을 묻는 When 의문문에 적합한 대답이다.

어휘 | workstation 다기능 컴퓨터, 단말기 lose 잃다 access 접속, 접근 password 비밀번호, 패스워드

13 What did you think of Lily's suggestions for the package design?
(A) Only recycled materials.
(B) Yes, I thought so.
(C) They were helpful.

릴리의 포장 디자인 제안은 어떠셨어요?
(A) 재활용 소재만요.
(B) 네, 그렇게 생각했어요.
(C) 도움이 되었어요.

해설 | **의견을 묻는 What 의문문**
(A) **연상 작용 오답:** 질문의 package design에서 연상 가능한 소재(recycled materials)를 이용한 오답이다.
(B) **Yes/No 대답 불가 오답:** 의견을 묻는 What 의문문에는 Yes/No로 대답할 수 없다.
(C) **정답:** 릴리의 제안에 대한 의견을 묻는 질문에 도움이 되었다(They were helpful)며 구체적인 의견을 밝혔으므로 정답이다.

어휘 | suggestion 제안 package 포장 recycled 재활용된 material 소재, 재료 helpful 도움이 되는, 유용한

14 Which application should I fill out to apply for a job in the warehouse?
(A) The contract was for six months.
(B) The first floor staff room.
(C) The one that's in the green box.

창고 업무에 지원하려면 어떤 지원서를 작성해야 합니까?
(A) 계약은 6개월간이었어요.
(B) 1층 직원실요.
(C) 녹색 상자에 있는 거요.

해설 | **작성해야 할 지원서를 묻는 Which 의문문**
(A) **연상 작용 오답:** 질문의 apply for a job에서 연상 가능한 계약(contract) 기간을 언급한 오답이다.
(B) **연상 작용 오답:** 질문의 warehouse에서 연상 가능한 staff room을 이용한 오답이다.
(C) **정답:** 작성해야 할 지원서를 묻는 질문에 대명사 one(=application)을 사용하여 녹색 상자에 있는 것(The one that's in the green box)이라고 답하고 있으므로 정답이다.

어휘 | application 지원, 지원서 fill out 기입하다, 작성하다 apply for ~에 지원하다 warehouse 창고 contract 계약

15 Why weren't you at the training session this morning?
(A) No, maybe next season.
(B) Show your identification card.
(C) My supervisor said it was optional.

왜 오늘 오전에 교육에 참가하지 않았죠?
(A) 아니요, 아마도 다음 시즌이요.
(B) 신분증을 제시해 주세요.
(C) 제 상사가 그건 선택이라고 말했거든요.

해설 | **이유를 묻는 Why 의문문**
(A) **Yes/No 대답 불가 오답:** 이유를 묻는 Why 의문문에는 Yes/No로 답변할 수 없다.
(B) **관련 없는 오답:** 질문과 상관 없는 답변이다.
(C) **정답:** Because를 생략하고, (필수가 아닌) 선택이어서 교육에 참가하지 않았다는 이유를 밝혔으므로 정답이다.

어휘 | training session 교육 과정 identification card 신분증
supervisor 감독관, 상사 optional 선택적인

16 How do I lower the projector screen?
(A) I owe her money for lunch.
(B) The control panel's by the door.
(C) Which shelf are they on?

어떻게 하면 영사기 화면을 낮출 수 있나요?
(A) 나는 그녀에게 점심값을 빚졌어요.
(B) 문 옆에 제어판이 있어요.
(C) 그것들이 어느 선반에 있지요?

해설 | **방법을 묻는 How 의문문**
(A) **유사 발음 오답:** 질문의 lower와 일부 발음이 유사한 owe를
이용한 오답이다.
(B) **정답:** 영사기 화면을 낮추는 방법을 묻는 질문에 문 옆에
제어판이 있다(The control panel's by the door)며
우회적으로 방안을 제시했으므로 정답이다.
(C) **인칭 오류 오답:** 대명사 they가 가리키는 대상이 질문에 없으며,
문맥적으로도 파악이 불가능하다.

어휘 | lower 낮추다 owe 빚지다 control panel 제어판

17 What did you decide about the marketing plan?
(A) We've hired a consultant to review it.
(B) It just opened for business.
(C) I'm definitely planning on it.

마케팅 계획에 대해 어떤 결정을 하셨나요?
(A) 그것을 검토할 자문위원을 채용했어요.
(B) 그 업체는 막 영업을 시작했어요.
(C) 저는 꼭 그것을 할 계획입니다.

해설 | **결정 사항을 묻는 What 의문문**
(A) **정답:** 마케팅 계획에 대한 결정 사항을 묻는 질문에 자문위원
채용이라고 구체적으로 답했으므로 정답이다.
(B) **연상 작용 오답:** marketing plan에서 연상 가능한
business를 이용한 오답이다.
(C) **다의어 오답:** 질문에 나오는 plan은 '계획'을, 보기의 plan은
'계획하다'를 의미한다.

어휘 | hire 채용하다 consultant 자문위원 definitely 분명히

18 Which parking area is closest to the client's
office?
(A) I usually take public transportation.
(B) Maybe around this time tomorrow.
(C) Wow—what a great view!

어느 주차장이 그 고객의 사무실에서 가장 가까운가요?
(A) 저는 보통 대중교통을 이용해요.
(B) 아마도 내일 이 시간쯤에요.
(C) 와, 전망이 훌륭하네요!

해설 | **가까운 주차장을 묻는 Which 의문문**
(A) **정답:** 가까운 주차장을 묻는 질문에 자신은 보통 대중교통을
이용한다(I usually take public transportation)며
모른다는 것을 우회적으로 드러내고 있으므로 정답이다.
(B) **관련 없는 오답:** 시점을 묻는 When 의문문에 적합한 응답이다.
(C) **연상 작용 오답:** 질문의 client's office에서 연상 가능한 사무실
전망에 대한 견해(what a great view)를 언급한 오답이다.

어휘 | client 고객 public transportation 대중교통 view 전망

19 Why don't you request an office with a window?
(A) Ten square meters.
(B) Would you like me to close it?
(C) I'm happy where I am now.

창문이 있는 사무실을 요청하지 그러세요?
(A) 10제곱미터요.
(B) 제가 그걸 닫아드릴까요?
(C) 지금 있는 곳에 만족해요.

해설 | **제안·권유의 Why 의문문**
(A) **연상 작용 오답:** 질문의 office에서 연상 가능한 사무실
크기(Ten square meters)를 언급한 오답이다.
(B) **연상 작용 오답:** 질문의 window에서 연상 가능한 창문을 닫는
상황(Would you like me to close it?)을 언급한 오답이다.
(C) **정답:** 창문이 있는 사무실을 요청하라는 제안에 지금 있는 곳에
만족한다(I'm happy where I am now)며 우회적으로 거절의
의사를 밝혔으므로 정답이다.

어휘 | request 요청하다 square meter 제곱미터

20 How long is the taxi ride to the train station?
(A) It depends on the traffic.
(B) Around fifty dollars.
(C) The first stop in town.

기차역까지 택시로 얼마나 걸리죠?
(A) 교통 상황에 따라 달라요.
(B) 50달러 정도요.
(C) 시내 첫 번째 정류장요.

해설 | **기간을 묻는 How 의문문**
(A) **정답:** 택시로 기차역까지 가는 데 걸리는 시간을 묻는 질문에
교통 상황에 따라 다르다(It depends on the traffic)는
우회적 답변을 하고 있으므로 가장 적절한 응답이다.
(B) **관련 없는 오답:** 택시 요금을 묻는 How much 의문문에
어울리는 대답이다.
(C) **연상 작용 오답:** 질문의 train station에서 연상 가능한
stop(정류장)을 이용한 오답이다.

어휘 | depend on ~에 달려 있다 traffic 교통

21 What's on the agenda for the staff meeting?
(A) Next to the lobby.
(B) Attendance was good.
(C) It hasn't been finalized.

직원 회의의 안건이 뭐죠?
(A) 로비 옆에서요.
(B) 출석률이 좋았어요.
(C) 확정되지 않았어요.

해설 | **회의 안건을 묻는 What 의문문**
(A) **관련 없는 오답:** Where 의문문에 대한 답변이다.
(B) **연상 작용 오답:** 질문의 staff meeting에서 연상할 수 있는
attendance를 이용한 오답이다.
(C) **정답:** 회의 안건을 묻는 질문에 아직 확정되지 않았다(It hasn't
been finalized)며 관련 상황을 언급하고 있으므로 가장
적절한 응답이다.

어휘 | agenda 안건 staff meeting 직원 회의 attendance
출석률 finalize 확정하다, 마무리짓다

22 Which candidate was chosen as the new software engineer?
(A) At a higher salary.
(B) It's a new version.
(C) We selected Claudia Fernandez.

새로운 소프트웨어 엔지니어로 어느 지원자가 선정되었나요?
(A) 더 높은 임금이에요.
(B) 그것은 새 버전이에요.
(C) 클라우디아 페르난데스 씨를 선택했어요.

해설 | **선정된 지원자를 묻는 Which 의문문**
(A) **연상 작용 오답**: 질문의 candidate에서 연상 가능한 salary를 이용한 오답이다.
(B) **연상 작용 오답**: 의미상 연결이 가능한 두 단어(software 소프트웨어/version 버전)를 이용한 오답이다.
(C) **정답**: 선정된 지원자를 묻는 질문에 사람 이름으로 잘 답변한 정답이다.

어휘 | candidate 지원자, 후보자 as (자격) ~으로서 salary 봉급, 급료 select 선택하다

23 Why hasn't our supply order come in yet?
(A) Ink for the printer.
(B) No, I don't need anything.
(C) Because we sent it late.

우리가 주문한 용품이 왜 아직 안 온 거지요?
(A) 프린터 잉크예요.
(B) 아니요, 아무것도 필요 없어요.
(C) 우리가 주문을 늦게 보내서 그래요.

해설 | **배송 지연 이유를 묻는 Why 의문문**
(A) **연상 작용 오답**: 질문의 supply order에서 연상 가능한 Ink for the printer를 이용한 오답이다.
(B) **Yes/No 대답 불가 오답**: 이유를 묻는 Why 의문문에는 Yes/No로 대답할 수 없다.
(C) **정답**: 주문품이 도착하지 않은 이유를 묻는 질문에 우리가 주문을 늦게 보냈다(Because we sent it late)는 구체적인 이유를 제시했으므로 정답이다.

어휘 | supply 용품, 물품 order 주문(품)

24 How often does the corporate newsletter come out?
(A) Four times a year.
(B) It's longer than usual.
(C) There are no color copies.

회사 소식지는 얼마나 자주 나와요?
(A) 1년에 네 번이요.
(B) 평소보다 더 오래 걸려요.
(C) 컬러 복사본이 없어요.

해설 | **발행 빈도를 묻는 How 의문문**
(A) **정답**: 회사 소식지의 발행 빈도를 묻는 질문에 구체적인 횟수(Four times a year)를 알려주었으므로 정답이다.
(B) **관련 없는 오답**: 소식지의 발행 빈도를 묻는 질문에 평소보다 더 오래 걸린다(It's longer than usual)라고 하는 것은 상황에 맞지 않는 대답이다.
(C) **연상 작용 오답**: 질문의 corporate newsletter에서 연상 가능한 color copies를 이용한 오답이다.

어휘 | corporate 회사의 newsletter 소식지 come out 나오다 than usual 평소보다 copy 복사(본)

25 What should we do to celebrate Ms. Chen's retirement?
(A) Eight years, I think.
(B) Let's go to the High Line Café.
(C) She's moving to Australia.

첸 씨의 은퇴를 기념하기 위해 뭘 해야 할까요?
(A) 8년인 것 같아요.
(B) 하이라인 카페에 가죠.
(C) 그녀는 오스트레일리아로 이사할 거예요.

해설 | **의견 제안을 요청하는 What 의문문**
(A) **관련 없는 오답**: 기간을 묻는 How long 의문문에 어울리는 대답이다.
(B) **정답**: 행사에 대한 아이디어를 요청하는 질문에 하이라인 카페에 가자(Let's go to the High Line Café)며 구체적인 의견을 제안했으므로 정답이다.
(C) **연상 작용 오답**: 질문의 Ms. Chen's retirement에서 연상 가능한 은퇴 후 계획(She's moving to Australia)을 언급한 오답이다.

어휘 | celebrate 기념하다, 축하하다 retirement 은퇴, 퇴직 move 이사하다

Unit 05 일반 / 부정 / 부가 의문문

① 일반 의문문

ETS 유형 연습

본책 p.050

| 1 (B) | 2 (C) | 3 (A) | 4 (A) | 5 (A) | 6 (A) |

1 Are you going to install the equipment yourself?
(A) A more efficient assembly line.
(B) No, the manufacturer will do that.
(C) Seven thousand dollars.

장비를 직접 설치하실 거죠?
(A) 더 효율적인 조립 라인요.
(B) 아니요, 그건 제조업체에서 할 겁니다.
(C) 7천 달러요.

해설 | **장비 설치의 주체를 확인하는 일반 의문문**
(A) **연상 작용 오답**: equipment에서 연상 가능한 assembly line을 사용한 오답이다.
(B) **정답**: 장비 설치를 직접 안 하고 제조업체(manufacturer)가 할 것이라고 주체를 밝혔으므로 정답이다.
(C) **관련 없는 오답**: 가격을 묻는 How much 의문문에 적절한 대답이다.

어휘 | install 설치하다 equipment 장비 efficient 효율적인 assembly line (공장) 조립 라인 manufacturer 제조업체

2 Does this job require a lot of traveling?
(A) I was there yesterday.
(B) Yes, he was very helpful.
(C) No, I don't think so.

이 일은 출장을 많이 다녀야 하나요?
(A) 저는 어제 거기 있었어요.
(B) 네, 그는 도움이 무척 많이 됐어요.
(C) 아니요. 그런 것 같지는 않아요.

027

해설 | **요구 조건을 확인하는 일반 의문문**
(A) **연상 작용 오답**: 질문의 traveling에서 연상 가능한 there을 이용한 오답이다.
(B) **인칭 오류 오답**: 대명사 he가 가리키는 대상이 질문에 없다.
(C) **정답**: 일이 잦은 출장을 요구하는지 묻는 질문에 먼저 No라고 응답한 후, 그런 것 같지 않다(I don't think so)며 한 번 더 부정의 의사를 덧붙였으므로 정답이다.

어휘 | require 요구하다, 필요로 하다 traveling 이동, 여행 helpful 도움이 되는, 유용한

3 Will Mr. Hong be back in time to attend the ceremony?
(A) He should be able to make it.
(B) Very ceremonial.
(C) Yes, it was an honor.

홍 씨가 행사 참석 시간에 맞춰 돌아올까요?
(A) 참석할 수 있을 거예요.
(B) 매우 의례적이었어요.
(C) 네, 영광이었어요.

해설 | **미래의 일을 묻는 일반 의문문**
(A) **정답**: 홍 씨가 행사 시간에 맞춰 돌아올지 묻는 질문에 참석할 수 있을 것(He should be able to make it)이라고 예측하고 있으므로 가장 적절한 응답이다.
(B) **파생어 오답**: 질문에 나오는 ceremony와 파생어 관계인 ceremonial을 이용한 오답이다.
(C) **연상 작용 오답**: 질문의 attend the ceremony에서 연상 가능한 honor를 이용한 오답이다.

어휘 | in time 시간에 늦지 않게 ceremony 행사, 의식 make it 참석하다 ceremonial 의식의 honor 명예, 영광

4 Have you watched our new promotional video yet?
(A) Yes—it was impressive!
(B) It's fifteen percent off.
(C) I'm not wearing a watch.

저희 새 홍보 동영상을 보셨나요?
(A) 네. 인상 깊었어요!
(B) 15퍼센트 할인입니다.
(C) 저는 시계를 차고 있지 않아요.

해설 | **시청 여부를 확인하는 일반 의문문**
(A) **정답**: 새 홍보 동영상을 봤는지 묻는 질문에 먼저 Yes라고 응답한 후, 인상 깊었다(it was impressive)는 의견을 덧붙였으므로 정답이다.
(B) **연상 작용 오답**: 질문의 promotional에서 연상 가능한 할인율(fifteen percent off)을 언급한 오답이다.
(C) **다의어 오답**: 질문의 watched는 '보다'라는 뜻의 동사이고, 보기의 watch는 '시계'라는 뜻의 명사이다.

어휘 | promotional 홍보의 impressive 감명 깊은, 인상적인

5 Excuse me, do you know where Marie LeDuke's office is?
(A) I'm sorry, I've just started working here.
(B) No, I don't think she is.
(C) That's an official document.

실례지만, 마리 리듀크 씨의 사무실이 어디에 있는지 아세요?
(A) 죄송하지만, 제가 이제 막 이곳에서 근무를 시작했어요.
(B) 아니요, 그녀가 그렇다고 생각하지 않아요.
(C) 그건 공문서입니다.

해설 | **장소를 묻는 간접 의문문**
(A) **정답**: 사무실의 위치를 묻는 질문에 미안하다고 한 후 모르는 이유(I've just started working here)를 설명하고 있으므로 가장 적절한 응답이다.
(B) **관련 없는 오답**: 질문의 사람 이름에서 연상할 수 있는 she가 포함되어 있으나, 전체 내용이 질문과 어울리지 않는다.
(C) **파생어 오답**: 질문에 나오는 office의 파생어 official을 이용한 오답이다.

어휘 | official document 공문서

6 Ling, do you have time to review this document with me?
(A) Could we go over it tomorrow?
(B) About ten pages long.
(C) Quite a few revisions.

링, 나랑 이 서류 좀 같이 검토할 시간 있어요?
(A) 내일 검토해도 될까요?
(B) 약 10페이지 길이에요.
(C) 꽤 수정이 많군요.

해설 | **가능 여부를 묻는 일반 의문문**
(A) **정답**: 서류를 함께 검토할 시간이 있느냐고 묻는 질문에 내일 하면 어떠냐고 되묻고 있으므로 가장 적절한 응답이다.
(B) **연상 작용 오답**: 질문의 document에서 연상 가능한 페이지 수(ten pages)를 언급한 오답이다.
(C) **연상 작용 오답**: 질문의 document에서 연상 가능한 revisions를 이용한 오답이다.

어휘 | review 검토하다 go over 검토하다 revision 수정

② 부정 의문문

ETS 유형 연습
본책 p.051

1 (C)	**2** (A)	**3** (C)	**4** (C)	**5** (A)	**6** (B)

1 Aren't you enjoying your meal?
(A) For the retirement party.
(B) A good business deal.
(C) No, it's undercooked.

식사를 즐기고 있지 않나요?
(A) 은퇴 기념 파티를 위해서요.
(B) 훌륭한 거래네요.
(C) 아니요. 덜 익었어요.

해설 | **의견을 묻는 부정 의문문**
(A) **연상 작용 오답**: 질문의 enjoying your meal에서 연상 가능한 식사를 하게 된 이유(For the retirement party)를 언급한 오답이다.
(B) **유사 발음 오답**: 질문의 meal과 발음이 유사한 deal을 이용한 오답이다.
(C) **정답**: 식사를 즐기고 있는지 확인하는 질문에 먼저 No라고 응답한 후, 이유(it's undercooked)를 덧붙였으므로 정답이다.

어휘 | retirement 은퇴, 퇴직 deal 거래 undercooked 덜 익은

2 Haven't you already been to that exhibition?
(A) I didn't see everything last time.
(B) No, I put it in the bin.
(C) I'd like to visit Egypt.

그 전시회에 이미 가보지 않았나요?
(A) 지난번에 전부 다 보지 못했어요.
(B) 아니요, 쓰레기통에 그것을 넣었어요.
(C) 저는 이집트를 방문하고 싶어요.

해설 | **사실 여부를 묻는 부정 의문문**
(A) **정답:** 전시회에 가봤는지 확인하는 질문에 Yes를 생략하고, (가봤지만) 다 관람하지 못했다는 추가 정보로 잘 답변한 정답이다.
(B) **유사 발음 오답:** 질문의 been과 발음이 동일한 bin을 이용한 오답이다.
(C) **연상 작용 오답:** 의미상 연결이 가능한 두 표현(have been to ~에 가본 적이 있다 / visit 방문하다)을 이용한 오답이다.

어휘 | exhibition 전시회, 전시 bin 쓰레기통

3 Shouldn't we post next month's work schedule?
(A) We can't go then.
(B) There's a letter here for you.
(C) Yes, I'll do it right away.

다음 달 업무 일정을 게시해야 하지 않나요?
(A) 우린 그때 갈 수가 없어요.
(B) 여기 당신에게 온 편지가 있어요.
(C) 네, 지금 바로 할 겁니다.

해설 | **필요 여부를 확인하는 부정 의문문**
(A) **연상 작용 오답:** 질문의 next month에서 연상 가능한 then을 이용한 오답이다.
(B) **연상 작용 오답:** 질문의 post를 '발송하다, 보내다'라는 뜻으로 잘못 이해했을 경우 연상 가능한 letter를 이용한 오답이다.
(C) **정답:** 업무 일정을 게시해야 하지 않는지 묻는 질문에 먼저 Yes라고 응답한 후, 지금 바로 하겠다(I'll do it right away)며 덧붙였으므로 정답이다.

어휘 | post 게시하다 schedule 일정 right away 곧바로

4 Why doesn't the bus to the city park ever arrive on time?
(A) Until the next one.
(B) No, you can't park here.
(C) It's frustrating, isn't it?

도심 공원행 버스는 왜 항상 정시에 도착하지 않을까요?
(A) 다음 것이 올 때까지요.
(B) 아니요, 여기에 주차할 수 없어요.
(C) 참 답답해요, 그렇지 않나요?

해설 | **불평을 하는 부정 의문문**
(A) **관련 없는 오답:** When 의문문에 가능한 대답이다.
(B) **Yes/No 대답 불가·다의어 오답:** 이유를 묻는 Why 의문문에는 Yes/No로 대답할 수 없으며, 질문의 park는 '공원'이라는 명사, 보기의 park는 '주차하다'라는 동사이다.
(C) **정답:** 버스가 왜 정시에 도착하지 않느냐고 답답한 심정을 나타낸 질문에 동감의 표현을 하고 있다.

어휘 | arrive on time 정각에 도착하다 frustrating 불만스러운, 실망하게 하는

5 Don't you think the Web site needs to be updated?
(A) A new design might attract more customers.
(B) Thanks, but I already have one.
(C) No, only once before.

웹사이트를 업데이트해야 하지 않을까요?
(A) 디자인을 새롭게 하면 고객들이 더 많이 올 거예요.
(B) 고맙지만, 저는 하나 있어요.
(C) 아니요, 전에 한 번만요.

해설 | **의견을 묻는 부정 의문문**
(A) **정답:** 새로운 디자인이 더 많은 고객들을 끌어들일 것이라는 말로 웹사이트 업데이트에 찬성하는 의견을 우회적으로 표현했다.
(B) **연상 작용 오답:** needs에서 연상 가능한 already have one을 언급한 오답이다.
(C) **관련 없는 오답:** 질문의 내용과 관련 없는 응답이다.

어휘 | update 새롭게 하다 attract 끌어들이다

6 Didn't Jay approve the expense report yesterday?
(A) That's expensive.
(B) No, he'll do it today.
(C) I didn't try it on.

제이가 어제 비용 보고서를 승인하지 않았나요?
(A) 그건 비쌉니다.
(B) 안 했어요, 오늘 할 겁니다.
(C) 저는 착용해 보지 않았어요.

해설 | **승인 여부를 확인하는 부정 의문문**
(A) **파생어 오답:** 질문의 expense와 파생어 관계인 expensive를 이용한 오답이다.
(B) **정답:** 보고서에 대한 승인 여부를 확인하는 질문에 부정(No)으로 대답한 뒤 오늘 할 것(he'll do it today)이라며 부연 설명하고 있으므로 정답이다.
(C) **단어 반복 오답:** 질문의 Didn't를 반복 이용한 오답이다.

어휘 | approve 승인하다 expense report 비용 보고서 try on ~을 착용해 보다

③ 부가 의문문

ETS 유형 연습 본책 p.052

1 (C)	2 (A)	3 (A)	4 (A)	5 (B)	6 (B)

1 That concert was really good, wasn't it?
(A) A new design concept.
(B) I wasn't sure I could.
(C) Yes, I think everyone enjoyed it.

그 음악회는 정말 좋았어요, 그렇죠?
(A) 새로운 디자인 컨셉입니다.
(B) 할 수 있을지 확신이 없었어요.
(C) 네, 모두가 즐겁게 본 것 같아요.

해설 | **동의를 구하는 부가 의문문**
(A) **유사 발음 오답:** 질문의 concert와 발음이 유사한 concept을 이용한 오답이다.
(B) **단어 반복 오답:** 질문의 wasn't를 반복 이용한 오답이다.

(C) **정답**: 음악회가 정말 좋았다며 동의를 구하는 질문에 먼저 Yes라고 응답한 후, 모두가 즐겁게 본 것 같다(I think everyone enjoyed it)며 동조하고 있으므로 정답이다.

2 You wanted these charts copied, didn't you?
(A) And then they should be refiled.
(B) I'll pour the coffee.
(C) At the top of the chart.

이 차트들이 복사되기를 원하셨죠, 그렇지 않나요?
(A) 그러고 나서 그것들을 다시 철해 놓아야 해요.
(B) 제가 커피를 따라 드릴게요.
(C) 차트 맨 위에요.

해설 | 의견을 재확인하는 부가 의문문
(A) **정답**: 차트 복사본을 원하지 않았느냐는 질문에 복사를 원했을 뿐 아니라 그것을 다시 철해 놓아야 한다고 대답하고 있다.
(B) **유사 발음 오답**: 질문의 copied와 발음이 유사한 coffee를 사용한 오답이다.
(C) **단어 반복 오답**: 질문의 chart를 반복 사용한 오답이다.

어휘 | copy 복사하다 refile (문서 등을) 다시 철하다

3 You've operated this equipment before, haven't you?
(A) Yes, many times.
(B) In the training manual.
(C) No, the factory.

이 장비를 전에 다뤄 봤죠, 그렇지 않나요?
(A) 네, 여러 번이요.
(B) 교육 지침서에서요.
(C) 아니요, 공장이요.

해설 | 경험을 확인하는 부가 의문문
(A) **정답**: 장비 작동 경험에 대한 질문에 먼저 Yes로 긍정 답변을 한 후, 여러 번이라는 말을 덧붙이고 있으므로 정답이다.
(B) **연상 작용 오답**: 질문의 operated this equipment에서 연상 가능한 manual을 이용한 오답이다.
(C) **연상 작용 오답**: 질문의 operated에서 연상 가능한 factory를 이용한 오답이다.

어휘 | operate 작동하다 equipment 장비 training manual 교육 지침서 factory 공장

4 The software training will end by four, won't it?
(A) It's supposed to.
(B) In the computer lab.
(C) No, I only sent three.

소프트웨어 교육이 4시 전에 끝날 예정이죠, 그렇지 않나요?
(A) 그러기로 되어 있어요.
(B) 컴퓨터실에서요.
(C) 아니요. 저는 세 개만 보냈어요.

해설 | 사실을 확인하는 부가 의문문
(A) **정답**: 소프트웨어 교육이 4시 전에 끝날 예정인지 확인하는 질문에 그러기로 되어 있다(It's supposed to)며 긍정의 응답을 하고 있으므로 정답이다.
(B) **연상 작용 오답**: 질문의 software에서 연상 가능한 computer를 이용한 오답이다.
(C) **연상 작용 오답**: 질문의 four에서 연상 가능한 three를 이용한 오답이다.

어휘 | be supposed to ~하기로 되어 있다

5 The project proposals are due tomorrow, right?
(A) Yes, I work from home.
(B) No, the deadline was moved.
(C) In conference room B.

프로젝트 제안서 기한이 내일이죠, 그렇죠?
(A) 네, 저는 재택근무를 해요.
(B) **아니요, 기한이 바뀌었어요.**
(C) B 회의실에서요.

해설 | 사실을 확인하는 부가 의문문
(A) **관련 없는 오답**: 프로젝트 제안서 기한이 내일인지 확인하는 질문에 재택근무를 한다(I work from home)라고 하는 것은 상황에 맞지 않는 대답이다.
(B) **정답**: 프로젝트 제안서 기한이 내일인지 확인하는 질문에 먼저 No라고 응답한 후, 기한이 바뀌었다(the deadline was moved)며 부연 설명하고 있으므로 정답이다.
(C) **연상 작용 오답**: 질문의 project proposals에서 연상 가능한 제안서 발표 장소(In conference room B)를 언급한 오답이다.

어휘 | proposal 제안서 due ~하기로 되어 있는, 예정된 work from home 재택근무하다 deadline 기한 conference room 회의실

6 I don't have to renew my security badge, do I?
(A) The guard at the front desk.
(B) No, the one you have is still valid.
(C) Tickets are seven dollars each.

제 보안 명찰을 갱신할 필요는 없지요, 그렇죠?
(A) 안내데스크에 있는 경비원이요.
(B) **그러실 필요 없어요, 지금 갖고 계신 게 아직 유효해요.**
(C) 티켓은 장당 7달러예요.

해설 | 필요 여부를 확인하는 부가 의문문
(A) **연상 작용 오답**: 질문의 security에서 연상 가능한 guard를 이용한 오답이다.
(B) **정답**: 갱신 필요 여부를 묻는 질문에, No로 부정한 후에 설명을 덧붙이고 있으므로 정답이다.
(C) **관련 없는 오답**: How much 의문문에 가능한 대답이다.

어휘 | renew 갱신하다 security badge 보안 명찰 guard 경비원 valid 유효한

● 실전 **도움닫기**   본책 p.053
----

1 (C) **2** (C) **3** (A) **4** (B) **5** (A)

1. Is the Italian restaurant open on Mondays?
(A) It was an excellent meal.
(B) No, it's across the street.
(C) Yes, but only for lunch.

그 이탈리아 식당은 월요일에 문을 여나요?
(A) 훌륭한 식사였어요.
(B) 아니요, 거긴 길 건너편이에요.
(C) 네, 하지만 점심만 돼요.

해설 | 사실을 확인하는 일반 의문문
(A) **연상 작용 오답**: restaurant에서 연상 가능한 meal을 사용한 오답이다.

(B) **연상 작용 오답**: restaurant의 위치로 연상할 수 있는 across the street를 사용한 오답이다.

(C) **정답**: 월요일에 영업한다고 Yes로 긍정한 후, 점심 시간 동안만이라고 부연 설명했다.

2. Do you know why I need to apply in person?
(A) I don't believe we've ever met.
(B) No, I don't need help.
(C) Maybe you need to show identification.

왜 직접 방문해서 지원을 해야 하는지 아세요?
(A) 제 생각엔 우리가 만난 적이 없어요.
(B) 아니요, 안 도와주셔도 됩니다.
(C) 아마 신분증을 보여줘야 할 거예요.

해설 | **이유를 묻는 간접 의문문**
(A) **연상 작용 오답**: 질문의 in person에서 연상 가능한 have ever met을 이용한 오답이다.
(B) **단어 반복 오답**: 질문의 need를 반복 사용한 오답이다.
(C) **정답**: 직접 방문해서 지원해야 하는 이유를 아느냐는 질문에 신분증을 제시해야 하기 때문일 것이라고 추측해 답했으므로 가장 적절한 응답이다.

어휘 | in person 손수, 직접 identification 신분증

3. Have you finished reading the report?
(A) Just two more pages.
(B) He reports to Mr. Garcia.
(C) Yes, the apartment is furnished.

보고서 다 읽었어요?
(A) 두 페이지만 더 읽으면 돼요.
(B) 그는 가르시아 씨에게 업무 보고를 합니다.
(C) 네, 그 아파트에는 가구가 갖춰져 있어요.

해설 | **완료 여부를 확인하는 일반 의문문**
(A) **정답**: 보고서를 다 읽지 못했다는 것을 우회적으로 드러내고 있으므로 가장 적절한 응답이다.
(B) **다의어 오답**: 질문의 report는 '보고서'라는 뜻의 명사이고, 보기의 report는 '보고하다'라는 뜻의 동사이다.
(C) **유사 발음 오답**: 질문의 finished와 발음이 유사한 furnished를 이용한 오답이다.

어휘 | report to ~에게 보고하다 furnish (가구 등을) 갖추다

4. Didn't Joe use to work in the shipping department?
(A) Please send it by overnight mail.
(B) Yes, but he was transferred.
(C) A lot of work today.

조가 발송부에서 일하지 않았나요?
(A) 그것을 빠른 우편으로 보내주세요.
(B) 네, 하지만 그는 부서를 옮겼어요.
(C) 오늘은 일이 많아요.

해설 | **부서를 확인하는 부정 의문문**
(A) **연상 작용 오답**: 질문의 shipping department에서 연상 가능한 overnight mail을 사용한 오답이다.
(B) **정답**: 조가 발송 부서에서 근무했었다고 Yes로 긍정한 후, 부서를 옮겼다고 부연 설명을 했다.
(C) **단어 반복 오답**: 질문의 work를 반복 사용한 오답이다.

어휘 | shipping department 발송부 overnight mail (다음 날 배달되는) 빠른 우편 transfer 인사이동하다

5. We won't be late for our appointment, will we?
(A) No, not if we hurry.
(B) What date works best for you?
(C) John's been appointed.

우리 약속에 늦지는 않겠죠, 그렇죠?
(A) 서두르면 그렇지 않을 거예요.
(B) 어떤 날짜가 당신에게 가장 좋은가요?
(C) 존이 임명됐어요.

해설 | **확인을 구하는 부가 의문문**
(A) **정답**: 약속에 늦지는 않을지 묻는 질문에 먼저 No라고 한 뒤, '서두르면(if we hurry)'이라는 조건을 덧붙이고 있으므로 정답이다.
(B) **연상 작용 오답**: 질문의 appointment에서 연상 가능한 date를 이용한 오답이다.
(C) **파생어 오답**: 질문의 appointment와 파생어 관계인 appointed를 이용한 오답이다.

어휘 | work best 가장 적합하다 appoint 임명[지정]하다

● ETS 실전문제

1 (A)	2 (A)	3 (A)	4 (C)	5 (B)
6 (C)	7 (C)	8 (B)	9 (A)	10 (C)
11 (A)	12 (A)	13 (B)	14 (B)	15 (C)
16 (A)	17 (C)	18 (C)	19 (A)	20 (B)
21 (A)	22 (C)	23 (B)	24 (B)	25 (A)

1 Is there any money left in our office supply account?
(A) Let me look and see.
(B) There's one nearby.
(C) I'd like that.

사무용품 계좌에 남아 있는 돈이 있나요?
(A) 제가 한번 살펴볼게요.
(B) 근처에 하나 있어요.
(C) 저는 그게 마음에 들어요.

해설 | **잔여 여부를 확인하는 일반 의문문**
(A) **정답**: 사무용품 계좌에 남은 돈이 있는지 묻는 질문에, 간접 응답으로 살펴보겠다(Let me look and see)고 하므로 적절한 대답이다.
(B) **단어 반복 오답**: 질문에 나온 Is there의 평서문 형태인 There's를 이용한 오답이다.
(C) **관련 없는 오답**: I'd like that은 무언가를 선호한다는 의사 표시이므로 확인을 요청하는 질문의 대답으로는 적합하지 않다.

어휘 | office supply 사무용품 nearby 인근에, 가까운 곳에

2 Have you renewed the office lease for another year?
(A) Yes, I signed it today.
(B) A performance review.
(C) A new product release.

사무실 임대차 계약을 한 해 더 갱신하셨나요?
(A) 네, 오늘 서명했어요.
(B) 인사 고과예요.
(C) 신제품 출시입니다.

LC

PART 2

(A) **정답**: 사무실 임대차 계약을 갱신했는지 묻는 질문에 먼저 Yes라고 응답한 후, 구체적인 시점(today)을 덧붙였으므로 정답이다.
(B) **유사 발음 오답**: 질문의 renewed와 발음이 유사한 review를 이용한 오답이다.
(C) **유사 발음 오답**: 질문의 lease와 일부 발음이 동일한 release를 이용한 오답이다.

어휘 | renew 갱신하다 lease 임대차 계약 performance review 인사 고과 release 출시

3 Will this package reach San Francisco by the end of the day?
(A) No, I don't think so.
(B) It's a wonderful city.
(C) The baggage claim area.

이 소포가 오늘이 가기 전에 샌프란시스코에 도착할까요?
(A) 아니요. 그럴 것 같지 않아요.
(B) 멋진 도시군요.
(C) 수하물 찾는 구역요.

해설 | **미래의 일을 묻는 일반 의문문**
(A) **정답**: 소포가 오늘이 가기 전에 도착할지 묻는 질문에 먼저 No라고 응답한 후, 그런 것 같지 않다(I don't think so)며 한 번 더 부정의 의사를 덧붙였으므로 정답이다.
(B) **연상 작용 오답**: 질문의 San Francisco에서 연상 가능한 도시에 대한 견해(It's a wonderful city)를 언급한 오답이다.
(C) **연상 작용 오답**: 질문의 reach에서 연상 가능한 baggage claim area를 이용한 오답이다.

어휘 | package 소포 baggage claim 수하물 찾는 곳

4 Didn't you complete your time sheet last week?
(A) If he has time.
(B) They ordered a complete set.
(C) Oh, I think I forgot.

지난주 근무 시간 기록표를 작성하지 않으셨나요?
(A) 그가 시간이 있다면요.
(B) 그들은 완전한 세트를 주문했어요.
(C) 아, 잊어버린 것 같아요.

해설 | **작성 여부를 확인하는 부정 의문문**
(A) **단어 반복 오답**: 질문의 time을 반복 이용한 오답이다.
(B) **다의어 오답**: 질문의 complete는 '작성하다'라는 뜻의 동사이고, 보기의 complete는 '완전한, 전부의'라는 뜻의 형용사이다.
(C) **정답**: 근무 시간 기록표를 작성했는지 묻는 질문에 잊어버린 것 같다(I think I forgot)며 작성하지 않았다는 사실을 우회적으로 드러내고 있으므로 정답이다.

어휘 | complete 기입하다, 작성하다:완전한 time sheet 근무 시간 기록표 order 주문하다 forget 잊다

5 The number ten bus runs all night, doesn't it?
(A) He left it on the bus.
(B) According to the schedule, yes.
(C) I don't know where the station is.

10번 버스는 밤새도록 운행하죠, 그렇지 않나요?
(A) 그는 그것을 버스에 두고 내렸어요.
(B) 시간표에 따르면 그러네요.
(C) 정류장이 어딘지 모르겠어요.

해설 | **사실을 확인하는 부가 의문문**
(A) **단어 반복 오답**: 질문의 bus를 반복 이용한 오답이다.
(B) **정답**: 버스가 밤새도록 운행하는지 확인하는 질문에 시간표에 따르면 그렇다(According to the schedule, yes)며 확인해 주었으므로 정답이다.
(C) **연상 작용 오답**: 질문의 bus에서 연상 가능한 station을 이용한 오답이다.

어휘 | leave 남겨두다 according to ~에 따라 station 정류장, 역

6 Have you looked over the expense reports I gave you?
(A) It isn't very expensive.
(B) In a scientific journal.
(C) I'll get to it this afternoon.

제가 드린 비용 보고서를 검토했나요?
(A) 그것은 그다지 비싸지 않아요.
(B) 과학 학술지에서요.
(C) 오늘 오후에 시작할게요.

해설 | **완료 여부를 묻는 일반 의문문**
(A) **파생어 오답**: expense의 파생어 expensive를 사용한 오답이다.
(B) **연상 작용 오답**: reports에서 연상 가능한 journal을 사용한 오답이다.
(C) **정답**: 보고서 검토 완료 여부를 묻는 질문에 오늘 오후에 시작할 것이라고 하며 아직 검토하지 않았음을 드러내고 있으므로 정답이다.

어휘 | look over 검토하다 expense 비용, 경비 get to ~을 시작하다

7 Do you know if all employees need to submit a time sheet?
(A) We had a really good time.
(B) In the benefits department.
(C) I'll ask Donna.

모든 직원들이 근무 시간 기록표를 제출해야 하는지 아세요?
(A) 우린 정말 즐겁게 보냈어요.
(B) 복리후생과에서요.
(C) 도나에게 물어봐야겠군요.

해설 | **정보를 확인하는 간접 의문문**
(A) **단어 반복 오답**: 질문에 나온 time을 반복 사용한 오답이다.
(B) **연상 작용 오답**: employees에서 연상 가능한 benefits department를 사용한 오답이다.
(C) **정답**: 근무 시간 기록표 제출 관련 질문에 도나에게 물어보겠다고 우회적인 답변을 했다.

어휘 | employee 직원 submit 제출하다 time sheet 근무 시간 기록표 benefits (급여 외의) 복리후생 department 과, 부서

8 Were you able to get in touch with all of the job candidates?
(A) I can get it for you.
(B) I contacted half of them.
(C) An online application.

모든 입사 지원자들과 연락이 됐나요?
(A) 제가 당신을 위해 그것을 구할 수 있어요.
(B) 그들 중 절반과 연락했어요.
(C) 온라인 지원서요.

해설 | **사실을 확인하는 일반 의문문**
- (A) **다의어 오답:** 질문의 get은 in touch와 함께 '연락하다'라는 뜻을 나타내고, 보기의 get은 '얻다, 구하다'라는 뜻이다.
- (B) **정답:** 모든 입사 지원자들에게 연락했는지 묻는 질문에 그들 중 절반과 연락했다(I contacted half of them)며 모두와 연락된 것은 아니라는 부정의 응답을 하고 있으므로 정답이다.
- (C) **연상 작용 오답:** 질문의 job candidates에서 연상 가능한 online application을 이용한 오답이다.

어휘 | get in touch with ~와 연락하다 job candidate 입사 지원자 contact 연락하다 half 절반 application 지원서

9 Don't I need manager approval to place this order?
(A) No, because it's less than 25 dollars.
(B) You can't turn left here.
(C) An additional twelve cases.

제가 이 주문을 하려면 관리자의 승인이 필요하지 않나요?
(A) 아니요, 25 달러 미만이라서요.
(B) 여기서 좌회전하시면 안 돼요.
(C) 추가로 케이스 12개요.

해설 | **필요 여부를 확인하는 부정 의문문**
- (A) **정답:** 승인이 필요하지 않는지 확인하는 질문에 먼저 No라고 응답한 후, 승인이 필요하지 않은 구체적인 이유(because it's less than 25 dollars)를 덧붙였으므로 정답이다.
- (B) **관련 없는 오답:** 승인이 필요한지 묻는 질문에 좌회전하면 안 된다(You can't turn left here)라고 하는 것은 상황에 맞지 않는 대답이다.
- (C) **연상 작용 오답:** 질문의 order에서 연상 가능한 추가 주문품(An additional twelve cases)을 이용한 오답이다.

어휘 | approval 승인 place an order 주문을 하다 additional 추가의

10 The Human Resources office is on the fourth floor, correct?
(A) I'll call Maintenance.
(B) Actually, we only need three.
(C) The building directory is behind you.

인사부 사무실이 4층에 있죠, 맞죠?
(A) 제가 관리부에 전화할게요.
(B) 사실, 우리는 세 개만 필요해요.
(C) 건물 안내도가 당신 뒤에 있어요.

해설 | **사실을 확인하는 부가 의문문**
- (A) **연상 작용 오답:** 질문의 Human Resources에서 연상 가능한 Maintenance를 이용한 오답이다.
- (B) **연상 작용 오답:** 질문의 fourth에서 연상 가능한 three를 이용한 오답이다.
- (C) **정답:** 인사부 사무실이 4층에 있는지 확인하는 질문에 건물 안내도(building directory)를 언급하며 우회적으로 확인 방법을 제시하고 있으므로 정답이다.

어휘 | Human Resources 인사부 Maintenance 관리부 actually 사실은 building directory 건물 안내도

11 Do you know who's planning Jane's going-away party?
(A) I think it's Tom Shields.
(B) It's on the twenty-third.
(C) No, he can't go.

제인의 송별회를 누가 계획하고 있는지 아세요?
(A) 톰 쉴즈인 것 같아요.
(B) 23일이에요.
(C) 아니요, 그는 못 가요.

해설 | **담당자를 묻는 간접 의문문**
- (A) **정답:** 제인의 송별회를 계획하고 있는 사람을 묻는 질문에 구체적인 인물(Tom Shields)을 언급했으므로 정답이다.
- (B) **연상 작용 오답:** 질문의 party 날짜로 연상 가능한 twenty-third를 이용한 오답이다.
- (C) **파생어 오답:** 질문의 going과 파생어 관계인 go를 이용한 오답이다.

어휘 | plan 계획하다 going-away party 송별회

12 Has the cooling system been checked today?
(A) Miguel has the inspection report.
(B) That tool on the shelf.
(C) I checked in to the hotel.

오늘 냉각 장치 점검을 받았나요?
(A) 미겔이 검사 보고서를 가지고 있어요.
(B) 선반 위에 있는 그 도구요.
(C) 저는 그 호텔에 체크인했어요.

해설 | **점검 여부를 확인하는 일반 의문문**
- (A) **정답:** 점검 여부를 묻는 질문에 미겔이 검사 보고서를 가지고 있다(Miguel has the inspection report)며 점검을 받았다는 사실을 우회적으로 드러내고 있으므로 정답이다.
- (B) **관련 없는 오답:** 점검 여부를 확인하는 질문에 특정 도구를 가리키는 대답은 어울리지 않는다.
- (C) **단어 반복 오답:** 질문의 checked를 반복 이용한 오답이다.

어휘 | cooling system 냉각 장치[방식] inspection 검사, 점검

13 Is the workshop mandatory for all employees?
(A) Yes, she was hired.
(B) No, only for managers.
(C) It's on Friday.

그 워크숍에 전 직원이 의무적으로 참석해야 하나요?
(A) 네, 그녀는 채용됐어요.
(B) 아니요, 관리자들만요.
(C) 금요일입니다.

해설 | **의무 여부를 묻는 일반 의문문**
- (A) **인칭 오류 오답:** 대명사 she가 가리키는 대상이 질문에 없다.
- (B) **정답:** 워크숍에 전 직원이 참석해야 하는지 묻는 질문에 먼저 No라고 응답한 후, 관리자들만(only for managers)이라며 부연 설명하고 있으므로 정답이다.
- (C) **연상 작용 오답:** 질문의 workshop에서 연상 가능한 워크숍 일정(It's on Friday)을 언급한 오답이다.

어휘 | mandatory 의무적인 employee 직원 hire 채용하다 manager 관리자

14 Hasn't the outgoing mail been picked up yet?
(A) I can give you a ride.
(B) Not that I know of.
(C) Usually by express mail.

발송 우편물을 아직 수거해 가지 않았나요?
(A) 제가 차로 태워 드릴 수 있어요.
(B) 제가 알기로는 아니에요.
(C) 대개는 빠른 우편으로요.

해설 | 완료 여부를 묻는 부정 의문문
(A) 연상 작용 오답: 질문에 나온 pick up을 '(차로 사람을) 태우러 가다'라는 의미로 이해할 때 연상할 수 있는 give someone a ride를 이용한 오답이다.
(B) 정답: 우편물의 수거 여부를 묻는 질문에 '내가 알기로는 아직 안 가져갔다'라고 적절히 대답하고 있으므로 정답이다.
(C) 단어 반복 오답: 질문에 나온 mail을 반복 이용한 오답이다.

어휘 | outgoing (우편물이) 발송 준비가 된 pick up 가져가다 give A a ride A에게 차를 태워 주다 express mail 빠른 우편

15 We really need to buy a new copy machine, don't you think?
(A) Fifty cents a cup.
(B) No, this one works fine.
(C) There's a copy on my desk.
복사기를 정말 새로 사야 해요, 그렇게 생각하지 않아요?
(A) 한 컵에 50센트예요.
(B) 아니요, 이건 잘 작동하잖아요.
(C) 제 책상 위에 한 부 있어요.

해설 | 동의를 구하는 부가 의문문
(A) 연상 작용 오답: copy를 coffee로 잘못 이해했을 때 연상 가능한 가격 정보를 언급한 오답이다.
(B) 정답: 복사기가 아직 쓸 만하다며 반대 의사를 나타내고 있으므로 정답이다.
(C) 단어 반복 오답: 질문의 copy를 반복 사용한 오답이다.

어휘 | copy machine 복사기 work 작동하다 copy 부, 권

16 Did Mr. Davis ask why the shipment of laboratory supplies was late?
(A) Yes, and I explained the problem.
(B) Just some cleaning materials.
(C) Check in the storage cabinet.
데이비스 씨가 실험실 장비가 왜 늦게 도착했는지 물었어요?
(A) 네, 그래서 문제가 뭔지 설명해 드렸어요.
(B) 청소 도구 몇 가지만 있으면 돼요.
(C) 물품 보관함을 확인해 봐요.

해설 | 사실 여부를 확인하는 일반 의문문
(A) 정답: 실험실 장비가 늦게 도착한 이유를 데이비스 씨가 물었냐는 질문에, 그렇다며 긍정으로 답하고 있으므로 정답이다.
(B) 관련 없는 오답: 질문의 내용과 논리적으로 연결되지 않는다.
(C) 연상 작용 오답: 질문의 supplies에서 연상 가능한 storage cabinet을 이용한 오답이다.

어휘 | shipment 배송품 laboratory supplies 실험실 장비 cleaning material 청소 도구 storage cabinet 물품 보관함

17 Has Mr. Kim's new design been tested?
(A) He used to have one.
(B) Check the signs.
(C) No, the testing begins next week.
김 씨의 새 디자인이 테스트를 받았나요?
(A) 그는 예전에 하나를 갖고 있었어요.
(B) 징후들을 확인해 봐요.
(C) 아니요, 테스트는 다음 주에 시작돼요.

해설 | 완료 여부를 확인하는 일반 의문문
(A) 관련 없는 오답: 질문의 내용과 관련 없는 응답이다.
(B) 유사 발음 오답: design과 발음이 비슷한 signs를 사용한 오답이다.

(C) 정답: 새 디자인을 테스트 해봤는지에 대해 No로 부정한 후, 다음 주에 시작된다고 올바른 정보를 알려 주었으므로 정답이다.

어휘 | used to do 예전에 ~했다 sign 징후, 조짐

18 Do you have time for a quick football game?
(A) Do you remember that one?
(B) I have seen them play.
(C) Should I bring my ball?
간단하게 축구 한 게임 할 시간 있나요?
(A) 저거 기억나세요?
(B) 그들의 경기를 본 적이 있어요.
(C) 제가 공을 가져올까요?

해설 | 시간이 있는지를 묻는 일반 의문문
(A) 관련 없는 오답: 축구 할 시간이 있는지 묻는 질문에 무언가를 기억하느냐고 되묻는 것은 어울리지 않는 대답이다.
(B) 연상 작용 오답: 질문의 game에서 연상 가능한 play를 이용한 오답이다.
(C) 정답: 축구 할 시간이 있는지 물어보는 질문에 공을 가져와야 하는지(Should I bring my ball?) 되물으며 관련 내용을 묻고 있으므로 가장 적절한 응답이다.

어휘 | quick 잠깐의

19 Weren't you going to fix your mobile phone?
(A) I replaced it instead.
(B) No, I'll send her an e-mail.
(C) You can leave a message.
휴대전화 수리하려고 하지 않았어요?
(A) 대신 바꿨어요.
(B) 아니요, 제가 그녀에게 이메일을 보낼게요.
(C) 메시지를 남기셔도 됩니다.

해설 | 수리 여부를 확인하는 부정 의문문
(A) 정답: 휴대전화를 수리하려고 하지 않았는지 묻는 질문에 대신 바꿨다(I replaced it instead)며 관련 상황을 설명하고 있으므로 정답이다.
(B) 인칭 오류 오답: 대명사 her가 가리키는 대상이 질문에 없다.
(C) 연상 작용 오답: 질문의 mobile phone에서 연상 가능한 leave a message를 이용한 오답이다.

어휘 | fix 수리하다, 고치다 replace 교체하다 instead 대신 leave a message 메시지를 남기다

20 You put the stamps in the top drawer, didn't you?
(A) OK, just give me a moment.
(B) Actually, I just used the last one.
(C) I've always liked to draw.
맨 위 서랍 안에 우표를 두었죠, 그렇지 않나요?
(A) 좋아요, 저에게 잠시만 시간을 주세요.
(B) 실은, 제가 마지막 것을 방금 써버렸어요.
(C) 저는 항상 그리기를 좋아했어요.

해설 | 사실 여부를 확인하는 부가 의문문
(A) 관련 없는 오답: 요청하는 질문에 적절한 대답이다.
(B) 정답: 특정 정보를 확인하는 상대의 말에 직접적으로 답하지는 않았지만, 상대방이 찾는 것이 남아 있지 않음을 알려주고 있으므로 가장 적절한 응답이다.
(C) 유사 발음 오답: drawer와 발음이 유사한 draw를 이용한 오답이다.

어휘 | stamp 우표 drawer 서랍 actually 사실은

21 Are the labor-cost projections for the next fiscal year done yet?
(A) Yes, we've just finished them.
(B) Heavy physical work.
(C) I have no objections.

내년 회계연도에 예상되는 인건비 산출이 끝났나요?
(A) 네, 저희가 막 끝냈어요.
(B) 힘든 육체 노동이에요.
(C) 저는 이의가 없습니다.

해설 | **완료 여부를 묻는 일반 의문문**
(A) **정답:** 인건비 산출의 완료 여부를 묻는 질문에 먼저 Yes로 긍정적 응답을 한 후, 방금 끝냈다(we've just finished them)고 부연 설명을 한 정답이다.
(B) **연상 작용 오답:** 질문의 labor에서 연상 가능한 work을 이용한 오답이다.
(C) **유사 발음 오답:** 질문의 projections와 부분적으로 발음이 유사한 objections를 이용한 오답이다.

어휘 | labor cost 인건비 projection 예상, 추정 fiscal year 회계 연도 done 완료된 heavy 힘든 physical work 육체 노동 objection 반대

22 Did you manage to get tickets to the art exhibition this weekend?
(A) My manager promoted me.
(B) Yes, that's an excellent article.
(C) No, it was sold out.

이번 주말 미술 전시회 표를 구할 수 있었나요?
(A) 제 관리자가 저를 승진시켰어요.
(B) 네, 훌륭한 기사네요.
(C) **아니요. 매진됐어요.**

해설 | **구매 여부를 확인하는 일반 의문문**
(A) **파생어 오답:** 질문의 manage와 파생어 관계인 manager를 이용한 오답이다.
(B) **유사 발음 오답:** 질문의 art와 일부 발음이 동일한 article을 이용한 오답이다.
(C) **정답:** 미술 전시회 표를 구했는지 묻는 질문에 먼저 No라고 응답한 후, 매진됐다(it was sold out)며 부연 설명하고 있으므로 정답이다.

어휘 | manage to 간신히 ~하다, 해내다 art exhibition 미술 전시회 promote 승진시키다 article 기사 sold out 매진된, 품절된

23 Do you think we should take extra product samples to the convention?
(A) I worked with her before.
(B) That's probably a good idea.
(C) It took me all day.

컨벤션에 여분의 제품 샘플을 가져가야 할까요?
(A) 예전에 그녀와 같이 일했어요.
(B) **아마도 그게 좋겠네요.**
(C) 그거 하는 데 저는 하루 종일 걸렸어요.

해설 | **의견을 묻는 간접 의문문**
(A) **인칭 오류 오답:** 보기의 대명사 her가 가리키는 대상이 질문에 없다.

(B) **정답:** 여분의 제품 샘플을 가져가야 하는지 묻는 질문에 대해 좋은 생각이라는 긍정적인 반응을 하고 있으므로 정답이다.
(C) **다의어 오답:** 서로 다른 의미의 take를 반복 이용한 오답이다. 질문의 take는 '가지고 가다'의 의미이고, 보기의 took은 '시간이 걸리다'라는 의미이다.

어휘 | extra 추가의, 여분의

24 Won't you need more time to finish all this paperwork?
(A) Six-thirty last night.
(B) No, I'm almost done.
(C) Hardcover and paperback.

이 서류 작업 전부 마치려면 시간이 더 필요하지 않겠어요?
(A) 어젯밤 6시 30분이요.
(B) **아니요, 거의 다 끝났어요.**
(C) 양장본과 문고판이요.

해설 | **필요 여부를 확인하는 부정 의문문**
(A) **관련 없는 오답:** When 의문문에 나올 수 있는 응답이다.
(B) **정답:** 서류 작업 마치는 데 시간이 더 필요한지 묻는 질문에, 부정으로 답하며 거의 다 끝났다고 말하므로 정답이다.
(C) **유사 발음 오답:** 질문의 paperwork와 일부 발음이 유사한 paperback을 이용한 오답이다.

어휘 | paperwork 서류 작업 hardcover 양장본 paperback 문고판

25 Dr. Yu is giving this afternoon's speech, isn't she?
(A) Dr. Abed's taking her place.
(B) We speak every day.
(C) I haven't gotten any.

유 박사님이 오늘 오후 연설을 하실 예정이죠, 그렇지 않나요?
(A) **아베드 박사님이 대신하실 겁니다.**
(B) 우리는 매일 이야기해요.
(C) 하나도 받지 못했어요.

해설 | **사실을 확인하는 부가 의문문**
(A) **정답:** 유 박사가 연설할 예정인지 확인하는 질문에 아베드 박사가 대신한다(Dr. Abed's taking her place)며 우회적으로 부정의 응답을 하고 있으므로 정답이다.
(B) **파생어 오답:** 질문의 speech와 파생어 관계인 speak을 이용한 오답이다.
(C) **연상 작용 오답:** 질문의 giving을 '주다'라는 뜻으로 잘못 이해했을 경우 연상 가능한 상황(I haven't gotten any)을 이용한 오답이다.

어휘 | give a speech 연설하다 take one's place ~를 대신하다, 대체하다

Unit 06 선택 / 요청·제안 의문문 / 평서문

① 선택 의문문

ETS 유형 연습

본책 p.056

1 (C)	**2** (C)	**3** (A)	**4** (B)	**5** (A)	**6** (C)

1 Will you be using a credit card or cash for your purchase?
(A) At the bank on Main Street.
(B) Thanks, I bought it online.
(C) I'll use my card.

결제를 신용카드로 하시겠어요, 현금으로 하시겠어요?
(A) 메인 가에 있는 은행에서요.
(B) 고마워요, 인터넷으로 샀어요.
(C) 카드로 할게요.

해설 | **지불 수단을 묻는 선택 의문문**
(A) **연상 작용 오답**: 질문의 credit card or cash에서 연상 가능한 bank를 이용한 오답이다.
(B) **연상 작용 오답**: 질문의 purchase에서 연상 가능한 bought를 이용한 오답이다.
(C) **정답**: 지불 수단으로 제시된 신용카드(credit card)와 현금(cash) 중 전자를 선택하여 답했으므로 정답이다.

어휘 | credit card 신용카드 purchase 구매(품)

2 Can I borrow that book, or are you still reading it?
(A) One of my favorite authors.
(B) They're stored on the bottom shelf.
(C) I'm only halfway through it.

그 책을 빌릴 수 있을까요, 아니면 아직 읽고 계신가요?
(A) 제가 가장 좋아하는 작가들 중 한 명이요.
(B) 그것들은 맨 아래 선반에 보관되어 있어요.
(C) 겨우 반 읽었어요.

해설 | **책을 다 읽었는지 묻는 선택 의문문**
(A) **연상 작용 오답**: book에서 연상 가능한 author를 사용한 오답이다.
(B) **연상 작용 오답**: book에서 연상 가능한 bottom shelf를 사용한 오답이다.
(C) **정답**: 두 가지 선택 사항(빌려줄 수 있다/아직 읽고 있다) 중 반만 읽었다는 우회적 응답으로 후자를 선택했다.

어휘 | author 저자, 작가 store 보관하다, 저장하다 bottom 맨 아래의 shelf 선반 halfway (시간·거리상으로) 중간쯤에

3 Would you rather be contacted by e-mail or by phone?
(A) Either is OK.
(B) I have the contract.
(C) In the evening.

이메일로 연락을 받고 싶으세요, 아니면 전화로 받고 싶으세요?
(A) 어느 쪽이든 괜찮아요.
(B) 저는 계약서를 갖고 있어요.
(C) 저녁에요.

해설 | **연락 방법을 묻는 선택 의문문**
(A) **정답**: 연락 방법으로 제시된 e-mail과 phone 중에서 직접 선택을 하지 않고 어느 쪽이든 상관없다는 응답을 하고 있으므로 정답이다.
(B) **유사 발음 오답**: 질문의 contacted와 발음이 유사한 contract를 이용한 오답이다.
(C) **연상 작용 오답**: 질문의 contacted에서 연상 가능한 연락 시점(In the evening)을 언급한 오답이다.

어휘 | would rather ~하고 싶다, (차라리) ~하겠다 contact 연락하다 either (둘 중) 어느 하나 contract 계약

4 Are we moving to the new building this month or next?
(A) For the past few months.
(B) We'll find out in today's meeting.
(C) Next to the parking garage.

새 건물로 이번 달에 이사를 가나요, 아니면 다음 달에 가나요?
(A) 지난 몇 개월간이요.
(B) 오늘 회의에서 알게될 겁니다.
(C) 주차장 옆이요.

해설 | **이사 시점을 묻는 선택 의문문**
(A) **단어 반복 오답**: 질문의 month를 반복 이용한 오답이다.
(B) **정답**: 이사 시점으로 제시된 this month와 next (month) 중 어느 것도 선택하지 않고 오늘 회의에서 알게될 것(We'll find out in today's meeting)이라며 관련된 상황을 언급하고 있으므로 가장 적절한 응답이다.
(C) **연상 작용 오답**: 질문의 new building에서 연상 가능한 건물의 위치(Next to the parking garage)를 언급한 오답이다.

어휘 | past 지나간, 지난 find out 알아내다 parking garage 주차장, 주차건물

5 Do you want to edit this letter now, or finish the monthly report first?
(A) Let's do the letter first.
(B) Every fourth Tuesday.
(C) Another version.

지금 이 서신을 편집하고 싶어요, 아니면 월례 보고서를 먼저 끝내고 싶나요?
(A) 서신 작업을 먼저 합시다.
(B) 매 넷째 주 화요일에요.
(C) 또 다른 버전이요.

해설 | **먼저 할 업무를 묻는 선택 의문문**
(A) **정답**: 두 가지 선택 사항(서신을 편집한다/월례 보고서를 끝낸다) 중 전자를 선택했다.
(B) **연상 작용 오답**: 질문의 monthly에서 연상 가능한 Every fourth Tuesday를 이용한 오답이다.
(C) **연상 작용 오답**: 질문의 edit에서 연상 가능한 version을 이용한 오답이다.

어휘 | edit 편집하다 monthly report 월례 보고서

6 Should we review our notes today, or is tomorrow OK?
(A) They got great reviews.
(B) Yes, I noticed.
(C) It doesn't matter to me.

우리가 필기 내용을 오늘 검토해야 하나요, 아니면 내일 해도 괜찮나요?
(A) 그들은 훌륭한 평가를 받았어요.
(B) 네, 제가 알았어요.
(C) 저는 상관없어요.

해설 | **업무 일정을 묻는 선택 의문문**
(A) **다의어 오답**: 서로 다른 의미의 review를 반복 이용한 오답이다. 질문의 review는 '검토하다'라는 동사이고, 보기의 review는 '평가'라는 의미의 명사이다.
(B) **유사 발음 오답**: 질문의 notes와 일부 발음이 유사한 noticed를 이용한 오답이다.
(C) **정답**: today와 tomorrow 중에서 선택하지 않고, 언제든 상관없다는 간접 응답으로 대화가 자연스럽게 연결되므로 정답이다.

어휘 | review 검토하다; 평가, 논평 matter 중요하다

② 요청·제안 의문문

ETS 유형 연습
본책 p.057

1 (B) 2 (B) 3 (B) 4 (C) 5 (C) 6 (B)

1 Could you turn on the air conditioner, please?
(A) The contract was fair.
(B) Sorry, it's not working.
(C) Make the next left.

에어컨 좀 켜 주실래요?
(A) 계약은 공정했어요.
(B) 죄송하지만 작동이 안 돼요.
(C) 다음에 좌회전하세요.

해설 | **부탁·요청의 의문문**
(A) **유사 발음 오답**: 질문의 air와 일부 발음이 동일한 fair를 이용한 오답이다.
(B) **정답**: 에어컨을 켜달라는 요청에 미안하지만 작동이 안 된다(Sorry, it's not working)며 우회적으로 거절의 의사를 드러내고 있으므로 정답이다.
(C) **연상 작용 오답**: 질문의 turn을 '방향을 바꾸다, 돌다'라는 뜻으로 잘못 이해했을 경우 연상 가능한 상황(Make the next left)을 이용한 오답이다.

어휘 | turn on 켜다 fair 공정한 make a left 좌회전하다

2 Can you organize a party for So-Hee's last day?
(A) To a sales position.
(B) Yes, I'd be happy to.
(C) The updated organization chart.

소희 씨의 마지막 날을 기념하는 파티를 준비해 줄래요?
(A) 영업직으로요.
(B) 네, 기꺼이 그렇게 하죠.
(C) 갱신된 조직도예요.

해설 | **부탁·요청의 의문문**
(A) **관련 없는 오답**: 파티를 준비해 달라는 요청에 직책으로 답하는 것은 어울리지 않는다.
(B) **정답**: 파티 준비 요청에 Yes라고 수락한 후, 기꺼이 하겠다(I'd be happy to)며 덧붙이고 있으므로 정답이다.
(C) **파생어 오답**: 질문의 organize와 파생어 관계인 organization을 이용한 오답이다.

어휘 | organize 준비[조직]하다 position 직책 organization 조직

3 Why don't we update our corporate Web site?
(A) Up at the top.
(B) I don't have time right now.
(C) Thanks for your cooperation.

회사 웹사이트를 업데이트하는 것이 어때요?
(A) 위쪽 꼭대기예요.
(B) 지금은 시간이 없어요.
(C) 협조해줘서 고마워요.

해설 | **제안·권유의 의문문**
(A) **유사 발음 오답**: 질문의 update와 발음이 유사한 up at을 이용한 오답이다.

(B) **정답**: 제안을 수락할 수 없는 이유를 말하며 간접적으로 거절의 뜻을 밝혔으므로 정답이다.
(C) **유사 발음 오답**: 질문의 corporate와 발음이 유사한 cooperation을 이용한 오답이다.

어휘 | update 최신화하다 corporate 기업의, 회사의 cooperation 협조, 협력

4 Would you like to borrow this book?
(A) A best-selling author.
(B) Let's book the flight tomorrow.
(C) Thanks, but I've already read it.

이 책 빌리실래요?
(A) 베스트셀러 작가입니다.
(B) 내일 항공편을 예약합시다.
(C) 감사하지만 이미 읽었어요.

해설 | **제안·권유의 의문문**
(A) **연상 작용 오답**: 질문의 book에서 연상 가능한 A best-selling author를 이용한 오답이다.
(B) **다의어 오답**: 질문의 book은 '책'이라는 뜻의 명사이고, 보기의 book은 '예약하다'라는 뜻의 동사이다.
(C) **정답**: 책을 빌리고 싶은지 묻는 질문에 고맙지만 이미 읽었다(Thanks, but I've already read it)며 우회적으로 거절의 의사를 밝혔으므로 정답이다.

어휘 | borrow 빌리다 author 작가 flight 항공편, 비행

5 Would you mind updating the meeting notes?
(A) I think the blue one is mine.
(B) We've already picked one out.
(C) Sure, how soon do you need them?

회의록을 업데이트해 줄 수 있나요?
(A) 파란색이 제 것 같아요.
(B) 우리는 벌써 하나를 골랐어요.
(C) 그럼요, 언제까지 필요하세요?

해설 | **부탁·요청의 의문문**
(A) **유사 발음 오답**: 질문의 mind와 발음이 유사한 mine을 이용한 오답이다.
(B) **관련 없는 오답**: 내용이 논리적으로 연결되지 않는다.
(C) **정답**: 회의록 업데이트를 부탁하는 요청에 긍정으로 응하면서 언제까지 해야 하는지를 묻고 있으므로 정답이다.

어휘 | mind 꺼려하다

6 How about a game of tennis this weekend?
(A) No, I'm afraid I didn't.
(B) Well, I do need the exercise.
(C) I bought ten of them.

이번 주말에 테니스 한 게임 어때요?
(A) 아니요, 유감스럽게도 안 했어요.
(B) 음, 전 정말 운동을 해야 해요.
(C) 제가 그것들 중 열 개를 샀어요.

해설 | **제안·권유의 의문문**
(A) **관련 없는 오답**: 어떤 일을 했는지 확인하는 질문에 적절한 대답이다.
(B) **정답**: 주말에 테니스 한 게임을 치자는 제안에 운동이 정말 필요하다(I do need the exercise)며 긍정적 반응을 하고 있으므로 정답이다.

(C) **유사 발음 오답**: 질문의 tennis와 부분적으로 발음이 유사한 ten을 이용한 오답이다.

어휘 | exercise 운동

③ 평서문

ETS 유형 연습
본책 p.058

1 (B)	2 (C)	3 (B)	4 (C)	5 (A)	6 (A)

1 Oakville Manufacturing is building a facility in Brazil.
(A) She's on a business trip.
(B) I just heard about that.
(C) The grand opening celebration.

오크빌 제조사는 브라질에 시설 하나를 설립할 것입니다.
(A) 그녀는 출장 중이에요.
(B) 방금 그것에 관해서 들었어요.
(C) 개관식이요.

해설 | **정보를 전달하는 평서문**
(A) **인칭 오류 오답**: 보기의 she가 가리키는 대상이 질문에 없다.
(B) **정답**: 오크빌 제조사가 브라질에 시설을 짓는다는 말에 대해, 방금 들었다(I just heard about that)며 자신도 알고 있음을 드러냈으므로 가장 적절한 응답이다.
(C) **연상 작용 오답**: 시설을 짓는다(building a facility)는 말에서 연상할 수 있는 개관식(grand opening celebration)을 이용한 오답이다.

어휘 | facility 시설, 공장 be on a business trip 출장 중이다
grand opening 개장, 개관 celebration 축하, 축하 행사

2 There are no more parking spaces on this street.
(A) It's a nice space for a park.
(B) No, I live on the next street.
(C) Try around the corner.

이 거리에는 더 이상 주차 공간이 없어요.
(A) 공원을 만들기에 좋은 공간이네요.
(B) 아니요. 저는 다음 거리에 살아요.
(C) 모퉁이를 돌아서 가 보세요.

해설 | **문제점을 언급하는 평서문**
(A) **단어 반복 오답**: 평서문의 space를 반복 이용한 오답이다.
(B) **단어 반복 오답**: 평서문의 street를 반복 이용한 오답이다.
(C) **정답**: 이 거리에 더 이상 주차 공간이 없다는 말에 모퉁이를 돌아가 보라(Try around the corner)며 주차 문제에 대한 대안을 제시하고 있으므로 가장 적절한 응답이다.

어휘 | parking space 주차 공간 around the corner 모퉁이를 돈 곳에

3 You really should try to attend Dr. Wong's talk.
(A) No, she wrote it herself.
(B) OK, but I may have to leave early.
(C) I wonder who the speaker was.

웡 박사님의 강연에 꼭 참석하셔야 해요.
(A) 아니요, 그녀가 직접 그것을 썼어요.
(B) 좋아요, 하지만 저는 아마 일찍 나와야 할 거예요.
(C) 연사가 누구였는지 궁금하네요.

해설 | **제안을 하는 평서문**
(A) **관련 없는 오답**: 특정 인물이 대필을 부탁했는지 확인하는 질문에 적절한 응답이다.
(B) **정답**: 강연회 참석을 제안하는 말에 좋다(OK)고 수락하면서 오래 있을 수는 없다는 내용을 덧붙였으므로 가장 적절한 응답이다.
(C) **연상 작용 오답**: 연설을 의미하는 talk에서 연상 가능한 speaker를 이용한 오답이다.

어휘 | attend 참석하다 talk 연설, 강연 wonder 궁금해 하다
speaker 연설자, 말하는 사람

4 The facilities manager is away on vacation.
(A) That building is vacant.
(B) It's bi-weekly.
(C) Who's covering for her?

시설 관리자는 휴가를 가고 없어요.
(A) 저 건물은 비어 있어요.
(B) 격주예요.
(C) 그녀의 일을 누가 대신하죠?

해설 | **정보를 전달하는 평서문**
(A) **파생어 오답**: 평서문의 vacation과 파생어 관계인 vacant를 이용한 오답이다.
(B) **관련 없는 오답**: 빈도를 묻는 질문에 적절한 응답이다.
(C) **정답**: 시설 관리자가 휴가를 가고 없다는 말에 그녀의 일을 누가 대신하는지(Who's covering for her?) 되물으며 관련된 상황을 확인하고 있으므로 가장 적절한 응답이다.

어휘 | facility 시설 on vacation 휴가 중인 vacant 비어 있는
bi-weekly 격주의 cover for ~의 일을 대신하다

5 I think the vice president should select the location.
(A) But she asked us to.
(B) A wide variety.
(C) We couldn't find them.

부회장님이 장소를 선택하셔야 할 것 같아요.
(A) 그렇지만 그녀가 우리보고 하라고 하셨잖아요.
(B) 아주 다양해요.
(C) 그것들을 찾을 수가 없었어요.

해설 | **의견을 제시하는 평서문**
(A) **정답**: 부회장이 장소를 선택해야 할 것 같다는 의견에 그녀(부회장)가 우리보고 결정하라고 했다며 우회적으로 반대 의견을 제시하고 있으므로 정답이다.
(B) **연상 작용 오답**: 평서문의 select(선택하다)에서 연상 가능한 variety(다양성)를 이용한 오답이다.
(C) **관련 없는 오답**: 질문의 내용과 논리적으로 맞지 않는다.

어휘 | vice president 부회장 location 장소, 위치

6 Let's see that museum exhibit together.
(A) Great—when should we go?
(B) No, the exit's on the left.
(C) I thought so, too.

그 박물관 전시회 같이 보시죠.
(A) 좋아요. 언제 갈까요?
(B) 아니요. 출구는 왼편에 있어요.
(C) 저도 그렇게 생각했어요.

해설 | **제안을 하는 평서문**
(A) **정답**: 박물관 전시회를 같이 보러 가자는 제안에 먼저
수락(Great)한 후, 언제 갈지(when should we go?) 되묻고
있으므로 정답이다.
(B) **유사 발음 오답**: 평서문의 exhibit와 발음이 유사한 exit를
이용한 오답이다.
(C) **관련 없는 오답**: 제시된 평서문은 대체로 의견이나 정보를
전달하는 평서문에 대한 동의를 나타내므로, 제안을 나타내는
평서문에 대한 응답으로는 적절하지 않다.

어휘 | exhibit 전시회 exit 출구 on the left 왼쪽에

● 실전 **도움닫기**   본책 p.059

1 (C) **2** (B) **3** (C) **4** (C) **5** (C)

1. Do you need to leave immediately, or can you
stay a little longer?
(A) The sleeves are too long.
(B) No thanks, I don't need one.
(C) I'd better go soon.
당장 가셔야 하나요, 아니면 좀 더 머무르실 수 있나요?
(A) 소매가 너무 길어요.
(B) 아니요, 괜찮아요. 전 필요 없어요.
(C) **곧 가봐야겠어요.**

해설 | **앞으로 할 행동을 묻는 선택 의문문**
(A) **유사 발음 오답**: 질문에 나온 leave와 발음이 유사한 sleeve를
이용한 오답이다.
(B) **단어 반복 오답**: 질문에 나온 need를 반복 이용한 오답이다.
(C) **정답**: 두 가지 선택 사항 중 당장 가야 한다는 내용의 전자를
선택한 응답이다.

어휘 | immediately 곧, 즉시 sleeve (옷의) 소매 had better
~하는 게 좋다[낫다]

2. Could you check these budget calculations for
me?
(A) No, I haven't.
(B) All right, put them on my desk.
(C) The quarterly sales figures.
이 예산 산정안을 검토해 주시겠어요?
(A) 아니요, 저는 그러지 않았어요.
(B) **알았어요, 제 책상 위에 놓아두세요.**
(C) 분기별 매출액이요.

해설 | **부탁·요청의 의문문**
(A) **관련 없는 오답**: 완료나 경험을 묻는 Have 의문문에 적절한
응답이다.
(B) **정답**: 예산 산정안을 검토해 달라는 요청에 수락(All right)한 후
책상에 두라고 했으므로 정답이다.
(C) **연상 작용 오답**: 질문의 budget에서 연상할 수 있는 sales
figures를 이용한 오답이다.

어휘 | budget calculation 예산 산정(안) quarterly 분기별의
sales figures 매출액

3. Please make sure to enter your hours on this
form.
(A) Until five on most days.
(B) Isn't this the right door?
(C) Thanks for reminding me.
이 양식에 반드시 당신의 근무 시간을 기입해 주세요.
(A) 대부분의 평일에 다섯 시까지요.
(B) 이게 맞는 문 아닌가요?
(C) **상기시켜 줘서 고마워요.**

해설 | **행동을 요청하는 명령문**
(A) **연상 작용 오답**: hours에서 연상 가능한 until five를 이용한
오답이다.
(B) **연상 작용 오답**: enter를 '들어가다'로 착각할 경우 연상 가능한
door를 이용한 오답이다.
(C) **정답**: 해야 할 일을 상기시켜 준 데에 대한 고마움을 표하고
있으므로 가장 적절한 응답이다.

어휘 | enter (내용 등을) 기입하다 form 서식, 양식 remind
상기시키다

4. The hotel was full and they couldn't find our
reservations.
(A) Did he have to replace it?
(B) The front row is reserved.
(C) So where did you stay?
그 호텔은 만원이었고, 우리는 예약이 안 되어 있더라고요.
(A) 그는 그것을 교체해야만 했나요?
(B) 앞줄은 예약돼 있어요.
(C) **그래서 어디에서 묵었어요?**

해설 | **문제 상황을 언급하는 평서문**
(A) **관련 없는 오답**: 호텔에서 겪은 문제점과는 관련이 없는
답변이다.
(B) **파생어 오답**: 평서문의 reservation과 파생어 관계인
reserve를 이용한 오답이다.
(C) **정답**: 호텔이 만원이었고 그곳에 예약이 안 되어 있었다는
상황을 들은 후 그래서 어떻게 되었냐고 결과를 묻고 있으므로
가장 적절한 응답이다.

어휘 | reservation 예약 replace 바꾸다, 교체하다 row 줄, 열

5. Why don't you finish that tomorrow when you're
not so tired?
(A) He wasn't tired this time.
(B) Whenever you have a minute.
(C) That's probably a good idea.
내일 많이 피곤하지 않을 때 그걸 끝내는 게 어때요?
(A) 그는 이번에 피곤하지 않았어요.
(B) 당신이 잠깐 시간이 있을 때면 언제든지요.
(C) **그게 좋은 생각인 것 같아요.**

해설 | **제안·권유의 의문문**
(A) **단어 반복·인칭 오류 오답**: 질문의 tired를 반복 이용한
오답이며, 보기의 He가 가리키는 대상이 질문에 없다.
(B) **유사 발음 오답**: 질문의 when과 부분적으로 발음이 같은
whenever를 사용한 오답이다.
(C) **정답**: 제안 의문문에 대한 전형적인 동의 표현 응답이다.

어휘 | minute (시간의) 분, 잠깐 동안

● ETS 실전문제

본책 p.060

1 (A)	2 (C)	3 (A)	4 (C)	5 (C)
6 (C)	7 (C)	8 (C)	9 (A)	10 (A)
11 (A)	12 (C)	13 (B)	14 (A)	15 (A)
16 (B)	17 (C)	18 (B)	19 (A)	20 (B)
21 (C)	22 (A)	23 (B)	24 (B)	25 (C)

1 Did the hiring committee choose Norman, or did they pick Heidi?
(A) Neither of them, actually.
(B) She didn't finish them.
(C) Yes, I'd prefer another date.

채용위원회는 노먼 씨를 선택했나요, 아니면 하이디 씨를 뽑았나요?
(A) 사실 두 명 다 아니에요.
(B) 그녀는 그것들을 끝내지 않았어요.
(C) 네, 저는 다른 날짜를 원합니다.

해설 | **고용 대상을 묻는 선택 의문문**
(A) **정답:** 고용 대상으로 제시된 노먼 씨와 하이디 씨 중 어느 누구도 뽑지 않았다(Neither of them)고 답하고 있으므로 정답이다.
(B) **관련 없는 오답:** 위원회가 노먼 씨와 하이디 씨 중 누구를 선택했는지 묻는 질문에 그녀가 그것들을 끝내지 않았다(She didn't finish them)라고 하는 것은 상황에 맞지 않는 대답이다.
(C) **연상 작용 오답:** 질문의 hiring committee에서 연상 가능한 면접 일정과 관련된 상황(I'd prefer another date)을 언급한 오답이다.

어휘 | hiring committee 채용 위원회 neither (둘 중) 어느 것도 아닌 actually 사실, 실제로 prefer 좋아하다, 선호하다

2 Do you mind if I borrow your stapler?
(A) In several different colors.
(B) Yes, last week.
(C) Not at all—here it is.

스테이플러를 빌려주실 수 있나요?
(A) 몇 가지 다양한 색으로요.
(B) 네, 지난주요.
(C) 그럼요. 여기 있어요.

해설 | **부탁·요청의 의문문**
(A) **관련 없는 오답:** 스테이플러를 빌려달라는 요청에 몇 가지 다양한 색(In several different colors)이라고 하는 것은 상황에 맞지 않는 대답이다.
(B) **연상 작용 오답:** 질문의 borrow에서 연상 가능한 빌린 시점(last week)을 언급한 오답이다.
(C) **정답:** 스테이플러를 빌려달라고 요청하는 Do you mind 질문에 꺼리지 않는다(Not at all)며 수락한 후, 여기 있다(here it is)고 덧붙이고 있으므로 정답이다.

어휘 | mind 꺼려하다 borrow 빌리다 several 몇몇의

3 Why don't you wait to see the survey results before making a decision?
(A) Oh, we've already taken them into account.
(B) I don't see the waiter anywhere.
(C) A select group of customers.

결정을 내리기 전에 설문 조사 결과를 기다려 보는 게 어때요?
(A) 아, 우리는 이미 그것을 참작했어요.
(B) 웨이터가 어디에도 안 보이네요.
(C) 엄선된 고객 단체요.

해설 | **제안·권유의 의문문**
(A) **정답:** 설문 조사 결과를 기다렸다가 결정을 내리라는 제안에, 이미 그 결과를 참작했다고 답하고 있으므로 가장 적절한 응답이다.
(B) **파생어 오답:** 질문에 나오는 wait의 파생어 waiter를 이용한 오답이다.
(C) **연상 작용 오답:** 설문 조사 결과를 기다려 보라는 제안과는 관련 없는 응답으로, 질문의 survey에서 연상 가능한 select group을 이용한 오답이다.

어휘 | survey 설문 조사 make a decision 결정하다 take A into account A를 고려하다 select 엄선된, 선발된

4 I'd like to discuss the project you just turned in.
(A) We just purchased that projector.
(B) Not very often.
(C) Could it wait until tomorrow?

당신이 방금 제출한 기획서에 대해 논의하고 싶습니다.
(A) 방금 그 영사기를 구입했습니다.
(B) 아주 자주는 아니에요.
(C) 내일 하면 안 될까요?

해설 | **바람을 나타내는 평서문**
(A) **파생어 오답:** 평서문의 project와 파생어 관계인 projector를 이용한 오답이다.
(B) **관련 없는 오답:** 빈도를 묻는 질문에 어울리는 응답이다.
(C) **정답:** 기획서(the project)에 대해 논의하고 싶다는 의견에 대해 내일 하면 안 되는지(Could it wait until tomorrow?) 되묻고 있으므로 가장 적절한 응답이다.

어휘 | discuss 논의하다 project 기획서, 안 turn in 제출하다 purchase 구입하다

5 Would you rather see a movie or go to a concert tonight?
(A) Thanks, I had a great seat.
(B) It was interesting.
(C) There is a new film I want to see.

오늘 저녁 영화를 보고 싶어요, 아니면 음악회에 가고 싶어요?
(A) 고마워요. 자리가 정말 좋았어요.
(B) 그것은 흥미로웠어요.
(C) 보고 싶은 신작 영화가 있어요.

해설 | **계획을 묻는 선택 의문문**
(A) **연상 작용 오답:** 질문의 movie 또는 concert에서 연상 가능한 seat를 이용한 오답이다.
(B) **연상 작용 오답:** 질문의 movie 또는 concert에서 연상 가능한 영화 및 음악회에 대한 견해(It was interesting)를 이용한 오답이다.
(C) **정답:** 계획으로 제시된 see a movie와 go to a concert 중 보고 싶은 신작 영화가 있다(There is a new film I want to see)며 우회적으로 전자를 선택하고 있으므로 정답이다.

어휘 | would rather ~하고 싶다, (차라리) ~하겠다 seat 자리, 좌석 film 영화

6 Please bring twelve copies of the agenda.
  (A) It's actually at 4:30.
  (B) There's an import tax.
  (C) OK, I'll be sure to do that.

회의 안건 사본을 12부 가져오세요.
(A) 사실은 4시 30분이에요.
(B) 수입 관세가 있어요.
(C) 좋아요. 꼭 그렇게 할게요.

해설 | **행동을 요청하는 명령문**
(A) **연상 작용 오답**: 제시문의 twelve를 시간으로 잘못 들었을 경우 연상 가능한 4:30을 이용한 오답이다.
(B) **관련 없는 오답**: 여자의 요청에 수입 관세가 있다는 대답은 논리적으로 맞지 않는다.
(C) **정답**: 요청을 수락한 후 꼭 하겠다고 덧붙이고 있으므로 정답이다.

어휘 | agenda 회의 안건, 의제 import tax 수입 관세

7 Would you like me to show you the way to the cafeteria?
  (A) I did like the show.
  (B) I wouldn't throw it away.
  (C) Actually, I've been there before.

제가 카페테리아로 가는 길을 알려드릴까요?
(A) 저는 그 공연이 참 좋았어요.
(B) 저는 그걸 버리진 않겠어요.
(C) 사실 전에 거기 가 본 적이 있어요.

해설 | **제안·권유의 의문문**
(A) **단어 반복·다의어 오답**: 질문의 like 및 show를 반복 이용한 오답이다. 또한 질문의 show는 '알려 주다, 안내하다'라는 뜻의 동사이고, 보기의 show는 '공연, 쇼'라는 뜻의 명사이다.
(B) **단어 반복·유사 발음 오답**: 질문의 Would를 반복 이용하고 있으며, 질문의 show you the way와 발음이 일부 유사한 throw it away를 이용한 오답이다.
(C) **정답**: 카페테리아로 가는 길을 알려 주겠다는 제안에 전에 거기 가 본 적이 있다(I've been there before)며 우회적으로 거절의 의사를 밝혔으므로 정답이다.

어휘 | throw away 버리다 actually 사실, 실제로

8 Will you help me move these chairs?
  (A) The fifth-floor conference room.
  (B) It's at the information desk.
  (C) Where do they need to go?

이 의자들 옮기는 걸 도와 주실래요?
(A) 5층 회의실요.
(B) 그건 안내 데스크에 있어요.
(C) 그것들은 어디로 가야 해요?

해설 | **부탁·요청의 의문문**
(A) **연상 작용 오답**: 질문의 move these chairs에서 연상 가능한 옮기는 장소(The fifth-floor conference room)를 언급한 오답이다.
(B) **연상 작용 오답**: 질문의 chairs에서 연상 가능한 desk를 이용한 오답이다.
(C) **정답**: 의자 옮기는 걸 도와 달라는 요청에 어디로 옮겨야 하는지(Where do they need to go?) 되물으며 관련 정보를 요청하고 있으므로 가장 적절한 응답이다.

어휘 | conference 회의 information 정보

9 Should I start by cleaning the lab equipment or organizing the new supplies?
  (A) Let's see what Mr. Park thinks.
  (B) To streamline the process.
  (C) Yes, they're much better.

실험 장비 청소부터 해야 할까요, 아니면 새 용품들 정리 먼저 해야 할까요?
(A) 박 씨의 생각을 알아보죠.
(B) 절차를 간소화하려고요.
(C) 네, 그것들이 훨씬 낫네요.

해설 | **일의 순서를 묻는 선택 의문문**
(A) **정답**: 먼저 해야 할 일로 제시된 cleaning the lab equipment와 organizing the new supplies 중 어느 것도 선택하지 않고 박 씨의 생각을 알아보자(Let's see what Mr. Park thinks)며 결정을 보류하고 있으므로 가장 적절한 응답이다.
(B) **연상 작용 오답**: 질문의 organizing을 '체계화하다'라는 뜻으로 잘못 이해했을 경우 연상 가능한 streamline the process를 이용한 오답이다.
(C) **Yes/No 대답 불가 오답**: cleaning the lab equipment와 organizing the new supplies 중 하나를 선택하라는 질문에는 Yes/No로 대답할 수 없다.

어휘 | lab 실험실 equipment 장비 organize 정리하다, 배열하다 supply 용품 streamline 간소화하다, 능률화하다 process 절차

10 Could I have a copy of last year's sales figures?
  (A) Angela has all the data.
  (B) Sorry, we don't sell photocopiers.
  (C) Sure, here's your coffee.

작년도 매출 기록 사본을 얻을 수 있을까요?
(A) 안젤라가 모든 자료를 가지고 있어요.
(B) 죄송해요, 저희는 복사기를 판매하지 않아요.
(C) 물론이죠, 여기 커피요.

해설 | **부탁·요청의 의문문**
(A) **정답**: 매출 기록 사본을 요청하는 질문에 수락이나 거절 대신, 다른 사람이 가지고 있다는 정보를 알려주며 잘 답변한 정답이다.
(B) **연상 작용 오답**: 질문의 copy에서 연상할 수 있는 photocopiers를 이용한 오답이다.
(C) **유사 발음 오답**: 질문의 copy와 발음이 유사한 coffee를 이용한 오답이다.

어휘 | figures (기록된) 수치 photocopier 복사기

11 Would you be willing to lead the new employee orientation?
  (A) Well, it depends on when it is.
  (B) Around twenty-five people.
  (C) No, I didn't read it.

신입사원 오리엔테이션 진행을 해 주시겠어요?
(A) 음, 언제인지에 따라서요.
(B) 약 25명요.
(C) 아니요. 저는 그것을 읽지 않았어요.

해설 | **부탁·요청의 의문문**
(A) **정답**: 신입사원 오리엔테이션을 진행해달라는 부탁에 언제인지에 달려있다(it depends on when it is)며 수락 여부를 보류하고 있으므로 가장 적절한 응답이다.

(B) **연상 작용 오답**: 질문의 new employee orientation에서 연상 가능한 참석 인원(Around twenty-five people)을 언급한 오답이다.

(C) **유사 발음 오답**: 질문의 lead와 발음이 유사한 read를 이용한 오답이다.

어휘 | be willing to 기꺼이 ~하다 lead 이끌다 employee 직원 depend on ~에 달려 있다

12 I think Marcy took the marketing report home with her.
  (A) Let's pick some up at the market.
  (B) A house on King's Road.
  (C) I guess I'll read it tomorrow.

마시가 마케팅 보고서를 집에 가지고 간 것 같아요.
  (A) 시장에서 좀 사 옵시다.
  (B) 킹스 가에 있는 집이에요.
  (C) 저는 내일 읽어 보면 될 것 같아요.

해설 | **상황을 설명하는 평서문**

(A) **유사 발음 오답**: 평서문의 marketing과 일부 발음이 동일한 market을 이용한 오답이다.

(B) **연상 작용 오답**: 평서문의 home에서 연상 가능한 house를 이용한 오답이다.

(C) **정답**: 마시가 보고서를 집에 가져간 것 같다는 말에 내일 읽어 보겠다(I'll read it tomorrow)라고 하며 상황을 받아들이고 있으므로 가장 적절한 응답이다.

어휘 | report 보고서 pick up 사다, 찾아오다

13 Are you leaving for lunch now, or do you have time to look over some paperwork?
  (A) I'll look for it over here.
  (B) I'm free until one-thirty.
  (C) Yes, he's at lunch.

지금 점심 먹으러 갈 거예요, 아니면 서류 검토할 시간이 있나요?
  (A) 여기서 그걸 찾아볼게요.
  (B) 1시 30분까지는 시간이 있어요.
  (C) 네, 그는 지금 점심을 먹고 있어요.

해설 | **지금 할 일을 묻는 선택 의문문**

(A) **단어 반복 오답**: 질문의 look과 over를 반복 사용한 오답이다.

(B) **정답**: 지금 점심 먹으러 갈 것인지 아니면 서류 검토할 시간이 있는지 묻는 선택 의문문이다. 1시 30분까지 시간이 있다는 말로 그때까지 서류 검토 작업을 하겠다는 것을 우회적으로 표현하고 있다.

(C) **단어 반복 오답**: 질문의 lunch를 반복 사용한 오답이다.

어휘 | look over ~을 검토하다 look for ~을 찾다

14 Could you proofread the translation before we send it to the Madrid office?
  (A) Sure, I'll have a look.
  (B) Not very recently.
  (C) It arrived on schedule.

번역문을 마드리드 사무소로 보내기 전에 교정 봐 줄 수 있어요?
  (A) 그럼요, 제가 볼게요.
  (B) 아주 최근은 아니에요.
  (C) 그건 예정대로 도착했어요.

해설 | **부탁·요청의 의문문**

(A) **정답**: 번역문을 교정 봐 달라는 요청에 대해, Sure라는 수락의 표현을 이용하여 답하고 있으므로 정답이다.

(B) **관련 없는 오답**: When 의문문에 어울리는 대답으로, 번역문 교정 요청과는 전혀 무관한 답변이다.

(C) **연상 작용 오답**: 질문의 send it to the Madrid office에서 연상 가능한 상황(arrived on schedule)을 이용한 오답이다.

어휘 | proofread 교정을 보다 translation 번역(문) recently 최근에 on schedule 예정대로

15 Shall I show you how to make the font size larger?
  (A) It is hard to read at this size.
  (B) Sure, I'd love to go.
  (C) Thanks for the letter.

글씨 크기를 더 크게 만드는 방법을 알려 드릴까요?
  (A) 이 크기로는 읽기가 어렵네요.
  (B) 물론이죠, 기꺼이 갈게요.
  (C) 편지 주셔서 감사합니다.

해설 | **제안·권유의 의문문**

(A) **정답**: 글씨 크기 확대 방법을 알려 주겠다는 제안에 '이 크기로는 읽기 어렵다(It is hard to read at this size)'며 방법을 알려 달라고 우회적으로 표현하고 있으므로 정답이다.

(B) **연상 작용 오답**: 질문의 show를 '공연'으로 잘못 이해했을 때 연상 가능한 I'd love to go를 이용한 오답이다.

(C) **관련 없는 오답**: 방법을 알려주겠다는 제안에 편지를 주어 고맙다고 하는 것은 어울리지 않는다.

어휘 | font 글씨(체)

16 The city council meeting has been postponed.
  (A) I've never visited there.
  (B) Thanks for letting me know.
  (C) She's on the phone.

시의회 회의가 연기됐어요.
  (A) 저는 거기 가 본 적이 없어요.
  (B) 알려줘서 고마워요.
  (C) 그녀는 통화 중입니다.

해설 | **정보를 전달하는 평서문**

(A) **관련 없는 오답**: 시의회 회의가 연기됐다는 말에 거기 가 본 적이 없다(I've never visited there)라고 하는 것은 상황에 맞지 않는 대답이다.

(B) **정답**: 시의회 회의가 연기됐다는 말에 알려줘서 고맙다(Thanks for letting me know)며 정보 전달에 대한 감사의 의사를 표현하고 있으므로 정답이다.

(C) **인칭 오류·유사 발음 오답**: 대명사 She가 가리키는 대상이 평서문에 없으며, 평서문의 postponed와 발음이 일부 유사한 phone을 이용한 오답이다.

어휘 | city council 시의회 postpone 미루다, 연기하다

17 Do you want to design your own business cards, or use a standard format?
  (A) Yes, they're very creative.
  (B) Great, here are some examples.
  (C) I'd prefer to design them myself.

본인의 명함을 직접 디자인하고 싶으세요, 아니면 표준 서식을 이용하고
싶으세요?
(A) 네, 그들은 매우 창의적이죠.
(B) 좋아요. 여기 몇 가지 예시가 있어요.
(C) 제가 직접 디자인하고 싶어요.

해설 | **명함 제작 방식을 묻는 선택 의문문**
(A) **Yes/No 대답 불가 오답:** design your own business
cards와 use a standard format 중 하나를 선택하라는
질문에는 Yes/No로 대답할 수 없다.
(B) **연상 작용 오답:** 질문의 design your own business
cards에서 연상 가능한 examples를 이용한 오답이다.
(C) **정답:** 명함 제작 방식으로 제시된 design your own
business cards와 use a standard format 중 직접
디자인하고 싶다며 전자를 선택하여 답했으므로 정답이다.

어휘 | business card 명함 standard 표준 규격의 creative
창의적인 prefer 좋아하다, 선호하다

18 I thought Mr. Watson's speech was very
entertaining.
(A) Next month, I think.
(B) It certainly was.
(C) We should make a reservation.
왓슨 씨의 연설이 매우 재미있다고 생각했어요.
(A) 다음 달인 것 같군요.
(B) 분명히 그랬죠.
(C) 우리는 예약을 해야 해요.

해설 | **의견을 표현하는 평서문**
(A) **파생어 오답:** 평서문에 나오는 과거형 thought의 현재형
think를 이용한 오답이다.
(B) **정답:** 왓슨 씨의 연설이 재미있었다는 의견에 대해 동의(It
certainly was)의 의사를 밝혔으므로 정답이다.
(C) **관련 없는 오답:** 연설이 재미있었다는 의견에 예약을 해야
한다며 제안하는 것은 어울리지 않는다.

어휘 | speech 연설 entertaining 재미있는 certainly 틀림없이,
분명히 make a reservation 예약하다

19 Let's try the new restaurant that opened near the
office.
(A) I've already eaten lunch.
(B) The office is closed today.
(C) It's by the copier.
사무실 근처에 개업한 새 식당에 가 봅시다.
(A) 저는 이미 점심 식사를 했는데요.
(B) 사무실은 오늘 닫았어요.
(C) 그건 복사기 옆에 있어요.

해설 | **제안을 하는 평서문**
(A) **정답:** 개업한 새 식당에 가보자는 제안에 이미 점심 식사를
했다(I've already eaten lunch)며 우회적으로 거절의 의사를
밝혔으므로 정답이다.
(B) **단어 반복 오답:** 평서문의 office를 반복 이용한 오답이다.
(C) **연상 작용 오답:** 평서문의 office에서 연상 가능한 copier를
이용한 오답이다.

어휘 | copier 복사기

20 Would you like some help with the mailing labels?
(A) On my desk.
(B) That would be great.
(C) Yes, I can.
주소 라벨 작업 좀 도와드릴까요?
(A) 제 책상 위에요.
(B) 그럼 너무 좋죠.
(C) 네, 가능해요.

해설 | **제안·권유의 의문문**
(A) **연상 작용 오답:** 질문의 mailing labels에서 연상 가능한 주소
라벨이 있는 장소(On my desk)를 언급한 오답이다.
(B) **정답:** 도움을 제안하는 질문에 그러면 좋겠다(That would be
great)며 수락의 의사를 밝혔으므로 정답이다.
(C) **관련 없는 오답:** 도움을 제안하는 질문에 가능하다(Yes, I can)
라고 하는 것은 상황에 맞지 않은 대답이다.

어휘 | mailing label 수신인 주소 성명용 라벨

21 Can you join Friday's conference call, or should I
find someone else?
(A) I'll look up the number.
(B) Someone left you a message.
(C) Can I let you know tomorrow?
금요일 화상 회의에 참석하실 수 있어요, 아니면 다른 분을 찾아야
할까요?
(A) 제가 번호를 찾아볼게요.
(B) 누군가 당신에게 메시지를 남겼어요.
(C) 내일 알려드려도 되나요?

해설 | **참석 여부를 묻는 선택 의문문**
(A) **연상 작용 오답:** 질문의 call에서 연상 가능한 number를
이용한 오답이다.
(B) **연상 작용 오답:** 질문의 call에서 연상 가능한 상황(Someone
left you a message)을 이용한 오답이다.
(C) **정답:** 화상 회의의 참석 여부를 묻는 질문에 내일 알려줘도
되는지(Can I let you know tomorrow?) 되물으며 선택을
보류하고 있으므로 가장 적절한 응답이다.

어휘 | conference call 화상회의 look up 찾아보다 leave a
message 메시지를 남기다

22 We finally got approval to hire more staff.
(A) That's good to hear.
(B) On a higher shelf.
(C) The monthly staff meeting.
마침내 직원 추가 채용 승인을 받았어요.
(A) 잘 됐네요.
(B) 더 위에 있는 선반에요.
(C) 월간 직원회의요.

해설 | **정보를 전달하는 평서문**
(A) **정답:** 마침내 직원 추가 채용 승인을 받았다는 말에 잘
됐다(That's good to hear)며 긍정적인 반응을 하고 있으므로
정답이다.
(B) **유사 발음 오답:** 평서문의 hire와 발음이 유사한 higher를
이용한 오답이다.
(C) **단어 반복 오답:** 평서문의 staff를 반복 이용한 오답이다.

어휘 | finally 마침내 get approval 승인을 받다 hire 채용하다
shelf 선반 monthly 월간의

23 Is the conference center on the north side of the highway or on the south side?
(A) I'm attending a two-day seminar.
(B) It's to the south, just past Exit 52.
(C) Within an hour or so.

그 회의장은 고속도로 북쪽에 있나요, 아니면 남쪽에 있나요?
(A) 저는 이틀간 열리는 세미나에 참석하고 있어요.
(B) 남쪽으로 52번 출구를 막 지나서 있어요.
(C) 한 시간 정도 이내에요.

해설 | 회의장의 위치를 묻는 선택 의문문
(A) 연상 작용 오답: 질문에 나온 conference center에서 연상 가능한 단어 seminar를 이용한 오답이다.
(B) 정답: 회의장의 방향이 고속도로 남쪽(It's to the south)이라면서 질문의 두 사항 중 하나를 택한 후, 52번 출구를 막 지나서 있다(just past Exit 52)고 덧붙였으므로 가장 적절한 대답이다.
(C) 관련 없는 오답: 회의장의 위치를 묻는 질문에 시간을 나타내는 말은 적절한 대답이 될 수 없다.

어휘 | conference center (대규모) 회의장 past ~을 지나서 exit 출구 or so ~정도

24 I would like to treat our staff to a nice dinner.
(A) We waited ten minutes for a table.
(B) We do have some money left in the budget.
(C) Just the vegetarian platter.

우리 직원들에게 맛있는 저녁을 대접하고 싶어요.
(A) 우리는 10분 동안 자리가 나기를 기다렸어요.
(B) 예산에서 남는 돈이 좀 있긴 해요.
(C) 그냥 채식 요리요.

해설 | 바람을 나타내는 평서문
(A) 연상 작용 오답: 평서문의 dinner에서 연상 가능한 table을 이용한 오답이다.
(B) 정답: 직원들에게 저녁을 대접하고 싶다는 말에 예산에 남은 돈이 있다(We do have some money left in the budget)며 가능성을 시사하고 있으므로 가장 적절한 응답이다.
(C) 연상 작용 오답: 평서문의 dinner에서 연상 가능한 vegetarian platter를 이용한 오답이다.

어휘 | budget 예산 vegetarian 채식의, 채식주의자 platter 모듬 요리, 큰 접시

25 Have you signed the contract, or do you need more time to review it?
(A) I didn't see the sign.
(B) Please address the letter to me.
(C) I'll need another day or two.

계약서에 서명하셨나요, 아니면 계약서를 검토할 시간이 더 필요하세요?
(A) 표지판을 못 봤어요.
(B) 그 편지를 저에게 보내주세요.
(C) 하루나 이틀 더 필요해요.

해설 | 서명 여부를 묻는 선택 의문문
(A) 다의어 오답: 질문의 signed는 '서명하다'라는 뜻의 동사이고, 보기의 sign은 '표지판'이라는 뜻의 명사이다.
(B) 관련 없는 오답: 계약서 서명 여부를 묻는 질문에 편지를 보내달라(Please address the letter to me)고 요청하는 응답은 어울리지 않는다.

(C) 정답: 계약서에 서명했는지 아니면 검토할 시간이 더 필요한지 묻는 질문에 하루나 이틀 더 필요하다(I'll need another day or two)며 후자를 선택하여 답했으므로 정답이다.

어휘 | sign the contract 계약(서)에 서명하다 review 검토하다 address (~앞으로 우편물을) 보내다

● ETS ACTUAL **TEST**   본책 p.062

7 (C)	**8** (B)	**9** (C)	**10** (A)	**11** (C)
12 (A)	**13** (B)	**14** (A)	**15** (B)	**16** (A)
17 (B)	**18** (B)	**19** (B)	**20** (B)	**21** (B)
22 (B)	**23** (C)	**24** (C)	**25** (A)	**26** (C)
27 (C)	**28** (A)	**29** (A)	**30** (C)	**31** (C)

7 Where can I buy fresh flowers this time of year?
(A) Ten thirty this morning.
(B) Yes, in July and August.
(C) Try the florist on North Avenue.

연중 이맘때쯤 싱싱한 꽃을 어디에서 살 수 있죠?
(A) 오늘 오전 10시 30분이요.
(B) 네, 7월과 8월이요.
(C) 노스 가에 있는 꽃집에 가보세요.

해설 | 구매 장소를 묻는 Where 의문문
(A) 관련 없는 오답: 시점을 묻는 When 의문문에 어울리는 응답이다.
(B) Yes/No 대답 불가 오답: Where 의문문에는 Yes/No로 대답할 수 없다.
(C) 정답: 꽃을 살 수 있는 장소를 묻는 질문에 특정 장소(the florist on North Avenue)를 제시했으므로 정답이다.

어휘 | florist 꽃집, 꽃집 직원

8 Marcela hasn't heard back from the Canadian distributors, has she?
(A) An equal distribution of funds.
(B) I don't think so, no.
(C) Can you help me move those boxes?

마르셀라는 캐나다의 배급사들로부터 연락을 못 받았죠, 받았나요?
(A) 자금의 공정한 배분이요.
(B) 아닌 것 같아요, 아니에요.
(C) 저 상자들을 옮기는 것 좀 도와주시겠어요?

해설 | 사실을 확인하는 부가 의문문
(A) 파생어 오답: 질문에 나오는 distributors와 파생어 관계인 distribution을 이용한 오답이다.
(B) 정답: 연락을 받았는지 확인하는 질문에 아닌 것 같다(I don't think so)고 한 후, 다시 한 번 no라고 말하며 확인해 주고 있으므로 정답이다.
(C) 관련 없는 오답: 사실을 확인하는 질문에 도움을 요청하는 것은 어울리지 않는다.

어휘 | distributor 배급사, 배포자 equal 동등한, 공정한 distribution 배분

9 Wouldn't you rather have a dark color for the carpet?
(A) Yes, it's made of wood.
(B) My car's right over there.
(C) That would look good in this room.

카펫을 어두운 색으로 하시겠어요?
(A) 네, 그건 나무로 만들어졌어요.
(B) 제 차는 바로 저기 있어요.
(C) 그게 이 방에 잘 어울리겠어요.

해설 | 의견을 확인하는 부정 의문문
(A) **관련 없는 오답:** 카펫을 어두운 색으로 하지 않을지 묻는 질문에 나무로 만들어졌다(it's made of wood)며 소재를 언급하는 것은 상황에 어울리지 않는다.
(B) **유사 발음 오답:** 질문의 carpet과 일부 발음이 동일한 car를 이용한 오답이다.
(C) **정답:** 카펫을 어두운 색으로 하지 않을지 묻는 질문에 방에 잘 어울리겠다(That would look good in this room)며 우회적으로 긍정의 응답을 하고 있으므로 정답이다.

어휘 | would rather ~하고 싶다, (차라리) ~하겠다 **be made of** ~로 만들어지다 **over there** 저쪽에

10 Who does the quality control tests on our company's products?
(A) Several people do them.
(B) Only the highest quality materials.
(C) Before Mr. Keith arrived.

우리 회사 제품의 품질 관리 시험은 누가 하나요?
(A) 여러 명이 해요.
(B) 최고급 소재만요.
(C) 키스 씨가 도착하기 전에요.

해설 | 담당자를 묻는 Who 의문문
(A) **정답:** 품질 관리 시험의 담당자를 묻는 질문에 여러 명이 한다(Several people do them)고 답하고 있으므로 가장 적절한 응답이다.
(B) **단어 반복 오답:** 질문의 quality를 반복 이용한 오답이다.
(C) **관련 없는 오답:** 시점을 묻는 When 의문문에 적절한 응답이다.

어휘 | quality control 품질 관리 **product** 제품 **several** 몇몇의 **material** 재료, 소재 **arrive** 도착하다

11 Why did you get here so early this morning?
(A) Not until the afternoon.
(B) Yes, I submitted it early.
(C) There was less traffic than usual.

오늘 아침엔 왜 이렇게 일찍 도착했어요?
(A) 오후나 되어서요.
(B) 네, 저는 일찍 제출했어요.
(C) 평소보다 교통량이 적었어요.

해설 | 일찍 도착한 이유를 묻는 Why 의문문
(A) **연상 작용 오답:** 질문의 morning에서 연상 가능한 afternoon을 이용한 오답이다.
(B) **단어 반복 오답:** 질문의 early를 반복 이용한 오답이다.
(C) **정답:** 일찍 도착한 이유를 묻는 질문에 평소보다 교통량이 적었다(There was less traffic than usual)며 구체적인 이유를 제시했으므로 정답이다.

어휘 | not until ~이후에야 비로소 **submit** 제출하다 **traffic** 교통 **than usual** 평소보다

12 You remembered to lock the office door, didn't you?
(A) I'll double-check.
(B) The road was blocked.
(C) I remember his name.

사무실 문 잠그는 거 기억했죠, 그렇지 않나요?
(A) 다시 한 번 확인할게요.
(B) 도로가 봉쇄됐어요.
(C) 저는 그의 이름을 기억해요.

해설 | 사실을 확인하는 부가 의문문
(A) **정답:** 사무실 문 잠그는 걸 기억했는지 확인하는 질문에 다시 한 번 확인하겠다(I'll double-check)고 답하고 있으므로 가장 적절한 응답이다.
(B) **유사 발음 오답:** 질문의 lock과 일부 발음이 동일한 blocked를 이용한 오답이다.
(C) **파생어 오답:** 질문에 나오는 과거형 remembered의 현재형 remember를 이용한 오답이다.

어휘 | lock 잠그다 **double-check** 다시 한 번 확인하다, 재확인하다 **blocked** 봉쇄된

13 I just heard a news report on the radio about seasonal farm work.
(A) Some homegrown vegetables.
(B) Which station was it on?
(C) For a music producer.

방금 라디오에서 계절에 따른 농장일에 대한 뉴스를 들었어요.
(A) 집에서 기른 채소들요.
(B) 어떤 방송에서 나왔어요?
(C) 음악 제작자를 위해서요.

해설 | 사실을 전달하는 평서문
(A) **연상 작용 오답:** 평서문의 farm에서 연상 가능한 vegetables를 이용한 오답이다.
(B) **정답:** 라디오에서 계절에 따른 농장일에 대한 뉴스를 들었다는 말에 어떤 방송에 나왔는지(Which station was it on?) 되물으며 관련된 정보를 확인하고 있으므로 가장 적절한 응답이다.
(C) **연상 작용 오답:** 평서문의 heard ~ on the radio에서 연상 가능한 music을 이용한 오답이다.

어휘 | news report 뉴스 보도 **seasonal** 계절의 **homegrown** 국내산의, 집에서 기른 **station** 방송국, 방송

14 When will the results of your research be published?
(A) In the July issue of the journal.
(B) A different case study.
(C) I hope you find it.

당신의 연구 결과는 언제 게재될 예정인가요?
(A) 7월호 학술지에서요.
(B) 다른 사례 연구요.
(C) 찾으시기를 바라요.

해설 | 게재 예정 시점을 묻는 When 의문문
(A) **정답:** 연구 결과가 게재될 시점을 묻는 질문에 7월호 학술지(In the July issue of the journal)라며 게재 예정 시점을 언급하고 있으므로 정답이다.
(B) **연상 작용 오답:** 질문의 research에서 연상 가능한 case study를 이용한 오답이다.
(C) **관련 없는 오답:** 연구 결과가 게재될 시점을 묻는 질문에 찾길 바란다(I hope you find it)고 하는 것은 상황에 맞지 않는 응답이다.

어휘 | result 결과 **research** 연구 **publish** 출판하다, 게재하다 **journal** 저널, 학술지 **case study** 사례 연구

15 Who suggested the changes to the meeting agenda?
(A) The last topic.
(B) It was Ms. Howell's idea.
(C) Wednesday afternoon.

회의 안건 변경은 누가 제안했죠?
(A) 마지막 주제요.
(B) 하웰 씨의 의견이었어요.
(C) 수요일 오후요.

해설 | 제안자를 묻는 Who 의문문
(A) 연상 작용 오답: 질문의 agenda에서 연상 가능한 topic을 이용한 오답이다.
(B) 정답: 회의 안건 변경의 제안자를 묻는 질문에 하웰 씨의 의견이었다(It was Ms. Howell's idea)며 제안자를 특정했으므로 정답이다.
(C) 관련 없는 오답: 회의 일정을 묻는 When 의문문에 적합한 대답이다.

어휘 | suggest 제안하다 agenda 안건, 의제

16 Can we listen to music at our desks while we're working?
(A) As long as you wear headphones.
(B) Yes, a new work desk.
(C) No, we didn't hear it.

일하면서 책상에서 음악을 들어도 되나요?
(A) 헤드폰을 착용하기만 한다면요.
(B) 네, 새 업무 책상이에요.
(C) 아니요, 저희는 못 들었어요.

해설 | 부탁·요청의 의문문
(A) 정답: 일하면서 책상에서 음악을 들어도 되는지 묻는 질문에 헤드폰을 착용하기만 한다면(As long as you wear headphones)이라는 조건을 제시하여 우회적으로 수락의 의사를 드러내고 있으므로 정답이다.
(B) 단어 반복·파생어 오답: 질문의 desk를 반복 이용하고 있으며, 질문의 working과 파생어 관계인 work를 이용한 오답이다.
(C) 연상 작용 오답: 질문의 listen to에서 연상 가능한 hear를 이용한 오답이다.

어휘 | as long as ~하기만 하면, ~하는 한

17 What should I bring to next week's orientation?
(A) I brought one too.
(B) Just a pen and a notebook.
(C) The theater is next to the station.

다음 주에 있을 오리엔테이션에 무엇을 가지고 가야 하나요?
(A) 저도 하나 가져왔어요.
(B) 펜과 공책이면 돼요.
(C) 그 극장은 역 바로 옆에 있어요.

해설 | 필요한 것을 묻는 What 의문문
(A) 파생어 오답: 질문에 나오는 bring의 과거형인 brought를 이용한 오답이다.
(B) 정답: 가지고 가야 할 것을 묻는 질문에 구체적인 물건(a pen and a notebook)을 알려 주었으므로 정답이다.
(C) 단어 반복 오답: 질문의 next를 반복 이용한 오답이다.

어휘 | theater 극장

18 Doesn't the cost of the movie ticket include a beverage?
(A) No, the entrance is around the corner.
(B) Only on weekdays.
(C) You can find one in the brochure.

영화표 값에는 음료가 포함되지 않나요?
(A) 아니요. 입구는 모퉁이를 돌면 있어요.
(B) 평일에만요.
(C) 안내책자에서 볼 수 있어요.

해설 | 포함 여부를 확인하는 부정 의문문
(A) 관련 없는 오답: 영화표 값에 음료가 포함되지 않는지 묻는 질문에 입구가 모퉁이를 돌면 있다(the entrance is around the corner)라고 하는 것은 상황에 맞지 않는 대답이다.
(B) 정답: 영화표 값에 음료가 포함되지 않는지 묻는 질문에 평일에만(Only on weekends)이라는 조건을 제시하여 답하고 있으므로 정답이다.
(C) 연상 작용 오답: 질문의 movie에서 연상 가능한 brochure를 이용한 오답이다.

어휘 | include 포함하다 beverage 음료 entrance 입구 weekday 평일 brochure 안내책자

19 Is Ms. Sanchez the new head of the sales department?
(A) We're ahead of schedule.
(B) Yes, she started last week.
(C) No, at a marketing meeting.

산체스 씨가 새로운 영업부장인가요?
(A) 우리는 예정보다 앞서 있어요.
(B) 네, 그녀는 지난주에 업무를 시작했어요.
(C) 아니요, 마케팅 회의에서요.

해설 | 사실을 확인하는 일반 의문문
(A) 유사 발음 오답: 질문의 head와 일부 발음이 유사한 ahead를 이용한 오답이다.
(B) 정답: 산체스 씨가 새로운 영업부장인지 묻는 질문에 먼저 Yes라고 응답한 후, 지난주에 업무를 시작했다(she started last week)며 부연 설명하고 있으므로 정답이다.
(C) 연상 작용 오답: 질문의 sales department에서 연상 가능한 marketing meeting을 이용한 오답이다.

어휘 | department 부서 ahead of schedule 예정보다 빨리

20 On which day will the store's return policy change?
(A) Here's your change and receipt.
(B) The manager has that information.
(C) Oh, I can work that day.

상점의 반품 정책이 바뀌는 게 언제인가요?
(A) 여기 거스름돈과 영수증 있습니다.
(B) 그것에 대해서는 관리자가 알아요.
(C) 아, 저는 그날 일할 수 있어요.

해설 | 변경 시점을 묻는 Which 의문문
(A) 다의어 오답: 질문의 change는 '바뀌다'라는 뜻의 동사이고, 보기의 change는 '거스름돈'이라는 뜻의 명사이다. 정책이 바뀌는 날짜를 묻는 질문에는 어울리지 않는 응답이다.
(B) 정답: 정책 변경 시점을 묻는 질문에 해당 정보를 제공할 수 있는 특정 인물(manager)을 언급하고 있으므로 가장 적절한 응답이다.
(C) 단어 반복 오답: 질문의 day를 반복 이용한 오답이다.

어휘 | return 반품 policy 정책 receipt 영수증

21 How can we attract more international clients?
(A) Sharon is picking them up at the airport.
(B) We should change our advertising strategy.
(C) It's a standard contract.

어떻게 하면 더 많은 해외 고객을 유치할 수 있을까요?
(A) 샤론이 공항에서 그들을 데려올 거예요.
(B) 우리는 광고 전략을 바꿔야 해요.
(C) 그건 표준 계약서입니다.

해설 | **방법을 묻는 How 의문문**
(A) **연상 작용 오답:** 질문의 international clients에서 연상 가능한 상황(Sharon is picking them up at the airport)을 언급한 오답이다.
(B) **정답:** 해외 고객 유치 방법을 묻는 질문에 광고 전략을 바꿔야 한다(We should change our advertising strategy)며 구체적인 방안을 제시했으므로 정답이다.
(C) **연상 작용 오답:** 질문의 clients에서 연상 가능한 contract를 이용한 오답이다.

어휘 | attract 유치하다 international 국제적인 advertising 광고 strategy 전략 standard 표준의 contract 계약(서)

22 Did someone report the broken window, or should I call maintenance?
(A) No, it won't close anymore.
(B) I just sent them an e-mail.
(C) On the third floor.

누군가 깨진 창문에 대해 보고했나요, 아니면 제가 유지보수팀에 전화할까요?
(A) 아니요. 더 이상 닫히지 않을 겁니다.
(B) 제가 방금 그들에게 이메일을 보냈어요.
(C) 3층이에요.

해설 | **보고 여부를 묻는 선택 의문문**
(A) **연상 작용 오답:** 질문의 window에서 연상 가능한 close를 이용한 오답이다.
(B) **정답:** 창문이 깨졌다고 알렸는지 아니면 자신이 유지보수팀에 전화할지 묻는 질문에 유지보수팀(them = maintenance)에게 이메일을 보냈다(I just sent them an e-mail)며 전자를 선택하여 답했으므로 정답이다.
(C) **관련 없는 오답:** 위치를 묻는 where 의문문에 적절한 대답이다.

어휘 | report 보고하다, 알리다 maintenance 유지보수

23 When are we supposed to present our design proposals?
(A) On the projection screen.
(B) The manager was present.
(C) At Wednesday's staff meeting.

우리의 디자인 제안서를 언제 발표하기로 되어 있나요?
(A) 영사기 화면에서요.
(B) 관리자는 참석했어요.
(C) 수요일 직원 회의에서요.

해설 | **발표 예정 시점을 묻는 When 의문문**
(A) **연상 작용 오답:** 질문의 present(발표하다)에서 연상 가능한 projection screen을 이용한 오답이다.
(B) **다의어 오답:** 질문의 present는 '발표하다'라는 뜻의 동사이고, 보기의 present는 '참석한'이라는 뜻의 형용사이다.
(C) **정답:** 디자인 제안서의 발표 예정 시점을 묻는 질문에 수요일 직원 회의(At Wednesday's staff meeting)라며 발표 예정 시점을 언급하고 있으므로 정답이다.

어휘 | be supposed to ~하기로 되어 있다, ~할 예정이다 present 보여주다; 참석한 proposal 제안(서)

24 Before we prepare the revised budget, let's break down last year's expenses.
(A) How did it break?
(B) That's a high price.
(C) I'll get the expense reports.

예산 수정안을 준비하기 전에 작년 경비를 분석해 봅시다.
(A) 그건 어떻게 고장 났죠?
(B) 가격이 높군요.
(C) 제가 비용 보고서를 가져올게요.

해설 | **제안을 하는 평서문**
(A) **다의어 오답:** 평서문의 break는 down과 함께 '분석하다'라는 뜻을 나타내고, 보기의 break는 '고장 나다'라는 뜻이다.
(B) **연상 작용 오답:** 평서문의 budget과 expenses에서 연상 가능한 price를 이용한 오답이다.
(C) **정답:** 예산 수정안을 준비하기 전에 작년 경비를 분석하자는 제안에 비용 보고서를 가져오겠다(I'll get the expense reports)며 우회적으로 수락 의사를 밝혔으므로 정답이다.

어휘 | prepare 준비하다 revised 수정된, 변경된 break down 분석[분류]하다 expense 경비, 비용

25 Where can I purchase parts for my motorcycle?
(A) Maria would know.
(B) The parts ship tomorrow.
(C) I'm afraid I haven't yet.

제 오토바이 부품은 어디서 살 수 있을까요?
(A) 마리아가 알 거예요.
(B) 부품은 내일 발송돼요.
(C) 저는 아직 안 한 것 같아요.

해설 | **구매 장소를 묻는 Where 의문문**
(A) **정답:** 오토바이 부품의 구매 장소를 묻는 질문에 마리아가 알 것(Maria would know)이라며 해당 정보를 제공할 수 있는 특정 인물을 언급하고 있으므로 가장 적절한 응답이다.
(B) **단어 반복 오답:** 질문의 parts를 반복 이용한 오답이다.
(C) **관련 없는 오답:** 오토바이 부품의 구매 장소를 묻는 질문에 아직 안 한 것 같다(I'm afraid I haven't yet)라고 하는 것은 상황에 맞지 않는 대답이다.

어휘 | purchase 구입하다 parts 부품 ship 발송되다, 출하되다

26 Could you give me a detailed list of the supplies we should buy?
(A) At least one hundred euros.
(B) An unlisted phone number.
(C) I have it right here.

구입해야 하는 용품 세부 목록을 주시겠어요?
(A) 적어도 100 유로요.
(B) 전화 번호부에 없는 번호요.
(C) 지금 저에게 있어요.

해설 | **부탁·요청의 의문문**
(A) 유사 발음·연상 작용 오답: 질문의 list와 발음이 유사한 least를 이용하고 있으며, 질문의 buy에서 연상 가능한 구매 금액(one hundred euros)을 이용한 오답이다.
(B) 파생어 오답: 질문의 list와 파생어 관계인 unlisted를 이용한 오답이다.
(C) 정답: 용품 세부 목록을 달라는 요청에 지금 자신이 가지고 있다(I have it right here)며 우회적으로 수락 의사를 드러내고 있으므로 정답이다.

어휘 | detailed 상세한 supply 용품 at least 최소한, 적어도 unlisted 전화 번호부에 올라 있지 않은

27 Ms. Walsh will be a consultant on the water conservation project.
(A) Next to the water cooler.
(B) Yes, the project went very well.
(C) I look forward to working with her.

월시 씨가 물 보존 프로젝트의 자문 위원이 되실 겁니다.
(A) 음료수 냉각기 옆이요.
(B) 네, 프로젝트는 아주 순조롭게 진행됐어요.
(C) 그녀와 함께 일하기를 고대하고 있어요.

해설 | **정보를 전달하는 평서문**
(A) 단어 반복 오답: 평서문의 water를 반복 이용한 오답이다.
(B) 단어 반복 오답: 평서문의 project를 반복 이용한 오답으로, 프로젝트(project)의 결과를 묻는 질문에 적합한 대답이다.
(C) 정답: 월시 씨가 물 보존 프로젝트의 자문 위원이 될 것이라는 소식에 함께 일하기를 고대하고 있다(I look forward to working with her)며 긍정적인 반응을 하고 있으므로 정답이다.

어휘 | consultant 자문 위원 conservation 보존, 보호 look forward to ~를 기대하다

28 What do you think about buying another printer?
(A) Why don't we wait until next quarter?
(B) A special type of paper.
(C) I printed plenty of copies.

프린터를 더 사는 걸 어떻게 생각하세요?
(A) 다음 분기까지 기다리면 어때요?
(B) 특수한 종류의 종이요.
(C) 저는 복사를 많이 했어요.

해설 | **의견을 묻는 What 의문문**
(A) 정답: 프린터를 더 구매하는 것에 대한 의견을 묻는 질문에 다음 분기까지 기다리면 어떨지(Why don't we wait until next quarter?) 되물으며 우회적으로 부정적인 의사를 드러내고 있으므로 정답이다.
(B) 연상 작용 오답: 질문의 printer에서 연상 가능한 paper를 이용한 오답이다.
(C) 파생어 오답: 질문의 printer와 파생어 관계인 printed를 이용한 오답이다.

어휘 | quarter 분기 plenty of 많은

29 Is it possible to get this picture framed now?
(A) I'll get to it in a few minutes.
(B) Usually about 25 or 30 centimeters.
(C) No, it's the same we've always used.

이 사진을 지금 액자에 넣을 수 있나요?
(A) 몇 분 후에 시작하겠습니다.
(B) 대개 약 25~30센티미터요.
(C) 아니요, 그건 우리가 항상 사용했던 것과 같아요.

해설 | **가능 여부를 묻는 일반 의문문**
(A) 정답: 지금 액자에 사진을 넣을 수 있는지 묻는 질문에 몇 분 후에 시작하겠다(I'll get to it in a few minutes)며 우회적으로 지금은 불가능하다는 응답을 하고 있으므로 정답이다.
(B) 연상 작용 오답: 질문의 framed를 frame(액자)으로 잘못 들었을 경우 연상 가능한 액자의 치수(about 25 or 30 centimeters)를 이용한 오답이다.
(C) 연상 작용 오답: 질문의 now에서 연상 가능한 always를 이용한 오답이다.

어휘 | possible 가능한 frame 액자에 넣다 get to ~에 착수하다, 시작하다 usually 보통, 대개

30 Why don't you set up the projector while we're waiting for everyone to arrive?
(A) I think he arrives at gate G6.
(B) For over three hours.
(C) OK, they should be here soon.

모두가 도착할 때까지 기다리는 동안 영사기를 설치하면 어때요?
(A) 그는 G6번 게이트로 도착하는 것 같아요.
(B) 3시간 넘게요.
(C) 좋아요. 그들이 곧 도착할 겁니다.

해설 | **제안·권유의 의문문**
(A) 인칭 오류·단어 반복 오답: 대명사 he가 가리키는 대상이 질문에 없으며, 질문의 arrive를 반복 이용한 오답이다.
(B) 단어 반복 오답: 질문의 for를 반복 이용한 오답으로, 설치(set up) 또는 대기(waiting) 시간을 묻는 질문에 적합한 대답이다.
(C) 정답: 모두가 도착할 때까지 기다리는 동안 영사기를 설치하라는 제안에 먼저 수락한 후, 그들이 곧 도착할 것(they should be here soon)이라고 덧붙이고 있으므로 정답이다.

어휘 | set up 설치하다 arrive 도착하다

31 Do you know how many guests are expected on Thursday?
(A) It's on the second floor.
(B) A weekly event.
(C) Definitely more than a hundred.

목요일에 손님이 몇 분 오시는지 알고 있나요?
(A) 그건 2층에 있어요.
(B) 주간 행사요.
(C) 틀림없이 100명이 넘을 거예요.

해설 | **방문 예상 인원을 묻는 간접 의문문**
(A) 관련 없는 오답: 장소나 위치를 묻는 Where 의문문에 적합한 대답이다.
(B) 연상 작용 오답: 질문의 guests에서 연상 가능한 event를 이용한 오답이다.
(C) 정답: 방문 예정인 손님의 수를 아는지 묻는 질문에 틀림없이 100명이 넘을 것(Definitely more than a hundred)이라며 인원을 예측하고 있으므로 정답이다.

어휘 | expect 예상하다, 기대하다 definitely 분명히, 틀림없이 more than ~이상의

PART 3 LC

Unit 07 주제·목적 / 화자·장소 문제

① 주제·목적 문제

공략포인트

본책 p.070

여	우리 회사 새 로고 디자인이 이렇게 힘들 줄은 몰랐어요. 도대체 끝이 날 것 같지 않았어요.
남	그러게요, 그래도 결과는 좋았어요. 그렇지 않아요? 우리 회사를 정확히 표현하고 있어요. 활동적이면서도 신뢰를 주는 것 같아요.
여	맞아요, 그리고 회사 편지지에 작게 나온 것과 매장 간판과 제품에 크게 나온 것 둘 다 잘된 것 같아요.

어휘 | come up with ~을 생각해 내다, 제안하다 take forever 시간이 오래 걸리다 result 결과 worthwhile ~한 보람이 있는 sum up 요약하다 exactly 정확히 stand for ~을 나타내다 sporty 화려한, 민첩한 dependable 믿음직한 come out well (일 등이) 잘되다 letterhead 편지지 위쪽의 인쇄문구, 문구가 적힌 편지지

문제 화자들은 무엇을 논의하고 있는가?
(A) 신형 자전거　　(B) 회사 로고
(C) 편지　　(D) 새 매장

● 실전 도움닫기

본책 p.071

1 (C)　**2** (B)　**3** (C)　**4** (D)

[1] M-Cn / W-Br

M	Thanks for meeting with me to revise the company budget, Georgia.
W	No problem.
M	With the increase in rent for office space this year, we're definitely over budget right now.
W	Yes, we'll have to find areas to cut back on.

남 회사 예산을 수정하기 위해 이렇게 만나 주셔서 고마워요, 조지아.
여 별말씀을요.
남 올해 사무실 임대료가 올라서 우리가 지금 확실히 예산을 초과하고 있거든요.
여 맞아요, 비용을 줄일 수 있는 부분을 찾아야 해요.

어휘 | revise 수정하다 budget 예산 rent 임대료 definitely 명백히, 분명히 cut back on ~을 줄이다

1 화자들은 무엇을 논의하고 있는가?
(A) 부동산 대출　　(B) 승차 공유 계획
(C) 회사 예산　　(D) 채용 계획

해설 | **전체 내용 - 대화의 주제**
남자가 첫 번째 대사에서 여자에게 회사 예산을 수정하기 위해 만나줘서 고맙다(Thanks for meeting with me to revise the company budget)고 했으므로 (C)가 정답이다.

어휘 | real estate 부동산 initiative 계획, 발전방안

[2] W-Br / M-Am

W	You've reached Dr. Franklin's office. How may I help you?
M	Yes, this is Martin Brown. I need to cancel my appointment for an eye exam on Wednesday.
W	OK. Would you like to reschedule? The doctor could see you at two o'clock on Friday.

여 프랭클린 병원입니다. 무엇을 도와드릴까요?
남 네, 저는 마틴 브라운이라고 합니다. **수요일의 눈 검사 예약을 취소하려고요.**
여 알겠습니다. 예약을 다시 잡으시겠어요? 의사 선생님께서 금요일 2시에 환자분을 진료하실 수 있는데요.

어휘 | reach (전화로) 연락하다 appointment 약속, 예약 eye exam 눈 검사 reschedule 일정을 변경하다, 스케줄을 다시 짜다

2 남자는 왜 전화했는가?
(A) 소매점 점원과 이야기를 하기 위해
(B) 예약을 취소하기 위해
(C) 면접 일정을 정하기 위해
(D) 구독을 갱신하기 위해

해설 | **전체 내용 - 전화의 목적**
남자가 첫 대사에서 자신의 이름을 밝힌 후 수요일에 있을 눈 검사 예약을 취소하려 한다(I need to cancel my appointment for an eye exam on Wednesday)고 했으므로 (B)가 정답이다.

어휘 | set up (일정을) 정하다 renew 갱신하다 subscription 구독

[3] W-Am / M-Au

W	I'm going to be out of town starting Monday, August first, and I'd like to put a hold on my mail, please.
M	Certainly. We can keep your mail here at the post office while you're away. Incidentally, did you know that you could have your mail forwarded to another address instead?
W	Well, I'm actually going to be traveling overseas, so I don't think that'd be possible.

여 제가 8월 1일 월요일부터 여기 없을 거예요. 그래서 **우편물을 보류해 주셨으면 해요.**
남 네, 안 계신 동안 이곳 우체국에서 우편물을 보관해 드릴 수 있어요. 그런데 우편물을 대신 다른 주소로 보내게 할 수 있는 건 알고 계세요?
여 음, 저는 사실 해외로 나갈 거라서 그건 불가능할 것 같아요.

어휘 | put a hold on ~를 보류하다, 중지하다 incidentally 그런데, 그건 그렇고 forward 전달하다 instead 대신 actually 사실은, 실제로 overseas 해외로

3 대화는 주로 무엇에 관한 것인가?

(A) 회의 준비하기

(B) 사무실 다시 꾸미기

(C) 우편물 배송 중단하기

(D) 분실된 소포 찾기

해설 | **전체 내용 - 대화의 주제**

여자가 첫 번째 대사에서 우편물을 보류해 줄 것(I'd like to put a hold on my mail)을 요청했는데, 이에 대해 남자가 우체국에서 우편물을 보관할 수 있다(We can keep your mail here at the post office)며 우편물 배송과 관련된 대화를 이어가고 있으므로 (C)가 정답이다.

어휘 | organize 조직하다, 준비하다 redecorate 다시 꾸미다, 실내장식을 새로 하다 delivery 배송

---

[4] M-Br / W-Am

M Hello. Jeffrey Hines speaking.

W This is Martha Benjamin. I'm calling to let you know I've put my research report in the interoffice mail. You should have it this afternoon. I hope you're still willing to review it for me.

M Of course. I'll be out of town on business for the next few days, but I'll take it with me.

남 네, 제프리 하인즈입니다.

여 저 마사 벤자민이에요. **제 연구 보고서를 사내 우편함에 넣어둔 걸 말씀 드리려고 전화했어요.** 오늘 오후에 받으실 거예요. 지금도 검토해 주실 의향이 있다면 좋겠네요.

남 물론이죠. 며칠 동안 출장을 떠날 거지만 그걸 가지고 갈게요.

어휘 | research report 연구 보고서 interoffice (조직 내에서) 부서간의, 사내의 be willing to 기꺼이 ~하다

4 마사가 제프리에게 전화를 한 목적은 무엇인가?

(A) 그녀가 지방에 간다고 말하기 위해서

(B) 추가 연구비를 지원해 줄 수 있는지 묻기 위해서

(C) 자신을 만나준 걸 감사하기 위해서

(D) 그에게 보고서를 보냈다고 말하기 위해서

해설 | **전체 내용 - 전화의 목적**

여자가 첫 번째 대사에서 자신의 연구 보고서를 사내 우편함에 넣어 뒀다는 사실을 알리려고 전화했다(I'm calling to let you know I've put my research report in the interoffice mail)고 했으므로, (D)가 정답이다.

어휘 | additional 추가의

---

② 화자·장소 문제

공략포인트 .... 본책 p.072

남 안녕하세요, 귀하의 미술용품점에서 강의를 한다는 TV 광고를 봤습니다. 어떤 과정들이 있나요?

여 지금은 데생과 회화, 조각에 대한 다양한 수업을 진행하고 있어요. 관심 있는 게 있으신가요?

남 조각을 해보고 싶어요. 그런데 미술에 관해서는 아무것도 배워본 적이 없어서 초급 수준의 수업을 듣고 싶어요.

어휘 | commercial 광고 art-supply store 미술용품점 course 과정, 과목 drawing 스케치, 소묘 sculpture 조각 introductory-level 초급 수준의

문제 여자는 어디에서 근무하는가?

(A) 미술용품점   (B) 대학교

(C) 사진관   (D) 주민 센터

● 실전 **도움닫기** .... 본책 p.073

1 (B) **2** (B) **3** (A) **4** (B)

[1] W-Am / M-Cn

W Hi, I'm checking in for the conference. My name's Melissa Han.

M Han... OK, I have your registration receipt here. Your hotel isn't listed. Are you staying here or somewhere else?

W I'm staying here, but I registered for the conference late.

여 안녕하세요, **회의 참가 수속을 하려 합니다.** 제 이름은 멜리사 한입니다.

남 한... 알겠습니다. **여기 등록 영수증이 있네요.** 묵고 계신 호텔이 기재되어 있지 않습니다. 여기에 묵고 계신가요, 아니면 다른 곳에 묵고 계신가요?

여 여기에 묵고 있습니다만, 회의에 늦게 등록했어요.

어휘 | check in 수속을 하다 registration 등록 list 목록에 기재하다, 포함시키다 conference (대규모) 회의

1 남자는 누구일 것 같은가?

(A) 기업주   (B) 회의 담당 직원

(C) 식당 매니저   (D) 여행사 직원

해설 | **전체 내용 - 남자의 신분**

회의 참가 수속을 하겠다는 여자의 말에, 등록 영수증이 있다(I have your registration receipt here)고 확인해 주고 있으므로 (B)가 정답이다.

W Here are my keys. Can you give me an idea of when I should come back to pick up the car?

M We need to rotate the tires, change the oil, and perform a safety inspection, so it'll probably be ready around 5 o'clock.

W I can be back here by five, but I'll need to get to and from my office today.

여 키 여기 있어요. 차를 찾으러 언제 와야 하는지 알려 주시겠어요?

남 타이어를 서로 바꿔 끼우고 오일도 교환해야 하며 안전 점검도 실시해야 합니다. 그러면 아마 5시경에는 준비될 겁니다.

여 제가 5시까지 올 수 있긴 하지만, 오늘 사무실로 왔다 갔다 해야 할 거예요.

어휘 | rotate tires (타이어의 균일한 마모를 위해) 타이어를 서로 바꿔 끼우다 safety inspection (자동차 등의) 안전 점검

2 이 대화는 어디에서 이루어지고 있는 것으로 보이는가?
(A) 극장 안 (B) 자동차 정비소
(C) 주차장 안 (D) 자동차 대여업체

해설 | 전체 내용 - 대화 장소
여자가 첫 대사에서 차를 언제 찾으러 와야 하느냐고 물었는데, 남자가 타이어를 서로 바꿔 끼우고 오일도 교환해야 하며 안전 점검도 실시해야 한다(We need to rotate the tires, change the oil, and perform a safety inspection)고 한 것으로 보아 (B)가 정답이다.

M Lucy, have you come up with any ideas for the print campaign for The Sawgrass Company's new line of spring clothing?

W Well, from the samples the client sent us, I think what really stands out is the fabric. The material is so lightweight. Plus, it's washable and wrinkle-resistant.

M Then why don't we market it as travel clothing?

남 루시, 소그래스 사의 봄 의류 신상품용 인쇄물 광고에 대한 아이디어 좀 생각해 봤나요?

여 음, 고객이 보낸 샘플을 보니까 눈에 확 띄는 게 옷감인 것 같아요. 소재가 아주 가벼워요. 게다가 물세탁도 가능하고 주름도 잘 가지 않아요.

남 그럼 여행용 의류로 마케팅하는 것은 어떨까요?

어휘 | line (상품의) 종류, 제품군 stand out 눈에 띄다 fabric 천, 옷감 material 소재 lightweight 가벼운 washable 물세탁 가능한 wrinkle-resistant 주름이 잘 안 가는

3 화자들은 누구일 것 같은가?
(A) 광고 책임자 (B) 의류 영업직원
(C) 패션 디자이너 (D) 잡지 편집자

해설 | 전체 내용 - 화자들의 신분
남자가 첫 번째 대사에서 여자에게 봄 의류 신상품용 인쇄물 광고에 대한 아이디어가 있는지(have you come up with any ideas for the print campaign for The Sawgrass Company's new line of spring clothing?) 물었고, 여자의 답변을 들은 후 여행용 의류로 마케팅하자며 의견을 제시했으므로, 화자들이 광고 책임자라는 것을 추론할 수 있다. 따라서 (A)가 정답이다.

M Hi. Welcome to Jerry's Salon. Do you have an appointment with us?

W No, I don't – I was hoping one of the stylists might be free. I just need to have my hair trimmed.

M Well, let me see… our senior stylist Teresa has an opening at eleven thirty, or you could see one of our newer stylists at two.

남 안녕하세요. 제리 살롱에 오신 것을 환영합니다. 예약이 되어 있나요?

여 아니요. 미용사 중 한 분이 시간이 되시면 좋겠네요. 머리를 다듬기만 하면 되거든요.

남 아, 한 번 볼게요. 저희 수석 미용사인 테레사 씨가 11시 30분에 시간이 비어 있어요. 아니면 2시에 경력이 더 짧은 미용사들 중 한 명에게 하실 수 있고요.

어휘 | appointment (특히 업무 관련) 약속, 예약 trim 다듬다, 손질하다 have an opening 자리가 나다

4 남자는 어디에서 일하겠는가?
(A) 호텔 (B) 미용실
(C) 드라이클리닝 업체 (D) 주택 개조 상점

해설 | 전체 내용 - 남자의 근무 장소
남자가 첫 번째 대사에서 제리 살롱에 온 것을 환영한다(Welcome to Jerry's Salon)며 자신의 근무지를 언급했고, 이어 여자가 머리를 다듬어야 한다고 했으므로, 남자가 미용실에서 근무한다는 것을 알 수 있다. 따라서 (B)가 정답이다.

어휘 | home improvement 주택 개조

● ETS 실전문제
본책 p.074

1 (D)	2 (C)	3 (A)	4 (C)	5 (B)	6 (A)
7 (B)	8 (A)	9 (C)	10 (A)	11 (A)	12 (B)
13 (B)	14 (C)	15 (A)	16 (A)	17 (C)	18 (B)
19 (B)	20 (D)	21 (C)	22 (D)	23 (B)	24 (A)

M Hey Mayumi, [1]didn't you go see the Johnny Clyde Jazz Trio last night? I was thinking of seeing them this Saturday—[1]how were they?

LC

PART 3

W [1]Actually, I was pretty disappointed. The band was really good, but [2]it was hard to hear them because the speaker system at the theater wasn't working well. I think some of the equipment may have been broken. We decided to leave halfway through the show.

M That's too bad. You know, [3]you should ask for your money back. I'm sure the theater doesn't want a lot of negative reviews.

남 마유미, [1]어젯밤 조니 클라이드 재즈 트리오 공연 보지 않았어요? 이번 토요일에 보려고 생각 중이거든요. [1]어땠나요?

여 [1]사실 정말 실망했어요. 악단은 정말 훌륭했는데 [2]공연장 스피커 시스템이 제대로 작동하지 않아서 잘 들리지 않았거든요. 장비 일부가 고장 났던 것일 수도 있어요. 그래서 공연 중간에 나오기로 결정했죠.

남 유감이네요. [3]환불해 달라고 요청하셔야 해요. 공연장 측에서는 나쁜 후기가 많은 것을 원치 않을 겁니다.

어휘 | disappointed 실망한 theater 극장 equipment 장비 be broken 고장 나다 halfway through ~의 중간쯤 negative 부정적인 review 후기, 평가

1 화자들은 주로 무엇에 대해 이야기하는가?
(A) 연극   (B) 운동 경기
(C) 영화 시사회   (D) 음악회

해설 | 전체 내용 - 대화의 주제
남자가 첫 번째 대사에서 조니 클라이드 재즈 트리오 공연(the Johnny Clyde Jazz Trio)이 어땠는지(how were they?) 물어봤는데, 이에 대해 여자가 정말 실망했다(Actually, I was pretty disappointed)며 공연과 관련된 대화를 이어가고 있으므로 (D)가 정답이다.

Paraphrasing
대화의 the Johnny Clyde Jazz Trio → 정답의 A concert

2 여자가 실망한 이유는?
(A) 표를 구할 수 없었다.
(B) 행사 시작 부분을 놓쳤다.
(C) 음향 시스템이 제대로 작동하지 않았다.
(D) 사람들 몇 명이 시야를 가렸다.

해설 | 세부 내용 - 여자가 실망한 이유
여자가 첫 번째 대사에서 공연에 실망했다고 한 후, 공연장 스피커 시스템이 제대로 작동하지 않아서 잘 들리지 않았다(it was hard to hear them because the speaker system at the theater wasn't working well)며 이유를 밝혔으므로 (C)가 정답이다.

어휘 | miss 놓치다 beginning 시작 block one's view ~의 시야를 가리다

Paraphrasing
대화의 the speaker system → 정답의 The sound system

3 남자는 여자가 무엇을 해야 한다고 생각하는가?
(A) 환불 요청하기   (B) 다른 공연 참석하기
(C) TV 프로그램 시청하기   (D) 후기 쓰기

해설 | 세부 내용 - 남자의 제안 사항
남자가 마지막 대사에서 환불해 달라고 요청할 것(you should ask for your money back)을 여자에게 제안했으므로 (A)가 정답이다.

어휘 | refund 환불 attend 참석하다 performance 공연

Paraphrasing
대화의 ask for your money back → 정답의 Ask for a refund

[4-6] 3인 대화 W-Br / M-Cn / M-Au

W [4]Tom, can I get past you to the fridge? I need some milk.

M1 Sure. Have you tried this tea?

W No, I'm not big on tea. [4]I like the coffee they give us, though.

M1 Yeah, [4/5]I love working here. There are so many great benefits! Did you hear about the new vacation policy?

W Yes, it's great, isn't it? Oh, hello Anil. Anil, have you met Tom? [6]Anil just started this week.

M2 Nice to meet you, Tom.

M1 You too, Anil. Glad to have you with us.

M2 Thanks. Oh, we're out of coffee?

W No, there's some here. Oops, I'm running late. Anil, I'll stop by later to show you how to use the time entry system.

여 [4]톰, 냉장고 쪽으로 지나가도 될까요? 우유가 좀 필요해서요.

남1 물론이죠. 이 차 드셔 보셨어요?

여 아니요, 차는 그다지 좋아하지 않아서요. [4]하지만 회사에서 주는 커피는 괜찮던데요.

남1 맞아요, [4/5]여기서 근무해서 정말 좋아요. 좋은 혜택이 아주 많잖아요! 새 휴가 방침에 대한 얘기 들었어요?

여 네, 좋더라고요, 그렇지 않아요? 오, 안녕하세요. 아닐. 톰을 예전에 본 적 있나요? [6]아닐은 이번 주에 근무를 시작했어요.

남2 만나서 반가워요, 톰.

남1 저도요, 아닐. 저희와 함께 근무하게 되어 기쁩니다.

남2 고마워요. 오, 커피가 떨어졌나요?

여 아니요, 여기 좀 있어요. 이런, 늦었네요. 아닐, 제가 나중에 들러서 시간 입력 시스템 사용법을 알려 드릴게요.

어휘 | get past 지나가다 fridge 냉장고 be big on ~을 아주 좋아하다 benefit 혜택 be out of ~이 떨어지다 be running late 늦어지다 stop by ~에 들르다 entry 입력

4 대화가 이루어지고 있는 곳은 어디일 것 같은가?
(A) 취업 박람회   (B) 회의실
(C) 사무실 주방   (D) 커피숍

해설 | 전체 내용 - 대화 장소
여자가 첫 번째 대사에서 남자 1에게 냉장고 쪽으로 지나가도 될지 (can I get past you to the fridge?) 물었고 이후 회사가 제공하는 음료 및 복리후생에 대해 이야기 하고 있으므로, (C)가 정답이다.

5 톰이 회사에 대해 암시하는 바는 무엇인가?

(A) 더 많은 사람들을 뽑아야 한다.

(B) 직원들에 대한 대우가 좋다.

(C) 곧 보수 공사를 할 것이다.

(D) 몇 가지 새로운 장비를 구입할 것이다.

해설 | 세부 내용 - 회사에 대해 암시하는 바

톰(남자 1)의 두 번째 대사에서 여기서 근무해서 정말 좋고 혜택도 아주 많다(I love working here. There are so many great benefits!)고 했으므로 (B)가 정답이다.

6 여자는 아닐에 대해 무엇이라고 말하는가?

(A) 최근에 입사했다.　　　(B) 여자의 직책에 지원했다.

(C) 톰에게 보고할 것이다.　(D) 휴가에서 막 복귀했다.

해설 | 세부 내용 - 아닐에 대한 언급

여자의 세 번째 대사에서 아닐이 이번 주에 근무를 시작했다(Anil just started this week)고 했으므로 (A)가 정답이다.

[7-9] W-Am / M-Au

> **W** I'm flying to London this Thursday, and **7**I'm calling to check on your baggage policy. It's been a while since I flew overseas — last time I went I could check two bags for free. Is that still the case?
>
> **M** Unfortunately, our policy has changed since your last trip. For international flights, we now allow you to check only one bag for free. **8**There's a 30 dollar charge for each additional bag.
>
> **W** **8**Oh, that's too bad. I guess I'll have to rethink my packing — maybe I can fit everything into one suitcase.
>
> **M** In that case, **9**you should be aware of our size restrictions. If you'd like, I can give you that information now.

> 여 이번 주 목요일에 비행기로 런던에 갈 건데요, **7귀사의 수하물 정책을 확인하려고 전화했어요.** 제가 해외로 나간 지 좀 됐거든요. 지난번에 갔을 때는 가방 두 개를 무료로 보낼 수 있었는데, 여전히 그런가요?
>
> 남 유감스럽게도, 고객님이 마지막으로 여행하신 이후로 저희 정책이 변경되었습니다. 국제선의 경우, 이제 가방 한 개만 무료로 보내실 수 있어요. **8가방 한 개가 추가될 때마다 30달러의 요금이 붙습니다.**
>
> 여 **8**아, 유감이네요. 짐 꾸리는 것을 다시 생각해 봐야 할 것 같아요. 아마 여행 가방 하나에 모든 짐을 넣을 수 있을 것 같아요.
>
> 남 그렇다면, **9크기 제한 규정에 대해 아셔야 합니다.** 원하신다면, 지금 그 정보를 드릴게요.

> **어휘 |** overseas 해외로 check (짐을) 물표를 받고 맡기다, 부치다 unfortunately 유감스럽게도 charge 요금 additional 추가의 in that case 그런 경우에는, 그렇다면 restriction 제한, 규제

7 전화의 목적은 무엇인가?

(A) 예약 확인하기　　　(B) 정책에 대해 질문하기

(C) 표 가격 확인하기　　(D) 출발일 변경하기

해설 | 전체 내용 - 전화의 목적

여자가 첫 대사에서 수하물 정책을 확인하기 위해 전화했다(I'm calling to check on your baggage policy)고 했으므로 (B)가 정답이다.

어휘 | confirm 확인하다 reservation 예약 check on 확인하다

8 여자는 왜 실망하는가?

(A) 새로운 요금이 추가되었다.

(B) 그녀의 여행 가방 하나가 없어졌다.

(C) 선호하는 좌석을 구할 수 없다.

(D) 도착 시간이 바뀌었다.

해설 | 세부 내용 - 여자가 실망하는 이유

남자의 첫 대사에서 가방 한 개가 추가될 때마다 추가 수수료가 있다고 하자, 여자가 "Oh, that's too bad"라고 하며 실망감을 나타내고 있다. 따라서 (A)가 정답이다.

어휘 | fee 요금, 수수료 seating preference 선호하는 좌석

9 남자는 무엇을 설명해 주겠다고 제안하는가?

(A) 선택 가능한 식사　　　(B) 비자 요구 조건

(C) 크기 제한　　　　　　(D) 결제 방법

해설 | 세부 내용 - 남자가 설명해 주겠다고 하는 것

남자가 마지막 대사에서 크기 제한 규정(size restrictions)을 알려주겠다고 했으므로 (C)가 정답이다.

어휘 | selection 선택 가능한 것들 requirement 필요 조건 limitation 제약, 제한

[10-12] M-Au / W-Br

> **M** Hi, you must be Rita. **10**I'm Min-Soo, with the real estate agency. We spoke on the phone. Let me show you the apartment now.
>
> **W** Thanks, Min-Soo. **11**I've been excited about seeing this place—it's in a great location, directly across from the park.
>
> **M** There's been a lot of interest because of that. And as you can see, this apartment has lots of space as well.
>
> **W** Hmm… but there's no washing machine in here?
>
> **M** Actually, **12**there's a laundry room on the first floor just for tenants. I can show you that now.

> 남 안녕하세요, 당신이 리타 씨군요. **10저는 부동산 중개소에서 나온 민수입니다.** 우리 통화했었지요. 이제 아파트를 보여드리겠습니다.
>
> 여 감사합니다, 민수 씨. **11이곳을 너무 보고 싶었어요.** 공원 바로 건너편이라서 위치가 아주 좋네요.
>
> 남 그 이유 때문에 관심 가지시는 분들이 아주 많아요. 그리고 보시는 바와 같이 이 아파트는 공간도 아주 넓습니다.
>
> 여 음… 하지만 여기 세탁기는 없네요?
>
> 남 실은 **12**1층에 세입자들만을 위한 세탁실이 있습니다. 지금 보여드릴 수 있어요.

> **어휘 |** real estate 부동산 laundry room 세탁실 tenant 세입자

10 남자는 누구인가?

(A) 부동산 중개인   (B) 집 주인

(C) 건축 감리사   (D) 인테리어 디자이너

해설 | 전체 내용 - 남자의 신분

남자의 첫 번째 대사에서 자신이 부동산 중개소(real estate agency)에서 나왔다며 아파트를 보여주겠다(Let me show you the apartment now)고 했으므로 (A)가 정답이다.

11 여자는 그 아파트에 대해 무엇이 마음에 든다고 말하는가?

(A) 공원 근처에 위치해 있다.

(B) 구조가 개방적이다.

(C) 가격이 합리적이다.

(D) 바닥이 목재로 되어 있다.

해설 | 세부 내용 - 여자가 마음에 든다고 말한 것

여자가 첫 번째 대사에서 해당 아파트가 너무 보고 싶었다며 공원 바로 건너편이라서 위치가 아주 좋다(it's in a great location, directly across from the park)고 했으므로, (A)가 정답이다.

어휘 | layout 구조 reasonably 합리적으로 priced 가격이 책정된

12 화자들은 다음에 어디로 갈 것인가?

(A) 옥상 정원   (B) 세탁 시설

(C) 창고   (D) 주차장

해설 | 세부 내용 - 화자들이 다음에 갈 곳

남자가 마지막 대사에서 1층에 세입자들만을 위한 세탁실(a laundry room)이 있다며 지금 보여줄 수 있다(I can show you that now)고 했다. 따라서 화자들이 세탁실에 갈 것임을 알 수 있으므로, (B)가 정답이다.

[13-15] W-Am / M-Au

W Hello. **13**I'm calling because I'm interested in having some landscaping done outside my home, at 19 Sycamore Street. Your company did a lot of work around my neighbor's house recently, and I'm very impressed with how beautiful everything looks.

M Yes, I remember that job — that's the Watson residence. I'll be in your neighborhood on Monday — would you like me to stop by so you can show me the property?

W Monday would be fine. But **14**I should mention that the job here would be much smaller than the one at my neighbor's. I just want some flower beds in front of the house.

M That's OK. We're happy to do small jobs as well. **15**After I've seen the front yard, I can draw up some design options for the flower beds and send them to you.

여 안녕하세요. **13**시커모어 가 19번지에 있는 저희 집 외부 조경 작업을 하고 싶어 전화 드립니다. 귀사에서 최근에 저희 이웃집 공사를 많이 하셨더라고요. 모든 게 아주 예뻐서 매우 깊은 인상을 받았습니다.

남 네, 그 공사 기억이 나네요. 왓슨 씨 댁이죠. 제가 월요일에 그 동네로 가는데, 잠깐 들를 테니 집을 좀 보여 주시겠습니까?

여 월요일이면 괜찮겠네요. 근데 **14**저희 집 공사 규모는 이웃집 공사보다 훨씬 작을 거예요. 저는 그냥 집 앞에 화단이 있었으면 하거든요.

남 괜찮습니다. 저희는 소규모 공사도 환영합니다. **15**제가 앞뜰을 보고 나서 화단 디자인 시안을 몇 가지 해서 보내 드리겠습니다.

어휘 | landscaping 조경 residence 거주지, 주택 property 집, 부동산 mention 언급하다 flower bed 화단 draw up 작성하다, 만들다

13 화자들은 무엇을 논의하고 있는가?

(A) 집 보수 공사   (B) 조경 계획

(C) 도로 보수   (D) 집 청소 서비스

해설 | 전체 내용 - 대화의 주제

여자가 첫 대사에서 자신의 집 외부 조경 작업을 하고 싶어 전화했다(I'm calling because I'm interested in having some landscaping done outside my home)고 했으므로 (B)가 정답이다.

14 여자는 진행하려고 하는 일에 관해 무엇이라고 하는가?

(A) 특별한 장비가 필요할 것이다.

(B) 다음 주에 시작해야 한다.

(C) 대규모 프로젝트가 아니다.

(D) 불편을 야기할 수도 있다.

해설 | 세부 내용 - 여자가 계획에 대해 말하는 것

여자는 두 번째 대사에서 자신이 계획하는 공사가 이웃집에서 했던 것보다 훨씬 소규모일(I should mention that the job here would be much smaller than the one at my neighbor's)이라고 했으므로 (C)가 정답이다.

15 두 사람이 만난 후에 남자는 여자에게 무엇을 보낼 것인가?

(A) 설계도   (B) 제품 카탈로그

(C) 수정한 계약서   (D) 현지 지도

해설 | 세부 내용 - 남자가 보낼 것

남자는 마지막 대사에서 앞뜰을 보고 난 후 디자인 시안을 몇 개 만들어 보내 주겠다(After I've seen the front yard, I can draw up some design options for the flower beds and send them to you)고 했으므로 (A)가 정답이다.

[16-18] M-Cn / W-Br

M Hala, **16/17**I've just come from the mixing room, and we seem to be having trouble with the chocolate again. **17**The consistency is too grainy to be made into candies.

W Oh no. I noticed yesterday that **17**the chocolate didn't seem quite as smooth as it usually is. I wasn't sure what was causing the problem. Do you think it's the mixer?

M Well, **18**that machine is pretty old, and we've already had it repaired in the past. **18**Maybe it's time to get a new one.

남 할라, **16/17지금 혼합실에서 오는 길인데요. 초콜릿에 다시 문제가 생긴 것 같아요. 17밀도가 너무 거칠어서 사탕으로 만들 수가 없어요.**

여 저런. 어제 초콜릿이 평소만큼 매끄러워 보이지 않는다는 걸 알았어요. 무엇 때문에 문제가 생긴 건지 잘 모르겠더라고요. 혼합기 때문인 것 같아요?

남 음, **18기계가 꽤 오래됐죠.** 예전에 이미 수리한 적도 있고요. **18새 기계를 사야 할 때인 것 같군요.**

어휘 | have trouble with ~에 문제가 생기다 consistency 농도, 밀도 grainy 거친 notice 알아차리다 repair 수리하다

---

16 화자들은 어떤 업계에서 일하겠는가?

(A) 식품 생산　　　　　　(B) 기계류 판매
(C) 행사 기획　　　　　　(D) 직물 제조

해설 | **전체 내용 - 화자들이 종사하는 업계**
남자가 첫 번째 대사에서 혼합실(the mixing room)에서 오는 길이라고 한 후, 초콜릿에 다시 문제가 생긴 것 같다(we seem to be having trouble with the chocolate again)며 밀도(consistency)를 언급했으므로, 화자들이 초콜릿 관련 식품 생산 업계에 종사한다는 것을 알 수 있다. 따라서 (A)가 정답이다.

어휘 | production 생산 machinery 기계류 textile 직물 manufacturing 제조

17 화자들은 어떤 문제에 대해 이야기하는가?

(A) 직원이 시간이 안 된다.
(B) 기기 청소를 안 했다.
(C) 제품 품질이 좋지 않다.
(D) 고객이 불만을 제기했다.

해설 | **세부 내용 - 문제점**
남자가 첫 번째 대사에서 초콜릿에 다시 문제가 생긴 것 같다고 한 후, 밀도가 너무 거칠어서 사탕으로 만들 수가 없다(The consistency is too grainy to be made into candies)는 부연 설명을 했다. 이에 여자도 초콜릿이 평소만큼 매끄러워 보이지 않는다(the chocolate didn't seem quite as smooth as it usually is)며 문제점을 언급하고 있으므로 (C)가 정답이다.

어휘 | available 시간이 되는 appliance 기기, 가전제품 complain 불평하다

18 남자는 무엇을 제안하는가?

(A) 경영진에게 알림
(B) 기계 교체
(C) 가격 인하
(D) 일부 상품 폐기

해설 | **세부 내용 - 남자의 제안 사항**
남자가 마지막 대사에서 기계가 꽤 오래됐다(that machine is pretty old)고 한 후, 새 기계를 사야 할 때인 것 같다(Maybe it's time to get a new one)는 의견을 밝혔으므로 (B)가 정답이다.

어휘 | alert (위험 등을) 알리다 management 경영진 replace 교체하다 lower 낮추다 discard 폐기하다, 버리다 merchandise 상품

Paraphrasing
대화의 get a new one → 정답의 Replacing a machine

[19-21] W-Br / M-Cn

W Hi, Gerhard. **19You wanted to talk to me about the strawberries that we're growing?**

M Yes. This year, **19our farm's doing better than last year. 20I'm glad we tried something different by using another brand of fertilizer on the strawberries.** Amazing results!

W That's great! Then we should use that brand on the blueberries, too.

M I was thinking the same thing, but **21we don't have enough fertilizer.** Should I go ahead and order some more?

W Let's do that. I think it's worth the money.

M All right, **21I'll call and order it now.** One hundred kilograms should be enough.

여 안녕하세요, 거하드. **19우리가 재배하는 딸기에 대해 이야기하고 싶다고 하셨죠?**

남 예. 올해 **19우리 농장은 지난해보다 수확이 좋아요. 20딸기에 다른 브랜드의 비료를 사용하는 색다른 시도를 했다는 게 기뻐요.** 그 결과가 놀랍네요!

여 잘됐네요! 그럼 블루베리에도 그 브랜드의 비료를 사용해야겠네요.

남 저도 같은 생각을 하고 있었지만, **21비료의 양이 충분하지 않아요.** 제가 더 주문할까요?

여 그렇게 하죠. 돈을 들일 가치가 있다고 생각해요.

남 좋아요, **22그럼 지금 전화해서 주문할게요.** 100킬로그램이면 충분할 거예요.

어휘 | fertilizer 비료 worth ~할 만한 가치가 있다

---

19 화자들은 어디서 일할 것 같은가?

(A) 공원　　　　　　(B) 농장
(C) 정원 용품 가게　　　　　　(D) 조경 회사

해설 | **전체 내용 - 화자들의 근무 장소**
여자가 첫 번째 대사에서 함께 재배하는 딸기(the strawberries that we're growing)를 언급했고, 남자가 첫 번째 대사에서 농장이 지난해보다 수확이 좋다(our farm's doing better than last year)고 했으므로, 화자들이 농장에서 일한다는 것을 알 수 있다. 따라서 (B)가 정답이다.

20 남자는 무엇에 대해 기뻐하는가?

(A) 추가 직원 채용　　　　　　(B) 운영 시간 확대
(C) 고객에게 할인 제공　　　　　　(D) 비료 브랜드 교체

해설 | **세부 내용 - 남자가 기뻐한 것**
남자가 첫 번째 대사에서 다른 브랜드의 비료를 사용하는 색다른 시도를 했다는 게 기쁘다(I'm glad we tried something different by using another brand of fertilizer)고 했으므로, (D)가 정답이다.

어휘 | additional 추가의 extend 연장하다

Paraphrasing
대화의 using another brand of fertilizer → 정답의 Changing a brand of fertilizer

LC

PART 3

21 남자는 다음에 무엇을 할 것인가?

(A) 장비 수리

(B) 소상공인 사업자 등록 신청

(C) 용품 주문

(D) 악천후에 대비

[22-24] W-Br / M-Cn

> W Mr. Howard, ²²thank you for agreeing to answer a few questions for the article I'm writing. We at *Architectural Art* magazine were surprised to hear that you'll be retiring soon. You've been leading your firm for the last thirty years. How will your decision affect your company?
>
> M It really won't. ²³At our firm, our mission is to build homes that families can afford. The new CEO will continue to be dedicated to the company's goal of building homes that are within the means of most people.
>
> W Well, I'm sure you're looking forward to having more free time. What are your plans for the future?
>
> M ²⁴I'll continue to pursue my architectural interests by giving lectures at different universities. That way, I can spend all my time doing what I love most—discussing architecture, rather than running a business.

여 하워드 씨, ²²제가 쓰고 있는 기사를 위한 몇 가지 질문에 답해 **주시기로 한 점 감사드립니다.** 저희 <건축 예술> 잡지사는 사장님께서 곧 은퇴하신다는 소식을 듣고 놀랐습니다. 지난 30년간 회사를 이끌어 오셨는데요. 사장님의 결정이 회사에 어떤 식으로 영향을 미칠까요?

남 큰 영향이 없을 겁니다. ²³저희 회사의 임무는 일반 가정에서 살 수 **있는 가격이 적당한 집을 짓는 것입니다.** 대부분 사람들의 자금 **범위 내에 있는 집을 짓겠다는 저희 회사의 목표를** 신임 CEO가 헌신적으로 계속 추진할 것입니다.

여 음, 분명히 더 많은 자유 시간을 기대하고 계실텐데요. 앞으로 계획은 어떻게 되나요?

남 ²⁴여러 대학에서 강의를 하면서 건축에 대한 관심을 이어갈 겁니다. 그렇게 하면서 모든 시간을 제가 가장 좋아하는 일, 즉 건축에 대한 논의를 하면서 보낼 겁니다. 회사를 운영하는 일은 하지 않고요.

22 여자는 누구일 것 같은가?

(A) 건축 감리사   (B) 경영 컨설턴트

(C) 건축가   (D) 기자

23 하워드 씨 회사의 목표는 무엇인가?

(A) 재활용 자재 이용

(B) 가격이 적당한 주택 건설

(C) 역사적인 건축물 보존

(D) 에너지 효율성 증대

24 하워드 씨는 앞으로 무엇을 할 계획인가?

(A) 대학 강의   (B) 책 출판

(C) 자원봉사 프로젝트 진행   (D) 해외 사무실 개업

Unit 08 세부 사항 / 문제점 · 걱정거리 문제

① 세부 사항 문제

공략포인트
본책 p.076

> 여 안녕하세요, 켄. 회의 준비는 어떻게 진행되고 있죠?
>
> 남 잘되고 있어요. 우리 부스에서 선보일 제품을 설명하는 자료집 초안 작성을 방금 끝냈어요.
>
> 여 좋습니다. 내게 이메일로 한 부 보내 줄래요? 직접 내용을 검수하고 싶어요.

문제 자료집에는 무엇이 들어 있는가?

(A) 회사 소개   (B) 부스 규정

(C) 회의 일정   (D) 제품 상세 설명

1 (A) **2** (B) **3** (C) **4** (D)

---

[1] M-Br / W-Am

> M　Welcome back, Flora! How was Spain?
> W　Wonderful, thanks. I went with a few friends— we stayed at a small hotel in Valencia for two weeks.
> M　Yeah, I really enjoyed Valencia when I visited my family there last year.

남　플로라, 돌아오셨군요! 스페인 어땠어요?
여　좋았죠, 고마워요. 친구 몇 명과 같이 갔어요. **2주 동안 발렌시아의 작은 호텔에 머물렀고요.**
남　그렇군요. 저도 작년에 가족을 방문하러 발렌시아에 갔을 때 정말 좋더라고요.

1 플로라는 발렌시아에서 어디에 머물렀는가?
　(A) 호텔　　　　　　　　(B) 친구 집
　(C) 친척들과 함께　　　(D) 야영지

해설 | **세부 내용 - 플로라가 머문 곳**
여자가 첫 대사에서 발렌시아의 작은 호텔에 2주간 머물렀다(we stayed at a small hotel in Valencia for two weeks)고 했으므로 (A)가 정답이다.

어휘 | relative 친척　campsite 캠프장, 야영지

---

[2] M-Au / W-Br

> M　Hi, Barbara. Nice to run into you! We've missed you since you left Allen Real Estate.
> W　Kevin! Yes, it's been a while. That was a big decision, to change companies. But I like my new job a lot.
> M　That's great. How's the work different from what you did with us?
> W　Well—I only handle commercial properties now. But I like being able to focus on one area.

남　안녕하세요, 바바라. 이렇게 만나게 돼서 반가워요! 앨런 부동산을 떠난 뒤로 보고 싶었어요.
여　케빈! 네, 오랜만이에요. 회사를 옮긴다는 게 큰 결정이긴 했죠. 하지만 새 직장이 정말 마음에 들어요.
남　잘됐네요. 우리와 일할 때와 업무가 어떻게 다른가요?
여　음, 저는 지금 상업용 부동산만 다뤄요. **그래도 한 분야에 집중할 수 있어서 좋아요.**

어휘 | commercial 상업용의　property 부동산

2 여자는 자신의 직업에 대해 무엇이 마음에 든다고 하는가?
　(A) 창의성을 활용하는 것　(B) 한 분야를 전문으로 다루는 것
　(C) 보너스 급여를 받는 것　(D) 출장 기회를 갖는 것

해설 | **세부 내용 - 여자가 마음에 들어 하는 점**
여자의 두 번째 대사에서 한 분야에 집중할 수 있어서 좋다(I like being able to focus on one area)고 했으므로 (B)가 정답이다.

어휘 | creativity 창의성　specialize in ~을 전문으로 하다

---

[3] W-Br / M-Au

> W　Hello, my name is Melissa Stein. I'm calling because I'm planning to sell my house. I was referred to you by a coworker. You helped her sell her house a while ago, and she was very pleased with your agency.
> M　I'd be happy to help you with that, Ms. Stein. Are you ready to put the house on the market immediately?

여　안녕하세요, 제 이름은 멜리사 스테인입니다. 집을 매매할 계획이라 전화드립니다. **제 동료가 소개해 주었어요.** 얼마 전에 제 동료의 집을 팔아주셨다는데 그쪽 부동산이 아주 만족스러웠다고 하네요.
남　기꺼이 도와드리죠, 스테인 씨. 집을 바로 매물로 내놓을 수 있나요?

어휘 | refer A to B A한테 B에게 문의하라고 하다　coworker 동료 put A on the market A를 (팔려고) 시장에 내놓다

3 여자는 남자의 부동산 중개소를 어떻게 알았는가?
　(A) 이웃으로부터　　　(B) 잡지에서
　(C) 동료로부터　　　　(D) 인터넷에서

해설 | **세부 내용 - 여자가 남자의 부동산 중개소를 알게 된 방법**
여자의 첫 번째 대사에서 집을 팔 생각인데 직장 동료가 소개를 해줘서(I was referred to you by a coworker) 전화를 한다고 했다. 따라서 (C)가 정답이다.

---

[4] M-Au / W-Am

> M　Hello. We're here to set up our booth for the electronics trade fair. Can you tell us where it's located? We're from Elmheart Electronics.
> W　Let me see… you're in booth number twelve, right by the service elevators. Do you need any assistance taking anything out of your vehicle? We have some staff available to help.
> M　Thanks, that would be great.

남　안녕하세요. 전자제품 무역 박람회에 부스를 설치하려고 왔습니다. 위치가 어디인지 알려주실 수 있나요? 저희는 엘름하트 일렉트로닉스에서 왔어요.
여　한 번 보죠. 업무용 승강기 바로 옆 12번 부스네요. **차량에서 물건을 꺼내는 데 도움이 필요하세요? 도와드릴 직원이 있습니다.**
남　감사합니다. 그렇게 해 주시면 좋겠어요.

어휘 | set up 설치하다　electronics 전자제품　trade fair 무역 박람회　service elevator 업무용 승강기　assistance 도움, 지원 vehicle 차량　available 시간이 되는

4 여자에 따르면 직원들은 어떤 도움을 줄 수 있는가?

(A) 비용 지불   (B) 행사 준비
(C) 제품 선택   (D) 물품 내리기

해설 | **세부 내용 - 직원들이 줄 수 있는 도움**
여자가 첫 번째 대사에서 차량에서 물건을 꺼내는 데 도움이 필요한지(Do you need any assistance taking anything out of your vehicle?) 물어본 후, 도와줄 수 있는 직원들이 있다(We have some staff available to help)고 했으므로 (D)가 정답이다.

어휘 | make a payment 지불하다 organize 준비하다, 조직하다 choose 선택하다 unload (짐을) 내리다

② 문제점·걱정거리 문제

공략포인트

> 여 혹시 로스앤젤레스로 가는 다음 비행기를 탈 방법이 있을까요? 뉴욕에서 타고 온 비행기가 정시에 도착하지 못하는 바람에 연결편을 놓쳤어요.
> 남 잠시만요. 직항편은 없지만 샌프란시스코에서 갈아타도 괜찮으시다면 20분 후에 떠나는 비행기가 하나 있어요.
> 여 로스앤젤레스로 갈 수만 있다면 탈게요.

문제 여자의 문제는 무엇인가?

(A) 수하물을 잃어버렸다.
(B) 비행기를 놓쳤다.
(C) 항공권을 안 가져왔다.
(D) 탑승구가 어디인지 모른다.

● 실전 도움닫기
본책 p.079

1 (B) **2** (B) **3** (A) **4** (B)

[1] M-Au / W-Am

> M Hi, my name's Ron Halberg. I checked in to the hotel earlier today. Do you have any messages for me? My luggage didn't arrive, so I've been expecting a call from Reyes Airlines.
> W Ah, Mr. Halberg—I'm sorry, but they haven't called yet. Is there any way I can help you?
> M Well, I'm attending an awards dinner this evening, and my only formal clothes are in my suitcase. Is there a place nearby where I can rent a nice suit?

> 남 안녕하세요, 저는 론 홀버그라고 합니다. 오늘 아까 호텔에 체크인 했는데요. 저에게 온 메시지가 있나요? **제 수하물이 도착하지 않아서 레예스 항공에서 오는 전화를 기다리고 있거든요.**
> 여 아, 홀버그 씨. 죄송하지만 아직 전화가 안 왔네요. 제가 도와드릴 일이 있나요?

> 남 음, 제가 오늘 저녁에 시상식 만찬에 참석하는데 딱 한 벌 있는 정장이 여행가방에 들어있어요. 괜찮은 정장을 빌릴 수 있는 곳이 근처에 있나요?

어휘 | luggage 수하물 expect 기대하다 attend 참석하다 awards 시상식 formal 격식을 차린 nearby 근처에 rent 빌리다, 대여하다

1 남자의 문제는 무엇인가?

(A) 계산서가 틀렸다.
(B) 수하물이 분실됐다.
(C) 예약이 취소됐다.
(D) 정장이 훼손됐다.

해설 | **세부 내용 - 남자의 문제**
남자가 첫 번째 대사에서 자신의 수하물이 도착하지 않아서(My luggage didn't arrive) 레예스 항공의 전화를 기다리고 있다고 했으므로 (B)가 정답이다.

어휘 | bill 고지서, 계산서 incorrect 맞지 않는 reservation 예약 cancel 취소하다 damage 손상을 주다, 훼손하다

[2] W-Am / M-Cn

> W I'm looking for the current issue of *Crafts Magazine*. Do you know if the library stopped subscribing to it? It wasn't in the section where I usually find it.
> M Oh, yes, I'm sorry. The library didn't renew its subscription from last year, so you won't see it on the shelves.

> 여 <크래프트 매거진> 이번 호를 찾고 있어요. 도서관에서 구독을 중단했는지 여부를 아세요? 보통 있었던 구역에 없거든요.
> 남 아, 네. 죄송합니다. 도서관에서 작년부터 구독 갱신을 하지 않았어요. **그래서 책장에 없을 겁니다.**

어휘 | craft 공예 current 현재의 issue 호 subscribe to ~를 구독하다 renew 갱신하다 subscription 구독

2 화자들은 어떤 문제에 대해 이야기하는가?

(A) 작품 한 점이 도착하지 않았다.
(B) 잡지를 이용할 수 없다.
(C) 도서관 카드가 만료됐다.
(D) 매장이 문을 닫는다.

해설 | **세부 내용 - 화자들이 언급한 문제점**
여자가 <크래프트 매거진> 이번 호가 보통 있었던 구역에 없다(It wasn't in the section where I usually find it)고 했는데, 이에 대해 남자가 도서관에서 작년부터 구독 갱신을 하지 않는다(The library didn't renew its subscription from last year)고 응답했으므로, 잡지를 이용할 수 없게 되었음을 알 수 있다. 따라서 (B)가 정답이다.

어휘 | arrive 도착하다 available 이용할 수 있는 expire 만료되다

058

M Hello. I'm calling about the notice I received today. It said that my apartment's been scheduled for some repairs on Wednesday 21.

W Yes, that's correct. The property managers have arranged to have new ceramic floor tiles put in all the kitchens in your building.

M Well, I usually work from home on Wednesdays, so I'm afraid that having my flooring changed while I'm there would make it too noisy for me to concentrate.

남 안녕하세요? 오늘 받은 안내문 관련해서 전화 드립니다. 21일 수요일에 제 아파트 수리 예정이라고 되어 있던데요.

여 네, 맞아요. 부동산 관리인들이 그 건물의 모든 주방에 세라믹 바닥 타일을 새로 깔도록 했거든요.

남 음, 저는 보통 매주 수요일에 재택 근무를 해요. 그래서 **제가 있는 동안 바닥재를 바꾸면 너무 시끄러워서 집중하기가 어려울 것 같은데요.**

어휘 | notice 안내문, 공고문 be scheduled ~할 예정이다 repair 수리 property 부동산, 건물 arrange 처리하다, 주선하다 work from home 재택근무하다 flooring 바닥재 concentrate 집중하다

3 남자는 무엇을 염려하는가?
(A) 소음 　　　　　　(B) 먼지
(C) 비용 　　　　　　(D) 안전

해설 | 세부 내용 - 남자의 우려 사항
남자가 마지막 대사에서 자신이 집에 있는 동안 바닥재를 바꾸면 너무 시끄러워서 집중하기가 어려울 것 같다(I'm afraid that having my flooring changed while I'm there would make it too noisy for me to concentrate)며 소음 발생을 우려하고 있으므로 (A)가 정답이다.

W Excuse me, I bought this jacket here last week, but when I got home, I realized that one of the buttons was missing. I'd like to exchange it for another one.

M I'm sorry about that. This jacket has been very popular this season and, unfortunately, we're sold out of them right now.

여 실례합니다, 제가 지난주 여기서 이 재킷을 샀는데 집에 와서 보니 단추 하나가 없더라고요. 다른 걸로 교환하고 싶은데요.

남 그 점에 대해 죄송합니다. 이 재킷은 이번 시즌에 매우 인기가 좋아서, **아쉽지만 지금 다 팔린 상태입니다.**

어휘 | get home 집에 도착하다 realize 깨닫다, 알아차리다 missing 빠진, 없는 exchange A for B A를 B로 교환하다 be sold out of ~을 다 팔았다

4 남자는 어떤 문제점을 언급하는가?
(A) 어떤 장비가 작동되지 않는다.
(B) 물건이 다 떨어졌다.
(C) 가격이 최근에 올랐다.
(D) 상점이 막 문을 닫으려 한다.

해설 | 세부 내용 - 남자가 언급한 문제점
여자가 재킷을 교환해 달라고 하자 남자는 아쉽게도 지금 물건이 다 팔렸다(unfortunately, we're sold out of them right now)고 했으므로 (B)가 정답이다.

어휘 | work 작동되다 out of stock 재고가 없는 *cf.* in stock 재고가 있는 recently 최근에 be about to do 막 ~하려 하다

● ETS 실전문제　　　　　　　　　본책 p.080

1 (C)	**2** (D)	**3** (B)	**4** (C)	**5** (D)	**6** (C)
7 (A)	**8** (C)	**9** (C)	**10** (C)	**11** (D)	**12** (A)
13 (D)	**14** (B)	**15** (A)	**16** (A)	**17** (B)	**18** (B)
19 (C)	**20** (A)	**21** (D)	**22** (A)	**23** (B)	**24** (C)

W Tim, I'm looking for a new fitness center to join. [1]The one I currently go to is convenient for me, but they just sent out an e-mail saying they're closing down in July.

M Why don't you join mine? The monthly fee is reasonable, and they just installed some new exercise machines. Personally, I just go there to swim. [2]I usually go first thing in the morning because the pool's practically empty then.

W Oh, that's good to know. I prefer going to the gym when it's less crowded too. Can I try out the equipment before signing up for a membership?

M Yes, they offer one-day trials. And [3]if you decide to sign up, mention my name, and you'll get a discount on the first month.

여 팀, 제가 새로 들어갈 피트니스 센터를 찾고 있는데요. **[1]지금 가는 곳이 편리하긴 한데, 7월에 문을 닫는다는 이메일을 보냈더라고요.**

남 제가 다니는 곳에 들어오지 그래요? 월 이용료도 적당하고 새 운동기구 몇 대를 이제 막 설치했어요. 개인적으로 저는 수영을 하러 가요. **[2]보통 아침에 일어나자마자 가죠. 그때는 사실상 수영장이 비어 있거든요.**

여 아, 좋은 정보군요. 저도 덜 붐빌 때 체육관에 가는 걸 좋아해요. 회원 가입을 하기 전에 장비를 이용해 볼 수 있나요?

남 네. 하루 시범 이용권을 제공해요. **[3]등록하기로 결정하시면 제 이름을 대세요. 그럼 첫 번째 달은 할인을 받게 돼요.**

어휘 | look for ~를 찾다 currently 현재 convenient 편리한 reasonable (가격 등이) 적당한, 합리적인 install 설치하다 personally 개인적으로 first thing 일어나자마자, 출근하자마자 practically 사실상 empty 비어 있는 prefer 선호하다 crowded 붐비는 equipment 장비 sign up for ~에 등록하다, 신청하다, 가입하다 trial 시험, 시범 get a discount 할인 받다

1 여자는 어떤 문제를 언급하는가?

(A) 일정이 몹시 바쁘다.
(B) 이용료가 인상됐다.
(C) 피트니스 센터가 문을 닫는다.
(D) 건물이 공사 중이다.

해설 | **세부 내용 - 여자가 언급한 문제점**
여자가 첫 번째 대사에서 지금 가는 피트니스 센터(The one I currently go to)에서 7월에 문을 닫는다는 이메일을 보냈다(they just sent out an e-mail saying they're closing down in July)고 했으므로 (C)가 정답이다.

어휘 | increase 증가하다 under construction 공사 중인

2 남자는 수영장에 대해 무엇이라고 말하는가?

(A) 다음 달에는 개장하지 않을 예정이다.
(B) 가르쳐 줄 수영 강사들이 있다.
(C) 최근 운영시간이 연장됐다.
(D) 아침에는 이용이 많지 않다.

해설 | **세부 내용 - 남자가 수영장에 대해 말한 것**
남자가 첫 번째 대사에서 보통 아침에 일어나자마자 수영을 간다(I usually go first thing in the morning)고 한 후, 그때는 사실상 수영장이 비어 있다(the pool's practically empty then)고 했으므로, 아침에는 수영장 이용이 많지 않다는 점을 알 수 있다. 따라서 (D)가 정답이다.

어휘 | instructor 강사 available 이용 가능한, 시간이 되는 extend 연장하다

Paraphrasing
대화의 practically empty → 정답의 not used a lot

3 여자는 어떻게 할인을 받을 수 있는가?

(A) 쿠폰 제시하기
(B) 친구 이름 대기
(C) 평일에만 시설 이용하기
(D) 여러 달 이용료를 선불로 내기

해설 | **세부 내용 - 여자가 할인 받는 방법**
남자가 마지막 대사에서 등록하기로 결정하면 자신의 이름을 댈 것(if you decide to sign up, mention my name)을 제안한 후, 그렇게 하면 첫 번째 달은 할인을 받게 된다(you'll get a discount on the first month)고 했다. 따라서 (B)가 정답이다.

어휘 | obtain 얻다 present 제시하다 facility 시설 in advance 미리

Paraphrasing
대화의 mention my name → 정답의 providing a friend's name

[4-6] W-Br / M-Cn

W Hi. The university registrar's office sent me here. ⁴I graduated from the nursing program two months ago, but I still haven't received a copy of my certificate. Can you help me?

M I'm sorry about that. You see, we haven't been able to get all the necessary signatures. We hope to have the certificates ready to mail by the end of August.

W Is there any way I could get mine sooner? ⁵The reason I ask is I'm looking for a job and an employer might want to see it.

M Well, ⁶if you can come to pick the certificate up in person, that would save you waiting for it to come in the mail. I could contact you as soon as it's ready.

여 안녕하세요. 대학교 교무처에서 이곳으로 저를 보냈어요. ⁴제가 두 달 전에 간호사 양성 과정을 졸업했는데, 아직 자격증을 받지 못해서요. 처리해 줄 수 있나요?

남 죄송합니다. 그게 말이죠, 필요한 서명들을 아직 다 받지 못해서요. 저희는 8월 말 즈음에 자격증 우편 발송 준비가 될 거라 봐요.

여 제 것을 좀 더 빨리 받을 방법이 있나요? ⁵지금 제가 구직 중인데, 혹시 회사에서 그것을 보고 싶어 할 수도 있기 때문이에요.

남 음, ⁶자격증을 직접 찾으러 올 수 있다면 우편 배달을 기다리는 시간이 절약될 거예요. 준비되는 즉시 연락 드리도록 할게요.

어휘 | registrar's office 교무처 graduate from ~을 졸업하다 nursing program 간호사 양성 과정 receive 받다 certificate 자격증, 면허증 signature 서명 employer 고용주, 회사 in person 직접 save 절약하다

4 여자는 최근에 무엇을 했는가?

(A) 수업에 등록했다.
(B) 병원에서 일을 시작했다.
(C) 대학교를 졸업했다.
(D) 소포를 보냈다.

해설 | **세부 내용 - 여자가 최근에 한 일**
여자가 첫 번째 대사에서 두 달 전에 간호사 양성 과정을 졸업했다(I graduated from the nursing program two months ago)고 했으므로, (C)가 정답이다.

어휘 | enroll in 등록하다 package 소포

5 여자는 왜 걱정하는가?

(A) 전근을 가게 될 것이다.
(B) 곧 교육을 시작한다.
(C) 기말시험을 치러야 한다.
(D) 자격증이 필요할 수도 있다.

해설 | **세부 내용 - 여자가 걱정하는 이유**
여자는 두 번째 대사에서 지금 구직 중인데, 회사에서 자격증을 보고 싶어할 수도 있다(The reason I ask is I'm looking for a job and an employer might want to see it)고 했다. 따라서 (D)가 정답이다.

어휘 | relocate 전근하다

6 남자는 여자에게 무엇을 하라고 제안하는가?

(A) 서면 요청서 보내기　　(B) 관리자와 이야기하기

(C) 서류 직접 가져가기　　(D) 이력서 업데이트하기

해설 | 세부 내용 - 남자의 제안 사항

남자가 마지막 대사에서 자격증을 직접 찾으러 오면 우편으로 오기를 기다리는 시간을 아낄 수 있다(if you can come to pick the certificate up in person, that would save you waiting for it to come in the mail)고 했다. 따라서 (C)가 정답이다.

[7-9] **3인 대화** W-Am / W-Br / M-Au

> **W1** ⁷Thabo and Michiko, I need help designing some pamphlets for our evening business courses. I'd like to have them ready before the end of April.
>
> **W2** Sure. Should we take a look at the ones from last year or make them different?
>
> **M** ⁸You know, I think the pamphlets last year had too many details. People can get dates and times from the Web site.
>
> **W1** I agree. Let's focus on the skills that people will learn in each class.
>
> **M** OK. ⁹I'll come up with a rough version of the text for the pamphlet by tomorrow and e-mail it to you. Then, next week we can start working on the design.
>
> 여 ⁷타보와 미치코, 저녁 비즈니스 수업용 팸플릿 디자인 좀 도와주세요. 4월 말 전에 준비해 놓고 싶거든요.
>
> 여2 네. 작년 것을 참고할까요, 아니면 다르게 만들어야 할까요?
>
> 남 ⁸아시겠지만, 작년 팸플릿에는 세부 사항이 너무 많이 들어갔어요. 사람들이 날짜와 시간은 웹사이트에서 볼 수 있거든요.
>
> 여 맞아요. 그럼 각 수업에서 사람들이 배우게 될 기술에 초점을 맞추죠.
>
> 남 좋아요. ⁹제가 내일까지 팸플릿에 들어갈 문구를 대략적으로 만들어서 이메일로 보내 드릴게요. 그럼 다음 주에 디자인 작업을 시작할 수 있을 겁니다.
>
> 어휘 | course 수업, 과정　take a look at ~을 보다, ~을 참고하다　details 세부 사항　focus on ~에 초점을 맞추다　come up with (계획이나 아이디어 등을) 제시하다, 생각해 내다　rough 대략적인　work on ~에 대해 작업하다

7 화자들은 무엇을 광고할 계획인가?

(A) 저녁 수업　　(B) 취업 기회

(C) 온라인 상점　　(D) 인쇄 시연

해설 | 세부 내용 - 광고하려고 하는 것

여자가 첫 번째 대사에서 저녁 비즈니스 수업용 팸플릿 디자인을 도와 달라(Thabo and Michiko, I need help designing some pamphlets for our evening business courses)고 했으므로 (A)가 정답이다.

Paraphrasing

대화의 evening business courses → 정답의 Evening classes

---

8 남자에 따르면, 작년 팸플릿의 문제점은 무엇이었는가?

(A) 정시에 준비되지 않았다.

(B) 크기가 잘못되었다.

(C) 정보가 너무 세부적이었다.

(D) 연락처가 빠졌다.

해설 | 세부 내용 - 작년 팸플릿의 문제점

남자의 첫 번째 대사에서 작년 팸플릿에는 세부 사항이 너무 많이 들어갔다(You know, I think the pamphlets last year had too many details)고 했으므로 (C)가 정답이다.

Paraphrasing

대화의 The pamphlets had too many details. → 정답의 The information was too specific.

9 남자는 여자에게 무엇을 보낼 것이라고 말하는가?

(A) 무료 제품 견본　　(B) 참가자 명단

(C) 문서 초안　　(D) 수정된 일정

해설 | 세부 내용 - 남자가 보내줄 것

대화 마지막에 남자가 내일까지 팸플릿에 들어갈 문구를 대략적으로 만들어서 이메일로 보내 주겠다(I'll come up with a rough version of the text for the pamphlet by tomorrow and e-mail it to you)고 했으므로 (C)가 정답이다.

Paraphrasing

대화의 a rough version of the text → 정답의 A draft of a document

[10-12] W-Am / M-Au

> **W** Hikaru, ¹⁰have you heard about how the company wants to make our buildings more energy-efficient? I see they're setting up a planning committee and asking for employees to participate.
>
> **M** I read about that in the weekly newsletter. It sounds like it might be interesting. ¹¹Are you thinking about signing up for the committee?
>
> **W** ¹¹I'm going to the first meeting on Thursday to see what's involved. I'm between projects right now, and I have a lot of ideas. Are you going?
>
> **M** ¹²I'd like to, but I'm going to be busy. I'm doing a sales presentation at the Alston Corporation, and I think it'll take most of the day. But maybe you could let me know what you find out at the meeting.
>
> 여 히카루, ¹⁰회사가 우리 건물을 더욱 에너지 효율적으로 만들려는 방안에 대해 들었어요? 기획위원회를 설립해서 직원들에게 참여하라고 요청하고 있어요.
>
> 남 주간 소식지에서 읽었어요. 흥미로운 얘기인 것 같아요. ¹¹위원회에 가입할 생각이에요?
>
> 여 ¹¹관련된 사항을 확인하기 위해 목요일 첫 회의에 가려고요. 지금은 프로젝트 종료 후 다음 프로젝트 시작 전이라 아이디어가 많거든요. 가실 건가요?

남 ¹²그러고 싶은데 바쁠 것 같아요. 앨스턴 코퍼레이션에서 영업 발표를 할 예정인데 거의 종일 걸릴 것 같네요. 가능하시면 회의에서 알게 되는 내용을 저에게 알려주세요.

어휘 | energy-efficient 에너지 효율적인 set up 설립하다, 수립하다 committee 위원회 participate 참여하다 involve 관련시키다, 수반하다 presentation 발표

10 회사의 계획은 무엇인가?
(A) 운송비 절감하기   (B) 신임 이사장 임명하기
(C) 에너지 효율성 높이기   (D) 해외 지점 열기

해설 | **세부 내용 - 회사의 계획**
여자가 첫 번째 대사에서 회사가 건물을 더욱 에너지 효율적으로 만들려는 방안(how the company wants to make our buildings more energy-efficient)에 대해 들었는지 물어보며 회사의 계획을 언급하고 있으므로 (C)가 정답이다.

어휘 | reduce 줄이다, 감소시키다 transportation cost 운송비, 교통비 appoint 임명하다 board president 이사장 overseas 해외에

Paraphrasing
대화의 make our buildings more energy-efficient
→ 정답의 increase energy efficiency

11 여자는 무엇을 고려하는가?
(A) 이메일 답신 보내기   (B) 설문조사 하기
(C) 전근 신청하기   (D) 위원회 들어가기

해설 | **세부 내용 - 여자의 고려 사항**
남자가 첫 번째 대사에서 위원회에 가입할 생각인지(Are you thinking about signing up for the committee?) 물어봤는데, 이에 대해 여자가 목요일 첫 회의에 가려고 한다(I'm going to the first meeting on Thursday)고 응답했으므로, 여자가 위원회에 들어가는 것을 고려하고 있음을 알 수 있다. 따라서 (D)가 정답이다.

어휘 | response 응답 conduct 실시하다 survey 조사 apply 신청하다 relocate 이전하다, 전근하다

Paraphrasing
대화의 signing up for the committee → 정답의 Joining a committee

12 남자는 왜 회의에 참석할 수 없는가?
(A) 발표를 할 예정이다.
(B) 동료를 태우러 갈 예정이다.
(C) 기사를 쓸 예정이다.
(D) 재고 조사를 할 예정이다.

해설 | **세부 내용 - 남자가 회의에 참석할 수 없는 이유**
남자가 마지막 대사에서 참석하고 싶은데 바쁠 것 같다(I'd like to, but I'm going to be busy)고 한 후, 앨스턴 코퍼레이션에서 영업 발표를 할 예정인데 거의 종일 걸릴 것 같다(I'm doing a sales presentation at the Alston Corporation, and I think it'll take most of the day)며 참석할 수 없는 이유를 밝혔으므로 (A)가 정답이다.

어휘 | colleague 동료 article 기사 take inventory ~의 목록표를 작성하다, 재고 조사를 하다

[13-15] **3인 대화** M-Au / W-Am / M-Cn

M1 ¹³I can't believe our contractor raised his prices again. This is the second time this year! I think we should find another contractor to manufacture pipes for us. What does everybody think?

W I agree with you. ¹⁴How about Small Plains Contracting? I've heard they do good work, and they have high ratings.

M1 Good idea. Please give them a call and get an estimate.

M2 We should also look into a few other contractors to compare prices.

M1 You're right, Luca. ¹⁵Could you make a list of other firms we can contact?

M2 ¹⁵Yes, I'll do that right now.

남1 ¹³협력업체에서 또 가격을 올렸다니 믿을 수가 없네요. 이번이 올해 들어 두 번째잖아요! 파이프를 생산해 줄 다른 협력업체를 찾아봐야 한다고 생각해요. 다들 어떻게 생각해요?
여 같은 의견이에요. ¹⁴스몰 플레인스 컨트랙팅은 어떨까요? 일을 잘하는 데다, 높은 평가를 받고 있다고 들었어요.
남1 좋은 생각이에요. 전화를 걸어서 견적을 받아보세요.
남2 가격을 비교하려면 다른 협력업체들도 조사해 봐야 해요.
남1 맞아요, 루카. ¹⁵우리가 연락할 수 있는 다른 업체들 명단을 만들어 줄래요?
남2 ¹⁵네, 지금 당장 할게요.

어휘 | contractor 협력업체, 하청업체[업자] raise 올리다 manufacture 제조하다 rating 평가 estimate 견적 compare 비교하다 firm 회사

13 현재 협력업체의 문제는 무엇인가?
(A) 일 처리가 너무 느리다.
(B) 제품이 손상되었다.
(C) 기계가 고장 났다.
(D) 비용이 너무 비싸다.

해설 | **세부 내용 - 문제점**
남자 1의 첫 번째 대사에서 협력업체가 가격을 또 올렸다(I can't believe our contractor raised his prices again)면서 다른 업체를 찾아야 한다고 했다. 따라서 (D)가 정답이다.

14 스몰 플레인스 컨트랙팅에 대해 여자는 무엇이라고 말하는가?
(A) 근처에 위치해 있다.
(B) 평판이 좋다.
(C) 최근에 직원을 늘렸다.
(D) 한 프로젝트를 거절했다.

해설 | **세부 내용 - 스몰 플레인스 컨트랙팅에 대해 여자가 말한 것**
여자의 대사에서 스몰 플레인스 컨트랙팅이 높은 평가를 받고 있다(How about Small Plains Contracting? I've heard they do good work, and they have high ratings)고 했다. 따라서 (B)가 정답이다.

어휘 | reputation 평판 expand 확대하다 decline 거절하다

Paraphrasing
대화의 high ratings → 정답의 good reputation

15 루카는 다음에 무엇을 하겠는가?

(A) 명단 작성　　　　　(B) 건설 현장 방문

(C) 파이프 회사에 전화　(D) 견적서 검토

해설 | 세부 내용 - 다음에 할 일

대화의 마지막 부분에서 루카(남자 2)는 연락할 수 있는 다른 업체들 명단을 만들어 달라(Could you make a list of other firms we can contact?)는 남자 1의 요청에 지금 당장 하겠다(Yes, I'll do that right now)며 수락했으므로 (A)가 정답이다.

어휘 | compile (자료를 모아) 작성하다 **construction site** 건설 현장

[16-18] W-Br / M-Cn

> **W** You've reached the Parks Department of Monroe City. How can I help you?
>
> **M** Hello. ¹⁶I moved to Monroe last month and I'm looking for volunteer opportunities. I thought that might help me get to know the area. Do you need any volunteers?
>
> **W** We do! In fact, right now ¹⁷we're conducting a census of native birds in our local parks. We need volunteers to count them so we have an idea of how many there are. Would you like to help with that?
>
> **M** Yes. ¹⁸My only concern is that I've never done anything like this before.
>
> **W** Don't worry. We'll pair you with a park ranger who'll show you how to identify the birds and count them.

> 여　먼로시 공원 관리부입니다. 무엇을 도와드릴까요?
>
> 남　안녕하세요. ¹⁶제가 지난달에 먼로시로 이사 왔는데요, 자원봉사를 할 기회를 찾고 있습니다. 이 동네를 알아가는 데 도움이 될 것 같아요. 자원봉사자가 필요하신가요?
>
> 여　필요해요! 실은, ¹⁷현재 우리 지역 공원에 서식하는 토종 새의 개체 수를 조사하고 있어요. 그 수가 얼마나 되는지 파악하기 위해 새의 개체 수를 세는 작업을 할 자원봉사자가 필요합니다. 그 일을 도와주시겠어요?
>
> 남　네. 그런데 ¹⁸한 가지 걱정되는 점은 제가 이런 일을 전에 해본 적이 없다는 거예요.
>
> 여　걱정 마세요. 토종 새를 구분해서 수를 세는 방법을 알려줄 공원 관리원과 짝을 지어드릴 거예요.

어휘 | opportunity 기회 **conduct** 실시하다, 수행하다 **census** 개체 수 조사, 인구조사 **park ranger** 공원 관리원 **identify** 구분하다, 밝혀내다

16 남자는 지난달에 무엇을 했다고 말하는가?

(A) 새로운 동네로 이사했다.　(B) 새로운 일을 시작했다.

(C) 과학 수업을 수강했다.　　(D) 공원을 방문했다.

해설 | 세부 내용 - 남자가 지난달에 한 일

남자가 첫 번째 대사에서 지난달에 먼로시로 이사 왔다(I moved to Monroe last month)고 했으므로, (A)가 정답이다.

17 여자는 남자에게 어떤 일을 도와 달라고 하는가?

(A) 하이킹 인솔　　　　(B) 새의 수 세기

(C) 나무 심기　　　　　(D) 공원 청소

해설 | 세부 내용 - 여자의 요청 사항

여자가 두 번째 대사에서 지역 공원의 토종 새의 개체 수(a census of native birds)를 조사하고 있다고 한 후 숫자를 세는 작업을 할 자원봉사자가 필요한데(We need volunteers to count them) 도와줄 수 있는지 물었다. 따라서 (B)가 정답이다.

18 남자가 걱정하는 것은 무엇인가?

(A) 바쁜 일정　　　　　(B) 경험 부족

(C) 근무지까지의 거리　(D) 참가 비용

해설 | 세부 내용 - 남자의 우려 사항

남자가 두 번째 대사에서 걱정되는 점이 이런 일을 전에 해본 적이 없다는 것(My only concern is that I've never done anything like this before)이라고 했으므로, (B)가 정답이다.

Paraphrasing
대화의 I've never done anything like this before
→ 정답의 His lack of experience

[19-21] W-Am / M-Cn

> **W** John, ¹⁹it seems like the launch of our newspaper's new Web site has been a great success. In just one week the site has already gotten very positive feedback from readers.
>
> **M** There *do* seem to be some issues with the mobile version of the site though—²⁰people who visit our Web site on their mobile phones are reporting that headlines and text aren't displayed correctly—lines can be completely cut off.
>
> **W** Oh, I wasn't aware of that problem—we'll need to address that right away. ²¹There's definitely a growing trend of reading news Web sites on a phone instead of on a computer, so this problem could be affecting a lot of readers.

> 여　존, ¹⁹우리 신문사 신규 웹사이트 개설이 큰 성공을 거둔 것 같아요. 1주일 만에 사이트가 독자들로부터 아주 긍정적인 평을 받았거든요.
>
> 남　그런데 사이트의 모바일 버전은 문제가 있는 듯합니다. ²⁰휴대전화로 웹사이트를 방문하는 사람들이 헤드라인과 본문이 정확하게 표시되지 않는다고 이야기해요. 끝이 완전히 잘리거든요.
>
> 여　아, 그 문제는 몰랐어요. 당장 해결해야겠어요. ²¹컴퓨터 대신 휴대전화로 뉴스 웹사이트를 보는 추세가 확실히 늘고 있으니 이 문제가 많은 독자에게 영향을 미칠 수 있어요.

어휘 | launch 출시, 시작 **positive** 긍정적인 **correctly** 정확하게, 바르게 **completely** 완전히 **be cut off** 잘리다 **be aware of** ~를 알다 **address** (문제 등을) 해결하다 **definitely** 분명히, 틀림없이 **instead of** ~대신에 **affect** 영향을 미치다

19 여자에 따르면, 회사는 최근에 무엇을 했는가?

(A) 합병 발표   (B) 편집자 채용
(C) 웹사이트 개설   (D) 워크숍 개최

해설 | **세부 내용 - 회사가 최근에 한 일**
여자가 첫 번째 대사에서 신문사 신규 웹사이트 개설이 큰 성공을 거둔 것 같다(it seems like the launch of our newspaper's new Web site has been a great success)고 했으므로, 회사가 최근에 웹사이트를 개설했음을 알 수 있다. 따라서 (C)가 정답이다.

어휘 | recently 최근에 announce 알리다, 발표하다 merger 합병 hire 채용하다 host 개최하다

20 남자는 어떤 문제를 언급하는가?

(A) 내용이 정확하게 보이지 않는다.
(B) 마감 시한을 놓쳤다.
(C) 판매량이 예상한 것보다 낮다.
(D) 장비가 구식이다.

해설 | **세부 내용 - 남자가 언급한 문제점**
남자가 첫 번째 대사에서 휴대전화로 웹사이트를 방문하는 사람들이 헤드라인과 본문이 정확하게 표시되지 않는다(headlines and text aren't displayed correctly)고 이야기한다며 문제점을 언급한 후, 끝이 완전히 잘린다(lines can be completely cut off)고 덧붙였다. 따라서 (A)가 정답이다.

어휘 | deadline 마감 기한 than expected 기대한 것보다, 예상보다 equipment 장비 outdated 구식인

21 여자는 무엇이 증가 추세라고 말하는가?

(A) 오디오북 청취
(B) 온라인 교육 개최
(C) 계약서 전자 서명
(D) 모바일 기기로 뉴스 읽기

해설 | **세부 내용 - 여자가 증가 추세라고 말한 것**
여자가 마지막 대사에서 컴퓨터 대신 휴대전화로 뉴스 웹사이트를 보는 추세가 확실히 늘고 있다(There's definitely a growing trend of reading news Web sites on a phone instead of on a computer)고 했으므로 (D)가 정답이다.

어휘 | contract 계약서 electronically 전자적으로, 컴퓨터로

Paraphrasing
대화의 on a phone → 정답의 on mobile devices

[22-24] W-Br / M-Cn

W ²²James, I still haven't seen the legal contract for the Cullens account. Did the delivery service happen to drop it off with you?

M No, I'm afraid not. ²³I have a tracking number for the package, but nothing showed up when I checked the online system this morning. We're scheduled to finalize the contract at our meeting tomorrow, so I'd better call the delivery company right now.

W I certainly would. ²⁴It's going to be a problem if the vice president can't sign the contract at the meeting. As soon as it's over, ²⁴he's leaving on a business trip and will be out of the country for several weeks.

여 ²²제임스, 제가 컬린스 건에 대한 법률 계약서를 아직 보지 못했어요. 혹시 택배회사에서 당신에게 그걸 주고 갔나요?

남 아니요, 안 왔어요. ²³제가 그 소포의 배송 추적 번호를 가지고 있는데, 오늘 오전에 온라인 시스템으로 확인해봤을 땐, 아무것도 뜨지 않았어요. 내일 회의 때 계약을 마무리 짓기로 되어 있으니 제가 지금 택배회사에 전화해보는 게 좋겠네요.

여 저라면 꼭 그렇게 하겠어요. ²⁴부회장님이 회의 때 계약서에 서명할 수 없다면 문제가 될 거예요. 회의가 끝나는 대로 ²⁴출장을 가시면 몇 주 간 해외에 계실 거니까요.

어휘 | legal 법률의 contract 계약서 account 고객사, 거래처, 계좌 drop A off with ~에게 A를 갖다 주다 tracking number (배송) 추적 번호 show up 나타나다 finalize 마무리짓다 vice president 부회장

22 화자들은 어떤 문제를 논의하고 있는가?

(A) 문서를 받지 못했다.
(B) 고객의 비행기가 도착하지 않았다.
(C) 동료가 회신 전화를 하지 않았다.
(D) 회의 공간이 예약되지 않았다.

해설 | **세부 내용 - 문제점**
여자가 첫 대사에서 법률 계약서를 보지 못했다(I still haven't seen the legal contract)는 문제점을 언급하고 남자가 이 문제에 대해 대답하고 있으므로 (A)가 정답이다.

어휘 | return a call 회신 전화하다

23 남자는 오늘 오전에 무엇을 했다고 말하는가?

(A) 자신의 음성 메시지를 들었다.
(B) 온라인 추적 시스템을 확인했다.
(C) 고객 서비스 직원과 이야기했다.
(D) 계약서를 준비했다.

해설 | **세부 내용 - 남자가 한 일**
남자가 첫 번째 대사에서 오늘 오전에 온라인 시스템을 확인했다(I checked the online system this morning)고 했으므로 (B)가 정답이다.

24 회의는 왜 내일 열려야 하는가?

(A) 분기 마지막 날이다.
(B) 사무실이 오늘 일찍 문을 닫는다.
(C) 임원 한 명이 출장을 간다.
(D) 보도자료가 배포될 예정이다.

해설 | **세부 내용 - 회의가 내일 열려야 하는 이유**
여자의 마지막 대사에서 부회장이 내일 회의에서 서명을 하지 못하면 문제가 될 것(It's going to be a problem if the vice president can't sign the contract at the meeting)이라며 회의 후 그가 출장을 떠난다고 했으므로, (C)가 정답이다.

어휘 | quarter 분기 executive 임원 press release 보도자료 distribute 배포하다

Unit 09 요청·제안/다음에 할 일 문제

① 요청·제안 문제

공략포인트
본책 p.082

> 여 제프, 궁금한 게 있는데... 이 책상 덮는 비닐은 누구를 위한 거예요?
> 남 우리를 위한 거예요. 기억해요? 건설업체에서 다음 주 화요일에 우리 사무 공간 개선 작업을 시작해요. 먼지가 많이 날 테니...
> 여 아, 그렇게 빨리 시작하는 줄 미처 몰랐네요. 그럼 우리가 다른 데서 일해야 할까요?
> 남 우린 여기 그대로 있을 거예요. 이건 작업자들이 일별로 어느 구역을 작업할지 보여 주는 일정표예요. 한번 보세요.
> 여 아, 좋아요. 제가 이것을 직원 게시판에 붙여 놓을게요.
>
> 어휘 | contractor 건설업체, 하청업체 timeline 일정표 crew 작업자들, 승무원 post 게시하다 bulletin board 게시판

문제 여자는 무엇을 해 주겠다고 제안하는가?
(A) 근무 시간 조정
(B) 사무용품 주문
(C) 일정표 게시
(D) 연수 프로그램 확대

● 실전 도움닫기
본책 p.083

1 (D) **2** (D) **3** (A) **4** (D)

[1] W-Am / M-Au

> W Mr. Young? I read about your innovative cooking techniques in *Good Food Magazine*, and I was wondering if you'd be interested in giving a demonstration in my class.
> M I'm definitely interested, but now's not a great time. I'm opening a second location of my restaurant, so things have been incredibly busy.
>
> 여 영 씨 되세요? <굿 푸드 매거진>에서 당신의 혁신적인 요리 기술에 대해 읽었는데요. 제 수업에서 시연하시는 일에 관심이 있으신지 궁금합니다.
> 남 물론 관심이 많지만, 지금은 적당한 때가 아니에요. 레스토랑 2호점을 개점할 예정이라서 엄청나게 바쁩니다.
>
> 어휘 | innovative 혁신적인 give a demonstration 시연하다 definitely 확실히 incredibly 엄청나게

1 여자는 남자에게 무엇을 해달라고 부탁하는가?
(A) 조리 기구 홍보
(B) 몇 번의 인터뷰 참석
(C) 잡지 기사 제출
(D) 시연

해설 | 세부 내용 - 여자의 요청 사항
여자가 첫 대사에서 남자에게 자신의 수업에서 시연하는 일에 관심이 있는지(I was wondering if you'd be interested in giving a demonstration in my class) 묻고 있으므로, (D)가 정답이다.

어휘 | promote 홍보하다 cookware 조리 기구

[2] M-Au / W-Br

> M Before I start scanning your items, did you bring any reusable bags for me to put your groceries in?
> W Oh, no—I didn't. Was I supposed to bring my own bags?
> M It is our store policy, but you could sign up for one of our membership cards. You'd receive a reusable bag for free with your membership, and it only takes a few minutes to register.
>
> 남 상품을 스캔하기 전에 여쭤보는데, 식료품을 담을 장바구니를 가지고 오셨나요?
> 여 아, 아니요. 가지고 오지 않았어요. 제 개인 가방을 가지고 와야 하나요?
> 남 그게 저희 가게 정책입니다만, **저희 회원 카드 중 하나를 신청하시면 돼요.** 회원 가입을 하시면 장바구니를 무료로 받게 되실 거예요. 그리고 가입하는 데 몇 분밖에 안 걸립니다.
>
> 어휘 | reusable 재사용할 수 있는 be supposed to ~하기로 되어있다 register 등록하다, 가입하다

2 남자는 여자에게 무엇을 할 것을 권하는가?
(A) 다음 날 다시 오기
(B) 미리 주문하기
(C) 인근 주차장에 주차하기
(D) 회원 카드 신청하기

해설 | 세부 내용 - 남자의 권유 사항
남자가 마지막 대사에서 회원 카드 중 하나를 신청하면(you could sign up for one of our membership cards) 장바구니를 무료로 받게 된다며, 여자에게 회원 카드 신청을 권유하고 있다. 따라서 (D)가 정답이다.

어휘 | following 다음의 in advance 미리

Paraphrasing
대화의 sign up for → 정답의 register for

[3] M-Cn / W-Am

> M Andrea, can I talk to you about a project we'd like you to work on? Management would like to see better communication between the sales department and the marketing department. We'd like you to lead this effort.
> W That sounds really interesting, Mark. But, what exactly would this project involve?
>
> 남 안드레아, 당신이 착수해 줬으면 하는 프로젝트에 대해 이야기를 좀 할 수 있을까요? 경영진은 영업부서와 마케팅부서가 더 원활히 소통하는 것을 원해요. 당신이 이 일을 이끌어 줬으면 해요.
> 여 마크, 정말 흥미로운 이야기군요. 하지만 이 프로젝트에 정확히 어떤 일이 포함되는 거죠?

LC

PART 3

3 남자는 여자에게 무엇을 해 달라고 요청하는가?

(A) 새 프로젝트 맡기

(B) 자문 위원 뽑기

(C) 임원 회의 참석하기

(D) 판촉 활동 보고하기

해설 | 세부 내용 - 남자의 요청 사항

남자가 여자에게 착수해 줬으면 하는 프로젝트에 대해 이야기할 수 있는지(can I talk to you about a project we'd like you to work on?) 물어본 후, 해당 프로젝트를 이끌어 줄 것(We'd like you to lead this effort)을 요청했으므로 (A)가 정답이다.

어휘 | take charge of ~를 맡다, 책임을 지다 recruit 모집하다, 뽑다 attend 참석하다 sales promotion 판촉 활동, 판촉

Paraphrasing

대화의 lead → 정답의 Take charge of

[4] W-Am / M-Cn

W I bought a chair from your store, and I was about to assemble it, but I don't think I have all of the parts I need.

M Oh, I'm sorry to hear that. Do you know what you're missing?

W Well, I have all the long bolts for the legs but none of the other bolts for the seat.

M OK, I have some replacement parts here at the store, and I can have the delivery driver drop them off at your house this afternoon.

여 제가 그쪽 가게에서 의자를 하나 사서 막 조립을 하려는데 필요한 부품이 다 있는 것 같지가 않아요.

남 아, 죄송합니다. 뭐가 빠졌는지 아세요?

여 음, 의자 다리용으로 긴 볼트는 전부 있는데 좌석용 볼트는 하나도 없어요.

남 그렇군요, 제가 여기 가게에 교체 부품을 좀 갖고 있으니까 **배달 기사를 통해 오늘 오후에 고객님 댁으로 갖다 드리겠습니다.**

4 남자는 무엇을 해 주겠다고 제안하는가?

(A) 주문 취소   (B) 기술자 고용

(C) 환불 제공   (D) 배달 조치

해설 | 세부 내용 - 남자의 제안 사항

남자의 마지막 대사에서 가게에 교체 부품이 있으니까 배달 기사를 통해 오늘 오후에 배달해 줄 수 있다(I can have the delivery driver drop them off at your house this afternoon)고 했으므로 (D)가 정답이다.

---

② 다음에 할 일 문제

공략포인트   본책 p.084

남 안녕, 캐시. 우리 오늘 밤 영화 보러 가자고 얘기했었지. 여전히 가고 싶어?

여 오, 이런, 까먹고 있었네. 미안한데, 오늘 밤엔 영화 보러 못 가. 사촌인 수잔이 뉴욕에서 비행기로 오는데 피아자로 저녁 먹으러 나갈 계획이야. 우리 집 근처에 새로 생긴 식당이야. 우리랑 같이 가지 않을래?

남 저녁 좋지! 또 네 사촌도 만나보고 싶고. 예약을 이미 해뒀어?

여 있지, 지금 당장 해야겠어. 거긴 비싼 식당은 아니지만 아주 인기 있거든.

문제 캐시는 다음에 무슨 일을 할 것인가?

(A) 수잔을 방문한다.   (B) 표를 좀 산다.

(C) 예약을 한다.   (D) 돈을 좀 구한다.

● 실전 도움닫기   본책 p.085

1 (B)   **2** (A)   **3** (B)   **4** (B)

[1] M-Am / W-Am

M Julie, when are you coming back from London?

W Well, if my meetings go really well, I could be back by next Tuesday, but I may stay through Friday. Why do you ask?

M Stephanie announced that she's moving to Boston for a new job. So I'm throwing her a party at Vega's Restaurant next Wednesday, and I was hoping you'd be able to come.

남 줄리, 런던에서 언제 돌아와요?

여 음, 회의가 아주 순조롭게 진행되면 다음 주 화요일쯤에 돌아올 수 있지만, 금요일까지 머물 수도 있어요. 그건 왜 물어요?

남 **스테파니가 새 직장때문에 보스턴으로 이사할 거라고 발표했어요. 그래서 다음 주 수요일 베가스 레스토랑에서 파티를 열어 주려고 하는데 당신도 오셨으면 해서요.**

1 다음 주 수요일에 무슨 일이 있겠는가?

(A) 고객과의 저녁 식사

(B) 직장 동료를 위한 송별회

(C) 신입 사원들을 위한 환영회

(D) 몇몇 친구들과의 점심 식사

해설 | 세부 내용 - 다음 주 수요일에 있을 일
남자가 두 번째 대사에서 스테파니가 보스턴으로 이사를 갈 예정이라 그녀를 위해 다음 주 수요일에 파티를 열 것(I'm throwing her a party at Vega's Restaurant next Wednesday)이라고 했으므로 (B)가 정답이다.

어휘 | client 고객 farewell party 송별회 coworker 직장 동료 reception 리셉션, 환영회

[2] W-Am / M-Au

W Amit, a new shipment of shoes came in, so I have to put price tags on them, but I don't think we have any more.

M I'm placing a supply order this afternoon so I'll add price tags to the list. They should arrive by tomorrow.

여 아미트, 새 신발 화물이 들어왔어요. 그래서 가격표를 붙여야 하는데 더 이상 없는 것 같아요.

남 오늘 오후에 용품을 주문할 예정이니 목록에 가격표를 추가할게요. 내일까지 도착할 겁니다.

어휘 | shipment 화물, 수송품 price tag 가격표 place an order 주문을 넣다

2 남자는 오늘 오후에 무엇을 하겠다고 말하는가?
  (A) 주문 넣기   (B) 관리자 만나기
  (C) 데이터베이스 업데이트하기   (D) 고객에게 전화하기

해설 | 세부 내용 - 남자가 할 일
남자가 오늘 오후에 용품을 주문할 예정(I'm placing a supply order this afternoon)이라고 했으므로 (A)가 정답이다.

어휘 | supervisor 관리자, 감독관

[3] W-Am / M-Cn

W Langfield Museum of Art. This is Karima speaking. How can I help you?

M Hi, I heard that the museum will be undergoing renovations in March. Will it still be open for visitors?

W The museum will be closed for the entire month, but the outdoor garden will still be open.

여 랭필드 미술관입니다. 저는 카리마라고 합니다. 무엇을 도와드릴까요?

남 안녕하세요, 미술관이 3월에 보수 공사를 할 거라고 들었습니다. 그래도 방문객들에게는 개방되나요?

여 미술관은 한 달 내내 문을 닫지만, 야외 정원은 개방될 겁니다.

어휘 | undergo (변화 등을) 겪다, 받다 renovation 보수 (공사)

3 3월에 어떤 일이 일어나겠는가?
  (A) 제품이 할인될 것이다.
  (B) 보수 공사로 건물이 폐쇄될 것이다.

  (C) 마케팅 캠페인이 시작될 것이다.
  (D) 학생들을 위한 교육 강좌가 열릴 것이다.

해설 | 세부 내용 - 3월에 있을 일
남자가 첫 번째 대사에서 3월에 있을 미술관 보수 공사(the museum will be undergoing renovations in March)를 언급했고, 여자가 두 번째 대사에서 미술관은 한 달 내내 문을 닫는다(The museum will be closed for the entire month)고 했으므로, (B)가 정답이다.

[4] W-Am / M-Au

W Excuse me, I'm planning to paint the walls of my kitchen white, but there are so many different paint types that I'm not sure which one to buy.

M Well, I'd suggest getting a high gloss paint, since it's going to be in your kitchen and it's easier to wash.

W Great—thanks! I'll need two cans of that, then. Also, can you show me where the paintbrushes are?

M Sure—those are in aisle ten. Let me take you there.

여 실례합니다, 주방 벽을 흰색으로 칠하려고 하는데 페인트 종류가 너무 많아서 어떤 걸 사야 할지 잘 모르겠어요.

남 음, 고광택 페인트를 추천해 드려요. 왜냐하면 주방용이고 또 씻어 내기도 더 쉽거든요.

여 좋네요, 고맙습니다! 그럼 그걸로 두 통 할게요. 또, 페인트 붓은 어디 있는지 알려주실래요?

남 네, 그건 10번 통로에 있어요. 제가 거기로 안내해 드릴게요.

어휘 | gloss 광택 aisle 통로

4 화자들은 다음에 무엇을 하겠는가?
  (A) 구매 주문을 검토한다.
  (B) 상점 내 다른 곳으로 간다.
  (C) 전문 페인트공 채용을 논의한다.
  (D) 상품을 시험 삼아 써 본다.

해설 | 세부 내용 - 화자들의 다음 행동
남자가 마지막 대사에서 여자가 찾는 페인트 붓이 10번 통로에 있다며 거기로 안내해 주겠다(Let me take you there)고 했으므로 (B)가 정답이다.

● ETS 실전문제
본책 p.086

1 (B)	**2** (D)	**3** (A)	**4** (B)	**5** (A)	**6** (C)
7 (B)	**8** (D)	**9** (D)	**10** (A)	**11** (D)	**12** (A)
13 (D)	**14** (B)	**15** (A)	**16** (D)	**17** (A)	**18** (B)
19 (B)	**20** (C)	**21** (A)	**22** (A)	**23** (D)	**24** (C)

> **M** Excuse me; I just bought a ticket for the eleven o'clock train to Chicago. ¹But my ticket doesn't show the platform number. ¹/²How will I know where to go?
>
> **W** ²You can just check the platform number on the display monitor. But it won't be posted until about fifteen minutes before the train is ready to leave.
>
> **M** Oh, OK. ³I guess I still have time to go get a cup of coffee before then.
>
> **W** Sure, our food court is right across from the waiting room. And actually, there's a display board over there as well.
>
> 남 실례합니다. 11시 시카고행 기차표를 샀는데요. ¹제 표에는 승강장 번호가 안 나와 있네요. ¹/²어디로 가야 하는지 어떻게 알 수 있죠?
>
> 여 ²전광판에서 승강장 번호를 확인하실 수 있습니다. 하지만 기차 출발 15분 전이나 되어야 표시될 거예요.
>
> 남 아, 알겠습니다. ³그 전에 커피 한 잔 마실 시간은 있을 것 같네요.
>
> 여 물론이죠. 저희 푸드코트가 대합실 바로 맞은편에 있어요. 사실 거기에도 전광판이 있어요.
>
> ---
>
> 어휘 | platform 승강장 display monitor 전광판 actually 사실 as well ~도, 또한

1 남자는 무엇을 알고 싶어하는가?
(A) 도착 시간　　　　(B) 탑승 장소
(C) 만료일자　　　　(D) 왕복 요금

해설 | **세부 내용 - 남자의 문의 사항**
남자가 첫 번째 대사에서 자신의 표에는 승강장 번호가 안 나와 있다(my ticket doesn't show the platform number)며 어떻게 알 수 있는지(How will I know where to go?) 문의했으므로, 탑승 장소를 알고 싶어 한다는 것을 알 수 있다. 따라서 (B)가 정답이다.

어휘 | arrival 도착 boarding 승차, 탑승 expiration 만료 round-trip 왕복 여행

2 여자는 남자에게 무엇을 하라고 권하는가?
(A) 안내 서비스에 전화하기
(B) 승무원과 이야기하기
(C) 표 영수증 모으기
(D) 전광판 확인하기

해설 | **세부 내용 - 여자의 제안 사항**
남자가 첫 번째 대사에서 어디로 가야 하는지 알 수 있는 방법(How will I know where to go?)을 문의했는데, 이에 대해 여자가 전광판에서 승강장 번호를 확인할 수 있다(You can just check the platform number on the display monitor)고 응답했으므로 (D)가 정답이다.

어휘 | conductor 승무원, 여행 안내원 receipt 영수증

3 남자는 다음으로 무엇을 하겠는가?
(A) 마실 것 사기　　　　(B) 매표기 이용하기
(C) 문자 메시지 보내기　　(D) 시간표 가져가기

해설 | **세부 내용 - 남자가 다음에 할 일**
남자가 마지막 대사에서 탑승 전에 커피 한 잔 마실 시간은 있을 것(I still have time to go get a cup of coffee before then) 같다고 했으므로 (A)가 정답이다.

Paraphrasing
대화의 go get a cup of coffee → 정답의 Buy something to drink

> **M** ⁴We're so glad you'll be joining the institute's staff of research scientists, Dr. Spencer. This laboratory on the right will be yours — here's the key. It's right next to the equipment storage room.
>
> **W** Thank you. Does this key open the storage room, too?
>
> **M** Actually, ⁵I'll have to ask the security office to have a storage room key made for you, but I'll need a copy of your company identification card to show them. ⁶Do you have your card yet?
>
> **W** No, but ⁶I have an appointment this afternoon to get one.
>
> 남 ⁴스펜서 박사님, 박사님께서 연구소의 연구원으로 합류하신다니 아주 기쁩니다. 오른쪽에 있는 실험실이 박사님이 쓰실 곳이고 여기 열쇠가 있습니다. 장비 창고 바로 옆입니다.
>
> 여 감사합니다. 이 열쇠로 창고도 열 수 있나요?
>
> 남 실은 ⁵박사님께서 사용하실 창고 열쇠를 경비실에 요청해야 하는데, 그들에게 보여줄 박사님의 사원증 복사본이 필요합니다. ⁶사원증은 이미 갖고 계신가요?
>
> 여 아니요, 하지만 ⁶오늘 오후에 수령할 예정이에요.
>
> ---
>
> 어휘 | institute 협회, 연구소 research scientist 연구원 laboratory 실험실 equipment 장비 storage room 창고 identification card 신분증

4 화자들은 어디에서 근무할 것 같은가?
(A) 의료용품점　　　　(B) 연구소
(C) 보안 회사　　　　(D) 지역 병원

해설 | **전체 내용 - 근무 장소**
남자가 첫 대사에서 여자가 연구소의 연구원으로 합류하는 것을 기쁘게 생각한다(We're so glad you'll be joining the institute's staff of research scientists, Dr. Spencer)고 했으므로 (B)가 정답이다.

5 남자는 무엇을 여자에게 주라고 경비실에 요청할 것인가?
(A) 창고 열쇠　　　　(B) 주차증
(C) 건물 견학　　　　(D) 안전 절차 목록

해설 | **세부 내용 - 남자가 요청할 것**
남자가 두 번째 대사에서 경비실에 여자가 쓸 창고 열쇠를 요청할 것(I'll have to ask the security office to have a storage room key made for you)이라고 했으므로 (A)가 정답이다.

6 여자는 오후에 무엇을 할 것이라고 말하는가?

(A) 보고서 복사하기   (B) 실험 수행하기

(C) 신분증 수령하기   (D) 업무용품 가지러 가기

해설 | 세부 내용 - 여자가 오후에 할 일

남자가 두 번째 대사에서 여자에게 사원증을 갖고 있는지(Do you have your card yet?)를 물었을 때, 여자는 아직 없지만 오늘 오후에 수령할 예정(I have an appointment this afternoon to get one)이라고 했으므로 (C)가 정답이다.

[7-9] W-Br / M-Au

> **W** Hello, Selwin Office Manufacturers. You've reached customer service. How may I help you today?
>
> **M** Yes, hello. I recently bought a used Selwin 6 label maker. The person I got it from no longer had the instructions, though, and I'm not sure how the machine works.
>
> **W** [7]Unfortunately, that's an earlier model that we no longer produce.
>
> **M** Oh, no. That's a problem.
>
> **W** No, it's OK, because the Selwin 10 has a similar design, and the instructions should be nearly the same.
>
> **M** Great! [8]Could you send me the instructions? My address is...
>
> **W** Actually, the manual for Selwin 10 is on our Web site. [9]I can send you the link so you can download it.

여 안녕하세요, 셀윈 오피스 제조사입니다. 귀하께서는 고객서비스로 연락하셨습니다. 오늘 어떻게 도와드릴까요?

남 네, 안녕하세요. 제가 최근에 중고로 셀윈 6 라벨 제조기를 샀습니다. 그런데 제게 물건을 판매한 분이 더 이상 설명서를 갖고 있지 않아서 기계 작동법을 잘 모르겠습니다.

여 [7]유감스럽게도, 그 제품은 저희가 더 이상 생산하지 않는 초기 모델입니다.

남 아, 이런. 문제네요.

여 아니요, 괜찮습니다. 셀윈 10이 비슷한 디자인이라서 설명서가 거의 똑같을 겁니다.

남 다행이네요! [8]제게 설명서를 보내 주실 수 있나요? 제 주소는...

여 사실 셀윈 10 매뉴얼은 저희 웹사이트에 있습니다. [9]고객님께서 설명서를 다운로드받으실 수 있게 제가 링크를 보내 드리겠습니다.

어휘 | used 중고의 instructions 설명서 though (문장 중간이나 끝에서) 그렇지만 work 작동되다 similar 유사한 nearly 거의

---

7 여자는 셀윈 6에 대해 무엇이라고 말하는가?

(A) 사용하기 쉽다.   (B) 초기 모델이다.

(C) 잘 만들어졌다.   (D) 매우 인기 있다.

해설 | 세부 내용 - 셀윈 6에 대한 여자의 언급

여자의 두 번째 대사에서 그 제품은 더 이상 생산하지 않는 초기 모델(Unfortunately, that's an earlier model that we no longer produce)이라고 했으므로 (B)가 정답이다.

---

8 남자는 무엇을 요청하는가?

(A) 보증서   (B) 상환

(C) 교체 부품   (D) 설명서

해설 | 세부 내용 - 남자의 요청 사항

남자의 세 번째 대사에서 설명서를 보내 달라(Could you send me the instructions?)고 했으므로 (D)가 정답이다.

9 여자는 무엇을 해 주겠다고 제안하는가?

(A) 비밀번호 재설정   (B) 방침 설명

(C) 주문의 일부분 확인   (D) 웹사이트 링크 제공

해설 | 세부 내용 - 여자의 제안 사항

여자가 마지막 대사에서 설명서를 다운로드받을 수 있게 링크를 보내주겠다(I can send you the link so you can download it)고 했으므로 (D)가 정답이다.

[10-12] **3인 대화** W-Am / W-Br / M-Au

> **W1** Hello, [10]I'm here to purchase the new Turbo X photo printer, but I couldn't find it on any of the shelves...
>
> **W2** Hmm, I thought we had one left, but my colleague would know—he manages the electronics section. Min-Soo, do we have a Turbo X in stock?
>
> **M** No, I sold our last one this morning.
>
> **W1** Hmm, can I order it online, then?
>
> **M** You can, but we already have an order on the way, so it'll be easier for you to pick it up here. [11]The shipment will arrive on Thursday. I can call you when it comes in.
>
> **W1** OK, that sounds good. [12]My name is Irina. Here's my business card with my number on it.

여1 안녕하세요, [10]저는 새로 나온 터보 X 사진 인화기를 사려고 왔는데요, 선반 어디에서도 찾을 수가 없네요...

여2 음, 저는 한 대 남아 있는 걸로 생각했는데요, 제 동료가 알 거예요. 그가 전자제품 쪽을 담당하고 있어서요. 민수, 우리 터보 X 재고가 있나요?

남 아니요, 오늘 아침에 마지막 남은 한 대를 팔았어요.

여1 음, 그럼 인터넷으로 주문할 수 있을까요?

남 하실 수 있어요. 그런데 저희가 이미 주문한 상태라서 여기서 받아가시는 게 더 편하실 거예요. [11]배송 상품은 목요일에 도착할 거예요. 제품이 들어오면 제가 전화 드릴 수 있고요.

여1 네, 그게 좋겠네요. [12]제 이름은 이리나예요. 여기 제 전화번호가 있는 명함을 드릴게요.

어휘 | purchase 구매하다 colleague 동료 manage 관리하다, 담당하다 shipment 배송품 business card 명함

---

10 화자들은 어떤 제품에 대해 이야기하고 있는가?

(A) 사진 인화기   (B) 헤드폰

(C) 편집 소프트웨어   (D) 잉크 카트리지

LC

PART 3

해설 | 세부 내용 - 이야기하고 있는 물건

여자 1이 첫 번째 대사에서 새로 나온 터보 X 사진 인화기를 사려고 왔는데(I'm here to purchase the new Turbo X photo printer) 찾을 수 없다(I couldn't find it)고 하자, 여자 2와 남자가 도와주고 있으므로, (A)가 정답이다.

11 남자는 무엇을 해 주겠다고 하는가?

(A) 교환 처리   (B) 다른 상점 추천

(C) 비품 보관실 확인   (D) 배송품 도착 시 전화

해설 | 세부 내용 - 남자가 자청한 일

남자가 두 번째 대사에서 배송 상품(shipment)이 들어오면 전화해 주겠다(I can call you when it comes in)고 제안했으므로, (D)가 정답이다.

Paraphrasing

대화의 comes in → 정답의 arrives

12 이리나는 남자에게 무엇을 주는가?

(A) 명함   (B) 상점 쿠폰

(C) 배송 주소   (D) 결제 정보

해설 | 세부 내용 - 이리나가 준 것

여자 1이 마지막 대사에서 자신의 이름(Irina)을 밝힌 후, 전화번호가 있는 명함(Here's my business card with my number on it)을 전달했으므로, (A)가 정답이다.

[13-15] 3인 대화 M-Cn / W-Am / W-Br

M Hi, Jee Soo. **13**We'd like to move up the press deadline for the spring catalog to the fourteenth. Do you think you'll have the pages about our Ralton furniture line ready by then?

W1 That shouldn't be a problem. I've completed most of the design work, but **14**we still need the product prices. Sasha, have you received the final product price list from marketing yet?

W2 No, not yet. It was due on Friday but I still haven't heard from anyone in marketing.

M Hmm. **15**Marlene's the head of marketing, let me call and ask her to get the listings to you so you can finish up the pages. The catalog is our top priority.

남 안녕하세요, 지수. **13**봄 카탈로그 인쇄 마감일을 14일로 당기고 싶은데요. 우리 랄튼 가구에 대한 페이지를 그때까지 준비하실 수 있을까요?

여 문제 없을 겁니다. 제가 디자인 작업은 대부분 끝냈습니다만 **14**아직도 제품 가격을 기다리고 있어요. 사샤, 마케팅부서에서 최종 제품 가격 표를 받았나요?

여2 아니요, 아직요. 기한이 금요일까지였는데 마케팅부서 직원 누구에게도 연락이 없네요.

남 음. **15**말린이 마케팅 부장이니까 제가 전화해서 페이지를 마무리 지을 수 있도록 가격표를 당신에게 주라고 할게요. 카탈로그를 제일 먼저 처리해야 해요.

어휘 | move up (일정을) 당기다 **press** 인쇄 **line** 제품군 **complete** 완성하다 **head** 책임자, 장 **listing** 명부, 일람표 **finish up** 마무리 짓다, 완전히 끝내다 **top priority** 가장 우선할 일

13 화자들은 어떤 작업을 하고 있는가?

(A) 동료 직원 교육   (B) 사무실 이전

(C) 예산 계획   (D) 카탈로그 제작

해설 | 세부 내용 - 작업 내용

남자의 첫 번째 대사에서 봄 카탈로그 인쇄 마감일을 14일로 당기고 싶다(We'd like move up the press deadline for the spring catalog to the fourteenth)고 한 후 여자들과 논의를 이어가고 있으므로 (D)가 정답이다.

14 여자들은 무엇을 기다리고 있는가?

(A) 프로젝트 제안서   (B) 가격 정보

(C) 공식 서명   (D) 몇 가지 견본품

해설 | 세부 내용 - 여자들이 기다리는 것

여자 1의 첫 번째 대사에서 아직도 제품 가격을 기다리고 있다(we still need the product prices)고 했으므로 (B)가 정답이다.

15 남자는 무엇을 하겠다고 하는가?

(A) 부서장에게 전화   (B) 조수 고용

(C) 발표   (D) 일정 업데이트

해설 | 세부 내용 - 남자의 할 일

남자의 마지막 대사에서 말린이 마케팅 부장이니까 전화해서 물어보겠다(Marlene's the head of marketing, let me call and ask her)고 했으므로 (A)가 정답이다.

[16-18] M-Cn / W-Br

M Barbara, um… do you have a second? **16**I've been noticing that a lot of our customers have been complaining about the long lines and wait times at the grocery checkout counters.

W Yes, a few other cashiers had also mentioned that to me. **17**I thought it over and decided that we should get a few automated checkout counters, where customers with only a few items can check out their own groceries. **17**They'll be installed next month.

M Oh, we had those machines at my previous job, and the receipts would get stuck in them a lot. **18**After they're delivered, you might want to assign someone to those checkout counters to assist customers who have problems.

남 바버라, 음… 잠시 시간 되세요? **16**많은 고객들이 식료품 계산대 줄과 대기 시간이 길다고 불만을 제기했다는 걸 알았어요.

여 네, 계산원 몇 명도 저에게 이야기했어요. 심사숙고해 봤는데, 물건이 몇 개 안 되는 고객이 자신의 물품을 스스로 계산할 수 있는 **17**자동 계산대 몇 대를 마련하기로 결정했어요. 다음 달에 설치될 겁니다.

남 아, 제 이전 직장에 그런 기계가 있었는데요. 영수증이 기계 안에서 많이 걸려요. **18**기계가 배송되면 자동 계산대에 사람을 배정해서 문제를 겪는 고객을 도와주도록 하는 게 좋을 겁니다.

어휘 | complain 불평하다 grocery 식료품 checkout counter 계산대 mention 언급하다 think over 심사숙고하다 automated 자동화된 install 설치하다 previous 이전의 get stuck in ~에 걸리다 assign 배정하다

16 남자가 여자에게 알린 것은 무엇인가?

(A) 제품 결함　　　　　(B) 안전 관련 우려 사항

(C) 청구서 오류　　　　(D) 고객 불만 사항

해설 | **세부 내용 - 남자가 여자에게 알린 것**

남자가 첫 번째 대사에서 많은 고객들이 식료품 계산대 줄과 대기 시간이 길다고 불만을 제기했다는 것(a lot of our customers have been complaining about the long lines and wait times at the grocery checkout counters)을 알게 됐다고 여자에게 말했으므로, (D)가 정답이다.

어휘 | bring A to someone's attention 누군가가 A를 알게 하다 defect 결함 concern 우려 invoice 청구서, 송장

17 다음 달에 어떤 변화가 있을 것인가?

(A) 새 장비가 설치될 것이다.

(B) 다른 공급업체를 이용할 것이다.

(C) 매장 영업시간이 연장될 것이다.

(D) 회계사가 새로 채용될 것이다.

해설 | **세부 내용 - 다음 달에 일어날 변화**

여자가 첫 번째 대사에서 자동 계산대(automated checkout counters) 몇 대를 마련하기로 했다면서 다음 달에 설치될 예정(They'll be installed next month)이라고 했으므로 (A)가 정답이다.

어휘 | take place 일어나다, 발생하다 supplier 공급업체, 공급자 extend 연장하다 accountant 회계사

Paraphrasing

대화의 automated checkout counters → 정답의 equipment

18 남자는 무엇을 제안하는가?

(A) 제품 진열 이동시키기

(B) 직원이 도울 수 있도록 하기

(C) 입구에 게시물 내걸기

(D) 가정 배달 서비스 제공하기

해설 | **세부 내용 - 남자의 제안 사항**

남자가 마지막 대사에서 자동 계산대에 사람을 배정해서 문제를 겪는 고객을 도와주도록 하는 게 좋을 것(you might want to assign someone to those checkout counters to assist customers who have problems)이라고 했으므로, (B)가 정답이다.

어휘 | available 이용 가능한 post a sign 게시물을 내붙이다 entrance 입구 provide 제공하다

Paraphrasing

대화의 assign someone ~ to assist customers
→ 정답의 Making a staff person available

[19-21] W-Br / M-Cn

W Hi, Bob. I just got the results back from the market testing on our new solar panels. **¹⁹**They were very popular with the technicians—they were very enthusiastic about how easy it was to install them.

M That's wonderful news! It was a smart idea to mount the solar panels on hinges so that they attach so easily. **²⁰**Do you think they'll be ready for us to present at the Solar Tech Trade Fair in September?

W Yes—we still have a few minor issues to fix, but I'm sure they'll be ready to introduce to the market by then. **²¹**You might want to give the fair's organizers a call right away though, to make sure we can still reserve a booth.

여 안녕하세요, 밥. 새 태양 전지판에 관한 시장성 조사 결과를 방금 받았어요. **¹⁹**기술자들에게 굉장히 인기가 많았는데요. 그들은 설치가 굉장히 쉽다는 점에 아주 열광했습니다.

남 좋은 소식이네요! 태양 전지판을 경첩 위에 설치해서 쉽게 부착되게 한 아이디어가 좋았어요. **²⁰**9월에 있을 솔라 테크 무역 박람회에서 선보일 준비가 될 것 같아요?

여 네. 아직 해결할 사소한 문제들이 좀 있지만 그때까지는 시장에 내놓을 준비가 될 겁니다. **²¹**박람회 주최측에 바로 전화해서 아직 부스를 예약할 수 있는지 알아보는 게 좋을 거예요.

어휘 | market testing 시장성 조사 solar panel 태양 전지판 technician 기술자 enthusiastic 열광적인, 열렬한 install 설치하다 mount 설치하다, 앉히다 hinge 경첩 attach 부착하다, 붙다 minor 작은, 가벼운 fix 고치다 organizer 주최자 reserve 예약하다

19 여자에 따르면 태양 전지판은 왜 인기가 많은가?

(A) 작다.　　　　　(B) 설치하기 쉽다.

(C) 멋지다.　　　　(D) 값이 싸다.

해설 | **세부 내용 - 태양 전지판이 인기 있는 이유**

여자가 첫 번째 대사에서 태양 전지판이 기술자들에게 굉장히 인기가 많았다(They were very popular with the technicians)고 한 후, 설치가 굉장히 쉽다는 점(how easy it was to install them)에 아주 열광했다고 덧붙였으므로 (B)가 정답이다.

어휘 | attractive 멋진, 매력적인 inexpensive 비싸지 않은, 값싼

20 9월에 무엇이 열리는가?

(A) 공장 견학　　　　　(B) 직원 교육

(C) 무역 박람회　　　　(D) 회사 합병

해설 | **세부 내용 - 9월에 열릴 행사**

남자가 첫 번째 대사에서 9월에 있을 솔라 테크 무역 박람회(the Solar Tech Trade Fair in September?)를 언급하고 있으므로, (C)가 정답이다.

Paraphrasing

대화의 the Solar Tech Trade Fair → 정답의 A trade show

LC

PART 3

21 남자는 다음으로 무엇을 하겠는가?

(A) 전화하기   (B) 보고서 읽기

(C) 절차 검토하기   (D) 대금 보내기

해설 | **세부 내용 - 남자가 다음에 할 일**

여자가 마지막 대사에서 남자에게 박람회 주최측에 바로
전화해서(You might want to give the fair's organizers a
call right away though) 아직 부스를 예약할 수 있는지 알아보는
게 좋을 거라고 했으므로, 남자가 이 말을 듣고 전화를 할 것임을
추론할 수 있다. 따라서 (A)가 정답이다.

어휘 | review 검토하다 procedure 절차

[22-24] W-Br / M-Am

> W ²²We haven't been happy with our current
> shipping company and are looking to find a
> new one. **That's why we asked you to come in
> today.**
>
> M ²²Well, I'll be happy to tell you about our
> services. I'm sure you'll find that our rates for
> air, ground, and sea shipments are all very
> competitive. But first, can you tell me a little
> about your needs?
>
> W ²³We manufacture construction machinery,
> like tractors and cranes, and we handle our
> own domestic deliveries—but for international
> orders we rely on an outside shipping
> company. That's what we're hoping you can do
> for us.
>
> M International deliveries are our specialty.
> ²⁴Now let's talk about your budget and typical
> delivery deadlines, and then we can start
> drafting a contract.
>
> 여 ²²저희는 현재 거래하는 운송회사가 만족스럽지 않아서 새 회사를
> 찾고 있어요. 그래서 오늘 여기 오시라고 부탁드린 거예요.
>
> 남 ²²음, 저희 서비스에 대해 말씀드릴 수 있게 되어 기쁩니다. 저희
> 항공, 육상, 해상 운송 요금이 정말 경쟁력 있다는 사실을 분명 알게
> 되실 거예요. 하지만 우선 무엇이 필요한지부터 말씀해주실 수
> 있나요?
>
> 여 ²³저희는 트랙터와 크레인 같은 건설 기계를 생산해요. 국내 운송은
> 직접 처리합니다만, 해외 발주 건에 대해서는 외부 운송회사에
> 의존하고 있어요. 그게 바로 저희가 요청 드리는 일이에요.
>
> 남 국제 운송은 저희 전문 분야죠. ²⁴이제부터 예산과 일반적인 배송
> 마감 시한에 대해 논의한 후, 계약서 초안 작성을 시작하시죠.
>
> 어휘 | shipping company 운송회사 competitive 경쟁력 있는
> manufacture 생산하다 construction machinery 건설 기계
> handle 다루다, 처리하다 domestic 국내의 specialty 전문 분야,
> 특산품 budget 예산 typical 전형적인, 일반적인 draft 초안; 초안을
> 작성하다

22 남자는 어디에서 일하는가?

(A) 운송회사   (B) 여행사

(C) 항공사   (D) 정부 기관

해설 | **전체 내용 - 남자의 근무처**

여자가 첫 번째 대사에서 현재 거래하는 운송회사가 별로 만족스럽지
않아서 새 회사를 찾는 중이라(We haven't been happy with
our current shipping company and are looking to find
a new one) 남자를 오라고 한 것이라고 했고, 이에 대해 남자가
자신의 회사 서비스(our services)를 말할 수 있어서 기쁘다고
했으므로, 남자가 운송회사에서 근무하고 있음을 알 수 있다. 따라서
(A)가 정답이다.

23 여자의 회사는 무엇을 만드는가?

(A) 화물기   (B) 외항선

(C) 포장재   (D) 건설 기계

해설 | **세부 내용 - 여자의 회사가 만드는 것**

여자의 두 번째 대사에서 트랙터와 크레인 같은 건설 기계를
생산한다(We manufacture construction machinery, like
tractors and cranes)고 했으므로 (D)가 정답이다.

24 화자들은 다음에 무엇을 할 것 같은가?

(A) 기계를 배송한다.

(B) 비행기에 탑승한다.

(C) 사업 계약서에 대해 논의한다.

(D) 건축 계획을 점검한다.

해설 | **세부 내용 - 화자들이 할 일**

남자가 마지막 대사에서 예산과 일반적인 배송 마감 시한에 대해
논의한 후 계약서 초안 작성을 시작하자(Now let's talk about
your budget and typical delivery deadlines, and then
we can start drafting a contract)고 했으므로 (C)가 정답이다.

Unit 10   의도 파악 / 시각 정보 연계 문제

① 의도 파악 문제

공략포인트

> 남 좋아요, 토레스 씨, 제게 가격 견적서가 있습니다. 울타리를 포함해 집
> 외부 전체를 칠하면 5천 달러가 들 겁니다.
>
> 여 저희 예상보다는 꽤 많이 나오네요. 그리고 사실 콜게이트 페인팅은
> 4천 달러에 그 작업을 하겠다고 했거든요…
>
> 남 음, 제가 말씀드린 견적가에는 페인트와 물품비가 포함되어 있어서
> 사실 아주 저렴하게 해 드리는 겁니다.

어휘 | price estimate 가격 견적서 exterior 외면, 외부 including
~을 포함해 fence 울타리 cost 비용이 ~이다 supplies 용품, 물품
quote A a price A에게 가격을 말하다 a good deal 유리한 거래

문제 여자가 "그리고 사실 콜게이트 페인팅은 4천 달러에 그 작업을
하겠다고 했거든요"라고 말한 의도는 무엇인가?

(A) 요청 사항을 명확하게 설명하기 위해

(B) 가격을 협상하기 위해

(C) 도움을 주기 위해

(D) 서비스를 권하기 위해

본책 p.089

1 (C) **2** (A) **3** (B) **4** (D)

---

[1] W-Am / M-Cn

> **W** Hi, Girolamo. I just got an e-mail from THY Incorporated. They're wondering when we can begin building their new headquarters. They want a start date.
>
> **M** I've been meaning to contact them, but I'm waiting to confirm some results from the soil analysis. There's a patch of ground that might be too moist and unstable to build on. Our analysts are doing a few more tests.
>
> 여 안녕하세요, 지롤라모. 제가 방금 THY 사로부터 이메일을 받았습니다. 그쪽에서 우리가 언제 자신들의 새 본사 건설을 시작할 수 있는지 궁금해하네요. 시작 날짜를 알고 싶어 해요.
>
> 남 제가 그 회사에 연락할 생각을 하고 있었는데, 몇 가지 토양 분석 결과에 대한 확인을 기다리는 중이에요. 건물을 짓기에 너무 습하고 불안정한 것 같은 구역이 있거든요. 우리 분석가들이 몇 가지 추가 검사를 하고 있는 중이에요.

어휘 | headquarters 본사 mean to ~할 셈이다 confirm 확인하다 soil 토양 analysis 분석 patch 작게 구획된 땅 ground 땅, 토양 moist 습한, 축축한 unstable 불안정한 build on ~의 위에 쌓다 analyst 분석가

1 남자가 "제가 그 회사에 연락할 생각을 하고 있었는데"라고 말한 의도는 무엇인가?
   (A) 프로젝트에 대한 논의를 기대하고 있다.
   (B) 진술을 명료히 할 필요가 있다.
   (C) 뭔가를 해야 한다는 점을 인식하고 있다.
   (D) 고객에게 연락하는 것을 잊었다.

해설 | **세부 내용 - 화자의 의도**
여자가 첫 번째 대사에서 THY 사가 건설 시작 날짜를 알고 싶어한다(They want a start date)고 하자, 이에 대해 남자가 그 회사에 연락할 생각을 하고 있었다(I've been meaning to contact them)고 한 후 연락을 미룬 이유를 덧붙였다. 이는 남자가 자신이 해야 할 일을 인식하고 있었다는 의미라고 볼 수 있으므로, (C)가 정답이다.

---

[2] M-Cn / W-Br

> **M** Hi, Gabriella. I wanted to talk to you about using the new online time reporting system… A lot of people have been asking about it.
>
> **W** Yes, well, I've been very busy. But I am planning the training session for early next week. That should make it quite clear to everyone.
>
> **M** OK.

> 남 안녕하세요, 가브리엘라. 새로 생긴 온라인 시간 보고 시스템에 대해 얘기하고 싶어요… 많은 사람들이 그것에 대해 물어보고 있거든요.
>
> 여 네, 음, 제가 아주 바빴어요. 하지만 다음 주 초에 직원 교육을 계획하고 있어요. 그럼 모든 사람이 명확하게 알 수 있을 겁니다.
>
> 남 좋아요.

어휘 | training session 교육 (과정) clear 명료한

2 남자가 "많은 사람들이 그것에 대해 물어보고 있거든요"라고 말한 의도는 무엇인가?
   (A) 직원들이 절차에 대해 혼란스러워 한다.
   (B) 사람들이 워크숍이 흥미롭다는 얘기를 들었다.
   (C) 직원들이 새로운 업무를 기다리고 있다.
   (D) 휴가 일정표가 아직 게시되지 않았다.

해설 | **세부 내용 - 화자의 의도**
남자가 첫 번째 대사에서 새로 생긴 온라인 시간 보고 시스템에 대해 얘기하고 싶다며 많은 사람들이 문의하고 있다(A lot of people have been asking about it)고 했다. 이에 여자가 직원 교육(training session)을 계획하고 있다고 답했으므로, 많은 직원들이 새 시스템에 대해 잘 모른다는 의미임을 알 수 있다. 따라서 (A)가 정답이다.

---

[3] M-Cn / W-Br

> **M** Hi, Elaine. It's almost twelve-thirty. I'm on my way to lunch with Sam if you'd like to come with us.
>
> **W** I have three payroll checks left to process.
>
> **M** Oh, OK. I'll see you at the department meeting this afternoon then.

> 남 안녕하세요, 일레인. 거의 12시 30분이네요. 샘하고 점심 먹으러 가는 길인데, 당신도 같이 갈래요?
>
> 여 처리해야 할 급여 명세서 세 건이 남아 있어요.
>
> 남 아, 알았어요. 그럼 오후에 부서 회의 때 봐요.

어휘 | payroll check 급여 명세서 process 처리하다

3 여자가 "처리해야 할 급여 명세서 세 건이 남아 있어요"라고 말하는 이유는 무엇인가?
   (A) 어떤 소프트웨어에 대해 불평하려고
   (B) 초대를 거절하려고
   (C) 자원봉사자를 요청하려고
   (D) 동료를 안심시키려고

해설 | **세부 내용 - 화자의 의도**
남자가 첫 번째 대사에서 점심 먹으러 같이 갈 것(I'm on my way to lunch with Sam if you'd like to come with us)을 제안했는데, 여자가 '처리해야 할 급여 명세서 세 건이 남아 있어요(I have three payroll checks left to process)'라고 응답했다. 이에 남자가 '그럼 부서 회의 때 봐요'라고 했으므로, 여자가 점심 초대를 거절한 것임을 알 수 있다. 따라서 (B)가 정답이다.

W Fred, the Regional Library Association is running a workshop in town called Managing Digital Content. It looks useful. I think our library's whole staff should attend, don't you?

M Oh, I've already inquired about that workshop. Uh… Most of the content will be rather technical.

W I see. OK. Then I should have only the data management team attend?

M That sounds like a much better plan.

여 프레드, 지역 도서관 협회가 우리 시에서 '디지털 콘텐츠 관리'라는 워크숍을 운영하는데요. 유용할 것 같아요. **우리 도서관의 모든 직원들이 참석해야겠죠?**

남 제가 그 워크숍에 대해 이미 물어봤어요. 음 … **내용 대부분이 다소 기술적이에요.**

여 그렇군요. 그러면 데이터 관리팀만 참석하도록 해야겠군요?

남 그게 훨씬 더 나은 계획 같아요.

어휘 | regional 지역의 association 협회 run 운영하다 manage 관리하다 content 내용, 주제 attend 참석하다 inquire 묻다 rather 약간, 다소 technical 기술적인 management 관리

4 남자가 "내용 대부분이 다소 기술적이에요"라고 말한 의도는 무엇인가?
(A) 워크숍의 내용을 수정하기를 원한다.
(B) 워크숍 참석을 고대한다.
(C) 워크숍 발표가 쉽지 않을 거라 생각한다.
(D) 워크숍이 모든 직원에게 유익하지 않을지도 모른다고 생각한다.

해설 | **세부 내용 - 화자의 의도**
여자가 첫 번째 대사에서 직원 전체가 워크숍에 참석해야 한다고 하자 남자가 내용 대부분이 기술적이라고 했고, 이에 여자가 데이터 관리팀만 참석시키겠다고 하자 적극 동의했다. 즉, 남자는 워크숍이 모든 직원에게 유용하지는 않을거라 생각한 것이므로, (D)가 정답이다.

어휘 | revise 수정하다 look forward to -ing ~하기를 고대하다 present 발표하다 challenging 도전적인 benefit 유익하다

② 시각 정보 연계 문제

공략포인트

본책 p.090

남 안녕하세요, 오늘 할 배달은 거의 끝냈는데 코튼 인더스트리스로 나갈 배달에 문제가 있습니다. 제가 그 회사 건물 앞에 있는데 도로가 혼잡해서 짐을 내릴 동안 주차할 만한 곳을 못 찾겠어요.

여 미안해요. 코튼 인더스트리스는 처음 거래하는 고객사라서 제가 배달 일정표에 주차 정보를 써 놓았어야 했는데요. 그 회사는 건물 뒤에 주차장이 있어요.

남 알겠습니다, 지금 거기로 갈게요.

어휘 | have trouble with ~에 어려움이 있다, 문제가 있다 office building 사무실[회사] 건물 unload 짐을 내리다 should have + p.p. ~을 했어야 했다

오늘의 배달 토탈리 제과점	
고객	주소
마틴스 슈퍼마켓	펜가 1700번지
코튼 인더스트리스	던바 가 270번지
패스트 숍 편의점	포브스 가 43번지

문제 시각 정보에 따르면, 남자는 어느 거리에 있는가?
(A) 토탈리   (B) 펜
(C) 던바   (D) 포브스

● 실전 도움닫기

본책 p.091

1 (C) **2** (A) **3** (D)

W Hi, Barry. I'm just checking in. How's everything going up here? Are you finished cleaning the Romano Construction offices yet?

M No, it's taking longer than expected. I vacuumed the carpet, but there are a lot of stains. So I decided to shampoo it. But then I had to go down and get the steam-cleaning machine and bring it up here.

W Well, before you start shampooing, could you come downstairs? I need some help moving a big table in one of the conference rooms.

여 안녕하세요, 배리. 제가 점검하고 있는데요. 여기 위층은 전체적으로 어떻게 진행되고 있나요? **로마노 건설 사무실 청소는 다 끝내셨어요?**

남 **아니요, 예상보다 더 걸리네요.** 카펫을 진공청소기로 밀었는데도 얼룩이 많이 남아 있네요. 그래서 세제로 닦아 보기로 했죠. 하지만 또 아래층으로 내려가서 증기 청소기를 가지고 여기로 올라와야 했거든요.

여 음, 세제로 닦기 전에 아래층으로 내려와 주실래요? 회의실 한 곳에 있는 대형 테이블을 옮기는 데 도움이 필요해서요.

어휘 | construction 건설, 공사 take longer than expected 예상보다 시간이 더 걸리다 vacuum ~을 진공 청소기로 청소하다 stain 얼룩, 자국 shampoo 세제로 청소하다 steam-cleaning machine 증기 청소기

사무실 안내판

1층: HLT 컴퍼니
2층: 노블 주식회사
3층: 로마노 건설
4층: 그레이턴 앤 선즈

1 시각 정보에 따르면, 남자는 현재 어디에서 일하고 있는가?

(A) 1층   (B) 2층

(C) 3층   (D) 4층

해설 | **세부 내용 - 시각 정보 연계**

여자가 첫 번째 대사에서 남자에게 로마노 건설 사무실 청소를 다 끝냈는지 물어봤고, 이에 대해 남자가 아니라고 하면서 예상보다 시간이 더 걸린다(No, it's taking longer than expected)고 했다. 사무실 안내판을 보면 로마노 건설은 3층에 있으므로 (C)가 정답이다.

---

[2] 대화 + 카탈로그 W-Am / M-Cn

> **W** Based on the eye exam I just conducted, your vision hasn't changed since last time, Mr. Mukherjee. So you can keep using the glasses you have now.
>
> **M** Great. But… I don't like my old frames anymore, so I was planning to order some new ones.
>
> **W** OK. You can see our selection of frames in this catalog.
>
> **M** Hmm… I like the ones with the small round lenses. Eighty dollars isn't too much to spend. I'll get those.
>
> **여** 제가 방금 해 드린 시력 검사에 따르면 무커지 씨의 시력은 지난번과 달라지지 않았습니다. 그래서 지금 갖고 계신 안경을 계속 쓰셔도 됩니다.
>
> **남** 잘 됐네요. 그런데 예전 안경테가 더 이상 마음에 들지 않아서 새 것으로 주문할 계획이었어요.
>
> **여** 알겠습니다. 이 카탈로그에서 저희 안경테들을 보실 수 있어요.
>
> **남** 음… 작고 둥근 렌즈가 있는 안경테가 좋아요. 80달러면 그리 비싸진 않네요. 그걸로 할게요.

어휘 | based on ~에 근거하여 eye exam 시력 검사 conduct (수행)하다 selection (선택 가능한 것들의) 집합

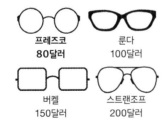

프레즈코 **80달러**

룬다 100달러

버켈 150달러

스트랜조프 200달러

2 시각 정보에 따르면, 남자는 어떤 안경테 모델을 구입할 것인가?

(A) 프레즈코   (B) 룬다

(C) 버켈   (D) 스트랜조프

해설 | **세부 내용 - 시각 정보 연계**

남자가 마지막 대사에서 작고 둥근 렌즈가 있는 안경테가 좋다(I like the ones with the small round lenses)고 한 후, 80달러면 그리 비싸진 않다(Eighty dollars isn't too much to spend)며 구매 의사를 밝혔다. 시각 정보에서 남자의 조건을 충족하는 안경테는 프레즈코(Prezko)이므로, (A)가 정답이다.

---

[3] 대화 + 메뉴 M-Au / W-Am

> **M** Hi, I'm calling to get some information about having an event catered at my company.
>
> **W** Sure. I'll need to know how many people you're expecting and what your budget is.
>
> **M** It's a retirement party for one of our directors. There'll be about thirty people, and we're on a budget of no more than $500.
>
> **W** We do have a package that fits your requirements. On our Web site, if you click on the Options tab, you can see the various menus there.
>
> **남** 안녕하세요, 저희 회사 행사 때 출장 요리를 이용하고 싶은데 몇 가지 알고 싶어 전화 드립니다.
>
> **여** 네. 예상 인원과 예산은 어떻게 되는지 알아야 합니다.
>
> **남** 이사님 한 분의 퇴직 송별회예요. 대략 30명 정도이고, 예산은 500달러 안쪽입니다.
>
> **여** 말씀하신 조건에 맞는 패키지가 있습니다. 저희 웹사이트 상에서 선택 항목 탭을 클릭하면 거기서 다양한 메뉴를 보실 수 있습니다.

어휘 | cater 음식을 제공하다 director 이사 be on a budget of 예산이 ~이다 requirement 요구 사항, 필요 조건

선택 사항	
해산물 모둠 요리	900달러
쇠고기 모둠 요리	750달러
닭고기 모둠 요리	600달러
채식 모둠 요리	450달러

3 시각 정보에 따르면, 남자는 어떤 선택 사항을 고르겠는가?

(A) 해산물 모둠 요리

(B) 쇠고기 모둠 요리

(C) 닭고기 모둠 요리

(D) 채식 모둠 요리

해설 | **세부 내용 - 시각 정보 연계**

남자의 두 번째 대사에서 예산은 500달러 안쪽 (we're on a budget of no more than $500)이라고 했는데, 표를 보면 채식 모둠 요리(Vegetarian platter)가 450달러이므로 (D)가 정답이다.

어휘 | platter 모둠 요리 vegetarian 채식주의자

● ETS 실전문제

본책 p.092

1 (A)	2 (B)	3 (D)	4 (C)	5 (D)	6 (C)
7 (C)	8 (A)	9 (B)	10 (C)	11 (A)	12 (C)
13 (B)	14 (B)	15 (D)	16 (A)	17 (C)	18 (D)
19 (C)	20 (A)	21 (B)	22 (B)	23 (C)	24 (D)

LC

PART 3

M Hello, thank you for calling Gatewater Architecture. This is Jung-Soo.

W Hi, I'm Amal Osman. [1]I work for *Business Mentor Magazine*. I'm writing an article about the top architecture firms in the city, and I'd like to interview the president of your company, Mr. Garcia.

M Well, [2]he has a very full schedule, but I could see if one of our department managers can speak with you for the article.

W I just have a few questions, and [2]Mr. Garcia's answers will really interest readers.

M Uhm… [2/3]why don't you call back tomorrow after I've spoken with Mr. Garcia. [2]He may have a few minutes available for a phone interview.

남 안녕하세요, 게이트워터 건축 사무소에 전화 주셔서 감사합니다. 저는 정수라고 합니다.

여 안녕하세요, 저는 아말 오스먼이라고 합니다. [1]저는 <비즈니스 멘토 매거진>에서 일하고 있습니다. 제가 우리 시 최고의 건축 설계 회사들에 관한 기사를 쓰고 있는데, 귀사의 사장님이신 가르시아 씨를 인터뷰하고 싶습니다.

남 글쎄요, [2]사장님은 일정이 꽉 차 있으셔서요, 부서장들 중 한 분이 기사를 위해 당신과 인터뷰할 수 있는지 알아봐 드릴 수는 있습니다.

여 [2]저는 몇 가지 질문만 드릴 겁니다. [2]독자분들은 가르시아 씨의 답변에 많은 관심을 가질 거예요.

남 음… [2/3]제가 가르시아 씨께 말씀드려 볼 테니 내일 다시 전화 주시는 게 어떠세요? [2]아마 몇 분 정도 전화로 인터뷰할 시간은 내실 수 있을 거예요.

어휘 | article 기사 architecture 건축 available 시간이 있는

1 여자는 누구이겠는가?
(A) 기자　　　　　(B) 광고주
(C) 출판인　　　　(D) 회계사

해설 | 전체 내용 - 여자의 신분
여자가 첫 번째 대사에서 <비즈니스 멘토 매거진>에서 일하고 있다 (I work for *Business Mentor Magazine*)고 한 후, 시의 최고 건축 설계 회사들에 관한 기사를 쓰고 있다(I'm writing an article about the top architecture firms in the city)고 했으므로, (A)가 정답이다.

2 여자가 "저는 몇 가지 질문만 드릴 겁니다"라고 말한 의도는 무엇인가?
(A) 과제에 대해 확신이 없다.
(B) 많은 시간이 필요하지 않다.
(C) 지체되는 이유를 설명할 수 없다.
(D) 어떤 설명이 명확하다고 생각한다.

해설 | 세부 내용 - 화자의 의도
남자가 두 번째 대사에서 사장님은 일정이 꽉 차 있어서(he has a very full schedule), 부서장이 인터뷰할 수 있는지 알아봐 주겠다고 제안했는데, 이에 대해 여자가 '저는 몇 가지 질문만 드릴

겁니다(I just have a few questions)'라고 응답한 후, 독자들이 많은 관심을 가질 것(Mr. Garcia's answers will really interest readers)이라고 부연 설명을 했다. 그러자 남자는 마지막 대사에서 가르시아 씨가 몇 분 정도는 시간을 낼 수 있을 것 같다고 답했다. 이를 통해 여자가 인터뷰에 많은 시간이 필요하지 않다는 점을 강조하려고 한 말임을 알 수 있으므로, (B)가 정답이다.

3 남자는 여자에게 무엇을 하라고 제안하는가?
(A) 대회에 참석하라고
(B) 양식에 서명하라고
(C) 다시 이메일을 보내라고
(D) 나중에 다시 전화하라고

해설 | 세부 내용 - 남자의 제안 사항
남자가 마지막 대사에서 내일 다시 전화 줄 것(why don't you call back tomorrow)을 제안했으므로, (D)가 정답이다.

Paraphrasing
대화의 call back tomorrow → 정답의 Call again later

M1 Hello. [4]Can I mail a package to Portugal here?

W I'm sorry, but this counter is for domestic services only.

M1 Oh, OK. So I should go…

M2 I can help you over here.

M1 Yes, hello. I'd like to mail this package.

M2 Of course. Would you like to send it by priority mail or regular mail? [5]Priority mail takes less time, but it costs more.

M1 [5]I'd prefer priority mail since I want it to get to Lisbon by Friday. [6]Is there a free tracking service so I can track my package in the delivery process?

M2 Unfortunately, no. [6]We do, however, offer package delivery notification for an additional fee.

남1 안녕하세요. [4]여기서 포르투갈로 소포를 부칠 수 있나요?

여 죄송합니다만, 이 창구는 국내 우편 전용입니다.

남1 아, 네. 그럼 제가 가야 할 곳은…

남2 이쪽에서 도와드리겠습니다.

남1 네, 안녕하세요. 이 소포를 부치고 싶습니다.

남2 알겠습니다. 빠른 우편으로 보내시겠습니까, 보통 우편으로 보내시겠습니까? [5]빠른 우편은 시간은 적게 걸리지만 요금이 더 비쌉니다.

남1 [5]금요일까지 리스본에 도착해야 하니까 빠른 우편으로 하겠어요. [6]배송 과정에서 제 소포를 추적할 수 있는 무료 추적 서비스가 있나요?

남2 안타깝지만, 없습니다. [6]하지만 추가 수수료를 내시면 소포 배송 완료 알림을 보내 드립니다.

어휘 | package 소포 domestic 국내의 priority mail 빠른 우편 regular mail 보통 우편 track 추적하다 notification 알림, 통지 additional fee 추가 수수료

4 여자가 "이 창구는 국내 우편 전용입니다"라고 말하는 이유는 무엇인가?

(A) 규칙을 비판하기 위해
(B) 혼동을 표현하기 위해
(C) 요청을 거절하기 위해
(D) 사실을 검증하기 위해

해설 | **세부 내용 - 화자의 의도**
포르투갈로 소포를 부칠 수 있는지(Can I mail a package to Portugal here?)를 묻는 남자 1의 질문에 국내 전용 창구라고 답하는 것은 포르투갈로 소포를 부칠 수 없다는 것이다. 따라서 (C)가 정답이다.

어휘 | criticize 비판하다 confusion 혼동 verify 검증하다

5 고객은 무엇을 하기로 결정하는가?

(A) 배송을 취소한다.
(B) 제품을 교환한다.
(C) 특별 포장재를 구매한다.
(D) 더 빠른 배송을 위한 요금을 지불한다.

해설 | **세부 내용 - 고객의 결정 사항**
빠른 우편이 시간은 적게 걸리지만 요금이 더 비싸다(Priority mail takes less time, but it costs more)는 직원의 말에 고객은 금요일까지 리스본에 도착해야 하니까 빠른 우편으로 하겠다(I'd prefer priority mail since I want it to get to Lisbon by Friday)고 했다. 따라서 (D)가 정답이다.

어휘 | cancel 취소하다 shipment 배송, 배송품 packaging 포장재

6 고객은 무엇을 위해 추가 수수료를 내겠는가?

(A) 파손 보험   (B) 익일 배송
(C) 배송 확인   (D) 규격 초과 소포

해설 | **세부 내용 - 추가 수수료를 지불하는 이유**
배송 과정에서 소포를 추적할 수 있는 무료 추적 서비스가 있는지(Is there a free tracking service so I can track my package in the delivery process?)를 묻는 말에 추가 수수료를 내면 소포 배송 완료 알림을 보내 준다(We do, however, offer package delivery notification for an additional fee)고 했다. 따라서 (C)가 정답이다.

어휘 | damage 손상 insurance 보험 overnight shipping 익일 배송 confirmation 확인 oversized 규격이 초과된 parcel 소포

[7-9] M-Cn / W-Br

M ⁷Nehal, how was Vancouver?

W Relaxing, thanks. ⁷Nice to do some sightseeing and take a break from work. Uh, how were things while I was away? How's the search for a new engineer going?

M I think we've found our person. I left you the paperwork here on your desk.

W Is this César Villa's résumé? ⁸He's a friend of mine. You're telling me he's applied for this job?

M That's who I was referring to. He really impressed everyone.

W I'm glad to hear that. ⁹I've known César since college. We had classes together. I've run into him over the years at conventions, but I had no idea he was applying for a job here.

남 ⁷네할, 밴쿠버는 어땠어요?
여 느긋하게 보냈어요, 고마워요. ⁷관광도 좀 하고 일에서 벗어나 휴식을 취할 수 있어 좋았어요. 참, 제가 없는 동안 별일 없었나요? 새 엔지니어를 찾는 일은 어떻게 진행되고 있나요?
남 적임자를 찾은 것 같아요. 여기 당신 책상 위에 서류를 올려놓았어요.
여 이거 세자 비야의 이력서인가요? ⁸그는 제 친구예요. 그가 이 자리에 지원했다고요?
남 그 사람이 제가 말했던 사람이에요. 그는 정말 모든 사람들에게 깊은 인상을 남겼어요.
여 다행이네요. ⁹저는 대학 때부터 세자를 알고 지냈어요. 수업도 같이 들었고요. 수년간 컨벤션에서 우연히 마주치곤 했지만 그가 여기에 지원할 거라는 생각은 전혀 못했어요.

어휘 | relaxing 편안한, 느긋한 take a break 쉬다 search 물색, 찾기 paperwork 서류 apply for 지원하다 refer to 언급하다, 가리키다 impress 깊은 인상을 주다 run into 우연히 마주치다 convention 대회

7 여자는 밴쿠버에서 무엇을 하고 있었는가?

(A) 구직자 면접   (B) 신규 고객 만나기
(C) 휴가 보내기   (D) 수업하기

해설 | **세부 내용 - 밴쿠버에서 여자가 한 일**
남자의 첫 번째 대사에서 밴쿠버가 어땠냐(Nehal, how was Vancouver?)고 묻자, 여자가 관광도 좀 하고 일에서 벗어나 휴식을 취할 수 있어 좋았다(Nice to do some sightseeing and take a break from work)고 했으므로 (C)가 정답이다.

어휘 | candidate 지원자, 후보자

8 여자가 "이거 세자 비야의 이력서인가요"라고 말한 의도는 무엇인가?

(A) 서류를 보고 놀랐다.
(B) 지원자를 추천하고 있다.
(C) 보안을 걱정하고 있다.
(D) 몇몇 글씨를 읽지 못한다.

해설 | **세부 내용 - 화자의 의도**
여자의 두 번째 대사에서 세자 비야가 자신의 친구(He's a friend of mine)라고 하면서 그가 입사 지원을 한거냐고(You're telling me he's applied for this job?) 물었다. 즉, 여자는 자신의 친구인 세자 비야의 이력서를 보고 놀라서 이렇게 반응한 것이므로 (A)가 정답이다.

9 여자는 세자 비야를 어떻게 아는가?

(A) 이웃이었다.   (B) 같은 대학에 다녔다.
(C) 같이 회의를 준비했다.   (D) 같은 회사에서 일했다.

해설 | **세부 내용 - 여자가 세자 비야를 알게 된 계기**
대화 마지막에 여자가 대학 때부터 세자를 알고 지냈다(I've known César since college)고 했으며, 수업도 같이 들었다(We had classes together)고 했으므로 (B)가 정답이다.

W **¹⁰**Thanks again for coming to look at the water damage to the floor in our office. **Can it be repaired, or do I need a new floor?**

M I'm sorry to tell you that the damage is too extensive. **¹¹**The whole floor will have to be replaced.

W Hmm… I have some important clients coming here next week.

M Oh, we can have it done by the end of this week. It'll take three days at the most.

W That's great. **¹²**Can you give me an estimate for what it'll cost?

M If you choose the same kind of flooring you have now, it'll probably be about 5,000 dollars.

여 **¹⁰**저희 사무실 바닥 누수 피해를 봐 주러 오신 것 다시 한 번 감사드립니다. 수리가 될까요, 아니면 새 바닥이 필요한가요?

남 손상 부분이 너무 광범위하다는 말씀을 드리게 되어 유감입니다. **¹¹**바닥 전체를 교체해야 할 겁니다.

여 음… 다음 주에 중요한 고객들이 오시는데요.

남 아, 이번 주말까지는 완료해 드릴 수 있습니다. 길어도 사흘 걸립니다.

여 좋아요. **¹²**비용이 얼마나 들지 견적서를 주실 수 있나요?

남 지금과 같은 바닥재를 선택하시면 5천 달러 정도 들 겁니다.

어휘 | repair 수리하다 extensive 광범위한, 매우 넓은 replace 교체하다 at the most 많아봐야, 기껏해야 estimate 견적 probably 아마

10 무엇이 손상됐는가?
(A) 가구　　　　　　　(B) 기기
(C) 바닥　　　　　　　(D) 창문

해설 | **세부 내용 - 손상된 것**
여자가 첫 번째 대사에서 사무실 바닥 누수 피해를 봐 주러 온 것(coming to look at the water damage to the floor in our office)에 대해 감사를 전하며, 사무실 바닥의 손상을 언급하고 있으므로 (C)가 정답이다.

Paraphrasing
대화의 the floor in our office → 정답의 Some flooring

11 여자가 "다음 주에 중요한 고객들이 오시는데요"라고 말한 이유는 무엇인가?
(A) 소요 기간에 대한 우려를 나타내기 위해
(B) 초대를 거절하기 위해
(C) 다른 장소를 선택하라고 제안하기 위해
(D) 행사 연기를 제안하기 위해

해설 | **세부 내용 - 화자의 의도**
남자가 첫 번째 대사에서 바닥 전체를 교체해야 한다(The whole floor will have to be replaced)고 했는데, 이에 대해 여자가 '다음 주에 중요한 고객들이 오시는데요(I have some important clients coming here next week)'라고 응답했다. 이는 여자가 바닥 전체 교체에 장시간이 걸리는 상황에 대한 우려를 나타내는 것이라고 볼 수 있으므로 (A)가 정답이다.

어휘 | express concern 우려를 표하다 time frame (소요) 기간, 시간 refuse 거절하다 suggest 제안하다 postpone 연기하다, 미루다

12 여자는 남자에게 무엇을 요청하는가?
(A) 영수증　　　　　　(B) 명함
(C) 비용 견적서　　　　(D) 카탈로그

해설 | **세부 내용 - 여자의 요청 사항**
여자가 마지막 대사에서 비용이 얼마나 들지 견적서를 줄 것 (Can you give me an estimate for what it'll cost?)을 요청했으므로 (C)가 정답이다.

M Hi, I enrolled in the introduction to human resources course that meets on Mondays starting in September, but I never received a confirmation e-mail about it.

W OK, let me check on that. What's your name?

M Yuri Solokov. S-O-L-O-K-O-V.

W Here it is. Ah, I see—**¹³**there's a typo on your registration form. You put in 145 instead of 1145. I just fixed that for you.

M Thanks! One more thing… **¹⁴**I'd like to apply for a student loan to help pay for my school expenses. Could you tell me about my loan options?

W Oh, you'll have to talk to Financial Assistance about that—please hold and **¹⁵**I'll transfer you to that department.

남 안녕하세요, 저는 9월부터 월요일마다 수업이 있는 인적 자원 입문 강좌를 신청했는데요, 그와 관련해 확인 이메일을 받지 못했습니다.

여 네, 확인해 볼게요. 성함이 어떻게 되시죠?

남 유리 솔로코브입니다. 철자는 S-O-L-O-K-O-V이고요.

여 여기 있네요. 아, 문제가 뭔지 알겠어요. **¹³**신청서에 오타가 있었네요. 1145가 아니라 145라고 입력하셨어요. 방금 제가 정정했습니다.

남 감사합니다! 한 가지 더 여쭤볼 게 있는데요… **¹⁴**학비를 지불하기 위해 학자금 대출을 신청하고 싶습니다. 어떤 대출 옵션이 있는지 말씀해 주시겠어요?

여 아, 그 부분에 관해서는 재정지원부에 문의하셔야 돼요. 끊지 마시고 기다려 주시면 **¹⁵**해당 부서로 전화를 연결시켜 드릴게요.

어휘 | enroll 등록하다 human resources 인적 자원 confirmation 확인 typo 오타 registration form 신청서, 등록서 loan 대출 transfer 이동시키다, 연결해주다

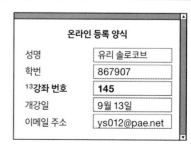

온라인 등록 양식	
성명	유리 솔로코브
학번	867907
¹³강좌 번호	**145**
개강일	9월 13일
이메일 주소	ys012@pae.net

13 여자의 말에 따르면, 시각 정보에서 어떤 정보가 틀렸는가?

(A) 학번   (B) 강좌 번호

(C) 개강일   (D) 이메일 주소

해설 | 세부 내용 - 시각 정보 연계

여자가 두 번째 대사에서 신청서에 오타(typo)가 있다고 한 후, 1145가 아니라 145라고 입력했다(You put in 145 instead of 1145)며 잘못 입력된 정보를 알렸다. 시각 정보에서 145는 강좌 번호이므로, (B)가 정답이다.

14 남자는 무엇에 관해 더 많은 정보를 요청하는가?

(A) 여름 인턴십   (B) 학자금 대출

(C) 개인 교습 서비스   (D) 자원봉사 기회

해설 | 세부 내용 - 남자의 요청 사항

남자가 마지막 대사에서 학자금 대출을 신청하고 싶다(I'd like to apply for a student loan)고 한 후, 대출 옵션(loan options)에 관한 정보를 요청했으므로, (B)가 정답이다.

15 여자는 다음에 무엇을 할 것인가?

(A) 안내 책자 찾기

(B) 청구서 프린트하기

(C) 신청서를 이메일로 보내기

(D) 전화 연결시켜 주기

해설 | 세부 내용 - 여자가 다음에 할 일

여자가 마지막 대사에서 해당 부서로 전화를 연결시켜 주겠다(I'll transfer you to that department)고 했으므로, (D)가 정답이다.

[16-18] 대화 + 영양 성분표 M-Cn / W-Br

> **M** Excuse me? ¹⁶I'm trying to change my diet and I want to eat something different for breakfast—you know, something healthier, like, maybe yogurt? Is there a yogurt that's low in calories but also has a lot of protein?
>
> **W** We have a lot of options you might like. Here's one of our most popular brands of blueberry yogurt. See, there's a lot of protein…
>
> **M** Mmm—nice! But ¹⁷my doctor told me I shouldn't eat a lot of sweet foods—and it would put me over the daily amount he recommended. That's more than 30 grams!
>
> **W** In that case, ¹⁸I'd suggest buying a plain version of this yogurt and adding your own fresh fruit.

남 실례합니다. ¹⁶제가 식단을 바꿀 생각인데 아침 식사로 뭔가 다른 걸 먹고 싶거든요. 몸에 좀 더 좋은 걸로, 말하자면 요구르트 같은 거랄까요? 칼로리는 낮지만 단백질은 풍부한 요구르트 있나요?

여 네, 좋아하실 만한 선택 품목이 많습니다. 가장 인기 있는 블루베리 요구르트 브랜드 중 하나인 거예요. 보시면 단백질이 풍부합니다…

남 음… 좋네요! 하지만 ¹⁷제 담당 의사가 단 음식은 많이 먹지 말라고 했는데 이건 의사의 일일 권장량을 넘기는 거예요. 30그램이 넘어요!

여 그럼 ¹⁸요구르트를 담백한 맛으로 구입하시고 따로 신선한 과일을 추가하시길 권해 드릴게요.

영양 정보	
제공량: 200그램	
칼로리	**150**
	1회분 당 함량
지방	5그램
단백질	11그램
¹⁷당분	**32그램**
나트륨	40밀리그램

16 남자는 왜 특정 제품을 찾고 있는가?

(A) 몸에 좋은 음식을 먹고 싶어 한다.

(B) 특정 성분에 알레르기가 있다.

(C) 할인 쿠폰을 가지고 있다.

(D) 가장 좋아하는 브랜드가 있다.

해설 | 세부 내용 - 남자가 특정 제품을 찾는 이유

남자의 첫 번째 대사에서 식단을 바꿀 생각이라 아침 식사로 뭔가 다른 걸 먹고 싶다며 몸에 좀 더 좋은 요구르트(something healthier, like, maybe yogurt?)를 찾고 있으므로 (A)가 정답이다.

17 시각 정보에 따르면, 남자는 어떤 성분에 우려를 나타내는가?

(A) 지방   (B) 단백질

(C) 당분   (D) 나트륨

해설 | 세부 내용 - 시각 정보 연계

남자의 두 번째 대사에서 담당 의사가 단 음식은 많이 먹지 말라고 했는데, 한 성분이 일일 권장량인 30그램이 넘는다(That's more than 30 grams!)고 했다. 표를 보면 당분(Sugar)이 32 grams로 표시되어 있으므로, (C)가 정답이다.

18 여자는 남자에게 무엇을 권하는가?

(A) 무료 샘플 맛보기

(B) 더 큰 지점으로 가기

(C) 의사와 상담하기

(D) 다른 품목을 구입하기

해설 | 세부 내용 - 여자의 추천 사항

대화 마지막에 여자가 남자에게 이 요구르트를 담백한 맛으로 구입하라(I'd suggest buying a plain version of this yogurt)고 했으므로 (D)가 정답이다.

[19-21] 대화 + 목록 M-Cn / W-Br

> **M** Hi Emiko, it's Makoto. ¹⁹I'm trying to decide which properties to show Ms. Wu. She wants to open a sandwich shop in the center of town.
>
> **W** Well, here are the listings. There are several properties available that might be suitable for a sandwich shop. ²⁰Is there any particular feature she's looking for?

M Well, ²⁰she really wants the shop to have its own parking area.

W OK, then you should probably show her this one.

M OK. ²¹I'll call her right now and set up an appointment.

남 안녕하세요, 에미코. 마코토예요. ¹⁹우 씨에게 어떤 부동산을 보여 드려야 할지 결정하려고 합니다. 그녀는 시내 중심부에 샌드위치 가게를 열고 싶어 하세요.

여 네, 여기 목록이 있어요. 샌드위치 가게에 어울릴 만한 가능한 부동산들이 여러 개 있어요. ²⁰그녀가 특별히 원하는 사항이 있나요?

남 음, ²⁰가게에 전용 주차장이 있는 걸 정말 원하세요.

여 네, 그러면 이걸 보여 드리면 될 것 같아요.

남 좋아요. ²¹지금 바로 전화 드려서 약속을 잡을게요.

어휘 | property 부동산 suitable 적합한 particular 특정한, 특별한 feature 특징, 사항 appointment 약속

상업용 부동산 임대

주소	부동산 특징
²⁰사우스 가 44번지	주차장
메인 가 20번지	보관 공간
콩그레스 가 11번지	가격
센터 가 35번지	크기

19 우 씨는 어떤 종류의 사업체를 개업하고자 하는가?

(A) 장난감 가게

(B) 회계 사무소

(C) 샌드위치 가게

(D) 법률 사무소

해설 | 세부 내용 - 우 씨의 사업체

남자가 첫 번째 대사에서 우 씨에게 보여 줄 부동산을 결정하려 한다고 한 후, 우 씨가 시내 중심부에 샌드위치 가게를 열고 싶어 한다(She wants to open a sandwich shop)고 했으므로, (C)가 정답이다.

20 시각 정보에 따르면, 어떤 부동산을 우 씨에게 보여 주겠는가?

(A) 사우스 가 44번지

(B) 메인 가 20번지

(C) 콩그레스 가 11번지

(D) 센터 가 35번지

해설 | 세부 내용 - 시각 정보 연계

여자가 첫 번째 대사에서 우 씨가 특별히 원하는 사항(feature)이 있는지 물었는데, 이에 대해 남자가 가게에 전용 주차장이 있는 것을 원한다(she really wants the shop to have its own parking area)고 했다. 시각 정보를 보면 주차장은 사우스 가 44번지에만 있으므로, (A)가 정답이다.

21 남자는 다음에 무엇을 할 것 같은가?

(A) 방의 치수를 잴 것이다.

(B) 고객에게 연락할 것이다.

(C) 운전 길 안내를 해 줄 것이다.

(D) 견적서를 줄 것이다.

해설 | 세부 내용 - 남자가 다음에 할 일

남자가 마지막 대사에서 지금 바로 전화해서 약속을 잡겠다(I'll call her right now and set up an appointment)고 했으므로, (B)가 정답이다.

Paraphrasing

대화의 call her → 정답의 Contact a client

[22-24] 대화 + 평면도 W-Br / M-Au

W Hi, I got a call about some malfunctioning computers?

M Well, they're not malfunctioning. ²²They're just not connected to our company network.

W Oh, I see. It should be easy to connect them. ²³Do you have the information for the network? Passwords and network addresses?

M Yes, our previous IT technician kept a detailed journal. Here.

W Great, thanks. So which computers do I need to look at?

M ²⁴They're in the Machine Room, next to the Training Department. Would you like me to show you?

W I know where the Machine Room is. Thanks, anyway.

여 안녕하세요, 고장 난 컴퓨터에 대한 전화를 받았는데요?

남 저, 고장이 아니고요. ²²회사 네트워크에 연결이 안 되어 있을 뿐이에요.

여 아, 그렇군요. 연결하는 일이라면 쉽죠. ²³네트워크 정보가 있으신가요? 암호와 네트워크 주소요?

남 네, 전에 일하던 IT 기술자가 상세한 일지를 적어 뒀어요. 여기요.

여 좋네요, 고맙습니다. 그럼 제가 어떤 컴퓨터들을 봐 드려야 하죠?

남 ²⁴교육부 옆의 기계실에 있는 것들이요. 제가 안내해드릴까요?

여 기계실이 어디 있는지 알아요. 아무튼, 고맙습니다.

어휘 | malfunctioning 고장 난, 오작동하는 connect 연결하다 previous 이전의 keep a journal 일기를 적다

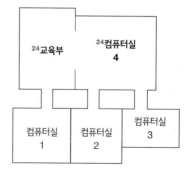

22 남자는 어떤 문제를 언급하는가?

(A) 물건이 엉뚱한 주소로 배송되었다.

(B) 일부 컴퓨터가 네트워크에 연결되어 있지 않다.

(C) 일부 직원들이 적절한 교육을 받지 못했다.

(D) 컴퓨터 기술자가 부재중이다.

해설 | **세부 내용 - 문제점**

컴퓨터 고장 전화를 받았다는 여자의 말에 남자는 고장이 아니라 회사 네트워크에 연결이 안 되어 있는(They're just not connected to our company network) 것뿐이라고 했다. 따라서 (B)가 정답이다.

23 여자는 무엇을 요구하는가?

(A) 기계 설명서   (B) 새 컴퓨터
(C) 보안 세부 정보   (D) 공장 견학

해설 | **세부 내용 - 여자가 요청하는 것**

여자가 두 번째 대사에서 네크워크 정보(Do you have the information for the network? Passwords and network addresses?)를 요청하고 있으므로, (C)가 정답이다.

어휘 | instruction 설명서 security 보안

24 시각 정보에 따르면, 여자는 어느 곳으로 가겠는가?

(A) 컴퓨터실 1   (B) 컴퓨터실 2
(C) 컴퓨터실 3   (D) 컴퓨터실 4

해설 | **세부 내용 - 시각 정보 연계**

어떤 컴퓨터를 봐야 하는지를 묻는 여자의 말에 남자는 교육부 옆의 기계실에 있는 것들(They're in the Machine Room, next to the Training Department)이라고 했다. 약도에서 교육부 옆에 있는 방은 컴퓨터실 4이므로 (D)가 정답이다.

● ETS ACTUAL TEST
본책 p.095

32 (C)	**33** (A)	**34** (C)	**35** (C)	**36** (C)	**37** (B)
38 (A)	**39** (C)	**40** (B)	**41** (D)	**42** (D)	**43** (A)
44 (C)	**45** (B)	**46** (A)	**47** (C)	**48** (B)	**49** (D)
50 (D)	**51** (C)	**52** (B)	**53** (B)	**54** (C)	**55** (A)
56 (C)	**57** (A)	**58** (C)	**59** (C)	**60** (C)	**61** (D)
62 (C)	**63** (D)	**64** (D)	**65** (C)	**66** (B)	**67** (B)
68 (B)	**69** (A)	**70** (B)			

[32-34] M-Au / W-Am

M   Hi, **³²I'm calling from Alan Tsao's office regarding your magazine's interview of Mr. Tsao on Thursday.** Is there anything else we need to arrange?

W   **³³I do have one request.** I would like to include some pictures of Mr. Tsao with our article. **³³Would you mind if I bring one of our photographers along to the interview?**

M   No, that's fine. **³⁴If you e-mail me your photographer's name, I can have both of your ID badges ready before you get here.** I'll leave your badges at the security desk just inside the main entrance to the building.

남   안녕하세요. **³²앨런 차오 씨 사무실에서 전화 드립니다. 목요일에 있을 차오 씨 잡지 인터뷰 관련해서요.** 저희가 준비해야 할 것이 있나요?

여   **³³한 가지 요청 사항이 있습니다.** 저희 기사에 차오 씨 사진을 좀 넣고 싶은데요. **³³인터뷰에 저희 사진기자를 한 명 데려가도 될까요?**

남   네, 좋습니다. **³⁴사진기자 분 성함을 이메일로 보내주시면 도착하시기 전에 두 분의 신분증을 준비해 둘 수 있습니다.** 건물 정문 바로 안쪽에 있는 보안 창구에 신분증을 두겠습니다.

어휘 | regarding ~에 관해 arrange 마련하다, 처리하다 request 요청 include 포함시키다 article 기사 security 보안 entrance 입구

32 남자에 따르면, 목요일에 어떤 일이 있을 것인가?

(A) 고객이 방문할 것이다.
(B) 사무실이 다시 문을 열 것이다.
(C) 직원이 인터뷰를 할 것이다.
(D) 잡지가 출간될 것이다.

해설 | **세부 사항 - 목요일에 있을 일**

남자가 첫 번째 대사에서 목요일에 있을 차오 씨 잡지 인터뷰 관련으로 전화한다(I'm calling ~ regarding your magazine's interview of Mr. Tsao on Thursday)고 했으므로, 그 날 인터뷰가 진행됨을 알 수 있다. 따라서 (C)가 정답이다.

어휘 | publish 출판하다

Paraphrasing

대화의 your magazine's interview of Mr. Tsao → 정답의 A staff member will be interviewed

33 여자는 무엇을 요청했는가?

(A) 동료를 데려가는 데 대한 허가
(B) 건물 위치 안내
(C) 시설 견학
(D) 제품 견본

해설 | **세부 내용 - 여자의 요청 사항**

여자가 첫 번째 대사에서 한 가지 요청 사항이 있다(I do have one request)고 한 후, 인터뷰에 사진기자를 데려가는 것(if I bring one of our photographers along to the interview)에 대한 허가를 요청했으므로 (A)가 정답이다.

어휘 | permission 허가 colleague 동료 directions 길 안내 facility 시설

Paraphrasing

대화의 one of our photographers → 정답의 a colleague

34 남자는 무엇을 준비하겠다고 말하는가?

(A) 서식   (B) 간식
(C) 신분증   (D) 사진

해설 | **세부 내용 - 남자가 준비할 것**

남자가 마지막 대사에서 사진기자의 이름을 이메일로 보내주면 도착하기 전에 여자와 사진기자의 신분증을 준비해 두겠다(I can have both of your ID badges ready)고 했으므로 (C)가 정답이다.

Paraphrasing

대화의 have ~ ready → 질문의 prepare

W Hi, Mr. Reynolds? This is Roberta Heinz from apartment 4B. I'm doing my laundry in the basement right now, and ³⁵the washing machine doesn't seem to be working properly. ³⁶I wanted to make sure building management was aware of the problem.

M ³⁶Oh, thanks for letting me know. I just had that machine installed, so I'm surprised that it's giving you trouble. What's the problem, exactly?

W Well, at the end of the wash cycle, the water doesn't drain out of the machine like it's supposed to. It's still completely full.

M OK — ³⁷I'll call an appliance repair service now and ask them to come take a look.

여 안녕하세요, 레이놀즈 씨죠? 저는 아파트 4B에 사는 로버타 하인즈라고해요. 지금 지하에서 세탁을 하고 있는데, ³⁵세탁기가 제대로 작동을 하지 않는 것 같아요. ³⁶건물 관리진이 이 문제에 대해 알고 계셨으면 했어요.

남 ³⁶오, 알려주셔서 감사해요. 그 기계를 설치한 지 얼마 안 됐는데 애를 먹인다니 놀랍네요. 정확히 뭐가 문제죠?

여 저기, 세탁 마지막 단계에서는 기계에서 물이 빠져야 되는데, 그러질 않네요. 아직도 물이 꽉 차 있어요.

남 알겠어요. ³⁷제가 지금 전자 제품 수리 서비스 센터에 전화해서 와서 점검해달라고 요청할게요.

어휘 | do the laundry 빨래하다 basement 지하 properly 제대로, 적절히 be aware of ~을 알다 install 설치하다 give A trouble A를 애먹이다 drain 물이 빠지다 be supposed to do ~하기로 되어 있다 appliance (가정용) 기기, 전자 제품 take a look 점검하다, 보다

35 여자는 어떤 문제로 전화를 하고 있는가?
(A) 파이프가 샌다.
(B) 문이 열리지 않는다.
(C) 세탁기가 제대로 작동하지 않고 있다.
(D) 난방기가 고장이다.

해설 | 세부 내용 - 문제점
여자가 첫 대사에서 세탁기가 제대로 작동하지 않는 것 같다(the washing machine doesn't seem to be working properly)고 했으므로 (C)가 정답이다.

어휘 | leak 새다 function 기능하다, 작용하다

36 남자는 누구일 것 같은가?
(A) 배관공   (B) 안전 검사관
(C) 건물 관리자   (D) 부동산 중개인

해설 | 전체 내용 - 남자의 신분
여자가 건물 관리진에게 문제를 알리고 싶어 전화했다고 하자, 두 번째 대사에서 남자가 알려줘서 고맙다(thanks for letting me know)고 했으므로 남자가 건물 관리자임을 추론할 수 있다. 따라서 (C)가 정답이다.

37 남자는 무엇을 하겠다고 말하는가?
(A) 설명서를 참고한다.
(B) 수리 서비스 센터에 연락한다.
(C) 서류를 작성한다.
(D) 교체 부품을 찾는다.

해설 | 세부 내용 - 남자가 할 일
마지막 대사에서 남자가 전자 제품 수리 서비스 센터에 연락할 것(I'll call an appliance repair service now)이라고 했으므로 (B)가 정답이다.

어휘 | consult 참고하다, 상담하다 replacement part 교체 부품

M Hi Marta. ³⁸I'm being sent to Madrid next month to cover an art show at the Ariza Gallery. I'm supposed to write an article about the show for our magazine. You were there recently, right?

W Yes, and my good friend is actually one of the artists whose work will be shown at that gallery next month. I could put you in touch with her.

M That'd be great. ³⁹I'd really like to learn as much as I can about the featured artists before attending the event.

W ⁴⁰Her business card is in my office. If you'll come with me, I can give it to you now.

남 안녕하세요, 마타. ³⁸저는 다음 달에 아리자 갤러리에서 있을 미술전 취재차 마드리드로 파견될 거예요. 잡지에 미술전 관련 기사를 써야 하거든요. 최근에 거기 다녀오셨죠, 그렇죠?

여 네. 사실 친한 친구가 다음 달 그 미술관에 작품이 전시될 화가 중 한 명이거든요. 그녀와 연락이 닿도록 해 드릴 수 있어요.

남 그래 주시면 좋죠. ³⁹행사에 참석하기 전에 참여 화가들에 대해 가능한 한 많이 알아두고 싶거든요.

여 ⁴⁰그녀의 명함이 제 사무실에 있어요. 지금 저랑 함께 가시면 드릴 수 있어요.

어휘 | cover 취재하다 be supposed to ~하기로 되어 있다, ~해야 한다 article 기사 recently 최근 actually 사실, 실제로 put A in touch with B A를 B와 연락이 닿게 하다 feature 특별히 포함하다 attend 참석하다

38 남자는 왜 마드리드에 가는가?
(A) 행사를 취재하기 위해
(B) 친지를 방문하기 위해
(C) 미술품을 구입하기 위해
(D) 대학교에서 공부하기 위해

해설 | 세부 내용 - 남자가 마드리드에 가는 이유
남자가 첫 번째 대사에서 다음 달에 아리자 갤러리에서 있을 미술전 취재차 마드리드로 파견될 것(I'm being sent to Madrid next month to cover an art show at the Ariza Gallery)이라며, 마드리드에 가는 이유를 밝혔으므로 (A)가 정답이다.

대화의 cover an art show at the Ariza Gallery
→ 정답의 report on an event

39 남자는 출장 가기 전 무엇을 하고 싶다고 말하는가?
(A) 강좌 등록
(B) 호텔 예약
(C) 화가들에 대해 조사
(D) 안내책자 구입

해설 | 세부 내용 - 남자가 출장 가기 전에 하고 싶은 일
남자가 두 번째 대사에서 행사에 참석하기 전에 참여 화가들에 대해 가능한 한 많이 알아두고 싶다(I'd really like to learn as much as I can about the featured artists before attending the event)고 했으므로 (C)가 정답이다.

Paraphrasing
대화의 learn as much as I can about the featured artists
→ 정답의 Research some artists

40 여자는 무엇을 하겠다고 제안하는가?
(A) 일정표 확인하기
(B) 연락처 찾기
(C) 전화하기
(D) 가격표 찾아보기

해설 | 세부 내용 - 여자의 제안 사항
여자가 마지막 대사에서 화가의 명함이 사무실에 있다(Her business card is in my office)고 한 후, 지금 함께 가면 명함을 주겠다(I can give it to you)고 했으므로 (B)가 정답이다.

Paraphrasing
대화의 Her business card → 정답의 some contact information

[41-43] M-Au / W-Br

M ⁴¹How are preparations going for the workshop on accounting spreadsheets, Maria? I assume a lot of employees will want to attend since the new software isn't very intuitive.
W ⁴¹There has been a lot of interest in the workshop. Now, I just need to find a place to hold it.
M ⁴²You can't use the meeting room downstairs? It'll hold twenty people.
W Thirty people plan to attend.
M Oh, I see. Well, you could always call the James Hotel—we hosted a training session there a couple of years ago.
W Good idea. ⁴³I'll set aside some time this afternoon to stop by the hotel and see what they have to offer.

남 ⁴¹회계 스프레드시트 워크숍 준비는 어떻게 되어 가나요, 마리아? 새 소프트웨어를 사용하기가 그리 쉽지 않아서 많은 직원들이 참여하고 싶어할 것 같은데요.
여 ⁴¹워크숍에 관심들이 많았어요. 이제 개최할 장소를 찾아야 합니다.
남 ⁴²아래층 회의실은 사용할 수 없나요? 20명을 수용할 수 있을 텐데요.
여 30명이 참석할 계획이에요.
남 아, 알겠어요. 제임스 호텔에 언제든 전화해도 돼요. 2년 전쯤 거기서 교육 강좌를 열었거든요.
여 좋은 생각이네요. ⁴³오늘 오후에 시간을 내서 호텔에 들러 거기서 무엇을 제공하는지 살펴볼게요.

어휘 | preparation 준비 accounting 회계 assume 추정하다 attend 참석하다 intuitive 직관적인, 사용하기에 쉬운 hold 수용할 수 있다 host 개최하다 set aside 확보하다

41 화자들은 어떤 행사에 대해 이야기하는가?
(A) 기자회견 (B) 보건 박람회
(C) 기념 행사 (D) 워크숍

해설 | 전체 내용 - 화자들이 논의하는 행사
남자가 첫 번째 대사에서 회계 스프레드시트 워크숍(the workshop on accounting spreadsheets) 준비의 진행 상황에 대해 문의했는데, 이에 대해 여자가 워크숍에 관심들이 많았다(There has been a lot of interest in the workshop)며 워크숍과 관련된 대화를 이어가고 있으므로 (D)가 정답이다.

42 여자가 "30명이 참석할 계획이에요"라고 말할 때, 그 의도는 무엇인가?
(A) 케이터링 업체에 연락을 해야 한다.
(B) 참석자 명단을 업데이트해야 한다.
(C) 기간이 너무 짧다.
(D) 회의실 크기가 충분치 않다.

해설 | 세부 내용 - 화자의 의도
남자가 두 번째 대사에서 아래층 회의실은 사용할 수 없는지(You can't use the meeting room downstairs?) 물은 후, 그 회의실이 20명을 수용할 수 있다(It'll hold twenty people)고 덧붙였는데, 이에 대해 여자가 '30명이 참석할 계획이에요(Thirty people plan to attend)'라고 응답했다. 이는 수용 가능 인원보다 참석 인원이 많다는 것, 즉 공간이 충분하지 않다는 의미이므로, (D)가 정답이다.

43 여자는 오늘 오후에 무엇을 하겠다고 말하는가?
(A) 호텔 방문
(B) 예산 검토
(C) 발표 준비
(D) 초대장 찾기

해설 | 세부 내용 - 여자가 할 일
여자가 마지막 대사에서 오늘 오후에 시간을 내서 호텔에 들러 보겠다(I'll set aside some time this afternoon to stop by the hotel)고 했으므로 (A)가 정답이다.

Paraphrasing
대화의 stop by → 정답의 Visit

W Thanks for catering our company dinner, Allen. **⁴⁴We were all really impressed with the wide variety of choices on the international buffet table.**

M I'm glad you enjoyed it. We try to include a range of food options because we serve customers from quite a number of different countries. Say, **⁴⁵would you mind writing a brief review for the client feedback page of my Web site?**

W I'd be happy to. And we'd like to book you now for next month's picnic. **⁴⁶Are you available the last Friday in May?**

M I might be, but **⁴⁶I'll need to check my calendar.** May is always a busy month for us.

여 앨런, 저희 저녁 회식 음식을 준비해 주셔서 감사합니다. **⁴⁴세계 뷔페 요리의 선택 폭이 굉장히 넓어서 저희 모두 깊은 인상을 받았어요.**

남 좋아하셨다니 다행입니다. 여러 나라의 고객들께 서비스를 제공하고 있어 다양한 음식을 포함시키려고 합니다. 저, **⁴⁵저희 웹사이트의 고객 후기 페이지에 간단한 평을 써 주실 수 있나요?**

여 그럼요. 그리고 다음 달 야유회를 지금 예약하고 싶습니다. **⁴⁶5월 마지막 금요일에 시간이 되시나요?**

남 그럴 것 같은데 **⁴⁶일정표를 확인해 봐야 해요.** 5월은 항상 바쁜 달이거든요.

어휘 | cater 음식을 공급하다 be impressed with ~에 깊은 인상을 받다, 감명받다 a wide variety of ~ 매우 다양한 include 포함시키다 a range of 다양한 different 다양한, 여러 가지의 book 예약하다 available 시간이 되는

44 여자는 행사의 어떤 점을 마음에 들어 했는가?

(A) 장식   (B) 객원 연설자
(C) 메뉴 선택권   (D) 오락거리

해설 | **세부 내용 - 여자가 행사에서 마음에 든다고 한 것**
여자가 첫 번째 대사에서 세계 뷔페 요리의 선택 폭이 굉장히 넓어서 깊은 인상을 받았다(We were all really impressed with the wide variety of choices on the international buffet table)고 했으므로, 여자가 메뉴 선택이 다양한 점을 마음에 들어 했다는 것을 알 수 있다. 따라서 (C)가 정답이다.

어휘 | decoration 장식 entertainment 오락

45 남자는 여자에게 무엇을 해 달라고 요청하는가?

(A) 계산 치르기
(B) 피드백 제공하기
(C) 일부 품목 반품하기
(D) 고객을 보내기

해설 | **세부 내용 - 남자의 요청 사항**
남자가 첫 번째 대사에서 웹사이트의 고객 후기 페이지에 간단한 평을 써 줄 것(would you mind writing a brief review for the client feedback page of my Web site?)을 요청했으므로 (B)가 정답이다.

어휘 | settle a bill 계산을 치르다 refer (다른 사람이나 기관에) 보내다, 추천하다

Paraphrasing
대화의 writing a brief review → 정답의 Give feedback

46 남자는 무엇을 하겠다고 말하는가?

(A) 시간이 되는지 확인하기
(B) 청구서 출력하기
(C) 새로운 조리법 시도하기
(D) 관리자에게 연락하기

해설 | **세부 내용 - 남자가 할 일**
여자가 마지막 대사에서 5월 마지막 금요일에 시간이 되는지(Are you available the last Friday in May?) 물었는데, 이에 대해 남자가 일정표를 확인해 봐야 한다(I'll need to check my calendar)고 응답했으므로, 남자가 시간이 되는지 확인할 것임을 알 수 있다. 따라서 (A)가 정답이다.

어휘 | availability (이용) 가능성 invoice 청구서, 송장 recipe 조리법 supervisor 관리자, 감독관

Paraphrasing
대화의 check my calendar → 정답의 Check his availability

W1 Next on the agenda... **⁴⁷we're spending a lot on transporting clothing from our warehouse to our stores.** I'd like to bring that cost down. Yan, you had an idea?

W2 Yes, currently, we transport clothes from our warehouse to the stores twice a week. **⁴⁷What about combining them into a single shipment per week?**

M **⁴⁷Yan's proposal sounds good, but ⁴⁸it could cause problems with inventory and storage at the stores if the shipments are twice as big.**

W1 OK. Let's check into that. **⁴⁹Yan, it's your idea... you'll need to find out what the store managers think.** I'd like a report on my desk by Friday.

여1 다음 안건은... **⁴⁷우리 창고에서 매장으로 의류를 운반하는 비용이 많이 듭니다.** 그 비용을 줄였으면 해요. 얀, 좋은 생각이 있다고요?

여2 네. 현재 1주일에 두 번 창고에서 매장으로 옷을 운송하는데요. **⁴⁷매주 1회 운송으로 합치면 어떨까요?**

남 **⁴⁷얀의 제안이 좋은 것 같은데, ⁴⁸적하물이 두 배가 되면 매장의 재고와 보관에 문제가 생길 수 있을 것 같아요.**

여1 좋아요. 한 번 확인해 보죠. **⁴⁹얀, 본인의 아이디어이니 매장 관리자들이 어떻게 생각하는지 알아보세요.** 금요일까지 제 책상에 보고서를 올려 두세요.

어휘 | agenda 회의 안건 transport 운송하다, 수송하다 warehouse 창고 currently 현재 combine A into B A를 B로 결합하다 shipment 수송품, 적하물 inventory 재고 storage 저장, 보관

47 화자들은 무엇에 대해 이야기하는가?

(A) 창고 직원 채용을 늘릴 시기
(B) 추가 매장을 열 장소
(C) 운송비 절감 방법
(D) 지역 관리자로 승진시킬 사람

해설 | **전체 내용 - 대화의 주제**
여자 1이 첫 번째 대사에서 창고에서 매장으로 의류를 운반하는 비용이 많이 든다(we're spending a lot on transporting clothing from our warehouse to our stores)는 문제점을 언급한 후, 운송비를 줄이는(bring that cost down) 방안이 있는지 얀에게 물었는데, 이에 대해 여자 2(얀)가 운송 횟수를 합치자고(What about combining them into a single shipment per week?) 제안했다. 남자 또한 여자 2(얀)의 제안에 대한 의견(Yan's proposal sounds good)을 밝히며 대화를 이어가고 있으므로 (C)가 정답이다.

어휘 | increase 증가시키다, 늘리다 staffing 직원 채용 additional 추가의 reduce 감소시키다 promote 승진시키다

Paraphrasing
대화의 bring that cost down → 정답의 reduce transportation costs

48 남자는 무엇에 대해 우려하는가?

(A) 믿을 만한 공급업체 찾기 (B) 충분한 보관 공간 확보
(C) 건설 프로젝트 연기   (D) 은행 대출 담보하기

해설 | **세부 내용 - 남자의 우려 사항**
남자가 첫 번째 대사에서 적하물이 두 배가 되면 매장의 재고와 보관에 문제가 생길 수 있을 것 같다(it could cause problems with inventory and storage at the stores)는 우려를 표하고 있으므로 (B)가 정답이다.

어휘 | reliable 믿을 만한 supplier 공급자 delay 미루다, 연기하다 secure a loan 대출을 담보하다

49 얀은 금요일까지 무엇을 하겠는가?

(A) 교육 워크숍 준비   (B) 패션쇼 참석
(C) 창고 점검   (D) 보고서 제출

해설 | **세부 내용 - 얀이 할 일**
여자 1이 마지막 대사에서 여자 2(얀)에게 매장 관리자들이 어떻게 생각하는지 알아보라고(you'll need to find out what the store managers think) 한 후, 금요일까지 자신의 책상에 보고서를 올려 둘 것(I'd like a report on my desk by Friday)을 요청했으므로, 얀이 금요일까지 보고서를 제출할 것임을 알 수 있다. 따라서 (D)가 정답이다.

어휘 | organize 준비하다, 조직하다 inspect 점검하다, 사찰하다 submit 제출하다

[50-52] M-Cn / W-Am

M Natalia, ⁵⁰did you hear that our company just hired a marketing specialist? It'll be interesting to see the specialist's plan for promoting our business.

W I agree. We definitely have the potential to grow—⁵¹there are hundreds of hotels and restaurants nearby, and they all need a service like ours to launder and fold their linens.

M Oh, that reminds me... ⁵²I didn't see the box of clean sheets and towels for the Forline Hotel in our delivery van. I know we deliver there every Friday, so I was wondering about that...

W Today's Thursday.

M Oh, that's right. Ugh—it's been a busy week.

남 나탈리아, ⁵⁰우리 회사에 마케팅 전문가를 채용했다는 소식 들었어요? 우리 회사 홍보를 위한 전문가의 계획을 본다는 것이 흥미로울 것 같아요.

여 맞아요. 우리 회사는 분명히 성장 잠재력이 있어요. ⁵¹근처에 수백 개의 호텔과 음식점이 있고, 그들 모두 우리가 제공하는 서비스처럼 리넨 제품을 세탁하고 개키는 서비스를 필요로 하니까요.

남 아, 그러니까 생각나는데요. ⁵²우리 배달 차량에서 포라인 호텔에 보내려고 세탁한 시트와 수건 상자를 못 봤어요. 매주 금요일에 배달하는 걸로 아는데요. 그래서 의아했어요.

여 오늘은 목요일인데요.

남 아, 그렇네요. 아... 이번 주에 너무 정신이 없어서요.

어휘 | specialist 전문가 promote 촉진하다, 홍보하다 business 사업(체) definitely 확실히, 분명히 potential 잠재력, 가능성 nearby 인근에 launder 세탁하다 fold 개키다 delivery 배송

50 최근 어떤 직책이 충원됐는가?

(A) 물류 담당자   (B) 고객 서비스 상담원
(C) 유지보수 기술자   (D) 마케팅 전문가

해설 | **세부 내용 - 최근에 충원된 직책**
남자가 첫 번째 대사에서 회사가 마케팅 전문가를 채용했다(our company just hired a marketing specialist)는 소식을 언급하고 있으므로 (D)가 정답이다.

어휘 | logistics 물류 coordinator 진행자, 조정자 representative 대리인, 안내 직원 maintenance 유지보수 technician 기술자

51 화자들은 어디에서 일하겠는가?

(A) 여행사   (B) 연회장
(C) 세탁 서비스 업체   (D) 직물 공장

해설 | **전체 내용 - 화자들의 근무 장소**
여자가 첫 번째 대사에서 호텔과 음식점들(they=hundreds of hotels and restaurants nearby)이 리넨 제품을 세탁하고 개키는 화자들 회사의 서비스 같은 것을 필요로 한다(they all need a service like ours to launder and fold their linens)고 했으므로, 화자들이 세탁 서비스 업체에서 일한다는 것을 알 수 있다. 따라서 (C)가 정답이다.

어휘 | travel agency 여행사 banquet 연회 textile 직물

52 여자가 "오늘은 목요일인데요"라고 말할 때, 그 의도는 무엇인가?

(A) 요청을 거절하려고   (B) 실수를 바로잡으려고
(C) 감사를 표하려고   (D) 마감시한을 제안하려고

남자가 두 번째 대사에서 매주 금요일에 포라인 호텔에 세탁한 시트와 수건을 배달하는 걸로(we deliver there every Friday) 알고 있는데 보지 못했다고 의아해 하자 여자가 '오늘은 목요일인데요(Today's Thursday)'라고 응답했다. 이는 요일을 착각한 남자의 실수를 바로잡으려는 의도라고 볼 수 있으므로 (B)가 정답이다.

어휘 | turn down 거절하다 request 요청 correct 바로잡다, 정정하다 appreciation 감사 deadline 기한, 마감 일자

[53-55] 3인 대화 W-Br / M-Cn / M-Au

W OK, **53**the annual budget proposals have to be submitted this week. Is there anything special our sales team needs?

M1 Well, **54**since the company just gave our team permission to work from home twice each week, **53**I think we should consider getting everyone a tablet computer.

M2 **53**Good idea. Then we won't need to use our personal computers when we work at home. Are there enough funds available within the budget?

W I think so, but **55**we might have to do some research to find ones that are reasonably priced. I'll take a look this afternoon and make a list of tablets we can suggest to management.

여 자, **53**연간 예산 제안서는 이번 주까지 제출해야 해요. 우리 영업팀에 특별히 필요한 것이 있나요?

남 음, **54**회사에서 우리 팀이 1주일에 두 번 재택근무할 수 있도록 허가를 해 줘서, **53**모두에게 태블릿 컴퓨터를 제공하는 걸 고려해 봐야 할 것 같아요.

남 **53**좋은 생각입니다. 그러면 집에서 일할 때는 개인 컴퓨터를 사용할 필요가 없겠군요. 예산 내에서 운용 가능한 자금이 충분히 있나요?

여 그런 것 같은데요. **55**하지만 가격이 적당한걸 찾으려면 조사를 좀 해야 할 겁니다. 오늘 오후에 한 번 보고 경영진에게 제안할 만한 태블릿의 목록을 작성할게요.

어휘 | annual 연간의 budget 예산 proposal 제안 submit 제출하다 permission 허가 work from home 재택근무하다 fund 자금 available 이용 가능한 reasonably priced 가격이 적정한 management 경영진, 임원진

53 화자들은 무엇에 대해 이야기하는가?
(A) 채용 결정　　　　(B) 예산 요청
(C) 컴퓨터 소프트웨어　(D) 판매 전략

해설 | 전체 내용 - 대화의 주제

여자가 첫 번째 대사에서 연간 예산 제안서는 이번 주까지 제출해야 한다(the annual budget proposals have to be submitted this week)고 한 후, 영업팀에 특별히 필요한 것이 있는지 물었는데, 이에 대해 남자 1이 모두에게 태블릿 컴퓨터를 제공하는 걸 고려해 봐야 한다(we should consider getting everyone a tablet

computer)며 예산과 관련된 의견을 제안했다. 남자 2 또한 남자 1의 제안에 대한 의견(Good idea)을 밝히며 대화를 이어가고 있으므로 (B)가 정답이다.

어휘 | decision 결정 tactic 전술, 전략

54 일부 직원들은 무엇을 하도록 허가받았는가?
(A) 사무실 장식　　　(B) 회의 참석
(C) 재택근무　　　　(D) 평상복 착용

해설 | 세부 내용 - 직원들이 허가 받은 사항

남자 1이 첫 번째 대사에서 회사에서 영업팀이 1주일에 두 번 재택근무할 수 있도록 허가했다(the company just gave our team permission to work from home twice each week)고 했으므로 (C)가 정답이다.

55 여자는 오늘 오후에 무엇을 하겠는가?
(A) 조사하기　　　　(B) 고객과 회의하기
(C) 장비 수리하기　　(D) 일정표 업데이트하기

해설 | 세부 내용 - 여자가 할 일

여자가 마지막 대사에서 가격이 적당한 태블릿 컴퓨터를 찾으려면 조사를 좀 해야 할 것(we might have to do some research to find ones that are reasonably priced)이라고 한 후, 오늘 오후에 한 번 살펴 보겠다(I'll take a look this afternoon)며 자원하고 있으므로 (A)가 정답이다.

어휘 | conduct 하다 repair 수리하다 equipment 장비

[56-58] W-Am / M-Au

W Hello, my name is Rachel Grant. I'm an administrative assistant in the research department. **56**I was hoping someone from Human Resources could answer a question for me about employee benefits.

M Of course. I'll be happy to help you if I can, Rachel. **57**Why don't you give me your employee ID number, so I can pull up your file?

W Sure, it's 904376. My question is about the school tuition reimbursement. I heard that our company will pay for full-time employees to attend university classes.

M Yes, it is company policy to pay for university classes for employees. **58**The first thing you'll need to do is talk to your manager and get her approval for the courses you intend to take.

여 안녕하세요, 저는 레이첼 그랜트입니다. 연구부서의 행정 보조 담당 직원이에요. **56**인사부서의 누군가가 직원 복리후생에 대한 질문에 답변해 주셨으면 하고요.

남 네. 제가 도움이 되면 좋겠네요, 레이첼. **57**직원 번호를 알려주시면 어떨까요? 그러면 파일을 찾을 수 있을 텐데요.

여 네, 904376입니다. 제 질문은 학교 수업료 환급에 관한 거예요. 우리 회사에서 상근직 직원에게 대학 강좌 수업료를 내 준다고 들었거든요.

남 네, 직원의 대학 강좌 비용을 지급하는 회사 정책입니다. **58**가장 먼저 관리자에게 이야기해서 들으려는 강좌에 대해 승인을 받으셔야 해요.

어휘 | administrative assistant 행정 보조 담당 직원 department 부서 human resources 인사부 employee benefit 직원 복리후생 tuition 수업료, 등록금 reimbursement 상환, 배상 full-time employee 상근직 직원 policy 정책 approval 승인

---

56 여자는 왜 전화했는가?

(A) 연구 프로젝트에 대해 논의하려고

(B) 제품 주문에 관해 문의하려고

(C) 직원 복리후생에 대해 물어보려고

(D) 회의 시간을 확정하려고

해설 | 전체 내용 - 여자가 전화한 이유

여자가 첫 번째 대사에서 인사부서의 누군가가 직원 복리후생에 대한 질문에 답변해 주기를 바란다(I was hoping someone from Human Resources could answer a question for me about employee benefits)고 했으므로, 여자가 직원 복리후생에 대해 문의하기 위해 전화했음을 알 수 있다. 따라서 (C)가 정답이다.

어휘 | inquire 묻다, 알아보다 confirm 확정하다

57 남자는 어떤 정보를 요청하는가?

(A) 식별 번호   (B) 이메일 주소

(C) 사무실 위치   (D) 전화번호

해설 | 세부 내용 - 남자가 요청한 정보

남자가 첫 번째 대사에서 여자에게 직원 번호를 알려줄 것(Why don't you give me your employee ID number)을 요청했으므로 (A)가 정답이다.

어휘 | identification 신원 확인, 신분 증명

Paraphrasing

대화의 your employee ID number → 정답의 An identification number

58 남자는 여자에게 무엇이 필요하다고 말하는가?

(A) 관리자 승인

(B) 고급 컴퓨터 능력

(C) 서명한 지원서

(D) 업데이트된 안건

해설 | 세부 내용 - 여자에게 필요한 것

남자가 마지막 대사에서 가장 먼저 관리자에게 이야기해서 들으려는 강좌에 대해 승인을 받아야 한다(The first thing you'll need to do is talk to your manager and get her approval for the courses you intend to take)고 했으므로 (A)가 정답이다.

어휘 | advanced 고급의, 상급의 application form 지원서

[59-61] W-Br / M-Cn

W Hassan, **59**I want to encourage you to attend the metalworking conference next month in New York. A number of the presentations will focus on new production processes for our industry.

M **59**Yes, I saw the program for the conference, and I'd like to go.

W Great. **60**You're very familiar with our manufacturing process, so I'm glad you'll be the one going. The company, of course, will cover your expenses for transportation and lodging. We'll just need to go over the details so we can make a budget.

M OK, **61**I'll estimate the costs associated with the trip and give you a list to look over.

여 핫산, **59**다음 달 뉴욕에서 있을 금속 세공 워크숍에 참석하실 것을 권해요. 많은 발표에서 우리 업계의 새로운 생산 공정을 집중적으로 다룰 거예요.

남 **59**네, 회의 프로그램을 봤는데 가고 싶더라고요.

여 좋아요. **60**우리 제조 공정을 아주 잘 알고 있는 당신이 간다니 기쁘네요. 당연히 회사에서 교통비와 숙박비를 댈 거예요. 세부 사항을 검토해 봐야 예산을 짤 수 있겠죠.

남 네. **61**출장 관련 비용을 추산해서 검토하실 목록을 드릴게요.

어휘 | encourage 장려하다, 권장하다 metalworking 금속 세공 presentation 발표 focus on ~에 초점을 맞추다 process 공정, 절차 industry 업계 be familiar with ~를 잘 알고 있다 manufacturing 제조 expense 비용 transportation 운송, 수송 lodging 숙소 budget 예산 estimate 추산하다, 추정하다 associated with ~와 관련된

---

59 대화는 주로 무엇에 관한 것인가?

(A) 위원회 가입   (B) 고객 방문 준비

(C) 행사 참석   (D) 안전 절차 변경

해설 | 전체 내용 - 대화의 주제

여자가 첫 번째 대사에서 다음 달 뉴욕에서 있을 금속 세공 워크숍에 참석하라(I want to encourage you to attend the metalworking conference next month in New York)고 남자에게 권했는데, 이에 대해 남자가 회의 프로그램을 봤다(I saw the program for the conference)고 한 후, 가고 싶다(I'd like to go)고 응답하며 행사 참석과 관련된 대화를 이어가고 있으므로 (C)가 정답이다.

어휘 | committee 위원회 procedure 절차

Paraphrasing

대화의 the metalworking conference → 정답의 an event

60 여자는 남자에 대해 무엇이라고 말하는가?

(A) 발표를 잘 한다.

(B) 생산 공정을 잘 알고 있다.

(C) 고객 대다수를 만나봤다.

(D) 회사에 오래 근속했다.

해설 | 세부 내용 - 여자가 남자에 대해 언급한 사항

여자의 두 번째 대사에서 남자가 회사의 제조 공정을 아주 잘 알고 있다(You're very familiar with our manufacturing process)고 했으므로 (B)가 정답이다.

어휘 | production 생산, 제작

Paraphrasing

대화의 are very familiar with our manufacturing process
→ 정답의 knows the production process well

61 남자는 여자에게 무엇을 줄 것인가?

(A) 신용카드 영수증   (B) 연설자 전기

(C) 제품 사양   (D) 출장비 견적서

해설 | 세부 내용 - 남자가 여자에게 줄 것

남자가 마지막 대사에서 출장 관련 비용을 추산해서 검토할 목록을 주겠다(I'll estimate the costs associated with the trip and give you a list to look over)고 했으므로 (D)가 정답이다.

어휘 | receipt 영수증 biography 전기 specification 사양 estimate 견적서

Paraphrasing

대화의 the costs associated with the trip → 정답의 Travel expense

[62-64] 대화 + 지도 M-Cn / W-Am

M Hi, I'd like to buy a ticket for the seven o'clock showing of the nature documentary. ⁶²Do you offer a student discount?

W Yes, we do—if you have your student ID, you're eligible for a ten percent discount.

M Great. Here it is.

W Thank you. That'll be twelve dollars. Also, we're running a special at our snack counter today. ⁶³You'll get a free beverage with the purchase of any food item.

M That sounds good, ⁶³but I actually just had dinner, so I'll head directly to the theater.

W OK. Here's your ticket—⁶⁴the movie is showing in the theater closest to the snack counter.

남 안녕하세요, 7시에 상영하는 자연 다큐멘터리 영화표를 사려고 합니다. ⁶²학생은 할인되나요?

여 네, 됩니다. 학생증을 지참하시면 10% 할인을 받으실 수 있습니다.

남 잘됐네요. 여기 있습니다.

여 감사합니다. 12달러입니다. 또한, 오늘 스낵 코너에서는 특별 서비스를 제공하고 있습니다. ⁶³어떤 것이든 먹거리를 구매하시면 음료가 무료로 제공됩니다.

남 그렇군요. ⁶³그런데 사실 저는 방금 저녁 식사를 하고 왔습니다. 그래서 상영관으로 바로 가려고요.

여 알겠습니다. 여기 표 있습니다. ⁶⁴영화는 스낵 코너에서 가장 가까운 상영관에서 상영됩니다.

어휘 | eligible ~의 자격이 있는 beverage 음료 directly 바로

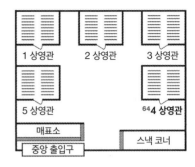

1 상영관	2 상영관	3 상영관
5 상영관		⁶⁴4 상영관

매표소   스낵 코너

중앙 출입구

62 남자는 여자에게 무엇에 대해 묻는가?

(A) 무료 주차   (B) 좌석 선택권

(C) 학생 할인   (D) 결제 방법

해설 | 세부 내용 - 남자의 문의 사항

남자가 첫 번째 대사에서 학생 할인(student discount)을 제공하는지 문의했으므로, (C)가 정답이다.

63 남자는 왜 제안을 거절하는가?

(A) 그는 극장에 거의 가지 않는다.

(B) 그는 친구를 만난다.

(C) 그는 온라인으로 표를 구매한다.

(D) 그는 방금 식사를 했다.

해설 | 세부 내용 - 남자가 거절한 이유

여자가 두 번째 대사에서 먹거리를 구매하면 음료가 무료로 제공된다(You'll get a free beverage with the purchase of any food item)고 했는데, 이에 대해 남자가 방금 저녁 식사를 하고 와서(but I actually just had dinner) 상영관으로 바로 가겠다(I'll head directly to the theater)고 했으므로, (D)가 정답이다.

64 시각 정보에 따르면, 남자는 다음에 어디로 갈 것인가?

(A) 1 상영관   (B) 2 상영관

(C) 3 상영관   (D) 4 상영관

해설 | 세부 내용 - 시각 정보 연계

여자가 마지막 대사에서 남자에게 티켓을 건네며 영화가 스낵 코너에서 가장 가까운 상영관에서 상영된다(the movie is showing in the theater closest to the snack counter)고 했다. 시각 정보를 보면 스낵 코너에서 가장 가까운 상영관은 4 상영관이므로, (D)가 정답이다.

[65-67] 대화 + 일정표 M-Cn / W-Br

M So, Anna, ^{65/67}when can we have a conference call with the coaching staff? ^{65/66}The board of directors wants me to give a report on our recent player acquisitions at their next meeting.

W Right, ⁶⁶recruiting those players was a big investment.

M And with the first game of the season coming up soon, ⁶⁶the board wants a progress report.

W OK. **⁶⁷**I'll set it up for next week—right after our regular meeting with the marketing team.

M Hmm... I'm not sure that will give us enough time? **⁶⁷**Can we schedule it for nine o'clock the next morning?

W **⁶⁷**That shouldn't be a problem. I'll take care of that now.

남 안나, **⁶⁵/⁶⁷**코칭 스태프와 화상 회의를 언제 할 수 있나요? **⁶⁵/⁶⁶**이사회에서 저에게 다음 회의 때 최근 선수 입단에 관한 보고서를 제출하라고 해서요.

여 맞아요. **⁶⁶**그 선수들을 뽑은 건 큰 투자였죠.

남 그리고 시즌 첫 경기가 곧 다가오니 **⁶⁶**이사회에서 경과 보고서를 요청하네요.

여 네. **⁶⁷**다음 주 마케팅팀과의 정기 회의 후에 바로 준비할게요.

남 음... 시간이 충분할지 모르겠는데요? **⁶⁷**다음 날 아침 9시 정각으로 일정을 잡을 수 있나요?

여 **⁶⁷**문제없을 겁니다. 지금 처리할게요.

어휘 | board of directors 이사회 acquisition 습득, 인수, 매입 recruit 모집하다, 뽑다 investment 투자 progress report 경과 보고서 set up 준비하다 regular 정기적인

---

⁶⁷월	3:30-4:30 마케팅팀 회의
화	11:00-12:00 미디어팀 회의
수	12:00-1:30 캐롤 스미스와 점심 식사
목	9:00-10:00 발몬트 은행과 화상 회의 4:00 병원 예약

65 화자들은 어떤 업계에서 일하겠는가?

(A) 금융 (B) 의류
(C) 스포츠 (D) 영화

해설 | 전체 내용 - 화자들이 종사하는 업계
남자가 첫 번째 대사에서 코칭 스태프와 화상 회의를 언제 할 수 있는지(when can we have a conference call with the coaching staff?) 문의한 후, 이사회에서 다음 회의 때 최근 선수 입단(our recent player acquisitions)에 관한 보고서 제출을 원한다고 했으므로, 화자들이 스포츠 관련 업계에서 일한다는 것을 알 수 있다. 따라서 (C)가 정답이다.

66 이사회는 무엇에 대해 듣고 싶어하는가?

(A) 미디어 캠페인 세부 사항
(B) 투자 진척 상황
(C) 예산 증액 계획
(D) 프로젝트 시각표

해설 | 세부 내용 - 이사회가 듣고 싶어하는 것
남자가 첫 번째 대사에서 이사회에서 최근 선수 입단에 관한 보고서를 제출할 것을 원한다(The board of directors wants me to give a report on our recent player acquisitions)고 했는데, 이에 대해 여자가 그 선수들을 뽑은 건 큰

투자였다(recruiting those players was a big investment)고 응답했다. 남자가 두 번째 대사에서 이사회에서 경과 보고서를 요청한다(the board wants a progress report)며 한 번 더 보고서에 대해 언급했으므로, 이사회가 선수 입단과 관련한 투자 진척 상황을 알고 싶어 한다는 것을 알 수 있다. 따라서 (B)가 정답이다.

67 시각 정보에 따르면, 화상 회의는 무슨 요일에 열릴 것인가?

(A) 월요일 (B) 화요일
(C) 수요일 (D) 목요일

해설 | 세부 내용 - 시각 정보 연계
여자가 두 번째 대사에서 마케팅과의 정기 회의 후에 바로(right after our regular meeting with the marketing team) 화상 회의를 준비하겠다(I'll set it up)고 했는데, 이에 대해 남자가 다음 날 아침 9시 정각으로 일정을 잡을 것(Can we schedule it for nine o'clock the next morning?)을 제안했고, 여자가 문제없을 거라며(That shouldn't be a problem) 남자의 제안을 수락했다. 시각 정보를 보면 마케팅팀과의 회의(Meeting w/Marketing Team)는 월요일에 진행되므로, 화상 회의는 다음 날인 화요일에 열리게 된다. 따라서 (B)가 정답이다.

[68-70] 대화 + 소장품 위치 M-Au / W-Am

M Welcome to the Lake City Art Museum. Have you been here before?

W No, I'm just in town for business. But I had some free time today, and **⁶⁸**the front desk manager at my hotel told me about your museum. Do you have any tours today?

M Yes, one starts in five minutes.

W Great. **⁶⁹**Where should I go for that?

M **⁶⁹**That tour begins in the wing that holds our Asian Art collection. Here's a pamphlet with the museum directory.

W Thank you. I'll head there now.

M If you enjoy your visit, **⁷⁰**please consider leaving a donation in our collection box before you leave.

남 레이크 시티 미술관에 오신 것을 환영합니다. 전에 방문하신 적이 있나요?

여 아니요. 출장으로 이 도시에 왔어요. 오늘은 비는 시간이 있었는데, **⁶⁸**호텔 안내 데스크 담당자가 미술관에 대해 이야기해 줬어요. 오늘 견학이 있나요?

남 네. 5분 후에 시작합니다.

여 잘됐네요. **⁶⁹**어디로 가야 하죠?

남 **⁶⁹**아시아 미술 소장품이 있는 동에서 시작합니다. 여기 미술관 안내 팜플렛이 있어요.

여 감사합니다. 지금 그쪽으로 가야겠어요.

남 즐겁게 관람하신다면 **⁷⁰**가시기 전에 저희 모금함에 기부를 해 주세요.

어휘 | directory 안내 (책자) head 향하다 donation 기부 collection box 모금함

소장품 위치	
69아시아 미술	북쪽 동
아프리카 미술	동쪽 동
남아메리카 미술	남쪽 동
유럽 미술	서쪽 동

68 여자는 미술관을 어떻게 알았는가?

(A) 업무상 고객으로부터

(B) 호텔 직원으로부터

(C) TV 광고에서

(D) 여행 잡지에서

해설 | **세부 내용 - 여자가 미술관에 대해 알게 된 방법**

여자가 첫 번째 대사에서 호텔 안내 데스크 담당자가 미술관에 대해 이야기해 줬다(the front desk manager at my hotel told me about your museum)고 했으므로 (B)가 정답이다.

Paraphrasing

대화의 the front desk manager at my hotel → 정답의 a hotel employee

69 시각 정보에 따르면, 여자가 참여할 견학은 어떤 동에서 시작하는가?

(A) 북쪽 동

(B) 동쪽 동

(C) 남쪽 동

(D) 서쪽 동

해설 | **세부 내용 - 시각 정보 연계**

여자가 두 번째 대사에서 견학을 위해 어디로 가야 할지(Where should I go for that?) 문의했는데, 이에 대해 남자가 아시아 미술 소장품이 있는 동에서 시작한다(That tour begins in the wing that holds our Asian Art collection)고 응답했다. 시각 정보에서 아시아 미술 소장품이 있는 동은 북쪽 동(North Wing)이므로 (A)가 정답이다.

70 남자는 여자에게 나중에 무엇을 하라고 제안하는가?

(A) 기념품점 들르기

(B) 기부하기

(C) 행사 참여하기

(D) 후기 쓰기

해설 | **세부 내용 - 남자의 제안 사항**

남자가 마지막 대사에서 여자에게 박물관을 떠나기 전에 모금함에 기부할 것(please consider leaving a donation in our collection box before you leave)을 권유했으므로 (B)가 정답이다.

Paraphrasing

대화의 leaving a donation → 정답의 Give a donation

PART 4   LC

Unit 11   전화 메시지

담화 흐름 파악하기   본책 p.106

안녕하세요, 월터스 씨에게 이 메시지를 남깁니다. 제 이름은 아니타 산체스입니다. 작은 연하장 제작 업체를 운영하고 있으며 사업 유통망을 확장하고자 합니다. 제 이웃 중 한 명이 귀하의 선물 가게를 언급하며 연락해 보라는 제안을 했습니다. 저희 카드를 귀하가 운영하는 가게에 추가하면 좋을 것 같은데, 저희 카드를 진열해 주실 수 있는지 궁금합니다. 제가 기꺼이 몇 가지 견본을 보내 드리겠습니다. 관심이 있으시다면, 우리가 이 문제를 좀 더 상세히 논의할 수 있도록 555-0112로 제게 전화 주십시오.

어휘 | business 사업(체) create 만들다 greeting card 연하장 expand 확장하다, 넓히다 distribution 유통, 분배 addition 추가 사항 be willing to do 기꺼이 ~하다 display 전시하다, 진열하다 discuss 논의하다

1 화자는 왜 전화를 걸고 있는가?

2 화자는 청자의 연락처를 어디에서 얻었는가?

3 화자는 무엇을 해주겠다고 제안하는가?

● 실전 도움닫기   본책 p.107

1 (A)   **2** (B)   **3** (A)   **4** (B)   **5** (B)   **6** (B)

[1-2]

Hello, this message is for Robert Costa in the radiology department. This is Dr. Mina Wilson from the Rosemont Medical Group. 1/2My patient, Sara Santos, had some x-rays taken of her foot at your office last week. It's been six days, and 2I'm still waiting for the films to be delivered to me. 1Could you please give me a call to let me know whether they've been sent? My direct number is 555-3156. Thank you.

안녕하세요, 이것은 방사선과 로버트 코스타 씨께 전하는 메시지입니다. 저는 로즈몬트 메디컬 그룹의 의사 미나 윌슨입니다. 1/2제 환자 사라 산토스 씨가 지난주 귀하 진료실에서 발 엑스레이를 몇 장 찍었습니다. 6일이 지났는데, 2저는 아직도 그 엑스레이 필름이 배달되기를 기다리고 있습니다. 1그 필름이 발송되었는지 전화로 제게 알려주시겠습니까? 제 직통 번호는 555-3156입니다. 감사합니다.

어휘 | radiology 방사선학 take an X-ray of ~의 엑스레이 촬영을 하다 deliver 배달하다 direct number 직통 번호

1 이 음성 메시지의 목적은 무엇인가?

(A) 정보를 요청하려고

(B) 사건을 보고하려고

해설 | **전체 내용 - 전화의 목적**

화자는 자신의 환자가 상대방(청자)의 방사선과에서 엑스레이를 찍었고 그 엑스레이 필름을 기다리는 중이라며 필름 발송 여부를 알려달라(Could you please give me a call to let me know whether they've been sent?)고 했으므로 (A)가 정답이다.

2 화자는 무엇을 기다리고 있는가?

(A) 보험 서류   (B) 엑스레이 필름

해설 | **세부 내용 - 화자가 기다리는 물건**

메시지 중반부에서 화자는 아직도 환자의 엑스레이 필름이 배달되기를 기다리고 있다(I'm still waiting for the films to be delivered to me)고 했으므로 (B)가 정답이다.

[3-4]

Hello, Ms. Hu. ³This is Mr. Hadid from Hadid Architects. You sent me your portfolio a couple of weeks ago. ⁴I apologize for not contacting you sooner. I was out of town on business. I'm very impressed with your designs and your work on the Stacy Building in Taipei, and I'd like to meet you to discuss potential projects. If you are still interested, please contact me at 555-0160 to set up a time.

안녕하세요, 후 씨. ³저는 하디드 건축의 하디드입니다. 몇 주 전에 저에게 포트폴리오를 보내 주셨는데요. ⁴더 일찍 연락 드리지 못해서 죄송합니다. 제가 일 때문에 다른 곳에 있었어요. 귀하의 디자인과 타이베이에 있는 스테이시 빌딩 작업이 아주 인상적이었어요. 향후 있을 프로젝트를 상의하기 위해 귀하를 만나고 싶습니다. 아직 관심이 있으면 시간 약속을 위해 555-0160번으로 연락 주십시오.

어휘 | portfolio 포트폴리오 apologize 사과하다 out of town 타 지역으로 potential 가능성 있는, 잠재적인

3 화자는 어디에서 일하겠는가?

(A) 건축 회사   (B) 미술관

해설 | **전체 내용 - 화자의 근무 장소**

메시지 초반부에서 화자는 자신을 하디드 건축에서 근무하는 하디드(This is Mr. Hadid from Hadid Architects)라고 소개하고 있다. 따라서 (A)가 정답이다.

4 화자가 "제가 일 때문에 타 지역에 있었어요"라고 말한 의도는 무엇인가?

(A) 타이베이 여행에 대해 설명하기 위해

(B) 전화 연락이 늦어진 이유를 설명하기 위해

해설 | **세부 내용 - 화자의 의도**

화자는 더 일찍 연락하지 못해 미안하다고 사과(I apologize for not contacting you sooner)를 한 후 일 때문에 타 지역에 있었다며 연락이 늦은 이유를 밝히고 있다. 따라서 (B)가 정답이다.

[5-6]

You have reached the Monroeville Fishing Museum. ⁵We are located on the riverfront in a restored nineteenth-century ship. Our hours of operation are 10 to 6, Tuesday through Sunday. ⁶Unfortunately, part of the museum will be closed this week, as a new interactive exhibit is being installed. We apologize for any inconvenience, and hope to see you here soon.

먼로빌 어업 박물관입니다. ⁵저희는 강변에 있는 복원된 19세기 선박 안에 있습니다. 개관 시간은 화요일부터 일요일까지 10시부터 6시까지입니다. ⁶아쉽게도, 새로운 참여형 전시품을 설치하고 있어서 박물관 일부가 이번 주에는 개관하지 않습니다. 불편을 끼쳐 드린 점에 대해 사과드리며 곧 이곳에서 뵙기를 바랍니다.

어휘 | riverfront 강기슭, 강변 hours of operation 운영 시간 interactive 직접 만지고 체험할 수 있는, 쌍방향의 exhibit 전시품

5 박물관은 어디에 있는가?

(A) 유서 깊은 집 안에   (B) 배 위에

해설 | **세부 내용 - 박물관의 위치**

메시지 초반부에 박물관이 강변에 있는 복원된 19세기 선박 안에 위치해 있다(We are located on the riverfront in a restored nineteenth-century ship)고 하므로 (B)가 정답이다.

6 왜 박물관 일부가 일시적으로 폐쇄되는가?

(A) 비디오 카메라를 설치하기 위해

(B) 전시품을 설치하기 위해

해설 | **세부 내용 - 박물관 일부 폐쇄 이유**

메시지 후반부에 새로운 참여형 전시품을 설치하고 있어서 박물관 일부가 이번 주에 개관하지 않을 것(Unfortunately, part of the museum will be closed this week, as a new interactive exhibit is being installed)이라고 하므로 (B)가 정답이다.

● **ETS 실전문제**   본책 p. 108

1 (D)	2 (B)	3 (A)	4 (C)	5 (B)	6 (D)
7 (D)	8 (B)	9 (A)	10 (B)	11 (C)	12 (D)
13 (B)	14 (D)	15 (C)	16 (C)	17 (A)	18 (D)
19 (B)	20 (D)	21 (C)			

[1-3] 전화 메시지

Good morning, this is a message for Mr. Lee. Mr. Lee, ¹I'm calling from the Grand Hotel in Parkville ²because you left your camera in your hotel room. I'm happy to mail the camera back to you—and I won't charge you the shipping cost, but ³I do need to confirm your address. Just give me a call back with this information, and I can send the camera back to you later today. Thanks, and have a nice day.

안녕하세요, 리 씨께 드리는 메시지입니다. **¹리 씨, 파크빌에 있는 그랜드 호텔에서 전화 드립니다. ²호텔 객실에 카메라를 두고 가셨어요.** 카메라를 우편으로 보내 드리겠습니다. 배송비는 청구하지 않을 예정이지만 **³주소를 확인해야 합니다.** 저에게 전화 주셔서 해당 정보를 알려주시면 오늘 이따가 카메라를 보내 드릴 수 있어요. 감사합니다. 좋은 하루 되세요.

어휘 | charge 청구하다 shipping cost 배송비 confirm 확인하다

1 화자는 어디에서 일하는가?
(A) 은행
(B) 전자제품 매장
(C) 우체국
(D) 호텔

해설 | **전체 내용 - 화자의 근무 장소**
전화 메시지의 초반부에서 파크빌에 있는 그랜드 호텔에서 전화한다(I'm calling from the Grand Hotel in Parkville)고 했으므로, (D)가 정답이다.

2 전화는 무엇에 관한 내용인가?
(A) 불량품
(B) 깜빡 잊은 물건
(C) 청구서 발부 문제
(D) 배송 지연

해설 | **전체 내용 - 전화의 주제**
전화 메시지의 초반부에서 호텔 객실에 카메라를 두고 갔다(you left your camera in your hotel room)고 알린 후, 카메라를 우편으로 보내 주겠다(I'm happy to mail the camera back to you)며 분실 물건과 관련된 이야기를 하고 있으므로 (B)가 정답이다.
어휘 | defective 결함이 있는 billing 청구서 발부 delay 지연

3 화자는 어떤 정보를 필요로 하는가?
(A) 우편 주소
(B) 신용카드 번호
(C) 추적 번호
(D) 물품 명세

해설 | **세부 내용 - 화자가 필요로 하는 정보**
전화 메시지의 후반부에서 배송을 위해 주소를 확인해야 한다(I do need to confirm your address)고 한 후, 전화해서 해당 정보를 알려줄 것을 요청했으므로 (A)가 정답이다.

[4-6] **전화 메시지**

Hello, this is Amal Singh and I'm calling at nine o'clock on Thursday morning. **⁴I live in apartment 3B in the Franklin Manor complex. ⁵With the heavy rain we had last night, a lot of water came in around the kitchen window.** Since this is just the beginning of the rainy season, I hope you can fix this problem today. **⁶Please phone me as soon as possible so I know when to expect you.** Thanks very much.

안녕하세요, 저는 아말 싱입니다. 지금은 목요일 아침 9시 정각이고요. **⁴프랭클린 매너 단지 3B 아파트에 살고 있어요. ⁵어젯밤 폭우로 주방 창문 근처에 물이 많이 들어왔어요.** 우기가 막 시작됐으니 이 문제를 오늘 해결해 주셨으면 합니다. **⁶가능한 한 빨리 저에게 전화 주셔서 언제 오실지 알려 주세요.** 감사합니다.

어휘 | beginning 시작 expect 기대하다, 예상하다

4 전화를 건 사람은 누구이겠는가?
(A) 집 청소부
(B) 목수
(C) 세입자
(D) 환자

해설 | **전체 내용 - 화자의 신분**
전화 메시지의 초반부에서 프랭클린 매너 단지 3B 아파트에 살고 있다(I live in apartment 3B in the Franklin Manor complex)고 했으므로, 화자가 세입자임을 추론할 수 있다. 따라서 (C)가 정답이다.

5 전화를 건 목적은?
(A) 조언을 하려고
(B) 문제를 알리려고
(C) 계산을 치르려고
(D) 약속을 취소하려고

해설 | **전체 내용 - 전화의 목적**
전화 메시지의 중반부에서 어젯밤 폭우로 주방 창문 근처에 물이 많이 들어왔다(With the heavy rain we had last night, a lot of water came in around the kitchen window)는 문제점을 언급했으므로, 화자가 문제를 알리기 위해 전화했다는 것을 알 수 있다. 따라서 (B)가 정답이다.
어휘 | report 알리다, 발표하다 appointment 약속

6 전화를 건 사람은 무엇을 요청하는가?
(A) 제품 카탈로그
(B) 할인 가격
(C) 추천서
(D) 회신 전화

해설 | **세부 내용 - 화자가 요청한 것**
전화 메시지의 후반부에서 가능한 한 빨리 전화해서 언제 올지 알려 줄 것(Please phone me as soon as possible so I know when to expect you)을 요청했으므로 (D)가 정답이다.

[7-9] **메시지**

Hi, Aaron. I just got out of my meeting with Janet Lin from product development. **⁷She liked our design for the company's new line of raincoats, but unfortunately, she wants us to use different colors than what we proposed.** I tried my best to convince her that a fresh, new look was needed, but she insisted on a more traditional approach. **⁸There wasn't much more I could do. You know ... she's the head of the department.** Anyway, I'm back at my desk now, so **⁹I'm going to find a time on our calendars tomorrow when we can get together and start on these changes.**

안녕하세요, 아론. 제가 방금 제품 개발과의 재닛 린과 회의를 마치고 나왔어요. **⁷재닛이 회사의 새 레인코트에 대한 우리 디자인을 마음에 들어**

했지만 아쉽게도 우리가 제안한 것과는 다른 색깔들을 사용하길 원하시네요. 신선하고도 새로운 모습이 필요하다는 점을 설득시키려고 최선을 다했지만 재닛은 좀 더 전통적인 접근을 고집하셨어요. **8제가 할 수 있는 게 많지 않았어요.** 아시겠지만... 재닛이 부서장이잖아요. 어쨌든 지금 제가 제 자리로 돌아왔으니까 **9만나서 이런 변경 작업을 시작할 수 있도록 내일 일정을 한 번 잡아 볼게요.**

어휘 | get out of a meeting 회의를 마치고 나오다 product development 제품 개발(과) line 종류, 제품 unfortunately 아쉽게도, 불행히도 convince 설득하다, 확신시키다 insist on ~을 고집하다 approach 접근 head 책임자, 장 get together 모이다, 만나다

7 화자는 재닛 린과 무엇을 논의했는가?

(A) 채용 계획 (B) 제품 디자인
(C) 물품 주문 (D) 여행 일정

해설 | 세부 내용 - 논의했던 주제
메시지 초반부에 '재닛이 회사의 새 레인코트에 대한 우리 디자인을 마음에 들어 했지만 아쉽게도 우리가 제안한 것과는 다른 색깔들을 사용하길 원하시네요(She liked our design for the company's new line of raincoats, but unfortunately, she wants us to use different colors than what we proposed)'라고 했으므로 (B)가 정답이다.

8 화자가 "재닛이 부서장이잖아요"라고 말한 의도는 무엇인가?

(A) 그는 직원을 소개하고 싶어 한다.
(B) 그는 최종 결정을 내릴 수 없다.
(C) 직함이 잘못되었다.
(D) 동료가 큰 성공을 거두었다.

해설 | 세부 내용 - 화자의 의도
메시지 중반부에 화자가 자신이 할 수 있는 게 많지 않았다(There wasn't much more I could do)고 했고 이어서 '재닛이 부서장이잖아요(she's the head of the department)'라고 했다. 이 말은 재닛이 부서장이라서 화자 입장에서는 최종 결정을 내릴 수 없다는 뜻이므로 (B)가 정답이다.

9 화자는 다음에 무엇을 하겠는가?

(A) 회의 마련 (B) 카탈로그 검토
(C) 양식 작성 (D) 고객에게 전화

해설 | 세부 내용 - 화자의 다음 행동
메시지 맨 마지막에 함께 만나서 변경 작업을 시작할 수 있도록 내일 일정을 한 번 잡아 보겠다(I'm going to find a time on our calendars tomorrow)고 했으므로 (A)가 정답이다.

[10-12] 전화 메시지

Hi Rose, it's Jennifer. **10**I just found out that I can't attend the information technology job fair, so I won't be able to drive you there on Monday morning. But I think José Morales is planning on going. **11**Why don't you give him a call to see whether he has space in his car for you? And since I'm not going, **12**I'll drop off the company

brochures we were planning to hand out at the fair. May I stop by your office tomorrow to give them to you?

안녕하세요, 로즈. 제니퍼예요. **10제가 정보통신 기술 취업박람회에 참석할 수 없다는 걸 방금 알게 됐어요. 그래서 월요일 아침에 차로 데려다 주지 못할 거예요.** 하지만 호세 모랄레스가 갈 계획인 것 같아요. **11그에게 전화해 차에 태워줄 자리가 있는지 확인해 보는 게 어때요?** 그리고 제가 가지 않으니, **12취업박람회에서 나눠주려고 했었던 회사 안내책자를 갖다 줄게요. 내일 당신 사무실에 가도 될까요?**

어휘 | attend 참석하다 information technology 정보통신 기술 job fair 취업박람회 drop off 갖다 놓다, 내려주다 hand out 나눠주다, 배포하다

10 화자가 전화를 건 이유는?

(A) 사무실 절차에 대해 설명하려고
(B) 출장 계획을 취소하려고
(C) 회의 장소에 대해 문의하려고
(D) 시간표를 요청하려고

해설 | 전체 내용 - 전화의 목적
전화 메시지의 초반부에서 정보통신 기술 취업박람회에 참석할 수 없다(I can't attend the information technology job fair)는 걸 방금 알게 됐다고 한 후, 월요일 아침에 차로 데려다 주지 못한다고 했으므로, 출장 관련 계획을 취소하기 위해 전화했다는 것을 알 수 있다. 따라서 (B)가 정답이다.

어휘 | procedure 절차 cancel 취소하다 inquire 물어보다, 알아보다

11 화자는 무엇을 제안하는가?

(A) 차량 대여하기 (B) 길 안내도 출력하기
(C) 동료에게 전화하기 (D) 더 일찍 출발하기

해설 | 세부 내용 - 화자의 제안 사항
전화 메시지의 중반부에서 모랄레스 씨에게 전화해 차에 태워줄 자리가 있는지 확인해 보라(Why don't you give him a call to see whether he has space in his car for you?)고 제안했으므로 (C)가 정답이다.

어휘 | rent 빌리다, 대여하다 directions 길 안내 coworker 동료

12 화자는 내일 무엇을 할 계획인가?

(A) 휴가 내기 (B) 화상 회의 참여하기
(C) 행사 등록하기 (D) 안내책자 가져다 주기

해설 | 세부 내용 - 화자의 내일 계획
전화 메시지의 후반부에서 취업박람회에서 나눠주려고 했었던 회사 안내책자를 갖다 주겠다(I'll drop off the company brochures we were planning to hand out at the fair)고 한 후, 내일 사무실에 가도 되는지(May I stop by your office tomorrow) 물었으므로 (D)가 정답이다.

어휘 | participate in ~에 참가하다 register for ~에 등록하다

Paraphrasing
담화의 drop off the company brochures → 정답의 Deliver some brochures

LC

PART 4

Hello, Ms. Johnson. ¹³I'm one of the organizers for next month's metropolitan conference on renewable energy. We're looking forward to your presentation on recent advances in solar power. In preparation for the conference, ¹⁴please don't forget to send me a short résumé of your professional experience. That information will appear in the conference program, and I'll use it to introduce you. ¹⁵I should add that although you've received a presentation time slot already, one of the other presenters is unable to attend. ¹⁵I'll be in touch about that soon.

안녕하세요, 존슨 씨. ¹³저는 다음 달에 있을 재생 에너지 관련 대도시 학회 주최자 중 한 명입니다. 최근에 이루어진 태양열 발전에 관한 귀하의 발표를 고대하고 있습니다. 학회 준비에 필요하니, ¹⁴저에게 경력이 담긴 간략한 이력서를 잊지 말고 보내주세요. 해당 정보는 학회 프로그램에 나올 예정이고, 제가 이를 이용해 존슨 씨를 소개할 겁니다. ¹⁵이미 발표 시간대를 받으셨겠지만 다른 발표자 중 한 명이 참석할 수 없다는 사실을 덧붙여 알려드려야 할 것 같네요. ¹⁵이 내용에 대해 곧 연락 드리겠습니다.

어휘 | organizer 주최자 metropolitan 대도시의 conference 학회, 회의 renewable 재생 가능한 look forward to ~를 고대하다, 기다리다 presentation 발표 recent 최근의 advance 진보, 발전 in preparation for ~의 준비를 위해, ~의 준비로 professional 전문적인, 직업의 appear 언급되다, 나오다 time slot 시간대 be in touch 연락하다

13 화자에 따르면, 학회는 무엇에 관한 것인가?
(A) 소셜 미디어 마케팅
(B) 재생 에너지
(C) 지구 과학
(D) 공공 도서관

해설 | **세부 내용 - 학회의 주제**
전화 메시지의 초반부에서 화자는 자신을 다음 달에 있을 재생 에너지 관련 대도시 학회 주최자 중 한 명이라고(I'm one of the organizers for next month's metropolitan conference on renewable energy) 소개하고 있다. 따라서 (B)가 정답이다.

어휘 | public 공공의, 대중의

14 화자는 청자에게 무엇을 하라고 상기시키는가?
(A) 이름표 찾기   (B) 사진 발송
(C) 등록 확인   (D) 이력서 제공

해설 | **세부 내용 - 청자에게 상기시키는 사항**
전화 메시지의 중반부에서 경력이 담긴 간략한 이력서를 잊지 말고 보내줄 것(please don't forget to send me a short résumé of your professional experience)을 요청했으므로 (D)가 정답이다.

Paraphrasing
담화의 send me a short résumé of your professional experience → 정답의 Provide a résumé

15 화자가 "다른 발표자 중 한 명이 참석할 수 없다"고 말할 때, 그 의도는 무엇인가?
(A) 장비 일부를 구입할 것이다.
(B) 초대장 일부가 늦게 수신됐다.
(C) 행사 시간표가 변경될 수도 있다.
(D) 제출 기한이 연장됐다.

해설 | **세부 내용 - 화자의 의도**
전화 메시지의 후반부에서 청자가 이미 발표 시간대를 받았겠지만 (you've received a presentation time slot already) 다른 발표자 중 한 명이 참석할 수 없다(one of the other presenters is unable to attend)며 다시 연락하겠다고 덧붙였다. 이는 청자에게 발표 시간이 변경될 수 있다는 점을 알리려는 의도라고 볼 수 있으므로, (C)가 정답이다.

어휘 | equipment 장비 purchase 구입하다 modify 수정하다, 변경하다 submission 제출 extend 연장하다

Hello, ¹⁶thank you for calling Fellspoint Electronics, the store for all your electronic needs! The store is now closed. And remember—¹⁷we will be closed this weekend, October twenty-fifth and twenty-sixth, due to the national holiday. The store will reopen for business on October twenty-seventh. If you're calling about your recent purchase of a Nightingale television set, we are aware that these may be defective. Because of this, the store is offering a five-year warranty on these televisions. ¹⁸Just bring in your receipt to register for the extended warranty.

안녕하세요, ¹⁶전자 제품에 대한 여러분의 모든 필요를 충족시켜 드리는 펠스포인트 전자에 전화해 주셔서 감사합니다. 매장은 현재 문을 닫았습니다. 그리고 기억해 주세요. ¹⁷이번 주말인 10월 25일과 26일은 국가 공휴일로 휴무입니다. 매장은 10월 27일에 다시 문을 열 것입니다. 고객님께서 최근에 구입하신 나이팅게일 텔레비전 세트 때문에 전화를 주신 것이라면, 제품의 결함 가능성에 대해 저희도 인지하고 있습니다. 이러한 이유로, 저희 매장에서는 이 텔레비전에 대해 5년 동안의 품질 보증을 제공합니다. ¹⁸품질 보증 기간 연장을 신청하시려면 영수증을 지참하여 매장에 방문해 주십시오.

어휘 | national holiday 국경일 purchase 구매(품) aware 인지하고 있는 defective 결함이 있는 warranty 품질 보증(서) extended 연장된

16 화자는 어디에서 일할 것 같은가?
(A) 변호사 사무실   (B) 철물점
(C) 전자 제품 매장   (D) 배송 회사

해설 | **전체 내용 - 화자의 근무 장소**
화자가 메시지 초반부에서 펠스포인트 전자에 전화해 주어 고맙다(thank you for calling Fellspoint Electronics)고 한 후, 매장 관련 안내를 이어 갔으므로, 화자가 전자 제품 매장에서 일한다는 것을 알 수 있다. 따라서 (C)가 정답이다.

17 화자는 이번 주말에 대해 무엇이라고 말하는가?
(A) 매장이 문을 닫을 것이다.
(B) 예약이 필요할 것이다.
(C) 할인 판매가 시작될 것이다.
(D) 주문 제품이 도착할 것이다.

해설 | **세부 내용 - 화자가 주말에 대해 말한 것**
메시지 초반부에서 매장이 주말에 문을 닫을 것(we will be closed this weekend)이라고 했으므로, (A)가 정답이다.

어휘 | require 요구하다, 필요로 하다

18 화자의 말에 따르면, 매장에서는 무엇을 제공하는가?
(A) 전화 상담
(B) 개인 맞춤 선물
(C) 할인 쿠폰
(D) 품질 보증 기간 연장

해설 | **세부 내용 - 매장에서 제공하는 것**
메시지 후반부에서 품질 보증 기간 연장을 신청하려면 영수증을 지참하여 매장을 방문할 것(Just bring in your receipt to register for the extended warranty)을 권유했으므로, (D)가 정답이다.

[19-21] 전화 메시지 + 할인 정보

Hi, **¹⁹**this is Rosa at Levenson Shoes. I'm calling to let you know that the winter boots you ordered have arrived. Please stop by at your convenience to complete your purchase. By the way, **²⁰**are you a member of our store's rewards program? If not, I'd recommend joining—it's free, and your membership will qualify you for a discount every time you shop with us. So, **²¹**you'd get a nice discount on the boots you ordered, considering they're 100 dollars. See you soon!

안녕하세요. **¹⁹**레벤슨 슈즈의 로사라고 합니다. 주문하신 겨울 부츠가 도착했다고 알려드리려 전화했습니다. 편하실 때 들르셔서 구매를 완료해 주세요. 그런데 **²⁰**저희 매장 보상 프로그램 회원이신가요? 아니시라면 가입을 권해드려요. 무료이고, 저희 제품을 사실 때마다 회원권으로 할인을 받으실 수 있습니다. **²¹**따라서 주문하신 부츠가 100달러인 것을 감안하면 할인을 많이 받으실 겁니다. 곧 뵙겠습니다.

어휘 | stop by 들르다 at one's convenience 편한 때에 complete 완료하다 purchase 구입, 구매 reward 보상 recommend 추천하다, 권장하다 qualify 자격을 주다 considering ~를 감안하면, 고려하면

독점 할인
25달러 구매 시 5달러 할인
50달러 구매 시 10달러 할인
²¹100달러 구매 시 15달러 할인
150달러 구매 시 20달러 할인

어휘 | exclusive 독점적인, 배타적인

19 매장에서 무엇을 판매하는가?
(A) 가구   (B) 신발
(C) 건축 자재   (D) 조경 장비

해설 | **세부 내용 - 매장에서 판매하는 제품**
전화 메시지의 초반부에서 화자가 자신을 레벤슨 슈즈의 로사(this is Rosa at Levenson Shoes)라고 소개한 후, 청자의 주문품인 겨울 부츠(the winter boots you ordered)를 언급했으므로, 매장에서 신발류를 판매한다는 것을 알 수 있다. 따라서 (B)가 정답이다.

Paraphrasing
담화의 Shoes/the winter boots → 정답의 Footwear

20 화자는 무엇을 하라고 제안하는가?
(A) 제품 사용 후기 작성   (B) 특별 행사 참석
(C) 다른 물건 선택   (D) 회원 등록

해설 | **세부 내용 - 화자의 제안 사항**
전화 메시지의 중반부에서 매장 보상 프로그램 회원(a member of our store's rewards program)인지 물어본 후, 아니라면 가입을 권한다(If not, I'd recommend joining)고 했으므로 (D)가 정답이다.

Paraphrasing
담화의 joining → 정답의 Registering for

21 시각 정보에 따르면, 청자는 구입 상품에 대해 얼마를 할인 받겠는가?
(A) 5달러
(B) 10달러
(C) 15달러
(D) 20달러

해설 | **세부 내용 - 시각 정보 연계**
전화 메시지의 후반부에서 주문한 부츠가 100달러인 것을 감안하면 할인을 많이 받게 될 것(you'd get a nice discount on the boots you ordered, considering they're 100 dollars)이라고 했다. 시각 정보를 보면 100달러 구매 시 15달러를 할인($15 off $100 purchase)해 준다고 하므로 (C)가 정답이다.

Unit 12   공지 / 회의

담화 흐름 파악하기
본책 p. 110

안녕하세요, 여러분. 업무를 시작하기 전에 짧은 공지 사항 전할게요. 이곳 우리 매장에서는 겉옷 판매가 잘되고 있지만, 우리 웹사이트에 문제가 몇 가지 있습니다. 자세히 말하자면, 남성용 재킷을 볼 수 있는 링크가 작동하지 않습니다. IT팀에서 이 문제를 살펴보고 있지만 언제 고쳐질지 모릅니다. 그러니, 온라인상에 있는 재킷을 찾는 고객들이 오시면 그분들을 우리 고객 서비스 관리자에게 보내세요. 그녀가 그분들을 도와드릴 거예요. 감사합니다!

어휘 | namely 자세히 말하자면, 예를 들면 look into 조사하다

1 청자들은 어디에서 일할 것 같은가?

2 화자는 어떤 문제를 언급하는가?

3 화자는 청자들에게 무엇을 하라고 요청하는가?

● 실전 도움닫기

본책 p.111

1 (B) **2** (A) **3** (B) **4** (B) **5** (A) **6** (B)

[1-2]

> [1]Good evening, library patrons. We'll be closing in 30 minutes. If you're working on a public computer, we ask that you shut it down before you leave. [2]If you would like to check out any books, please proceed to the service desk near the front entrance. Also, we'd like to remind you that we will be showing a free movie tomorrow evening at six o'clock called *Life in Tuscany*. Please join us for this wonderful film.
>
> [1]안녕하세요, 도서관 이용객 여러분. 저희는 30분 후에 문을 닫습니다. 공용 컴퓨터를 쓰시고 계시면 나가시기 전에 전원을 꺼 주세요. [2]만약 대출하고 싶은 책이 있으면 정문 입구 근처의 안내 데스크로 가 주시기 바랍니다. 또한, 내일 저녁 6시에 영화 <토스카나에서의 삶>을 무료로 상영할 예정임을 다시 알려 드립니다. 오셔서 이 멋진 영화를 감상하시기 바랍니다.
>
> 어휘 | patron 고객, 이용객 check out (책을) 대출하다 proceed to ~으로 가다

1 이 안내 방송은 어디에서 나오고 있는가?
(A) 영화관에서
(B) 도서관에서

해설 | **전체 내용 - 장소**
안내 방송을 시작하면서 화자가 '안녕하세요, 도서관 이용객 여러분 (Good evening, library patrons)'이라고 했으므로 (B)가 정답이다.

2 청자들은 안내 데스크에서 무엇을 할 수 있는가?
(A) 자료를 대출한다.
(B) 컴퓨터를 사용하기 위해 등록한다.

해설 | **세부 내용 - 안내 데스크에서 할 수 있는 일**
중반부에서 만약 대출하고 싶은 책이 있으면 입구 근처의 안내 데스크로 가 달라(If you would like to check out any books, please proceed to the service desk near the front entrance)고 했으므로 (A)가 정답이다.

[3-4]

> Good morning. [3]This is an announcement for all passengers on Soar Wings Air flight 113 to Chicago. There will be a slight departure delay. Your new departure time is 10:05. [4]We apologize for this inconvenience due to the late arrival of the aircraft from the previous leg of its journey, and we thank you for your patience. Also, this flight has been overbooked, so we are offering

complimentary meal vouchers for passengers who are willing to be rebooked onto a later flight.

> 좋은 아침입니다. [3]시카고행 소어 윙스 항공 113편을 이용하시는 모든 승객 여러분께 안내 말씀드립니다. 다소 출발 지연이 있을 예정입니다. 변경된 출발 시각은 10시 5분입니다. [4]이전 여정에서 들어오는 항공기의 연착으로 인해 불편을 끼쳐드려 죄송합니다. 그리고 양해해 주셔서 감사드립니다. 아울러 이 항공기는 초과 예약되었습니다. 따라서 다음 항공편으로 예약 변경을 희망하시는 승객께는 무료 식사권을 제공해드릴 예정입니다.
>
> 어휘 | delay 지연 inconvenience 불편 due to ~때문에 leg (여정의) 구간 patience 인내심 overbook 초과 예약을 받다 complimentary 무료의 meal voucher 식사권

항공편	목적지	탑승 시각
542	오클랜드	9시 20분
[3]113	시카고	**9시 40분**
302	두바이	10시 5분
737	상하이	10시 35분

3 시각 정보에 따르면, 지연된 항공편의 원래 탑승 시각은 언제인가?
(A) 9시 20분   (B) 9시 40분

해설 | **세부 내용 - 시각 정보 연계**
안내 방송 초반부에서 시카고행 소어 윙스 항공 113편(Soar Wings Air flight 113 to Chicago) 출발이 지연될 예정(There will be a slight departure delay)이라고 했다. 표지판에서 시카고행 항공편을 보면 원래 탑승 시각은 9시 40분임을 알 수 있으므로, (B)가 정답이다.

4 항공편은 왜 지연되었는가?
(A) 항공기에 기계 결함이 있었다.
(B) 들어오는 비행기가 제시간에 도착하지 못했다.

해설 | **세부 내용 - 항공편 지연 이유**
안내 방송 중반부에서 이전 여정에서 들어오는 항공기의 연착으로 인해(due to the late arrival of the aircraft from the previous leg of its journey) 항공편이 지연된다고 했으므로 (B)가 정답이다.

어휘 | mechanical problem 기계 결함 incoming 들어오는 on time 제시간에

[5-6]

> Hello everyone, this will be a quick meeting, and I'll be very brief. [5]I just wanted to let you know of a change in policy. It used to be that when a customer called to get technical support and we couldn't solve the problem during the call, we'd ask the customer to call back. From now on, when you come across that kind of situation, [6]you need to give the customer a case number before hanging up. This will help us track each customer's problem much more efficiently.

여러분 안녕하세요. 오늘 회의는 아주 짧게, 제가 간단히 설명드리는 형식으로 진행하겠습니다. ⁵**정책 변경 사항 한 가지만 알려드리면 됩니다.** 고객이 기술 지원을 받기 위해 전화했는데 전화상으로 문제를 해결할 수 없을 때, 우리는 고객에게 나중에 다시 전화를 걸어 달라고 요청했습니다. 지금부터는 그러한 상황에 직면하면, ⁶**전화를 끊기 전에 고객에게 접수 번호를 주어야 합니다.** 이렇게 하면 각 고객의 문제를 훨씬 더 효율적으로 추적하는 데 도움이 될 것입니다.

어휘 | brief 간단한 policy 정책, 방침 technical support 기술 지원 solve 해결하다 come across ~을 우연히 만나다 situation 상황 case number 접수 번호 hang up 전화를 끊다 track 추적하다 efficiently 효율적으로

5 회의의 목적은 무엇인가?
(A) 정책 변경을 발표하는 것
(B) 신기술을 소개하는 것

해설 | **전체 내용 - 회의의 목적**
회의 초반부에서 정책 변경 사항에 관해 알려 주겠다(I just wanted to let you know of a change in policy)고 했으므로 (A)가 정답이다.

6 화자가 직원들에게 요청하는 것은 무엇인가?
(A) 고객의 전화에 회신할 것
(B) 각 고객에게 접수 번호를 줄 것

해설 | **세부 내용 - 직원들에게 요청하는 사항**
회의 후반부에서 전화상으로 고객의 문제를 해결할 수 없는 상황에 직면했을 때 앞으로는 전화를 끊기 전에 고객에게 접수 번호를 주라(you need to give the customer a case number before hanging up)고 했으므로 (B)가 정답이다.

● ETS 실전문제

본책 p.112

1 (C)	**2** (A)	**3** (D)	**4** (A)	**5** (B)	**6** (C)
7 (C)	**8** (A)	**9** (B)	**10** (C)	**11** (A)	**12** (C)
13 (C)	**14** (B)	**15** (A)	**16** (B)	**17** (A)	**18** (D)
19 (B)	**20** (C)	**21** (C)			

[1-3] 회의 발췌

Good morning. ¹At today's meeting, I'll be training everyone on how to use the new videoconferencing system. We're hoping this new software will make it much easier to communicate with colleagues at our international branches. ²Now, I see you've all brought your laptops as I requested. By now you should all have the new videoconferencing software installed on them. So, let's get started. The first thing I'm going to do is pass out an attendance sheet. Your name and phone number should already be there, but ³please add your e-mail address in the space provided.

안녕하세요. ¹**오늘 회의에서는 제가 모든 분께 새로운 화상회의 시스템 사용법을 가르쳐 드릴 겁니다.** 이 새 소프트웨어로 해외 지점에 있는 동료들과 훨씬 수월하게 소통할 수 있길 바랍니다. ²**지금 보니 여러분 모두 제가 요청 드린 대로 노트북을 가져오셨네요.** 지금쯤 모두들 새로운 화상회의 소프트웨어를 노트북에 설치하셨을 겁니다. 자, 그럼 시작하죠. 제가 제일 먼저 하려고 하는 것은 출석부를 나눠 드리는 겁니다. 거기에 여러분 이름과 전화번호는 이미 있습니다만 ³**빈 공간에 여러분의 이메일 주소를 추가해 주세요.**

어휘 | videoconferencing system 화상회의 시스템 communicate with ~와 소통하다 colleague 동료 install 설치하다 pass out 나누어 주다 attendance sheet 출석부

1 회의의 목적은 무엇인가?
(A) 회사 합병을 알리기 위해
(B) 신입직원을 소개하기 위해
(C) 직원들에게 교육을 제공하기 위해
(D) 국제 회의를 기획하기 위해

해설 | **전체 내용 - 회의 목적**
회의 초반부에서 청자들에게 새로운 화상회의 시스템 사용법을 가르쳐 줄 것(I'll be training everyone on how to use the new videoconferencing system)이라고 했으므로, (C)가 정답이다.

어휘 | merger 합병

2 청자들은 회의 때 무엇을 가져오라는 요청을 받았는가?
(A) 노트북 컴퓨터　　　(B) 사원증
(C) 현재 이력서　　　(D) 경과 보고서

해설 | **세부 내용 - 청자들에게 가져오라고 요청한 것**
회의 중반부에서 '여러분 모두 제가 요청 드린 대로 노트북 컴퓨터를 가져오셨네요(you've all brought your laptops as I requested)'라고 했으므로, (A)가 정답이다.

3 청자들은 다음에 무엇을 하라는 요청을 받는가?
(A) 다른 회의실로 이동　　　(B) 비밀번호 변경
(C) 설명서 보기　　　(D) 추가 연락 정보 제공

해설 | **세부 내용 - 청자들이 요청 받은 일**
회의 후반부에서 청자들에게 빈 공간에 이메일 주소를 추가해 달라(please add your e-mail adress)고 요청했으므로 (D)가 정답이다.

Paraphrasing
담화의 add your e-mail address → 정답의 Provide additional contact information

[4-6] 안내 방송

May I have everyone's attention, please? ⁴Thank you for coming to the Science Theater at the Brinkley Museum. And ⁵thank you all for waiting so patiently in line. Unfortunately, we have just filled all the seats for the three o'clock showing of today's documentary film. However, ⁶there will be another showing at five o'clock, and we usually have fewer attendees at that time. **We hope you'll return then. In the meantime, feel free to continue exploring the museum's exhibits, cafeteria, and gift shop.**

모두 주목해 주시겠습니까? **4브링클리 박물관 과학 극장에 와 주셔서 감사합니다. 5아울러 줄을 서서 참을성 있게 기다려 주셔서 감사드립니다.** 안타깝게도 오늘 다큐멘터리 영화 3시 상영 좌석이 모두 찼습니다. 하지만 **65시 정각에 다시 상영하며, 해당 시간에는 보통 참석자가 더 적습니다.** 그 때 다시 와 주시기 바랍니다. 그동안 박물관 내 전시실, 카페테리아, 기념품점 등을 자유롭게 계속 둘러보십시오.

어휘 | attention 주의, 주목 patiently 참을성 있게, 끈기 있게 attendee 참석자 in the meantime 그동안 explore 답사하다

4 안내 방송은 어디에서 이뤄지는가?
(A) 박물관 (B) 대학교
(C) 가구점 (D) 도서관

해설 | **전체 내용 - 안내 방송 장소**
안내 방송 초반부에서 브링클리 박물관의 과학 극장(Science Theater at the Brinkley Museum)와주어 감사하다고 했으므로 (A)가 정답이다.

5 청자들은 어디에 참석하려고 기다리는가?
(A) 강의 (B) 영화
(C) 전시회 (D) 음악회

해설 | **세부 내용 - 청자들이 참석을 기다리는 행사**
안내 방송의 중반부에서 청자들에게 줄을 서서 참을성 있게 기다려 준 것(waiting so patiently in line)에 감사를 전한 후, 오늘 다큐멘터리 영화 3시 상영은 좌석이 모두 찼다(we have just filled all the seats for the three o'clock showing of today's documentary film)고 했으므로, 청자들이 다큐멘터리 영화의 상영을 기다리고 있었음을 알 수 있다. 따라서 (B)가 정답이다.

6 화자는 5시 행사에 대해 무엇이라고 말하는가?
(A) 더 저렴하다. (B) 더 짧다.
(C) 덜 붐빈다. (D) 간식이 포함되어 있다.

해설 | **세부 내용 - 화자가 5시 행사에 대해 언급한 사항**
안내 방송의 중반부에서 영화는 5시 정각에 다시 상영한다(there will be another showing at five o'clock)고 한 후, 해당 시간에는 보통 참석자가 더 적다(we usually have fewer attendees at that time)고 했으므로 (C)가 정답이다.

Paraphrasing
담화의 fewer attendees → 정답의 less crowded

[7-9] 회의 발췌

Good morning, everyone. As you know, this past year has been very successful. **7We filled orders for many large events, and everyone loved our cakes, cookies, and pastries.** Because the profits are higher than I expected, **8I am very happy to announce that you'll all be getting a pay raise.** I've been revising the pay scale this week, and

I'll send you an email explaining the details later today. But **9please read your next paychecks carefully. Because we've had so many orders to fill this week, I've been working late every night.**

안녕하세요, 여러분. 아시다시피 작년에는 매우 큰 성공을 거뒀습니다. **7다수의 대형 행사 주문을 처리했고, 모두가 우리 케이크, 쿠키, 제과류에 만족했어요.** 제 예상보다 수익이 더 많아서, **8여러분 모두 급여를 인상받게 되었다는 사실을 알리게 되어 기쁩니다.** 이번 주에 급여표를 수정했고 오늘 늦게 세부 사항을 설명하는 이메일을 보낼 예정입니다. 그래도 **9다음 번 급여를 주의 깊게 살펴보세요.** 이번 주에 처리할 주문건이 너무 많아서 제가 매일 밤늦게까지 일했거든요.

어휘 | successful 성공적인 fill an order 주문을 충족시키다 profit 이윤, 수익 announce 발표하다, 알리다 pay raise 급여 인상 revise 수정하다 pay scale 급여 체계, 급여표 paycheck 급료

7 청자들은 어디에서 일하겠는가?
(A) 해산물 식당 (B) 농장
(C) 제과점 (D) 아이스크림 가게

해설 | **전체 내용 - 청자들의 근무 장소**
회의의 초반부에서 대형 행사 주문 고객 모두가 우리 케이크, 쿠키, 제과류에 만족했다(We filled orders for many large events, and everyone loved our cakes, cookies, and pastries)며 회사의 취급 품목을 언급하고 있으므로, 화자와 청자 모두 제과점에서 일한다는 것을 알 수 있다. 따라서 (C)가 정답이다.

8 화자는 무엇을 알리게 되어 기뻐하는가?
(A) 직원들에게 급여 인상을 해 줄 수 있다는 것
(B) 새 메뉴를 추가할 수 있는 것
(C) 회사가 새 지점을 열었다는 것
(D) 회사가 상을 탔다는 것

해설 | **세부 내용 - 화자가 알리게 되어 기쁜 사항**
회의의 중반부에서 모두가 급여 인상을 받게 되었다는 사실을 알리게 되어 기쁘다(I am very happy to announce that you'll all be getting a pay raise)고 했으므로 (A)가 정답이다.

어휘 | employee 고용인, 직원 increase 증가, 인상 win a prize 상을 타다

Paraphrasing
담화의 a pay raise → 정답의 a pay increase

9 화자가 "제가 매일 밤 늦게까지 일했거든요"라고 말할 때, 그 의도는 무엇인가?
(A) 승진할 자격이 있다.
(B) 실수했을 지도 모른다.
(C) 자원 봉사자를 구하고 있다.
(D) 다른 근무 시간대에 일하고 있다.

해설 | **세부 내용 - 화자의 의도**
회의의 후반부에서 다음 번 급여를 주의 깊게 살펴볼 것(please read your next paychecks carefully)을 권고한 후, 이번 주에 처리할 주문 건이 너무 많아서(Because we've had so many orders to fill this week) 자신이 밤늦게까지 일했다고 덧붙였다. 이는 급여 산정에 실수가 있을 수 있다는 점에 대해 미리 양해를 구하려는 의도라고 볼 수 있으므로, (B)가 정답이다.

어휘 | deserve ~할 자격이 있다, ~할 만하다 promotion 승진 volunteer 자원 봉사자 shift 교대 근무 (시간)

[10-12] 안내 방송

Good evening, passengers, and [10]thank you for choosing Tate Airways for your trip to Portland. We'll arrive at our final destination in just over an hour. We're happy to inform you that [11]we're now offering free wireless Internet to our passengers. This will allow you to get some work done or just check the news headlines. [12]All we ask is that you remember to use headphones when listening to audio on your personal devices so that you don't disturb those around you.

승객 여러분, 안녕하십니까? [10]포틀랜드까지의 여정에 테이트 항공을 선택해 주셔서 감사합니다. 한 시간 남짓이면 최종 목적지에 도착합니다. 승객 여러분께 [11]무선 인터넷을 무료로 제공해 드리고 있다는 점을 알려 드립니다. 이를 이용해 업무를 완료하시거나 뉴스 헤드라인을 확인하실 수 있습니다. [12]개인 기기로 오디오를 청취하실 때는 잊지 말고 헤드폰을 사용하셔서 주변 승객을 방해하지 않도록 해 주십시오.

어휘 | passenger 승객 destination 목적지 inform 알리다 offer 제공하다 wireless 무선의 device 기기 disturb 방해하다

10 화자는 누구이겠는가?
(A) 전기 기사 　　　　　(B) 기자
(C) 비행기 승무원 　　　(D) 여행사 직원

해설 | **전체 내용 - 화자의 신분**
안내 방송의 초반부에서 포틀랜드까지의 여정에 테이트 항공을 선택한 것(choosing Tate Airways for your trip to Portland)에 대해 감사를 전한 후, 한 시간 남짓이면 최종 목적지에 도착한다고 했으므로, 화자가 기내 승무원(flight attendant)임을 알 수 있다. 따라서 (C)가 정답이다.

11 화자는 어떤 무료 서비스를 언급하는가?
(A) 무선 인터넷 　　　　(B) 가정 배달
(C) 공항 교통편 　　　　(D) 기술 지원

해설 | **세부 내용 - 화자가 언급한 무료 서비스**
안내 방송의 중반부에서 승객에게 무선 인터넷을 무료로 제공한다(we're now offering free wireless Internet to our passengers)는 점을 알린다고 했으므로 (A)가 정답이다.

Paraphrasing
담화의 free → 질문의 complimentary

12 청자들은 무엇을 하라는 이야기를 들었는가?
(A) 영수증 보관 　　　　(B) 좌석벨트 착용
(C) 헤드폰 착용 　　　　(D) 고객 설문조사 작성

해설 | **세부 내용 - 청자들이 주의 받는 사항**
안내 방송의 후반부에서 주변 승객을 방해하지 않기 위해 개인 기기로 오디오를 청취할 때 헤드폰을 사용하라(you remember to use headphones when listening to audio on your personal devices)고 요청했으므로 (C)가 정답이다.

[13-15] 회의 발췌

Before we end this morning's staff meeting, [13]please note that the relocation to our new headquarters building will begin at eight o'clock on Monday morning. The moving company we've hired, Takeda Transport, will take care of all office furniture and electronic equipment. Employees are responsible for packing up their own personal belongings before leaving the office on Friday. [14]Please remember to write your name and new office number clearly on each of your boxes so that nothing gets lost. [15]If you have any questions, please contact the move coordinator, Don Brooks. Don's in the facilities department, so he can answer any questions you might have.

오늘 아침 직원 회의를 마치기 전에 [13]새 본사 건물로의 이전이 월요일 아침 8시 정각에 시작됨을 알려드립니다. 우리가 고용한 이사업체인 다케다 트랜스포트에서 모든 사무용 가구와 전기 장비를 처리할 겁니다. 직원들은 금요일 퇴근 전에 자신의 개인 물품을 포장해야 합니다. [14]상자마다 이름과 새 사무실 번호를 명확하게 기입하셔서 물품을 분실하지 않도록 하십시오. [15]질문 있으시면 이사 담당자인 돈 브룩스에게 연락하시기 바랍니다. 돈은 시설 부서에 있어 여러분의 모든 질문에 답변해 드릴 수 있습니다.

어휘 | relocation 이전 headquarters 본사 take care of ~를 처리하다 furniture 가구 equipment 장비 be responsible for ~에 책임이 있다 belongings 소유물, 재산 facility 시설 department 부서

13 담화는 무엇에 관한 것인가?
(A) 건물 보수 　　　　　(B) 컴퓨터 교체
(C) 곧 있을 사무실 이사 　(D) 회사 합병

해설 | **전체 내용 - 담화의 주제**
회의의 초반부에서 새 본사 건물로의 이전이 월요일 아침 8시 정각에 시작된다(the relocation to our new headquarters building will begin at eight o'clock on Monday morning)는 점을 알린다고 한 후, 이전과 관련된 내용을 안내하고 있으므로 (C)가 정답이다.

어휘 | renovation 수선, 보수 replacement 교체 upcoming 다가오는, 곧 있을 merger 합병

Paraphrasing
담화의 relocation → 정답의 office move

14 화자는 청자들에게 무엇을 하라고 말하는가?
(A) 금요일까지 물품 주문하기
(B) 개인 물품에 이름표 붙이기
(C) 모든 장비 끄기
(D) 사무실을 잠가 두기

해설 | **세부 내용 - 청자들에게 상기시키는 사항**
회의의 중반부에서 물품을 분실하지 않도록 상자마다 이름과 새 사무실 번호를 명확하게 기입하라(to write your name and new office number clearly on each of your boxes)고 했으므로 (B)가 정답이다.

어휘 | supply 용품 locked 잠긴

15 청자들은 왜 돈 브룩스에게 연락해야 하는가?

(A) 지시 사항에 대한 명확한 설명을 듣기 위해

(B) 컴퓨터 식별 번호를 제공하기 위해

(C) 프로젝트 진행을 자원하기 위해

(D) 새 사무실 가구를 요청하기 위해

해설 | **세부 내용 - 청자들이 돈 브룩스에게 연락해야 하는 이유**

회의의 후반부에서 이전 관련 질문이 있으면 이사 담당자인 돈 브룩스에게 연락하라고(please contact the move coordinator, Don Brooks) 권고한 후, 시설 부서(the facilities department)에 있어 모든 질문에 답변해 줄 수 있다(he can answer any questions you might have)며 권고의 이유를 덧붙였으므로 (A)가 정답이다.

어휘 | clarification 명확한 설명 instruction 지시 사항 identification 식별, 신원 확인 volunteer 자원하다 request 요청하다

[16-18] 공지

Welcome to this month's all-staff meeting. To begin, I have some great news. As the editor in chief of *Science and You* magazine, [16]I am pleased to announce the finalization of our company's merger with Stonewell Publishing. This means many exciting things for us, namely that [17]we can take advantage of Stonewell's incredible technology department so we can make the online version of our magazine better. And why wouldn't we? Our data shows that sixty percent of our magazine subscribers use their mobile phones to read articles online. Now, Stonewell has already granted all of us access to their publications. [18]So, please use some time over the next few weeks to familiarize yourselves with their Web sites.

이번 달 전 직원 회의에 오신 것을 환영합니다. 우선 몇 가지 좋은 소식이 있습니다. 저는 <과학과 당신> 잡지의 편집장으로서 [16]우리 회사가 스톤웰 출판사와의 합병을 마무리지었다는 점을 알리게 되어 기쁩니다. 이것은 우리에게 많은 흥미로운 점을 시사하는데, 한 가지 예를 들면 [17]우리가 스톤웰의 훌륭한 기술부서를 통해 우리 잡지의 인터넷판을 더 잘 만들 수 있다는 겁니다. 그러니 우리가 왜 마다하겠습니까? 저희 자료에 따르면, 우리 잡지 구독자 중 60퍼센트가 휴대 전화로 인터넷 기사를 읽고 있습니다. 자, 스톤웰이 벌써 우리 모두가 그들의 출판물을 이용할 수 있게 해 주었습니다. [18]그러니 앞으로 몇 주간 시간을 내서 그들의 웹사이트를 잘 익혀두시기 바랍니다.

어휘 | editor in chief 편집장 finalization 완결, 마무리 짓기 merger 합병 take advantage of ~을 이용하다 incredible 믿기지 않는 subscriber 구독자 grant 주다 access 접근(권), 이용 publication 출판물 familiarize oneself with ~을 잘 익히다

16 공지의 목적은 무엇인가?

(A) 예산 제안서 검토

(B) 곧 있을 합병에 대한 논의

(C) 몇 가지 설문조사 결과 설명

(D) 신입직원 소개

해설 | **전체 내용 - 공지의 목적**

공지 초반부에 회사가 스톤웰 출판사와의 합병을 마무리지었다는 점을 알린다(I am pleased to announce the finalization of our company's merger with Stonewell Publishing)고 했으므로 (B)가 정답이다.

어휘 | budget proposal 예산 제안서 upcoming 다가오는, 곧 있을

17 여자가 "그러니 우리가 왜 마다하겠습니까"라고 말한 의도는 무엇인가?

(A) 결정을 지지한다.

(B) 전근을 희망한다.

(C) 청자들이 의견을 공유하길 원한다.

(D) 선적물이 걱정스럽다.

해설 | **세부 내용 - 화자의 의도**

공지 중반부에 스톤웰의 훌륭한 기술부서를 통해 잡지의 인터넷판을 더 잘 만들 수 있을 것(we can take advantage of Stonewell's incredible technology department so we can make the online version of our magazine better)이라고 했다. 그런 다음 우리가 왜 마다하겠느냐(And why wouldn't we)고 말했는데, 이는 회사의 합병 결정을 지지한다는 의미라고 볼 수 있으므로 (A)가 정답이다.

18 여자는 청자들에게 무엇을 하라고 요청하는가?

(A) 교육 참석   (B) 몇 가지 서류에 서명

(C) 질문 목록 수거   (D) 온라인으로 몇 가지 정보 검토

해설 | **세부 내용 - 여자의 요청 사항**

공지의 마지막 부분에 청자들에게 앞으로 몇 주간 시간을 내서 그 회사의 웹사이트를 잘 익혀두라(So, please use some time over the next few weeks to familiarize yourselves with their Web sites)고 했으므로 (D)가 정답이다.

[19-21] 회의 발췌 + 매출 그래프

I have one final issue to discuss at today's staff meeting. [19]I just handed out a graph summarizing our shoe store's annual sales data. And, well...I think this information is particularly interesting since we relocated to a different neighborhood this year. As you might have expected, the relocation decreased our sales significantly at first. [20]During the quarter we moved, we experienced the lowest shoe sales of the entire year. That was largely because people in the new neighborhood didn't know about us. [21]However, thanks to the newspaper advertisements and radio commercials we put out, business picked up quickly, and we ended the year by making a record number of sales.

오늘 직원 회의에서 마지막으로 논의할 사항이 한 가지 있습니다. **¹⁹제가 방금 우리 신발 가게의 연간 매출 자료를 요약한 그래프를 나눠 드렸습니다.** 그리고 음.. 제 생각에 이 정보는 특히나 흥미로운데 왜냐하면 우리가 올해 다른 지역으로 이전했기 때문입니다. 예상하셨겠지만 이전하면서 처음에는 매출이 상당히 하락했습니다. **²⁰한 해 전체를 통틀어 우리가 이전한 해당 분기 동안 신발 매출이 가장 저조했습니다.** 대체로 새 주민들이 우리에 관해 몰랐기 때문입니다. **²¹하지만 우리가 낸 신문과 라디오 광고로 사업이 빠르게 호전되었고 기록적인 매출을 달성하며 한 해를 마무리했습니다.**

어휘 | hand out 나누어 주다 summarize 요약하다 annual sales 연매출 relocate to ~로 이전하다 neighborhood 인근 지역, 이웃 significantly 상당히 largely 대체로 commercial (TV나 라디오) 광고 put out 내놓다 business 사업, 거래 pick up 개선되다, 회복되다 a record number of 기록적인, 최고치의

연매출

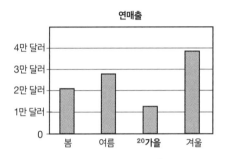

19 회사는 어떤 종류의 상품을 판매하는가?
(A) 옷　　　　　　　(B) 신발
(C) 가전기기　　　　(D) 소프트웨어

해설 | **세부 내용 - 판매 상품**
회의 초반부에 신발 가게의 연간 매출 자료(our shoe store's annual sales data)를 요약한 그래프를 나눠주었다고 했으므로 (B)가 정답이다.

Paraphrasing
담화의 shoe → 정답의 Footwear

20 시각 정보에 따르면, 회사는 어느 계절에 이전했는가?
(A) 봄　　　　　　　(B) 여름
(C) 가을　　　　　　(D) 겨울

해설 | **세부 내용 - 시각 정보 연계**
회의 중반부에 한 해 전체를 통틀어 이전한 분기에 신발 매출이 가장 저조했다(During the quarter we moved, we experienced the lowest shoe sales of the entire year)고 했다. 표를 보면 가을 매출이 가장 저조하므로, (C)가 정답이다.

21 회사는 이전 후 무엇을 했는가?
(A) 물품 목록을 확장했다.　　(B) 직원을 추가 고용했다.
(C) 광고를 했다.　　　　　　(D) 개업식을 준비했다.

해설 | **세부 내용 - 이전 후 회사가 한 일**
회의 후반부에 이전 후 매출이 저조했지만 신문과 라디오 광고로(thanks to the newspaper advertisements and radio commercials we put out) 사업이 빠르게 호전되었다고 했으므로 (C)가 정답이다.

어휘 | expand 확장하다, 늘리다 inventory 재고품, 물품 목록 additional 추가의 inauguration 개업, 취임

Unit 13　설명 / 소개

담화 흐름 파악하기
본책 p.114

환영합니다, 여러분. 제 이름은 이소벨이고, 여러분들과 오늘 저녁 요리 수업을 함께 할 강사입니다. 제가 여러분들께 고급 빵 굽는 법을 가르쳐 드릴 텐데요. 자, 필요한 재료는 이미 조리대 위에 놓아두렸지만, 여러분 모두 앞으로 나오셔서 큰 그릇과 빵틀을 하나씩 가져가시겠어요? 아, 그건 그렇고, 한 30분 후에 사진 작가가 새 홍보 책자용 사진을 찍으러 들를 겁니다. 사진에 찍히고 싶지 않으시다면 그에게 알려주세요.

어휘 | instructor 강사 artisanal 고급의 ingredient 재료 counter 조리대 loaf pan 빵틀 promotional 홍보의

1 청자들이 참석하고 있는 것은?
2 화자가 청자들에게 요청하는 것은?
3 여자는 30분 뒤에 무슨 일이 일어날 거라고 말하는가?

● 실전 **도움닫기**
본책 p.115

1 (B)　**2** (A)　**3** (A)　**4** (B)　**5** (B)　**6** (B)

[1-2]

¹Welcome to the sixth annual Corzell Technology Convention. I know you're looking forward to a weekend filled with software demonstrations, workshops, and some fantastic exhibits of the latest computer technology. **²Those of you who participated in previous conventions will notice something new this year—we now have Internet access in all our meeting rooms.** One final note: if you're planning to attend the computer networking workshop, there's been a change. It will be held in the Hudson Room, not the Bayside Center.

¹제6회 연례 코젤 기술 대회에 오신 것을 환영합니다. 여러분께서는 소프트웨어 시연과 워크숍, 환상적인 최신 컴퓨터 기술 전시로 가득 찬 주말을 고대하고 계실 것입니다. **²이전 대회 참가자분들은 올해 새로워진 점을 알아차리실 텐데요, 이제 모든 회의실에서 인터넷 사용이 가능하다는 겁니다.** 마지막으로 컴퓨터 네트워킹 워크숍에 참석하실 분들께 변동사항을 알려 드립니다. 워크숍은 베이사이드 센터가 아니라 허드슨 룸에서 열립니다.

어휘 | convention 대회 demonstration 시연 notice 알아차리다

1 화자는 어디에 있는가?

(A) 컴퓨터 판매점

(B) 기술 대회

해설 | **전체 내용 - 화자의 장소**

초반부에서 기술 대회에 온 것을 환영한다(Welcome to the sixth annual Corzell Technology Convention)고 했으므로, (B)가 정답이다.

2 화자가 언급한 새로운 특징은 무엇인가?

(A) 인터넷 접속이 되는 방

(B) 특가 소프트웨어

해설 | **세부 내용 - 새로운 특징**

중반부에서 올해 새로워진 점은 회의실마다 인터넷 접속이 가능하다는 것(we now have Internet access in all our meeting rooms)이라고 했으므로, (A)가 정답이다.

[3-4]

Our next speaker is Dr. Clarissa Trevor, a marine biologist who has greatly impacted the scientific world. ³The evidence is on the walls of her office, which are lined with numerous awards and plaques. This past year, Dr. Trevor found a new species of turtle in the Galapagos Islands. So I think it's safe to tell her—make sure you leave some room on those walls. Her findings are documented in her new book, *The Unknown Turtle*. ⁴Today, she will be reading a chapter and discussing her amazing discovery. Please join me in welcoming Dr. Clarissa Trevor.

다음에 모실 연사는 과학계에 엄청난 영향을 미친 해양 생물학자인 클라리사 트레보 박사입니다. ³그 증거는 박사님 사무실 벽에 있습니다. 벽에는 수많은 상과 명판이 줄줄이 붙어 있습니다. 작년에 트레보 박사는 갈라파고스 군도에서 새로운 바다거북 종을 발견했습니다. 따라서 저는 그녀에게 그 벽에 공간을 남겨두었는지 확인해 보라고 말하는 편이 좋을 것 같습니다. 조사 결과는 그녀의 신간 <알려지지 않은 바다거북>에 기록되어 있습니다. ⁴오늘 그녀는 책의 한 챕터를 낭독하고 자신의 놀라운 발견에 대해 토론할 예정입니다. 그럼 저와 함께 클라리사 트레보 박사를 환영해 주십시오.

어휘 | marine biologist 해양 생물학자 impact 영향을 주다 scientific world 과학계 evidence 증거 be lined with 줄줄이 늘어서 있다 numerous 수많은 plaque 명판 species 종(種) turtle 바다거북 finding 조사 결과 document 기록하다 discovery 발견

3 화자가 "그 벽에 공간을 남겨두었는지 확인해 보라"고 말한 의도는 무엇인가?

(A) 감탄을 표현하기 위해   (B) 경고를 해주기 위해

해설 | **세부 내용 - 화자의 의도**

앞서 트레보 박사의 사무실 벽에 수많은 상과 명판(numerous awards and plaques)이 붙어 있다고 했으며, 작년에 갈라파고스 군도에서 새로운 바다거북 종을 발견했으니 벽에 상을 더 붙일

공간을 남겨두었는지 확인하라고 한 말이므로, 감탄을 표현하려는 의도임을 알 수 있다. 따라서 (A)가 정답이다.

어휘 | admiration 감탄, 존경 warning 경고

4 트레보 박사는 오늘 무엇을 할 것인가?

(A) 갈라파고스 군도로 날아갈 것이다.

(B) 자신의 책 일부분을 공유할 것이다.

해설 | **세부 내용 - 트레보 박사가 오늘 할 일**

소개 후반부에서 트레보 박사가 자신이 저술한 책을 낭독할 것(she will be reading a chapter)이라고 했으므로 (B)가 정답이다.

[5-6]

I know you've all been waiting to find out who our board of directors selected to receive the Graystone Achievement Award. ⁵This award recognizes an employee who's really contributed a lot to our work here at LC Sportswear. This year we're proud to present the award to ⁶Juan Mendez from the graphic design department. He did an outstanding job creating our new company logo. This image is what consumers see on every one of our athletic products, and Juan's striking design is sure to attract more attention.

여러분 모두 그레이스톤 공로상을 누가 받게 될지 우리 이사회의 결정을 기다리고 계실 겁니다. ⁵이 상은 여기 LC 스포츠웨어에서 업무상 많은 공헌을 한 직원의 노고를 치하하기 위한 것입니다. 올해는 자랑스럽게도 ⁶그래픽 디자인 부서의 후안 멘데즈 씨에게 이 상을 수여합니다. 그는 탁월한 능력을 발휘하여 우리 회사의 새로운 로고를 만들었습니다. 이 이미지는 우리의 모든 스포츠 제품 하나하나에서 고객들이 보게 될 것이며, 후안 씨의 인상적인 디자인은 확실히 더 많은 관심을 끌 것입니다.

어휘 | board of directors 이사회 recognize 표창하다, 공로를 인정하다 contribute 공헌하다 outstanding 우수한, 뛰어난 consumer 소비자 striking 눈에 띄는, 인상적인 attract (마음·관심을) 끌다

5 주로 무엇에 관한 발표인가?

(A) 신규 계약   (B) 직원의 성과

해설 | **전체 내용 - 주제**

초반부에 그레이스톤 공로상은 LC 스포츠웨어에서 업무상 많은 공헌을 한 직원에게 수여된다(This award recognizes an employee who's really contributed a lot to our work here at LC Sportswear)고 한 후 수상자를 소개하고 있으므로 (B)가 정답이다.

6 후안 멘데즈 씨는 누구인가?

(A) 회사 고객   (B) 그래픽 디자이너

해설 | **세부 내용 - 특정 인물의 신분**

중반부에 수상자를 그래픽 디자인 부서의 후안 멘데즈 씨(Juan Mendez from the graphic design department)라고 소개했으므로, (B)가 정답이다.

1 (D)	**2** (C)	**3** (A)	**4** (A)	**5** (D)	**6** (A)
7 (C)	**8** (B)	**9** (D)	**10** (A)	**11** (D)	**12** (B)
13 (B)	**14** (A)	**15** (A)	**16** (C)	**17** (A)	**18** (D)
19 (C)	**20** (A)	**21** (D)			

[1-3] 설명

> ¹Since today is your first day on the job, let's briefly review some information for cleaning the hospital rooms. During this morning's training session, you were given procedure manuals. Does everyone have one? On the first page, there's a chart showing the process for cleaning each room, and a checklist of cleaning products you'll need. ²Please read the instructions carefully and keep them with you because I'll be in meetings the rest of the day. Everyone has been assigned a cleaning cart. ³Follow your checklists to fill your carts with cleaning supplies from the storage room.
>
> ¹오늘은 여러분의 첫 근무일이니 병실 청소에 대한 정보를 간략히 **검토하시죠.** 오늘 아침 교육 중에 절차 설명서를 받으셨을텐데요. 모두 갖고 계시죠? 첫 번째 장에 각 병실 청소 과정을 보여주는 도표와 필요한 청소용품 점검표가 있습니다. ²설명서를 잘 읽고 가지고 다니세요. 제가 오늘 나머지 시간 동안 회의에 들어가야 해서요. 모두에게 청소 카트를 배정했습니다. ³점검표에 따라 보관실에 있는 청소용품으로 카트를 채우세요.

어휘 | briefly 간단히 review 검토하다 procedure 절차 manual 설명서 checklist 점검표 instruction 설명, 지시 assign 배정하다 cleaning supplies 청소용품 storage 보관, 저장

1 화자는 누구에게 말하고 있는가?
(A) 조사관   (B) 기술자
(C) 창고 인부   (D) 청소 직원

해설 | 전체 내용 - 청자들의 신분
담화의 초반부에서 청자들의 첫 근무일이니 병실 청소에 대한 정보를 함께 간략히 검토해 보자(let's briefly review some information for cleaning the hospital rooms)는 제안을 하며, 청자들이 신입 청소 직원임을 드러내고 있으므로 (D)가 정답이다.

2 화자가 "제가 오늘 나머지 시간 동안 회의에 들어가야 해서요"라고 말할 때, 그 의도는 무엇인가?
(A) 자신의 일정이 불만스럽다.
(B) 회의실에서 연락을 받을 수 있다.
(C) 질문에 대답할 시간이 없을 것이다.
(D) 자신의 임무를 넘길 사람이 필요하다.

해설 | 세부 내용 - 화자의 의도
담화의 중반부에서 설명서를 잘 읽고 가지고 다닐 것(Please read the instructions carefully and keep them with you)을

권고한 후, '제가 오늘 나머지 시간 동안 회의에 들어가야 해서요(I'll be in meetings the rest of the day)'라며 그 이유를 덧붙였다. 이는 회의로 인해 청자들의 업무 관련 질문에 대답할 시간이 없다는 점을 알리려는 의도라고 볼 수 있으므로 (C)가 정답이다.

어휘 | reach 연락하다 available 시간이 되는 assignment 임무

3 청자들은 다음으로 무엇을 할 것인가?
(A) 용품 챙기기   (B) 시연 보기
(C) 유니폼 착용하기   (D) 근무 일지 작성하기

해설 | 세부 내용 - 청자들이 다음에 할 일
담화의 마지막에서 점검표에 따라 보관실에 있는 청소용품으로 카트를 채울 것(Follow your checklists to fill your carts with cleaning supplies from the storage room)을 지시하며, 청자들이 다음에 해야 할 일을 언급하고 있으므로 (A)가 정답이다.

어휘 | gather 모으다, 챙기다 demonstration 시연, 설명 fill out 작성하다, 기입하다 timesheet 근무 시간 기록표

Paraphrasing
담화의 fill your carts with cleaning supplies
→ 정답의 Gather supplies

[4-6] 소개

> ⁴It's great to see such a large crowd gathered at this retirement celebration for our colleague Nathan Milo. It's not surprising, though, that so many of us want to honor Nathan for his contributions to our company. Although he has many talents, I think ⁵what I've appreciated most is Nathan's ability to lead. When he took over as our chief creative director, our company Main Stay Advertising was a small local business, but due to his leadership, ⁶it is now one of the best-known companies in the country. I think I speak for us all when I say thank you, Nathan. We wish you all the best in your retirement.
>
> ⁴동료인 네이든 마일로의 퇴임식에 이렇게 많은 분들이 모여 주셔서 **기쁩니다.** 하지만 우리 중 다수가 네이든이 회사에 한 공헌을 기념하고 싶어한다는 것은 그리 놀라운 일이 아닙니다. 많은 재능을 갖췄지만 ⁵제가 가장 인정하는 부분은 네이든의 통솔력입니다. 그가 광고 제작 수석 감독을 맡았을 때, 우리 메인 스테이 애드버타이징은 소규모 지역 업체였지만 그의 리더십 덕분에 ⁶현재는 국내에서 가장 **이름난 회사 중 하나가 됐습니다.** 네이든, 제가 감사하다고 이야기하는 것은 우리 모두를 대신해서 하는 말입니다. 은퇴 후 모든 것이 잘되기를 바랍니다.

어휘 | crowd 군중 gather 모이다 retirement 은퇴, 퇴직 celebration 기념 행사 colleague 동료 contribution 기여, 공헌 appreciate 진가를 알아보다, 인정하다 take over as ~를 맡다

4 담화의 목적은?
(A) 은퇴하는 직원을 기리기 위해
(B) 행정상의 변동을 설명하기 위해
(C) 새로운 광고 캠페인을 발표하기 위해
(D) 수상자를 소개하기 위해

해설 | **전체 내용 - 담화의 목적**
담화의 초반부에서 동료인 네이든 마일로의 퇴임식에 많은
사람들이 모여서 기쁘다(It's great to see such a large
crowd gathered at this retirement celebration for our
colleague Nathan Milo)고 한 후, 퇴임하는 직원을 소개하고
있으므로 (A)가 정답이다.

어휘 | administrative 행정상의, 관리상의 announce 발표하다,
알리다 present 소개하다

5 화자는 네이든 마일로에 대해 무엇을 인정한다고 말하는가?
(A) 예술적인 재능   (B) 재무 경험
(C) 기술적인 역량   (D) 통솔력

해설 | **세부 내용 - 화자가 네이든 마일로에 대해 인정한 것**
담화의 중반부에서 화자가 가장 인정하는 부분은 네이든의
통솔력(what I've appreciated most is Nathan's ability to
lead)이라고 했으므로 (D)가 정답이다.

어휘 | artistic 예술의 financial 금융의, 재무의 technical
기술적인

Paraphrasing
담화의 Nathan's ability to lead → 정답의 His leadership
ability

6 화자는 회사에 대해 무엇이라고 말하는가?
(A) 전국적으로 잘 알려져 있다.
(B) 내년에 이전할 예정이다.
(C) 직원을 더 채용할 계획이다.
(D) 신문 기사에 나왔다.

해설 | **세부 내용 - 화자가 회사에 대해 언급한 사항**
담화의 후반부에서 회사가 현재는 국내에서 가장 이름난 회사 중
하나가 됐다(it is now one of the best-known companies in
the country)고 했으므로 (A)가 정답이다.

어휘 | relocate 이전하다, 이동하다 feature 특별히 포함하다

Paraphrasing
담화의 one of the best-known companies in the country
→ 정답의 well-known throughout the country

[7-9] 설명

> [7]Welcome to the Oakbridge Museum of Art. My
> name is Josh Wilson, and I will be showing you
> around today. Throughout the museum you will
> see many examples of the very old and the very
> new. For example, how many of you know that
> this is the oldest building in the city? Would it
> surprise you to hear, in that case, that [8]we've got
> a very modern security system? And think about
> how the artwork is organized. Most of you know
> that the museum has three floors. Did you know
> that all of our artwork is displayed according to
> date? That's right. [9]The oldest works are on the
> ground floor and the newest works are located on

> the top floor. We will start our tour at the
> "Highlights of the Museum" exhibit, which is near
> the rear entrance to the ground floor.

[7]오크브리지 미술관에 오신 것을 환영합니다. 제 이름은 조쉬 윌슨이며,
오늘 여러분의 안내를 맡을 예정입니다. 여러분은 미술관 곳곳에서
아주 오래된 것과 가장 새로운 것의 다양한 예를 보게 되실 텐데요.
가령, 이 미술관이 이 도시에서 가장 오래된 건물이라는 것을 여러분
가운데 몇 분이나 알고 계신가요? 그렇다면 [8]이곳에 아주 현대적인 보안
시스템이 갖추어져 있다는 사실을 들으시면 놀라시겠죠? 미술품이 어떤
방식으로 정리되어 있는지도 생각해 보세요. 미술관이 3층으로 이루어져
있다는 사실은 대부분 알고 계십니다. 미술품이 전부 연대순으로
전시되어 있다는 사실도 알고 계셨나요? 맞습니다. [9]가장 오래된 작품은
1층에 있고 가장 최근의 작품은 맨 위층에 있습니다. 그럼 1층 후문
근처에서 전시되고 있는 '미술관의 하이라이트' 전시회부터 관람을
시작하겠습니다.

어휘 | throughout ~의 도처에 security system 보안 장치
artwork 미술품 organize 정리하다 display 전시하다 according
to date 연대순으로 ground floor 1층 exhibit 전시회 rear
entrance 후문

7 화자는 누구인가?
(A) 여행사 직원   (B) 건축가
(C) 박물관 견학 가이드   (D) 사서

해설 | **세부 내용 - 화자의 신분**
담화 초반부에서 화자가 미술관을 방문한 청자들에게 환영의
인사를 한 다음, 자신이 조쉬 윌슨이며 오늘 안내를 담당할 것(My
name is Josh Wilson, and I will be showing you around
today)이라고 했으므로 (C)가 정답이다.

8 화자는 건물에 관해 무엇이라고 말하는가?
(A) 도심에 위치하고 있다.
(B) 최신 보안 시스템을 갖추고 있다.
(C) 원래 1층짜리 건물이었다.
(D) 출입구가 한 개밖에 없다.

해설 | **세부 내용 - 건물에 관해 말하는 것**
담화 중반부에서 미술관이 오래되었지만 아주 현대적인 보안
시스템을 갖추고 있다(we've got a very modern security
system)고 했으므로 (B)가 정답이다.

어휘 | advanced 진보한 originally 원래

9 가장 오래된 작품은 어디에 보관되어 있는가?
(A) 창고   (B) 맨 위층
(C) 후문 근처   (D) 1층

해설 | **세부 내용 - 보관 장소**
담화 후반부에서 가장 오래된 작품들은 1층에 있다(The oldest
works are on the ground floor)고 했으므로 (D)가 정답이다.

[10-12] 행사 안내

> Good evening, and thank you all for attending
> this dinner. [10]We're here to honor the recent
> graduates of the Akron carpenters' association

apprenticeship program. **It takes years of persistence and hard work for apprentices to graduate from this program and become certified carpenters, so this accomplishment is certainly worth celebrating. I'm sure that** [11]**many of the friends and family who have come tonight are curious about what kind of training the apprentice program involves. So, before we eat,** [11]**I'll show you a video depicting a typical day in the life of our apprentices. And** [12]**after dinner, join us for dancing in the ballroom.**

안녕하세요. 오늘 저녁 식사에 와 주셔서 감사합니다. [10]오늘은 아크론 목수협회 인턴십 프로그램의 최근 졸업자들을 축하하기 위해 여기 모였습니다. 인턴들이 이 프로그램을 졸업하고 공인된 목수가 되는 데 수 년간의 끈기와 노고를 들였으니, 이번 성취는 분명 축하할 만한 가치가 있습니다. [11]오늘 오신 많은 친구와 가족 여러분께서는 인턴십 프로그램에 어떤 종류의 교육이 수반되는지 궁금해하실 거라 생각합니다. 그래서 식사에 앞서 [11]인턴들의 전형적인 하루 일과를 묘사한 동영상을 보여드리려고 합니다. [12]저녁 식사 후에는 무도회장에서 함께 춤을 추시죠.

어휘 | attend 참석하다 recent 최근의 graduate 졸업생 association 협회 apprenticeship 수습직, 인턴십 certified 공인된 accomplishment 성취 worth -ing ~할 가치가 있다 involve 수반하다, 포함하다 depict 그리다, 묘사하다 typical 일반적인, 전형적인

10 행사의 목적은?
  (A) 새로운 졸업자들을 기념하기 위해
  (B) 건물을 봉헌하기 위해
  (C) 직원의 은퇴를 기념하기 위해
  (D) 단체 기금 조성을 위해

  해설 | 세부 내용 - 행사의 목적
  담화의 초반부에서 아크론 목수협회 인턴십 프로그램의 최근 졸업자들을 축하하기 위해 여기 모였다(We're here to honor the recent graduates of the Akron carpenters' association apprenticeship program)고 했으므로 (A)가 정답이다.

  어휘 | dedicate 바치다, 봉헌하다 retirement 은퇴, 퇴직 raise fund 기금을 모으다

  Paraphrasing
  담화의 the recent graduates → 정답의 new graduates

11 동영상은 무엇에 관한 것인가?
  (A) 새 자선 단체
  (B) 회사 발전
  (C) 역사적 장소
  (D) 교육 프로그램

  해설 | 세부 내용 - 동영상의 내용
  담화의 중반부에서 참석한 친구와 가족이 인턴십 프로그램에 어떤 종류의 교육이 수반되는지 궁금해할 것이라고 한 후, 인턴들의 전형적인 하루 일과를 묘사한 동영상을 보여주겠다(I'll show you a video depicting a typical day in the life of our apprentices)고 했으므로, 동영상이 인턴십 프로그램 관련 내용을 담고 있음을 알 수 있다. 따라서 (D)가 정답이다.

12 식사 후에는 어떤 일이 있을 것인가?
  (A) 건물 견학   (B) 댄스 파티
  (C) 회장 연설   (D) 단체 사진

  해설 | 세부 내용 - 식사 후에 있을 일
  담화의 마지막에서 저녁 식사 후에 무도회장에서 함께 춤을 추자(after dinner, join us for dancing in the ballroom)고 제안했으므로 (B)가 정답이다.

[13-15] 설명

Thank you for inviting me to your guitar manufacturing plant. My name is Ingrid Weber, and I'm the president of LVC Materials. [13/14]**I'm here to tell you about a new material we produce that can be used to make musical instruments.** [14]**LVC has developed an innovative wood-like product made from the materials of linen and resin.** [13/14]**It looks like real wood but is lighter and more durable.** And just so you know, we've already partnered with several other instrument makers. [15]Now, I'd like to show you one of our musical instruments. I brought a guitar so you can hear its excellent sound quality.

귀사의 기타 제조 공장에 저를 초대해 주셔서 감사합니다. 저는 LVC 머티리얼의 잉그리드 웨버 회장입니다. [13/14]악기 제조가 가능한 저희의 새로운 생산 소재에 대해 말씀드리러 왔습니다. [14]LVC는 리넨과 수지 소재로 나무와 같은 혁신적인 제품을 개발했습니다. [13/14]진짜 나무처럼 보이지만 더 가볍고 내구성이 더욱 좋습니다. 참고로, 저희는 이미 여러 악기 제조업체와 제휴하고 있습니다. [15]이제 여러분께 저희 악기 중 하나를 보여드리고자 합니다. 기타를 가져왔으니 훌륭한 음질을 들어 보실 수 있습니다.

어휘 | manufacturing 제조 plant 공장 material 재료, 소재 musical instrument 악기 develop 개발하다 innovative 혁신적인 resin 수지 durable 내구성이 있는 partner with ~와 제휴하다, 협력하다 just so you know 참고로 말하자면

13 화자는 소재의 어떤 점이 특별하다고 말하는가?
  (A) 제조하는 데 비용이 적게 든다.
  (B) 천연 나무와 비슷하다.
  (C) 환경 친화적이다.
  (D) 다양한 색상이 있다.

  해설 | 세부 내용 - 화자가 소재에 대해 특별하다고 언급한 사항
  담화 초반부에서 화자가 회사의 새로운 생산 소재에 대해 알려주기 위해 왔다(I'm here to tell you about a new material we produce)고 한 후, 이 소재가 진짜 나무처럼 보이지만 더 가볍고 내구성이 더욱 좋다(It looks like real wood but is lighter and more durable)고 했으므로, (B)가 정답이다.

  어휘 | inexpensive 저렴한 resemble 닮다, 비슷하다 environmentally friendly 환경 친화적인

  Paraphrasing
  담화의 looks like real wood → 정답의 resembles natural wood

14 화자가 "저희는 이미 여러 악기 제조업체와 제휴하고 있습니다"라고 말할 때, 그 의도는 무엇인가?

(A) 청자들이 자신들과 거래하도록 장려하기 위해

(B) 지연되는 이유를 대기 위해

(C) 청자들을 행사에 초대하기 위해

(D) 동료의 제안을 거절하기 위해

해설 | 세부 내용 - 화자의 의도

담화의 초반부에서 화자는 기타 제조 공장(your guitar manufacturing plant)을 방문한 목적과 새로운 생산 소재에 대해 설명한 후, '저희는 이미 여러 악기 제조업체와 제휴하고 있습니다(we've already partnered with several other instrument makers)'라고 덧붙였다. 이는 청자들이 자신의 회사와 거래하도록 설득하려는 의도라고 볼 수 있으므로 (A)가 정답이다.

어휘 | encourage 격려하다, 장려하다 do business with ~와 거래하다 delay 지연 reject 거절하다 colleague 동료 suggestion 제안

15 화자는 다음으로 무엇을 할 것인가?

(A) 시연하기　　　　　(B) 조사하기

(C) 과정 설명하기　　　(D) 안내책자 나눠 주기

해설 | 세부 내용 - 화자가 다음에 할 일

담화의 후반부에서 악기 하나를 보여주겠다(I'd like to show you one of our musical instruments)고 한 후 기타의 훌륭한 음질을 들을 수 있을 거라고 했으므로 (A)가 정답이다.

[16-18] 소개

> As chairman of the International Health Convention, it's my pleasure to introduce Mr. Tadashi Yamada. **16**Mr. Yamada comes to us with nearly three decades of experience in the medical profession. **17**He's just created a computer program that combines patients' health records with other important information into one single program. This means that health care professionals can better keep track of their patients' medical history—no matter where those patients received care in the past. So **18**now Mr. Yamada will demonstrate how his program works and explain its various features.

국제보건협의회 의장으로서 타다시 야마다 씨를 소개하게 되어 기쁩니다. **16**야마다 씨는 의료 직종에서 거의 30년의 경력을 갖고 있는데요. **17**환자의 의료 기록과 다른 주요 정보를 결합해 단일 프로그램화하는 컴퓨터 프로그램을 만들었습니다. 이는 전문 의료진들이 환자가 과거에 어디에서 치료를 받았는지에 관계없이 그들의 병력을 더 잘 파악할 수 있게 된다는 뜻입니다. **18**이제 야마다 씨가 프로그램 작동법을 시연하고 다양한 기능을 설명해 주시겠습니다.

어휘 | chairman 의장 convention 협의회 nearly 거의 decade 10년 profession 직업, 직종 combine 결합하다 keep track of ~를 기록하다, ~을 파악하다 demonstrate 실증하다, 보여주다 feature 특성, 기능

16 야마다 씨는 어떤 업계에서 일하는가?

(A) 금융　　　　　　　(B) 건축

(C) 의료　　　　　　　(D) 소셜미디어

해설 | 세부 내용 - 야마다 씨가 종사하는 업계

소개의 초반부에서 야마다 씨는 의료 직종에서 거의 30년의 경력을 갖고 있다(Mr. Yamada comes to us with nearly three decades of experience in the medical profession)고 했으므로 (C)가 정답이다.

Paraphrasing

담화의 the medical profession → 정답의 Health care

17 야마다 씨는 어떤 주요 업적을 인정받고 있는가?

(A) 컴퓨터 프로그램 개발　　(B) 자선 단체 창설

(C) 공교육 교과 과정 개선　　(D) 조사 결과 발표

해설 | 세부 내용 - 야마다 씨가 인정받는 주요 업적

소개의 중반부에서 야마다 씨가 환자의 의료 기록과 다른 주요 정보를 결합해 단일 프로그램화하는 컴퓨터 프로그램을 만들었다(He's just created a computer program that combines patients' health records with other important information into one single program)고 했으므로 (A)가 정답이다.

어휘 | accomplishment 업적 be recognized for ~로 인정받다 charitable organization 자선 단체 improve 개선시키다, 향상시키다 publish 발표하다, 공개하다

18 화자에 따르면, 야마다 씨는 다음으로 무엇을 할 것인가?

(A) 시설 견학하기　　　(B) 기자들에게 이야기하기

(C) 상 받기　　　　　　(D) 시연하기

해설 | 세부 내용 - 야마다 씨가 다음에 할 일

소개의 후반부에서 이제 야마다 씨가 프로그램 작동법을 시연하고 다양한 기능을 설명해 줄 것(Mr. Yamada will demonstrate how his program works and explain its various features)이라고 했으므로 (D)가 정답이다.

Paraphrasing

담화의 demonstrate → 정답의 Give a demonstration

[19-21] 설명+지도

> Hello—welcome to the Visitors Center at Mountainside Park. **19**My name's Josephine and I'll be guiding your hike today. **20**Normally we'd be taking the Heron Trail to the Picnic Area, but the second part of that trail is closed for maintenance this week. So instead, we'll be starting out on the Heron Trail and changing over midway to the Pine Trail, as you can see here on the map. We'll break for our lunch at the end of the Pine Trail, and then we'll take the Sunset Trail back to our starting point. **21**It's supposed to be sunny today, so it's a good idea to put on some sunscreen and wear a hat.

안녕하세요, 마운틴사이드 공원 방문자 센터에 오신 것을 환영합니다. **¹⁹제 이름은 조세핀이며 오늘 여러분의 하이킹을 안내해드릴 겁니다.** **²⁰우리는 보통 헤론길을 이용해 피크닉장으로 갑니다만, 그 길의 두 번째 구역이 이번 주 보수 작업 때문에 폐쇄되었습니다. 그래서 대신 여기 지도상에서 보시는 것처럼 우리는 헤론길에서 출발해 중간쯤에서 파인길로 빠질 겁니다.** 파인길 끝에서 점심 휴식 시간을 가진 다음 선셋길을 이용해 다시 출발 지점으로 돌아오겠습니다. **²¹오늘은 햇볕이 내리쬘 것이므로 자외선 차단제를 바르고 모자를 쓰는 것이 좋습니다.**

어휘 | hike 하이킹 take (길을) 이용하다 maintenance 정비, 보수 관리 midway 중간에, 도중에 break 쉬다 starting point 출발 지점 put on (화장품 등을) 바르다 sunscreen 자외선 차단제

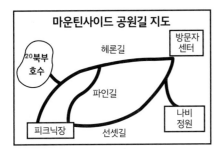
마운틴사이드 공원길 지도
북부 호수 / 헤론길 / 방문자 센터 / 파인길 / 피크닉장 / 선셋길 / 나비 정원

19 청자들은 누구일 것 같은가?
(A) 관리 직원들   (B) 버스 기사들
(C) 관광객들   (D) 공원 경비원들

해설 | **전체 내용 - 청자의 신분**
안내 초반부에 화자가 청자들에게 자신은 조세핀이며 오늘 하이킹을 안내할 것(My name's Josephine and I'll be guiding your hike today)이라고 했으므로 청자들이 관광객임을 추론할 수 있다. 따라서 (C)가 정답이다.

20 시각 정보에 따르면, 청자들은 오늘 어디에 갈 수 없을 것인가?
(A) 북부 호수   (B) 피크닉 구역
(C) 나비 정원   (D) 방문자 센터

해설 | **세부 내용 - 시각 정보 연계**
안내 초반부에 보통은 헤론길을 이용해 피크닉장으로 가지만 그 길의 두 번째 구역이 이번 주 정비 작업 때문에 폐쇄되었다(Normally we'd be taking the Heron Trail to the Picnic Area, but the second part of that trail is closed for maintenance this week)고 했다. 그리고 헤론길에서 출발해 중간에서 파인길로 빠지겠다(So instead, we'll be starting out on the Heron Trail and changing over midway to the Pine Trail)고 했다. 따라서 지도를 보면 청자들이 북부 호수에는 갈 수 없다는 것을 알 수 있으므로 (A)가 정답이다.

21 여자는 청자들에게 무엇을 하도록 권장하는가?
(A) 지도 지참   (B) 일기예보 확인
(C) 소지품 보관   (D) 자외선 차단제 사용

해설 | **세부 내용 - 권장 사항**
안내 후반부에 오늘은 햇볕이 내리쬘 것이므로 자외선 차단제를 바르고 모자를 쓰는 것이 좋다(It's supposed to be sunny today, so it's a good idea to put on some sunscreen and wear a hat)고 했으므로 (D)가 정답이다.

어휘 | belonging 소유물, 소지품

Unit 14 광고 / 방송

담화 흐름 파악하기   본책 p.118

시티 악기사가 새 매장을 열었습니다! 십 년 이상 시티 악기사는 굉장히 저렴한 가격에 악기를 제공해 왔으며, 이를 자랑스럽게 생각하고 있습니다. 최근에 저희는 도심에 있는 지점에 이어 스카일러빌 쇼핑센터에도 새로운 매장을 열었습니다. 새로운 지점에 방문하시는 고객님들을 환영하는 의미에서, 한정된 기간 동안 어떤 악기를 구입하시든 간에 해당 악기에 대한 한 달 무료 음악 수업을 제공해 드리려고 합니다. 그리고 이번 주 토요일에만, 여러분의 쇼핑 편의를 위해 늦게까지 문을 열어둘 것입니다.

1 광고되고 있는 것은?
2 제공되는 특별 혜택은?
3 토요일에 일어날 일은?

● 실전 도움닫기   본책 p.119

1 (B) **2** (B) **3** (A) **4** (B) **5** (A) **6** (B)

[1-2]

¹This is Ken Harrison with a special traffic report. If you are driving southbound on Clover Street, you should be ready for delays. **²**There is a break in a water pipe between Morris Boulevard and Ridge Avenue, which has caused the right lane to be closed down. The police are now on the scene directing traffic, but things are still moving quite slowly on Clover. We recommend avoiding Clover Street altogether and taking an alternate route. Our next traffic report will be in fifteen minutes, so keep listening.

¹특별 교통 방송을 보내드리는 켄 해리슨입니다. 클로버 가 남행 노선에서 운전하고 계시다면, 지체에 대비하셔야겠습니다. **²모리스 대로와 리지 가 사이에 수도관이 파열되어 오른쪽 차선이 폐쇄되었습니다.** 지금 경찰이 현장에서 교통 정리를 하고 있지만, 여전히 클로버 가의 진행이 상당히 느립니다. 저희는 클로버 가를 완전히 피하고 우회로로 가실 것을 추천합니다. 저희 다음 교통 방송은 15분 후에 있습니다. 계속 청취해 주십시오.

어휘 | southbound 남행의 delay 지체 water pipe 수도관 lane 차선 close down 폐쇄하다 direct traffic 교통 정리를 하다 recommend 추천하다 altogether 완전히, 전적으로 alternate route 우회로

1 이 방송은 누구를 대상으로 하는가?
(A) 교통 경찰
(B) 차량 운전자들

해설 | **전체 내용 - 방송 대상**
화자가 자신을 특별 교통 방송을 전하는 켄 해리슨(This is Ken Harrison with a special traffic report)이라고 소개했으므로 방송 대상은 차량 운전자들이다. 따라서 (B)가 정답이다.

2 문제가 발생한 원인은 무엇인가?
(A) 고장 난 교통신호등　　(B) 파열된 수도관

해설 | **세부 내용 - 문제의 원인**
방송 초반부에서 모리스 대로와 리지 가의 수도관이 파열되어(There is a break in a water pipe between Morris Boulevard and Ridge Avenue) 교통이 정체된다고 했으므로 (B)가 정답이다.

어휘 | defective 결함이 있는

[3-4]

Welcome back to Zahara's FM Radio. Before we get to the weather forecast, I want to remind all our listeners that at ten o'clock ³Ms. Beatrice Vince will be stopping by our studio. She doesn't usually give radio interviews. ⁴Ms. Vince, famous for building her own shoe company, will be giving our listeners tips on how to build your own business. Don't miss this talk. OK. And now, here's the week's weather.

다시 자하라의 FM 라디오입니다. 일기예보로 넘어가기 전에 모든 청취자 여러분께 10시 정각에 ³베아트리체 빈스 씨가 스튜디오에 나올 예정임을 다시 한 번 알려드립니다. 그녀는 라디오 인터뷰를 잘 안 하는 분이시죠. ⁴신발 회사를 창업한 것으로 유명한 빈스 씨가 청취자 여러분께 창업하는 방법에 대한 조언을 드릴 겁니다. 이 이야기를 놓치지 마세요. 좋습니다. 자, 이제 이번 주 날씨를 들어봅니다.

어휘 | remind 상기시키다　stop by ~에 들르다　build 세우다, 설립하다

3 화자가 "그녀는 라디오 인터뷰를 잘 안 하는 분이시죠"라고 말한 의도는 무엇인가?
(A) 기회의 중요성을 보여 주기 위해
(B) 행사의 확정 여부에 의문을 던지기 위해

해설 | **세부 내용 - 화자의 의도**
베아트리체 빈스 씨가 스튜디오에 출연할 예정이라고 알리면서 그녀는 라디오 인터뷰를 잘 안 하는 사람이라고 했다. 이는 이번 방송이 귀한 사례라는 것을 강조하려는 의도라고 볼 수 있으므로, (A)가 정답이다.

어휘 | value 가치, 중요성　opportunity 기회　certainty 확실성

4 빈스 씨는 무엇에 대해 이야기할 것인가?
(A) 날씨 상태　　　　　(B) 사업 조언

해설 | **세부 내용 - 이야기 주제**
신발 회사 창업자로 유명한 빈스 씨가 청취자들에게 창업하는 방법에 대한 조언을 할 것이다(Ms. Vince, famous for building her own shoe company, will be giving our listeners tips on how to build your own business)라고 했으므로 (B)가

정답이다.

[5-6]

⁶Come to Endwell Shoes this weekend for our annual winter sale! Friday through Sunday, we're taking twenty percent off our entire inventory as we make room for our new styles. ⁵The discount even applies to Ella Bancroft designer boots, which style experts on the Forward Fashion television network say are this season's most popular line of footwear. You'll be sure to find something you like—and at a price that can't be beat. Remember, ⁶the sale ends Sunday, so come take advantage of these great deals while they last!

⁶연례 겨울 할인 행사가 있으니 이번 주말에 엔드웰 슈즈로 오십시오! 신상품을 위한 공간을 마련하기 위해, ⁶금요일부터 일요일까지 전 재고 품목을 20퍼센트 할인해 드립니다. ⁵이 할인 행사는 엘라 밴크로프트 디자이너 부츠에도 적용됩니다. 이 부츠는 포워드 패션 TV 방송에서 스타일 전문가들이 이번 시즌에 가장 인기 있는 신발류로 지목한 품목입니다. 마음에 드는 제품을 꼭 찾으실 수 있을 겁니다. 게다가 가격도 이보다 더 저렴할 수 없습니다. 기억하십시오. ⁶할인 행사는 일요일에 끝납니다. 그러니 행사가 끝나기 전에 엄청난 할인 혜택을 누리세요!

어휘 | annual 연례의　entire 전체의　inventory 재고(품) make room for ~을 위한 공간을 만들다　apply 적용되다　expert 전문가(specialist)　a line of ~ 상품군　beat 더 낫다, 능가하다 take advantage of ~을 이용하다　deal 흥정, 거래

5 스타일 전문가들은 엘라 밴크로프트 상품에 대해 무엇이라고 말했는가?
(A) 이번 시즌에 인기가 있다.
(B) 천연 재료로 만들어졌다.

해설 | **세부 내용 - 전문가들의 의견**
광고 중반부에서 엘라 밴크로프트 부츠에도 할인이 적용된다고 한 후 스타일 전문가들이 이 회사의 부츠를 이번 시즌에 가장 인기 있는 신발류로 지목했다(style experts on the Forward Fashion television network say are this season's most popular line of footwear)고 했으므로 (A)가 정답이다.

6 판촉 행사는 언제 끝나는가?
(A) 토요일
(B) 일요일

해설 | **세부 내용 - 판촉 행사 종료 시점**
광고 초반부에서 상품 할인 행사 기간이 금요일부터 일요일까지 (Friday through Sunday)라고 했으며, 후반부에서도 할인 행사가 일요일에 끝난다(the sale ends Sunday)고 했으므로 (B)가 정답이다.

어휘 | promotion 홍보, 판촉 (행사)

1 (B)	**2** (D)	**3** (A)	**4** (D)	**5** (D)	**6** (C)
7 (D)	**8** (A)	**9** (C)	**10** (B)	**11** (D)	**12** (A)
13 (A)	**14** (B)	**15** (D)	**16** (D)	**17** (C)	**18** (A)
19 (C)	**20** (A)	**21** (B)			

[1-3] 방송

Thanks for tuning in for tonight's business report. Today, **1/2**Ashton Holt, a locally based company with over twenty years of experience designing and manufacturing clothing, announced its much-anticipated merger with MW Incorporated. MW Incorporated will provide an online platform for selling Ashton Holt's clothing. **3**Make sure to tune in at this time tomorrow for an exclusive interview with the president of Ashton Holt. She'll give us more details about what this merger will mean to the local economy.

오늘 저녁 비즈니스 뉴스를 청취해 주셔서 감사합니다. 오늘, **1/2**20년 이상 의류를 디자인하고 제조해 온 지역 업체 애쉬튼 홀트가 고대해 온 MW 주식회사와의 합병을 발표했습니다. MW 주식회사는 애쉬튼 홀트의 의류 사업에 필요한 온라인 플랫폼을 제공할 것입니다. **3**내일 이 시간 애쉬튼 홀트 회장과의 독점 인터뷰가 방송되니 꼭 청취해 주시기 바랍니다. 애쉬튼 홀트 회장은 이번 합병이 지역 경제에 어떤 의미인지를 더 자세히 설명할 예정입니다.

어휘 | tune in 시청하다, 청취하다 locally based 현지에 기반을 둔 manufacture 제조하다 announce 발표하다, 알리다 incorporated 주식회사의, 유한 책임의 much-anticipated 많이 기다려 온 merger 합병 exclusive 독점적인, 배타적인

1 방송의 목적은?
(A) 매장 개점을 광고하기 위해
(B) 업체 합병을 발표하기 위해
(C) 신상품에 대해 이야기하기 위해
(D) 규정 변경을 보고하기 위해

해설 | **전체 내용 - 방송의 목적**
방송의 초반부에서 지역 업체 애쉬튼 홀트가 MW 주식회사와의 합병을 발표했다(Ashton Holt ~ announced its much-anticipated merger with MW Incorporated)고 했으므로, 두 업체의 합병 소식을 발표하기 위한 방송임을 알 수 있다. 따라서 (B)가 정답이다.

어휘 | grand opening 개장, 개점 regulation 규정

2 애쉬튼 홀트는 어떤 종류의 업체인가?
(A) 건설회사   (B) 인테리어 디자인 회사
(C) 광고대행사   (D) 의류업체

해설 | **세부 내용 - 애쉬튼 홀트의 업종**
방송의 초반부에서 20년 이상 의류 디자인과 제조를 해 온 지역 업체(a locally based company with over twenty years of experience designing and manufacturing clothing)로

애쉬튼 홀트를 소개했으므로 (D)가 정답이다.

Paraphrasing
담화의 company with ~ experience designing and manufacturing clothing → 정답의 A clothing company

3 화자는 청자들에게 무엇을 하라고 권하는가?
(A) 인터뷰 청취   (B) 웹사이트 방문
(C) 일자리 지원   (D) 대회 참가

해설 | **세부 내용 - 화자의 권장 사항**
방송의 후반부에서 내일 이 시간 애쉬튼 홀트 회장과의 독점 인터뷰가 방송되니 꼭 청취해 주기를 바란다(Make sure to tune in at this time tomorrow for an exclusive interview with the president of Ashton Holt)고 했으므로 (A)가 정답이다.

어휘 | apply for ~에 지원하다 enter a contest 대회에 참가하다

Paraphrasing
담화의 tune in ~ for an exclusive interview → 정답의 Listen to an interview

[4-6] 광고

Do you love to read? Then the Pace E-Reader is for you. **4**The Pace E-Reader is an electronic reading device that can hold up to one thousand books. **5**And the best part is that it's lightweight and fits into any bag! So, now you don't need to worry about carrying several heavy books to get you through a vacation. Just download your favorite books to the Pace E-Reader, put it in your bag, and travel light! And what's more, **6**if you buy a Pace E-Reader this month, you'll receive a coupon for a free download of an electronic book of your choice.

독서를 좋아하세요? 그렇다면 페이스 E-리더가 바로 여러분을 위한 것입니다. **4**페이스 E-리더는 최대 1,000권의 책을 저장할 수 있는 전자 독서기입니다. **5**그리고 최고의 장점은 가볍고 어떤 가방에도 들어간다는 것입니다! 그러니 이제 휴가를 보내기 위해 무거운 책 여러 권을 가지고 다닐 걱정은 할 필요가 없습니다. 그냥 가장 좋아하는 책들을 페이스 E-리더에 다운로드받아서 가방에 넣고 가볍게 여행하시기 바랍니다! 그리고 또한 **6**이번 달에 페이스 E-리더를 구입하면 원하시는 전자책 한 권을 무료로 다운받을 수 있는 쿠폰을 받게 됩니다.

어휘 | electronic 전자의, 온라인의 device 장치, 기기 hold 담다, 저장하다 up to 최대 lightweight 가벼운 fit into ~에 꼭 들어맞다 get through (시간, 계절 등을) 보내다 of one's choice 원하는, 선택하는

4 무엇을 위한 광고인가?
(A) 여행가방   (B) 에너지 음료
(C) 옷   (D) 전자기기

해설 | **전체 내용 - 광고 상품**
광고 초반부에 페이스 E-리더는 최대 1,000권의 책을 저장할 수 있는 전자 독서기(an electronic reading device)라고 했으므로 (D)가 정답이다.

LC

PART 4

109

5 화자는 제품의 어떤 특징을 강조하는가?

(A) 소재   (B) 색깔
(C) 비용   (D) 무게

해설 | 세부 내용 - 제품에 대한 강조점
광고 초반부에 제품의 가장 큰 장점(the best part)은 가볍고(it's lightweight) 어떤 가방에도 들어간다는 것이라고 했으므로, (D)가 정답이다.

6 화자에 따르면 구입품과 함께 제공되는 것은 무엇인가?

(A) 제품 견본   (B) 무료 선물 포장
(C) 쿠폰   (D) 잡지 구독권

해설 | 세부 내용 - 구입품과 함께 제공되는 것
광고 후반부에 이번 달에 페이스 E-리더를 구입하면 원하는 전자책 한 권을 무료로 다운받을 수 있는 쿠폰을 받게 된다(you'll receive a coupon for a free download of an electronic book of your choice)고 했으므로 (C)가 정답이다.

[7-9] 뉴스 보도

> Making headlines today is the City Art Museum. **7**After two months of renovations, the museum is finally reopening to the public! To celebrate, they're presenting a temporary exhibition titled *Art of Today*. **8**This show will feature artworks by some of the most acclaimed contemporary Canadian artists, including Soo-Min Lee, recipient of the Canadian Artist of the Year Award. **9**This Saturday, the mayor will give an address at the opening ceremony. Visit the City Art Museum's Web site for more details.
>
> 오늘의 헤드라인을 장식하는 것은 시립 미술관입니다. **7**2개월의 보수공사가 끝나고 미술관이 마침내 일반인들에게 다시 개방됩니다! 박물관은 기념 행사로 '오늘날의 예술'이라는 주제의 임시 전시회를 개최합니다. **8**이번 전시회는 올해의 캐나다 미술가상 수상자인 이수민 씨를 포함해 가장 높이 평가 받는 현대 캐나다 미술가들 몇몇의 작품을 선보일 것입니다. **9**이번 주 토요일 시장이 개관식에서 연설을 합니다. 더 자세한 내용은 시립 미술관의 웹사이트를 방문해 주시기 바랍니다.
>
> 어휘 | make headlines 화제가 되다, 헤드라인을 장식하다 renovation 보수공사 celebrate 축하하다 present 제시하다 temporary 임시의 exhibition 전시회 feature ~을 특징으로 하다 artwork 미술품 acclaimed 호평을 받고 있는 contemporary 현대의, 동시대의 recipient 수령인 mayor 시장 give an address at ~에서 연설하다

7 뉴스 보도의 주제는 무엇인가?

(A) 미술 대회   (B) 모금 행사
(C) 시청 보수공사   (D) 미술관 재개관

해설 | 전체 내용 - 뉴스 보도의 주제
뉴스 보도 초반부에 2개월의 보수공사가 끝나고 미술관이 마침내 일반인들에게 다시 개방된다(the museum is finally reopening to the public)고 했으므로 (D)가 정답이다.

8 이수민은 누구인가?

(A) 미술가   (B) 큐레이터
(C) 학생   (D) 정치인

해설 | 세부 내용 - 이수민의 신분
뉴스 보도 중반부를 보면 임시 전시회에 이수민 씨를 포함한 캐나다 미술가들(contemporary Canadian artists, including Soo-Min Lee)의 작품이 전시된다고 했으므로 (A)가 정답이다.

9 시장은 토요일에 무엇을 할 것인가?

(A) 다른 도시 방문   (B) 토론회 참석
(C) 행사 연설   (D) 수상자 발표

해설 | 세부 내용 - 시장의 토요일 계획
뉴스 보도 후반부에 이번 주 토요일 시장이 개관식에서 연설을 한다(the mayor will give an address)고 했으므로 (C)가 정답이다.

Paraphrasing
담화의 give an address → 정답의 Give a speech

[10-12] 광고

> **10**My Star Health is thrilled to announce the opening of our newest health center, Pond Springs Wellness—a combination health clinic and fitness facility. In addition to our state-of-the-art fitness equipment and exercise classes, we will also have a full team of doctors. **11/12**Please join us for our grand opening on May second from ten A.M. to six P.M., when all visitors will receive a free reusable water bottle. **12**If you'd like to schedule an appointment with one of our physicians in advance of the center's official opening, please call our scheduling line at 555-0190. We hope to see you on May second!
>
> **10**마이 스타 헬스는 병원과 피트니스 시설을 결합한 폰드 스프링즈 웰니스 의료 센터의 개장을 알리게 되어 기쁩니다. 최첨단 피트니스 장비와 운동 강좌뿐 아니라 완벽한 의료진도 갖추고 있습니다. **11/12**5월 2일 오전 10시부터 오후 6시까지 열리는 저희 개장 행사에 함께해 주십시오. 모든 방문객은 재사용이 가능한 물병을 무료로 받으실 수 있습니다. **12**센터의 공식 개장에 앞서 저희 의사 중 한 명에게 진료 예약을 하고 싶으시면 일정 예약 전용선인 555-0190으로 전화하세요. 5월 2일에 뵙겠습니다!
>
> 어휘 | be thrilled to ~하게 되어 신이 나다 combination 결합 facility 시설 in addition to ~뿐 아니라, ~에 더해 equipment 장비 reusable 재사용이 가능한 appointment (진료 등의) 예약, 약속 physician 의사, 내과 의사 in advance of ~보다 앞에 official 공식적인

10 곧 무엇이 문을 열 예정인가?

(A) 의과 대학   (B) 의료 센터
(C) 댄스 스튜디오   (D) 스포츠 용품 매장

것으로 보이는데, 이는 연중 이맘때의 평균 기온에 해당됩니다. 지금 시각은 7시입니다. ¹⁵다음 일기 예보는 정확히 한 시간 후에 오늘의 최신 교통 정보와 함께 전해드립니다.

어휘 | hourly 매 시간의 unseasonably 철에 맞지 않게, 때 아니게 approach 다가가다, 근접하다 degree (온도 단위) 도 Celsius 섭씨의 high-pressure 고기압의 system 대기 상황 things 형편, 상황 break down 붕괴하다, 약화되다 average 평균(의) this time of the year 연중 이맘때 along with ~와 함께 traffic update 최신 교통 정보

해설 | 세부 내용 - 곧 문을 열 예정인 곳
광고의 초반부에서 폰드 스프링즈 웰니스 의료 센터의 개장(the opening of our newest health center, Pond Springs Wellness)을 알리게 되어 기쁘다고 했으므로 (B)가 정답이다.

11 행사에서 무엇을 나눠줄 것인가?
(A) 티셔츠   (B) 회원권
(C) 체력 평가   (D) 물병

해설 | 세부 내용 - 행사에서 나눠줄 것
광고의 중반부에서 개장 행사에 오면 재사용 가능한 물병을 무료로 받을 수 있다(all visitors will receive a free reusable water bottle)고 했으므로 (D)가 정답이다.

어휘 | evaluation 평가

12 청자들은 5월 2일 이전에 무엇을 할 수 있는가?
(A) 예약 잡기   (B) 강좌 등록하기
(C) 장비 주문하기   (D) 강사와 이야기하기

해설 | 세부 내용 - 청자들이 5월 2일 전에 할 수 있는 것
광고의 중반부에서 5월 2일이 센터의 개장 행사일임을 언급했는데, 후반부에서 센터의 공식 개장에 앞서 의사 중 한 명에게 진료 예약을 하고 싶다면 일정 예약 전용선으로 전화하라고(If you'd like to schedule an appointment ~, please call our scheduling line) 했으므로 (A)가 정답이다.

어휘 | register for ~에 등록하다 instructor 강사

[13-15] 일기 예보

Good morning, this is Rebecca Melaney in the weather room with your hourly weather report. ¹³We'll have more unseasonably warm weather today. Although spring is still a month away, we can expect sunny skies and temperatures approaching 20 degrees Celsius in the city today. The National Weather Center reports that a high-pressure system over the western part of the country is keeping the usual winter rains and clouds well to the north of us. ¹⁴Things are likely to change early next week, though. The weather center expects the high-pressure system to begin breaking down on Sunday. ¹⁴The clouds will return and high temperatures should drop to around 12 degrees, which is right around average for this time of the year. It's seven o'clock now; ¹⁵we'll have the next weather report in exactly one hour, along with the daily traffic update.

좋은 아침입니다. 저는 매시간 날씨를 전해드리는 기상 상황실의 레베카 멜라니입니다. ¹³오늘은 때 아니게 날씨가 덥겠습니다. 봄이 되려면 아직 한 달이 더 있어야 하지만, 오늘은 도시의 날씨가 화창하고 기온이 섭씨 20도에 육박할 것으로 예상됩니다. 국립 기상 센터는 우리 나라의 서부 지역에 형성된 고기압이 통상적인 겨울비와 구름을 북쪽 지역에 묶어 두고 있다고 전합니다. ¹⁴하지만 다음 주 초에는 이런 상황이 변할 것 같습니다. 기상 센터는 일요일에 고기압이 약화되기 시작할 것이라고 예상합니다. ¹⁴구름이 다시 돌아오고 높은 기온은 약 12도로 떨어질

---

13 화자가 오늘의 날씨에 대해 시사하는 것은 무엇인가?
(A) 이례적으로 따뜻할 것이다.
(B) 하루 종일 비가 올 것이다.
(C) 교통 문제를 일으킬 것이다.
(D) 오늘 이따가 변할 것이다.

해설 | 세부 내용 - 오늘의 날씨 정보
방송 초반부에 오늘은 철에 맞지 않게 날씨가 따뜻할 것(We'll have more unseasonably warm weather today)이라고 했으므로 (A)가 정답이다.

어휘 | unusually 유별나게, 이례적으로

14 다음 주에 무슨 일이 일어나겠는가?
(A) 봄이 시작될 것이다.
(B) 기온이 내려갈 것이다.
(C) 기상 센터가 문을 닫을 것이다.
(D) 날마다 날씨가 매우 화창할 것이다.

해설 | 세부 내용 - 다음 주에 일어날 일
방송 중반부에서 다음 주에 상황이 변할 것이라고 한 후, 높은 기온이 약 12도로 떨어질 것(high temperatures should drop to around 12 degrees)이라고 했으므로 (B)가 정답이다.

어휘 | decrease (온도 등이) 내려가다

15 다음 일기 예보는 언제 있겠는가?
(A) 12분 후   (B) 20분 후
(C) 30분 후   (D) 1시간 후

해설 | 세부 내용 - 다음 일기 예보 시점
방송 후반부에서 다음 일기 예보는 정확히 한 시간 후에 최신 교통 정보와 함께 전하겠다(we'll have the next weather report in exactly one hour, along with the daily traffic update)고 했으므로 (D)가 정답이다.

[16-18] 광고

If your office needs renovating, why not choose a company you trust? ¹⁶Yang Brothers is the number-one commercial remodeling contractor in the Springbridge area. From reception areas to offices, conference rooms and amenities… we do it all! Not only do we offer complete design-and-build services, but we also guarantee long-term quality. ¹⁷Unlike our competitors, we offer a free one-year inspection program: one year after the project is completed, we will come check that everything in your renovated space is working as it should. **¹⁸Visit our Web site at www.yangbrothers.com to see pictures of other commercial spaces we've remodeled.** You're sure to be impressed by the creativity and quality of our past projects. No matter the workspace, Yang Brothers has a solution for you.

귀하의 사무실을 보수해야 한다면 신뢰하는 업체를 선택해야 하지 않을까요? **¹⁶양 브라더스는 스프링브리지 지역 최고의 상가 리모델링 건설업체입니다.** 안내 구역부터 사무실, 회의실, 편의 시설에 이르기까지 모든 작업을 해 드립니다. 완벽한 설계 및 건축 서비스를 제공할 뿐 아니라 장기적인 품질도 보장합니다. **¹⁷경쟁업체와는 달리 1년 점검 프로그램을 무료로 제공합니다.** 작업 완료 후 1년이 되면 저희가 가서 보수한 공간이 모두 제대로 돌아가고 있는지 확인해 드립니다. **¹⁸웹사이트 www.yangbrothers.com을 방문하셔서 저희가 리모델링한 상업 공간의 사진들을 살펴보세요.** 지난 작업들의 창의성과 품질에 감동하실 겁니다. 어떤 업무 공간이든 양 브라더스가 해결책을 제시해 드립니다.

어휘 | renovate 보수하다, 수선하다 commercial 상업적인 contractor 건설업체, 도급업체 reception 접수, 안내, 환영 conference 회의 amenities 편의 시설 complete 완벽한 guarantee 보장하다, 약속하다 long-term 장기적인 competitor 경쟁자 inspection 점검, 검사 impress 깊은 인상을 주다, 감동시키다 creativity 창의성

16 어떤 종류의 업체를 광고하고 있는가?
(A) 웹디자인 회사　　　(B) 철물점
(C) 부동산 중개업체　　(D) 리모델링 회사

해설 | **전체 내용 - 광고하는 업체의 종류**
광고의 초반부에서 양 브라더스는 스프링브리지 지역 최고의 상가 리모델링 건설업체(Yang Brothers is the number-one commercial remodeling contractor in the Springbridge area)라고 소개했으므로 (D)가 정답이다.

17 업체는 어떤 특별 서비스를 제공하는가?
(A) 무료 설치　　　　　(B) 융통성 있는 결제 방식
(C) 후속 점검　　　　　(D) 긴급 수리

해설 | **세부 내용 - 업체가 제공하는 특별 서비스**
광고의 중반부에서 경쟁업체와는 달리 1년 점검 프로그램을 제공한다(Unlike our competitors, we offer a free one-year inspection program)고 한 후, 작업 완료 후 1년이 되면 방문하여 보수한 공간이 모두 제대로 돌아가고 있는지 확인한다(one year after the project is completed, we will come check that everything in your renovated space is working as it should)고 덧붙였으므로 (C)가 정답이다.

어휘 | installation 설치 flexible 융통성 있는, 유연한 payment plan 결제 방식 follow-up 후속 조치

18 화자는 청자들에게 온라인에서 무엇을 하라고 제안하는가?
(A) 작업 견본 보기　　　(B) 의견 남기기
(C) 상담 요청하기　　　(D) 업체 위치 찾기

해설 | **세부 내용 - 화자의 제안 사항**
광고의 후반부에서 웹사이트를 방문하여 자신의 회사가 리모델링한 상업 공간의 사진들을 살펴볼 것(Visit our Web site ~ to see pictures of other commercial spaces we've remodeled)을 제안했으므로 (A)가 정답이다.

어휘 | request 요청하다 consultation 상담, 협의, 진찰

Paraphrasing
담화의 see pictures of other commercial spaces we've remodeled → 정답의 View work samples

[19-21] 라디오 방송 + 편성표

You're listening to 105.2 Cam's Money Corner. Welcome back from the commercial break. I know all our listeners are excited to hear from Ms. Cheryl Graves during this week's segment on Ask an Expert. **¹⁹Unfortunately, Ask an Expert will start a few minutes late due to a technical problem.** We are currently having trouble with Ms. Graves' microphone. While we wait, I want to remind all the listeners that **²⁰she'll be discussing practical tips on how to keep better track of your earnings and your spending.** **²¹Ms. Graves will also answer questions from our listeners, so call in if you're struggling with money management or have other questions.**

105.2 <캠의 자금 관리 코너>를 듣고 계십니다. 중간 광고를 듣고 오셨습니다. 모든 청취자 여러분께서 이번 주 <전문가에게 물어보세요> 시간에 셰릴 그레이브스 씨의 이야기를 기대하고 계시다는 점을 알고 있습니다. **¹⁹안타깝게도 <전문가에게 물어보세요>가 기술적인 문제로 몇 분 늦게 시작할 예정입니다.** 현재 그레이브스 씨의 마이크에 문제가 있습니다. 기다리는 동안 청취자 여러분께 **²⁰그녀가 소득과 지출을 더 잘 관리하는 법에 대한 실용적인 조언을 해드릴 예정임을** 다시 한 번 알려 드리고 싶네요. **²¹그레이브스 씨는 청취자들의 질문도 받을 예정이오니,** 자금 관리에 어려움을 겪고 계시거나 다른 질문이 있으시다면 전화 주십시오.

어휘 | commercial break 중간 광고 segment 부분 due to ~때문에 technical 기술적인 practical 실용적인 earning 소득 spending 지출 struggle with ~로 씨름하다 management 관리

라디오 편성표

오후 2시 - 2시 55분	키스의 투자 조언
오후 2시 55분 - 3시	중간 광고
¹⁹오후 3시 - 4시 30분	**전문가에게 물어보세요**
오후 4시 30분 - 4시 35분	최신 교통 정보

19 시각 정보에 따르면, 편성표에서 어떤 시작 시각이 더 이상 정확하지 않은가?
(A) 오후 2시　　　　　(B) 오후 2시 55분
(C) 오후 3시　　　　　(D) 오후 4시 30분

해설 | 세부 내용 - 시각 정보 연계
방송 중반부에서 '전문가에게 물어보세요'가 기술적인 문제로 몇 분
늦게 시작할 예정(Unfortunately, Ask an Expert will start
a few minutes late due to a technical problem)이라고
했는데, 편성표를 보면 '전문가에게 물어보세요'가 원래 3시에 시작할
예정이었다는 것을 알 수 있다. 따라서 (C)가 정답이다.

20 셰릴 그레이브스 씨는 무엇에 대해 이야기할 것인가?
(A) 자금을 관리하는 방법
(B) 은행가가 되는 방법
(C) 주택 구매에 대한 조언
(D) 경영 연수생을 위한 워크숍

해설 | 세부 내용 - 셰릴 그레이브스가 할 이야기의 주제
후반부에서 셰릴 그레이브스 씨가 소득과 지출을 더 잘 관리하는
법에 대한 실용적인 조언을 할 것(she'll be discussing
practical tips on how to keep better track of your
earnings and your spending)이라고 했다. 따라서 (A)가
정답이다.

21 화자는 청자들에게 무엇을 하라고 요청하는가?
(A) 음악을 들으라고   (B) 질문이 있으면 전화하라고
(C) 웹사이트를 방문하라고   (D) 퀴즈 대회에 출전하라고

해설 | 세부 내용 - 요청 사항
마지막에 자금 관리에 어려움을 겪고 있거나 다른 질문이 있다면
전화를 달라(call in if you're struggling with money
management or have other questions)고 했으므로, (B)가
정답이다.

어휘 | enter 출전하다 trivia contest 퀴즈 대회

● **ETS ACTUAL TEST**   본책 p.122

71 (C)	**72** (D)	**73** (B)	**74** (D)	**75** (C)	**76** (A)
77 (D)	**78** (D)	**79** (A)	**80** (B)	**81** (D)	**82** (A)
83 (A)	**84** (B)	**85** (D)	**86** (C)	**87** (A)	**88** (B)
89 (D)	**90** (B)	**91** (C)	**92** (C)	**93** (B)	**94** (B)
95 (A)	**96** (C)	**97** (B)	**98** (D)	**99** (D)	**100** (B)

[71-73] 공지

> [72]I called this meeting to discuss a serious
> problem. As you are all aware, [71/72]Winslow
> Publications has published many top-selling
> books and has an excellent reputation. So [71/72]we
> were surprised to learn that two manuscripts of
> unpublished books have disappeared. To prevent
> this from occurring again, [73]you will be required
> to fill out a form asking for permission when you
> take a manuscript out of the office so that we
> know where documents are at all times. If you
> have any questions about this, please see your
> department head.

[72]심각한 문제를 논의하고자 이 회의를 소집했습니다. 모두 알다시피
[71/72]윈슬로우 출판사는 많은 베스트셀러 도서를 출판했고 평판이 매우
좋습니다. 그래서 [71/72]미출판 도서 두 권의 원고가 사라졌다는 것을
알고는 모두 놀랐죠. 이런 일이 다시 일어나는 것을 막기 위해 [73]여러분이
사무실에서 원고를 가지고 나갈 때 허가를 구하는 서식을 작성하게
해서 항상 문서의 위치를 알 수 있게끔 하겠습니다. 여기에 관한 질문이
있으시면 부서장과 면담하십시오.

어휘 | be aware 알다 publish 출판하다 reputation 명성, 평판
manuscript 원고 unpublished 미출판된 disappear 사라지다
prevent 막다 occur 발생하다 fill out a form 서식을 작성하다
permission 허가 department 부서

71 화자는 어디서 일하겠는가?
(A) 서점   (B) 도서관
(C) 출판사   (D) 광고회사

해설 | 전체 내용 - 화자의 근무 장소
공지의 초반부에서 윈슬로우 출판사는 많은 베스트셀러 도서를
출판했다(Winslow Publications has published many
top-selling books)고 한 후, 미출판 도서 두 권의 원고가
사라졌다는 것을 알고 모두 놀랐다(we were surprised to
learn that two manuscripts of unpublished books have
disappeared)고 했으므로, (C)가 정답이다.

72 화자는 어떤 문제에 대해 이야기하는가?
(A) 부정적인 보도 자료
(B) 최근 고객 불만 사항
(C) 인원이 부족한 부서
(D) 없어진 문서

해설 | 세부 내용 - 화자가 논의하는 문제점
공지의 중반부에서 미출판 도서 두 권의 원고가 사라졌다(two
manuscripts of unpublished books have
disappeared)는 문제점을 언급했으므로 (D)가 정답이다.

어휘 | negative 부정적인 complaint 불만, 불평 understaffed
인원이 부족한 missing 없어진

Paraphrasing
담화의 two manuscripts of unpublished books have
disappeared → 정답의 Some missing documents

73 직원들은 앞으로 무엇을 해야 하는가?
(A) 구매 승인 받기
(B) 허가서 작성하기
(C) 사전에 휴가 신청하기
(D) 주간 목표량 달성하기

해설 | 세부 내용 - 직원들이 요구받은 사항
공지의 중반부에서 직원들에게 사무실에서 원고를 가지고 나갈
때 허가를 구하는 서식을 작성할 것(you will be required to
fill out a form asking for permission when you take a
manuscript out of the office)을 요구했으므로 (B)가 정답이다.

어휘 | approval 승인 purchase 구입 complete a form 서식을
작성하다 in advance 미리 meet a target 목표를 달성하다

Paraphrasing
담화의 fill out a form asking for permission
→ 정답의 Complete a permission form

LC

PART 4

[74-76] 광고

⁷⁴Natural Earth Magazine is now offering a year-long subscription for only 15 Euros. When you subscribe to our spectacular magazine, each month you'll receive news of the latest nature discoveries and stories of awe-inspiring locations around the world. And ⁷⁵for a limited time only, when you subscribe to Natural Earth Magazine you'll receive two free admission tickets to one of the many national parks our magazine supports. You'll be able to see some of the most spectacular plants and animal species the world has to offer. So ⁷⁶go to our Web site and type in the number 8632 to take advantage of this limited-time offer.

⁷⁴<내추럴 어스 매거진>은 현재 단 15유로로 연간 구독권을 제공하고 있습니다. 이 멋진 잡지를 구독하시면, 최신 자연 발견 및 전 세계의 장엄한 장소에 관한 소식을 매월 받으실 수 있습니다. 아울러 ⁷⁵한정된 기간 동안 <내추럴 어스 매거진> 구독 시, 저희 잡지에서 후원하는 많은 국립공원 중 한 곳의 무료 입장권 2매를 받으시게 됩니다. 지구상에서 가장 인상적인 동식물을 보실 수 있을 겁니다. ⁷⁶이번 한정 판매 혜택을 받으시려면 웹사이트를 방문하셔서 숫자 8632를 입력하십시오.

어휘 | year-long 일 년 내내 계속되는 subscription 구독 spectacular 장관을 이루는, 화려한, 인상적인 discovery 발견 awe-inspiring 경외심을 불러일으키는, 장엄한 limited 한정된 admission ticket 입장권 support 지원하다 species 종 take advantage of ~를 이용하다

74 무엇을 광고하고 있는가?
(A) 음악회 시리즈   (B) 과학관
(C) 반려동물 가게   (D) 월간지

해설 | 전체 내용 - 광고하는 것
광고의 초반부에서 <내추럴 어스 매거진>은 단 15유로에 연간 구독권을 제공하고 있다고 한 후, 잡지를 구독하면 매월 소식을 받을 수 있다(When you subscribe to our spectacular magazine, each month you'll receive news)고 했으므로, (D)가 정답이다.

75 신규 고객은 한정 기간 동안 무엇을 받게 되는가?
(A) 무료 견본 식품   (B) 강좌 초청장
(C) 공원 입장권   (D) 기념 티셔츠

해설 | 세부 내용 - 신규 고객이 한정 기간 동안 받을 것
광고의 중반부에서 한정된 기간 동안(for a limited time only) <내추럴 어스 매거진> 구독 시, 많은 국립공원 중 한 곳의 무료 입장권 2매를 받게 된다(you'll receive two free admission tickets to one of the many national parks)고 했으므로 (C)가 정답이다.

어휘 | lecture 강좌, 강의 entry ticket 입장권 souvenir 기념품

Paraphrasing
담화의 admission tickets → 정답의 Entry tickets

76 청자들은 웹사이트에서 무엇을 하라고 요청 받았는가?
(A) 판촉 번호 사용하기
(B) 사진 보기
(C) 우편물 수신자 목록에 등록하기
(D) 대회 참가하기

해설 | 세부 내용 - 청자들이 요청 받은 사항
광고의 마지막에서 한정 판매 혜택을 받으려면 웹사이트를 방문해서 숫자 8632를 입력할 것(go to our Web site and type in the number 8632 to take advantage of this limited-time offer)을 요청했으므로 (A)가 정답이다.

어휘 | promotional code 판촉 번호 mailing list 우편물 수신자 목록 enter a contest 대회에 참가하다

[77-79] 전화 메시지

Hello, Ms. Yamamoto. ⁷⁷I'm calling from Rivers Medical Center. In your voicemail message from this morning, ⁷⁸you asked to have your annual health checkup with Dr. Hamam. Well, I have to tell you that he recently moved to New York. ⁷⁸We do have several other doctors in our practice. ⁷⁹They all have professional profiles on our Web site, so I'd encourage you to read them. I'm sure the information in the profiles will help you decide who you'd like to see.

안녕하세요, 야마모토 씨. ⁷⁷리버스 의료 센터에서 전화 드립니다. 오늘 아침에 남기신 음성 메시지에 ⁷⁸하맘 선생님께 연례 건강 검진을 받고 싶다고 하셨는데요. 음, 선생님께서 최근에 뉴욕으로 이사를 가셨다는 말씀을 드려야겠네요. ⁷⁸저희 병원에는 다른 의사 선생님들이 여러분 계십니다. ⁷⁹저희 웹사이트에 선생님들의 이력 사항이 모두 나오니 그것들을 읽어 보시기를 권합니다. 이력 사항의 정보가 어느 분께 검진을 받고 싶은지 결정하시는 데 분명 도움이 될 겁니다.

어휘 | annual 연례의 health checkup 건강 검진 practice (의사·변호사 등의) 업무, 사무실 professional profile (전문적인) 이력 encourage 권고하다

77 화자는 어디에서 일하는가?
(A) 회계 사무소에서
(B) 인터넷 서비스 제공업체에서
(C) 부동산 중개소에서
(D) 의료 센터에서

해설 | 전체 내용 - 화자의 근무 장소
메시지의 초반부에서 리버스 의료 센터에서 전화한다(I'm calling from Rivers Medical Center)고 했으므로, 화자가 의료 센터에서 일한다는 것을 알 수 있다. 따라서 (D)가 정답이다.

78 화자가 "선생님께서 최근에 뉴욕으로 이사를 가셨다"라고 말할 때 무엇을 의미하는가?
(A) 채용 결정이 놀랍다.
(B) 장소가 매우 인기 있다.
(C) 어쩔 수 없이 지체되었다.
(D) 요청을 수용할 수 없다.

해설 | **세부 내용 - 화자의 의도**

화자는 야마모토 씨가 하맘 선생님에게 연례 건강 검진을 받고 싶다고 요청한(you asked to have your annual health checkup with Dr. Hamam) 메시지를 받았다는 사실을 언급한 직후 '선생님께서 최근에 뉴욕으로 이사를 가셨다(he recently moved to New York)'라며 다른 의사 선생님들이 있다고 덧붙였다. 이는 야마모토 씨의 요청이 이루어질 수 없음을 알리려는 의도라고 볼 수 있으므로, (D)가 정답이다.

어휘 | accommodate 수용하다, (요구 등에) 부응하다

79 화자가 웹사이트 방문을 권하는 이유는?

(A) 이력 사항을 읽으라고
(B) 양식을 다운로드받으라고
(C) 결제를 하라고
(D) 주소를 찾으라고

해설 | **세부 내용 - 웹사이트 방문을 권하는 이유**

전화 메시지의 후반부에서 웹사이트에 선생님들의 이력 사항이 모두 나오니 읽어 볼 것을 권한다(They all have professional profiles on our Web site, so I'd encourage you to read them)고 했으므로, (A)가 정답이다.

[80-82] 공지

> ^{80}I wanted to give you all an update on the new software program we'll soon begin using here at the clinic. As you know, we're making this upgrade because our current software takes a long time to load, and that causes delays when we input our patients' information. Well, you'll be happy to know that the new software is very fast. But… it's not software you're familiar with. ^{81}I'd like to find time outside of our regular business hours for you to learn the basics. I'm passing around a calendar—^{82}please write down which times you're available to come in.
>
> ^{80}우리가 이 병원에서 곧 사용하게 될 새로운 소프트웨어 프로그램에 대한 최신 정보를 여러분 모두에게 알려주려고 합니다. 여러분도 알다시피, 이 업그레이드를 하고 있는 이유는 현재 소프트웨어가 로딩하는 데 시간이 오래 걸리고 이로 인해 환자 정보를 입력할 때 시간이 지연되기 때문입니다. 음, 새 소프트웨어가 매우 빠르다는 것을 알면 기쁠 겁니다. 하지만 여러분들이 잘 아는 소프트웨어가 아니에요. ^{81}정규 업무 시간 외에 별도로 여러분이 기본기를 배울 수 있는 시간을 가질까 합니다. ^{82}지금 달력을 돌리고 있는데요, 몇 시에 들어올 수 있는지 적어 주세요.
>
> 어휘 | current 현재의 cause 야기하다 familiar 익숙한, 잘 아는 regular 정규의 pass around (여러 사람이 보도록) 돌리다 available 시간이 되는, 이용 가능한

80 청자들은 어디에서 일하는가?

(A) 기술회사에서 (B) 의료기관에서
(C) 회계법인에서 (D) 제조공장에서

해설 | **전체 내용 - 청자들의 근무지**

공지 초반부에서 청자들에게 새로 사용할 소프트웨어 프로그램에 대해 알려주겠다고 한 후, '이곳 병원에서(here at the clinic)'라며 직접적으로 근무지를 언급했다. 따라서 (B)가 정답이다.

81 화자가 "여러분들이 잘 아는 소프트웨어가 아니에요"라고 말한 의도는 무엇인가?

(A) 회사의 발표가 잘못되었다.
(B) 프로젝트 제안서가 성공을 거두지 못할 것이다.
(C) 일부 소프트웨어가 아직 개발 중이다.
(D) 약간의 교육이 필요할 것이다.

해설 | **세부 내용 - 화자의 의도**

공지 중반부에서 '여러분들이 잘 아는 소프트웨어가 아니에요'라고 한 직후, 정규 업무 시간 외에 청자들이 기본기를 배울 수 있는 시간을 가지려 한다(I'd like to find time outside of our regular business hours for you to learn the basics)고 했다. 따라서 (D)가 정답이다.

어휘 | announcement 발표 proposal 제안(서) work 효과가 있다, 성공하다 develop 개발하다

82 청자들은 다음에 무엇을 할 것인가?

(A) 가능한 시간 표시
(B) 관리자에게 전화하기
(C) 데이터 분석하기
(D) 약속 확인해 주기

해설 | **세부 내용 - 청자들이 할 일**

공지 후반부에서 청자들에게 교육에 올 수 있는 시간을 표시해달라(please write down which times you're available to come in)고 했으므로, (A)가 정답이다.

어휘 | indicate 표시하다 availability 가능성 analyze 분석하다 confirm 확인하다

[83-85] 전화 메시지

> Hello, this message is for Lisa Cheng. Ms. Cheng, I'm calling on behalf of the Canadian Association of Nurses. $^{83/84}$We're having our annual conference on November fifteenth in Calgary, and I'd like to invite you to give a lecture about your research on proper nutrition for hospital patients. I know ^{84}you've written a book about healthy eating habits, and I think our audience would benefit a lot from your expertise. ^{85}We would, of course, be happy to pay for all your transportation expenses for getting to and from the conference. Please give me a call to discuss the details. Thanks Ms. Cheng, and have a nice day.

115

안녕하세요. 리사 청 씨께 메시지 남깁니다. 청 씨, 제가 캐나다 간호사협회를 대표해 전화 드립니다. **83/84**11월 15일에 캘거리에서 연례 회의가 열리는데요. 병원 환자에게 적절한 영양에 관해 연구하신 바를 강의해 주셨으면 합니다. **84**건강한 식습관에 대해 책을 쓰신 것도 알고 있으며, 청중들이 당신의 전문 지식에서 많은 것을 얻을 수 있을 거라 생각합니다. **85**물론 회의 장소를 오가는 데 발생하는 여비는 전액 지급해 드릴 것입니다. 전화 주셔서 세부 사항을 논의하시죠. 청 씨, 감사합니다. 좋은 하루 되세요.

어휘 | on behalf of ~를 대표하여 association 협회 annual 매년의, 연례의 conference 회의 lecture 강좌, 강의 research 연구 proper 적절한 nutrition 영양 expertise 전문 지식 transportation expense 교통비

83 메시지의 목적은?
(A) 청자를 행사에 초청하려고
(B) 입사지원서에 대한 후속 조치를 취하려고
(C) 곧 있을 출판에 대해 논의하려고
(D) 전문 기관을 광고하려고

해설 | **전체 내용 - 메시지의 목적**
전화 메시지의 초반부에서 11월 15일에 캘거리에서 연례 회의가 열린다(We're having our annual conference on November fifteenth in Calgary)고 한 후, 청 씨의 연구에 대해 강의해 줄 것(I'd like to invite you to give a lecture about your research)을 요청했으므로, (A)가 정답이다.

어휘 | follow up on ~를 끝까지 하다, 후속 조치를 하다 upcoming 다가오는 publication 출판 advertise 광고하다

Paraphrasing
담화의 annual conference → 정답의 event

84 리사 청의 전문 영역은 무엇인가?
(A) 소셜미디어 마케팅
(B) 식이와 영양
(C) 병원 관리
(D) 도시 계획

해설 | **세부 내용 - 리사 청의 전문 영역**
전화 메시지의 중반부에서 병원 환자에게 적절한 영양에 관한 청 씨의 연구에 대해 강의(a lecture about your research on proper nutrition for hospital patients)해줄 것을 부탁한 후, 청 씨가 건강한 식습관에 대해 책을 썼다(you've written a book about healthy eating habits)는 사실을 언급했으므로, (B)가 정답이다.

어휘 | management 경영, 관리 urban 도시의

85 화자는 무엇을 해 주겠다고 제안하는가?
(A) 연구 자료 공유   (B) 광고 제작
(C) 동료에게 연락   (D) 출장비 지급

해설 | **세부 내용 - 화자가 자청한 일**
전화 메시지의 후반부에서 회의 장소를 오가는 데 발생하는 여비는 전액 지급할 것(We would ~ pay for all your transportation expenses for getting to and from the conference)이라고 했으므로 (D)가 정답이다.

어휘 | colleague 동료 travel cost 출장비

Paraphrasing
담화의 transportation expenses → 정답의 travel costs

[86-88] 방송

This is KTVX Radio. **86**We've just heard "Forgotten Moments," the latest song from Erika Bauer. She's one of the most successful contemporary jazz singers, and she's performed with some of the world's top musicians. If you're interested in learning more about her rise to stardom, **87**be sure to tune in this evening. She'll be the guest on our program "Musical Chat." During the interview, Ms. Bauer will tell us about her fascinating life. **88**We'll be accepting questions from listeners at home, so you can e-mail those to us here at the station.

KTVX 라디오입니다. **86**에리카 바우어의 최신곡 '잊혀진 순간들'을 들어봤습니다. 당대 최고의 성공적인 재즈 가수 중 한 명으로, 세계 최고의 음악가들과 공연한 바 있죠. 그녀가 스타로 발돋움한 과정을 더 자세히 알고 싶으시다면 **87**오늘 저녁 채널을 고정해 주세요. '음악 이야기' 프로그램에 초대손님으로 나옵니다. 인터뷰 중 바우어 씨가 그녀의 매력적인 삶에 대해 이야기해 줄 겁니다. **88**댁에 계신 청취자들께 질문을 받을 예정이니 이메일을 통해 방송국으로 질문을 보내주세요.

어휘 | forgotten 잊혀진, 망각된 contemporary 동시대의, 당대의 perform 공연하다 rise to stardom 스타가 됨 tune in 청취하다, 라디오의 채널을 맞추다 fascinating 매력적인 accept 받아들이다 station 방송국

86 에리카 바우어는 누구인가?
(A) 작가
(B) 배우
(C) 가수
(D) 기자

해설 | **세부 내용 - 에리카 바우어의 신분**
방송의 초반부에서 에리카 바우어의 최신곡을 들어봤다(We've just heard ~ the latest song from Erika Bauer)고 한 후, 그녀를 당대 최고의 성공적인 재즈 가수 중 한 명(She's one of the most successful contemporary jazz singers)이라고 소개했으므로 (C)가 정답이다.

87 화자에 따르면, 에리카 바우어는 오늘 저녁 무엇을 할 것인가?
(A) 자신의 삶에 대해 이야기하기
(B) 현재 행사에 대해 논의하기
(C) 책 비평하기
(D) 직업에 관한 조언하기

해설 | **세부 내용 - 에리카 바우어가 오늘 저녁에 할 일**
방송의 중반부에서 오늘 저녁에 채널을 고정해달라(be sure to tune in this evening)고 한 후, 바우어 씨가 초대손님(the guest on our program)으로 나와서 자신의 매력적인 삶에 대해

이야기해 줄 것(Ms. Bauer will tell us about her fascinating life)이라고 했으므로 (A)가 정답이다.

어휘 | current 현재의 career 직업, 사회생활

88 청자들은 무엇을 하라고 권유받는가?

(A) 노래 신청
(B) 질문 제출
(C) 대회 참가
(D) 방송국 방문

해설 | 세부 내용 - 청자들이 권유받은 사항
방송의 마지막에서 청취자들에게 질문을 받을 예정(We'll be accepting questions from listeners)이라고 한 후, 질문을 이메일로 방송국에 보내주면 된다(you can e-mail those to us here at the station)고 했으므로 (B)가 정답이다.

어휘 | request 요청하다 submit 제출하다 enter a contest 대회에 참가하다

[89-91] 주주 회의

> [89]Welcome to the annual shareholder meeting for Local Fresh Foods. As you know, we've expanded recently by offering home delivery of groceries, and we're grateful for your support during this process. Now, [90]the first item on the agenda is the recent decline in our profits. It's important to remember that we just installed new refrigeration units on all our delivery trucks. [91]We've prepared a short video on how this investment will improve our business in the long term. Let's take a look.
>
> [89]로컬 프레시 푸드 연례 주주회의에 오신 것을 환영합니다. 아시는 대로, 저희는 최근 식료품 가정 배달 서비스를 제공하며 사업을 확장했습니다. 이 과정을 지지해 주셔서 감사합니다. [90]자, 첫 번째 안건은 최근의 수익 감소입니다. 꼭 기억하실 점은 저희가 모든 배송 트럭에 새 냉장 장치를 설치했다는 것입니다. [91]이번 투자가 장기적으로 우리 사업을 어떻게 향상시킬지에 관해 짧은 동영상을 준비했습니다. 한 번 보시죠.
>
> 어휘 | annual 매년의, 연례의 shareholder 주주 expand 확장하다 recently 최근 groceries 식료품 process 과정 decline 감소, 하락 profit 이윤, 수익 install 설치하다 refrigeration 냉각, 냉장 delivery 배달, 배송 investment 투자 improve 개선하다, 향상시키다 in the long term 장기적으로 take a look 보다

89 화자는 어디에 있는가?

(A) 지점 개업식
(B) 무역박람회
(C) 고객과의 저녁 식사
(D) 주주회의

해설 | 전체 내용 - 담화의 장소
담화의 초반부에서 로컬 프레시 푸드 연례 주주회의에 온 것을 환영한다(Welcome to the annual shareholder meeting for Local Fresh Foods)고 했으므로, 화자가 주주회의에 있다는 것을 알 수 있다. 따라서 (D)가 정답이다.

90 화자가 "저희가 모든 배송 트럭에 새 냉장 장치를 설치했다"고 말한 의도는 무엇인가?

(A) 차량 검사에 대해 보고하기 위해
(B) 재정적 손실에 대해 설명하기 위해
(C) 채용 결정을 해명하기 위해
(D) 투자에 이의를 제기하기 위해

해설 | 세부 내용 - 화자의 의도
담화의 중반부에서 첫 번째 안건이 최근의 수익 감소(the first item on the agenda is the recent decline in our profits)라고 한 후, 모든 배송 트럭에 새 냉장 장치를 설치했다(we just installed new refrigeration units on all our delivery trucks)는 사실을 꼭 기억해야 한다(It's important to remember)고 덧붙였다. 이는 화자가 최근 수익 감소의 이유를 설명하려는 의도라고 볼 수 있으므로 (B)가 정답이다.

어휘 | inspection 점검, 검사 financial 재정적인, 금융의 loss 손실 justify 정당화하다, 해명하다 decision 결정, 결심

91 화자는 다음으로 무엇을 하겠는가?

(A) 객원 연설자 소개하기 　(B) 재고 조사하기
(C) 동영상 보여주기 　(D) 견본 나눠 주기

해설 | 세부 내용 - 화자가 다음에 할 일
담화의 후반부에서 짧은 동영상을 준비했다(We've prepared a short video)고 한 후, 함께 볼 것(Let's take a look)을 제안했으므로, (C)가 정답이다.

어휘 | take inventory 재고 조사를 하다 distribute 분배하다, 나누어 주다

[92-94] 소개

> Before we end today's tour of the art museum, [92]I'd like to tell you about an upcoming exhibit that will be opening in July. The exhibit is called International Jewels and it will feature pieces by fifty well-known jewelry artists. This exhibit has already been shown in Rome, Paris, and London, and it has received excellent reviews. Plus, [93]our gift shop is going to be selling affordable reproductions of some of the most prominent pieces of jewelry. These replicas have been especially made to be sold during this exhibit. So if you're interested in this unique exhibit, [94]I encourage you to buy your tickets today, as we're expecting them to sell out quickly.
>
> 오늘 미술관 견학을 마치기 전에 [92]여러분께 곧 7월에 열릴 전시회에 대해 말씀드리고 싶습니다. 전시회 제목은 국제 보석전으로, 유명한 보석 예술가 50인의 작품이 전시될 예정입니다. 본 전시회는 이미 로마, 파리, 런던에서 열렸으며 훌륭한 평을 받았습니다. [93]아울러 저희 기념품점에서는 가장 인기있는 보석 몇 점을 적정한 가격의 복제품으로 제작하여 판매할 겁니다. 이 모조품들은 이번 전시회 동안 판매하기 위해 특별히 제작된 것입니다. 이 특별 전시회에 관심이 있으시다면 [94]오늘 표를 구입하십시오. 빠르게 매진될 것으로 예상됩니다.

92 담화의 목적은?

(A) 객원 연설자를 소개하려고

(B) 견학 일정을 제공하려고

(C) 새로운 전시회를 홍보하려고

(D) 미술관 역사를 설명하려고

해설 | **전체 내용 - 담화의 목적**

담화의 초반부에서 7월에 열릴 전시회에 대해 안내해 주고 싶다(I'd like to tell you about an upcoming exhibit that will be opening in July)고 했으므로, 전시회 홍보를 위한 안내임을 알 수 있다. 따라서 (C)가 정답이다.

Paraphrasing

담화의 tell you about an upcoming exhibit

→ 정답의 promote a new exhibit

93 화자는 기념품점에 대해 무엇이라고 말하는가?

(A) 보수 공사로 문을 닫을 것이다.

(B) 특별 상품을 판매할 것이다.

(C) 무료 지도를 비치하고 있다.

(D) 오늘 할인을 한다.

해설 | **세부 내용 - 화자가 기념품점에 대해 언급한 사항**

담화의 중반부에서 기념품점에서 가장 인기있는 보석 몇 점을 적정한 가격의 복제품으로 제작하여 판매할 예정(our gift shop is going to be selling affordable reproductions of some of the most prominent pieces of jewelry)이라고 한 후, 특별 제작된 것이라 덧붙였으므로, (B)가 정답이다.

어휘 | renovation 보수, 수리 merchandise 상품, 물품

Paraphrasing

담화의 affordable reproductions of some of the most prominent pieces of jewelry → 정답의 merchandise

94 화자는 청자들에게 무엇을 하라고 권하는가?

(A) 미술관에서 자원 봉사하기

(B) 예매권 구입하기

(C) 연간 회원 등록하기

(D) 참석하는 예술가 만나보기

해설 | **세부 내용 - 화자의 권고 사항**

담화의 후반부에서 곧 있을 특별 전시회에 관심이 있으면 오늘 표를 구입할 것(I encourage you to buy your tickets today)을 권고한 후, 빠르게 매진될 것으로 예상된다고 덧붙였으므로 (B)가 정답이다.

어휘 | volunteer 자원 봉사하다 purchase 구입하다 advance ticket 예매권 register for ~에 등록하다

Paraphrasing

담화의 buy your tickets today → 정답의 Purchase advance tickets

[95-97] 공지+투표 결과

[95]Before your shifts start this evening, I wanted to update you on our restaurant's menu. [96]At our pizza tasting event last week, we introduced four new pizza toppings, and asked attendees to vote for the one they liked the best. Take a look at the results I'm passing around now—as you can see, figs received the most votes. However, as you know, the prices of figs have gone up. So, [97]we've decided to add the second most popular topping instead. The new menus will be ready next week and [97]for the time being we'll just write it on the specials board. Please remember to let diners know that it's available.

[95]오늘 저녁 근무를 시작하기 전에 여러분께 우리 식당 메뉴에 대해 새로운 소식을 알려 드리겠습니다. [96]지난주 피자 시식 이벤트에서 네 가지 새로운 피자 토핑을 소개했고 참석자들에게 가장 마음에 드는 것에 투표해 달라고 요청했습니다. 제가 지금 나눠 드리는 결과를 봐 주세요. 보시는 대로 무화과가 가장 많은 표를 받았습니다. 하지만 아시다시피 무화과의 가격이 인상되었습니다. 그래서 [97]우리는 대신 두 번째로 인기 있는 토핑을 추가하기로 결정했습니다. 새로운 메뉴는 다음 주에 준비될 예정이고 [97]당분간은 그것을 특별 요리 게시판에 그냥 써 놓기만 하겠습니다. 식사 손님들에게 새 토핑을 이용할 수 있다고 알려 주시기 바랍니다.

어휘 | shift 교대 근무 tasting event 시식회 attendee 참석자 vote for ~에 찬성 투표를 하다 fig 무화과 go up 올라가다, 인상되다 add 추가하다 instead 대신 for the time being 당분간 special 특별 요리 diner 식사 손님 available 이용 가능한

피자 토핑	득표 수
무화과	42
[97]고구마	**40**
호두	33
가지	30

95 청자들은 누구이겠는가?

(A) 식당 종업원

(B) 요리 강사

(C) 식품 담당 기자

(D) 포커스 그룹 참여자

해설 | **전체 내용 - 청자의 신분**

담화 초반부에 '오늘 저녁 근무를 시작하기 전에 여러분께 우리 식당 메뉴에 대해 새로운 소식을 알려 드리겠습니다(Before your shifts start this evening, I wanted to update you on our restaurant's menu)'라고 했으므로, (A)가 정답이다.

96 화자에 따르면 지난주에 무슨 일이 있었는가?

(A) 책 출시

(B) 주방 보수공사

(C) 시식 행사

(D) 교육

해설 | **세부 내용 - 지난주에 발생한 일**

담화 초반부에 지난주에 있었던 피자 시식 이벤트(At our pizza tasting event last week)를 언급했으므로 (C)가 정답이다.

97 시각 정보에 따르면, 어떤 토핑이 특별 요리 게시판에 나타나겠는가?

(A) 무화과

(B) 고구마

(C) 호두

(D) 가지

해설 | **세부 내용 - 시각 정보 연계**

담화 후반부에 '당분간은 그것을 특별 요리 게시판에 그냥 써 놓기만 하겠습니다(for the time ~ specials board)'라고 했는데, 여기서 it은 앞에서 언급된 두 번째로 인기 있는 토핑을 말한다. 표를 보면 두 번째로 인기 있는 토핑은 고구마(Sweet potatoes)이므로, (B)가 정답이다.

[98-100] 회의 발췌+평면도

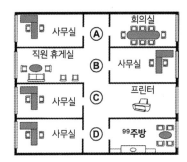

Hi everyone. The first item on the meeting agenda is a new company initiative. ⁹⁸To promote employee health, we're encouraging everyone to drink more water. ⁹⁸/⁹⁹As part of this plan, we'll be installing a new water dispenser. There's already one in the employee lounge, but ⁹⁹we'll be adding one in the hallway, right across from the kitchen. And to encourage you to use the dispensers, we're giving each employee a reusable water bottle. ¹⁰⁰You'll have a choice of either metal or glass, so please put a check next to the one you'd prefer on the sheet I'm passing around.

안녕하세요, 여러분. 회의 의제 중 첫 번째 안건은 새로운 사내 계획입니다. ⁹⁸우리는 직원 건강을 증진시키기 위해 전 임직원에게 물을 더 마실 것을 권합니다. ⁹⁸/⁹⁹이 계획의 일환으로 새로운 식수대를 설치할 것입니다. 이미 직원 휴게실에 하나 있지만, ⁹⁹주방 바로 맞은편 복도에 하나 더 설치할 예정입니다. 또한 식수대 사용을 독려하기 위해 재사용 가능한 물병을 직원 개개인에게 지급할 것입니다. ¹⁰⁰금속제와 유리병 중에 선택할 수 있으니 제가 지금 나눠 드릴 용지에 자신이 선호하는 것 옆에 체크 표시를 해 주세요.

어휘 | agenda 안건 initiative 계획 promote 촉진하다, 증진하다 water dispenser 식수대 reusable 재사용 가능한

98 회사는 무엇을 하려고 하는가?

(A) 재활용 권장

(B) 비용 절감

(C) 사업장 안전 개선

(D) 직원 건강 증진

해설 | **세부 내용 - 회사의 계획**

회의의 초반부에서 직원 건강을 증진시키기 위해(To promote employee health) 전 임직원에게 물을 더 마실 것을 권한다고 한 후, 이 계획의 일환으로 새로운 식수대를 설치할 것이라고 했으므로, (D)가 정답이다.

99 시각 정보에 따르면, 새 식수대는 어디에 설치될 것인가?

(A) A 위치에

(B) B 위치에

(C) C 위치에

(D) D 위치에

해설 | **세부 내용 - 시각 정보 연계**

회의의 중반부에서 주방 바로 맞은편 복도에 하나 더 설치할 예정(we'll be adding one in the hallway, right across from the kitchen)이라고 했다. 시각 정보를 보면 주방 바로 맞은편 복도는 D 위치에 해당하므로, (D)가 정답이다.

100 청자들은 무엇을 하라고 요청 받는가?

(A) 영수증을 보관하라고

(B) 선호하는 것을 표시하라고

(C) 사용 설명서를 읽으라고

(D) 문제점을 즉시 보고하라고

해설 | **세부 내용 - 요청 받은 사항**

회의의 후반부에서 금속제 물병과 유리 물병 중에 선택할 수 있다(You'll have a choice of either metal or glass)고 한 후, 용지에 자신이 선호하는 것 옆에 체크 표시할 것(please put a check next to the one you'd prefer on the sheet)을 요청했으므로, (B)가 정답이다.

어휘 | indicate 표(시)하다 preference 선호 (사항)

Paraphrasing

담화의 put a check next to the one you'd prefer

→ 정답의 Indicate a preference

PART 5 & 6 RC

Unit 01 품사와 문장 구조

① 주어와 동사

ETS 유형 연습　　　　　　　　本책 p. 136

| 1 (B) | 2 (C) | 3 (C) |

1 (B)

번역 | 에스컬레이터가 일시 고장이어서 게이트 H에 도착하는 승객은 메인 터미널까지 계단으로 걸어 올라가야 했다.

해설 | 빈칸은 접속사 because가 이끄는 절의 주어 자리이다. 문맥상 '에스컬레이터가 고장 났다'라는 의미가 적절하므로 (B) escalator가 정답이다.

어휘 | passenger 승객, 탑승객 temporarily 일시적으로 out of order 고장인, 작동이 되지 않는 escalate 상승하다 escalation 상승, 확대

2 (C)

번역 | 토목 기사인 로렌조 라스팔로 씨가 다음 달 열리는 제5회 연례 교량관리학회의 초청 연사로 확정되었다.

해설 | Civil engineer Lorenzo Raspallo가 주어이고 빈칸이 동사인 문장이다. 따라서 문장에서 동사 역할을 할 수 있는 (C) has been confirmed가 정답이다.

어휘 | civil engineer 토목 기사 guest speaker 초청 연사 annual 연례의, 일년마다의 conservation 관리, 보호 colloquium 학회, 세미나 confirm 확정하다, 확인하다

3 (C)

번역 | 직원 교육 시간을 줄일 새로운 소프트웨어가 개발되고 있다.

해설 | 주어 뒤의 수식어구(that ~ time)를 묶어 보면 빈칸은 문장의 동사가 필요한 자리이다. 따라서 문장에서 동사 역할을 할 수 있는 (C) is being developed가 정답이다.

어휘 | reduce 줄이다, 감소시키다 develop 개발하다

② 목적어

ETS 유형 연습　　　　　　　　本책 p. 137

| 1 (C) | 2 (C) | 3 (B) |

1 (C)

번역 | 야마모토 씨는 최근 캠페인 기간 동안 광고부의 노고와 헌신에 감사를 표했다.

해설 | 동사 voiced의 목적어 역할을 하며 소유격 his의 수식을 받는 자리이므로, 명사인 (C) appreciation이 정답이다.

어휘 | voice ~을 말로 표현하다; 목소리 dedication 헌신, 열성 recent 최근의 appreciate 고맙게 생각하다, 감사하다 appreciation 감사, 고마움

2 (C)

번역 | 대부분의 정부 기관 및 상업 시설들은 독립기념일을 기념하여 월요일에 문을 닫을 것이다

해설 | 빈칸은 전치사 in의 목적어 자리이므로, 전치사의 목적어 역할을 할 수 있는 동명사 (B) observing과 명사 (C) observance 중 하나를 선택해야 한다. 구조상 빈칸 앞의 in과 빈칸 뒤의 of와 결합하여 'in observance of(~을 기념하여, 준수하여)'로 쓰이는 (C) observance가 정답이다. (B) observing은 타동사 observe의 동명사형이므로 빈칸 뒤에 바로 목적어가 있어야 한다.

어휘 | commercial 상업의 establishment 기관, 시설 observe 관찰하다, 준수하다 observant 관찰력 있는, 준수하는

3 (B)

번역 | 송 씨가 부서장으로 승진했다고 오늘 아침 직원 회의에서 발표되었다.

해설 | division과 결합하여 전치사 of의 목적어 역할을 하는 자리이므로, 명사인 (B) manager가 정답이다. division manager는 '부서장'이라는 뜻의 복합명사이다.

어휘 | promotion 진급, 승진 division 부서 staff meeting 직원 회의 manageable 처리할 수 있는, 관리할 수 있는

③ 보어

ETS 유형 연습　　　　　　　　本책 p. 138

| 1 (D) | 2 (C) | 3 (B) |

1 (D)

번역 | 회의 첫날 소개된 조사 연구의 범위는 매우 인상 깊었다.

해설 | 빈칸은 be동사(was)의 보어 자리이면서 부사 very의 수식을 받을 수 있어야 하므로 형용사인 (D) impressive가 정답이다. (A) impressed도 형용사 역할을 할 수 있지만 의미상 부적절하다.

어휘 | range 범위, 영역 present 발표하다, 소개하다 impress 깊은 인상을 주다 impressive 인상적인 impressed 감명 받은

2 (C)

번역 | 애쉬포드 상공회의소에서는 방문객들에게 도시 해변가에 있는 식당과 극장을 애용해 달라고 당부한다.

해설 | 목적어 visitors를 보충 설명하는 목적격 보어 자리로 목적어의 동작을 나타내는 to부정사 (C) to patronize가 정답이다. 동사 invite는 주로 <invite + 목적어 + to부정사>의 구조로 쓰인다.

어휘 | Chamber of Commerce 상공회의소 waterfront 강변, 해안지구, 부두 patronize 애용하다

3 (B)

번역 | 금융 시장의 변화로 투자자들은 양질의 조언과 정보에 더욱 의존하게 되었다.

해설 | make는 5형식 동사로 <make + 목적어 + 목적격 보어>의 구조로 쓰인다. 문제에서 목적어는 investors이므로 그 뒤에는 목적격 보어가 필요하다. 따라서 보기 중 make의 목적격 보어 역할을 할 수 있는 형용사 (B) dependent(의존하는)가 정답이다.

어휘 | financial market 금융 시장 investor 투자자 quality 고급의, 양질의 dependency 의존, 의지

④ 수식어

ETS 유형 연습

본책 p. 139

1 (A)	2 (A)	3 (D)

1 (A)

번역 | 모든 코드 숫자가 확실히 전송되게 하려면 키패드를 강하게 눌러야 한다.

해설 | 빈칸 앞에 있는 수동형 동사인 should be pressed를 수식할 수 있는 품사는 부사이므로 (A) firmly가 정답이다.

어휘 | keypad 키패드 press 누르다 ensure 확실하게 하다 digit (아라비아) 숫자 transmit 보내다, 전송하다

2 (A)

번역 | 산 페드로 계곡의 송수관 확장 계획이 진행되고 있다.

해설 | 일단 문장이 under way에서 완전히 끝나므로, 뒤에 the extension이라는 명사를 수식어구로 만들 전치사가 필요하다. 보기 중 전치사는 (A)와 (D)인데(next는 형용사, while은 접속사), 문맥을 보면 '송수관 확장을 위한 계획(plans)'이므로 (A) for가 정답이다.

어휘 | under way 진행 중인 extension 확장, 확대 pipeline 파이프라인, 수송관

3 (D)

번역 | 사원들의 전문성 개발을 위한 프로그램에 예산이 편성되었음에도 불구하고, 이사는 진행하기를 꺼리고 있다.

해설 | 빈칸 뒤에 <주어(money)+동사(has been budgeted)>가 있고, 콤마 뒤에도 <주어(the director)+동사(is)>가 있으므로 빈칸에는 두 개의 절을 이어주는 부사절 접속사가 필요하다. 따라서 (D) Although가 정답이다. (A) In spite of(~에도 불구하고)와 (C) Because of(~ 때문에는)는 전치사이므로 <주어+동사> 앞에 놓일 수 없고 (B) Therefore(그러므로)는 접속부사이므로 절을 이끌 수 없다.

어휘 | budget 예산을 세우다; 예산 professional 전문(가)의; 전문가, 전문직 종사자 director (회사의) 중역, 이사 be reluctant to ~하기를 꺼리다 proceed 계속하다, 진행하다

● ETS 실전문제

본책 p. 140

1 (B)	2 (D)	3 (A)	4 (A)	5 (A)	6 (A)
7 (D)	8 (B)	9 (C)	10 (D)	11 (B)	12 (C)
13 (D)	14 (C)	15 (D)	16 (A)	17 (C)	18 (D)

1 (B)

번역 | 유행의 첨단을 걷는 새 옷가게 스트릿소는 유명한 그라피티 예술가가 손으로 그린 티셔츠를 제공할 것이다.

해설 | The trendy new clothing shop Streetso가 주어, 빈칸이 동사, T-shirts가 목적어인 문장이다. 따라서 문장에서 동사 역할을 할 수 있는 (B) will offer가 정답이다.

어휘 | well-known 잘 알려진 offer 제공하다

2 (D)

번역 | 이사가 마무리되면 인사부의 탱 씨에게 새 집주소를 알려주세요.

해설 | 빈칸은 소유격 your 뒤에 오는 명사 자리로, 해당 절에서 주어 역할을 한다. 따라서 명사인 (D) relocation이 정답이다.

어휘 | relocation 이전, 재배치 finalize 마무리짓다 human resources 인사부

3 (A)

번역 | 연례 회의에서 경영진은 뛰어난 일을 해낸 직원들을 표창할 것이다.

해설 | 빈칸이 조동사 will과 목적어 역할을 하는 명사 employees 사이에 있으므로, 동사원형인 (A) recognize가 정답이다.

어휘 | recognize 인정하다, 표창하다 outstanding 뛰어난

4 (A)

번역 | 우리 투자자들을 위한 재정 브리핑은 정확히 목요일 오전 9시 30분에 시작할 것이다.

해설 | 문제에서 동사 begin은 '(브리핑이) 시작한다'라는 의미의 자동사로 쓰였다. 따라서 빈칸은 부사 자리이므로 (A) precisely가 정답이다.

어휘 | financial 재정적인, 경제의 briefing 브리핑, 간단한 보고 investor 투자자 precisely 정확히, 명확히 precise 정확한 precision 정확, 정밀

5 (A)

번역 | 어제자 <시프널 데일리 에코>에 광고된 할인은 주방 가전에는 적용되지 않는다.

해설 | 빈칸은 정관사 The 뒤에 오는 명사 자리로, 동사 do not apply의 주어 역할을 한다. 따라서 do와 수가 일치하는 복수명사 (A) discounts가 정답이다.

어휘 | advertise 광고하다 apply to ~에 적용되다 appliance 가전제품

6 (A)

번역 | 새 건물에 제안된 몇몇 모델이 이번 주 남은 기간 동안 로비에 전시될 것이다.

해설 | 빈칸은 전치사 for의 목적어 역할을 하며 정관사 the의 수식을 받는 명사 자리이므로, (A) remainder가 정답이다.

어휘 | proposed 제안된 on display 전시하는, 전시 중인 remainder 잔여 기간, 나머지

7 (D)

번역 | 사용 설명서는 그 프로그램을 처음 사용할 때 직면하는 문제들을 해결하는 데 아주 도움이 될 것이다.

해설 | 빈칸 앞에 주어와 동사를 갖춘 절이 왔으므로 빈칸에는 동사인 (A), (B), (C)가 올 수 없다. 따라서 '~함에 있어서'라는 의미의 <in+-ing> 구문에 해당하는 (D) in solving이 정답이다.

어휘 | manual 매뉴얼, 사용 설명서 encounter 우연히 만나다, 직면하다

8 (B)

번역 | 응답자들의 참여를 독려하기 위해 거제도 여성 클럽은 설문지 작성자 전원에게 25,000원짜리 기프트 카드를 제공하고 있다.

RC

PART 5&6

121

해설 | 타동사 encourage(독려하다, 권장하다) 뒤의 목적어
자리로 명사가 필요하다. 그러므로 '참여'라는 뜻의 명사인
(B) participation이 정답이다.

어휘 | respondent 응답자 complete a survey 설문지를 작성하다
participate 참여하다 participatory 참여의

9 (C)
번역 | 최근 조사에 따르면 조립 공정의 근로자들은 야근하는 동안
집중력이 훨씬 떨어질 가능성이 높은 것으로 밝혀졌다.

해설 | 빈칸은 주어 assembly-line workers를 설명하는 주격
보어 자리로, less와 함께 부사 much의 수식을 받는 형용사가
들어가야 한다. 따라서 (C) attentive가 정답이다.

어휘 | assembly-line 조립 공정의 be likely to do ~할 것 같다,
~할 가능성이 있다 overtime 야근(의), 초과 근무(의) shift 근무조,
교대제 근무시간 attentive 집중하는 attentiveness 조심성

10 (D)
번역 | 전체 프로젝트가 완료될 때까지 팀원들은 모든 휴가를
연기하라는 요청을 받고 있다.

해설 | 빈칸 앞뒤에 <주어＋동사>를 갖춘 완전한 절이 있으므로,
빈칸에는 접속사가 들어가야 한다. 문맥상 '프로젝트가 완료될
때까지'라는 의미가 되어야 자연스러우므로 (D) until이 정답이다.

어휘 | postpone 연기하다 vacation 휴가 entire 전체의
complete 완료하다

11 (B)
번역 | 브룩스 컴퓨터 사의 매출은 지난 몇 달간 실적이 비교적
저조했지만 이번 달에는 나아질 것 같다.

해설 | 빈칸은 전치사 after의 목적어 역할을 하며 형용사 poor의
수식을 받는 명사 자리이므로, (B) performance가 정답이다.

어휘 | relatively 비교적 performance 성과, 실적; 공연

12 (C)
번역 | 플리트 호텔은 웹사이트에서 직접 객실을 예약한 고객에게
가장 저렴한 요금을 보장한다.

해설 | 빈칸은 who가 이끄는 관계사절에서 동사 book을 수식하는
역할을 하므로, 부사인 (C) directly가 정답이다.

어휘 | guarantee 보장하다, 약속하다 rate 요금 book 예약하다
directness 단순명쾌함 directly 직접

13 (D)
번역 | 만약 이사하신다면 회사 안내 책자에 있는 당신의 연락처를
최대한 빨리 업데이트하세요.

해설 | 빈칸은 your contact information을 목적어로 취하는
동사 자리로, 주어 you가 생략된 명령문을 이끈다. 따라서
동사원형인 (D) update가 정답이다.

어휘 | directory 안내 책자 as soon as possible 가능한 한 빨리

14 (C)
번역 | 손테라 투어링 컴퍼니는 아마존 정글로 떠나는 여러 가지 고급
여행 상품을 운영하는 업체다.

해설 | 빈칸은 정관사 the 뒤에 오는 명사 자리로, 주어 Sonterra
Touring Company의 주격 보어 역할을 한다. 따라서 주어와 동격
관계를 이루며 '운영자, 운영업체'라는 뜻을 나타내는 단수명사

(C) operator가 정답이다.

어휘 | deluxe 고급의 excursion 여행 operation 사업(체), 영업
operational 운영상의

[15-18] 이메일

발신: 오스트레일리아 웨스트 항공사
수신: 마거릿 번햄
날짜: 6월 5일
제목: 비행기 예약

번햄 씨께,

귀하의 다음 항공편을 위해 오스트레일리아 웨스트 항공사를
선택해 주시고, 저희 온라인 예약 및 체크인 시스템을 이용해 주셔서
감사합니다. ¹⁵귀하의 비행기 예약이 확정되었습니다. 수하물 수속 및
보안 검색대 통과 절차를 빠르게 진행하기 위해서, 댁에서 탑승권을
출력해 오실 것을 권해 드립니다. 그렇게 하시면 출발 탑승구에 확실히
¹⁶제때 도착하실 것입니다.

공항에 계시는 동안, 저희 웨스트워드 라운지에서 호주 달러로 단돈
10달러에 보안 무선 네트워크를 ¹⁷이용해 보세요. 출발일 전에 저희
예약 시스템에서 이 ¹⁸서비스를 준비해 두실 수 있습니다.

오스트레일리아 웨스트 항공사 팀

어휘 | reservation 예약 check-in 체크인, 수속 process 과정,
절차 security checkpoint 보안 검색대[지점] suggest 제안하다,
권하다 ensure 확실히 하다, 보장하다 take advantage of ~을
이용하다 secure 안전한, 보안이 철저한 available 이용 가능한
arrange 준비하다, 마련하다

15 (D)
번역 | (A) 로그인해서 절차를 시작하세요.
(B) 저희는 여섯 개 대륙에 취항합니다.
(C) 비행기에서 인터넷에 접속할 수 있습니다.
(D) 귀하의 비행기 예약이 확정되었습니다.

해설 | 빈칸 앞 문장에서 온라인 예약 및 체크인 시스템 이용(using
our online reservations and check-in system)에
감사하다고 했고, 뒤 문장에서 집에서 탑승권을 출력해 올
것(passengers print their boarding passes at home)을
권한다고 했다. 따라서 빈칸에도 예약 관련 안내 사항이 들어가야
문맥상 자연스러우므로, (D)가 정답이다.

어휘 | continent 대륙 access 이용, 접속 confirm 확정하다,
확인하다

16 (A)
해설 | 빈칸은 동사원형 ensure의 목적어 역할을 하는 명사
arrival을 수식하는 형용사 자리이다. 문장의 주어인 Doing so는
미리 탑승권을 출력해 오는 행위를 가리키므로, 문맥상 '그렇게 하면
탑승구에 제때 도착할 것이다'라는 내용이 되어야 자연스럽다. 따라서
(A) timely(제때의, 시기적절한)가 정답이다.

17 (C)
해설 | 빈칸은 advantage를 목적어로 취하는 동사 자리로, 주어
you가 생략된 명령문을 이끈다. 따라서 동사원형인 (C) take가
정답이다.

18 (D)

해설 | 빈칸이 앞 문장에서 언급한 보안 무선 네트워크(secure wireless network)를 가리키므로, '서비스'라는 의미의 (D) service가 정답이다.

어휘 | repair 수리 inspection 점검 journey 여정, 여행

Unit 02 명사

① 명사의 자리

ETS 유형 연습
본책 p. 142

1 (C) **2** (D) **3** (D)

1 (C)

번역 | 스프링데일 지역 시장에서는 직접 재배한 다양한 유기농 과일과 채소뿐만 아니라 수공예품과 장신구도 구입할 수 있다.

해설 | 빈칸은 전치사구 of homegrown and organic fruits and vegetables의 수식을 받으며 주어 역할을 하는 명사 자리이므로, '품종, 종류'라는 의미의 (C) Varieties가 정답이다.

어휘 | organic 유기농의 handmade 손으로 만든, 수제의 craft 공예품, 수공예 available 구할 수 있는, 살 수 있는 community 지역사회 variant 다른; 변종 various 다양한, 여러 가지의

2 (D)

번역 | 나오미 다케다 씨는 지난 화요일 회의에 참석할 수 없었지만, 클레어 마스터스 씨가 그녀에게 논의한 내용을 요약해 주었다.

해설 | 빈칸이 관사 a 뒤이며, 동사 gave 다음에 간접목적어인 her가 있다. give는 두 개의 목적어를 취하는 동사이므로 직접목적어 역할을 하는 명사인 (D) summary가 정답이다.

어휘 | attend 참석하다 summarily 간소하게, 간략하게 summarizer 요약하는 사람 summary 요약, 개요

3 (D)

번역 | 사이런 제조와 본페이트 해운의 관계는 협력과 존중에 기초를 두고 있다.

해설 | 전치사 on의 목적어 역할을 하는 단어가 필요한데 and 뒤에 명사 respect가 왔으므로 빈칸에도 같은 품사인 명사가 들어가야 한다. 따라서 명사인 (D) cooperation이 정답이다.

어휘 | relationship 관계 shipping 선적, 운송, 배송 be based on ~에 기초를 두다 cooperate 협력하다, 협동하다 cooperatively 협력하여, 협조적으로 cooperation 협력, 협조

② 명사의 앞뒤

ETS 유형 연습
본책 p. 143

1 (D) **2** (C) **3** (C)

1 (D)

번역 | <스타 워치>지에 따르면, 가수 겸 작곡가인 카일리 노턴 씨는 다가오는 자선음악회에 참가할 것이라고 발표했다.

해설 | 빈칸은 동사 has announced의 목적어 자리로 소유격 her와 형용사 upcoming의 수식을 받는 명사 자리이다. 따라서 (D) participation이 정답이다.

어휘 | upcoming 다가오는 charity 자선 (행위) participate 참여[참가]하다 participation 참가, 참석

2 (C)

번역 | 르로이-봉탕은 저칼로리 음료 제품 개발의 일환으로 전국 소비자들의 기호를 조사했다.

해설 | consumer와 결합해서 타동사 researched의 목적어가 될 수 있는 명사가 필요하므로 (C) preferences가 정답이다. consumer preferences는 '소비자 기호'라는 뜻의 복합명사로 researched의 목적어 역할을 한다.

어휘 | research 연구(하다), 조사(하다) consumer 소비자, 고객 beverage 음료 preference 기호, 좋아함

3 (C)

번역 | 경 디자인스는 최근에 호텔과 레스토랑 소유주들을 겨냥하기 위해 마케팅 전략을 변경했다.

해설 | to target의 목적어 자리로, hotel and restaurant과 결합하여 '호텔과 레스토랑의 소유주들'이라는 의미를 나타내는 명사인 (C) owners가 정답이다.

③ 명사의 종류

ETS 유형 연습
본책 p. 144

1 (A) **2** (B) **3** (D)

1 (A)

번역 | 재무팀 자리에 대한 지원서 제출 마감일은 다음 주 화요일이다.

해설 | 부정관사 a 뒤에는 단수 가산명사를 써야 하므로 (A) position이 정답이다.

어휘 | submit 제출하다 application 신청(서), 지원(서) finance 재무, 재정

2 (B)

번역 | 오노 씨는 프레젠테이션 동안 나눠준 모든 문서의 복사본을 요청했다.

해설 | 빈칸 앞뒤로 전치사가 있어서 빈칸에는 명사가 들어가야 하는데 빈칸 앞에 관사가 없으므로 복수형인 (B) duplicates가 정답이다.

어휘 | document 문서, 서류 pass out ~을 나눠주다 duplicate 사본, 복사; 복사하다; 사본의

3 (D)

번역 | 이 지역의 주요 산업에는 식품 가공과 항공기 제조가 포함된다.

해설 | food processing과 병렬 구조를 이루는 명사구를 완성하는 자리인데, 앞에 한정사가 없으므로 '제조'라는 뜻의 불가산명사인 (D) manufacture가 정답이다.

어휘 | industry 산업, 업계 district 지역, 구역 processing (가공) 처리 aircraft 항공기 manufacture 제조(하다), 제작(하다) manufacturer 제조사

④ 명사의 형태

ETS 유형 연습

본책 p. 145

1 (A) 2 (D) 3 (B)

1 (A)

번역 | 로우자 씨는 전 직원들이 솔선해서 잠재 고객들과 관계를 발전시켜 나가는 것을 보고 싶어 한다.

해설 | 빈칸에는 타동사 take의 목적어가 필요하므로 명사인 (A) initiative가 정답이다.

어휘 | contact 접촉, 교제, 관계 potential client 잠재 고객 initiative 솔선, 주도권 initiate 착수하다, 시작하다

2 (D)

번역 | 드레브노 바닥재 제품들은 산업 현장에서 사용하기 위해 고안되었다.

해설 | 전치사 for의 목적어 자리로 '사용을 위해'라는 의미를 나타내는 명사 (D) use가 정답이다. 가산명사의 단수형 (A) user는 관사 없이 쓸 수 없다.

어휘 | flooring 마루 (재료), 바닥 industrial 산업의

3 (B)

번역 | 마닐라 웰니스 센터에는 마카티 지점에서 근무할 시간제 및 임시직 공인 간호 조무사 자리에 공석이 있다.

해설 | 빈칸에는 앞의 employment와 함께 복합명사를 이루는 명사가 와야 한다. 문맥상 '채용(employment)을 위한 빈자리'라는 의미가 적절하며 앞에 한정사가 없으므로 복수 명사 (B) openings가 정답이다.

어휘 | temporary 임시의, 임시직의 certified 자격증[면허증]을 가진, 공인된 attendant 돌보는 사람, 간호인 opening 공석, 결원 openness 솔직함 opener 개시자, 여는 도구

● ETS 실전문제

본책 p. 146

1 (C)	2 (A)	3 (D)	4 (D)	5 (D)	6 (A)
7 (D)	8 (A)	9 (B)	10 (B)	11 (A)	12 (B)
13 (A)	14 (B)	15 (A)	16 (B)	17 (D)	18 (A)

1 (C)

번역 | 최근 졸업생들은 취업 박람회에 참여함으로써 다양한 업계의 취업 기회에 대해 알 수 있다.

해설 | 빈칸은 형용사 Recent의 수식을 받는 명사 자리로, 동사 can learn의 주어 역할을 한다. learn의 주체는 사람이어야 하므로, '졸업생들'이라는 의미의 (C) graduates가 정답이다.

어휘 | employment 취업, 고용 opportunity 기회 a wide range of 다양한 attend 참가하다 career fair 취업 박람회 graduate 졸업하다; 졸업생 graduation 졸업

2 (A)

번역 | 웨리버 빌딩 2층에 있는 전구들은 이번 주에 교체될 예정이다.

해설 | 빈칸은 전치사 on의 목적어 역할을 하는 명사 자리로, the Werriver Building's second의 수식을 받는다. 따라서 보기에서 '층'을 뜻하는 (A) floor와 (B) floors 중 하나가 들어가야 하는데, 특정 건물의 2층은 하나이므로, 단수명사 (A) floor가 정답이다.

어휘 | replace 교체하다 flooring 바닥재

3 (D)

번역 | 판프라덥 그래픽 디자인 사는 직원들에게 수많은 컴퓨터 프로그램에 대한 능숙함을 포함하여 고급 전문 기술을 갖추기를 요구한다.

해설 | 빈칸은 동사 possess의 목적어 역할을 하며 형용사 technical의 수식을 받는 명사 자리이다. 직원들이 갖추어야 하는 것을 나타내는 명사가 들어가야 하므로, (D) expertise(전문 지식, 전문 기술)가 정답이다.

어휘 | advanced 진보된, 첨단의 proficiency 능숙, 노련 numerous 수많은, 다수의 expert 전문가

4 (D)

번역 | 사장은 작년에 생산성이 가장 높았던 공장 부서에 보너스를 지급할 것이라고 발표했다.

해설 | 동사 has demonstrated의 목적어 역할을 하는 명사가 필요하다. 문맥상 '가장 높은 생산성'이라는 의미가 되어야 자연스러우므로, (D) productivity(생산성)가 정답이다.

어휘 | president 사장 award 주다, 수여하다 demonstrate (능력을) 보여주다, 시연하다 product 상품, 제품 produce 생산하다; 농산물

5 (D)

번역 | 야린 컨설팅은 고객이 현명한 투자 결정을 하도록 돕는 쌍방향 온라인 툴을 제공한다.

해설 | 빈칸은 investment와 복합명사를 이루어 동명사 making의 목적어 역할을 하는 명사 자리로, 형용사 smart의 수식을 받는다. 따라서 명사인 (D) decisions가 정답이다.

어휘 | interactive 쌍방향의, 대화형의 assist 돕다 make a decision 결정하다 investment 투자

6 (A)

번역 | 국제 엔지니어 협회의 위원들은 내년에 열릴 회의를 기획하기 위해 지난주에 모였다.

해설 | 빈칸은 동사 met의 주어 역할을 하는 명사 자리이다. 따라서 만남의 주체가 될 수 있는 사람 명사 (A) Representatives가 정답이다.

어휘 | conference 회의, 대회 representative 대표, 위원, 직원 represent 대표하다

7 (D)

번역 | 데이터베이스에 접속하려면 온라인 교육 모듈 수료 및 쿠퍼 씨의 서면 승인이 필요하다.

해설 | 빈칸은 과거분사 written의 수식을 받는 명사 자리로, completion of an online training module과 함께 동사 requires의 목적어 역할을 한다. 따라서 명사 (D) authorization이 정답이다.

어휘 | access 접근, 접속 require 필요로 하다 completion 완료 authorize 승인하다 authorization 승인

8 (A)

번역 | 3월 21일자 회람에서 언급된 대로 장비는 업무와 무관한 목적으로 사용되어서는 안 된다.

해설 | 빈칸은 전치사 for의 목적어 역할을 하며 형용사 non-work related의 수식을 받는 명사 자리이다. '목적'이라는 뜻의 purpose는 가산명사인데 앞에 한정사가 없으므로, 빈칸에는 복수형이 들어가야 한다. 따라서 (A) purposes가 정답이다.

어휘 | memo 회람, 공지 사항 equipment 장비, 기기 purposeful 의도적인

9 (B)

번역 | 기사는 건축 변경 사항을 승인했는데, 그 이유는 비용 면에서 크게 절감할 수 있었기 때문이다.

해설 | 빈칸은 부정관사 a와 형용사 dramatic의 뒤에 오는 명사 자리로, 동사 represented의 목적어 역할을 한다. 따라서 명사인 (B) reduction이 정답이다.

어휘 | approve 승인하다 represent 나타내다, 해당하다 dramatic 극적인 reduce 감소시키다 reduction 감소 reducible 축소시킬 수 있는

10 (B)

번역 | 하잘랍 사의 개선된 더마로스 세안제는 2년간의 추가 개발 후 시장에 출시되어 판매 중이다.

해설 | 빈칸은 형용사 further의 수식을 받는 명사 자리로, 전치사 of의 목적어 역할을 한다. 앞에 한정사가 없으며 문맥상 '2년간의 추가 개발 후'라는 의미가 되어야 자연스러우므로, (B) development가 정답이다.

어휘 | further 추가의, 더 이상의 be on the market 출시되다, 판매 중이다 developer 개발자

11 (A)

번역 | 옘 씨는 설문 조사의 응답을 분석하여 통계적으로 타당한 결론을 이끌어낼 수 있었다.

해설 | 빈칸은 survey와 복합명사를 이루어 전치사 of의 목적어 역할을 하는 명사 자리이므로, (A) responses(응답, 답변)가 정답이다.

어휘 | draw a conclusion 결론을 이끌어내다 statistically 통계(학)상으로 valid 유효한, 타당한 analysis 분석

12 (B)

번역 | 우리는 9월에 새 인사부 이사를 적극적으로 찾기 시작할 것으로 예상한다.

해설 | 빈칸이 관사 an과 명사 search 사이에 있으며 '적극적인 찾기'라는 의미가 적절하므로, 형용사인 (B) active가 정답이다.

어휘 | human resources director 인사부 이사 active 적극적인 activate 활성화하다 activity 활동

13 (A)

번역 | 이베시 일렉트로닉스는 제품의 우수한 품질을 보장하기 위해 필요한 조치들을 취하고 있다.

해설 | 의미상 '필요한 조치를 취하고 있다'라는 내용이 되어야 자연스러우므로, (A) measures(조치, 방안)가 정답이다.

어휘 | take a measure 조치를 취하다 guarantee 보장하다 superior 우수한 degree 정도

14 (B)

번역 | 직원들은 건물에서 기밀 문서를 가지고 나가기 전에 관리자의 허가를 받아야 한다.

해설 | 직원들이 기밀 문서를 가지고 나가기 전에 받아야(obtain) 하는 것을 나타내는 명사가 들어가야 자연스러우므로, (B) permission(허가)이 정답이다.

어휘 | obtain 얻다, 받다 remove 제거하다, 가져가다 confidential 기밀의

[15-18] 편지

9월 4일

라켈 테일러
오클랜드 웨이 105번지
웨스트필드, 미주리 63999

테일러 씨께,

귀하가 요청한 건축 허가증 신청서가 동봉되어 있습니다. 귀하가 식당 뒤쪽에 대규모 테라스 공사를 시작하기 ¹⁵전에 반드시 허가증 승인을 받아 저희 사무실에 보관되도록 해야 합니다. 신청서를 제출하실 때 자격증을 소지한 엔지니어에게 검토 및 인증을 받은 건물 설계도를 포함하기 바랍니다. 승인 과정은 ¹⁶대략 8주 정도 소요된다고 예상하면 됩니다.

아울러 공개 ¹⁷사용을 하기 전에 완성된 구조물을 공식적으로 점검 받아야 한다는 점을 기억해 주십시오. ¹⁸이러한 최종 단계의 일정을 잡을 준비가 되면 저희에게 알려 주시기 바랍니다.

헨리 벨링스워스, 매니저
건축법규준수국, 웨스트필드 지방자치 센터

동봉

어휘 | permit 허가(증) enclose 동봉하다 patio 테라스 rear 뒤쪽 approve 승인하다 on file 철하여 정리된 certify 인증하다 licensed 자격증[면허증]을 소지한 anticipate 예상하다 approval 승인 completed 완성된 officially 공식적으로 inspect 점검하다 compliance 준수 municipal 지방자치의, 시의 enclosure 동봉 (자료)

15 (A)

해설 | 뒤에 동명사가 왔고 문맥상 '대규모 테라스 공사를 시작하기 전에 먼저 허가증 승인을 받아야 한다'라는 내용이 되어야 자연스러우므로, '~ 전에'라는 뜻의 전치사 (A) Prior to가 정답이다.

어휘 | In spite of ~에도 불구하고 In addition 게다가

16 (B)

해설 | 수량 표현 eight을 수식해 주는 자리이므로, '대략'이라는 의미의 부사 (B) approximately가 정답이다.

어휘 | approximated 짐작된 approximate 근접한; 어림잡다 approximation 추정, 어림짐작

17 (D)

해설 | 전치사 before의 목적어 역할을 하면서 형용사 public(공공의, 공개의)의 수식을 받는 명사 자리이므로, (D) use(사용)가 정답이다. (A) users(사용자들)도 명사이지만 의미상 부적절하므로 오답이다.

18 **(A)**

번역 | (A) 이러한 최종 단계의 일정을 잡을 준비가 되면 저희에게
알려 주시기 바랍니다.
(B) 아쉽게도 저희 사무실은 내일 문을 닫습니다.
(C) 곧 있을 회의에 대한 상세한 내용을 준비해서 제게 연락
주십시오.
(D) 그 이후 귀하에게 공사 허가증이 발급될 예정입니다.

해설 | 빈칸 앞 문장에서 완성된 구조물을 공식적으로 점검 받아야
한다(the completed structure will need to be officially
inspected)고 했으므로, 빈칸에도 점검과 관련된 내용이 들어가는
것이 자연스럽다. 따라서 점검 일정을 언급한 (A)가 정답이다.

어휘 | step 단계, 절차 issue 발급하다

Unit 03 대명사

① 인칭 / 소유대명사

ETS 유형 연습
본책 p. 148

1 (A) **2** (B) **3** (B)

1 **(A)**

번역 | 카토 씨는 수하물이 발견되면 공항 직원이 그에게 연락할 수
있도록 호텔 전화 번호를 남겼다.

해설 | notify의 목적어가 들어갈 자리이고 문맥상 Mr. Kato를
가리키므로 목적격 인칭대명사 (A) him이 정답이다. 재귀대명사인
(B) himself는 행위(notify)의 주체(they)와 일치하지 않아 답이 될
수 없다.

어휘 | staff 직원 notify 알리다, 통지하다 luggage 수하물, 짐

2 **(B)**

번역 | 우리 회사에 바친 일레인 탕 씨의 뛰어난 노고를 인정하여,
인사부 이사는 오늘 밤에 열릴 사원 시상식에서 그녀를 기릴 것이다.

해설 | 명사 company를 수식해 주는 자리이므로 소유격 (B) our가
정답이다. (A) ours는 소유대명사임에 유의한다.

어휘 | in recognition of ~을 인정하여; ~의 답례로 exceptional
특별한, 예외적인, 뛰어난 honor 경의를 표하다, 명예를 주다 awards
ceremony 시상식

3 **(B)**

번역 | 거대 패스트푸드 기업인 누트루 사는 우리 로고가 그들의
로고를 형편없이 표절한 것이라고 주장한다.

해설 | 소유의 의미를 강조할 때는 <one's own + 명사>나 <명사 +of
one's own>을 쓸 수 있으므로 소유격 인칭대명사 (B) their가
정답이다.

어휘 | giant 거대 기업, 대가 claim 주장하다 disguised 변장한

② 재귀대명사

ETS 유형 연습
본책 p. 149

1 (D) **2** (D) **3** (D)

1 **(D)**

번역 | 실험실 기술자들은 외부 분석가를 채용하는 것이 비용이 너무
많이 들기 때문에 자신들이 직접 통계를 분석하기로 결정했다.

해설 | 빈칸이 없어도 완전한 문장이므로 빈칸에는 강조적 용법의
재귀대명사가 들어가야 한다. 따라서 주어인 The laboratory
technicians를 강조하는 (D) themselves가 정답이다.

어휘 | laboratory 실험실, 연구실 technician 전문가, 기술자
statistical 통계의, 통계(학)상의 analysis 분석 analyst 분석가
costly 비용이 많이 드는

2 **(D)**

번역 | 손님들은 미라벨 주방장이 기념일 연회에서 제공한 식사에
아주 만족하는 것처럼 보였다.

해설 | 동사 served의 목적어 자리로 The guests를 대신하는
목적격 인칭대명사 (D) them이 정답이다.

어휘 | chef 주방장 banquet 연회, 축연

3 **(D)**

번역 | 다른 프로그래머의 비밀번호에 문제가 있어서 신 씨는 회사
웹사이트를 혼자서 업데이트했다.

해설 | by oneself는 '혼자서'라는 뜻으로, 웹사이트를 업데이트하는
주체가 Mr. Shin이므로 (D) himself가 정답이다.

③ 지시대명사

ETS 유형 연습
본책 p. 150

1 (C) **2** (C) **3** (A)

1 **(C)**

번역 | 컨퍼런스 숙박 신청서를 받지 못한 분들은 가능한 한 빨리 등록
창구에 알려 주세요.

해설 | 주격 관계대명사 who가 이끄는 절의 수식을 받으면서 '~하는
사람들'의 의미를 나타내는 지시대명사 (C) Those가 정답이다.

어휘 | form 양식, 서식 registration desk 등록 창구

2 **(C)**

번역 | 조립 구역에서 근무하는 직원들은 항상 보호 장비를 착용해야
한다.

해설 | 명사구 Those employees(사람)를 수식하는 수식어 자리로
'일을 하는 직원들'이라는 의미를 나타내는 현재분사 (C) working이
정답이다. 문장에 이미 동사(must wear)가 있으므로, (A), (B),
(D)는 빈칸에 들어갈 수 없다.

어휘 | assembly 조립 protective gear 보호 장비 at all times
항상

3 **(A)**

번역 | 주요 자동차 대여 업체들의 올해 수입액은 지난 4년간의
수입액과 매우 비슷하다.

해설 | 빈칸은 앞에 나온 revenue figures라는 복수명사를 받아야
하므로 (A) those가 정답이다.

어휘 | revenue 수익, 수입 figure 수치 be similar to ~와 비슷하다
remarkably 현저히, 매우 preceding 이전의, 먼저의

④ 부정대명사

ETS 유형 연습

1 (A) **2** (B) **3** (D)

1 (A)

번역 | 이 소프트웨어 개발에 관여한 사람 중 어느 누구도 그것이 아주 인기 있을 것이라고는 짐작하지 못했다.

해설 | 의미상 '아무도 짐작하지 못했다'라는 뜻의 부정문이 되어야 하므로 (A) None이 정답이다.

어휘 | involved in ~에 관련된, 참가한 develop 개발하다

2 (B)

번역 | 카펫 전시실 공사는 이번 주말까지 완공될 것이지만, 영업은 한 달 더 지난 후에 개시될 것이다.

해설 | (A) other 뒤에는 복수명사와 불가산명사, (B) another 뒤에는 단수 가산명사가 온다. 빈칸 뒤에 단수 가산명사인 month가 있으므로 (B) another가 정답이다.

어휘 | construction 건설, 공사 showroom 진열실, 전시실 operation 운영, 조업

3 (D)

번역 | 코발트 연구상의 공동 수상자인 히마나 박사와 웨어햄 박사는 오클랜드에서 대학생 시절부터 서로 아는 사이였다.

해설 | 문맥상 '서로 아는 사이였다'라는 의미가 되려면 빈칸에는 (D) each other를 써야 한다. (A) other one은 '다른 것', (B) another one은 '또 다른 것'이라는 의미이므로 정답으로 적절하지 않다. (C) any other는 '뭔가 다른 (것), 누군가 딴 (사람)'을 지칭하는 형용사나 명사이므로 적절하지 않다.

어휘 | joint recipients 공동 수상자

● ETS 실전문제

1 (A)	**2** (D)	**3** (C)	**4** (D)	**5** (C)	**6** (B)
7 (A)	**8** (A)	**9** (B)	**10** (C)	**11** (D)	**12** (B)
13 (B)	**14** (D)	**15** (C)	**16** (A)	**17** (D)	**18** (B)

1 (A)

번역 | 스탠윅 앤 어소시에이츠에서는 각각의 고객에게 맞춤형 자산 관리 플랜을 제공하는 것을 자랑스럽게 생각합니다.

해설 | 빈칸은 giving의 간접목적어 역할을 하는 자리로, 전치사구 of our clients의 수식을 받는다. 따라서 목적어 자리에 들어갈 수 있는 부정대명사 (A) each가 정답이다. (D) every는 바로 뒤에 단수 명사가 와야 한다.

어휘 | pride oneself on ~를 자랑하다 personalized 개인 맞춤형의 wealth management 자산 관리

2 (D)

번역 | 프라샤드 씨는 채용 절차의 전반적인 효성을 검토하는 시간을 가진 후에 채용 절차를 대폭 개정할 계획이다.

해설 | 빈칸은 (overall) effectiveness를 한정 수식하는 자리이므로, 소유격 (D) its가 정답이다. 참고로 its는 our hiring procedure's를 뜻한다.

어휘 | revision 개정, 수정 hiring procedure 채용 절차 overall 전반적인, 종합적인 effectiveness 효과성

3 (C)

번역 | 얀 씨는 이번 주 금요일에 자신과 세 명의 고객이 사무실에서 새 공장 부지로 갈 때 이용할 교통편을 요청했다.

해설 | three clients와 함께 전치사 for의 목적어 역할을 하는 자리이다. 문맥상 주어 Ms. Yan과 세 명의 고객을 위한 교통편이 되어야 하므로, Ms. Yan을 대신하는 재귀대명사 (C) herself가 정답이다.

어휘 | request 요청하다 transportation 교통, 수송 plant 공장

4 (D)

번역 | 시상식 만찬을 성황리에 치러 주셔서 더할 나위 없이 감사 드린다고 뒤퐁 씨에게 전해 주세요.

해설 | 동사 could thank 앞의 주어 자리로 주격 인칭대명사 (D) we가 정답이다.

어휘 | there is no way 방법이 없다 thank 감사하다 award dinner 시상 만찬 success 성공

5 (C)

번역 | 사무실 관리자인 스티븐 브래드는 모든 직원에게 새로운 용품 주문 관련해서는 그와 직접 소통해 달라고 요청한다.

해설 | that이 이끄는 명사절에서 전치사 with의 목적어 역할을 하는 자리이다. 문맥상 직원들이 소통할 대상은 앞서 언급된 Steven Brad이므로, 목적격 (C) him이 정답이다.

어휘 | request 요청하다 supply 용품

6 (B)

번역 | 비록 팀에서 협력하여 이 보고서의 그래픽을 개발했지만, 문구는 주로 내가 작업한 것이다.

해설 | 빈칸은 is의 보어가 되어야 하며 의미상 my text를 줄인 단어가 필요하므로 소유대명사인 (B) mine이 정답이다.

어휘 | text 문서, 본문 primarily 주로, 기본적으로

7 (A)

번역 | 직원 여러분은 워렌 씨에게 이메일을 보내 변경된 점심 메뉴에 대한 의견을 알려 주세요.

해설 | 빈칸은 to express의 목적어 역할을 하는 명사 opinions를 한정 수식하는 자리이므로, 소유격 (A) their가 정답이다.

어휘 | express one's opinion 의견을 표하다 revise 변경하다

8 (A)

번역 | 최근 한 연구는 규칙적으로 아침을 먹는 사람들이 아침을 거르는 사람들보다 더 건강한 경향이 있다고 밝혔다.

해설 | 주격 관계대명사 who가 이끄는 절의 수식을 받으면서 '~하는 사람들'의 의미를 나타내는 지시대명사 (A) those가 정답이다.

어휘 | reveal 드러내다, 공개하다 tend to ~하는 경향이 있다 skip 건너뛰다

9 (B)

번역 | 주택 매매 및 임대 시장은 대개 지역 경제가 호전되면 덕을 보니 곧 활기를 찾을 것이다.

해설 | 빈칸은 접속사 as가 이끄는 절의 주어가 들어갈 자리인데, 동사가 복수(benefit)이고 문맥상 home sales and rental markets를 가리키므로 '둘 다'를 의미하는 (B) both를 써야 한다.

어휘 | rental 임대(의), 임대료 strengthen 강화하다, 증강하다 benefit 이익을 얻다, 덕을 보다

10 (C)

번역 | 제출된 세 가지 주차장 계획안 중에서 두 가지는 받아들여질 수 없고 나머지 하나는 25,000달러의 추가 예산이 책정되야만 가능하다.

해설 | 세 가지 계획안 중에 두 가지는 받아들여질 수 없다고 했으므로, while절의 주어 자리에는 '나머지 하나'를 뜻하는 말이 들어가야 한다. 따라서 (C) the other가 정답이다.

어휘 | garage 주차장 unacceptable 받아들일 수 없는 additional 추가의, 추가적인 budget 예산; 예산으로 잡다

11 (D)

번역 | 카타쿠라 교수는 여러 번 실험을 했지만 그 결과가 동료들의 결과와 다르다.

해설 | 빈칸은 전치사 from의 목적어 역할을 하는 자리로, 전치사구 of his colleagues의 수식을 받는다. 문장이 카타쿠라 교수와 동료들의 실험 결과(results)를 비교하고 있으므로, results를 대신하는 지시대명사 (D) those가 정답이다.

어휘 | perform 수행하다 experiment 실험 colleague 동료

12 (B)

번역 | 직원들은 연수 기간 동안 고객의 문의 사항을 처리하는 과정을 완벽하게 숙달하는 데 서로에게 도움이 되도록 2인 1조로 근무해야 한다.

해설 | 빈칸 앞에는 준동사 to help가, 뒤에는 동사원형 master가 온 <help + 목적어 + 동사원형> 구문이므로 빈칸은 목적어 자리이다. 앞에서 둘씩 짝을 지어 활동한다는(work in pairs) 내용이 나오므로 '서로'를 의미하는 부정대명사 (B) each other가 정답이다.

어휘 | staff member 직원 master 숙달하다 procedure 절차 handle 처리하다 inquiry 질문, 문의

13 (B)

번역 | 최근 고객 설문조사는 많은 사람들이 자신들의 호텔 식사 경험에 대해 불만족스러웠다는 것을 보여준다.

해설 | that이 이끄는 명사절에서 동사 were의 주어 역할을 하는 자리이므로, were와 수가 일치하는 부정대명사 (B) many가 정답이다.

어휘 | survey 설문 조사 indicate 나타내다, 보여주다 be dissatisfied with ~을 불만스럽게 여기다

14 (D)

번역 | 이사는 전 직원을 외부 (위탁) 교육 과정에 보내서 새로운 소프트웨어를 배우도록 하는 대신에 자신이 직접 모두를 교육하기로 결정했다.

해설 | 의미상 the entire staff를 대신하는 단어가 필요하므로 (D) everyone이 정답이다.

어휘 | director 이사, 국장

[15-18] 기사

> ### 얼루어웨어 신임 CFO 임명
>
> 밀라노에 본사를 둔 소매업체인 얼루어웨어 주식회사는 파이퍼 셰이 씨를 신임 최고재무책임자(CFO)로 임명했다. 최근에 카리나스 스포츠웨어에서 6년[15]간 CFO로 근무한 셰이 씨는 12월 1일부터 새로운 직책을 맡는다. [16]이 역할에서 그녀는 재무, 회계, 부동산을 책임지게 된다. "파이퍼 씨를 얼루어웨어의 가족으로 맞게 되어 기쁩니다." 얼루어웨어 CEO인 유지니아 리날디 씨는 한 성명에서 말했다. "[17]그녀의 탄탄한 재무 분야 경력과 소매업 관련 전문 지식은 의심의 여지 없이 우리 회사의 성장을 도울 것입니다. 그녀의 긍정적인 공헌을 기대합니다." 셰이 씨는 세군 시모네 씨의 [18]후임이 될 예정이다. 얼루어웨어의 현 CFO인 시모네 씨는 11월 말일 자로 퇴직한다.
>
> ---
> **어휘 |** appoint 임명하다 -based ~에 본사를 둔 chief financial office 최고재무책임자(CFO) serve as ~의 역할을 하다 position 일자리, 직책 statement 성명, 진술 background 배경, 경험, 경력 expertise 전문 지식[기술] undoubtedly 의심의 여지 없이 growth 성장 contribution 공헌 current 현재의 retire 퇴직하다

15 (C)

해설 | 빈칸 뒤의 six years(기간) 앞에 쓰여 '~ 동안'이라는 의미를 나타내는 전치사 (C) for가 정답이다.

16 (A)

번역 | (A) 이 역할에서 그녀는 재무, 회계, 부동산을 책임지게 된다.
　　　(B) 리날디 씨는 20여 년 전에 얼루어웨어에서 근무하기 시작했다.
　　　(C) 이 중 한 가지는 여성용 스포츠웨어 신규 제품군을 만드는 것이었다.
　　　(D) 그녀는 근무 첫날이 "굉장히 건설적"이었다고 묘사했다.

해설 | 빈칸 앞 문장에서 셰이 씨가 12월 1일부터 새로운 직책을 맡는다(Hsieh, ~ will start her new position on December 1)고 했으므로, 빈칸에는 이 직책에 대한 추가 설명이 들어가는 것이 자연스럽다. 따라서 (A)가 정답이다.

어휘 | be responsible for ~에 책임이 있다 finance 재무 extremely 극도로 constructive 건설적인

17 (D)

해설 | 빈칸 앞에서 Piper Hsieh에 대해 계속 언급하고 있었으므로 Piper Hsieh를 가리키는 소유격 인칭대명사 (D) Her가 정답이다.

18 (B)

해설 | 빈칸 뒤 문장에서 현 CFO인 시모네 씨가 11월 말에 퇴직한다(Simone, Allure Wear's current CFO, will retire at the end of November)고 했으므로, 셰이 씨가 시모네 씨의 후임이 될 예정이라는 내용이 되어야 자연스럽다. 따라서 (B) replace(대체하다)가 정답이다.

어휘 | supervise 감독하다 assist 돕다

Unit 04 형용사

① 형용사의 자리

ETS 유형 연습

본책 p.154

1 (C) **2** (A) **3** (C)

1 **(C)**

번역 | 다니엘 윈드미어 사에서 해외 업무 담당 직원들은 거주지를 구할 때 전폭적인 재정 지원을 받는다.

해설 | 빈칸 뒤에 <형용사+명사>가 있는데 보통 이런 자리에는 형용사를 수식하는 부사가 답이지만, 보기 중에는 부사가 없다. 문맥상 빈칸 뒤의 명사 support를 수식하는 형용사가 필요하므로 (C) extensive가 정답이다.

어휘 | assignment 일, 업무 financial support 재정 지원 extend 확대하다 extent 정도 extensive 광범위한

2 **(A)**

번역 | 팔라우 베이 은행의 대출 신청 과정은 아주 효율적이다.

해설 | 빈칸은 주격 보어 자리로 부사 very의 수식을 받으므로, 형용사인 (A) efficient가 정답이다.

어휘 | loan application 대출 신청 process 과정 efficient 효율적인, 효과적인 efficiency 효율성 efficiently 효율적으로

3 **(C)**

번역 | 비평가들은 미셸 자오의 최근 영화 줄거리가 너무 뻔하다고 평했다.

해설 | call A B는 'A를 B라고 부르다[말하다]'라는 뜻이다. 빈칸에는 목적격 보어가 필요하므로, 부사 too의 수식을 받으면서 목적어 the plot을 보충 설명하는 형용사 (C) predictable이 정답이다.

어휘 | critic 비평가 plot 줄거리, 구상 predictable 예측 가능한, 새로운 게 없는

② 수량 / 부정형용사

ETS 유형 연습

본책 p.155

1 (D) **2** (B) **3** (D)

1 **(D)**

번역 | 안도 생물학 실험실의 모든 표본은 적정한 온도에서 보관되어야 한다.

해설 | all, most, other 뒤에는 복수 가산명사나 불가산명사가 와야 하므로 모두 오답이다. 반면 every는 '모든'이라는 뜻으로 뒤에 단수 가산명사가 올 수 있으므로 (D) Every가 정답이다.

어휘 | biology 생물학 lab 실험실(= laboratory) temperature 온도

2 **(B)**

번역 | 비용이 듦에도 불구하고, 많은 직원들이 강당을 수리하는 것에 찬성했다.

해설 | 빈칸이 복수명사 staff members 앞에 있으므로 (B) many가 정답이다. (A) mass는 '대중의, 대량의'라는 뜻으로

의미상 적합하지 않다. (C) much는 불가산명사 앞에 써야 한다. (D) plenty는 of가 없으므로 정답이 될 수 없다.

어휘 | despite ~에도 불구하고 in favor of ~에 찬성하여, 선호하여 renovate 수리하다, 개조하다 auditorium 강당

3 **(D)**

번역 | 델무어 사는 오용, 부적절한 관리, 또는 기타 고객 부주의로 인한 파손에 대해서는 책임지지 않습니다.

해설 | 빈칸이 불가산명사인 consumer negligence 앞에 있으며 의미상 '(그 밖의) 다른'이라는 뜻이 필요하므로 (D) other가 정답이다. (B) <the other+명사>는 정해진 범위에서 일부를 제외하고 '(남은) 다른 것'이라는 뜻인데 이 문장에서는 consumer negligence의 정해진 범위가 없으므로 의미상 옳지 않다.

어휘 | be responsible for ~에 대한 책임이 있다 misuse 오용, 남용 improper 부적절한 consumer 소비자, 고객 negligence 무시, 부주의

③ 형용사의 형태

ETS 유형 연습

본책 p.156

1 (C) **2** (C) **3** (C)

1 **(C)**

번역 | 헤일 밸리의 다양한 관광 명소는 방문객들과 주민들에게 꾸준히 즐거움을 선사한다.

해설 | 빈칸은 명사 attractions 앞에서 명사를 수식하는 형용사 자리로 (C) diverse가 정답이다. (B) diversifying은 '다양하게 만드는, 다각화하는'이라는 뜻으로 의미상 옳지 않다.

어휘 | attraction 인기물, 명소 delight 기쁘게 하다 resident 주민 diverse 다양한 diversity 다양성

2 **(C)**

번역 | 모든 승객들은 다른 사람을 배려하여 휴대전화로 통화할 때 작게 말해야 한다.

해설 | '모든 승객들은 다른 사람들을 배려해야 한다'라는 의미가 되어야 하므로 '배려하는, 사려 깊은'이라는 뜻의 (C) considerate이 정답이다. <be considerate of+사람>을 '(사람)을 배려하다'라는 뜻으로 기억해두자. (A) considerable은 '상당한'이라는 뜻이므로 의미상 옳지 않다.

어휘 | passenger 승객, 탑승객 mobile phone 휴대전화 consideration 고려, 숙고

3 **(C)**

번역 | 우리 회사의 전문 컨설팅 서비스를 이용하는 명망 있는 회사 및 단체의 최신 목록을 동봉합니다.

해설 | 빈칸 뒤의 명사구 companies and institutions를 수식하는 자리로 형용사 역할을 할 수 있는 과거분사 (C) distinguished가 정답이다.

어휘 | enclosed 동봉한 listing 목록, 명단 institution 단체, 기관 firm 회사 specialized 전문화된, 전문적인 consulting service 자문 서비스 distinguishably 구별 가능하여 distinguishability 구별 가능성 distinguished 유명한, 뛰어난 distinguish 구별하다, 분간하다

④ 형용사 어휘

ETS 유형 연습

본책 p. 157

> **1** (D)　**2** (A)　**3** (C)

1 (D)

번역 | 회사 지침에 따르면, 신입 사원들은 3개월간 상근으로 근무한 후에 휴가를 받을 수 있다.

해설 | '휴가 혜택을 받을 자격이 있다'가 적합하므로 (D) eligible이 정답이다. eligible은 <eligible for + 명사>나 <eligible to + 동사원형>의 형태로 주로 쓰인다. (A) capable(할 수 있는)은 뒤에 <of + (동)명사>가 온다.

어휘 | guideline 지침 benefits 복리 후생 full-time 상근의, 전시간 근무제의 variable 변하기 쉬운 flexible 유연한, 탄력적인

2 (A)

번역 | 모든 승객들은 출발 전에 적절한 여행 서류를 구비할 책임이 있다.

해설 | 'be responsible for(~할 책임이 있다)'를 적용시키는 문제로 전치사 (A) for가 정답이다.

어휘 | passenger 승객 proper 적절한 document 문서, 서류

3 (C)

번역 | 저희 영업부에서 훌륭히 업무를 수행하고 계신 점 진심으로 감사드립니다.

해설 | 형용사 어휘 문제이므로, 빈칸 뒤의 명사를 살펴본다. 문맥상 '진심 어린 감사'가 적절하므로 (C) sincere가 정답이다.

어휘 | sales department 영업부 sincere 진심에서 우러난 estimated 어림 잡은 completed 완료된

● ETS 실전문제

본책 p. 158

> **1** (D)　**2** (D)　**3** (A)　**4** (A)　**5** (B)　**6** (D)
> **7** (A)　**8** (D)　**9** (A)　**10** (A)　**11** (B)　**12** (A)
> **13** (B)　**14** (A)　**15** (A)　**16** (B)　**17** (C)　**18** (B)

1 (D)

번역 | 가르시아 씨는 밀레 병원에서 모든 환자에 마음을 쓰는 헌신적이고 열정적인 병원 간부이다.

해설 | 과거분사 devoted와 함께 복합명사 hospital executive를 수식하는 형용사 자리이다. 따라서 형용사인 (D) enthusiastic이 정답이다.

어휘 | devoted 헌신적인 executive 경영진, 간부, 중역 enthusiast 열렬한 지지자 enthusiasm 열정, 열의 enthusiastic 열정적인

2 (D)

번역 | 지역 제조업체들은 생산성이 향상될 때까지 직원을 추가로 채용하길 주저했다.

해설 | 빈칸은 주어 Local manufacturers를 보충 설명하는 주격 보어 자리로, to부정사와 어울려 쓰이는 형용사가 들어가야 한다. 따라서 '~하기를 주저하다'라는 의미를 완성하는 (D) hesitant가

정답이다.

어휘 | manufacturer 제조업체, 생산자 additional 추가적인, 부가적인 productivity 생산성

3 (A)

번역 | 행정 비서직 지원자는 강력한 조직력을 갖춰야 한다.

해설 | 빈칸은 명사 skills를 수식하는 형용사 자리이다. 따라서 형용사 (A) organizational이 정답이다.

어휘 | candidate 지원자, 후보자 administrative 행정상의, 관리상의 organizational skills 조직력

4 (A)

번역 | 건물에서 나가기 전에 반드시 문이 확실히 닫혀 있는지 확인하세요.

해설 | 빈칸은 closed라는 과거분사를 수식하는 자리이므로 부사인 (A) securely가 정답이다. <be + ------- + 과거분사>의 구조에서 빈칸에는 부사가 들어가야 한다는 점을 기억해두자.

어휘 | make sure 반드시 ~하도록 하다 securely 확실히, 단단히 security 보안, 안전, 무사 secure 안전하게 하다; 안전한

5 (B)

번역 | 지역 내 최고의 IT 지원업체로 항상 순위에 오르는 엑스트리넷 코퍼레이션은 믿을 수 있는 기술 지원을 제공한다.

해설 | 빈칸은 동사 provides의 목적어 역할을 하는 technical assistance를 수식하는 형용사 자리이다. 문맥상 기술 지원의 특징을 묘사하는 형용사가 빈칸에 들어가야 하므로, '믿을 만한'이라는 의미의 (B) dependable이 정답이다.

어휘 | consistently 끊임없이, 항상 provide 제공하다 technical 기술의 dependability 믿을 수 있음 depend 의존하다

6 (D)

번역 | 브라이트먼 파트너스 주식회사의 건축가들은 실용적일 뿐 아니라 우아한 건물을 설계한다.

해설 | 명사 buildings를 수식하는 관계사(that)절에서 형용사 elegant와 함께(as well as) 건물에 대해 보충 설명하는 주격 보어 자리이다. 따라서 '실용적인'이라는 의미의 형용사 (D) functional이 정답이다.

어휘 | architect 건축가 elegant 우아한, 품격 있는 function 기능; 작동하다 functionality 기능성

7 (A)

번역 | 비즈니스 작문 세미나에 등록한 사람들이 거의 없었기 때문에, 그 세미나는 9월로 연기되었다.

해설 | 복수명사인 people을 수식할 수 있는 수량형용사 (A) few가 정답이다. (C) less는 불가산명사와 함께 쓰인다.

어휘 | register for ~에 등록하다 postpone 연기하다, 미루다

8 (D)

번역 | 그 프로그램의 신규 버전은 현재 리얀 소프트웨어 다운로드 사이트에서 손쉽게 이용할 수 있다.

해설 | 빈칸은 부사 readily의 수식을 받는 형용사 자리로, 주어 A new version of the program을 보충 설명하는 주격 보어 역할을 한다. 따라서 (D) accessible이 정답이다.

어휘 | readily 손쉽게 accessibility 접근하기 쉬움 access 접근, 접속; 접근하다 accessible 접근 가능한, 이용할 수 있는

9 (A)

번역 | 여러 관리자들은 계획에 없던 유지보수 작업이 차량 조립에 지장을 줬다고 불평했다.

해설 | 빈칸은 that절의 주어 the unscheduled maintenance를 보충 설명하는 주격 보어 자리로, 전치사구 to vehicle assembly와 함께 의미를 완성한다. 계획에 없던 유지보수 작업이 차량 조립에 미치는 영향을 묘사하는 형용사가 빈칸에 들어가야 하므로, '지장을 주는'이라는 의미의 (A) disruptive가 정답이다.

어휘 | supervisor 감독관, 관리자 unscheduled 계획에 없던 maintenance 유지 assembly 조립 disruptive 지장을 주는 disruption 중단, 분열 disrupt 지장을 주다, 방해하다

10 (A)

번역 | 적정 가격을 유지하기 위해 킴스 제과점은 빵과 케이크를 점포에서 만들기 시작할 것이다.

해설 | keep은 목적어가 필요한 타동사이므로 빈칸에는 prices와 함께 복합명사를 이루는 명사가 올 수도 있고 <keep + 목적어 + 목적격 보어>의 형식으로 쓰여 형용사가 올 수도 있다. 복합명사의 경우 (C) reasoning과 (D) reason을 생각해 볼 수 있는데, 둘 다 prices와 함께 썼을 때 뜻이 통하지 않는다. '가격을 적정하게 유지하기 위해서'라는 의미가 되어야 자연스러우므로, 형용사인 (A) reasonable(합리적인, 비싸지 않은)이 정답이다.

어휘 | on the premises 점포 내에서 reasonably 합리적으로 reasoning 추론

11 (B)

번역 | 제3자에 의해 실시되는 어쿠슈티컬 사의 임상 실험실 검사는 3개월마다 실시된다.

해설 | 의미상 '3개월마다'라는 뜻이 되어야 하므로 (B) every가 정답이다. 일정한 주기를 나타내는 <every + 기수 + 복수명사 (~마다)>를 기억해 두자.

어휘 | third-party 제3자의 inspection 점검, 검사 clinical 병상의, 병실에서 사용되는, 임상의 laboratory 실험실 every three months 3개월마다

12 (A)

번역 | 전 세계의 수많은 고대 기념물들의 상태가 나빠지고 있으며, 숙련된 보존전문가들의 도움을 필요로 한다.

해설 | 빈칸이 전치사 in과 명사 condition 사이에 있으며, 문맥상 '나빠지는 상태'라는 의미가 되어야 자연스러우므로, (A) deteriorating(악화되는, 나빠지는)이 정답이다.

어휘 | monument 기념물 skilled 숙련된, 능숙한 preservationist 보존주의자[전문가], 보호주의자 deterioration 악화 deteriorate 나빠지다

13 (B)

번역 | 그래프 센터 안내원들은 문이 열리기 전, 충분한 수의 콘서트 프로그램을 손에 갖추어 놓아야 한다.

해설 | concert programs를 수식하는 a number of와 어울리는 형용사가 빈칸에 들어가야 하므로, '충분히 많은'이라는 의미를 완성하는 (B) adequate가 정답이다.

어휘 | usher 좌석 안내원 opposite 반대의 adequate 충분한, 적절한 intensive 집중적인, 철두철미한 eligible ~할 자격이 되는

14 (A)

번역 | 예정된 의류 부문 확대안은 필요 예산 배정의 최종 승인 여부에 달려 있다.

해설 | 동사 remain, 전치사 on과 결합하여 '~에 달려 있다'는 의미를 나타내는 형용사 (A) contingent가 정답이다. remain 대신 be, become을 써도 되고, contingent 대신 dependent로 바꾸어 쓸 수 있다는 것도 참고로 알아두자.

어휘 | projected 예상된 expansion 확장, 확대 apparel 옷, 의류 final approval 최종 승인 budget 예산(안) allocation 할당, 배정, 배분(액) contingent ~의 여부에 따라 eventual 궁극적인 speculative 투기적인, 추측에 근거한

[15-18] 이메일

발신: 맥스 모아나 <mmoana@egmontflooring.co.nz>
수신: 데비나 하토노 <dhartono@hartonogroup.co.nz>
제목: 새 카펫
날짜: 3월 3일

하토노 씨께,

저희 카펫 설치 서비스에 관한 **15**문의사항에 답변 드립니다. 불편을 최소화하기 위해 정규 업무시간을 피해서 작업할 수 있습니다. 아울러 인테리어 장식에 전문 지식을 갖춘 저희 직원들이 멋진 바닥재들을 다양하게 **16**보여드릴 수 있습니다.

에그몬트 플로어링은 천연 소재뿐 아니라 합성 소재로도 이용 가능한 매우 다양한 카펫 스타일, 무늬, 디자인을 제공합니다. 우수한 저희 카펫은 산뜻하고 **17**매력적인 분위기를 조성하며 어떤 일터든 완전히 바꿔 놓을 수 있습니다.

18착수하시려면 저희 미드우드 애비뉴 전시장을 방문해 주십시오. 연락해 주셔서 감사합니다. 서비스를 제공해 드릴 수 있기를 바랍니다.

맥스 모아나
에그몬트 플로어링 영업관리자

어휘 | respond to ~에 응답하다, 대응하다 installation 설치 definitely 분명히, 틀림없이 work around ~를 피해서 일하다 regular 정기적인 minimize 최소화하다 inconvenience 불편 in addition 게다가 expertise 전문 지식 decorating 장식 a wide variety of 다양한 available 이용 가능한 synthetic 합성한, 인조의 transform 변형시키다, 완전히 바꿔 놓다 atmosphere 분위기 look forward to -ing ~하기를 고대하다

15 (A)

해설 | 두 번째 문장부터 회사가 제공하는 다양한 서비스에 대해 설명을 이어가고 있으므로, 빈칸에 들어갈 응답(responding to)의 대상은 카펫 설치 서비스(carpet installation service)와 관련된 '질문' 또는 '문의사항'이라고 볼 수 있다. 따라서 (A) inquiry가 정답이다.

어휘 | article 글, 기사 evaluation 평가

16 (B)

해설 | 빈칸은 주어 members of our staff의 동사 자리이다. 전문 지식을 갖춘 직원들이 제공할 수 있는 서비스를 설명하고 있으므로, '능력, 가능성'을 나타내는 조동사 can을 포함한 (B) can show가 정답이다.

17 (C)

해설 | 형용사 fresh와 함께 명사 atmosphere를 수식하는 형용사 자리이다. 문맥상 분위기(atmosphere)를 묘사하는 형용사가 들어가야 하므로, '매력적인'이라는 의미의 (C) inviting이 정답이다.

18 (B)

번역 | (A) 이번에는 더 나은 제품을 제공해 드리지 못해 죄송합니다.
(B) 착수하시려면 저희 미드우드 애비뉴 전시장을 방문해 주십시오.
(C) 제 동료인 페이 씨가 일정 변경사항을 알려드릴 것입니다.
(D) 마지막으로 저희가 제공해 드린 관리 지침을 따라주십시오.

해설 | 빈칸 앞에서는 하토노 씨의 카펫 설치 서비스 문의에 답변한 후 제품을 소개했고, 뒤에서는 서비스를 제공할 수 있길 바란다(We look forward to serving you)고 했다. 따라서 빈칸에도 이와 관련된 내용이 들어가야 문맥상 자연스러우므로, 매장 방문을 권유한 (B)가 정답이다.

어휘 | showroom 전시실 associate 동료 finally 마지막으로, 마침내 instruction 지침, 설명

Unit 05 부사

① 부사의 자리

ETS 유형 연습
본책 p. 160

1 (D) **2** (B) **3** (C)

1 (D)

번역 | 귀하가 분명하게 서면으로 하지 말라고 요청하지 않는 한 저희는 마케팅 목적으로 귀하의 우편 주소를 저희 계열사와 공유할 수도 있습니다.

해설 | 주어(you)와 본동사(request) 사이에 들어갈 수 있는 품사는 동사를 수식하는 부사뿐이므로 (D) specifically가 정답이다.

어휘 | mailing address 우편 주소 subsidiary 계열사, 자회사 in writing 서면으로 specification 명세, 제목 specifically 분명히, 구체적으로

2 (B)

번역 | 납세 지위에 변동이 있는 경우에는 제때 수정할 수 있도록 즉시 급여 관리부에 신고하셔야 합니다.

해설 | 빈칸 바로 앞의 구조를 보면 수동태(should be reported)와 수식어인 전치사구(to the payroll division)로 되어 있어 완전한 문장을 이루고 있다. 따라서 빈칸은 뒤에서 동사를 수식하는 부사 자리이므로 (B) promptly(즉시)가 정답이다.

어휘 | status 지위, 상태 payroll division 급여 관리부 cf. payroll 급료 지불 명부 make a correction 수정하다, 고치다 in a timely fashion 제때에, 알맞은 시기에 prompt 즉각적인; 촉발하다

3 (C)

번역 | 새로운 생산 장비 덕분에 제조업자들은 완전히 플라스틱으로만 전자 디스플레이를 만드는 것에 한 걸음 더 다가갔다.

해설 | 빈칸은 바로 뒤의 부사구 out of plastic(플라스틱으로)을 수식하는 부사 자리이므로, (C) totally가 정답이다.

어휘 | device 장치, 설비 manufacturer 제조업체, 생산자 electronic display 전자 디스플레이 totally 완전히, 전적으로

② 부사 어휘 1

ETS 유형 연습
본책 p. 161

1 (D) **2** (B) **3** (B)

1 (D)

번역 | 본사 경리부에서는 아직도 작년의 연간 지출액을 공개하지 않았다.

해설 | '아직도 공개하지 않았다'라는 의미가 가장 적절하므로 부사 (D) still(아직도)이 정답이다. (A) once(한 때, 한 번), (B) soon(곧), (C) almost(거의)는 모두 의미상 부적절하다.

어휘 | accounting office 경리부 release 발표하다, 공개하다 annual spending figures 연간 지출액

2 (B)

번역 | 기술적인 문제로 인해, 넬슨스 일렉트로닉 옥션스에서는 현재 이메일로 어떠한 사진 제출도 받지 않습니다.

해설 | '기술적인 문제로 인해 지금은 사진 제출을 받고 있지 않다'라는 내용이 되어야 자연스러우므로, 현재진행 동사와 어울리는 (B) currently(지금, 현재)가 정답이다.

어휘 | technical 기술상의, 기술적인 submission 제출(물)

3 (B)

번역 | 많은 투자자들은 금융 시장에 영향을 끼칠 수 있는 시사를 따라잡기 위해 뉴스 프로그램을 자주 시청한다.

해설 | 의미상 '뉴스 프로그램을 자주 시청한다'라고 하는 것이 가장 적절하므로 (B) often(자주)이 정답이다. (A) shortly(곧), (C) soon(곧), (D) hardly(거의 ~아닌)는 모두 의미상 적합하지 않다.

어휘 | investor 투자자 in order to do ~하기 위해 keep up with (뉴스·유행 등을) 알다, ~를 따르다 impact 영향; 영향을 끼치다 financial market 금융 시장

③ 부사 어휘 2

ETS 유형 연습
본책 p. 162

1 (C) **2** (B) **3** (C)

1 (C)

번역 | X200의 또렷하고 필름같은 이미지는 그것이 시장에서의 최첨단 디지털 카메라임을 입증해 준다.

해설 | 빈칸에는 형용사 advanced를 수식하는 부사가 필요하다. 부사인 (A) high(높이)와 (C) highly(매우, 대단히) 중에서 advanced와 결합해 '대단히 발전된'이라는 뜻이 되어야 하므로 부사 (C) highly가 정답이다.

어휘 | crisp 또렷한 film-like 필름과 같은 prove 입증하다 advanced 발전된, 앞선

2 (B)

번역 | 몽고메리 대학에서는 거의 모든 과정의 자료를 인터넷으로 이용할 수 있도록 할 것이라고 발표했다.

해설 | 빈칸 뒤에 수량을 나타내는 all이 있으므로 이를 수식할 수 있는 '거의'라는 뜻의 부사 (B) nearly가 정답이다.

어휘 | material 자료 available 이용할 수 있는, 구할 수 있는

3 (C)

번역 | 만약 회사들이 동일한 제품을 서로 다른 버전으로 제공하지 않고 표준화한다면 회사 비용을 상당히 줄일 수 있을 것이다.

해설 | 빈칸 앞쪽에 reduce라는 동사가 있으므로 '상당히'라는 뜻으로 증가나 감소의 동사를 수식할 수 있는 부사인 (C) significantly가 정답이다.

어휘 | standardize 표준화하다 instead of ~ 대신에, ~하지 않고 reduce 줄이다 expense 비용

④ 부사 어휘 3

ETS 유형 연습

본책 p.163

| 1 (D) | 2 (D) | 3 (A) |

1 (D)

번역 | 서마브라이트의 신형 소형 온도계 시제품에 대한 시장 조사 결과들은 아주 고무적이었다.

해설 | 형용사 encouraging(고무적인)을 수식하는 부사 자리이므로, 정도를 나타내는 부사가 들어가야 자연스럽다. 따라서 (D) very가 정답이다.

어휘 | market research 시장 조사 handheld 손에 쥐고 사용할 수 있는, 포켓용의 thermometer 온도계 prototype 시제품, 모델

2 (D)

번역 | 6월 30일자로 끝나는 기간 동안 호라이즌 스타디움 사는 티켓 판매로 전례 없는 수익을 기록했는데, 광고로는 훨씬 더 많은 수익을 기록했다.

해설 | 빈칸 뒤의 비교급 more가 힌트로, 보기들 중 비교급을 강조할 수 있는 부사 (D) even이 정답이다. 이때 even은 '심지어'가 아니라 '훨씬'이라는 의미로 해석된다. 참고로, (B) very는 원급과 쓰인다.

어휘 | unprecedented 전례가 없는 revenue 수익

3 (A)

번역 | 노나카 컨설팅 사의 강점은 뛰어난 데이터 분석가 팀을 갖추고 있다는 것이고, 그러므로 그 회사에서는 신규 고객을 찾을 때 분석적인 서비스를 강조한다.

해설 | 두 절을 연결하는 접속사 and가 있으므로, 빈칸은 없어도 되는 부사 자리이다. 보기 중 접속사인 (B), (C)를 제외하면 부사는 (A)와 (D)가 남는다. 문맥상 '뛰어난 데이터 분석가 팀이 있어 분석적인 서비스를 강조한다'라는 내용이 되어야 자연스러우므로, (A) therefore(그러므로)가 정답이다.

어휘 | consultancy 컨설팅 회사 strength 장점, 강점 accomplished 뛰어난, 우수한 analyst 분석가 highlight 두드러지게 하다, 강조하다 analytic 분석적인

● ETS 실전문제

본책 p.164

1 (D)	2 (A)	3 (C)	4 (B)	5 (C)	6 (A)
7 (D)	8 (C)	9 (D)	10 (B)	11 (A)	12 (B)
13 (C)	14 (A)	15 (C)	16 (D)	17 (D)	18 (A)

1 (D)

번역 | 우편물 수신자 목록의 정기적인 업데이트는 정확한 시장을 겨냥하려는 TNI 컴퍼니의 노력을 성공적으로 뒷받침했다.

해설 | 빈칸은 현재완료 have supported 사이에서 supported를 수식하는 부사 자리이므로, (D) successfully가 정답이다.

어휘 | regular 정기적인 mailing list 우편물 수신자 목록 effort 노력 target 겨냥하다, 목표로 삼다

2 (A)

번역 | 산텐 섬은 아름다운 해변과 맛있는 음식과 더불어 여행객들에게 수많은 야외 활동을 제공한다.

해설 | 빈칸 뒤에 있는 명사구 outdoor activities를 수식할 수 있는 형용사가 필요하므로 형용사 (A) numerous가 정답이다. numerous 뒤에는 항상 복수 가산명사가 온다는 점도 기억해 두자.

어휘 | along with ~와 함께 numerous 수많은, 다수의

3 (C)

번역 | 그 분석은 아주 자세해서 독자들이 최근 그린뷰의 경기 침체를 이해할 수 있게 해줄 것이다.

해설 | 빈칸 뒤에 있는 형용사 thorough를 수식할 수 있는 부사 (C) extremely가 정답이다.

어휘 | analysis 분석 thorough 철저한, 완벽한 downturn (경기) 침체, 후퇴 extremity 극한 extremely 아주, 몹시

4 (B)

번역 | 시그마 테크놀로지스는 최근 고객의 요구사항에 더 부합하는 새 회계 소프트웨어를 구입했다.

해설 | 빈칸은 주어 Sigma Technologies와 동사 bought 사이에서 bought를 수식하는 부사 자리이다. '최근에 구매했다'라는 내용이 되어야 자연스러우므로, (B) recently가 정답이다. (D) the most recently는 구조상 빈칸에 들어갈 수 없다.

어휘 | accounting 회계 meet the needs of ~의 요구에 부응하다 recent 최근의 recently 최근에

5 (C)

번역 | 펠레넴 대학교를 졸업한 직후 동급생인 트레버 토슨과 하이디 스미스는 컨설팅 회사를 공동 창립했다.

해설 | 빈칸은 전치사구 after graduating from Pellenem University를 강조하는 부사 자리로, 전치사 after와 어울려 '바로 직후'라는 의미를 완성하는 (C) Shortly가 정답이다.

어휘 | graduate from ~를 졸업하다 cofound 공동 창립하다 provided that ~라면 despite ~에도 불구하고

6 (A)

번역 | 저명한 작가인 네하 디후리 씨는 일요일에 글로스터 대학 서점에서 비평가들의 격찬을 받은 자신의 저서인 <잊혀진 것들>에 사인을 해줄 것이다.

133

해설 | 빈칸 앞에는 소유격 her, 뒤에는 형용사 acclaimed가 있으므로 형용사를 수식하는 부사 (A) critically가 정답이다.

어휘 | noted 저명한, 유명한(= famous) acclaimed 호평받고 있는 critically 비평적으로 criticism 비평 critic 비평가, 평론가 criticize 비평하다, 비난하다

7 (D)

번역 | 올해 원자재 부족 때문에 마호가니 가구 가격이 상당히 올랐다.

해설 | 완전한 절에서 자동사 rose를 수식하는 부사 자리이다. 따라서 '상당히'라는 뜻으로 증가의 동사를 수식하는 부사 (D) considerably가 정답이다.

어휘 | rise 오르다 due to ~ 때문에 shortage 부족 raw material 원자재, 원료 consider 고려하다 considering ~를 고려하면

8 (C)

번역 | 부동산 소유주들은 자신들의 건물을 방수 처리하는 것의 중요성에 대해 충분히 공부해야 한다.

해설 | 빈칸은 should educate 사이에서 educate를 수식하는 부사 자리이므로, '충분히, 완전히'라는 의미의 (C) fully가 정답이다.

어휘 | property 부동산 value 가치, 중요성

9 (D)

번역 | 요코하마 오케스트라의 하계 음악회는 오후 7시에 시작되어 약 2시간 동안 계속될 것이다.

해설 | 빈칸은 숫자 표현 two (hours)를 수식하는 부사 자리이다. 따라서 '대략'이라는 의미의 부사 (D) approximately가 정답이다.

어휘 | last 지속되다 approximate 거의 정확한; 비슷하다 approximation 근사치, 비슷한 값

10 (B)

번역 | 회원 가입을 하시려면 단지 협회 웹사이트에서 지원서를 작성하시기만 하면 됩니다.

해설 | 빈칸 뒤 명령문을 수식하여 회원 가입 과정(=웹사이트에서 지원서 작성)이 간단하다는 것을 강조하는 부사가 들어가야 하므로, (B) simply가 정답이다.

어휘 | apply for ~을 신청하다, 지원하다 society 협회, 학회 simply 그저, 단지 simplify 단순화하다 simplicity 단순(성)

11 (A)

번역 | 현 씨는 한결같이 인상 깊은 직업 의식을 보이면서, 종종 자신의 정규 업무 외에도 추가 프로젝트를 맡는다.

해설 | 빈칸 뒤에 온 분사 demonstrating을 수식하는 자리이므로, 부사 (A) Consistently가 정답이다.

어휘 | demonstrate 보여주다 impressive 인상적인, 인상 깊은 work ethic 직업 (윤리) 의식, 직업관 take on ~을 맡다, 책임지다 in addition to ~에 추가로, ~외에도 consistently 한결같이, 일관성 있게 consistency 한결같음, 일관성 consistent 한결같은, 일관된

12 (B)

번역 | 인터넷 쇼핑은 고객들이 실제 점포에 전시 공간이 주어질 정도로 인기가 있지는 않은 제품들을 접할 수 있도록 해 준다.

해설 | 빈칸 앞 형용사 popular를 수식하는 부사 자리이다. 문맥상 '공간이 주어질 정도로 충분히 인기 있는'이 자연스러우므로 부사

(B) enough가 정답이다. 참고로 부사 enough는 형용사나 부사를 뒤에서 수식한다.

어휘 | have access to ~에 접근할 수 있다 be given 주어지다

13 (C)

번역 | 방문객들은 박물관 입구 근처에 주차할 공간이 거의 없다고 불평했다.

해설 | 방문객들의 불평(Visitors have complained)을 유발한 부정적인 상황을 적절히 묘사하는 부사가 빈칸에 들어가야 한다. 따라서 '주차할 공간이 거의 없다'라는 뜻을 완성하는 (C) hardly가 정답이다.

어휘 | complain 불평하다 entrance 입구 normally 보통 hardly 거의 ~않다 openly 터놓고, 솔직하게

14 (A)

번역 | 신입 사원들은 질문하려고 인사부서에 연락하기 전 직원 안내서를 면밀히 검토해야 한다.

해설 | 직원 안내서를 검토하는(review) 정도 또는 방식을 적절히 묘사하는 부사가 빈칸에 들어가야 하므로, '철저히, 면밀히'라는 의미의 (A) thoroughly가 정답이다.

어휘 | new hire 신입 사원 human resources 인사부 incidentally 부수적으로, 우연히 relatively 비교적, 상대적으로 previously 이전에

[15-18] 정보문

펀 레이크 지역 사회 센터는 펀 레이크 지역 사회에 기여하고 있으며 전적으로 자원봉사자들에 의해 운영되는 기관입니다. 지역 주민들 사이에서 **15**일반적으로 '더 펀'으로 알려진 저희 센터는 지역 내 맞벌이 부모의 자녀들을 위해 우수한 방과 후 돌봄 서비스를 제공합니다. 또한 쿠엔틴 가에 있는 저희 건물에서 모든 연령을 대상으로 한 교육 프로그램들을 **16**진행합니다. **17**이 프로그램에는 춤과 그림 수업도 있습니다.

또한 지역 사회 센터는 연중 내내 여러 **18**야외 행사도 제공합니다. 가장 규모가 크고 유명한 것은 연례 펀 박람회입니다. 모든 주민들이 올해 4월 12일 브로드 가 부두에서 저희와 함께 시원한 봄바람을 느끼며 지역 최고의 음식과 공예품, 음악 공연을 즐기실 수 있습니다.

더 많은 정보를 원하시면 www.fernlakecc.com/fair를 방문해 주십시오.

어휘 | entirely 완전히 volunteer-run 자원봉사자들에 의해 운영되는 local 지역 주민 high-quality 고품질의, 수준 높은 working parents 맞벌이 부모 in addition 추가로, 아울러 throughout ~ 동안 쭉, 내내 annual 연례의 fair 박람회 craft 공예품 savor 음미하다, 감상하다 breeze 산들바람, 미풍

15 (C)

해설 | 과거분사 known을 수식하는 부사 자리로 문맥상 '일반적으로 ~라고 알려진'이라는 의미가 되어야 자연스럽다. 따라서 (C) Popularly가 정답이다.

어휘 | cooperatively 협력해서 mutually 상호간에 essentially 필수적으로

16 (D)

해설 | 빈칸 뒤의 educational programs를 목적어로 취해 '교육 프로그램들을 진행하다'라는 뜻이 되어야 하므로 타동사 (D) host가 정답이다. 자동사인 (A) participate(참여하다)는 전치사 in과 쓰여야 하고, (B) claim(주장하다)과 (C) enroll(등록시키다)은 의미상 부적절하므로 정답이 될 수 없다.

17 (D)

번역 | (A) 저희는 현재 자원봉사자들을 구하고 있지 않습니다.
(B) 중앙 홀을 빌리시려면 저희 사무실로 연락해 주세요.
(C) 이런 프로그램의 대부분은 더 이상 제공되지 않습니다.
(D) 이 프로그램에는 춤과 그림 수업도 있습니다.

해설 | 빈칸 앞 문장에서 교육 프로그램을 진행한다(We also host educational programs ~ on Quentin Street)고 했으므로, 빈칸에도 진행하는 교육 프로그램과 관련된 내용이 들어가야 자연스럽다. 따라서 (D)가 정답이다.

어휘 | available 이용 가능한, 시간이 있는 include 포함하다

18 (A)

해설 | 지문 첫 번째 단락에서 건물 내부에서 진행하는 교육 프로그램에 대해 안내했는데, 두 번째 단락에서는 추가로(In addition) 다른 프로그램을 안내하며 외부에서 진행되는 행사(Fern Fair ~ on the Broad Street Pier)에 대해 설명했으므로, '야외의'라는 뜻의 (A) outdoor가 정답이다.

어휘 | exclusive 배타적인 athletic 운동의 formal 공식적인

Unit 06 동사의 형태와 종류

① 동사의 활용

ETS 유형 연습

본책 p. 166

1 (A) **2** (D) **3** (B)

1 (A)

번역 | 수석 프로젝트 매니저는 다음 주 목요일에 현장을 방문할 예정인데 편집자들에게 오전 9시 30분에 자신의 사무실에서 만나자고 요청했다.

해설 | ask, require, request, insist, suggest, recommend처럼 주장, 제안, 요구의 동사 뒤에 오는 명사절 접속사 that이 이끄는 절에는 <should + 동사원형>이 오는데, 이때 should는 생략 가능하다. 따라서 동사원형인 (A) meet가 정답이다.

어휘 | senior 선임의, 고참의 on-site 현지에, 현장에서 editor 편집자

2 (D)

번역 | 많은 기업들이 새 정부의 조세안에 있는 여러 조항을 강력히 비판했다.

해설 | 빈칸 앞에는 have가, 뒤에는 목적어(several provisions)가 있으므로 완료형을 완성하는 과거분사가 필요하다. 따라서 (D) criticized가 정답이다.

어휘 | provision 조항 criticize 비난하다

3 (B)

번역 | 드소르보 사는 가을 카탈로그에 신상품 가죽 부츠를 소개할 것이다.

해설 | 동사 will be 뒤에는 현재분사(-ing)와 과거분사(p.p.)가 올 수 있다. 빈칸 뒤에 its new leather boots라는 목적어를 취하면서 '소개하고 있다'는 능동적 의미를 나타내므로 현재분사 (B) introducing이 정답이다. (A) introduce와 (C) introduces는 will be 뒤에 올 수 없고, (D) introduced는 수동적 의미를 나타내므로 정답이 될 수 없다.

어휘 | leather 가죽 catalog 카탈로그, 목록

② 자동사와 타동사

ETS 유형 연습

본책 p. 167

1 (D) **2** (A) **3** (D)

1 (D)

번역 | 임원은 예산안을 준비하면서 행동 방침을 결정하기 전에 여러 선택사항을 검토하게 된다.

해설 | 빈칸 뒤에 several options라는 목적어가 왔으며, 문맥상 '여러 선택사항을 검토하다'가 적합하므로 타동사 (D) examine이 정답이다.

어휘 | budget 예산(안) encourage ~를 하게 하다, 촉진하다 executive 간부, 임원 option 옵션, 선택사항 course of action 행동 방침

2 (A)

번역 | 고객들이 지역 쇼핑객 할인을 받기 위해서는 거주 증명서를 제시해야 한다.

해설 | 뒤의 전치사 for와 함께 쓰여 '지역 쇼핑객 할인의 자격이 있다'라는 의미를 나타내는 자동사 (A) qualify가 정답이다. '~의 자격이 있다'라는 의미의 표현으로 be eligible for도 함께 알아 두자.

어휘 | discount 할인 proof of residency 거주 증명서 award 수여하다 certify 증명하다, 보증하다

3 (D)

번역 | 신입 사원들은 사흘간 진행되는 오리엔테이션에 전원 참석해야 한다.

해설 | 빈칸 뒤의 in과 결합하여 '~에 참석하다'라는 뜻을 갖는 자동사 (D) participate가 정답이다. (A) attend 뒤에는 전치사 없이 바로 목적어인 the three-day orientation이 와야 하므로 오답이다.

어휘 | be required to do (반드시) ~해야 한다

③ 주의해야 할 타동사

ETS 유형 연습

본책 p. 168

1 (C) **2** (B) **3** (B)

1 (C)

번역 | 어느 누구도 두고 가지 않도록, 여행 안내원은 모든 방문객들에게 오전 7시까지 정문 로비에 와 있으라고 일러두었다.

해설 | <동사+사람 목적어(all the visitors)+to부정사> 구조로 쓰일 수 있는 동사를 선택해야 한다. 따라서 '사람들이 ~하도록 일러두다'라는 표현을 완성하는 (C) reminded가 정답이다. 참고로, <remind+사람 목적어+that절> 구조로도 자주 쓰인다.

어휘 | leave behind ~을 뒤에 남기다 tour operator 여행 안내원 front lobby 정문 로비 recall 회상하다 memorize 암기하다 remind 일러두다, 상기시키다 identify 확인하다, 알아보다

2 (B)

번역 | 가와노 씨는 직원들이 매장 전시 가구에서 발견하는 모든 결함을 그에게 알려주기를 바란다.

해설 | 사람 목적어를 취하고, 전치사 of와 어울려 쓰이는 타동사를 선택해야 한다. 따라서 '알리다, 통지하다'라는 의미의 (B) inform이 정답이다. 참고로 (A) supply는 supply A with B 구조로 쓰인다.

어휘 | flaw 결함 display 전시 supply 제공하다 reply 응답하다 notice 주목하다, 알아차리다

3 (B)

번역 | 조립 구역에서 작업하는 직원들은 모두 기계 조작에 관한 교육을 받아야 할 것이다.

해설 | 문맥상 주어인 employees가 '교육을 받도록 요구 받는다'라는 의미를 나타내므로 (B) required가 정답이다. 참고로 <be asked/requested/required+to부정사>는 모두 '~하도록 요구 받다'라는 의미로 쓰인다.

어휘 | assembly 조립 (부품) operation 조작, 운전

④ 동사 어휘

ETS 유형 연습

본책 p.169

1 (A)	2 (C)	3 (C)

1 (A)

번역 | 1월 셋째 주 동안에 매년 실시하는 인사 고과가 있음을 명심하세요.

해설 | that절의 주어 자리로, 문맥상 '업무능력 평가'가 적합하므로 명사 (A) reviews가 정답이다. review는 동사와 명사로 모두 쓰인다는 사실을 명심한다. (C) reviewer와 (D) reviewers도 명사이지만, '사람'을 나타내는 명사이기 때문에 문맥에 맞지 않다.

어휘 | be aware that ~을 알다 annual 연례의, 1년마다 performance 성과, 실적 take place 발생하다, 열리다

2 (C)

번역 | 우리의 최고 운영 책임자는 최근 매출액에 아주 감명받았다.

해설 | 사람 주어인 Our chief operating officer는 감동을 받는 대상이므로 수동적 의미를 나타내는 과거분사 (C) impressed가 정답이다.

어휘 | chief operating officer 최고 운영 책임자 sales figures 매출 수치[액] impress 깊은 인상을 주다

3 (C)

번역 | 모든 출장 연회 업체에서는 부패하기 쉬운 음식이 상하지 않도록 냉장 보관한다.

해설 | 상하기 쉬운 음식을 냉장 보관하는 것은 부패를 방지하기 위함이라고 볼 수 있다. 따라서 <prevent A from -ing>

구조로 쓰여 'A가 ~하는 것을 방지하다'라는 의미를 완성하는 (C) prevent가 정답이다.

어휘 | commercial 상업상의 catering 출장 연회 refrigerate 냉장 보관하다 perishable 썩기 쉬운, 부패하기 쉬운 spoil (음식이) 상하다 oppose 반대하다 forbid 금지하다

● ETS 실전문제

본책 p.170

1 (A)	2 (A)	3 (C)	4 (D)	5 (A)	6 (D)
7 (A)	8 (C)	9 (A)	10 (A)	11 (C)	12 (D)
13 (A)	14 (D)	15 (A)	16 (D)	17 (B)	18 (C)

1 (A)

번역 | 405번 고속도로의 새 주유소 개장은 초기 연료 수송이 제시간에 도착하지 못해 연기됐다.

해설 | 빈칸이 did not 뒤에 있으므로, 동사원형이 들어가야 한다. 따라서 (A) arrive가 정답이다.

어휘 | automotive 자동차의 service station (고속도로의) 휴게소, 주유소 initial 초기의 shipment 수송 on time 시간을 어기지 않고 arrival 도착

2 (A)

번역 | 이번에는 귀하에게 일자리를 제안할 수 없게 되었지만, 다음 기회를 위해서 귀하의 이력서를 보관해 두겠습니다.

해설 | 빈칸은 have와 결합하여 현재완료를 이루는 과거분사 자리이므로, (A) decided가 정답이다. 빈칸 뒤의 not은 to부정사 to offer를 부정하여 '제안하지 않기로'라는 뜻을 나타낸다.

어휘 | offer 제공[제안]하다 position 직책, 일자리 keep A on file A를 철하다, (기록을) 보관하다 opening 결원, 공석

3 (C)

번역 | 오사키 씨는 전 직원이 협력해서 마감일까지 그 업무를 끝내기를 원한다.

해설 | 목적어의 동작을 보충 설명하는 목적격 보어 자리로 (C) to work가 정답이다. 문장에 이미 동사 would like가 있으므로 빈칸에 (A), (D)와 같은 동사는 올 수 없다. <would like+목적어+목적격 보어(to부정사)>의 구조를 기억하자.

어휘 | entire staff 전 직원 deadline 마감일

4 (D)

번역 | 세계 보건의 날을 기념하여 모든 직원들은 설탕이 들어간 간식을 과일과 채소로 대체하라고 권장받는다.

해설 | 빈칸 앞에 be, 뒤에 to부정사가 있으므로 5형식 동사 encourage의 수동태 구문임을 알 수 있다. 따라서 과거분사 (D) encouraged가 정답이다.

어휘 | celebrate 기념하다, 축하하다 replace 대체하다, 대신하다 sugary 설탕이 든, 설탕 맛이 나는 encourage 격려하다, 권장하다

5 (A)

번역 | 소기업들은 협업하는 데서 이득을 볼 수 있기 때문에 많은 소유주들이 지역 사업 조합에 가입하는 것이 도움이 된다고 생각한다.

해설 | 전치사 from과 어울려 쓰이는 자동사를 선택하는 문제이다. 따라서 from과 함께 '~로부터 이익을 얻다'라는 의미를 완성하는 (A) benefit이 정답이다.

어휘 | local 지역의 association 협회 assist 돕다

6 (D)

번역 | 벡커 스트리트 일렉트로닉스는 7월 할인 행사의 일환으로 TX266 카메라의 배송비를 한시적으로 면제할 예정이다.

해설 | 회사가 할인 행사의 일환으로 배송비(shipping costs)와 관련해 취할 수 있는 조치를 나타내는 타동사가 필요하다. 따라서 '면제하다, (권리 등을) 포기하다'라는 의미의 타동사 (D) waive가 정답이다.

어휘 | limited 제한된, 한정된 shipping cost 배송비 proceed 진행하다 hesitate 주저하다 displace 대신하다, 대체하다

7 (A)

번역 | 해외로 배송되는 섬유 제품은 모든 국제 라벨 표시 요건을 준수해야 한다.

해설 | 전치사 with와 결합하여 요건(requirements), 규정 등의 명사와 어울려 쓰이는 자동사를 선택해야 한다. 따라서 with와 함께 '~을 준수하다, 지키다'라는 의미를 완성하는 (A) comply가 정답이다.

어휘 | textile 직물, 섬유 overseas 해외로 requirement 요건 confront 직면하다 assign 맡기다, 배정하다

8 (C)

번역 | 오시예크 시스템즈의 직원들은 사샤 바실레프 씨를 신임 부사장으로 정한 이사진의 결정에 놀랐다.

해설 | 동사 were의 주어인 Employees를 보충 설명하는 주격 보어 자리로, '직원들은 놀랐다'라는 수동적 의미를 나타내야 한다. 따라서 과거분사 (C) surprised가 정답이다. surprised는 수동의 의미를 지닌 채 '놀란'이란 뜻의 형용사 어휘로 굳어져 쓰이니 참고하자.

어휘 | the board of directors 이사진 decision 결정 vice president 부사장 surprise 놀라게 하다

9 (A)

번역 | 주디스 쿡 영업부장이 내일 아침까지 정확한 발송 날짜를 알려 드릴 것입니다.

해설 | <inform + A + of + B(A에게 B를 알리다)>를 적용시키는 문제이므로 전치사 (A) of가 정답이다. 동사가 특정 전치사와 결합할 때는 동사와 전치사를 함께 기억해 두어야 한다.

어휘 | sales department 영업부 shipment 발송, 선적

10 (A)

번역 | 래퍼티 씨의 추천인들은 그녀의 확고한 직업 의식을 언급했지만, 중역들은 그녀에게 그 직책에 필요한 기술이 부족하다고 여긴다.

해설 | but이 앞뒤 절을 연결하고 있으므로, 래퍼티 씨의 추천인(references)과 중역들(directors)의 의견은 상반되는 내용이어야 한다. 따라서 '기술이 부족하다'라는 부정적인 표현을 완성하는 (A) lacks가 정답이다.

어휘 | reference 추천서, 추천인 pretend ~인 체하다 remove 제거하다 vacate 비우다

11 (C)

번역 | 마부르크 일렉트로 사는 올해 상당한 수익 증가를 발표할 것으로 예상된다.

해설 | 빈칸 앞에 be, 뒤에 to부정사가 있으므로 빈칸에는 자동사의 과거분사가 들어가야 한다. 문맥상 '상당한 수익 증가를 발표할 것으로 예상된다'라는 내용이 되어야 자연스러우므로, (C) expected가 정답이다.

어휘 | significant 상당한 profit 수익 earn 벌다 outgrow ~보다 커지다 rise 오르다

12 (D)

번역 | 진료 예약을 취소하거나 일정을 조정하시려면 최소 24시간 전에 병원에 알려 주세요.

해설 | 주어 없이 시작하는 명령문의 동사원형 자리이다. 문맥상 '진료 예약을 취소 또는 변경하려면 24시간 전에 통지하라'라는 의미가 적합하므로 (D) notify가 정답이다. 참고로, (B) report는 보고 사항을 직접 목적어로 취한다.

어휘 | in advance 미리, 사전에 cancel 취소하다 reschedule 일정을 다시 잡다 appointment 약속 arrange 준비하다, 마련하다

13 (A)

번역 | 투자자인 조 기무라는 에이헌 매뉴팩처링의 모든 자산을 인수하면서 회사의 부채도 모두 떠맡았다.

해설 | 투자자로서 회사의 자산(assets)을 인수하며 부채도 모두 떠맡았다(also assumed ~ debts)는 내용이 되어야 자연스러우므로, '취득했다, 인수했다'라는 의미의 (A) acquired가 정답이다.

어휘 | investor 투자자 asset 자산 assume 맡다 debt 빚, 부채 deliver 배달하다 maintain 유지하다 analyze 분석하다

14 (D)

번역 | 새로운 디자인은 매우 혁신적이지만 이번에 우리가 개발을 진행하기에는 비용이 너무 많이 든다.

해설 | 전치사 with와 어울려 쓰이는 자동사를 선택하는 문제이다. 따라서 with와 함께 '~을 계속하다, 진행하다'라는 의미를 완성하는 (D) proceed가 정답이다. (A), (B), (C)는 모두 타동사이다.

어휘 | innovative 혁신적인 costly 많은 비용이 드는 development 개발 examine 조사하다 treat 대하다 urge 촉구하다

[15-18] 이메일

수신: info@kathyscaterers.com
발신: jberthel@berthetech.com
날짜: 12월 1일
제목: 행사 케이터링 문의

관계자께,

저는 현재 저희 회사의 연례 휴가 파티를 계획하고 있습니다. 케이터링 업체인 귀사에 대해 제가 ¹⁵본 모든 후기가 매우 긍정적이네요. 하지만 최종 결정을 내리기 전에 몇 가지 ¹⁶질문이 있습니다.

12월 16일 금요일에 25인분 음식을 제공해 주실 시간이 되나요? 행사는 래링턴 애비뉴 138번지에 있는 저희 회사 건물에서 개최될 예정입니다. 그날 오후 2시까지 간식을 배달해 주실 수 있습니까? 귀사의 스몰 바이츠 메뉴가 파티에 완벽하게 맞을 것 같아요.

¹⁷맛있는 음식 종류가 다양하게 제공된다는 점이 좋습니다. 모두의 음식 기호를 만족시킬 가장 쉬운 방법인 것 같네요.

¹⁸마지막으로, 남은 음식을 낭비하는 것에 대해 많은 사람들이 염려하는데요. 남은 음식을 집에 가져갈 사람들을 위해 포장용 상자를 제공해 주실 수 있나요?

감사합니다.

제임스 버텔, 버텔 테크놀로지스

어휘 | inquiry 문의 to whom it may concern 관계자에게 currently 현재 annual 연례의, 매년의 positive 긍정적인 make a final decision 최종 결정을 하다 available 이용 가능한, 시간이 되는 take place 개최되다 refreshments 간식 satisfy 만족시키다 preference 선호 be concerned about ~에 대해 우려하다 leftover 남은 음식 carryout 사서 들고 가는, 포장해서 가는

15 (A)

해설 | 빈칸은 have와 함께 현재완료를 이루는 과거분사 자리이므로, (A) seen이 정답이다.

16 (D)

해설 | 빈칸 뒤에서 궁금한 점들에 대해 문의하고 있으므로, 해당 문장은 최종 결정 전(before I make a final decision)에 질문을 하고 싶다는 내용이 되어야 문맥상 자연스럽다. 따라서 (D) questions가 정답이다.

17 (B)

번역 | (A) 저희는 친환경적인 컵, 접시, 기구를 사용합니다.
(B) 맛있는 음식 종류가 다양하게 제공된다는 점이 좋습니다.
(C) 숙련된 서빙 직원으로만 보내주세요.
(D) 최종 비용은 음료를 포함해야 합니다.

해설 | 빈칸 뒤에서 모두의 음식 기호를 만족시킬 가장 쉬운 방법인 것 같다(This would ~ satisfy everyone's food preferences)고 했으므로, 빈칸에서 먼저 이 판단의 근거가 제시되어야 문맥상 자연스럽다. 따라서 다양한 음식 종류를 언급한 (B)가 정답이다.

어휘 | environmentally friendly 친환경적인 utensil (가정에서 사용하는) 도구, 기구 a variety of 다양한 experienced 숙련된 beverage 음료

18 (C)

해설 | 콤마 뒤 문장을 수식하는 부사 자리이다. 빈칸 앞에서 몇 가지 문의사항을 나열했고, 빈칸 뒤에서 포장용 상자 제공(provide carryout boxes for people to take any leftovers)이 가능한지 문의하며 끝맺었으므로, '마지막으로'라는 의미의 (C) Finally가 정답이다.

어휘 | meanwhile 당분간, 그 동안 otherwise 그렇지 않으면

Unit 07 수 일치와 태

① 주어와 동사의 수 일치

ETS 유형 연습

본책 p.172

1 (A) **2** (A) **3** (B)

1 (A)

번역 | 백스터 씨는 멕시코 시티로 전근을 갔지만, 뉴욕 지사에서 근무하는 예전 동료들과 계속 연락하고 지낸다.

해설 | 주어가 Ms. Baxter and her former colleagues (at the New York branch), 빈칸이 동사인 절이다. 따라서 복수주어와 수가 일치하는 (A) remain이 정답이다. remain in contact는 '연락을 유지하다, 계속 연락하며 지내다'라는 의미이다.

어휘 | transfer 전근시키다 former 이전의, 전의 branch 지점, 지사

2 (A)

번역 | 현재 프린터에 필요한 잉크 카트리지를 구할 수 없으니, 컬러 프린터를 아껴 사용해 주세요.

해설 | since절의 주어는 it requires의 수식을 받는 the ink cartridges이므로 복수동사 (A) are가 정답이다. 참고로, it requires 앞에는 목적격 관계대명사 that이 생략되어 있다.

어휘 | sparingly 절약하여 currently 현재, 지금 unavailable 이용할 수 없는, 구할 수 없는

3 (B)

번역 | 우리가 비교해 보았던 커피 메이커들은 가격, 크기 및 내구성 면에서 다양하다.

해설 | 관계대명사 목적격이 생략된 수식 구조((that) we compared)를 묶어 보면 주어가 복수명사(The coffee makers)이므로 복수동사인 (B) vary가 정답이다.

어휘 | compare 비교하다 in terms of ~에 관하여, ~의 관점에서 durability 튼튼함, 내구성 vary 다양하다, 다르다 variable 변하기 쉬운, 일정치 않은

② 단수주어 복수주어

ETS 유형 연습

본책 p.173

1 (D) **2** (B) **3** (D)

1 (D)

번역 | 나는 사전 조사를 하는 동안에, 지난 10년간 미호 아오키의 시에 관해 쓰인 글이 거의 없다는 것을 알게 되었다.

해설 | 불가산명사인 research를 대신 받으면서, 단수동사인 has와 수가 일치하는 주어인 부정대명사 (D) little이 정답이다. (B) few는 복수명사를 대신 받아서 복수동사와 함께 써야 한다.

어휘 | perform 수행하다 preliminary 예비의, 준비의 decade 10년

2 (B)

번역 | 센트리 사진 현상소 직원들의 절반 가량은 버스로 출퇴근한다.

해설 | half of the employees (at Century Photo Labs)가 문장의 주어이고, 빈칸은 문장의 동사 자리이다. half of와 같은 부분을 나타내는 표현은 of 뒤의 명사에 수를 일치한다. 여기서는 복수명사인 the employees가 왔으므로 복수동사인 (B) commute가 정답이다.

어휘 | roughly 대충, 대략 photo lab (사진) 현상소 commute 통근하다

3 (D)

번역 | 스텔렌 박물관의 폭넓은 소장품은 다양한 문화권에서 온 고대 공예품과 그림으로 어우러져 구성되어 있다.

해설 | 빈칸은 The Stellen Museum's extensive의 수식을 받는 주어 자리이므로 명사가 들어가야 한다. 따라서 동사 consist와 수가 일치하는 복수명사 (D) holdings가 정답이다.

어휘 | extensive 광대한, 다방면에 걸친 consist of ~으로 구성되다 artifact 공예품 various 다양한 holdings (도서관 등의) 장서, 소장품

③ 동사의 수동태

ETS 유형 연습
본책 p. 174

1 (B) **2** (B) **3** (C)

1 (B)

번역 | 해외 여행객들에 대한 새로운 규제로 인해, 대부분의 나라에서 특정 종류의 식물은 허가 없이 반입될 수 없다.

해설 | 조동사(cannot) 뒤에는 동사원형이 와야 하며, 주어인 certain types of plants는 bring의 행위자가 아니라 대상이므로 수동태인 (B) be brought가 정답이다. 빈칸 뒤에 목적어가 없으니 수동태로 접근하는 것도 좋다.

어휘 | restriction 규제, 제한 plant 식물 permit 허가, 인가

2 (B)

번역 | 기한 내에 책을 반납하지 않은 도서관 이용객들에게는 연체료가 부과될 것이다.

해설 | 문장의 동사 자리로 시간상 미래의 일을 나타내고, 의미상 '이용객이 연체료를 부과받는' 수동의 개념이므로 (B) will be charged가 정답이다.

어휘 | patron 이용객, 단골 손님 due date 기한, 지급 기일 fee 요금, 수수료 charge 청구하다

3 (C)

번역 | 대표단은 오전 9시에 대사관에서 출발할 것이며, 체육부 장관이 공항까지 동행할 것이다.

해설 | 빈칸은 주어 The delegation의 동사 자리인데, 문맥상 대표단이 체육부 장관의 수행을 받을 것(by the Minister of Sports)이라는 내용이 되어야 자연스러우므로, 수동태인 (C) will be accompanied가 정답이다.

어휘 | delegation 대표단 embassy 대사관 minister 장관 accompany 동반하다, 동행하다

④ 여러 가지 수동태

ETS 유형 연습
본책 p. 175

1 (A) **2** (A) **3** (A)

1 (A)

번역 | 매달 다섯 명의 우수 직원을 선발하여 회사의 성과에 크게 기여한 것에 대해 시상을 할 것이다.

해설 | '~에 대한 공로로 표창을 받다'라는 뜻은 be honored for 형태로 써야 하므로 전치사 (A) for가 정답이다. 이때 for는 이유/원인을 나타낸다. at은 보통 장소나 시점에 쓰이고, across는 '(도로가 다리 따위를) 건너서', over는 '(기간에) 걸쳐서', 혹은 '~에 관한'이란 뜻으로 사용된다.

어휘 | outstanding 뛰어난, 탁월한 honor 경의를 표하다, 명예를 주다 exceptional 특별한, 예외적인 contribution 공헌, 기여 performance 성과, 실적

2 (A)

번역 | 침대차 승객들에게는 여정에 필요한 침구류가 제공될 것이다.

해설 | 동사 provide는 전치사 with와 함께 provide A with B의 형태로 'A에게 B를 제공하다'라는 의미로 자주 쓰이고, 이 문장은 수동태가 되면서 A의 자리에 있어야 할 목적어가 문장의 주어(Sleeping-car passengers)로 문장 맨 앞에 나와 있는 상태이므로 전치사 (A) with가 정답이다.

어휘 | sleeping-car 침대차(의) passenger 승객 bedding 침구류

3 (A)

번역 | 저층 아파트들은 먼지와 도로의 소음에 더 많이 노출되기 때문에 값이 더 싸다.

해설 | 빈칸 앞에 온 exposed와 결합하여 '~에 노출되다'라는 의미를 나타내는 전치사 (A) to가 정답이다. <be exposed to + 명사>의 관용적 표현으로 기억하자.

어휘 | dust 먼지 noise 소음

● ETS 실전문제
본책 p. 176

1 (A)	**2** (B)	**3** (B)	**4** (D)	**5** (A)	**6** (D)
7 (B)	**8** (B)	**9** (D)	**10** (A)	**11** (B)	**12** (D)
13 (A)	**14** (B)	**15** (A)	**16** (B)	**17** (C)	**18** (C)

1 (A)

번역 | 왓칠 비스트로의 새 메뉴는 아몬드가 덮인 연어, 소고기 안심, 버섯 리조토를 포함한다.

해설 | 빈칸은 전치사구 for the Watchill Bistro의 수식을 받는 주어 The new menu의 동사 자리이다. 따라서 단수명사 menu와 수가 일치하는 (A) includes가 정답이다.

어휘 | -crusted ~가 덮인 tenderloin 안심 inclusion 포함

2 (B)

번역 | 소매부가 마감 일자를 앞두고 있어서 부서 영업보고서는 주말까지 완료되어야 한다.

해설 | 특정 기한까지 요구되는 대상은 '부서 영업보고서'이므로, 빈칸에는 sales와 함께 복합명사를 이루는 명사가 들어가야 한다. 빈칸이 동사 are required의 주어 역할을 하므로, are와 수가 일치하는 복수명사 (B) reports가 정답이다.

어휘 | retail 소매 division 분과, 부 deadline 마감 department 부서 require 요구하다

3 **(B)**

번역 | 향상된 품질 덕분에 지난 몇 년간 환불을 요청하는 고객들의 수가 감소했다.

해설 | 단수 주어 The number와 수가 일치하는 (A) declined와 (B) has declined 중 하나를 선택해야 하는데, 뒤에 over the last few years(지난 몇 년간)라는 표현이 있으므로 현재완료 시제가 빈칸에 들어가야 자연스럽다. 따라서 (B) has declined가 정답이다.

어휘 | request 요청하다 decline 감소하다 improved 향상된

4 **(D)**

번역 | 회사 자선 모금 운동에 기부하고자 하는 직원들은 잭 엘리엇 씨의 사무실에 있는 상자에 기증품을 넣어 주세요.

해설 | 관계사절(who ~ charity drive)의 수식을 받는 주어 Employees의 동사 자리이다. 직원들이 '상자에 기증품을 넣어달라'는 요청을 받는 상황이므로, 수동태 동사가 쓰여야 한다. 따라서 (D) are invited가 정답이다. invite는 to부정사를 목적격 보어로 취하는 5형식 동사로, 수동태로 바꾸면 <be invited to부정사>의 형태가 된다.

어휘 | contribute 기부하다, 기여하다 charity drive 자선 모금 (운동) donation 기부(금), 기증(품)

5 **(A)**

번역 | 콤코 사는 지난해 컴퓨터 부품 공급업체 중 선도적인 회사가 되었는데, 당시 그 회사는 설립된 지 10년도 채 되지 않았었다.

해설 | 단수 주어 it(Comco, Inc.)은 설립되는 대상이므로 수동태 단수동사인 (A) was founded가 정답이다. 나머지 (B) founds, (C) have founded, (D) founded는 모두 능동태 동사이다.

어휘 | leading 선도하는 supplier 공급업체 found 설립하다

6 **(D)**

번역 | 수백 명의 기술 전문가들이 지난달 취리히에서 열렸던 총회에 참석했다.

해설 | 모든 문장에는 동사가 있어야 하는데 동사가 없는 문장이다. 동사를 갖추고 '~이 있다'라는 의미를 나타내는 (D) There were가 정답이다.

어휘 | technical specialist 기술 전문가 convention 회의, 총회

7 **(B)**

번역 | 제일슨 오피스 타워의 난방 시스템이 시 건물 안전 부서에 의해 점검되고 있다.

해설 | 빈칸은 주어 Jalesen Office Tower's heating system의 동사 자리이다. 주어 heating system은 점검되는 대상이자 단수명사이므로, 수동태 단수동사인 (B) is being inspected가 정답이다.

어휘 | inspect 검사[점검]하다 inspection 검사, 점검

8 **(B)**

번역 | 호토 프러덕션 플랜트의 상근 직원들은 4시간씩 교대 근무 때마다 15분간 휴식을 취할 권리가 있다.

해설 | 복수동사 are의 주어 자리로 복수명사인 (B) employees (직원들)가 정답이다.

어휘 | be entitled to do ~할 자격이[권리가] 있다 shift 교대 근무 (시간) employ 고용하다

9 **(D)**

번역 | 공항 셔틀은 한 시간 간격으로 호텔 정문에서 출발한다.

해설 | 일반적인 사실을 나타낼 때는 현재 시제를 쓰는데, 주어가 단수인 The airport shuttle이므로 단수동사인 (D) departs가 정답이다.

어휘 | front entrance 정문 depart 출발하다

10 **(A)**

번역 | 악천후와 인력 감원으로 인해 컨 사이언스 센터 보수 공사는 가장 큰 어려움을 겪게 되었다.

해설 | 주어가 'A and B'일 때는 복수동사를 써야 한다. 또한, 빈칸 뒤에 목적어 the greatest challenges가 있으므로 능동태 복수동사인 (A) have posed가 정답이다.

어휘 | inclement weather 악천후, 나쁜 날씨 reduced 줄어든 workforce 노동 인력, 전직원 challenge 난제, 도전 renovation 수리, 보수 공사 pose 일으키다, 유발하다

11 **(B)**

번역 | 앨핀타 간호직 유니폼에 쓰인 천은 일상적인 사용으로 발생하는 마모에는 강한 것으로 확인되었다.

해설 | 빈칸은 used in Alpinta nursing uniforms의 수식을 받는 주어 The fabric의 동사 자리이다. fabric은 확인되는 대상이자 단수명사이므로, 수동태 단수동사인 (B) has been confirmed가 정답이다.

어휘 | fabric 천, 직물 withstand (잘) 견뎌내다 wear and tear 마모, 손상 confirm 사실임을 보여주다, 확인하다

12 **(D)**

번역 | 아이언캐슬 하드웨어는 다음 주 월요일부터 매장 영업시간을 매일 밤 9시까지 연장할 것이다.

해설 | Ironcastle Hardware가 주어, 빈칸이 동사, its store hours가 목적어인 능동태 문장으로, 미래 시간을 나타내는 Starting next Monday가 문장 전체를 수식하고 있다. 따라서 능동태 미래 동사인 (D) will be extending이 정답이다.

어휘 | store hour 매장 영업시간 extend 연장하다, 확대하다

13 **(A)**

번역 | 신제품 비트롤럭스 X500 카메라는 내장형 플래시와 간단한 제어판이 장착되어 출시됩니다.

해설 | 자동사 become, remain, get, go, come 등의 성격을 이해하고 있어야 한다. 원래는 be equipped with(~가 갖추어져 있다)란 숙어인데 be가 come으로 바뀐 것으로, (A) equipped가 정답이다.

어휘 | integrated 통합[융화]된 advanced 발달된 captured 포착된

14 **(B)**

번역 | 이 도시는 시민들이 친절하기로 유명한 곳이라고 윌리엄스 시장은 자랑스럽게 말했다.

해설 | 빈칸 뒤의 전치사 for와 결합하여 '~으로 유명한'이라는 의미를 나타내는 과거분사 (B) known이 정답이다.

어휘 | mayor 시장 proudly 자랑스럽게 hospitality 환대, 친절함

[15-18] 이메일

수신: 전 직원 <staff@bensonwellslegal.com>
발신: 압둘라 알하르비 <a.alharbi@bensonwellslegal.com>
날짜: 9월 10일
제목: 의무 교육

전 직원에게,

기술의 지속적 발전은 우리 회사의 정보 관리에 끊임없는 도전 과제를 ¹⁵줍니다. 벤슨 웰스 리걸 솔루션즈에서는 우리 회사의 자료와 우리 고객의 자료 ¹⁶모두를 안전하게 지키기 위해서 항상 노력합니다. 이런 이유로 우리는 북미에서 선도적인 데이터 보안 회사 중 하나인 컨시더 더 클릭과 제휴를 맺고 있습니다. 이 회사에서 이번 ¹⁷보안 교육을 해 줄 것이고, 전 직원은 이미 등록돼 있습니다. 우리가 더 많이 알수록 회사는 더욱 안전해지고, 궁극적으로 더 성공할 수 있습니다.

교육을 위해 최소 45분을 비워 두십시오. 교육은 12월 1일에 끝날 것입니다. ¹⁸교육을 시작하기 위한 링크가 포함된 이메일을 곧 받게 될 것입니다.

압둘라 알하르비
정보기술 이사

어휘 | regular advance 지속적인 발전[발달] constant 끊임없는 challenge 어려움, 도전 과제 manage 관리하다, 다루다 leading 선도적인 enroll 등록하다 ultimately 궁극적으로 reserve 예약하다, 따로 잡아[남겨] 두다 complete 완성하다, 완료하다

15 (A)
해설 | 빈칸은 주어 Regular advances in technology의 동사 자리로, 명사구 constant challenges를 목적어로 취한다. 따라서 능동태 동사인 (A) present가 정답이다. to부정사인 (B) to present와 동명사/현재분사인 (D) presenting은 동사 자리에 들어갈 수 없다.
어휘 | present 주다, 야기하다

16 (B)
해설 | 빈칸에는 and와 짝을 이루어 our company's data와 our clients' data를 연결하는 단어가 들어가야 하므로, (B) both가 정답이다. (A) either는 or와, (C) not only는 but (also)와 짝을 이루어 쓰인다. '마치 ~처럼'이라는 의미의 부사절 접속사인 (D) as though 뒤에는 절이 와야 한다.

17 (C)
해설 | 빈칸이 지시형용사 this와 명사 training 사이에 있으므로, 빈칸에는 training을 수식하는 형용사 또는 training과 복합명사를 이루는 명사가 들어갈 수 있다. 빈칸 앞에서 선도적인 데이터 보안 회사 중 하나(one of the leading data safety firms)인 컨시더 더 클릭을 언급했고, 이 회사가 교육을 제공한다고 했으므로, 빈칸에는 safety와 유사한 의미의 단어가 들어가야 한다. 따라서 '보안'이라는 의미의 명사 (C) security가 정답이다. (A) financial은 '재정의', (D) electrical은 '전기의'라는 뜻의 형용사이고, (B) fitness는 '건강, 적합'이라는 뜻의 명사이므로 문맥상 빈칸에 적절하지 않다.

18 (C)
번역 | (A) 이 프로그램은 전적으로 각 직원의 선택에 달려 있습니다.
(B) 당신의 도움으로, 우리 웹사이트는 더 마음을 끄는 이미지를 제시할 수 있습니다.
(C) 교육을 시작하기 위한 링크가 포함된 이메일을 곧 받게 될 것입니다.
(D) 우리는 수집한 정보를 최대한 이용해야만 번영할 수 있습니다.
해설 | 빈칸 앞 문장에서 교육 시간 및 교육 종료일(Please reserve at least 45 minutes for the training, which is to be completed by December 1)을 언급했으므로, 빈칸에도 교육과 관련된 내용이 들어가야 문맥상 자연스럽다. 따라서 (C)가 정답이다.
어휘 | completely 완전히 optional 선택적인 present 제시하다 contain 포함하다 prosper 번영하다

Unit 08 시제

① 단순 시제

ETS 유형 연습
본책 p.178

| 1 (B) | 2 (B) | 3 (B) |

1 (B)
번역 | 보고르 스타디움의 좌석은 모든 방문객들이 경기를 잘 관람할 수 있도록 경기장을 완전히 둘러싸고 있다.
해설 | 문장의 동사가 필요한 자리이고 주어인 Seating이 단수명사이므로 (B) surrounds, (C) surrounded가 답이 될 수 있는데, 문맥상 일반적인 사실을 나타내므로 현재 시제 동사인 (B) surrounds가 정답이다.
어휘 | seating 좌석 completely 완전히 afford ~할 수 있다, (기회를) 주다 view 전망, 경치

2 (B)
번역 | 새로운 발견이 작동 모델을 구식으로 만들었을 때 기술자들은 겨우 문제를 분석하기 시작했던 참이었다.
해설 | 접속사 when이 이끄는 부사절의 동사 자리이다. 주절에 과거완료 시제(had begun)가 쓰였으므로, 빈칸에는 과거 시제가 들어가야 한다. 따라서 (B) rendered가 정답이다.
어휘 | analyze 분석하다 working model 작동 모델 obsolete 못쓰게 된, 구식의 render ~을 (어떠한 상태가) 되게 하다

3 (B)
번역 | 현재 연식 이후에 자동차 제조업체인 CFG는 구형 모델 세 개를 단종하고 새로운 모델 두 개를 출시할 것이다.
해설 | 단수 주어인 the automobile manufacturer CFG 뒤의 동사 자리이다. 시제를 고려해야 하는데, 등위접속사인 and 뒤에 나오는 introduce가 동사원형인 것으로 미루어 보아 앞에 나오는 동사는 <조동사 + 동사원형>이 되어야 하므로 미래 시제 동사 (B) will discontinue가 정답이다. 빈칸에 (C) discontinued가 오려면, 문두의 수식어구가 없어야 하고, and 뒤에 과거형인 introduced가 나와야 한다.
어휘 | model year 연식 automobile manufacturer 자동차 제조업체 discontinue 중지하다, 중단하다

141

② 진행 시제

ETS 유형 연습
본책 p. 179

1 (A)   **2** (D)   **3** (D)

1 (A)

번역 | LTD 엔터프라이지즈 사에서 현재 이달 말에 퇴직할 현 이사를 대신할 우수한 인재를 찾고 있습니다.

해설 | 빈칸 앞에 온 is currently가 문제 해결의 단서로, currently는 '현재, 지금'이라는 의미로 현재 시제와 어울려 쓸 수 있는 부사이다. 따라서 현재진행형 시제를 만들 수 있는 (A) seeking이 정답이다. (B) seeks는 currently 앞에 is가 왔으므로 정답이 될 수 없다는 것에 유의한다.

어휘 | accomplished 뛰어난 replace 대신하다, 대체하다 retire 은퇴하다, 퇴직하다

2 (D)

번역 | 윤 씨는 목요일에 돌아왔을 때 시차로 인해 피곤했고, 그래서 회의는 다음 주로 연기되었다.

해설 | when이 이끄는 부사절의 동사 returned가 과거를 나타내고 있다. 따라서 주절 또한 과거 시제가 되어야 하므로 과거진행 시제 동사 (D) was suffering이 정답이다.

어휘 | jet lag (비행기 여행) 시차로 인한 피로 postpone 연기하다, 미루다 suffer 겪다

3 (D)

번역 | 다음 6월에 아티탬 씨가 휴가를 갈 동안, 알 자므리 씨가 뭄바이 납품업체와의 계약 협상을 맡게 될 것이다.

해설 | While Ms. Atitam is on vacation next June이 미래 시점을 나타내므로, 빈칸에도 미래 시제 동사가 들어가야 한다. 따라서 미래진행 동사 (D) will be taking이 정답이다.

어휘 | on vacation 휴가 중인 contract 계약(서) negotiation 교섭, 협상 vendor 납품업체 take over 인계 받다, 떠맡다

③ 완료 시제

ETS 유형 연습
본책 p. 180

1 (B)   **2** (B)   **3** (A)

1 (B)

번역 | 지난 15년 동안 매틀록 사는 항상 전국 상위 10대 장난감 제조업체 안에 들었다.

해설 | '지난 15년 동안 (등급·순위를) 차지했다'라는 의미이므로 has와 결합하여 현재완료 시제를 나타내는 과거분사 (B) ranked가 정답이다.

어휘 | consistently 끊임없이, 항상 leading 일류의, 주도하는 manufacturer 제조업체, 생산자

2 (B)

번역 | 채용 위원회는 지원자들을 직접 면접하는 가능성에 대해 논의했지만, 그 대신 전화 인터뷰를 하기로 결정했다.

해설 | 채용 위원회가 전화 인터뷰를 하기로 결정했던 과거 시점 이전에 논의가 이뤄졌으므로 과거완료 (B) had discussed가 정답이다.

어휘 | hiring committee 채용 위원회 possibility 가능성 candidate 후보자, 지원자 in person 직접

3 (A)

번역 | 클리어 블레이즈 테크놀러지 사의 워드 프로세서 프로그램이 시판될 무렵이면, 소프트웨어 엔지니어들은 남아 있는 결함을 수정했을 것이다.

해설 | '~할 즈음, ~할 무렵'이라는 의미의 <By the time + 주어 + 현재 시제> 표현이 주절을 수식해 주고 있으므로, 빈칸에는 미래의 특정 시점에 완료될 일을 나타내는 미래완료 시제가 들어가야 자연스럽다. 따라서 (A) will have corrected가 정답이다.

어휘 | word processing program 워드 프로세서[문서 처리] 프로그램 go on the market 시장에 나오다, 팔리기 시작하다 flaw 결점, 결함

④ 시제 일치의 예외

ETS 유형 연습
본책 p. 181

1 (B)   **2** (A)   **3** (A)

1 (B)

번역 | 계정에 접속하길 원하신다면 적절한 칸에 비밀 번호를 입력하세요.

해설 | 빈칸은 When이 이끄는 부사절의 동사 자리이다. 시간/조건의 부사절에서는 미래의 일을 나타내더라도 현재 시제를 사용하므로, (B) want가 정답이다.

어휘 | access 접속하다 account 계좌, 계정 password 비밀 번호 appropriate 적절한, 알맞은 field 영역, 칸

2 (A)

번역 | 화재 위험에 대비한 창고 조사가 끝나는 대로, 정상적인 조업을 재개할 수 있다.

해설 | 빈칸은 As soon as가 이끄는 부사절의 동사 자리이다. 시간/조건의 부사절에서는 미래의 일을 나타내더라도 현재 시제를 사용하므로, 현재완료 (A) has been이 정답이다.

어휘 | warehouse 창고 hazard 위험, 모험 resume 재개하다 normal 정상적인 operation 운영, 조업

3 (A)

번역 | 라지브 커티 전무 이사는 스리니바산 푸드 공장의 품질 관리 절차를 검토하라는 주주들의 요청에 응했다.

해설 | that이 이끄는 절 앞에 requests(요청)라는 명사가 있으므로, that절의 동사는 <(should) + 동사원형>이 되어야 한다. 주어인 he는 절차를 검토하는 주체이므로, 능동태 동사원형인 (A) review가 정답이다.

어휘 | executive director 전무 이사 comply with ~의 요구에 응하다 shareholder 주주 quality control 품질 검사, 품질 관리 procedure 절차 facility 시설, 공장

● ETS 실전문제

본책 p.182

1 (A)	**2** (B)	**3** (D)	**4** (B)	**5** (B)	**6** (C)
7 (D)	**8** (A)	**9** (C)	**10** (D)	**11** (D)	**12** (B)
13 (D)	**14** (B)	**15** (A)	**16** (D)	**17** (D)	**18** (B)

1 (A)

번역 | 매년 여름 브라이튼의 상점 주인들은 관광객들을 더 많이 유치하려는 노력의 일환으로 쇼윈도를 독특하게 진열한다.

해설 | Brighton store owners가 주어, 빈칸이 동사, unique window displays가 목적어인 문장이다. 따라서 복수 주어와 수가 일치하는 능동태 동사가 들어가야 하므로, (A) create가 정답이다.

어휘 | owner 소유자, 주인 unique 독특한, 특이한 window display 쇼윈도의 상품 진열 attract 끌다, 유치하다 tourist 관광객 create 만들다

2 (B)

번역 | 매그넘 플러스 사의 카메라는 아주 사용하기 쉬워서 지금 매우 인기가 많다.

해설 | Magnum Plus cameras가 주어, 빈칸이 동사, very popular가 주격 보어인 문장이다. 뒤에 right now라는 표현이 있으므로, 빈칸에는 현재 시점에 진행되는 일을 나타내는 동사가 들어가야 자연스럽다. 따라서 현재진행형인 (B) are becoming이 정답이다.

어휘 | popular 인기 있는

3 (D)

번역 | 중역실에 페인트를 칠하고 있어서 오늘 오후 회의는 4층 회의실에서 열릴 예정이다.

해설 | 조동사 will의 뒤에는 동사원형이 온다. 문맥상 '회의가 열리다'라는 수동적 의미를 나타내므로 수동태 동사원형인 (D) be held가 정답이다.

어휘 | boardroom 중역실, (이사) 회의실 conference room 회의실

4 (B)

번역 | 리 씨가 조정을 좀 한 후에 엔진은 이전보다 더 부드럽게 작동했다.

해설 | 빈칸은 After가 이끄는 부사절의 주어인 Mr. Li의 동사 자리이므로, 보기에서 동사 자리에 들어갈 수 있는 (B) made와 (C) is making 중 하나를 선택해야 한다. 조정을 한 후 더 부드럽게 작동했다(worked)고 볼 수 있으므로, 빈칸에는 과거완료 또는 과거 시제가 들어갈 수 있다. 따라서 (B) made가 정답이다.

어휘 | adjustment 수정, 조정 smoothly 부드럽게

5 (B)

번역 | 라퍼 페인팅 사는 아바게일 가에 개장한 새 매장을 축하하기 위해 특별 할인 행사를 할 것이다.

해설 | Larper Painting이 주어, 빈칸이 동사, a special sale이 목적어인 문장이다. 라퍼 페인팅 사가 다음 달(next month)에 할인 행사를 진행할 것이라는 내용이므로, 능동태 미래 시제인 (B) will be running이 정답이다.

어휘 | celebrate 축하하다

6 (C)

번역 | 데릭 씨가 팀에 합류한 이후 자파타 씨와 콜먼 씨는 훌륭한 성과를 거둔 마케팅 팀에게 찬사를 보내 오고 있다.

해설 | 빈칸 앞에 have, 뒤에 목적어 the marketing team이 있으며, 과거부터 현재까지의 기간을 나타내는 since 부사절이 문장 전체를 수식하고 있다. 따라서 '데릭 씨가 합류한 이후로 마케팅 팀을 칭찬해 오고 있다'라는 내용이 되어야 자연스러우므로, have와 결합하여 능동태 현재완료(진행) 동사를 완성하는 (C) been praising이 정답이다.

어휘 | join 합류하다 praise 칭찬하다, 찬사를 보내다

7 (D)

번역 | 리톡 엔지니어링은 새 세입자들이 이사올 때까지 그 건물의 모든 전기 배선 점검을 마칠 것이다.

해설 | '~할 즈음, ~할 무렵'이라는 뜻의 <by the time + 주어(new tenants) + 현재 시제(move in)> 표현이 주절을 수식해 주고 있으므로, 미래의 특정 시점에 완료될 일을 나타내는 미래완료 시제가 쓰여야 자연스럽다. 따라서 과거분사 checked와 결합하여 '점검을 마칠 것이다'라는 의미를 완성하는 (D) will have가 정답이다.

어휘 | electrical wiring 전기 배선 tenant 세입자, 임차인

8 (A)

번역 | 럼 박사는 오늘 나온 결과를 입증하기 위해 내일 두 번째 연구 그룹이 실험을 반복할 것을 요청하고 있다.

해설 | 요청의 동사 is requesting의 목적어 역할을 하는 that절의 동사 자리로, <(should) + 동사원형>이 들어가야 한다. 주어 experiment는 반복되는 대상이므로, 수동태 동사원형 (A) be repeated가 정답이다.

어휘 | validate 입증하다 request 요청하다 experiment 실험 research 연구

9 (C)

번역 | 만약 배관 문제가 지속되면 제품 제조업체에 연락하시길 권해 드립니다.

해설 | 빈칸은 If가 이끄는 부사절의 동사 자리이다. 조건의 부사절에서는 미래의 일을 나타내더라도 현재 시제를 사용하므로 (C) persists가 정답이다. to부정사인 (A) to persist와 명사인 (D) persistence는 동사 자리에 올 수 없고, (B) was persisting은 과거진행형이므로 시제 면에서 부적절하다.

어휘 | plumbing 배관 recommend 권하다 manufacturer 제조업체 persist 지속되다 persistence 끈기, 고집

10 (D)

번역 | 양 씨가 타이베이에서 열리는 해외여행 회의에서 돌아올 때까지 우 씨가 모든 호텔 예약을 처리할 것이다.

해설 | Until이 이끄는 시간의 부사절에서 현재 시제(returns)를 사용하여 미래의 상황을 나타내고 있으므로, 주절에 미래 시제가 쓰여야 한다. 주어 Mr. Woo는 호텔 예약을 처리하는 주체이므로, 능동태 미래 시제인 (D) will handle이 정답이다.

어휘 | conference 회의, 대회 reservation 예약 handle 다루다, 처리하다

11 (D)

번역 | 고객 서비스 부서에 접수되는 불만 건수가 지난해 급격히 줄어들었다.

해설 | 과거부터 현재까지의 기간을 나타내는 over the past year의 수식을 받는 문장의 동사 자리로, 뒤의 목적어 a dramatic decrease와 결합하여 '지난해 동안 급격히 줄어들었다'라는 의미를 나타내는 현재완료 시제 동사 (D) has seen이 정답이다.

어휘 | dramatic 급격한 complaint 불만, 불평 see 보다, 겪다

12 (B)

번역 | 오카다 씨가 영업 회의를 위해 인천에 도착했을 무렵, 그녀는 이미 전화상으로 사전 협상을 마친 상태였다.

해설 | 주절의 동사가 과거 이전의 일을 나타내는 과거완료 시제(had completed)이므로, 빈칸에는 '~했을 즈음에'라는 표현을 완성하는 과거 시제가 들어가야 한다. 따라서 (B) arrived가 정답이다.

어휘 | sales meeting 영업 회의 preliminary 예비의, 준비의 negotiation 협상

13 (D)

번역 | 실비아 조 씨는 지난주에 프리오 카운티 동물병원에서 교육을 마쳤고, 수의 간호사로서 일을 시작할 것이다.

해설 | Sylvia Cho가 등위접속사 and 앞뒤 절의 공통 주어이다. and 뒤에는 미래 시제가 쓰였지만 and 앞에는 과거를 나타내는 last week가 동사를 수식하므로 과거 시제 동사 (D) concluded가 정답이다.

어휘 | training 훈련, 교육 veterinary technician 동물병원[수의] 간호사 conclude 끝내다, 마치다

14 (B)

번역 | 문서를 고객들에게 발송하기 전에 반드시 꼼꼼하게 검토해야 한다.

해설 | <It(가주어) ~ that절(진주어)> 구문으로, that절이 반드시 해야 하는 일을 나타내면서 동사는 원형(be examined)을 사용했다. 따라서 '필수적인, 중요한'이라는 뜻의 (B) imperative가 정답이다. imperative, important, essential과 같은 형용사 뒤에 오는 that절의 동사는 <(should)+동사원형>이 된다.

어휘 | meticulously 세심하게, 꼼꼼하게 examine 살펴보다, 검토하다 immediate 즉각적인 ultimate 궁극적인 conclusive 결정적인

[15-18] 이메일

발신: 레티나, 소니아
날짜: 6월 18일 월요일 오전 9시 28분
수신: 회사 전 직원
제목: 환급 요청서 및 신용카드 영수증

안녕하세요, 여러분.

출장 경비 환급 요청서를 제출할 때 상세한 구매 영수증을 첨부해야 한다는 점을 기억해 주시기 바랍니다. 이 정책은 식사, 호텔, 비행기, 지상 교통수단 등의 비용에 ¹⁵적용됩니다. 신용카드 영수증만으로는 여러분이 구매한 실제 상품이나 서비스에 대한 전체 ¹⁶내역서를 제공하지 못합니다. 우리는 최근 출장 중에 개인 신용카드를 이용한 ¹⁷직원들의 환급 요청서를 여러 건 받았습니다. ¹⁸유감스럽게도, 그들은 신용카드 영수증만 제출했습니다. 우리는 이 구매 건들에 대한

항목별 영수증이 없는 한 환급 수표를 발행할 수 없습니다. 이 점을 유념해 주시기 바랍니다.

소니아 레티나, 회계 이사

어휘 | reimbursement 환급 request 요청 submit 제출하다 purchase 구입하다; 구입한 것 expense 비용 transportation 교통(편) goods 상품, 제품 issue 발급[발행]하다 itemized receipt 항목별 영수증

15 (A)

해설 | 빈칸은 주어인 This policy의 동사 자리이다. 출장 경비 환급 요청과 관련된 정책을 나타내는 문장이므로, 일반적인 사실을 설명할 때 쓰이는 단순 현재 시제 동사가 들어가야 자연스럽다. 따라서 This policy와 수가 일치하는 (A) applies가 정답이다.

16 (D)

해설 | 빈칸은 동사원형 provide의 목적어 역할을 하며 형용사 full의 수식을 받는 명사 자리이다. 앞에 한정사가 없으므로, 빈칸에는 불가산명사나 복수명사가 들어가야 한다. 따라서 '서류, 내역서'라는 의미의 불가산명사인 (D) documentation이 정답이다.

17 (D)

해설 | 빈칸은 전치사 from의 목적어 역할을 하는 명사 자리로, 관계사절 who used their personal credit cards의 수식을 받는다. 회사 직원(To: Company staff)을 대상으로 출장 경비 환급 요청서 제출 방법을 설명하는 과정에서 최근에 받았던 요청서에 대해 언급하고 있으므로, 빈칸에도 '직원'을 뜻하는 단어가 들어가야 자연스럽다. 따라서 (D) employees가 정답이다.

18 (B)

번역 | (A) 그러나 회사에서는 접대비를 환급해 주지 않습니다.
(B) 유감스럽게도, 그들은 신용카드 영수증만 제출했습니다.
(C) 대부분의 비용은 사무용품에 관한 것이었습니다.
(D) 직원들은 보통 출장 중에 개인 신용카드를 사용합니다.

해설 | 빈칸 앞 문장에서 최근 환급 요청서를 여러 건 받았다(We have received several reimbursement requests recently)고 했고, 뒤 문장에서 항목별 영수증이 없는 한 환급 수표를 발행할 수 없다(We cannot issue reimbursement checks ~ for these purchases)고 했다. 따라서 빈칸에는 서류가 미비한 환급 요청과 관련된 내용이 들어가야 문맥상 자연스러우므로, (B)가 정답이다.

어휘 | pertain to ~와 관련되다, ~에 속하다

Unit 09 to부정사와 동명사

① to부정사의 용법

ETS 유형 연습

1 (A) **2** (A) **3** (C)

1 (A)

번역 | 이 정부 프로그램의 목적은 학교에서 새로운 학습 기술을 더 잘 이용할 수 있도록 하는 것이다.

해설 | The purpose (of this government program)가 문장의 주어이고, is가 동사이며, 빈칸은 is의 보어 자리이다. 따라서 '~하는 것'의 의미로 is의 보어 역할을 할 수 있는 to부정사 (A) to provide가 정답이다.

어휘 | purpose 목적 access 접근, 이용 provide A with B A에게 B를 제공하다

2 (A)

번역 | 오늘 테노피 테크는 키토와 카라카스에서 태양 전지판을 제조하기 위해 셰플라이 에너지 시스템즈와의 제휴 계획을 발표했다.

해설 | 동사 announced의 목적어인 its plans를 수식하는 자리로 '제휴할 계획'이라는 의미를 나타내는 (A) to partner가 정답이다. 문장의 동사인 announced가 있기 때문에 동사인 (C), (D)는 오답이다.

어휘 | solar panel 태양 전지판 partner with ~와 제휴[협력]하다

3 (C)

번역 | 해외 고객들의 편의를 도모하기 위해 머제스키 그룹은 유럽과 아시아에 지사를 개설할 것이다.

해설 | in order to(~하기 위하여)는 '목적'을 나타내는 to부정사 표현이므로 동사원형 (C) accommodate가 정답이다. <so as to 동사원형>이나 <to 동사원형>을 써도 같은 의미이다.

어휘 | overseas 해외의 accommodation 숙박 시설, 편의 제공 accommodate ~의 편의를 도모하다

② to부정사의 활용

ETS 유형 연습
본책 p.185

1 (A) **2** (D) **3** (A)

1 (A)

번역 | 애니스크 제약은 임상 연구에 참가한 모든 사람들의 비밀을 유지하고자 모든 노력을 기울인다.

해설 | 문장의 동사 makes가 있으므로 동사인 (B), (C), (D)는 들어갈 수 없다. 문맥상 '~하기 위해 모든 노력을 한다'가 적합하므로 to부정사 형태인 (A) to maintain이 정답이다.

어휘 | make every effort to 동사원형 ~하기 위해 온갖 노력을 다하다 confidentiality 기밀성, 비밀성 clinical study 임상 연구 maintain 유지하다

2 (D)

번역 | 귀하의 청구를 신속히 처리할 수 있도록 모든 서신에 귀하의 고객 번호를 기입하여 주십시오.

해설 | 빈칸 뒤의 the processing을 목적어로 취하면서, '신속히 처리하기 위해서'라는 의미를 완성하는 (D) To expedite가 정답이다.

어휘 | processing 처리 claim 주장, 청구 customer identification number 고객 번호 correspondence 서신, 편지 expedite 신속히 처리하다

3 (A)

번역 | 그 이사는 전문성 개발 세미나가 다양한 분야에 종사하는 직원들의 견문과 전문 지식을 넓히는 데 도움이 될 수 있다고 확신하고 있다.

해설 | 동사 help는 목적어로 to부정사 또는 원형부정사를 취할 수 있다. 보기 중에서는 동사 help의 목적어 역할을 하는 동시에 뒤에 the knowledge and expertise를 목적어로 취할 수 있는 원형부정사 (A) broaden이 정답이다.

어휘 | professional 직업의, 전문적인 expertise 전문 지식[기술] area 분야, 부문 broaden 넓히다 broadly 대체로, 대체로 말해서 broad 넓은

③ 동명사

ETS 유형 연습
본책 p.186

1 (C) **2** (D) **3** (C)

1 (C)

번역 | 여러 해 동안 그 지방 정부는 레드 밸리를 야생 공원으로 지정하는 것을 고려해 왔다.

해설 | Red Valley를 목적어로 취하는 동시에 has considered의 목적어가 될 수 있는 동명사 (C) designating이 정답이다. consider(고려하다)는 동명사를 목적어로 취하는 타동사이다.

어휘 | consider 고려하다 wilderness 미개지, (자연이 보존된) 야생 지역 designate 지정하다, 선정하다 designation 지정, 지명

2 (D)

번역 | 발표 중에 청중의 주의력을 흐트러뜨리는 것을 피하기 위해 복잡한 레이아웃을 사용하지 마십시오.

해설 | to avoid의 목적어 자리로 빈칸에는 명사와 동명사 둘 다 올 수 있다. 빈칸 뒤에 your audience를 목적어로 취하는 동시에 avoid의 목적어 역할을 할 수 있는 동명사 (D) distracting이 정답이다. avoid는 동명사를 목적어로 취하는 타동사이다.

어휘 | avoid 피하다 complex 복잡한 layout 레이아웃, 지면 배정; 배치(도) distraction 마음이 흐트러짐, 주의 산만 distract (주의력을) 흐트러뜨리다, 산만하게 하다

3 (C)

번역 | 백스터 씨는 지원자들의 면접을 본 후 고용위원회의 모든 구성원들을 다시 만나고 싶어 한다.

해설 | after는 접속사와 전치사로 모두 쓰이지만 빈칸 뒤에 주어가 없으므로 이 문장에서는 전치사로 쓰인 것이다. 따라서 candidates를 목적어로 취하는 동시에 전치사 after의 목적어 역할을 할 수 있는 동명사 (C) interviewing이 정답이다.

어휘 | hiring committee 고용위원회 candidate (일자리의) 후보자, 지원자 interview 면접을 보다

④ to부정사 / 전치사 to

ETS 유형 연습
본책 p.187

1 (A) **2** (C) **3** (D)

1 (A)

번역 | 스위트니스 초콜릿은 8월 1일자로 공공증권거래소에 상장된다는 사실을 발표하게 되어 기쁩니다.

해설 | 앞의 pleased를 수식하는 자리로 문맥상 '발표하게 되어 기쁘다'라는 의미가 적절하므로 (A) to announce가 정답이다. <be pleased to 동사원형>의 형태로 기억하자.

어휘 | list (증권거래소에) 상장하다 as of ~일자로

2 (C)

번역 | 그 신문의 판매국은 훌륭한 서비스를 제공하는 데 전력을 다하고 있다.

해설 | be committed to(~에 전념[헌신]하다)의 to는 전치사이므로 뒤에 명사나 동명사가 올 수 있다. 따라서 뒤에 있는 excellent service를 목적어로 취하는 동시에 전치사 to의 목적어 역할을 할 수 있는 동명사 (C) providing이 정답이다.

어휘 | circulation department 판매국 provision 공급, 준비, 예비 provide 제공하다

3 (D)

번역 | 페어몬트 파이낸스 직원들 몇 명은 회사 구내에서 주차비를 청구하는 것에 반대한다.

해설 | object는 전치사 to와 함께 쓰이는 자동사로 to 뒤에 명사나 동명사가 올 수 있다. 문장의 주어인 employees는 청구를 받는 대상이므로 수동태 동명사인 (D) being charged가 정답이다.

어휘 | object to ~에 반대하다 parking 주차 premises (토지를 포함한) 건물, 구내 charge (요금을) 청구하다

● ETS 실전문제

본책 p.188

1 (B)	**2** (A)	**3** (D)	**4** (B)	**5** (D)	**6** (D)
7 (A)	**8** (C)	**9** (A)	**10** (A)	**11** (C)	**12** (B)
13 (B)	**14** (C)	**15** (A)	**16** (D)	**17** (B)	**18** (B)

1 (B)

번역 | 편집장 카이라 데일리는 <하넷 타임즈>의 배포 지역을 확장해 윌스턴 카운티를 포함시키도록 하는 계획을 확정했다.

해설 | 빈칸은 명사 Wilston County를 목적어로 취하면서, 동사 confirmed를 수식하는 역할을 한다. 따라서 '포함시키도록'이라는 의미를 나타내는 to부정사 (B) to include가 정답이다.

어휘 | editor-in-chief 편집장 expand 확장하다, 확대하다 distribution 배포, 보급, 배분 inclusive 포괄적인, 폭넓은 inclusion 포함

2 (A)

번역 | 모든 야외 프로그램은 사전 통보 없이 취소될 수 있다는 점에 유의하세요.

해설 | '~되기 쉽다, ~될 수 있다'라는 의미를 나타내는 be subject to에서 to는 전치사이므로 뒤에 명사나 동명사를 써야 한다. 빈칸 뒤에 목적어가 없으므로 명사 (A) cancellation이 정답이다. (B) canceling은 목적어가 필요한 타동사의 동명사이므로 오답이다.

어휘 | prior notice 사전 통보

3 (D)

번역 | 매출 증가를 처리하고자 인사부는 다수의 신입 사원을 모집할 계획이다.

해설 | a number of new employees를 목적어로 취하는 동시에 intends의 목적어 역할을 할 수 있는 to부정사 (D) to recruit가 정답이다.

어휘 | handle 다루다, 처리하다 increase in sales 매출[판매] 증가 human resources department 인사부 intend to ~할 작정이다 recruit (신입 사원 등을) 모집하다, 뽑다

4 (B)

번역 | 1,000명 이상의 참가자를 위한 국제 회의를 준비하는 것이 그 팀에게 가장 어려운 임무였다.

해설 | 빈칸 뒤의 명사구 an international conference를 목적어로 취하면서 동사 was의 주어 역할을 할 수 있는 동명사 (B) Preparing이 정답이다.

어휘 | challenging 까다로운, 어려운 assignment 임무, 과제

5 (D)

번역 | 유로산 엔터프라이지즈의 경영진은 고객 서비스를 위한 일련의 새로운 지침들을 마련하는 중이다.

해설 | 빈칸 뒤의 a new set of guidelines를 목적어로 취하면서 전치사 of의 목적어 역할을 할 수 있는 동명사 (D) establishing이 정답이다.

어휘 | be in the process of ~하는 중이다, ~하는 과정이다 guideline 지침, 정책 establish 제정하다, 확립하다

6 (D)

번역 | 아투어 사이틀링 임원진은 노르딕 자전거 라인 생산을 중단하기로 결정한 이유로 판매 부진을 들었다.

해설 | 빈칸은 명사구 the Nordique bicycle line을 목적어로 취하면서, 앞에 있는 명사 decision을 수식하는 역할을 한다. 따라서 '중단하려는 결정'이라는 의미를 완성하는 to부정사 (D) to discontinue가 정답이다.

어휘 | executive 경영진, 임원진 cite (이유·예를) 들다 slow sale 판매 부진 decision 결정 discontinue (생산을) 중단하다

7 (A)

번역 | 작가 유니스 킴은 11월 말에 턴햄에서 다섯 번째 강연을 하기로 예정되어 있다.

해설 | 빈칸 앞에 동사 is scheduled가 있고, 뒤에 목적어 her fifth lecture가 있다. 따라서 be scheduled와 함께 '~할 예정이다'라는 표현을 완성하는 to부정사 (A) to give가 정답이다.

어휘 | author 저자, 작가 give a lecture 강연하다

8 (C)

번역 | 그 컨설팅 회사는 소규모 회사들에게 맞춤형 마케팅 해결책들을 제공하는 책임을 맡고 있다.

해설 | 전치사 for의 목적어 자리에는 명사와 동명사가 올 수 있다. 빈칸 뒤의 customized marketing solutions를 목적어로 취하는 동시에 전치사의 목적어 역할을 할 수 있는 동명사 (C) offering이 정답이다.

어휘 | customized 맞춤형의 solution 해결책

9 (A)

번역 | 참석자들에게 미리 회의 의제를 배포하는 것이 대체로 가장 효과적이다.

해설 | 주어인 It은 가짜 주어로 빈칸 이하의 진짜 주어를 대신하고 있으므로 진짜 주어 역할을 할 수 있는 (A) to circulate가 정답이다.

어휘 | effective 효과적인 agenda 의제, 안건 attendee 참석자 in advance 미리, 사전에 circulate 배포하다, 배부하다

10 (A)

번역 | 영업부장은 팀원들과 신입사원들의 교육에 상당한 시간을 들인다.

해설 | spend는 <spend + 시간 / 돈 + (in) 동명사>의 구조로 쓰이므로, 빈칸은 생략된 전치사 in의 목적어 자리이다. 따라서 목적어 his team members and new employees를 취하면서 전치사의 목적어 역할을 할 수 있는 동명사 (A) training이 정답이다.

어휘 | considerable 상당한

11 (C)

번역 | 벤토 화장품의 최고경영자는 최근 해외 매출에서 발생한 문제점들이 그 회사의 장기적인 수출 계획에 영향을 미치지 않도록 했다.

해설 | 사역동사 let의 목적어인 the recent problems with foreign sales를 보충 설명하는 목적격 보어 자리이다. 사역동사는 동사원형을 목적격 보어로 취하므로 동사원형 (C) affect가 정답이다.

어휘 | CEO 최고경영자(Chief Executive Officer) cosmetics 화장품 long-term 장기적인 affect 영향을 미치다

12 (B)

번역 | 회사 정관은 중역들이 회사에 가장 이익이 되는 쪽으로 행동할 것을 요구한다.

해설 | 타동사 requires의 목적어인 its executives의 동작을 보충 설명하는 목적격 보어 자리이다. require는 to부정사를 목적격 보어로 취하므로 (B) to act가 정답이다.

어휘 | corporate charter 회사 정관 require 요구하다 in the best interest of ~의 이익을 최우선시하여, ~의 가장 큰 이익을 위해

13 (B)

번역 | 모든 무용수는 시립 발레단에 고려되기 위해서 최소 2년의 사전 경력이 있어야 한다.

해설 | 빈칸 앞에 완전한 절이 왔고, 뒤에는 동사원형이 있으므로, 빈칸에는 to부정사의 to가 들어가야 한다. 따라서 '고려되기 위해서는'이라는 의미를 완성하는 (B) in order to(~하기 위해)가 정답이다. (A) likewise와 (C) currently는 부사, (D) only if는 부사절 접속사이므로 구조상 빈칸에 들어갈 수 없다.

어휘 | prior 이전의 consider (채용 등에) 고려하다 currently 현재

14 (C)

번역 | 마셀로 앤 불 목공사는 공예를 배우는 데 관심이 많은 하계 견습생을 찾고 있다.

해설 | 빈칸은 명사구 the craft를 목적어로 취하면서, 전치사 in의 목적어 역할을 한다. 따라서 동명사 (C) learning이 정답이다.

어휘 | carpentry 목공업 seek 찾다 apprentice 수습생, 도제 craft 공예

[15-18] 광고

귀하는 사업주로서 상업 부동산과 물품에 대한 포괄적인 보장 보험을 갖고 있을 것입니다. 하지만 귀하나 귀하의 직원들이 출장을 가야 할 때 상업 자동차 보험도 필요하실 겁니다. 미란다 브라더스 자동차 보험은 귀사의 요구사항에 가장 잘 맞는 보험 약정을 ¹⁵설계할 수 있는 역량에 자부심을 갖고 있습니다. ¹⁶차량 보험에 가입함으로써 사고 시 차량 수리 또는 교체를 보장받으실 수 있습니다.

¹⁷모든 규모의 사업체들이 저희의 자동차 보장 보험으로 비용을 절약합니다. 보험 보장 약정은 직원들이 업무 목적으로 회사 차량을 이용하는지, 아니면 개인 차량을 이용하는지에 따라 달라집니다. ¹⁸두 가지 모두 허용하는 회사를 위한 약정도 제공합니다.

어휘 | probably 아마 comprehensive 포괄적인 insurance 보험 coverage 보장 (범위) commercial 상업적인 property 건물, 부동산, 재산 inventory 재고, 물품 목록 purpose 목적 pride oneself on ~를 자랑하다 meet the needs of ~의 요구에 부응하다 insure 보험을 들다 guarantee 보장하다 replace 교체하다 depending on ~에 따라

15 (A)

해설 | 빈칸은 명사구 an insurance plan을 목적어로 취하면서, 명사 ability를 수식하는 역할을 한다. 문맥상 '보험 약정을 설계할 수 있는 역량'이라는 의미가 되어야 자연스러우므로, to부정사 (A) to design이 정답이다. 참고로 ability, plan과 같은 명사는 to부정사의 수식을 받는다.

16 (D)

해설 | 광고하는 주체가 미란다 브라더스 자동차 보험사(Miranda Brothers' Auto Insurance)이므로, 이 회사의 보험 가입(insuring) 대상은 자동차여야 한다. 따라서 '차량'이라는 의미의 (D) vehicles가 정답이다.

어휘 | antique 골동품

17 (B)

번역 | (A) 미란다 형제는 20년 전 회사를 설립했습니다.
(B) 모든 규모의 사업체들이 저희의 자동차 보장 보험으로 비용을 절약합니다.
(C) 저희는 10년 전 우수상을 받았습니다.
(D) 저희는 최근 마케팅 부서장을 새로 채용했습니다.

해설 | 빈칸 뒤에서 업무용 차량의 소유주에 따라 보장 약정이 달라진다(Coverage plans vary depending on whether employees use company cars or their own cars for work purposes)고 했으므로, 빈칸에서 먼저 보험 관련 내용이 언급되어야 문맥상 자연스럽다. 따라서 (B)가 정답이다.

어휘 | found 설립하다 win an award 상을 받다

18 (B)

해설 | 명사 options를 한정 수식하는 형용사 자리이다. 앞에서 보험 보장 약정이 직원들이 업무 목적(work purposes)으로 회사 차량(company cars)을 이용하는지, 아니면 개인 차량(their own cars)을 이용하는지에 따라 달라진다는 두 가지 선택사항(options)을 언급했으므로, '둘 다'라는 의미의 (B) both가 정답이다.

어휘 | limited 한정된

Unit 10 분사와 분사구문

① 분사의 자리

ETS 유형 연습

| **1** (D) | **2** (A) | **3** (D) |

1 (D)

번역 | 에이브러햄 컨설팅 사는 중소기업들에게 맞춤형 인력 채용 방안을 제공하는 일을 전문으로 하고 있다.

해설 | 빈칸은 복합 명사를 수식하는 형용사 자리이므로 분사가 와야 한다. '맞춤화된 인력 채용 방안'이라는 수동적 의미를 나타내므로 과거분사 (D) customized가 정답이다. 문장에 동사 specializes가 있으므로 동사 (A), (B)는 오답이며, 동명사 또는 현재분사인 (C) customizing은 의미상 부적합하다.

어휘 | corporation 회사, 법인 specialize in ~을 전문으로 하다 staffing solution 인력 채용 방안 business 기업 customize 주문 제작하다 customized 주문 제작한, 맞춤형의

2 (A)

번역 | 우리 사무실 비서가 컴퓨터 파일을 백업해두었기 때문에 정전된 후에도 정보가 성공적으로 복구되었다.

해설 | be동사 뒤의 주격 보어 자리로, 주어인 the information은 복구되는 대상이므로 수동의 의미를 나타내는 과거분사 (A) recovered가 정답이다. 뒤에 목적어가 없으니 수동태로 접근하는 것도 좋다. 참고로, 이 문장에서 recover는 '복구하다'라는 타동사로 쓰여 수동태가 가능하지만, <recover from + 병(~로부터 회복하다)>과 같은 자동사 용법은 수동태가 불가능하다는 것도 알아두자.

어휘 | make a backup of ~을 백업해 두다 power failure 정전 recover 되찾다, 회복하다

3 (D)

번역 | 늦은 오후쯤 북동 지역에 거센 바람을 동반한 뇌우가 도달할 것으로 예상됩니다.

해설 | 빈칸은 전치사구 by gusty winds와 결합해 주어 A thunderstorm을 수식하는 자리이다. 따라서 수동의 의미를 내포한 과거분사 (D) accompanied가 정답이다.

어휘 | thunderstorm 뇌우, (우레를 동반한) 폭우 gusty (바람이) 거센, 갑자기 불어닥치는 accompany 동반하다, 딸리다

② 분사의 종류

ETS 유형 연습

| **1** (C) | **2** (C) | **3** (D) |

1 (C)

번역 | 엄청난 수의 티켓 예매에 근거하여, 올해 도니골 축제의 참석자가 기록적인 수치에 이를 것으로 예상된다.

해설 | 빈칸 뒤의 명사 number를 수식하는 자리로 '압도적인 수치'라는 능동 관계가 성립하므로 현재분사 (C) overwhelming이 정답이다.

어휘 | based on ~에 근거[입각]하여 advance ticket sales 티켓 예매 record 기록적인, 공전의 attendance 참석, 참석자 수 overwhelm 압도하다, 제압하다 overwhelming 압도적인, 엄청난 overwhelmingly 압도적으로

2 (C)

번역 | 사이먼 고급 가구점의 전화는 회사 제품들에 대해 해박한 지식을 갖춘 헌신적인 직원들이 받고 있습니다.

해설 | 빈칸은 명사 representatives를 수식해 주는 자리로, 문맥상 '헌신적인 직원'이라는 내용이 되어야 자연스럽다. 따라서 과거분사형 형용사인 (C) dedicated가 정답이다. 빈칸을 전치사 by 뒤의 동명사 자리로 착각하여 (D) dedicating을 선택하지 않도록 의미를 잘 따져 보아야 한다.

어휘 | phone line 전화선 house (회사명으로) 상점, 회사 staff ~에 직원을 두다, ~의 직원으로 근무하다 representative 대리인, (회사의) 직원 thorough 빈틈없는, 철저한 dedicate (시간·노력을) 바치다, 헌납[헌정]하다 dedicated 헌신적인, 전념하는

3 (D)

번역 | 쿠퍼 씨 부부는 시의 엄격한 건축 법규가 수용할 수 없을 정도로 좌절감을 주자 시의 경계를 벗어난 곳에 집을 짓기로 결정했다.

해설 | 빈칸은 2형식 동사 became의 주격 보어 역할을 하는 형용사 자리이다. (A) frustrated와 (D) frustrating이 각각 과거분사, 현재분사로 형용사 역할을 할 수 있지만, 주어인 사물명사 building codes는 감정을 유발하는 주체이므로 현재분사 (D) frustrating이 정답이다.

어휘 | city limits 시의 경계 rigid 엄격한 building code 건축 법규 accommodate 수용하다, 받아들이다 frustrate 좌절감을 주다 frustrating 좌절감을 주는, 짜증스럽게 하는

③ 분사의 활용

ETS 유형 연습

| **1** (D) | **2** (A) | **3** (D) |

1 (D)

번역 | 자재를 대량 생산하는 기업들에게는 충분한 창고 공간이 매우 중요하다.

해설 | large quantities of materials를 목적어로 취하는 동시에 빈칸 앞의 명사 companies를 수식할 수 있는 현재분사 (D) producing이 정답이다.

어휘 | adequate 충분한, 적당한 storage 저장, 보관, 창고 large quantities of 대량의 material 재료, 소재, 자재 produce 생산하다

2 (A)

번역 | <인터내셔널 데일리> 신문기자인 매튜스 씨는 추후 통보가 있을 때까지 특별 취재 임무를 수행하게 된다.

해설 | 빈칸 앞에는 전치사 on이 있고 뒤에는 전치사의 목적어인 명사 assignment가 있으므로 명사를 수식하는 형용사 (A) special이 정답이다. (D) specializing도 분사로서 형용사 역할을 할 수 있지만, '전문으로 하고 있는'이란 뜻으로 문맥에 어울리지 않는다.

어휘 | assignment 과제, (기자에게) 할당된 임무 further 추가의, 더 이상의 notice 공지, 통지 special 특별한, 특수한 specialize (in) ~을 전공하다, 전문으로 다루다

3 (D)

번역 | 오늘 오전에 우리가 전화 통화에서 논의했던 바와 같이, 폭스 씨는 3월 14일 수요일 오후 2시에 귀사의 공장에 도착할 것입니다.

해설 | 부사절 접속사 as가 과거분사와 결합하면 '~된 대로'라는 의미의 관용표현으로 쓰인다. '전화 통화에서 논의된 대로'라는 의미를 완성하는 과거분사 (D) discussed가 정답이다.

어휘 | discuss 논의하다, 상의하다 discussion 논의, 상의

④ 분사구문

ETS 유형 연습   본책 p.193

1 (D) **2** (A) **3** (A)

1 (D)

번역 | 올해 이 도시에는 이례적으로 많은 양의 비가 내려서 도로공사 계획들이 제때에 완료되기 어려워졌다.

해설 | 문장의 본동사인 has experienced가 있기 때문에 동사인 (B), (C)는 오답이고, 결국 분사인 (A)와 (D) 중에서 선택해야 하는 분사구문 문제이다. 빈칸 뒤에 목적어 it이 있으므로 능동태 구조의 현재분사인 (D) making이 정답이다.

어휘 | unusually 평소와는 달리, 이례적으로 rainfall 강우(량) road project 도로공사 계획 on time 제때에

2 (A)

번역 | 지난주 제품 설명회에 깊은 인상을 받은 운영부장은 핸디메이드의 가전제품 여러 개를 주문하기로 결정했다.

해설 | 콤마 앞에서 문장 전체를 수식하는 분사구문의 분사 자리로 주절의 주어인 the operations manager는 감명받는 대상이므로 과거분사 (A) Impressed가 정답이다. 부사절인 <Because he was impressed by ~>를 분사구문으로 바꾸면, <Being impressed by ~>의 형태가 되는데, 이때 Being은 생략 가능하다.

어휘 | product demonstration 제품 설명회 operations manager 운영부장 several 몇몇, 몇 개 appliance 가전제품 impressed 감명받은, 좋은 인상을 받은 impressive 인상적인 impression 인상, 느낌

3 (A)

번역 | 회계학 학위를 땄기 때문에 사카이 씨는 관리직의 가장 유력한 후보 중의 한 명으로 여겨진다.

해설 | 콤마 앞에서 문장 전체를 수식하는 분사구문의 분사 자리다. 빈칸 뒤에 목적어(a degree)가 있으며, 주절의 시제(is considered)보다 한 시제 앞서므로 능동태 완료 분사구문인 (A) Having earned가 정답이다. (C) Being earned는 수동태 분사구문으로 목적어를 취할 수 없다.

어휘 | degree 학위 accounting 회계(학) consider A B A를 B로 여기다 candidate (일자리의) 후보자, 지원자 management position 관리직 earn 얻다, 획득하다

● ETS 실전문제   본책 p.194

1 (C)   **2** (A)   **3** (A)   **4** (D)   **5** (B)   **6** (B)
7 (A)   **8** (C)   **9** (B)   **10** (C) **11** (C) **12** (A)
13 (C) **14** (D) **15** (A) **16** (D) **17** (D) **18** (C)

1 (C)

번역 | 챈두 박물관 정책에 따라, 건물에 두고 가서 1주일 이내에 찾아가지 않은 개인 물품은 모두 폐기될 것이다.

해설 | 빈칸은 that이 이끄는 관계사절의 주격 보어 자리로, 앞에 나온 선행사 any personal items를 보충 설명한다. 수거되지 않은 개인 물품은 폐기될 것이라는 내용이므로, 수동의 의미를 내포한 과거분사 (C) claimed가 정답이다.

어휘 | in accordance with ~에 따라, ~에 부합하여 policy 정책 claim (소유권 등을) 요구하다 discard 폐기하다, 버리다

2 (A)

번역 | 신입사원들은 아침 8시에 필요한 모든 서류를 가지고 배정된 교육 장소로 출근해야 한다.

해설 | 빈칸은 소유격 their와 복합명사 training locations 사이에서 training locations를 수식하는 형용사 자리다. '교육 장소'는 배정되는 대상이므로, 수동의 의미를 내포한 과거분사 (A) assigned가 정답이다.

어휘 | necessary 필요한 paperwork 서류 assign 배치하다, 배정하다

3 (A)

번역 | 해리슨 씨는 그 분야에서 뛰어난 업적으로 인정받은 경력이 오래된 인사 전문가다.

해설 | 빈칸은 명사구 a long-time human resources professional을 수식하는 역할을 한다. '인사 전문가'는 인정을 받는 대상이므로, 수동의 의미를 내포한 과거분사 (A) recognized가 정답이다.

어휘 | long-time 오랜 professional 전문직 종사자 outstanding 뛰어난, 두드러진 achievement 성취, 업적 recognize 인정하다

4 (D)

번역 | 고객들 대부분은 우리의 전시실이 더 큰 공간으로 이전한다는 기대감에 들떠 있다.

해설 | 빈칸은 주어 Most of our clients를 보충 설명하는 보어 자리이다. 전시실 이전으로 고객들이 기대감을 느끼게 된 것이므로, 수동의 의미를 내포한 과거분사 (D) excited가 정답이다.

어휘 | prospect 전망, 기대 showroom 전시실

5 (B)

번역 | 다음 주에 이 지역 시 의회 선거 출마자들이 TV에 출연하여 자신들의 구상을 발표할 것이다.

해설 | 빈칸 뒤의 their ideas를 목적어로 취하며 수식어 역할을 하는 현재분사 (B) introducing이 정답이다. 명사인 (A)를 쓰면 복합명사가 된다고 생각할 수 있지만, 빈칸 뒤에 소유격 their가 있으므로 어순상 적절하지 않다.

어휘 | candidate 출마자, 후보자 local 해당 지역의, 현지의 city council 시 의회 introduce 소개하다, 발표하다

6 (B)

번역 | 라벨 병원 방침에는 서면 동의 없이 환자의 개인 정보가 공개되지 않는다고 명시되어 있다.

해설 | 전치사 without의 목적어인 명사 consent를 수식하는 형용사 자리로 '서면으로 된 동의'라는 수동적 의미를 나타내는 과거분사 (B) written이 정답이다.

어휘 | state 진술하다, 표명하다 release 공개[발표]하다 consent 동의

7 (A)

번역 | 글로버 사의 경영진이 개편된 이후로 그 회사 제품의 품질이 많이 개선되었다.

해설 | 동사 has been의 주어인 the quality를 보충 설명하는 주격 보어 자리로 품질(quality)은 향상되는 대상이므로 수동적 의미를 나타내는 과거분사 (A) improved가 정답이다.

어휘 | restructure (조직·제도 등을) 개편하다, 구조 조정하다 improve 개선하다, 향상시키다 improvement 개선, 향상

8 (C)

번역 | 한 독자적인 여론조사 회사가 실시한 조사를 인용하며, <더 타운 보이스>는 주민들의 70퍼센트가 새 경기장 건설을 지지했다고 보도했다.

해설 | 빈칸은 by an independent polling firm과 결합하여 현재분사 Citing의 목적어인 a survey를 수식해주는 자리이다. 설문 조사는 실시되는 대상이므로, 수동의 의미를 내포한 과거분사 (C) conducted가 정답이다.

어휘 | cite 인용하다 survey 조사, 설문 조사 polling firm 여론조사 회사 in favor of ~을 찬성[지지]하여 stadium 경기장, 스타디움 conduct 실시하다, 수행하다 conductor 안내자, 지휘자

9 (B)

번역 | 귀하의 갤럭시 유리 접시류를 박스에 담아 보관할 때는 긁힌 자국이 생기지 않도록 먼저 부드러운 화장지로 감싸 주세요.

해설 | 부사절 접속사 When 다음에 주어가 생략되고 목적어 your Galaxy glass dishware가 왔으므로, 빈칸에는 능동적 의미를 내포한 현재분사가 들어갈 수 있다. 따라서 (B) storing이 정답이다.

어휘 | dishware 접시류, 식기류 wrap (포장지 등으로) 싸다, 포장하다 scratch 긁힌 자국[상처] store 보관하다

10 (C)

번역 | 고객들이 구매한 물건에 만족하지 못하면 30일 이내에 어떤 물품이든 반품할 수 있게 하는 것이 앨린튼 하드웨어 사의 정책이다.

해설 | 동사 are의 사람주어인 they(customers)를 보충 설명하는 주격 보어 자리로 사람은 주로 감정을 느끼는 대상이므로 과거분사 (C) satisfied(만족한)가 정답이다. (A) satisfactory (만족스러운, 만족시키는)는 주로 감정을 유발하는 주체인 사물명사와 함께 쓴다.

어휘 | purchase 구매(물품) satisfaction 만족 satisfy 만족시키다

11 (C)

번역 | 광화문 호텔의 숙박 시설과 서비스는 뛰어나서 연례회의 주최자들을 매우 기쁘게 했다.

해설 | 빈칸은 the organizers를 목적어로 취하는 동시에 콤마 앞에 있는 절을 수식하는 역할을 한다. 숙박 시설과 서비스가 훌륭해 주최자들을 기쁘게 했다는 내용이므로, 능동의 의미를 내포한 현재분사 (C) delighting이 정답이다.

어휘 | accommodation 숙박 시설 stellar 뛰어난 organizer 주최자 delight 매우 기쁘게 하다

12 (A)

번역 | 비행기가 연착되는 바람에 메디나 씨는 예정대로 기자들과의 간담회를 열 수 없었다.

해설 | 문맥상 '예정된 대로'라는 내용이 되어야 자연스러우므로, 수동의 의미를 내포한 과거분사 (A) scheduled가 정답이다. as 뒤에 (C), (D)와 같은 명사가 오는 경우에는 '~로서'라고 해석한다.

어휘 | due to ~ 때문에 arrival 도착 flight 비행, 항공편 as scheduled 예정대로, 계획대로 schedule 일정; 일정을 잡다

13 (C)

번역 | 윈튼 지역에서 이뤄지는 양질의 직업 교육 프로그램들이 그 지역 회사들에 적합한 인력을 확충시키고 있다는 고무적인 신호들이 많이 있다.

해설 | 동사 are의 사물주어인 signs를 수식하는 수식어 자리로 사물명사 signs는 주로 격려하는 주체이므로 현재분사 (C) encouraging이 정답이다. 과거분사 (B) encouraged는 격려를 받는 대상인 사람명사와 함께 쓴다.

어휘 | high-quality 양질의 qualified 적격인 encourage 장려하다

14 (D)

번역 | 주문이 제때에 도착하지 않을 것을 우려해서 챙 씨는 속달을 요청했다.

해설 | 콤마 앞에서 문장 전체를 수식하는 분사구문으로 원래의 부사절인 <Because she was concerned that ~>을 분사구문으로 바꾼 것이므로 과거분사 (D) Concerned가 정답이다. (C) Concerning은 '걱정을 시키는(형용사)', '~에 관하여(전치사)'라는 뜻으로 빈칸에 적절하지 않다.

어휘 | on time 시간에 맞게, 정각에 express delivery 속달

[15-18] 공지

개발 제안 관련 공지

셸턴 시는 미첼 브라더스 빌더스로부터 노스 컬럼비아 대로 6410번지에 ¹⁵위치한 부지에 아파트를 세우겠다는 건축 허가 신청서를 받았습니다. 건축 계획에는 환경 보호 구역과 겹치는 송전선 연결이 포함됩니다. 본 공지의 목적은 컬리 인근 거주자 및 제안된 행위와 이해관계가 있는 사람들에게 알리고자 하는 것입니다.

셸턴 시 환경 구역 내 모든 ¹⁶건축 행위는 용도지역제 조례 33.430장에 나오는 환경 개발 기준을 준수할 것입니다. 대중의 모든 의견과 질문은 헤이 가 62번지, 셸턴, 테네시 주 37201의 셸턴 시청

도시계획가 자라 웡에게 제출해 주시면 됩니다. ¹⁷또는 웡 씨의 사무실 615-555-0163으로 연락할 수 있습니다. ¹⁸제안 내용에 대한 대중의 모든 의견은 10월 31일까지입니다.

> 어휘 | development 개발 permit 허가 application 신청서 erect 세우다, 만들다 include 포함하다 utility line 송전선 overlap 겹치다, 포개어지다 protected 보호받는 environmental 환경의 purpose 의도, 목적 resident 거주자 neighborhood 인근 interested 이해관계가 있는 adhere to ~를 고수하다, 잘 지키다 standard 기준 zoning (도시 계획의) 지대 설정, 용도지역제 code 법규, 조례 submit 제출하다

15 (A)

해설 | 빈칸은 명사구 the site를 뒤에서 수식하는 역할을 한다. 건물 부지는 위치가 정해지는 대상이므로, 수동의 의미를 내포한 과거분사 (A) located가 정답이다.

16 (D)

해설 | 앞에서 셸턴 시가 건축 허가 신청서(a building permit application)를 받았다고 한 후, 해당 작업에 포함된 송전선이 환경 보호 구역과 겹치는 문제를 언급했다. 따라서 빈칸에는 환경 개발 기준(environmental development standards)을 준수해야 하는 행위를 나타내는 명사가 들어가야 하므로, (D) construction(건설, 건축)이 정답이다.

17 (D)

해설 | 빈칸 앞에서 대중의 의견과 질문은 웡 씨에게 제출되어야 한다며 우편 주소를 알려줬는데, 빈칸 뒤에서는 웡 씨의 사무실에 전화로도 연락할 수 있다며 또 다른 방안을 제시하고 있다. 따라서 대안을 제시할 때 쓰이는 '또는, 양자택일로'라는 의미의 (D) Alternatively가 정답이다.

18 (C)

번역 | (A) 부지는 6월부터 비어 있습니다.
　　　(B) 계획은 셸턴 시에 서면으로 제출되어야 합니다.
　　　(C) 제안 내용에 대한 대중의 모든 의견은 10월 31일까지입니다.
　　　(D) 미첼 브라더스는 6년 전 영업을 시작했습니다.

해설 | 빈칸 앞에서 대중이 의견과 질문(All comments and questions from the public)을 제출할 수 있는 방법을 나열했으므로, 빈칸에도 이와 관련된 내용이 언급되어야 문맥상 자연스럽다. 따라서 제출 기한을 언급한 (C)가 정답이다.

어휘 | vacant 비어 있는 in writing 서면으로 due ~하기로 되어 있는, 예정된

Unit 11　전치사와 접속사

① 전치사 어휘 1

ETS 유형 연습
본책 p.196

> **1** (A)　**2** (B)　**3** (A)

1 (A)

번역 | 클럽 회원들은 건강한 생활 세미나에 무료로 참석할 수 있다.

해설 | 전치사 문제이므로, 뒤에 오는 명사와 어울리는 것을 고른다. '무료로'에 해당하는 표현은 at no cost이므로 전치사 (A) at이 정답이다.

어휘 | allow 허용[허락]하다 attend 참석하다

2 (B)

번역 | 다니엘은 그룹 관리자에게 제출하기 전에 보고서에 실수가 있는지 점검할 것이다.

해설 | 빈칸의 목적어인 mistakes는 보고서를 점검하는(checking the report) 이유 / 목적이라고 볼 수 있으므로, 전치사 (B) for가 정답이다. <check A for B>는 'B에 대비해 A를 점검하다'라는 뜻으로 덩어리로 암기해 두는 것이 좋다.

어휘 | mistake 실수, 오류 submit 제출하다

3 (A)

번역 | 마리아 고메즈 씨는 새 환승 시스템에 대한 자신의 계획안을 시 이사회에 검토해 달라고 제출했다.

해설 | 의미상 '이사회에 계획안을 제출했다'라는 내용이 되어야 자연스러우므로, '~에(게)'라는 뜻의 (A) to가 정답이다.

어휘 | submit 제출하다 transit 통과, 환승 review 검토

② 전치사 어휘 2

ETS 유형 연습
본책 p.197

> **1** (B)　**2** (C)　**3** (C)

1 (B)

번역 | 그로브즈버그 역사 협회는 일요일을 제외하고 매일 현지의 사적지 견학을 실시한다.

해설 | 빈칸 뒤의 명사 Sunday를 목적어로 취하면서 문맥상 '일요일을 제외한 매일'을 의미하는 전치사 (B) except가 정답이다.

어휘 | historical site 사적지

2 (C)

번역 | 와타나신 씨를 제외한 그 팀의 모든 팀원들은 웹 디자인 지침서를 완성하는 데 추가 시간이 필요했다.

해설 | Ms. Wattanasin을 목적어로 취하면서 '와타나신 씨를 제외한'이라는 의미를 나타내는 전치사 (C) Apart from이 정답이다. 유사한 뜻의 except도 답이 될 수 있다.

어휘 | additional 추가적인 tutorial 지침서

3 (C)

번역 | 회사 환급 절차에 관한 정보를 받지 못했다면 인사과의 블랙웰 씨에게 연락하세요.

해설 | 빈칸 앞에 have not received라는 동사가 있기 때문에, 동사로 쓰일 수 있는 (A) regard와 (B) regards는 정답에서 제외한다. 빈칸 뒤에 company reimbursement procedures를 목적어로 취하면서 '~에 관하여'라는 의미를 나타내는 분사 형태의 전치사인 (C) regarding이 정답이다.

어휘 | personnel office 인사과 reimbursement 환급, 상환 procedure 절차, 방법 regard 여기다, 간주하다

③ 전치사와 접속사

ETS 유형 연습

1 (B) **2** (B) **3** (D)

1 **(B)**

번역 | 상세한 여행 일정표가 청구서와 함께 제출되지 않는다면 직원들은 출장 비용의 상환을 요청할 수 없다.

해설 | 빈칸 뒤에 <주어(a detailed itinerary) + 동사(is submitted)>가 있으므로 접속사인 (B) unless와 (D) while 중 하나를 선택해야 한다. 문맥상 '~하지 않는다면'이라는 뜻의 접속사가 필요하므로, (B) unless가 정답이다.

어휘 | repayment 상환(금) detailed 상세한 itinerary 여행 일정표 claim 청구 (신청)

2 **(B)**

번역 | 지난 6개월 동안 수익 감소를 겪었음에도 불구하고 모리 앤 맥키 사는 내년에 3명의 특허 전문 변호사를 신규 채용할 계획이다.

해설 | 전치사인 Despite 뒤에는 명사나 동명사가 올 수 있으므로 동명사 (B) having experienced가 정답이다. 동사인 (A), (C), (D)는 전치사 뒤에 올 수 없다.

어휘 | despite ~에도 불구하고 decline 감소, 하락 revenue 수익 intend to do ~하려고 의도하다 patent 특허

3 **(D)**

번역 | 일단 3개월의 수습 기간이 끝나면 직원들은 회사의 모든 복리후생 혜택을 누릴 자격이 생긴다.

해설 | 빈칸 뒤에 <주어 + 동사>가 있으므로 빈칸은 접속사 자리로 '일단 ~하면'이라는 의미의 부사절 접속사 (D) Once가 정답이다. 나머지 보기들은 모두 부사이다.

어휘 | probationary 수습의 complete 완성하다; 완전한 be eligible for ~할 자격이 있다 benefits 혜택, 복리후생

④ 등위 / 상관접속사

ETS 유형 연습

1 (A) **2** (C) **3** (A)

1 **(A)**

번역 | 해외용 카탈로그는 포괄적이지만, 특정 물품의 경우 모든 나라에서 이용 가능하지는 않을 수도 있다.

해설 | 절과 절을 연결하는 접속사가 필요한데, 앞뒤 내용이 역접 관계이므로 등위접속사 (A) but이 정답이다.

어휘 | comprehensive 종합적인, 포괄적인 available 이용할 수 있는, 얻을 수 있는

2 **(C)**

번역 | 회의 참가자들은 기차나 버스로 와이엇 호텔에 갈 수 있다.

해설 | or와 호응을 이루는 상관접속사 (C) either가 정답이다. <either A or B>는 'A 또는 B'라는 뜻이다. (B) both는 and와 어울려 쓰인다. (A) unless는 접속사이므로 뒤에 절이 필요하고, (D) without은 전치사이므로 뒤에 명사가 와야 한다.

어휘 | conference 회의, 학회 participant 참가자

3 **(A)**

번역 | 새로운 의료 보험 계약 조건에 대해 논의한 결과, 경영진과 직원 모두 만족했다.

해설 | and와 짝을 이루는 상관접속사 (A) both가 정답이다. (C)의 either는 <either A or B(A 또는 B 둘 중 하나)> 구문으로 쓰인다.

어휘 | terms 조건, 조항 health-benefits 의료 혜택(의), 의료보험(의) contract 계약, 약정 management 경영(진) satisfied 만족한

● ETS 실전문제

1 (B) **2** (D) **3** (C) **4** (B) **5** (A) **6** (C)
7 (C) **8** (B) **9** (C) **10** (D) **11** (B) **12** (B)
13 (B) **14** (A) **15** (C) **16** (B) **17** (D) **18** (C)

1 **(B)**

번역 | 개조 프로젝트 동안 A 건물 직원들은 B 건물 3층으로 옮겨갈 것이다.

해설 | 빈칸은 명사구 the renovation project를 목적어로 취하여 수식어 덩어리를 만드는 자리이므로, '~ 동안'이라는 의미의 전치사 (B) During이 정답이다.

어휘 | renovation 개조, 수리 relocate 이동시키다, 이전시키다

2 **(D)**

번역 | 마가렛 넬슨은 조직의 구조조정이라는 복잡한 과정 내내 회사를 이끌도록 고용되었다.

해설 | 빈칸 뒤의 목적어 the complicated process와 결합하여 '복잡한 과정 내내'라는 의미를 나타내는 전치사 (D) through가 정답이다.

어휘 | hire 고용하다 complicated 복잡한 process 과정 organizational 조직의 restructuring 구조조정

3 **(C)**

번역 | 피드백이나 제안을 보내고 싶은 고객은 동봉된 서식을 기입함으로써 그렇게 할 수 있다.

해설 | 동봉된 서식을 기입하는 것(filling out the enclosed form)은 피드백이나 제안을 제공하는 방법이므로, '~함으로써'라는 의미의 전치사 (C) by가 정답이다.

어휘 | provide 제공하다 suggestion 제안 fill out a form 서식을 기입하다, 양식을 작성하다 enclosed 동봉된

4 **(B)**

번역 | 구매자들은 검사비뿐만 아니라 부동산 거래를 완료하는 데 관련된 다른 비용들도 지불해야 한다.

해설 | 빈칸은 두 명사구 inspection fees와 other expenses를 연결하는 역할을 하므로, '~뿐만 아니라 ~도'라는 의미의 상관접속사 (B) as well as가 정답이다. (A) although는 부사절 접속사이므로 빈칸에 들어갈 수 없고, (C) according to(~에 따르면)는 문맥상 어색하므로 정답이 될 수 없다. (D) that is를 <주격 관계대명사 + be동사>로 보더라도 선행사인 fees와 동사 is의 수가 일치하지 않으므로 오답이다.

어휘 | inspection 검사 property transaction 부동산 거래

5 (A)

번역 | 그 세 가지 자선 프로그램은 공통점이 많음에도 불구하고 모금 방식에는 명백한 차이점이 존재한다.

해설 | 콤마 앞의 완전한 절을 이끄는 부사절 접속사 자리로 콤마 앞 부사절의 내용과 주절의 내용이 서로 상반되므로 양보의 부사절 접속사 (A) Although(~임에도 불구하고)가 정답이다. (B) Despite의 경우 의미는 같지만 전치사이므로 절을 이끌 수 없어 오답이다.

어휘 | unmistakable 명백한, 틀림없는 exist 존재하다 funding 자금, 자금 제공

6 (C)

번역 | 브리그 카운티 히스토리컬 컬렉션 내 대부분의 지도는 출판사의 허가 없이도 복사 가능하다.

해설 | 지도의 복사 가능 여부는 출판사의 허가(permission) 유무와 관련이 있으므로, '~ 없이'라는 의미의 (C) without이 정답이다.

어휘 | permission 허가 publisher 출판인[사] except ~를 제외하고 besides ~ 외에도, 게다가

7 (C)

번역 | 귀하의 행사에 앞서 저희 동료 중 한 명이 메뉴 선택 및 손님 수 확인 차 연락을 드릴 것입니다.

해설 | 빈칸은 명사구 your event를 목적어로 취하여 수식어 덩어리를 만드는 자리이다. 메뉴 선택 및 손님 수 확인(confirm menu choices and the guest count)은 행사 전에 이루어지는 행위이므로, '~에 앞서, ~ 전에'라는 의미의 전치사 (C) Prior to가 정답이다.

어휘 | associate 동료 confirm 확인해 주다 as long as ~하는 한

8 (B)

번역 | 보고서는 불충분한 광고나 노력 부족 모두 감소하는 판매량의 요인이 아니었음을 나타내고 있다.

해설 | 빈칸 앞에 neither와 짝을 이루어 'A와 B 둘 다 아니다'라는 의미를 나타내는 (B) nor가 정답이다.

어휘 | insufficient 불충분한 lack 부족 effort 노력 factor 요소

9 (C)

번역 | 그 장비는 설명서대로 작동하지 않았기 때문에 기술부서로 반송되었다.

해설 | 콤마 앞의 완전한 절을 이끄는 부사절 접속사 자리로 내용상 '장비가 작동하지 않았기 때문에'라는 이유를 나타내는 부사절 접속사 (C) Because가 정답이다. (D) Due to도 같은 뜻이지만 전치사이므로 뒤에 명사가 와야 한다.

어휘 | function 작동하다 specification 설명서 ship 보내다, 배송하다 engineering (공학) 기술

10 (D)

번역 | 하모니 홈 굿즈의 할인 및 프로모션 관련 정보를 받고 싶지 않은 고객은 계정 설정을 변경하면 된다.

해설 | 빈칸은 명사구 sales and promotions를 목적어로 취하면서 앞에 나온 명사 information을 수식하는 역할을 하므로, 현재분사 또는 전치사가 들어갈 수 있다. 따라서 '~에 관한'이라는 의미의 분사형 전치사 (D) regarding이 정답이다.

어휘 | account 계정

11 (B)

번역 | 멜링턴 어소시에이츠 사무실 관리자는 복사기를 대여하는 대신 구입하기로 결정했다.

해설 | 복사기의 구매(to purchase)와 대여(leasing) 중 하나를 선택하는 상황에 어울리는 전치사가 빈칸에 들어가야 하므로, '~ 대신에'라는 의미의 (B) instead of가 정답이다.

어휘 | decide 결정하다, 결심하다 purchase 구입하다 photocopier 복사기 lease 임대하다, 대여하다 with regard to ~에 관해 according to ~에 따르면 on behalf of ~를 대표하여

12 (B)

번역 | 그 지역 중심부에 위치한 몬카르크 마을은 아름다운 자연과 매력적인 건축물을 모두 지니고 있다.

해설 | 빈칸 뒤의 and와 짝을 이루어 'A와 B 모두'라는 의미를 나타내는 (B) both가 정답이다.

어휘 | province 지방, 지역 architecture 건축물

13 (B)

번역 | 후르비츠 여행복은 가벼운 소재의 의류를 제공하는 것 외에도 멋진 여행 가방과 액세서리를 판매한다.

해설 | 빈칸 뒤의 동명사 구문 offering lightweight clothing을 목적어로 취하면서 문장 전체를 수식하는 전치사 자리로 '가벼운 소재의 의류를 제공하는 것 외에도'라는 의미를 나타내는 전치사 (B) Besides가 정답이다.

어휘 | lightweight 가벼운 stylish 유행을 따르는, 멋진 luggage 여행 가방 accessory 액세서리, 부속물

14 (A)

번역 | 도급업체 직원은 건축 장비가 부족함에도 불구하고 코스트랜드 파크웨이에서의 작업을 완료할 수 있었다.

해설 | 빈칸은 명사구 the shortage of construction equipment를 목적어로 취하여 수식어 덩어리를 만드는 자리이다. 장비가 부족했음에도 작업을 완성했다는 내용이므로, '~에도 불구하고'라는 의미의 전치사 (A) despite가 정답이다.

어휘 | contractor 계약자, 도급업체 complete 완료하다 shortage 부족 equipment 장비

[15-18] 정보문

> **자원봉사자 구인**
>
> 공공보건서비스(PHS)에서는 그레이어슨 대학교 주말 취업박람회 [15]동안 안내 부스에서 자원봉사를 할 12명의 직원을 구합니다. 행사는 4월 13일과 14일 오전 10시부터 오후 6시까지 열립니다. 자원봉사자들은 4시간 교대 근무로 일하며 [16]학생들에게 취업 기회, 학력 요건, 승진 기회 등에 관해 알려줄 것입니다. 또한 PHS의 활동에 대해 논의하고 [17]그들의 일상적인 업무에 관해 설명할 것입니다. [18]자원봉사자는 무료 점심을 제공받게 됩니다. 행사 전에 1시간의 교육이 있을 겁니다. 관심이 있는 직원은 htpps://phs.employees.site.com/grayerson_cfw에서 찾을 수 있는 양식을 작성하면 됩니다.

어휘 | volunteer 자원봉사자; 자원봉사를 하다 seek 찾다, 구하다
career fair 취업박람회 opportunity 기회 educational
교육의, 교육과 관련된 requirement 요건 possibility 가능성
advancement 발전, 승진 activity 활동 describe 설명하다
typical 일상적인 in advance of ~에 앞서

15 (C)

해설 | 빈칸이 목적어로 취하는 행사명(Grayerson University's Career Fair Weekend)에 기간을 나타내는 단어가 있으며, 문맥상 '취업박람회 동안'이라는 내용이 되어야 자연스러우므로, (C) during(~ 동안)이 정답이다.

16 (B)

해설 | 그레이어슨 대학교 주말 취업박람회에서 자원봉사 하는 직원들의 역할을 설명하고 있으므로, 정보를 제공받는(inform) 대상은 학생들이 되어야 문맥상 자연스럽다. 따라서 (B) students가 정답이다.

어휘 | contestant 대회 참가자

17 (D)

해설 | 빈칸은 전치사 in의 목적어 역할을 하는 명사 job을 한정 수식하는 자리이다. 자원봉사자들이 자신들의 일상적인 업무를 설명할 것이므로, 복수형 소유격인 (D) their가 정답이다.

18 (C)

번역 | (A) 자원봉사자는 발표 후에 제안을 할 것입니다.
(B) 자원봉사자는 정책을 읽었음을 명시해야 합니다.
(C) 자원봉사자는 무료 점심을 제공받게 됩니다.
(D) 자원봉사자는 해마다 온라인으로 재등록해야 합니다.

해설 | 빈칸 앞에서 자원봉사자가 행사에서 할 일을 언급했고, 뒤에서는 전에 자원봉사자를 대상으로 하는 교육(coaching session)이 있을 것이라고 했으므로, 빈칸에도 행사와 관련된 일반적인 공지가 들어가야 문맥상 자연스럽다. 따라서 자원봉사자들에게 제공되는 식사 혜택을 안내한 (C)가 정답이다. 발표/정책/등록 관련 내용은 앞서 언급되지 않았으므로, (A), (B), (D)는 부적절하다.

어휘 | suggestion 제안 following ~ 후에 presentation 발표 indicate 명시하다 policy 정책 complimentary 무료의 re-register 재등록하다

Unit 12 부사절 접속사

① 시간, 조건의 부사절

ETS 유형 연습

본책 p.202

1 (C)   2 (A)   3 (A)

1 (C)

번역 | 댓웨일러 앤 어소시에이츠의 보험 전문가들은 고객들과 일을 시작하기 전에 3개월간 집중 교육을 받는다.

해설 | 빈칸의 앞뒤에 주어와 동사를 갖춘 두 개의 절이 각각 나오므로 이 두 절을 연결할 접속사가 필요하다. 따라서 부사인 (A) rather와 (D) nearly는 답에서 제외시킨다. (B) whereas는 서로 상반되는 두 절을 연결하는 접속사인데, 이 문장에서는 보험 전문가가 집중

교육을 받는 것과 고객과 일을 시작하는 것이 상반된 내용이라고 볼 수 없다. 따라서 '~하기 전에'라는 뜻의 부사절 접속사 (C) before가 정답이다.

어휘 | insurance 보험 specialist 전문가 intensive 집중적인 client 고객 rather 오히려, 차라리 whereas ~이지만, ~인 반면에 nearly 거의

2 (A)

번역 | 교육 기간이 지속되는 동안 신입 사원들은 초봉의 60퍼센트를 받을 것이다.

해설 | 빈칸 뒤에 <주어(the training period)+동사(continues)>가 나오므로 절을 이끄는 부사절 접속사 (A) As long as(~하는 한)가 정답이다.

어휘 | training (직업상의) 교육, 연수 starting salary 초봉

3 (A)

번역 | 어떤 조치가 취해지지 않는 한, 윈필드 파크웨이의 교통 혼잡은 계속 악화될 것이다.

해설 | 빈칸 뒤에 <주어(something)+동사(is done)>가 나오므로, 절을 이끌 수 있는 부사절 접속사 (A) Unless가 정답이다. (C) Except (that)도 절을 이끌 수 있지만 문맥상 어색하다.

어휘 | traffic congestion 교통 혼잡 worsen 악화되다 unless ~하지 않는 한 except ~을 제외하고 therefore 그러므로

② 양보, 이유, 목적의 부사절

ETS 유형 연습

본책 p.203

1 (A)   2 (B)   3 (D)

1 (A)

번역 | 켄달 사는 단 9개월밖에 영업하지 않았지만 아주 빠르게 수익을 내고 있다.

해설 | 완전한 절을 이끌면서 '9개월밖에 안 되었음에도 불구하고'라는 양보의 의미를 나타내는 부사절 접속사 (A) Although가 정답이다.

어휘 | profitable 수익이 나는

2 (B)

번역 | 그 밴드에서 마침내 가능하다고 확인해 주었으므로 야외 공연은 6월 11일 일요일에 열릴 예정이다.

해설 | 완전한 절을 이끌면서 '확인해 주었으므로'라는 이유를 나타내는 부사절 접속사 (B) Now that이 정답이다. (C) So that도 부사절 접속사로 사용하지만, 목적을 나타내므로 문맥상 이 문장의 첫머리에서는 사용할 수 없다.

어휘 | confirm 확인하다 availability 가용성, 이용할 수 있음

3 (D)

번역 | 박 씨는 테크니플렉스 사에서 5년간 근무하면서 어려운 일에 직면했을 때 탁월한 능력을 발휘한다는 점을 거듭 보여주었다.

해설 | when 뒤에 <주어(he)+be동사(is)>가 생략된 구문으로, 전치사 with와 함께 '~에 직면하다'라는 표현을 완성하는 과거분사 (D) faced가 정답이다. 참고로, 타동사 face는 직접목적어를 취하거나, <be faced with A> 구조로 쓰인다.

어휘 | demonstrate 입증하다, 보여주다 repeatedly 반복해서, 거듭 excel 능력이 뛰어나다, 탁월하다 challenge 도전, 어려운 일

● ETS 실전문제

본책 p. 204

1 (D)	**2** (A)	**3** (B)	**4** (B)	**5** (A)	**6** (D)
7 (A)	**8** (B)	**9** (B)	**10** (D)	**11** (A)	**12** (B)
13 (B)	**14** (B)	**15** (C)	**16** (B)	**17** (A)	**18** (D)

1 (D)

번역 | 콜드웰 컴퓨터스는 상품이 포장재에서 꺼내지지 않았다면 반품을 받아준다.

해설 | 문맥상 '상품이 포장재에서 꺼내지지 않았다면'이라는 조건을 나타내야 자연스러우므로 '~하는 한, ~이면 하면'이라는 뜻의 접속사 (D) as long as가 정답이다. (A) in order that(~을 위해)과 (C) in case(~인 경우에 대비해)는 의미상 부적절하다. (B) such as(~와 같은)는 목적어를 취하는 전치사 기능을 하므로 빈칸에 들어갈 수 없다.

어휘 | accept 받다, 수락하다 remove 꺼내다, 제거하다 packaging 포장재

2 (A)

번역 | 첸 씨에게 내일 해외 사무소에서 오는 방문객들이 참석할 수 있도록 회의 일정이 변경되었다고 통보해 주세요.

해설 | 완전한 절을 이끄는 접속사 that과 결합하여 '참석할 수 있도록'이라는 목적을 나타내는 (A) so가 정답이다. '~하기 위해서'란 의미의 <so that+주어+동사>는 <in order that+주어+동사>로 바꿔 쓸 수 있다.

어휘 | notify 통보하다 reschedule 일정을 변경하다 overseas 해외의 concerning ~에 관한

3 (B)

번역 | 오늘 오후의 바로셀로나행, 런던행, 로마행 비행편은 목적지의 악천후 때문에 모두 연착했다.

해설 | 빈칸 뒤의 명사 inclement weather를 목적어로 취하면서 앞의 have been delayed를 수식하는 전치사 자리로 '악천후 때문에'라는 의미를 나타내는 전치사 (B) due to가 정답이다. 부사절 접속사 (C) now that(~ 때문에)과 (D) only if(~의 경우에 한해서)는 뒤에 완전한 절이 이어져야 한다. 전치사 (A) as for(~에 관해서)는 의미상 적합하지 않다.

어휘 | flight 비행편 delay 미루다, 연기하다; 지연, 지체 inclement (날씨가) 험한 destination 목적지, 도착지

4 (B)

번역 | 퍼스트 리저널 은행은 주니퍼에서 아주 좋은 성과를 내었기 때문에 파인우드와 노스 헤이븐에 지점을 열 예정이다.

해설 | 빈칸은 완전한 절을 이끄는 접속사 자리로, 해당 절은 콤마 뒤 주절을 수식한다. 주니퍼에서 아주 좋은 성과를 낸 것이 원인, 지점을 추가로 여는 것은 결과라고 볼 수 있으므로, '~ 때문에'라는 의미로 쓰일 수 있는 부사절 접속사 (B) Since가 정답이다.

어휘 | rather 오히려, 차라리 therefore 그러므로

5 (A)

번역 | 디어필드 오케스트라 지휘자가 은퇴한다는 공지를 받은 이후로, 이사회에서는 후임자를 찾고 있다.

해설 | 빈칸 뒤의 분사구문 receiving notice를 이끌면서 콤마 뒤의 완전한 문장을 수식하는 부사절 접속사 자리로 '통지를 받은 이래로'라는 의미를 나타내는 (A) Since가 정답이다. 참고로, 해당 부분은 <전치사 Since+동명사> 구문으로 볼 수도 있다.

어휘 | notice 공지, 안내문 director 감독, 지휘자 retire 은퇴하다 board of directors 이사회 replacement 대신할 사람, 후임자

6 (D)

번역 | 윈스럽 씨가 비록 영업 분야에서의 경험은 적지만, 활동적이고 단호하며 논리정연한 사람이어서 성공할 것이다.

해설 | 완전한 절을 이끌면서 '제한된 경험에도 불구하고'라는 양보의 의미를 나타내는 부사절 접속사 (D) even though가 정답이다. 부사 (A) already와 (B) perhaps는 절을 이끌 수 없다. 부사절 접속사 (C) as far as(~하는 한)는 의미상 적합하지 않다.

어휘 | dynamic 활동적인, 활력 있는 determined 결연한, 단호한 articulate 명료한, 논리정연한 limited 제한된, 한정된

7 (A)

번역 | 현재 릿지 제조사 지점에서 근무하는 직원들은 일단 건물이 완공되면 새로 지은 본사로 이사할 것이다.

해설 | 완전한 절을 이끌면서 '건물이 완공되면'이라는 조건의 의미를 나타내는 부사절 접속사 (A) once가 정답이다. (B) even(평평한; 심지어)은 형용사/부사, (D) moreover(더욱이)는 부사, (C) besides(~ 외에도; 게다가)는 전치사/부사로 뒤에 완전한 절을 이끌 수 없다.

어휘 | currently 현재 branch 지사 headquarters 본사

8 (B)

번역 | 이번 달 소식지는 직원들이 아직 새 출판 소프트웨어 사용을 배우고 있어서 미뤄질 예정이다.

해설 | 빈칸은 완전한 절을 이끄는 접속사 자리로, 해당 절이 앞에 나온 주절을 수식한다. 직원들이 아직 사용 방법을 배우고 있는 것(staff members are still learning to use)은 소식지가 지연되는 원인이라고 볼 수 있으므로, (B) because가 정답이다.

어휘 | newsletter 소식지 delay 미루다, 지연시키다 publishing 출판, 발행 in case of ~의 경우

9 (B)

번역 | 휴가 기간이 직무 분류에 따라 미리 결정되지 않는 한, 휴가 요청서 제출 마감기한은 1월 15일입니다.

해설 | 빈칸은 완전한 절을 이끄는 접속사 자리로, 해당 절이 콤마 앞 주절을 수식한다. 따라서 빈칸에는 부사절 접속사가 들어가야 하므로, '~하지 않는 한'이라는 의미의 (B) unless가 정답이다.

어휘 | submit 제출하다 request 요청 predetermine 미리 결정하다 based on ~에 따라 classification 분류 thus 그러므로 besides 게다가 despite ~에도 불구하고

10 (D)

번역 | 회사가 초기에는 난관에 직면했지만 지금은 전국 최대의 식물성 화장품 제조업체로 성공을 거두었다.

해설 | 완전한 절을 이끌면서 '초기에 난관에 직면했다 하더라도'라는 양보의 의미를 나타내는 부사절 접속사 (D) Although가 정답이다. 부사절 접속사 (B) Unless(~가 아니라면), (C) Whatever(어떤 ~라도)는 의미상 적합하지 않다. 부사인 (A) Instead(대신에)는 주어와 동사가 두 개씩 있는 문장의 맨 앞에는 올 수 없으므로 오답이다.

어휘 | face 직면하다 hardship 난관, 곤경 initially 초기에, 처음에 find success 성공을 거두다 manufacturer 제조업체 plant-based 식물성의 cosmetics 화장품

11 (A)

번역 | 트럭 적재량은 처음에 너무 무겁다고 생각됐지만 주 지침에 충분히 부합하고도 남았다.

해설 | 부사절 접속사 Although 다음에 <주어(the truck's load)+be동사(was)>가 생략된 구문으로, 빈칸에는 분사가 들어갈 수 있다. '적재량이 너무 무겁다고 생각됐지만'이라는 내용이 되어야 자연스러우므로, 수동의 의미를 내포한 과거분사 (A) believed가 정답이다.

어휘 | initially 처음에 state 국가(의), 주(의) guideline 지침

12 (B)

번역 | 저희 회사는 고객 문의를 많이 받기 때문에 귀하의 문의에 응답하기 전에 2~3일 정도 소요될 수 있습니다.

해설 | 완전한 절을 이끌면서 '응답하기 전에'라는 시간의 의미를 나타내는 부사절 접속사 (B) before가 정답이다. 부사절 접속사 (A) if(~한다면)와 (C) while(~ 동안, ~인 반면에)은 의미상 적합하지 않다.

어휘 | volume 양, 분량 inquiry 문의 respond to 응답하다

13 (B)

번역 | 탑승객은 국경을 넘는 기차를 탈 때 사진이 부착된 신분증을 제시해야 한다.

해설 | 빈칸은 분사구문(boarding trains)을 이끄는 부사절 접속사 자리로, 빈칸 뒤에 <주어(they)+be동사(are)>가 생략되어 있다. 신분증 제시(present photo identification)는 탑승할 때 행해지는 것이므로, (B) when이 정답이다.

어휘 | passenger 승객 present 제시하다, 보여주다 identification 신분증, 신원 증명 board 탑승하다 border 국경

14 (B)

번역 | 허브 엠포리엄 온라인에서 주문한 상품들은 전액 완납 시까지 운송되지 않는다는 점에 유의하시기 바랍니다.

해설 | 완전한 절을 이끌면서 '수령될 때까지'라는 시간의 의미를 나타내는 부사절 접속사 (B) until이 정답이다. <not ~ until...>은 '...하고 나서야 ~하다'라는 의미로 주로 쓰이므로 한 덩어리로 외워 두자.

어휘 | note 유의하다, 주목하다 payment 지불 (금액)

[15-18] 사용 설명서

CM200 전자레인지는 여러분의 주방, 거실, 또는 사무실에 손쉽게 둘 수 있습니다. 전자레인지를 주방 조리대나 튼튼한 탁자와 같은 평평한 표면에 올려 놓으십시오. 중요한 점은 공기가 전자레인지 주변으로 ¹⁵막힘없이 흐르도록 하는 것입니다. 전자레인지의 측면, 상단 및 후면 주변으로 적어도 10cm의 공간이 있어야 합니다. 전자레인지를 폐쇄된 공간에 ¹⁶설치하지 마십시오. 가스레인지나 전기레인지 위에 놓지 마십시오. ¹⁷요리하는 동안 모든 통풍구를 열어두십시오. 이렇게 하는 이유는 전자레인지가 켜진 ¹⁸후 공기가 빠져 나갈 곳이 막히게 되면 자동으로 꺼지기 때문입니다.

어휘 | microwave oven 전자레인지 family room 거실 flat 평평한 countertop 조리대 sturdy 튼튼한, 단단한 flow 흐르다 at least 적어도 enclosed 폐쇄된, 둘러싸인 electric 전기의 blocked 막힌 air exit 공기 출구 shut down 꺼지다 turn on 켜다

15 (C)

해설 | 빈칸 앞의 동사 flow를 수식할 부사가 필요하므로 (C) freely가 정답이다. 나머지 (A) freedom(자유)은 명사, (B) freer(더 자유로운)는 형용사의 비교급, (D) freeing(자유롭게 하기)은 동명사이므로 모두 품사 면에서 부적합하다.

16 (B)

해설 | 빈칸 앞에서 공기가 막힘없이 흐르는 것이 중요하다며 전자레인지 주변에 공간이 필요하다는 점을 강조했다. 따라서 해당 부분은 폐쇄된 공간(enclosed space)에 설치하지 말라는 내용이 되어야 자연스러우므로, (B) install(설치하다)이 정답이다.

17 (A)

번역 | (A) 요리하는 동안 모든 통풍구를 열어 두십시오.
(B) 포장 음식을 조리할 때 모든 지시사항을 지켜 주십시오.
(C) 어떤 액체라도 전자레인지를 사용해 끓이지 마십시오.
(D) 한 번에 두 개 이상의 접시를 전자레인지에 넣지 마십시오.

해설 | 빈칸 뒤에서 '이렇게 하는 이유는 공기가 빠져나갈 곳이 막히게 되면 자동으로 꺼지기 때문이다(The reason for this is that ~ the oven to shut down automatically)'라고 주의를 주었으므로, 빈칸에서 '이렇게 하는 것', 즉 통풍을 원활하게 하는 방법이 언급되어야 문맥상 자연스럽다. 따라서 (A)가 정답이다.

어휘 | vent 통풍구 follow 지키다, 따르다 packaged meal 포장 음식 boil 끓이다 liquid 액체

18 (D)

해설 | 빈칸은 완전한 절을 이끄는 접속사 자리이다. 문맥상 '켜진 후에'라는 내용이 되어야 자연스러우므로, (D) after가 정답이다. (A) from은 전치사, (B) next는 형용사/부사로 완전한 절을 이끌 수 없다. (C) like의 경우 '~대로, ~인 것처럼'이라는 뜻의 접속사로 쓰일 수 있지만 의미상 어색하다.

Unit 13 관계대명사

① 관계대명사의 종류

ETS 유형 연습   본책 p.206

1 (D) **2** (B) **3** (D)

1 (D)

번역 | 새로운 경비 보고 절차에 의문이 있는 관리자들은 예산 담당 사무실에 연락해 도움을 요청해야 한다.

해설 | 빈칸은 문장의 주어 Supervisors를 수식하는 관계사절을 이끄는 동시에, 관계사절에서는 동사 have의 주어 역할을 한다.

따라서 사람을 대신하는 주격 관계대명사 (D) who가 정답이다.

어휘 | supervisor 감독자, 관리자 expense 경비 process 과정, 절차 budget 예산 assistance 지원, 도움

2 (B)

번역 | 풍 앤 하스 사는 생산 시간의 절반 이상을 차지했던 치약 혼합 공정을 자동화했다.

해설 | 빈칸은 문장의 목적어 its toothpaste mixing processes에 대해 부연 설명하는 관계사절을 이끄는 동시에, 관계사절에서는 동사 used to take up의 주어 역할을 한다. 따라서 사물을 가리키는 주격 관계대명사 (B) which가 정답이다.

어휘 | automate 자동화하다 toothpaste 치약 process 공정, 과정

3 (D)

번역 | 메트로폴리탄 아트웍스는 트윈 강 지역의 공공 미술 프로젝트를 지원하는 것이 임무인 단체이다.

해설 | 빈칸은 문장의 보어 organization을 수식하는 관계사절을 이끄는 동시에, 관계사절의 주어 mission을 한정 수식하는 역할을 한다. organization과 mission은 '조직의 임무'라는 소유 관계를 나타내므로, 소유격 관계대명사 (D) whose가 정답이다.

어휘 | mission 임무, 사명 support 지원하다

② 관계대명사의 생략

ETS 유형 연습
본책 p.207

1 (A) **2** (B) **3** (C)

1 (A)

번역 | 프로빈스 은행 고객들은 온라인 뱅킹 이용에 사용하는 암호를 매년 갱신하시기 바랍니다.

해설 | 빈칸 앞에 명사, 뒤에는 타동사와 전치사구가 있으므로 빈칸 앞에 목적격 관계대명사가 생략되어 있음을 알 수 있다. 따라서 관계사절에서 동사 use의 주어 역할을 하는 대명사가 빈칸에 들어가야 하므로, (A) they가 정답이다.

어휘 | be requested to do ~하도록 요청받다 update 업데이트하다, 갱신하다 annually 매년 password 패스워드, 암호

2 (B)

번역 | 마케팅 부장에 의해 검토된 모든 사업 계획서 중에서 마틴 씨의 안이 가장 인상적이다.

해설 | 빈칸은 by the marketing manager와 결합해 수동의 의미를 나타내며 명사 plans를 수식해주는 자리이다. 따라서 '검토된'이라는 뜻의 과거분사 (B) reviewed가 정답이다. 참고로, 빈칸 앞에는 <주격 관계대명사(that / which)+be동사(were)>가 생략된 것으로 볼 수 있다.

어휘 | impressive 인상 깊은

3 (C)

번역 | 스프링든 정부는 임대 부동산 소유주들이 세입자들에게 재활용 서비스를 제공하도록 요구하는 규정을 공표했다.

해설 | 빈칸은 owners를 목적어로 취하며, 앞의 명사 regulations를 수식하는 자리이다. 따라서 '소유자들에게

요구하는 규정'이라는 능동적 의미를 나타내는 현재분사 (C) requiring이 정답이다.

어휘 | publish 공표하다, 발행하다 regulation 규칙, 규정 rental 임대 property 부동산, 재산 recycling 재활용 tenant 세입자 require 요구하다

③ 관계대명사의 활용

ETS 유형 연습
본책 p.208

1 (B) **2** (C) **3** (D)

1 (B)

번역 | 월간 보고서를 받을 부서장들의 이름은 직원 편람 마지막 장에 적혀 있다.

해설 | 빈칸 앞의 to부터 sent까지가 명사구 department heads를 수식하며 '보고서를 받을 부서장들'이라는 의미를 나타낸다. 따라서 빈칸에는 전치사 to의 목적어 역할을 하며 사람을 가리키는 관계대명사가 들어가야 하므로, (B) whom이 정답이다.

어휘 | department head 부서장 be located 위치해 있다

2 (C)

번역 | 지원자들은 자신이 일하고 싶은 프로젝트 옆에 있는 네모칸에 체크하여 연구 관심사를 표시해 주십시오.

해설 | 빈칸 앞의 on부터 work까지가 명사 projects를 수식하며 '일하고 싶은 프로젝트'라는 의미를 나타낸다. 따라서 빈칸에는 전치사 on의 목적어 역할을 하며 사물을 가리키는 관계대명사가 들어가야 하므로, (C) which가 정답이다.

어휘 | candidate 지원자, 후보자 indicate 나타내다

3 (D)

번역 | 벡토 디자인 회사는 12명의 그래픽 디자이너를 고용하고 있는데, 그들 모두 적어도 3년 이상의 경력이 있는 노련한 디자이너들이다.

해설 | 문장에 절이 두 개지만 접속사가 없기 때문에, 빈칸을 포함한 절이 콤마 앞의 graphic artists에 대해 부연 설명을 하는 관계사절임을 알 수 있다. 따라서 빈칸에는 of의 목적어 역할을 하며 사람을 가리키는 관계대명사가 들어가야 하므로, (D) whom이 정답이다.

어휘 | skilled 능숙한, 노련한 at least 적어도

④ 관계부사

ETS 유형 연습
본책 p.209

1 (D) **2** (A) **3** (D)

1 (D)

번역 | 모든 운송품은 하역장으로 도착하는데, 그곳에서 창고 담당자가 추적 라벨을 확인한다.

해설 | 빈칸 뒤의 완전한 절을 이끌면서 앞의 장소 명사 the receiving dock를 수식하는 관계부사 (D) where가 정답이다.

어휘 | shipment 운송품, 선적물 receiving dock 하역장 warehouse 창고 tracking 추적

2 **(A)**

번역 | 그 시설 관리자는 사무용품이 보관되어 있는 창고 열쇠를 가지고 있다.

해설 | 빈칸 뒤의 완전한 절을 이끌면서 앞의 장소 명사 the storage room을 수식하는 관계부사 (A) where가 정답이다. (B) how는 방법, (C) when은 시간, (D) why는 이유를 나타내는 관계부사이므로 적절치 않다.

어휘 | facility 시설 storage room 창고, 보관실 office supply 사무용품

3 **(D)**

번역 | 김 박사의 수상 연설은 대략 10분 정도 지속되리라 예상되며 그 후에 디저트가 제공될 것이다.

해설 | 연설이 대략 10분 정도 지속될 예정이며, 이후에 디저트가 제공될 예정이라는 내용이 되어야 자연스럽다. 따라서 빈칸에는 after의 목적어 역할을 하며 사물을 가리키는 관계대명사가 들어가야 하므로, (D) which가 정답이다.

어휘 | acceptance 수락; 수상 last 지속되다, 계속하다

● ETS 실전문제
본책 p.210

1 (C)	2 (A)	3 (A)	4 (D)	5 (B)	6 (C)
7 (C)	8 (C)	9 (D)	10 (B)	11 (A)	12 (A)
13 (B)	14 (C)	15 (B)	16 (C)	17 (A)	18 (C)

1 **(C)**

번역 | 치앙마이 오페라 하우스의 로비 카펫은 관리하기 더 쉬운 소재로 교체될 것이다.

해설 | 빈칸은 명사 material을 수식하는 관계사절을 이끄는 동시에, 관계사절에서는 동사 is의 주어 역할을 한다. 따라서 주격 관계대명사로 쓰일 수 있는 (C) that이 정답이다. (A) what은 선행사 뒤에 쓰일 수 없으므로 오답이다.

어휘 | be replaced with ~로 교체되다 material 소재, 옷감 maintain 관리하다, 유지하다

2 **(A)**

번역 | 그 가구점은 공장제 제품들뿐만 아니라 수제품도 판매하는 재능 있는 목공이 소유하고 있다.

해설 | 빈칸은 사람 명사 carpenter를 수식하는 관계사절을 이끄는 동시에, 관계사절에서는 동사 sells의 주어 역할을 한다. 따라서 사람을 가리키는 주격 관계대명사 (A) who가 정답이다.

어휘 | own 소유하다 talented 재능 있는 carpenter 목공

3 **(A)**

번역 | 톰슨 박사는 수많은 학술지에 연구가 게재된 선도적인 생물학자로, 다음 주 학회 때 특별 연사로 나올 것이다.

해설 | 빈칸은 명사구 a leading biologist를 수식하는 관계사절을 이끄는 동시에, 관계사절의 주어 work를 한정 수식하는 역할을 한다. biologist와 work는 '생물학자의 연구'라는 소유 관계를 나타내므로, 소유격 관계대명사 (A) whose가 정답이다.

어휘 | leading 선두의, 선도적인 biologist 생물학자 publish 게재하다, 발표하다 numerous 수많은 featured speaker 특별

연사 conference 회의, 학회

4 **(D)**

번역 | 존슨 박사는 효율적인 시간 관리에 대한 견해를 공유할 세 시간짜리 워크숍을 개최한다.

해설 | 빈칸 앞의 during부터 management까지가 명사 workshop을 수식하며 '시간 관리에 대한 견해를 공유할 워크숍'이라는 의미를 나타낸다. 따라서 빈칸에는 전치사 during의 목적어 역할을 하며 사물을 가리키는 관계대명사가 들어가야 하므로, (D) which가 정답이다

어휘 | offer 제공하다, 개설하다 share 나누다, 공유하다 perspective 견해, 관점 effective 효율적인 time management 시간 관리

5 **(B)**

번역 | 귀하가 주문하신 재킷의 경우 요청하신 색상으로는 현재 재고가 없지만 나머지 주문품들은 신속히 보내드리겠습니다.

해설 | 빈칸은 you와 함께 앞에 있는 명사 color를 수식한다. 문맥상 '요청했던 색상'이라는 내용이 되어야 자연스러우므로, 과거 시제인 (B) requested가 정답이다. 참고로, you 앞에는 목적격 관계대명사가 생략되어 있다.

어휘 | currently 현재 rest 나머지

6 **(C)**

번역 | 콘텐츠 전략가 로나 포지올리는 업계를 형성하는 동향에 박식한 전문가다.

해설 | 빈칸은 명사구 the business world를 목적어로 취하면서 앞에 있는 trends를 수식하는 역할을 한다. 따라서 능동의 의미를 내포한 현재분사 (C) shaping이 정답이다. 참고로, 빈칸 앞에는 <주격 관계대명사(that / which) + be동사(are)>가 생략된 것으로 볼 수 있다.

어휘 | strategist 전략가 expert 전문가 shape 어떤 모양으로 만들다, 형성하다

7 **(C)**

번역 | 동기부여 강연으로 유명한 엘라 포르토피노 씨가 6월에 열릴 ORIL 리더십 회의의 초청 연사가 될 예정이다.

해설 | 빈칸은 사람 명사 Ella Portofino에 대해 부연 설명하는 관계사절을 이끄는 동시에, 관계사절에서는 동사 is의 주어 역할을 한다. 따라서 사람을 가리키는 주격 관계대명사 (C) who가 정답이다.

어휘 | motivational speech 동기부여 강연 guest speaker 초청 연사

8 **(C)**

번역 | 모든 운전자는 차선이 다시 칠해지고 있는 5번 가 지역을 피해야 한다.

해설 | 빈칸 뒤의 완전한 절을 이끌면서 앞의 장소명사 Fifth Street를 수식하는 관계부사 (C) where가 정답이다.

어휘 | motorist 운전자 avoid 피하다

9 **(D)**

번역 | 외국 대표단이 라 플루어 레스토랑을 방문했을 때, 그들은 특별한 버섯 애피타이저를 제공받았다.

해설 | 빈칸 뒤의 동사 were served의 주어 자리로 주격 인칭대명사인 (D) they가 정답이다. 앞에 접속사 When이 있기 때문에 관계대명사인 (A) who는 빈칸에 들어갈 수 없고, (B) theirs는 '그들의 것'이란 의미로 문맥상 어색하다.

어휘 | delegate 대표단 serve 제공하다

10 (B)

번역 | 지난주 드림 타운 스튜디오스에서 공개한 <레드 샌드 가든>은 30대인 사람들에게 인기가 있었다.

해설 | 빈칸은 사물 명사 *Red Sand Garden*에 대해 부연 설명하는 관계사절을 이끄는 동시에, 동사 was released의 주어 역할을 한다. 따라서 사물을 가리키는 주격 관계대명사 (B) which가 정답이다.

어휘 | release 공개하다, 출시하다

11 (A)

번역 | 산업 장비를 조작하는 공장 직원은 1년에 한 번 안전 교육에 참석해야 한다.

해설 | 빈칸은 명사구 Factory personnel을 수식하는 관계사절을 이끄는 동시에, 관계사절의 주어 job을 한정 수식하는 역할을 한다. Factory personnel과 job은 '직원의 일/직무'라는 소유 관계를 나타내므로, 소유격 관계대명사 (A) whose가 정답이다.

어휘 | personnel (조직의) 직원 operate (기계를) 조작하다 industrial machinery 산업 장비 attend 참석하다 safety 안전

12 (A)

번역 | 부아클레르 로보틱스는 효율성을 향상시키기 위해 공장 내 조립 공정 전체를 감시할 수 있는 기계를 고안했다.

해설 | 빈칸은 명사 machine을 수식하는 관계사절을 이끄는 동시에, 관계사절에서는 동사 can monitor의 주어 역할을 한다. 따라서 주격 관계대명사로 쓰일 수 있는 (A) that이 정답이다.

어휘 | improve 향상시키다, 개선하다 efficiency 효율성 monitor 감시[관찰]하다 entire 전체의 assembly 조립

13 (B)

번역 | 관리자들은 종종 몇 가지 행동 방침들 사이에서 결정을 해야 하는데, 어느 것도 전적으로 옳거나 틀리지 않다.

해설 | 문장에 절이 두 개지만 접속사가 없기 때문에, 빈칸을 포함한 절이 콤마 앞의 several courses of action에 대해 부연 설명을 하는 관계사절임을 알 수 있다. 따라서 빈칸에는 of의 목적어 역할을 하며 사물을 가리키는 관계대명사가 들어가야 하므로, (B) which가 정답이다.

어휘 | course of action 행동 방침

14 (C)

번역 | 2주 이내에 답신을 받지 못한 서빙 직책 지원자는 후속 이메일을 보내야 한다.

해설 | 빈칸은 동사 should send의 주어 역할을 하는 명사 자리로, 사람 명사를 수식하는 관계사절(who have not received a response within two weeks)의 수식을 받는다. 따라서 '지원자들'이라는 의미의 명사 (C) Applicants가 정답이다.

어휘 | response 대답, 응답 follow-up 후속 조치 application 지원(서)

[15-18] 이메일

수신: 멜리사 하트<melissahart@hmail.com>
발신: 마일스 윈터스<mwinters@fivestarsrestaurantonline.com>
제목: 보조 요리사 직
날짜: 11월 2일

하트 씨께,

파이브 스타즈 레스토랑의 보조 요리사 직에 지원해 주시고 면접에 와 주셔서 감사합니다. 저희는 예상외로 많은 지원서를 받았습니다. ¹⁵그 결과, 총 일곱 명의 잠재 후보들을 면접하기로 결정했습니다. 모든 면접을 마친 후, 저희는 저명한 요리상을 많이 ¹⁶수상한 경력이 아주 많은 요리사를 채용했습니다.

¹⁷하지만, 저희는 귀하가 갖춘 자격에 아주 깊은 인상을 받았습니다. 저희 주방의 다른 직책에 관해 귀하와 다시 한번 이야기하고 싶습니다. ¹⁸관심이 있으시면, 518-555-2213으로 제게 전화 주시거나 이 이메일에 회신을 보내 주시기 바랍니다.

감사합니다.

마일스 윈터스

어휘 | unexpectedly 예상외로 application 지원서 potential 잠재적인 candidate 후보, 지원자 in the end 결국, 모든 일이 끝난 후 exceptionally 특별히, 대단히 experienced 경험이 많은 prestigious 저명한 culinary 요리의 regarding ~에 관해

15 (B)

해설 | 빈칸 앞에서 예상외로 많은 지원서를 받았다(We unexpectedly received a large number of applications)고 했고, 뒤에서 총 일곱 명의 잠재 후보들을 면접하기로 결정했다(we decided to interview a total of seven potential job candidates)고 했다며 앞 문장에 따른 후속 조치를 언급했다. 따라서 빈칸에는 선후관계/인과관계의 내용을 이어주는 접속부사가 들어가야 문맥상 자연스러우므로, '결과적으로, 그 결과'라는 의미의 (B) As a result가 정답이다.

16 (C)

해설 | 빈칸은 명사구 a number of prestigious culinary awards를 목적어로 취하면서 빈칸 앞 명사 chef를 수식하는 역할을 한다. 따라서 보기에서 (A) that is receiving과 (C) who has received 중 하나를 선택해야 한다. 문맥상 '이미 다수의 상을 받은 요리사'라는 내용이 되어야 자연스러우므로, (C) who has received가 정답이다.

17 (A)

번역 | (A) 하지만, 저희는 귀하가 갖춘 자격에 아주 깊은 인상을 받았습니다.
(B) 저희 주방 직원들은 당신과 만나기를 고대하고 있었습니다.
(C) 게다가, 저희는 식사 공간 개조를 계획하고 있습니다.
(D) 저희는 곧 식사 메뉴 선택 폭을 확대할 것입니다.

해설 | 빈칸 앞에서 경력이 아주 많은 요리사를 채용했다(we hired an exceptionally experienced chef)며 불합격 소식을 전했는데, 빈칸 뒤 문장에서 다른 직책에 관해 다시 한번 이야기하고 싶다(We would like to speak with you again regarding a different position in our kitchen)고 했으므로, 빈칸에는 하트

159

씨에게 주어질 새로운 고용 기회와 관련된 내용이 들어가야 문맥상 자연스럽다. 따라서 (A)가 정답이다.

어휘 | impressed 감명을 받은 credential 자격, 훌륭한 경력

18 (C)

해설 | 문맥상 앞에서 언급한 고용 기회(a different position in our kitchen)에 관심이 있으면 연락을 하라는 내용이 되어야 자연스러우므로, (C) interested(관심이 있는)가 정답이다.

어휘 | occupied 점유된, 사용 중인 determined 단호한, 결정된

Unit 14 명사절 접속사

① 명사절 접속사의 이해

ETS 유형 연습 본책 p.212

1 (A) **2** (A) **3** (A)

1 (A)

번역 | 특히 당시 겨우 26세였다는 점을 고려하면 생화학 분야에서 후아 허징 씨의 업적은 놀라웠다.

해설 | 빈칸 이하가 considering의 목적어 역할을 하며, '~라는 점을 고려하면'이라는 의미가 되어야 자연스러우므로, 명사절 접속사 (A) that이 정답이다.

어휘 | biochemistry 생화학 remarkable 놀라운, 주목할 만한

2 (A)

번역 | 많은 사람들은 아사노 씨가 5년 임기에 재선임되리라 예상한다.

해설 | 대명사 It은 가짜 주어이고 빈칸 이하가 진짜 주어 자리이다. 따라서 '~라는 것'을 의미하는 명사절 접속사 (A) that이 정답이다.

어휘 | widely 널리 nominate 지명하다, 임명하다 term 임기

3 (A)

번역 | 방침은 박물관 내 식음료 반입이 허용되지 않음을 분명히 명시하고 있다.

해설 | 빈칸은 states의 목적어 역할을 하는 명사절을 이끈다. 문맥상 '~라고 분명히 명시하다'라는 내용이 되어야 자연스러우므로, (A) that이 정답이다.

어휘 | policy 정책, 방침 state 명시하다, 발표하다

② 명사절 접속사 that / what

ETS 유형 연습 본책 p.213

1 (A) **2** (C) **3** (C)

1 (A)

번역 | <뉴스 업데이트> 지를 구독하시면, 최신 정치와 경제 동향에 대한 신뢰할 만한 분석을 받아 볼 것임을 확신할 수 있습니다.

해설 | 빈칸 앞에 온 be confident가 문제 해결의 단서로, 뒤의 완전한 절을 이끌면서 be confident와 결합하여 '~에 대해 확신하다'라는 의미를 나타내는 명사절 접속사 (A) that이 정답이다.

어휘 | subscribe to ~을 구독하다 be confident that ~을 확신하다 reliable 신뢰할 만한

2 (C)

번역 | 홀리아 오피스 파크 관리소는 공사가 진행되는 동안 업무가 최소한으로만 영향을 받을 것이라고 확언했다.

해설 | 빈칸은 has assured의 직접목적어 역할을 하는 명사절을 이끈다. 따라서 '~라는 것을 확언했다'라는 의미를 완성하는 명사절 접속사 (C) that이 정답이다.

어휘 | administration 관리, 집행 assure 확실히 하다, 보증하다 minimally 최소한으로 impact 영향을 주다

3 (C)

번역 | 고객들을 가장 기쁘게 한 것은 모라돈 은행이 제공한 효과적인 고객 서비스였다.

해설 | 빈칸부터 most까지가 주어, was가 동사인 문장이다. 따라서 빈칸에는 명사절을 이끌면서 pleased의 주어 역할을 하는 명사절 접속사가 들어가야 하므로, '~하는 것'이라는 의미를 나타내는 (C) What이 정답이다. 참고로, What(=the thing which)은 선행사를 포함한 관계대명사라고 볼 수도 있다.

어휘 | effective 효과적인

③ 명사절 접속사 whether / if

ETS 유형 연습 본책 p.214

1 (A) **2** (A) **3** (D)

1 (A)

번역 | 팩스 기계가 고장 나서, 수리가 가능한지 여부를 알아보기 위해 숙련된 기술자를 호출했다.

해설 | 빈칸 이하가 to see의 목적어 역할을 하므로, 빈칸에는 명사절 접속사가 들어가야 한다. 문맥상 '수리가 가능한지 (아닌지) 알아보기 위해'라는 내용이 되어야 자연스러우므로, (A) if(~인지 아닌지)가 정답이다.

어휘 | out of service 고장 난 experienced 숙련된 call in 불러들이다

2 (A)

번역 | 웨스트헤이븐 글래스웍스의 한은성 사장은 파인포드 트럭킹과의 계약을 연장할지 말지를 놓고 숙고하고 있다.

해설 | 빈칸 이하는 considering의 목적어 역할을 한다. 따라서 빈칸에는 to부정사와 함께 사용될 수 있는 접속사가 필요한데, 문맥상 '계약을 연장할지 (말지) 숙고하다'라는 내용이 되어야 자연스러우므로, (A) whether(~인지 아닌지)가 정답이다. whether는 <whether+주어+동사> 또는 <whether+to부정사> 구조로 쓰인다.

어휘 | glassworks 유리 공장 consider 고려하다, 숙고하다 renew (계약 등을) 갱신하다, 연장하다 trucking 트럭 수송(업)

3 (D)

번역 | 하모니 디자인 컨설턴트들은 고객들이 창을 장식할 때 커튼을 이용할지 블라인드를 이용할지 결정하는 데 도움을 줄 수 있다.

해설 | whether와 어울려 상관접속사로 쓰이는 (D) or가 정답이다. curtains와 blinds가 use의 목적어 역할을 하고 있다.

④ 의문사와 복합관계대명사

ETS 유형 연습
본책 p. 215

1 (A) **2** (C) **3** (D)

1 **(A)**
번역 | 좋은 이력서는 지원자의 자격요건이 어떻게 책무에 적합한지를 고용주에게 보여준다.

해설 | 동사 tells의 직접목적어 역할을 하는 완전한 절을 이끌면서 '어떻게 적합한지를'이라는 의미를 나타내는 의문부사 (A) how가 정답이다.

어휘 | qualification 자격요건 match 어울리다

2 **(C)**
번역 | 포스터 시티 역사학회의 회원들은 법원 청사 유적에 남아 있는 독창적인 건축학적 요소들이 보존되도록 청원하고 있다.

해설 | 빈칸부터 elements까지가 to have의 목적어 역할을 하며, preserved는 목적격 보어로 쓰였다. 따라서 빈칸에는 불완전한 명사절을 이끌며 remains의 주어 역할을 하는 명사절 접속사가 들어가야 하므로, (C) what이 정답이다.

어휘 | historical society 역사학회 petition 탄원하다, 청원하다 remain 남다, 잔존하다 courthouse 법원 청사 original 독창적인 architectural 건축학의 preserve 보존하다

3 **(D)**
번역 | 그로튼 그림을 누가 얻든 아마도 경매 최고가액의 미술품을 구매한 셈이 될 것이다.

해설 | 빈칸부터 painting까지가 문장의 주어 역할을 하므로, 빈칸에는 불완전한 절(acquires ~ painting)을 이끄는 명사절 접속사가 들어가야 한다. 문맥상 '~하는 사람은 누구든지'라는 의미가 되어야 자연스러우므로, (D) Whoever가 정답이다. Whoever는 Anyone who로 바꿔 쓸 수 있다.

어휘 | artwork 미술품 auction 경매

● ETS 실전문제
본책 p. 216

1 (D) **2** (C) **3** (B) **4** (A) **5** (D) **6** (D)
7 (A) **8** (B) **9** (D) **10** (D) **11** (A) **12** (A)
13 (C) **14** (D) **15** (B) **16** (D) **17** (C) **18** (D)

1 **(D)**
번역 | 비행기 여행객들이 자주 하는 한 가지 불평은 머리 위 짐칸이 너무 작다는 것이다.

해설 | 빈칸 이하가 동사 is의 주격 보어 역할을 하므로, 빈칸에는 완전한 절을 이끄는 명사절 접속사가 들어가야 한다. 문맥상 '머리 위 짐칸이 작다는 것이다'라는 내용이 되어야 자연스러우므로, (D) that이 정답이다.

어휘 | complaint 항의 overhead 머리 위의 compartment 선반, 짐칸

2 **(C)**
번역 | 미요 테크놀로지스는 팀이 생산하는 것에 대해 관리자들이 책임지도록 독려한다.

해설 | 빈칸부터 produce까지가 전치사 for의 목적어 역할을 한다. 따라서 빈칸에는 명사절 접속사가 들어가야 하는데, 뒤에 목적어가 없는 불완전한 절이 왔으므로 (C) what이 정답이다.

어휘 | encourage A to do A에게 ~하도록 권장하다 take responsibility for ~에 대해 책임을 지다

3 **(B)**
번역 | 리버풀 지역 공항에서 승객들을 가장 감동시키는 것은 천갈이를 한 좌석의 편안함이다.

해설 | 빈칸부터 most까지가 주어, is가 동사, the comfort 이하가 보어인 문장이다. 따라서 빈칸에는 명사절을 이끌면서 should impress의 주어 역할을 하는 명사절 접속사가 들어가야 한다. 문맥상 '승객들을 가장 감동시키는 것'이라는 내용이 되어야 자연스러우므로, (B) What이 정답이다.

어휘 | impress 감동시키다 comfort 편안함 upholster (의자 등의 가구에) 천을 씌우다

4 **(A)**
번역 | 송 씨는 3명의 지원자 중 누가 제품 수석 개발자 직책에 적합한지 아직 결정하지 못했다.

해설 | 빈칸은 decided의 목적어 역할을 하는 명사절을 이끄는 접속사 자리로, 명사절에서는 주어 역할을 한다. 따라서 전치사구 of the three candidates의 수식을 받아 '세 명의 지원자 중 어떤 사람'이라는 의미를 완성하는 (A) which가 정답이다.

어휘 | decide 결정하다, 결심하다 candidate 후보자, 지원자 developer 개발자

5 **(D)**
번역 | 그 제조업체는 자사에서 제조한 화장품이 3년 또는 제품 용기에 표시된 유효 기간 중 더 빠른 날짜까지 사용 가능하다고 보장한다.

해설 | 빈칸은 불완전한 절(is sooner)을 이끌어 앞에 있는 절을 수식한다. 따라서 해당 절에서 주어 역할을 하며, 앞서 언급된 for three years or until the expiration date on the package를 가리켜 '둘 중 어느 것이든지'라는 의미를 나타내는 복합관계대명사 (D) whichever가 정답이다.

어휘 | manufacturer 제조업체 guarantee 보장[보증]하다 cosmetic product 화장품 good 유효한, 사용 가능한 expiration date 유통 기한 package 포장, 용기

6 **(D)**
번역 | 요한슨 씨는 곧 은퇴할 것인지 질문받았을 때 자신은 일하는 것을 결코 멈추지 않을 것이라고 말했다.

해설 | 빈칸 이하는 앞의 과거분사 asked의 직접목적어 역할을 한다. 따라서 완전한 절을 이끌면서 '~인지 아닌지'라는 의미를 나타내는 명사절 접속사 (D) whether가 정답이다.

어휘 | retire 은퇴하다 while ~인 반면에, ~인 한편 whereas ~인 반면에 whenever 언제 ~든지

7 **(A)**
번역 | <워킹 트렌즈 투데이> 지에 발표된 한 최근 연구는 왼손잡이인 사람들이 사업에 성공할 가능성이 더 높다는 점을 시사한다.

해설 | 빈칸 이하는 동사 suggests의 목적어 역할을 한다. 따라서 완전한 절을 이끌면서 '~라는 것'이라는 의미를 나타내는 명사절 접속사 (A) that이 정답이다.

어휘 | publish 게재하다, 발표하다 suggest 시사하다 left-handed 왼손잡이인

8 (B)

번역 | 시장 조사 부서는 사람들이 운전하면서 얼마나 자주 라디오를 듣는지에 관한 조사를 실시했다.

해설 | 빈칸 이하는 전치사 on의 목적어 역할을 한다. 따라서 빈칸에는 부사 often과 결합하여 '얼마나 자주'라는 의미를 나타내며 완전한 절을 이끄는 명사절 접속사가 들어가야 하므로, 의문부사 (B) how가 정답이다.

어휘 | market-research 시장 조사 conduct 실시하다

9 (D)

번역 | 트래넬린 인더스트리스의 임원진은 어떤 부서들이 내년에 웨스트 코스트로 옮길지 판단하는 중이다.

해설 | 빈칸은 determining의 목적어 역할을 하는 명사절을 이끄는 접속사 자리로, 명사절에서는 주어 divisions를 수식하는 한정사 역할을 한다. 따라서 '어떤 부서들이 웨스트 코스트로 옮길지(which divisions will transfer to the West Coast)'라는 의미를 완성하는 (D) which가 정답이다.

어휘 | executive team 임원진 determine 결정하다, 판단하다 division 부서 transfer to ~로 옮기다

10 (D)

번역 | 오늘날에는 적당한 운동조차도 심장에 도움이 된다고 알려져 있다.

해설 | 동사 is의 주어 자리로, 진짜 주어인 that이 이끄는 명사절을 대신할 수 있는 가짜 주어 (D) it이 정답이다.

어휘 | moderate 보통의, 적당한 beneficial 유익한, 도움이 되는

11 (A)

번역 | 지원을 하거나 지원 절차 관련 정보를 구하는 데 도움이 필요한 사람은 누구든지 인사부로 오십시오.

해설 | 빈칸부터 assistance까지가 문장의 주어 역할을 하므로, 빈칸에는 불완전한 절(needs assistance)을 이끄는 명사절 접속사가 들어가야 한다. 문맥상 '~하는 사람은 누구든지'라는 의미가 되어야 자연스러우므로, (A) Whoever가 정답이다.

어휘 | assistance 지원, 도움 procedure 절차

12 (A)

번역 | 많은 독자들이 일간 신문의 사설면이 더 계몽적이라고 말하지만 그들이 처음 읽는 것은 스포츠면이라는 점을 인정한다.

해설 | 빈칸부터 first까지가 주어, is가 동사, the sports page가 보어인 절이다. 따라서 빈칸에는 목적어가 없는 불완전한 절(they read first)을 이끄는 명사절 접속사가 들어가야 하므로, '~하는 것'이라는 의미의 (A) what이 정답이다.

어휘 | state 말하다 editorial 사설 enlightening 계몽적인, 교육적인

13 (C)

번역 | 많은 연구가 시장 조사 단체들에 의해 실시되었지만, 고객들이 기꺼이 인터넷을 통해 식료품을 구입하는지 여부는 여전히 불확실하다.

해설 | 대명사 it은 가짜 주어이고 빈칸 이하가 진짜 주어 자리이다. 따라서 완전한 절을 이끌면서 '~인지 아닌지'라는 의미를 나타내는 명사절 접속사 (C) whether가 정답이다.

어휘 | multiple 많은, 다양한 uncertain 불확실한 grocery 식료품

14 (D)

번역 | 스프링 플라워 기프츠는 모든 소매점 관리자들에게 고객의 문의사항을 어떻게 처리해야 하는지 교육한다.

해설 | 전치사 in의 목적어 자리로, 빈칸 뒤의 완전한 절을 이끄는 명사절 접속사가 들어가야 한다. 따라서 '~하는 방법, 어떻게'라는 의미를 나타내는 의문부사 (D) how가 정답이다. 의문부사 how는 형용사 또는 부사와 결합하여 명사절 접속사로 쓰일 수 있다.

어휘 | retail store 소매점 deal with ~을 처리하다 inquiry 문의

[15-18] 공지문

3월 3일 게시

프놈펜 외국어대학교에서 불어학과를 15이끌어 주실 경험 많은 불어 강사를 찾고 있습니다. 16불어학과에는 현재 세 명의 전임 강사가 있습니다. 적임자는 이 작은 팀의 팀장으로 관리자 역할을 하고, 새로운 강사들을 교육할 수 있어야 합니다. 지원자의 교육학 학위 소지 17여부가 경력보다 중요하지는 않습니다. 이상적인 지원자는 최소 5년 이상의 강의 경험이 있어야 합니다. 관심 있으신 분은 chastain@ppsfl.ca.ed를 통해 이력서와 자기소개서를 루벤 채스테인 씨 앞으로 18제출하십시오. 추천인 명단은 현 채용 단계에서는 필요하지 않습니다.

어휘 | seek 구하다, 찾다 experienced 경험 많은, 숙련된 instructor 강사 department 학과, 부서 successful candidate 적임자, 합격자 assume 추정하다 managerial 관리자의 applicant 지원자 ideal 이상적인 résumé 이력서 a letter of introduction 자기소개서 reference 추천인, 신원 보증인 recruitment 채용

15 (B)

해설 | 문맥상 '우리 불어학과를 이끌어 줄 경험 많은 강사'라는 내용이 되어야 자연스러우므로, (B) lead가 정답이다.

어휘 | assess 평가하다 meet 충족시키다

16 (D)

번역 | (A) 우리 학생들은 다양한 배경을 갖고 있습니다.
(B) 불어는 세계 언어로서 중요성이 점점 커지고 있습니다.
(C) 우리는 이네즈 로버트 씨가 새로운 직책을 맡은 것을 축하합니다.
(D) 불어학과에는 현재 세 명의 전임 강사가 있습니다.

해설 | 빈칸 앞에서 불어학과를 이끌어 줄 강사를 찾고 있다고 했고, 뒤에서는 적임자(successful candidate)가 이 소규모 팀(this small team)의 팀장이 될 것이라고 했다. 따라서 빈칸에는 소규모 팀에 대한 내용이 들어가야 자연스러우므로, (D)가 정답이다.

어휘 | diverse 다양한 increasingly 점점 더 congratulate 축하하다

17 **(C)**

해설 | 빈칸부터 education까지가 주어이므로, 빈칸에는 완전한 절(an applicant ~ education)을 이끄는 명사절 접속사가 들어가야 한다. 따라서 '지원자가 교육학 학위를 소지했는지 아닌지를'이라는 의미를 완성하는 (C) Whether가 정답이다.

18 **(D)**

해설 | '관심 있는 사람은 이력서와 자기소개서를 제출해야 한다'라는 지원 방식을 안내하고 있으므로, (D) should send가 정답이다.

Unit 15   비교 / 도치 구문

① 원급 비교

ETS 유형 연습
본책 p. 218

1 (A)   **2** (B)   **3** (D)

1 **(A)**

번역 | 신형 FRI-25 디지털 카메라 모델은 시중의 많은 표준 모델들과 동일한 최첨단 기능들을 갖추고 있다.

해설 | 빈칸 앞에 온 the same이 문제 해결의 단서로, '~와 똑같은'이라는 원급 비교 표현을 완성하는 (A) as가 정답이다.

어휘 | feature 특징, 기능

2 **(B)**

번역 | 한 소비자 보고서는 저렴한 세탁용 세제가 더 비싼 제품과 똑같이 효과적일 수 있다고 밝혔다.

해설 | 원급 비교 구문 <as+원급+as>를 강조하는 부사 자리로 '꼭 ~만큼 효과적인'이라는 내용이 되는 것이 자연스러우므로 (B) just가 정답이다.

어휘 | consumer 소비자 reveal 밝히다 less 덜 laundry detergent 세탁용 세제 effective 효과적인

3 **(D)**

번역 | 디스크 드라이버가 설치된 후, 먼지가 쌓이는 것을 막기 위해 보호용 커버는 가능한 한 빨리 교체되어야 한다.

해설 | as 사이에서 동사 should be replaced를 수식하는 원급 부사가 필요하므로, (D) quickly가 정답이다. 참고로 <as+원급+as possible>은 '가능한 한 ~하게'라는 의미를 나타낸다.

어휘 | replace 교체하다 prevent 막다, 예방하다 accumulation 축적, 쌓임

② 비교급

ETS 유형 연습
본책 p. 219

1 (C)   **2** (B)   **3** (A)

1 **(C)**

번역 | 오피스 서플라이 웨어하우스의 고객 설문 조사에서 대다수 고객들은 전화보다는 웹사이트에서 더 효율적으로 주문할 수 있었다고 응답했다.

해설 | 앞의 동사 could order를 수식하는 부사 자리로, 빈칸 뒤쪽의 than과 결합하여 '~보다 더 효율적으로'의 의미를 나타내는 비교급 부사 (C) more efficiently가 정답이다.

어휘 | survey 설문 조사 majority 대다수 report 응답하다, 보고하다 order 주문하다 over the phone 전화상으로 efficient 효율적인 efficiently 효율적으로

2 **(B)**

번역 | 송 씨 그룹이 자료 수집 프로젝트를 제때 완수하려면 우리에게 훨씬 더 많은 행정적인 지원이 필요할 것이다.

해설 | 빈칸은 비교급 형용사 more administrative를 강조하는 부사 자리이므로, 비교급 강조 부사 (B) even이 정답이다. 비교급 앞에서 '훨씬 더'라는 의미로 비교급을 강조하는 부사에는 even, still, a lot, much, far 등이 있다.

어휘 | complete 완수하다 administrative 행정의, 관리의

3 **(A)**

번역 | 새로운 음료수 쿨 피즈의 광고 캠페인은 가격보다는 맛을 강조할 것이다.

해설 | 동사 will feature의 목적어인 flavor와 price를 비교하고 있으므로 '~라기보다는'이라는 의미를 나타내는 (A) rather than이 정답이다. 이 문장에서 feature는 '~을 중점적으로 다루다'란 뜻이다.

어휘 | advertising campaign 광고 캠페인 flavor 맛 in the event of ~하는 경우에 except for ~을 제외하고는 as for ~에 관해서는

③ 최상급

ETS 유형 연습
본책 p. 220

1 (B)   **2** (B)   **3** (D)

1 **(B)**

번역 | 중심 상업 지구에 정차하는 지하철 노선들 중에서 초록 노선이 프랭클린 건물에서 걸어가기가 가장 쉽다.

해설 | 빈칸은 동사 is의 주격 보어 자리이므로, 보기들 중 부사는 일단 탈락된다. 이때 비교 대상이 없으면 원급, 비교 대상이 여러 개이면 최상급을 답으로 한다. 맨 앞에 of the subway lines(지하철 노선들 중에서)를 보면 비교 대상이 여러 개이므로 최상급 형용사인 (B) easiest가 정답이다.

어휘 | central 중심의, 중앙의 business district 상업 지구

2 **(B)**

번역 | 그 일자리에 지원한 5명의 지원자 중에서 우리는 당연히 그 자리를 채울 최적임자를 고용할 것이다.

해설 | From among the five applicants를 통해 이야기하는 대상이 셋 이상임을 알 수 있다. 빈칸은 명사 candidate를 수식하는 형용사 자리이므로, 정관사 the와 결합하여 '가장 적임의'라는 의미를 나타내는 최상급 형용사 (B) most qualified가 정답이다.

어휘 | applicant 지원자 naturally 당연히 hire 고용하다 candidate 지원자, 후보자 fill a position 자리를 채우다 qualified 자격을 갖춘 qualify 자격을 주다

3 (D)

번역 | 올해 예산에서 신제품 개발에 할당된 자금은 최근 몇 년 만에 가장 넉넉한 액수가 될 것으로 예상된다.

해설 | 빈칸은 명사 amount를 수식하는 형용사 자리로, 문장 끝의 in recent history와 결합하여 '최근 몇 년 만에 가장 넉넉한'이라는 의미를 나타내는 최상급 형용사 (D) the most generous가 정답이다.

어휘 | funds 자금 allocate 할당하다 budget 예산 in recent history 최근 몇 년 만에, 최근 역사에서 generous 넉넉한, 관대한

④ 도치 구문

ETS 유형 연습

1 (D) **2** (A) **3** (C)

1 (D)

번역 | 박 씨는 제품 소개 발표에 참석할 수 없는데, 제퍼슨 씨 역시 참석할 수 없을 것이다.

해설 | 긍정/부정 동의를 나타내는 so/neither 도치 구문은 <so/neither+동사+주어>의 어순이 된다. 빈칸 뒤에 동사(will)와 주어(Mr. Jefferson)가 도치되어 있고 앞절에 부정어 not이 있으므로 부정 동의를 나타내는 (D) neither가 정답이다.

어휘 | sales presentation 제품 소개 발표

2 (A)

번역 | 신규 주택을 구매하기에 시장 여건이 이보다 더 이상적이었던 적은 드물었다.

해설 | 빈칸 뒤 어순이 <조동사(have)+주어(market conditions) +과거분사(been)>이므로, 보기 중에서 문장을 도치시킬 수 있는 부정부사 (A) Seldom이 정답이다.

어휘 | condition 여건, 상황, 조건 ideal 이상적인

3 (C)

번역 | 주민들이 공공 수영 시설에 방문하는 횟수가 증가함에 따라, 그들을 감독하는 안전 요원에 대한 수요도 증가한다.

해설 | 문두에 접속사가 있으므로 빈칸 이하도 절이 되어야 하는데, 동사가 없고 주어만 있다. 따라서 동사를 포함하며 긍정 동의를 나타내는 도치 구문 (C) so does가 정답이다.

어휘 | facility 시설, 설비 climb 올라가다, 증가하다 demand 수요

● ETS 실전문제

본책 p. 222

1 (C) **2** (A) **3** (D) **4** (D) **5** (C) **6** (A)
7 (B) **8** (D) **9** (C) **10** (C) **11** (D) **12** (C)
13 (A) **14** (A) **15** (D) **16** (A) **17** (D) **18** (B)

1 (C)

번역 | 비용 상승은 현재의 경쟁적인 시장 여건에서 중소기업들이 수익을 유지하기 한층 더 어렵게 만든다.

해설 | 동사 have made의 가짜 목적어인 it을 보충 설명하는 목적격 보어 자리로, 뒤의 than ever와 결합하여 '여느 때보다 더 어려운'이라는 의미를 나타내는 비교급 형용사 (C) harder가 정답이다.

어휘 | profitable 수익이 나는 competitive 경쟁적인

2 (A)

번역 | 전국 최대 에너지 공급업체인 오론 에너지는 거의 2천만 고객들에게 전기를 제공한다.

해설 | 전치사 of의 목적어인 energy supplies를 수식하는 형용사 자리로, '가장 큰 에너지 공급업체 중 하나'라는 의미를 나타내는 최상급 형용사 (A) largest가 정답이다. <one of the+최상급+복수명사> 표현을 기억하자.

어휘 | electricity 전기

3 (D)

번역 | 페레이라 컨설팅 사에 지원하는 구직자들은 가능한 한 정확하게 지원서 질문 사항에 답변해야 한다.

해설 | 동사 should answer를 수식하는 부사 자리로, 앞의 as 및 뒤의 as possible과 결합하여 '가능한 한 정확하게'라는 의미를 나타내는 원급 부사 (D) accurately가 정답이다.

어휘 | candidate 후보자, 지원자 position 근무처, 직장 application form 신청서, 지원서

4 (D)

번역 | 잘 안 빠지는 얼룩은 펄 글로우의 초강력 세탁용 세제로 보다 쉽게 제거될 수 있다.

해설 | 동사 be removed를 수식하는 부사 자리로, more와 결합하여 '더 쉽게'라는 의미를 나타내는 부사 (D) easily가 정답이다.

어휘 | tough 힘든, 골치 아픈 stain 얼룩 extra-strength 아주 강력한 laundry detergent 세탁용 세제

5 (C)

번역 | 이용 가능한 교통 수단 중에서 지하철을 타는 것이 웨스트 애프터톤 컨벤션 센터에서 공항으로 가는 가장 빠른 방법이다.

해설 | 빈칸은 명사 way를 수식하는 형용사 자리이다. 정관사 the와 결합하여 '이용 가능한 교통 수단 중에서(Among the available transportation options) 가장 빠른'이라는 의미를 나타내는 최상급 형용사 (C) quickest가 정답이다.

어휘 | option 선택

6 (A)

번역 | 우리 매장은 주요 경쟁업체들만큼 많은 가전제품을 구비하고 있다.

해설 | 명사 household appliances를 수식하는 형용사 자리로, 앞뒤에 있는 as와 결합하여 '~만큼 많은 가전제품'이라는 의미를 나타내는 원급 형용사 (A) many가 정답이다. '~만큼이나 많은 ...'이라는 뜻의 <as many/much+명사+as>의 원급 구조도 기억하자.

어휘 | competitor 경쟁업체, 경쟁자

7 (B)

번역 | 트렌텔 비즈니스 컨설팅 사는 신규 고객을 유치하는 것보다 충성도 높은 고객을 지키는 것이 더 중요하다고 강조한다.

해설 | 빈칸 뒤의 than과 어울리는 비교급 형용사가 필요하므로 형용사 important의 비교급을 만드는 (B) more가 정답이다.

어휘 | stress 강조하다 retain 간직하다, 보유하다 loyal 충성스러운

8 (D)

번역 | 문자, 숫자, 기호의 조합을 이용한 비밀번호가 가장 강력한 보안을 만들어 낸다.

해설 | 정관사 the와 명사 security 사이에서 security를 수식하는 형용사 자리이다. 따라서 the와 결합하여 '가장 강력한'이라는 최상급 표현을 완성하는 (D) strongest가 정답이다.

어휘 | utilize 이용하다 combination 조합 symbol 기호 security 보안

9 (C)

번역 | 다코 모터스와 케슬러 오토모티브의 합병은 분석가들이 예측한 것보다 더 많은 제조상의 문제를 초래했다.

해설 | 빈칸 앞의 비교급 표현 more production problems와 어울리는 (C) than이 정답이다. 여기서 more는 형용사 many의 비교급이다.

어휘 | merger 합병 automotive 자동차의 result in ~을 초래하다 analyst 분석가 predict 예측하다

10 (C)

번역 | 기술부는 단지 월말에만 그 프로젝트의 경과 보고서가 발행될 것이라고 발표했다.

해설 | that이 이끄는 명사절에서 only at the end of the month가 강조되어 절 앞에 있으므로 주어 a progress report of the project와 동사가 도치되어야 한다. 빈칸은 도치된 주어 앞의 동사 자리로, 뒤의 동사원형 be published와 어울리는 조동사 (C) will이 정답이다.

어휘 | engineering department 기술부 progress report 경과 보고서 publish 발행하다

11 (D)

번역 | 조기 등록 할인을 받으려면 신청서에 10월 28일 금요일자 이전의 소인이 찍혀야 한다.

해설 | Friday, October 28를 목적어로 취해 수식어 덩어리를 만들어 동사구 must be postmarked를 수식하는 자리이다. 따라서 전치사를 포함하며 '금요일보다 더 늦지 않게'라는 비교급 표현을 완성하는 (D) no later than이 정답이다. (A) in advance, (B) beforehand, (C) previously는 부사로 품사상 빈칸에 들어갈 수 없다.

어휘 | registration 등록, 기재 postmark 소인을 찍다 in advance 사전에 beforehand 미리, 사전에 previously 이전에

12 (C)

번역 | 황 씨의 결혼식 피로연을 위한 꽃 배달은 늦어도 5월 12일 금요일까지 완료될 것이다.

해설 | 배달이 완료되는 시점(by Friday, May 12)을 강조하는 부사 자리로, '늦어도'라는 뜻의 최상급 표현인 (C) at the latest가 정답이다.

어휘 | delivery 배달 complete 완료하다

13 (A)

번역 | 비알로보스 씨는 새로 구입한 휴대전화들이 그 부서에서 이제껏 구입한 것들 중 가장 가볍다고 보고했다.

해설 | 최상급 표현 the lightest를 강조하는 부사 자리로, '이제까지, 지금까지'라는 의미를 나타내는 (A) ever가 정답이다.

14 (A)

번역 | 마케팅 관리자인 하와 압델라는 사무실을 비워, 1월 12일 전에는 복귀하지 않을 예정이다.

해설 | 빈칸은 비교급 표현 than January 12와 함께 동사구 will not return을 수식하는 역할을 하므로, 복귀 시간과 어울리는 비교급 부사가 들어가야 한다. 따라서 '1월 12일 전에'라는 내용을 완성하는 (A) earlier(더 일찍)가 정답이다.

어휘 | recently 최근에 frequently 자주

[15-18] 이메일

발신: deaneckhart@gbhosp.org
수신: amanpour@sevcon.org
제목: 외과 과장직
날짜: 12월 10일

아만푸어 씨께,

귀하와 저를 함께 아는 **15**지인 글로리아 매닝 씨를 통해 귀하의 이력서를 받았습니다. **16**귀하의 폭넓은 경험이 참으로 인상적이군요. 그레이스 베스 병원의 외과 과장직이 공석임을 알고 계시는지 궁금합니다. 저희는 그 자리에 귀하와 같은 실력 있는 외과 의사를 찾고 있습니다. 규모 면에서 그레이스 베스는 의료 경영 경력을 쌓기에 아주 좋은 곳입니다. 사실 그레이스 베스 병원은 지역 내 4개 병원 중에서 **17**가장 규모가 큰 병원입니다. 저는 이 직책이 귀하의 **18**특유한 임상 경험에 가장 알맞은 자리임을 알게 되실 거라고 믿습니다. gbhosp.org/openpositions.htm에서 채용 공고를 확인해 보시고, 더 알고 싶은 내용이 있으시면 저에게 연락 주세요.

딘 에크하르트

그레이스 베스 병원 채용 담당자

어휘 | chief of surgery 외과 과장 curriculum vitae 이력서 mutual acquaintance 서로 알고 지내는 지인 be aware of ~을 인식하다, 알다 open position 공석 seek 구하다, 찾다 talented 재능이 있는 surgeon 외과 의사 enhance 향상하다 management 경영, 관리 match 아주 잘 어울리는 사람[것] clinical 임상의

15 (D)

해설 | 전치사 from의 목적어 자리로 빈칸 앞의 형용사 mutual의 수식을 받을 수 있는 명사 (D) acquaintance(지인)가 정답이다.

어휘 | acquaint 숙지시키다, 알게 하다 acquainted 정통한, 잘 알고 있는

16 (A)

번역 | (A) 귀하의 폭넓은 경험이 참으로 인상적이군요.
(B) 매닝 박사가 현재 외과 과장입니다.
(C) 그녀의 지원서를 신중하게 검토해 보시기 바랍니다.
(D) 저희는 또한 지원자들에게 추천서를 요구합니다.

RC

PART 5&6

165

해설 | 빈칸 앞에서 함께 아는 지인 글로리아 매닝 씨를 통해 이력서를 받았다(I received your curriculum vitae)고 했고, 뒤에서는 공석(open position)을 언급했다. 따라서 빈칸에도 야만 푸어 씨의 이력서와 관련된 내용이 들어가야 자연스러우므로, (A)가 정답이다.

어휘 | extensive 폭넓은, 광범위한 currently 현재 application 지원서, 신청서 applicant 지원자

17 (D)

해설 | 문장의 주어인 Grace Beth Hospital을 보충 설명하는 주격 보어 자리로, 정관사 the 및 전치사구 of the region's four hospitals와 결합하여 '지역 내 4개의 병원 중에 가장 큰 (병원)'의 의미를 나타내는 최상급 형용사 (D) largest가 정답이다.

18 (B)

해설 | 소유격 your와 명사 clinical background 사이에서 명사를 수식하는 형용사 자리로 문맥상 '귀하의 특유한 임상 경험'이라는 의미가 자연스러우므로 (B) particular(특유한, 특별한)가 정답이다. 나머지 (A) opaque(불투명한, 이해하기 힘든), (C) forthright(솔직한, 직설적인), (D) generic(일반적인)은 모두 의미상 적합하지 않다.

Unit 16 어휘

● ETS 실전문제 1
본책 p.232

1 (D)	2 (B)	3 (B)	4 (D)	5 (A)	6 (B)
7 (D)	8 (A)	9 (D)	10 (D)	11 (B)	12 (D)

1 (D)

번역 | 포드햄 문구는 밸리 제지가 지속적으로 주문 배송에 늦어서 최근 공급업체를 교체하기로 결정했다.

해설 | late를 수식하는 부사를 선택하는 문제이다. 문맥상 '지속적으로 늦어서 업체를 바꾸었다'는 내용이 되어야 자연스러우므로, (D) consistently가 정답이다. (A) steadily는 '꾸준하게, 성실하게'란 좋은 의미이므로 맞지 않다.

어휘 | switch 바꾸다 supplier 공급업체 shipping 선적, 배송 sensibly 현저히, 현명하게 exactly 정확하게

2 (B)

번역 | 회사 정책을 검토한 후 동봉된 계약서에 서명해서 7월 1일 이전에 보내주십시오.

해설 | 서명해야 하는 계약서(contract)의 상태를 적절히 묘사하는 형용사가 들어가야 하므로, '동봉된'이라는 뜻의 과거분사 (B) enclosed가 정답이다.

어휘 | review 검토하다 corporate 회사의 policy 정책 contract 계약서 surrounding 인근의, 주위의 concerned 염려하는 accepting 흔쾌히 받아들이는

3 (B)

번역 | 농산물 재배자 협회는 비타민이 가장 많이 든 과일과 채소 목록이 있는 소책자를 지역 슈퍼마켓들에 배포했다.

해설 | 전치사 with의 목적어 자리로 '비타민이 최고로 농축된'이라는 의미가 적합하므로 (B) concentrations(농축, 집중)가 정답이다.

어휘 | produce 농작물 grower 재배자 association 협회 distribute 배포하다, 배급하다 list 기록하다, 목록으로 만들다; 목록 attraction 매력 beneficiary 수혜자, 수익자 command 명령, 지휘

4 (D)

번역 | 제이슨 주지사는 세금을 줄이고 학교들에 더 많은 자금을 할당하겠다고 공약했기 때문에 선거에서 승리했다.

해설 | 빈칸에는 to부정사구를 목적어로 취하며, 제이슨 주지사(she)가 선거에서 승리한 이유를 나타내는 동사가 들어가야 한다. 따라서 '약속했다'라는 의미의 (D) promised가 정답이다. (A) followed(뒤따랐다), (B) predicted(예측했다), (C) invented(발명했다)는 구조상/문맥상 빈칸에 적절하지 않다.

5 (A)

번역 | 여름철에는 관광객이 아주 많으므로 그에 따라 여행객들은 계획을 세우고 일찍 예약해야 한다.

해설 | 동사 should plan을 수식하는 부사 자리로 문맥상 '(앞에서 언급한 내용에) 따라'라는 의미가 적합하므로 (A) accordingly가 정답이다. accordingly는 <according to + 명사>의 줄임말로, 앞의 말을 받아서 '그에 따라서'란 뜻이다.

어휘 | subsequently 결과적으로 conversely 거꾸로, 반대로 assuredly 확실히, 틀림없이

6 (B)

번역 | 퀼른의 웰버 기계 공장 엔지니어들은 복잡한 천공 시스템의 설계도에 있는 사소한 결함을 바로잡는 작업을 한다.

해설 | 천공 시스템의 특성을 설명하는 형용사가 들어가야 자연스러우므로, '복잡한'이라는 뜻의 (B) complex가 정답이다. (A) confused(헷갈리는), (C) informative(유익한), (D) cautious(신중한)는 의미상 부적절하다.

어휘 | correct 바로잡다, 정정하다 minor flaw 사소한 결함 drilling 구멍 뚫기, 천공

7 (D)

번역 | 판매원 카를로스 디아즈는 잠재 고객이 밸리 스트림 가구 전시장에 들어설 때 적극적으로 이끌어 진취성을 보여주었다.

해설 | 잠재 고객을 적극적으로 이끌며(by actively engaging potential customers) 보여준 태도를 나타내는 명사가 들어가야 자연스러우므로, '진취성, 주도권'이라는 의미의 (D) initiative가 정답이다.

어휘 | actively 적극적으로, 활발하게 engage 끌다 potential 잠재적인 showroom 전시실 objective 목적, 목표 reliance 의존, 의지

8 (A)

번역 | 아직 한 달이 남았는데 애초에 예상했던 분기 예상 수입액이 이미 초과되었다.

해설 | 주어인 Initial projections와 결합하여 '초기 예상 수입액이 초과되었다'라는 의미를 나타내므로 (A) exceeded가 정답이다.

어휘 | initial 처음의, 초기의 projection 예상, 예측 quarterly 연 4회의, 분기마다의 outdate 시대에 뒤처지게 하다 overdraw (수표나 어음을) 잔액 이상으로 초과 발행하다 impress 깊은 인상을 주다

9 (D)

번역 | 전 세계 스포츠 팬들은 연례 테니스 선수권 대회의 결과를 간절히 기다린다.

해설 | 스포츠 팬들이 결과를 기다리는(await the results) 심정을 적절히 묘사하는 부사가 들어가야 하므로, '간절히, 열심히'라는 의미의 (D) eagerly가 정답이다.

어휘 | perfectly 완벽하게 evenly 균등하게 rapidly 신속히

10 (D)

번역 | 피어플레인 사는 새로운 비행기 시제품이 모든 예비 검사를 통과했다고 어제 발표했다.

해설 | 동사 has passed의 목적어인 testing을 수식하는 형용사 자리로, '예비 검사를 통과했다'라는 내용이 되어야 자연스러우므로 (D) preliminary(예비의)가 정답이다.

어휘 | state 언급하다 prototype 원형, 표본 undeveloped 개발되지 않은 foregone 이미 정해진 subordinate 종속된, 부하의

11 (B)

번역 | 물류 컨설턴트를 고용한 결과 우리 매장들에 상품이 더 빠르게 배부되었다.

해설 | 물류 컨설턴트의 고용(Hiring a logistics consultant)이 가져올 수 있는 결과를 나타내는 명사가 들어가야 하므로, '상품의 더 빠른 배부'라는 의미를 완성하는 (B) distribution(분배, 배부)이 정답이다.

어휘 | founding 설립 treatment 취급, 치료 revision 수정, 개정

12 (D)

번역 | 스와비안 모터스는 경쟁사와 합병한 후에도 현 사명을 그대로 유지할 것이다.

해설 | 목적어 its current name과 결합하여 '현재의 이름을 계속 유지하다'라는 의미를 나타내는 (D) retain이 정답이다.

어휘 | even 심지어 merge with ~와 합병하다 rival 경쟁하는 inquire 문의하다, 묻다 grant 주다, 수여하다

● ETS 실전문제 2
본책 p.233

| 1 (B) | 2 (D) | 3 (A) | 4 (A) | 5 (D) | 6 (B) |
| 7 (A) | 8 (C) | 9 (C) | 10 (B) | 11 (D) | 12 (C) |

1 (B)

번역 | 이 문서에 기술된 계약 조건들은 사전 공지 없이 변경될 수 있다.

해설 | 동사 are의 주어인 The terms and conditions를 보충 설명하는 주격 보어 자리로 빈칸 뒤의 to change와 결합하여 '변경될 수 있는'이라는 의미를 나타내는 형용사 (B) subject가 정답이다. <be subject to + 명사> 구조는 암기해 두자.

어휘 | terms and conditions (거래·계약 등의) 조건 outline (개요를) 서술하다, 기술하다 without notice 예고 없이 dependent 의존하는 immediate 즉각적인

2 (D)

번역 | 신임 공장장인 천하재 씨는 타마린도 시설에서 관리비를 줄이는 업무를 담당할 것이다.

해설 | '관리비를 줄이는 업무를 담당하다'라는 내용이 되어야 자연스러우므로, 전치사 for와 함께 쓰여 '~을 책임지다, 맡다'라는 뜻을 완성하는 (D) responsible이 정답이다.

어휘 | plant director 공장장 reduce 줄이다 maintenance cost 관리비, 유지비 fortunate 운이 좋은 senseless 무의미한

3 (A)

번역 | 다바토 산업에서 나온 최신 전자레인지는 스테인리스강 내부와 10개의 가열 메뉴가 특징이다.

해설 | 빈칸 뒤의 목적어인 a stainless steel interior and ten different heat settings와 결합하여 '~를 특징으로 하다'라는 의미를 나타내는 (A) features가 정답이다.

어휘 | microwave oven 전자레인지 imply 암시하다 appoint 임명하다, (시간·장소 등을) 정하다

4 (A)

번역 | 보드너 체육관 클럽의 플래티넘 회원들만 이용할 수 있는 서비스를 지금 신청하시기 바랍니다.

해설 | '플래티넘 회원들만 이용할 수 있는'이라는 내용이 되어야 자연스러우므로, '오로지, ~만'이라는 뜻의 (A) exclusively가 정답이다.

어휘 | deal 거래 (상품, 서비스) available 이용 가능한 platinum 백금 financially 재정적으로 relatively 비교적 productively 생산적으로

5 (D)

번역 | XT1000은 시판되는 가장 민감한 주방용 저울 중 하나로 밀리그램 단위까지 정확한 측정값을 제공합니다.

해설 | 전치사 of의 목적어인 scales를 수식하는 형용사 자리로 '민감한(정확한) 저울'이라는 의미를 나타내는 (D) sensitive가 정답이다.

어휘 | scale 저울 on the market 시장에 나와 있는, 시판 중인 measurement 측정(값), 측량 tentative 잠정적인 deliberate 고의의, 신중한 investigative 조사의, 연구의

6 (B)

번역 | 예약한 지 2시간 내에 니코야 호텔에서 귀하의 여행 계획을 확정하는 확인 이메일을 받으실 겁니다.

해설 | '확인 이메일을 받을 것이다'라는 내용이 되어야 자연스러우므로, (B) confirmation(확인)이 정답이다.

어휘 | sponsor 후원자 margin 여백, 수익 permit 허가증; 허가하다

7 (A)

번역 | 새로운 조명 시스템이 총무과에 설치되어, 낡고 덜 효율적인 조명을 대체했다.

해설 | 빈칸 뒤의 목적어인 the older, less efficient one과 결합하여 '낡고 덜 효율적인 것을 대체한다'라는 의미를 나타내는 현재분사 (A) replacing이 정답이다.

어휘 | compare A with[to] B A를 B에 비교[비유]하다 brighten 밝게 하다 repair 수리하다

8 (C)

번역 | 데일 백화점은 연휴 직전에 보석류에 대한 특별 할인에 들어갈 것이다.

해설 | before와 결합하여 '~ 직전에'라는 표현을 완성하는
(C) immediately(바로)가 정답이다.

어휘 | department store 백화점 holiday 휴가, 공휴일
sensitively 민감하게 extremely 극도로 figuratively 비유적으로

9 (C)

번역 | 어젯밤 채널 5 뉴스에서 뛰어난 배우인 샌디 소여와의 독점
인터뷰를 방영했다.

해설 | 빈칸이 정관사 the와 명사 actor 사이에 있으므로, actor를
수식하는 형용사 또는 actor와 복합명사를 이루는 명사가 들어갈 수
있다. 문맥상 배우를 묘사하는 형용사가 들어가야 자연스러우므로,
'뛰어난'이라는 의미의 (C) accomplished가 정답이다.

어휘 | accomplish 성취하다 accomplishment 업적, 성취

10 (B)

번역 | 웰본 과학박물관의 새로운 천문 극장은 250명을 수용할 수
있는 좌석 규모를 갖추었다.

해설 | 동사 has의 목적어 자리로 앞의 seating과 결합하여 '좌석
규모'라는 의미를 나타내는 (B) capacity가 정답이다.

어휘 | astronomy 천문학 aptitude 소질, 적성 demonstration
시연 compliance 준수, 따름

11 (D)

번역 | 환경에 더욱 책임을 다하기 위해서, IKM사는 종이를 쓰지 않는
비용 상환 시스템을 시작했다.

해설 | 빈칸은 has와 함께 현재완료 시제를 이루며 명사구 a
paperless expense reimbursement system을 목적어로
취한다. 문맥상 환경을 위해 종이를 쓰지 않는 비용 상환 시스템을
시작했다는 내용이 되어야 자연스러우므로, (D) initiated(시작했다,
착수했다)가 정답이다.

어휘 | reimbursement 상환 confide 신뢰하다 resolve 해결하다,
결심하다 surround 둘러싸다

12 (C)

번역 | 건물 입구에 있는 인상적인 꽃 장식은 주로 파란 꽃으로
이루어져 있고, 빨간 꽃 몇 송이가 구석구석에 솜씨 있게 배치되었다.

해설 | 과거분사 made up of를 수식하는 부사 자리로 '주로
만들어지다, 이루어지다'라는 의미가 적합하므로 (C) primarily
(주로)가 정답이다. 동의어인 largely, mostly, mainly도 답이 될
수 있다.

어휘 | impressive 인상적인 floral display 꽃 장식 artfully 기교
있게

● **ETS 실전문제 3**   본책 p. 234

1 (D)   2 (C)   3 (D)   4 (C)   5 (C)   6 (D)
7 (D)   8 (D)   9 (D)   10 (D) 11 (C) 12 (C)

1 (D)

번역 | 재미슨 단지의 건물들은 평일에 저녁 7시까지 열려 있지만,
적절한 허가증이 있는 직원들은 언제든지 들어올 수 있다.

해설 | 전치사 with의 목적어 자리로, 언제든지 건물에 들어오기
위해서는 '적절한 허가증'이 필요하다는 내용이므로
(D) authorization이 정답이다.

어휘 | complex 복합 건물, (건물) 단지 proper 적절한
reinforcement 강화 participation 참여 competency 능숙함
authorization 허가(증)

2 (C)

번역 | 윈코트 항공사는 자사의 스카이 플라이어 클럽 회원에게는
15파운드의 수하물 비용을 면제해 줄 것이라고 발표했다.

해설 | 목적어 the £15 baggage fee와 결합하여 클럽
회원들에게는 '비용을 면제해 준다'는 내용이므로 (C) waive가
정답이다.

어휘 | prove (to be) ~라는 것이 입증되다 cost A B A에게 B의
비용이 들다 waive (규칙 등을) 적용하지 않다 align 정렬하다

3 (D)

번역 | 더 이상 판촉 할인 광고를 받고 싶지 않으시다면 허글랜드
마켓은 귀하의 이름을 우편물 수신인 목록에서 즉시 삭제할
것입니다.

해설 | 동사 delete를 수식하는 자리로, '귀하의 이름을 즉시
삭제할 것입니다'라는 내용이 되어야 자연스럽다. 따라서
(D) promptly(즉시, 신속하게)가 정답이다.

어휘 | promotional 홍보의, 판촉의 mailing list 우편물 수신인 목록
previously 이전에 overall 전체의; 종합적으로

4 (C)

번역 | 두 공연 사이에는 15분간의 짧은 중간 휴식 시간이 있을
것이다.

해설 | 15분간의 중간 휴식 시간(intermission)을 적절히 묘사하는
형용사가 들어가야 하므로, '짧은, 간결한'이라는 의미의 (C) brief가
정답이다.

5 (C)

번역 | 자너그 사의 신형 냉장고 모델들은 그 회사의 구형 모델들이
사용하는 에너지 양의 극히 일부만을 사용한다.

해설 | 앞의 a, 뒤의 of와 함께 use의 목적어인 energy를
수식하는 자리로, '극히 적은 양의 에너지'라는 의미를 완성하는
(C) fraction(아주 조금, 일부)이 정답이다.

어휘 | refrigerator 냉장고 relation 관계 moderation 적당, 온건,
절제 correction 정정, 수정

6 (D)

번역 | 회계부는 종이 사용을 줄이기 위해서 새로운 정책을 시행했다.

해설 | 빈칸은 has와 현재완료 동사를 이루며 명사구 a new
policy를 목적어로 취한다. '새로운 정책을 시행했다'라는 내용이
되어야 자연스러우므로, (D) implemented(시행했다)가 정답이다.

어휘 | preoccupy 선점하다 represent 나타내다, 대표하다
characterize 특징짓다

7 (D)

번역 | 객실은 호텔 고객이 체크아웃한 후 2시간 이내에 완전히
청소되어야 한다.

해설 | cleaned를 수식하는 자리로, 객실이 청소되는 방식이나

정도를 나타내는 부사가 들어가야 자연스럽다. 따라서 '완전히, 철저히'라는 의미의 (D) thoroughly가 정답이다.

어휘 | patron 고객 widely 널리 highly 매우 sturdily 억세게, 기운차게

8 (D)

번역 | 해외 마케팅 매니저는 널리 출장 다니는 것이 요구되므로, 익숙하지 않은 상황에 잘 적응할 수 있어야 한다.

해설 | 동사 must be의 주어인 The Global Marketing Manager를 보충 설명하는 주격 보어 자리로, to unfamiliar situations와 결합하여 '익숙하지 않은 상황에 적응할 수 있는'이라는 의미를 완성하는 (D) adaptable이 정답이다.

어휘 | extensively 광범위하게 unfamiliar 익숙하지 않은 be opposed to ~에 반대하다 versatile 다용도의, 다재 다능한 relative 상대적인

9 (D)

번역 | 3월 12일 교육에 참석할 수 없는 직원은 대체 가능한 날짜로 편성될 예정이다.

해설 | 3월 12일 교육에 참석할 수 없는 직원은 다른 날짜에 참석할 수 있게 해 주겠다는 내용이므로, '대체 가능한, 대안적인'이라는 의미의 (D) alternative가 정답이다.

어휘 | attend 참석하다 be scheduled for ~로 예정되다, 편성되다 unoccupied 비어 있는, 점령되지 않은 irreplaceable 대체 불가능한

10 (D)

번역 | 페일스 북스토어스는 올해 순익이 20퍼센트 하락했다고 발표했는데, 이 회사는 이것을 율 북셀러스 사와의 치열한 경쟁에서 기인한 결과로 보았다.

해설 | 빈칸은 목적격 관계대명사 which가 이끄는 절의 동사 자리로, which가 가리키는 a 20 percent decrease in net profit이 의미상 직접목적어 역할을 한다. 따라서 전치사구 to fierce competition과 결합하여 '순익 감소는 치열한 경쟁 때문이다'라는 의미를 완성하는 (D) attributed가 정답이다. 'A를 B의 탓으로 돌리다'라는 뜻의 <attribute A to B> 구조를 암기해두자.

어휘 | accuse 고발하다, 비난하다 present 증정하다, 제출하다 disapprove 못마땅해 하다, 불만을 나타내다

11 (C)

번역 | 환경 오염 예방은 소기업과 대기업 모두에게 중요한 고려 사항이 되었다.

해설 | 빈칸 앞의 and와 결합하여 '둘 다 똑같이, 모두'의 의미를 나타내는 부사 (C) alike가 정답이다. <A and B alike>는 <both A and B>의 형태로도 쓸 수 있다.

어휘 | prevention 예방, 방지 environmental 환경의 pollution 오염 consideration 고려 사항 forth ~에서 멀리, 밖으로

12 (C)

번역 | 마이어 컴퍼니의 계약 조건이 매년 변경될 수 있다는 점을 알아 두십시오.

해설 | 계약 조건(terms and conditions)이 변경될 수 있다는 점을 고지하는 내용이므로, '알아 두십시오'라는 의미를 완성하는 (C) aware(~를 알고 있는)가 정답이다. Please be aware that, Please note that 등과 같은 표현은 암기해두는 것이 좋다.

어휘 | terms and conditions 조건, 약관 contract 계약 be subject to ~될 수 있다, ~에 달려 있다 annually 매년, 일 년에 한 번

● **ETS 실전문제 4**   본책 p.235

- -

| 1 (C) | 2 (B) | 3 (D) | 4 (D) | 5 (D) | 6 (B) |
| 7 (C) | 8 (A) | 9 (C) | 10 (A) | 11 (A) | 12 (B) |

1 (C)

번역 | 새롭게 웹사이트를 개선해서, 힐 스트리트 디자인 고객들은 최근 구매품의 간략한 내역을 볼 수 있을 것이다.

해설 | 빈칸은 동사 view의 목적어 자리로 '최근 구매품들의 내역이 간략하게 정리된 것'을 나타내는 명사가 들어가야 자연스럽다. 따라서 (C) summary(요약, 개요)가 정답이다.

어휘 | enhancement 향상, 상승 purchase 구매(품) voucher 상품권, 쿠폰 payment 지불(금)

2 (B)

번역 | 내 의견으로는, 이 회사의 주가는 연간 수익과 비교해 상대적으로 낮다.

해설 | 형용사 low를 강조하는 부사 자리로, 뒤의 compared to와 결합하여 '~에 비해서 상대적으로 낮은'이라는 의미를 나타내는 (B) relatively가 정답이다.

어휘 | in my opinion 내 의견으로는 stock price 주가 compared to ~와 비교하여 earnings 소득, 이익 audibly 들을 수 있게 plentifully 풍부하게 anonymously 익명으로

3 (D)

번역 | 스텔라스 제과점의 교대 근무 시간은 8시간이며 점심시간 30분이 포함된다.

해설 | 근무 시간(work shifts)에 점심시간 30분이 포함되어 있다는 내용이 되어야 자연스러우므로, (D) include(포함하다)가 정답이다.

어휘 | confectionary 제과, 제과 회사 prepare 준비하다 release 공개하다, 출시하다 assemble 조립하다

4 (D)

번역 | 반스 씨는 신입 영업사원을 위한 교육 프로그램을 검토한 후에, 관계망 형성 기술에 좀 더 주안점을 두어야 한다고 결론 내렸다.

해설 | 빈칸 뒤 동사 should be placed와 함께 '강조되어야 한다'라는 의미를 완성하는 (D) emphasis가 정답이다. <place[put] an emphasis on 명사>는 '~에 주안점을 두다, ~를 강조하다'라는 의미로 사용된다.

어휘 | conclude 결론 내리다 networking 네트워킹, 개인적 인맥[정보망]의 형성 appeal 애원, 호소 analysis 분석 distinction 구별

5 (D)

번역 | 피츠턴 갤러리는 워딩턴에서 주요 예술 기획사였으며 많은 공개 행사를 후원해 왔다.

해설 | 많은 공개 행사를 후원한 기획사(promoter)를 적절히 수식하는 형용사가 들어가야 하므로, '주요한, 제1의'라는 뜻의 (D) primary가 정답이다.

어휘 | sponsor 후원하다 public event 공개[공공] 행사 precise 정확한 separate 분리된 certain 확실한, 어떤

6 (B)

번역 | 달리 명시되어 있지 않다면, 사진과 관련 서류들은 저자에 의해 제공된 것이다.

해설 | 빈칸 뒤의 과거분사 noted를 수식하는 부사 자리로 unless와 함께 '달리 명시되어 있지 않다면'이라는 의미를 완성하는 (B) otherwise(~와 다르게)가 정답이다. <unless otherwise 과거분사> 구문은 암기해두는 것이 좋다.

어휘 | document 문서, 서류

7 (C)

번역 | 노구치 인베스트먼트는 고객에게 최상의 서비스를 제공하기 위해 정기적으로 철저한 업계 현재 동향 분석을 실시한다.

해설 | 정기적으로 실시되는 분석들(analyses)의 특징을 묘사하는 형용사가 들어가야 하므로, '철저한, 빈틈없는'이라는 의미의 (C) thorough가 정답이다.

어휘 | regularly 정기적으로 conduct 실시하다 analysis 분석 current 현재의 spacious 널찍한 eventual 궁극적인, 최종적인 probable 개연성이 있는

8 (A)

번역 | 우리 직원들이 배송 양식에 정확한 주소를 쓰지 않았지만, 기계 부품들은 예정대로 낙농장에 도착했다.

해설 | 전치사 on과 결합하여 '일정대로'라는 의미를 나타내는 명사 (A) schedule이 정답이다. '예정보다 늦게'라는 의미의 <behind schedule>, '예정보다 빨리'라는 의미의 <ahead of schedule>도 알아두자.

어휘 | form 서식, 양식 part 부품 dairy farm 낙농장 appointment 약속 authority 지휘권, 권한 condition 상태

9 (C)

번역 | 메리 번역회사는 통역사를 통해 사업 관계자와 의사소통할 때 예의 바르게 주의를 기울일 것을 제안한다.

해설 | 빈칸 뒤 전치사 with와 어울려 쓰여 '~와 의사소통하다'라는 의미를 완성하는 (C) communicating이 정답이다.

어휘 | suggest 제안하다 associate 동료, 관계[제휴]자 interpreter 통역사 focus one's attention on ~에 주목하다, 주의를 기울이다 regulate 규제하다, 조정하다 acquaint 숙지시키다 contemplate 고려하다, 생각하다

10 (A)

번역 | 도시 계획 책임자에 따르면, 애들레이드의 구도심 지역은 신도심 건설 작업이 시작하기 전에 완전히 철거되어야 한다.

해설 | 동사 must be demolished와 의미상 잘 어울리는 부사 어휘를 선택하는 문제로, '완전히 철거되어야 한다'라는 내용이 되어야 가장 자연스러우므로 (A) completely가 정답이다.

어휘 | city planning 도시 계획 director 책임자, 관리자 civic center 도심, 관청가 demolish 철거하다 construction 건설 new center 신도심 defectively 불완전하게 plentifully 많이, 풍부하게 richly 화려하게, 풍부하게

11 (A)

번역 | TV 뉴스 프로그램인 플림튼 리포트는 세계의 사건들을 신뢰성

있게 보도하는 것으로 알려져 있다.

해설 | 전치사 for의 목적어 역할을 하는 coverage(보도)를 수식하는 형용사 자리로, 문맥상 '신뢰할 만한 보도'라는 내용이 되어야 자연스럽다. 따라서 '믿을 만한'이라는 의미의 형용사 (A) reliable이 정답이다.

어휘 | coverage 보도 reliance 의존, 의지

12 (B)

번역 | 사누라이프 웹사이트는 여러분께 의학 연구 분야의 모든 최신 발전에 대한 소식을 알려 드립니다.

해설 | 전치사 of의 목적어 자리로, 앞의 all the latest와 결합하여 '최신 발전'이라는 의미를 나타내는 (B) advances가 정답이다. 참고로 명사 advance는 주로 전치사 in과 함께 쓰인다.

어휘 | novelty 새로움, 신기함 elevation 격상, 높이 formation 형성, 대형

● ETS 실전문제 5

1 (B)	2 (B)	3 (A)	4 (A)	5 (D)	6 (D)
7 (D)	8 (D)	9 (B)	10 (D)	11 (B)	12 (C)

1 (B)

번역 | 직원 편람은 경비 보고서 제출 절차를 명확히 설명한다.

해설 | 빈칸 뒤의 목적어 the procedure와 결합하여 '절차를 설명하다'라는 의미를 나타내므로 (B) outlines(서술하다, 설명하다)가 정답이다.

어휘 | procedure 절차 file (증서나 서류를) 정식으로 제출하다 purchase 구입하다 ration 배급하다 invest 투자하다

2 (B)

번역 | 전화 상담원은 전화를 받을 때 합당한 범위 내에서 고객의 우려사항을 처리하기 위해 가능한 것들을 해야 한다.

해설 | 빈칸 앞 전치사 within과 어울려 쓰이는 명사를 선택하는 문제이다. 고객의 우려사항을 처리하기 위해(to address customer concerns) 하는 일은 합당한 범위 내에서 이루어져야 한다는 내용이므로, '합리적인 범위(sensible limits)'를 뜻하는 (B) reason이 정답이다. within reason은 고정된 표현으로 암기해 두는 것이 좋다.

어휘 | representative 대리인, 담당자 address 고심하다, 다루다 concern 우려 (사항)

3 (A)

번역 | 밤새도록 비가 내려 다행히 최근 가뭄을 완화해 주었다.

해설 | 비가 밤새(throughout the night) 내린 모습을 적절히 묘사하는 부사가 빈칸에 들어가야 하므로, '계속해서, 끊임없이'라는 의미의 (A) continuously가 정답이다.

어휘 | relief 안도, 경감 recent 최근의 dry spell 가뭄, 건기 mutually 상호간에, 서로 needlessly 쓸데없이, 불필요하게 optimistically 낙관적으로

4 (A)

번역 | 직원들은 최소 12개월 이상 근무했다면 육아 휴직과 병가를 낼

자격이 있다.

해설 | 주어인 Employees를 보충 설명하는 주격 보어 자리로, to 부정사와 결합하여 '~할 자격이 있는'이라는 의미를 나타내는 형용사 (A) eligible이 정답이다.

어휘 | leave 휴가 desirable 바람직한, 호감이 가는 preferred 우선의 suitable 적합한

5 (D)

번역 | 누노카와 씨의 기조연설 후 컨벤션 센터 중앙 로비에서 환영 연회가 이어질 것이다.

해설 | 기조연설(keynote speech)과 환영회(reception)가 진행되는 순서를 나타내는 과거분사가 들어가야 자연스러우므로, be동사 및 by와 함께 '이어지다'라는 의미를 완성하는 과거분사 (D) followed가 정답이다.

어휘 | keynote speech 기조연설 reception 환영 연회 acquire 획득하다, 얻다 detail 상세히 열거하다

6 (D)

번역 | 퀴브테크 디자인은 최근 구직자의 적합성을 평가하기 위한 절차를 개선했다.

해설 | 구직자에 대해 회사가 평가하는(measuring) 항목을 나타내는 명사가 들어가야 자연스러우므로, '적합성'이라는 의미의 (D) suitability가 정답이다.

어휘 | recently 최근 process 과정, 절차 measure 판단하다, 평가하다 job applicant 구직자 resource 자원

7 (D)

번역 | 새로운 품질보장 정책은 하루에 불량품이 5개 이상 나올 경우 모든 기계를 점검할 것을 요구한다.

해설 | 기계 점검(all machines be inspected)의 원인이 되는 상품의 상태를 묘사하는 형용사가 들어가야 하며, '결함이 있는'이라는 의미의 (D) defective가 정답이다.

어휘 | quality assurance 품질보장 policy 정책 inspect 점검하다, 검사하다 collective 집단의 efficient 효율적인 immediate 즉각적인

8 (D)

번역 | 상인들이 <위클리 라운드업> 지에 게재한 광고들이 반드시 저희 경영진의 보증을 받은 것임을 암시하지는 않습니다.

해설 | imply를 수식하는 부사 자리로 not과 결합하여 '반드시 암시하지는 않는다'라는 의미를 나타내는 (D) necessarily가 정답이다. '반드시 ~하지는 않는'이라는 부분 부정의 의미를 나타내는 not necessarily는 고정된 표현으로 암기해 두는 것이 좋다.

어휘 | merchant 상인, 무역상 imply 암시하다 endorsement 지지, (유명인이 광고에 나와 하는 상품에 대한) 보증, 홍보 barely 간신히, 가까스로 gradually 서서히

9 (B)

번역 | 로즈 패션 부티크는 이번 주 토요일에 모든 구매 고객에게 20퍼센트 할인을 제공할 예정이다.

해설 | 할인과 관련하여 회사가 구매 고객에게 할 수 있는 행위를 나타내는 동사가 필요하므로, '제공하다'는 의미의 (B) offering이 정답이다. 참고로, (A) notifying은 통지를 받는 대상인 사람 명사를 직접목적어로 취한다.

어휘 | notify 알리다 perform 수행하다, 공연하다

10 (D)

번역 | 부서 관리자는 강 씨에게 완성된 직원 평가서를 보내야 한다.

해설 | 관리자가 보낼 직원 평가서(employee evaluations)의 상태를 적절히 묘사하는 형용사가 들어가야 하므로, '작성된, 완성된'이라는 뜻의 (D) completed가 정답이다.

어휘 | department 부서 evaluation 평가 steady 꾸준한 skillful 숙련된 turned 돌려진

11 (B)

번역 | 이 웹사이트 이용은 우리의 약관에 동의함을 의미합니다.

해설 | 동사 implies의 목적어 자리로, 빈칸 뒤 with our terms and conditions와 결합하여 '약관에 대한 동의'라는 의미를 나타내는 (B) agreement가 정답이다.

어휘 | imply 의미하다, 암시하다 terms and conditions 약관[조건] contentment 만족 placement 설치 development 발달

12 (C)

번역 | 전시 중이 아닐 경우, 희귀 필사본은 보존에 가장 적합한 환경에 보관되어 있다.

해설 | 원고 보존을 위한 보관 환경의 상태(conditions)를 적절히 묘사하는 형용사가 들어가야 하므로, '최적의, 가장 좋은'이라는 의미의 (C) optimal이 정답이다.

어휘 | be on display 전시 중이다 rare 진기한, 드문 manuscript 필사본, 원고 preservation 보존 attentive 주의를 기울이는 credible 믿을 수 있는 competent 능숙한

● ETS 실전문제 6
본책 p.237

| 1 (D) | 2 (C) | 3 (D) | 4 (C) | 5 (B) | 6 (C) |
| 7 (B) | 8 (B) | 9 (B) | 10 (D) | 11 (C) | 12 (B) |

1 (D)

번역 | 패티슨 씨는 3년간 일하면서 한 번도 마감 기한을 어긴 적이 없는 것으로 상을 받았다.

해설 | 빈칸 이하는 상을 받은 근거를 나타내므로, '마감 기한을 어긴 적이 없다'는 내용이 되어야 자연스럽다. 따라서 (D) never(결코 ~않는)가 정답이다.

어휘 | receive an award 상을 받다 miss a deadline 기한을 놓치다

2 (C)

번역 | 와튼 가 구역에 더 많은 업체를 유치하자는 시 의회의 제안서는 이 달 중으로 마무리될 것이다.

해설 | 제안서(proposal)와 시점(later this month)을 의미상 적절히 연결하는 과거분사가 빈칸에 들어가야 하므로, '마무리된, 완성된'이라는 의미의 (C) finalized가 정답이다.

어휘 | city council 시 의회 attract 끌어 모으다 remind 상기시키다 reduce 줄이다, 축소하다 confuse 혼란스럽게 하다

3 (D)

번역 | 목요일에 약한 비가 내릴 가능성이 있는 가운데, 이번 주 내내 온화한 날씨가 계속될 것 같다.

해설 | be동사 및 to부정사와 어울려 쓰이는 형용사를 선택하는 문제로, '~할 것 같다'는 의미를 완성하는 (D) likely가 정답이다. (A) probable도 비슷한 의미이지만 구조상 빈칸에 들어갈 수 없다. 참고로, likely와 probable은 <It is probable/likely that절>의 구조로 가능성 있는 상황을 묘사할 수 있다.

어휘 | with a chance of ~할 가능성이 있는 probable 개연성 있는 frequent 빈번한 considerable 상당한, 많은

4 (C)

번역 | 실험실 테스트는 세정제가 효과적이기 위해서는 다양한 원료들의 정확한 배합이 필요하다는 것을 보여 준다.

해설 | 전치사 of의 목적어 자리로, 앞의 combination과 결합하여 '다양한 원료들의 배합'이라는 의미를 완성하는 (C) ingredients(재료, 원료)가 정답이다.

어휘 | precise 정확한 combination 결합 compound 혼합물, 화합물 effective 효과적인 division 분할, 부문 prospect 가능성 compartment 칸막이, 구획

5 (B)

번역 | 장식용 식물 품종에 대한 수요가 곧 늘어날 것으로 예상되니 정원사들은 이를 비축해 두는 것이 좋다.

해설 | 늘어날 것이 예상되는(is expected to rise) 미래 상황과 어울리는 부사가 들어가야 자연스러우므로, (B) soon(곧)이 정답이다.

어휘 | demand 수요 decorative 장식용의 variety 품종 be encouraged to do ~할 것이 장려되다 stock up 비축하다 eagerly 열심히, 간절히

6 (C)

번역 | 우리는 선라이즈 팜즈처럼 현지의 환경 친화적 업체로부터 재료를 구하는 것을 선호한다.

해설 | 현지의 환경 친화적인 업체로부터 나온 재료(ingredients)와 관련하여 할 수 있는 행위를 나타내는 동사가 필요하므로, '구하다, 얻다'라는 의미의 (C) obtain이 정답이다.

어휘 | environmentally friendly 환경 친화적인 comprise 구성하다 achieve 달성하다

7 (B)

번역 | 멜로 어드버타이징은 색이 밝고 눈길을 끄는 로고, 전단 및 기타 홍보물로 잘 알려져 있다.

해설 | 광고 회사가 제작하는 자료(material)의 목적을 나타내는 형용사가 들어가야 자연스러우므로, '판촉의, 홍보의'라는 의미의 (B) promotional이 정답이다.

어휘 | eye-catching 눈길을 끄는 flyer 전단 conditional 조건부의 promotional material 홍보물

8 (B)

번역 | 크로스 코브는 많은 뉴질랜드 예술가들의 고향인데, 그중에 특히 프란시스 슈어드 씨와 카일 매킨타이어 씨가 유명하다.

해설 | 빈칸 뒤의 명사구를 강조하는 자리로, '그중에서도 특히 가장 유명한'이라는 의미를 완성하는 (B) notably(특히 ~한)가 정답이다.

어휘 | separately 각각, 개별적으로 commonly 공통적으로

9 (B)

번역 | 헤스턴 부동산 관리는 현재 진행되는 개조 공사가 세입자들에게 줄 수 있는 불편에 대해 사과드립니다.

해설 | 사과(apologizes)의 이유가 되는 명사가 들어가야 하므로, '불편'이라는 의미의 (B) inconvenience가 정답이다.

어휘 | apologize 사과하다 current 현재의 renovation 개조, 수리 tenant 세입자 resolution 해결 improvement 개선, 향상 distinction 차이

10 (D)

번역 | 내일 회의 말미에 시간이 있으면 실라 샘슨이 토론토 아트 페스티벌에 대해 간략히 이야기할 것이다.

해설 | 회의 말미에 시간이 있을 경우(If there is time) 특정 주제에 대해 간략하게 이야기할 것이라는 내용이 되어야 자연스러우므로, '간략히'라는 의미의 (D) briefly가 정답이다.

어휘 | rarely 드물게 slightly 약간

11 (C)

번역 | 도시의 스트레스에서 멀리 떨어진 곳에 있는 코즈칼 호텔은 고객에게 편안한 휴가 경험을 제공하는 것에 대해 자부심을 갖고 있습니다.

해설 | 호텔이 제공하는 휴가 경험(vacation experience)의 특성을 적절히 묘사하는 형용사가 들어가야 하므로, '편안한'이라는 의미의 (C) relaxing이 정답이다.

어휘 | pride oneself on ~를 자랑하다 reclining 기대는 restored 회복된 retired 은퇴한

12 (B)

번역 | 하트윅 운송의 아템브 씨는 화물 운송에 대한 고객들의 우려를 해결해 줄 가장 좋은 방법들에 관한 워크숍을 열 것이다.

해설 | 목적어인 concerns와 결합하여 '우려를 해결하다'라는 의미를 나타내는 (B) address(처리하다, 해결하다)가 정답이다. 참고로, address는 issue나 problem과도 자주 쓰인다.

어휘 | inform A of B A에게 B에 대해 알리다 supervise 관리[감독]하다

● ETS 실전문제 7   본책 p.238

1 (A) 2 (C) 3 (D) 4 (A) 5 (A) 6 (D)
7 (C) 8 (B) 9 (B) 10 (C) 11 (A) 12 (B)

1 (A)

번역 | 크래독 서지컬 프로덕트 사에서의 고용 관련 문의는 인사부서로 보내져야 한다.

해설 | '고용 관련 문의'라는 의미가 되어야 자연스러우므로, (A) Inquiries(문의, 문의 사항)가 정답이다.

어휘 | regarding ~에 관한 employment 고용 direct 보내다 influence 영향 occasion 경우, 때 qualification 자질, 자격

2 **(C)**

번역 | 경영 분석가들은 젬퀴스트 주식회사가 보류 중인 합병 결정을 곧 내리기를 기대한다.

해설 | 합병 결정(merger decision)이 아직 내려지지 않은 상황을 나타내므로, '보류 중인, 미결정인'이라는 의미의 (C) pending이 정답이다.

어휘 | analyst 분석가 merger 합병 decision 결정 sparse 드문, 희박한 related 관련된 attentive 주의를 기울이는

3 **(D)**

번역 | 고객들은 퍼포먼스 와이어리스의 낮은 요금과 훌륭한 고객 서비스 때문에 흔히 돌아온다.

해설 | 긍정적인 요인으로 인해 고객들이 돌아오는 경우가 많다는 내용이 되어야 자연스러우므로, '자주, 흔히'라는 의미의 (D) frequently가 정답이다.

어휘 | moderately 적당히 mutually 상호간에, 서로

4 **(A)**

번역 | 리넬라 미디어 그룹은 작년에 새로운 미디어 분야의 수익 성장이 텔레비전 광고의 감소를 상쇄하도록 도와주었음을 시사했다.

해설 | 빈칸 뒤의 목적어 a decrease in television advertising과 결합하여 '감소·하락을 메우다, 상쇄하다'라는 의미를 나타내므로 타동사 (A) offset(상쇄하다)이 정답이다.

어휘 | growth 성장, 발전 revenue 수입 outplay 패배시키다 input 입력하다 overact 지나치게 행동하다

5 **(A)**

번역 | 프린델 커뮤니케이션즈의 복잡한 신규 시간 보고 지침은 직원들에게 혼란을 야기했다.

해설 | 복잡한 지침(The complicated new time-reporting guidelines)으로 인해 직원들이 겪게 될 문제점을 나타내는 명사가 들어가야 자연스러우므로, '혼란, 혼동'이라는 의미의 (A) confusion이 정답이다.

어휘 | complicated 복잡한 guideline 지침 attention 주의, 주목 impression 인상

6 **(D)**

번역 | 슈 잉 장 박사는 분자생물학 분야에 중요한 공헌을 해 명망 있는 로랜드 메달을 받았다.

해설 | 로랜드 메달(Loland Medal)의 위상을 적절히 묘사하는 형용사가 들어가야 하므로, '명망 있는, 일류의'라는 의미의 (D) prestigious가 정답이다.

어휘 | be awarded 상을 받다 significant 중요한 contribution 공헌 molecular biology 분자생물학 dominant 우세한 cooperative 협력하는

7 **(C)**

번역 | 오크만 코퍼레이션은 8월 6일에 신임 회장 임명을 발표했다.

해설 | 회사에서 신임 회장의 임명을 발표했다는 내용이 되어야 자연스러우므로, '발표했다, 알렸다'라는 의미의 (C) announced가 정답이다. 참고로, (A) informed는 알림의 대상인 사람 명사를 목적어로 취한다.

어휘 | appointment 임명 announce 발표하다, 알리다

8 **(B)**

번역 | 윌트셔 오케스트라의 콘서트는 대략 3시간 길이였고, 밤 11시가 막 지나서 끝났다.

해설 | 숫자 표현 three (hours)를 수식하는 부사 자리로 '대략'이란 의미의 (B) approximately가 정답이다.

어휘 | just after ~ 직후에 attentively 세심하게 endlessly 끝없이 comparatively 비교적

9 **(B)**

번역 | 피셔 카페테리아는 평일 오후 3시부터 10시까지 저녁 교대조를 감독할 상근직 부지배인을 찾고 있다.

해설 | 평일 오후 3시부터 10시까지 부지배인이 감독할 대상을 나타내는 명사가 들어가야 하므로, '교대조'라는 의미의 (B) shift가 정답이다.

어휘 | oversee 감독하다 practice 실행, 연습 effect 영향, 효과

10 **(C)**

번역 | 동료 간의 빈번하고 긍정적인 상호작용은 연중 생산성 향상과 관련이 있었다.

해설 | 빈칸 뒤 productivity와 결합하여 '증가된 생산성'이라는 의미를 완성하는 (C) increased가 정답이다.

어휘 | frequent 빈번한, 잦은 positive 긍정적인 coworker 동료 be associated with ~와 관련되다 productivity 생산성 licensed 허가를 받은, 면허를 소지한

11 **(A)**

번역 | 오스왈트 인터내셔널은 200개가 넘는 개발 프로젝트를 성공적으로 완수했기 때문에 현재 서비스 수요가 높다.

해설 | 서비스 수요가 높은 이유를 언급한 부분이므로, 개발 프로젝트를 성공적으로 완수했다(has completed)는 내용이 되어야 자연스럽다. 따라서 (A) successfully가 정답이다.

어휘 | complete 완료하다 development 개발 be in high demand 수요가 높다 instantly 즉각, 즉시 financially 재정적으로

12 **(B)**

번역 | 효과적인 감시 없이 안전 규정을 시행하기는 어려울 것이다.

해설 | 목적어 the safety regulations와 결합하여 '안전 규정을 시행하다'라는 의미를 나타내는 (B) enforce(시행하다)가 정답이다.

어휘 | safety regulations 안전 규정 effective 효과적인 monitor 모니터하다, 감시하다 entrust (일을) 맡기다 imply 암시하다, 내포하다 implore 애원하다, 간청하다

● **ETS 실전문제 8**　　　　　　　　본책 p. 239

| 1 (C) | 2 (C) | 3 (A) | 4 (B) | 5 (A) | 6 (C) |
| 7 (D) | 8 (A) | 9 (A) | 10 (B) | 11 (B) | 12 (B) |

1 **(C)**

번역 | 목요일 회의에 참석할 수 없는 직원은 에버렛 왓슨에게 알려야 한다.

해설 | be동사 및 to부정사와 함께 쓰여 '~할 수 없다'라는 의미를 완성하는 (C) unable이 정답이다.

어휘 | personnel 직원들, 인원 attend 참석하다 unpleasant 불쾌한

2 (C)

번역 | 핼리건 윈도우 드레싱에서 만든 블라인드는 색상이 다양하게 나오며 대부분의 창문에 맞도록 주문 제작될 수 있다.

해설 | 전치사 in과 어울려 쓰이는 자동사를 선택해야 한다. 블라인드가 다양한 색상(a variety of colors)으로 시장에 출시된다는 내용을 완성하는 자동사 (C) come(나오다)이 정답이다.

어휘 | a variety of 다양한 customize 주문 제작하다

3 (A)

번역 | 새 수영장 공사는 현재 진행 중으로 5월 1일까지 완료될 것으로 예상된다.

해설 | 5월 1일 완공 예정인 수영장 공사의 현황을 나타내는 명사가 빈칸에 들어가야 하므로, 전치사 in과 함께 '진행 중인'이라는 의미를 완성하는 (A) progress가 정답이다.

어휘 | construction 건설, 공사 currently 현재 complete 완료하다 in place 제자리에 있는 demand 수요

4 (B)

번역 | 대너 코퍼레이션은 3년 연속 신입사원 채용 목표를 이루었다.

해설 | 명사 year를 수식하는 형용사 자리로, the third 및 year와 결합하여 '3년 연속'이라는 의미를 나타내는 형용사 (B) consecutive(연속적인)가 정답이다. 참고로, <for the +서수(third) +consecutive year> 혹은 <for +기수(three) +consecutive years>로 표현할 수 있는데, 이때 year의 단복수 차이에 유의해야 한다.

어휘 | meet (기준·목표를) 맞추다, 충족시키다 recruitment 신입사원 모집[채용] following 그 다음의 approximate 거의 정확한, 대략의 absolute 절대적인

5 (A)

번역 | 크레숑 공원의 나무 일부는 조경 전문가들이 의도적으로 심은 반면 대부분은 씨앗에서 자연적으로 성장했다.

해설 | '조경 전문가(landscaping professionals)에 의해 의도적으로 심어진'이라는 내용이 되어야 자연스러우므로, (A) intentionally(의도적으로)가 정답이다.

어휘 | plant 심다 landscaping 조경 seed 씨앗 intentionally 일부러, 의도적으로 highly 매우 profoundly 완전히, 극심하게 indefinitely 무기한으로

6 (C)

번역 | 손더가드 난방기기는 매우 효율적이어서 주택 소유자들의 난방비를 줄여준다.

해설 | 난방비를 줄여주는 기기의 특성을 적절히 묘사한 형용사가 들어가야 하므로, '효율적인'이라는 의미의 (C) efficient가 정답이다.

어휘 | result in 그 결과로 ~이 되다 heating cost 난방비 reasonable 합리적인, 가격이 적정한 preferred 우선의

7 (D)

번역 | 고객이 긴급 서비스를 선택하지 않는 한, 주문은 보통 처리되는

데 사흘이 걸린다.

해설 | 긴급 서비스가 아닌 일반 주문은 통상 사흘이 걸린다는 내용이 되어야 자연스러우므로, '보통, 통상적으로'라는 의미의 (D) typically가 정답이다.

어휘 | expedited 긴급의 process 처리하다 substantially 상당히, 주로 perpetually 영구히 familiarly 스스럼없이, 친근하게

8 (A)

번역 | 피에르 던 씨는 델번 제조사의 사장으로 근무할 때, 회사를 변화시킨 여러 정책을 실시했다.

해설 | 목적어 several policies와 결합하여 '여러 정책을 실시[실행]하다'라는 의미를 나타내는 (A) instituted (실시했다)가 정답이다.

어휘 | transform 바꾸다 relieve A of B A에게서 B(짐, 부담, 책임)를 덜어 주다 fabricate 조립하다, 제작하다

9 (A)

번역 | WHJ 연구 목적은 윌밍데일 업무지구에 자전거 도로를 추가하는 것의 실행 가능성을 알아내는 것이다.

해설 | 자전거 도로 추가 계획과 관련하여 연구에서 알아내야 (determine) 하는 사항을 나타내는 명사가 들어가야 하므로, '실행 가능성'이라는 의미의 (A) feasibility가 정답이다.

어휘 | purpose 의도, 목적 determine 알아내다, 판단하다, 결정하다 district 지구 dependency 의존, 종속 intensity 강도 accuracy 정확성

10 (B)

번역 | 윈 대학교 연구원들은 모조와르노 자연보호구역 내 식물 종을 기록하면서 몇 개월을 보냈다.

해설 | 명사구 the plant species를 목적어로 취하며 '종을 기록하면서'라는 의미를 완성하는 (B) documenting이 정답이다. 참고로, (A) experimenting과 (C) commenting은 자동사로 전치사 on과 함께 쓰인다.

어휘 | species 종 nature preserve 자연보호구역 experiment 실험하다 document 기록하다 comment 견해를 밝히다, 논평하다 accomplish 성취하다, 완수하다

11 (B)

번역 | 구 씨의 원고 마감 기한은 6개월이나 남았지만, 그녀는 초고를 거의 완성했다.

해설 | 마감 기한이 아직 많이 남았지만 초고가 완성되었다는 내용으로, 빈칸에는 완성 정도를 나타내는 부사가 들어가야 자연스럽다. 따라서 (B) nearly(거의)가 정답이다.

어휘 | due 제출해야 하는 complete 완료하다 draft 초안, 원고 rarely 드물게, 좀처럼 ~하지 않는

12 (B)

번역 | 가구 운송 절차를 간소화함으로써, 우리는 비용을 낮추고 배송 시간을 절반으로 줄일 수 있다.

해설 | 목적어인 the furniture shipping process와 결합하여 '절차를 간소화함으로써'라는 의미를 나타내는 동명사 (B) streamlining이 정답이다.

어휘 | outpace ~을 능가하다 persevere 인내하다 forestall 미연에 방지하다

Unit 17   편지 / 이메일

지문 구성과 독해 전략   본책 p. 244

> 수신: 레이첼 모스 <rmorse@mailnet.com>
> 발신: 프랭크 오토 리페어 <cs@franksautorepair.com>
> 제목: 차량 서비스
> 날짜: 7월 1일
>
> 모스 씨께,
>
> 저희 기록에 의하면 귀하의 차량이 서비스 예약을 할 시기가
> 되었습니다. 다음 사항 점검 시 20퍼센트 할인을 받으시려면 앞으로
> 30일 이내에 예약을 잡으세요.
>
> • 엔진   • 타이어
> • 오일 양   • 배터리
>
> 다음의 링크를 클릭해 쿠폰을 출력하시고, 예약에 맞춰 오셔서 비용
> 지불 시 함께 제출해 주십시오.
> www.franksautorepair.com/inspectioncoupon.
> 예약 날짜를 잡으려면 (206) 555-0117로 전화하세요.
> 곧 뵙기를 바랍니다!
>
> 고객서비스 부서
> 프랭크 오토 리페어

> 어휘 | due ~하기로 되어 있는, 예정된 inspection 점검 fluid 유동체,
> (자동차의) 오일 submit 제출하다

Q1 이메일의 목적은?
(A) 환불되었음을 확인하기 위해
(B) 고객에게 지불을 요청하기 위해
(C) 고객에게 예약을 잡으라고 상기시키기 위해
(D) 예약 날짜가 잡혔음을 확인해 주기 위해

어휘 | issue a refund 환불해 주다, 환불금을 지불하다 remind
상기시키다 confirm 확인하다, 확정하다

Q2 모스 씨에 대해 명시된 것은?
(A) 최근에 새로 차를 구입했다.
(B) 차가 현재 수리 중이다.
(C) 운전면허증이 만료되었다.
(D) 할인을 받을 자격이 있다.

어휘 | recently 최근 purchase 구입하다 currently 현재
expired 만료된 eligible 자격이 있는

● 실전 **도움닫기**   본책 p. 245

1 (A)   **2** (B)   **3** (B)   **4** (B)

[1-2] 편지

> 코빈 씨께,
>
> 저희 기록을 보니 〈투데이즈 트렌드〉 [1]**6월호를 끝으로 귀하의
> 구독이 종료될 예정인데 아직 갱신을 안 하셨습니다.** 귀하의 갱신을
> 장려하고자 〈투데이즈 트렌드〉를 할인 가격으로 제공해 드리고자
> 합니다. [2]**귀하께서는 현재 호당 3달러를 내시는데,** 앞으로 6개월간
> 호당 2.25달러에 드리겠습니다. 즉 구독을 갱신하시면 7월부터
> 12월까지 총 4.5달러를 할인받으시는 겁니다.
>
> 월요일부터 금요일은 오전 9시부터 오후 5시까지, 토요일은 오전
> 10시부터 오후 3시까지 사무실 전화 888-555-3214번으로 연락해
> 주십시오. 일요일은 휴무입니다. 그럼 앞으로도 계속 서비스를 제공해
> 드릴 수 있기를 고대하겠습니다.
>
> 마샤 클레민스
> 영업이사

> 어휘 | issue (간행물의) 호 renew 갱신하다 subscription 구독(료)
> encourage 장려하다, 권장하다 reduced 할인한 currently 현재
> save 구하다, 절약하다

1 코빈 씨의 현재 구독은 언제 끝나는가?
(A) 6월   (B) 12월

해설 | **세부 사항**
첫 번째 단락에서 6월호를 끝으로 코빈 씨의 구독이 종료될 예정(the
June issue of *Today's Trends* will be your last)이라고
했으므로, (A)가 정답이다.

2 코빈 씨가 현재 지불하는 월 구독료는 얼마인가?
(A) 2.25달러   (B) 3달러

해설 | **세부 사항**
첫 번째 단락에서 코빈 씨가 현재 호당 3달러를 지불한다(You
are currently paying $3.00 per issue)고 했으므로, (B)가
정답이다.

Paraphrasing
지문의 per issue → 질문의 per month

[3-4] 이메일

> 발신: mburnes@worldstore.com
> 수신: wpitts@pma.net
>
> 피츠 씨께:
>
> [3]**기상 악화로 인해 월드 스토어TM 분류 시설이 위치한 중서부의
> 많은 공항을 오가는 항공 교통이 큰 지장을 받았습니다.** 그 결과
> 상당수 배송이 약 24-48시간 동안 지연될 예정입니다.
>
> 월드 스토어TM은 최상의 서비스를 제공하기 위해 최선을
> 다하고 있습니다. [4]**배송 상황에 관한 최신 정보를 알고 싶으시면
> Worldstore.com의 "내 정보"를 방문하세요.** 이곳에서 배송 상황을
> 조회하실 수 있습니다.
>
> 저희가 이 문제를 해결하는 동안 넓은 아량으로 참고 이해해 주시면
> 감사하겠습니다.

마이클 번스 드림
사장
Worldstore.com

---

3 이메일을 쓴 목적은 무엇인가?
(A) 여행 계획을 연기하기 위하여
(B) 발송 지연에 관한 정보를 제공하기 위하여

해설 | **주제/목적**
첫 번째 단락에서 기상 악화(Severe weather conditions)로
인해 항공 교통에 지장이 있어 배송이 지연될 것임(As a result,
many deliveries will be delayed by approximately 24 to
48 hours)을 알리고 있으므로, (B)가 정답이다.

4 번스 씨는 피츠 씨에게 무엇을 하라고 제안하는가?
(A) 운송 회사에 즉시 연락할 것
(B) 자세한 정보를 얻기 위해 웹사이트를 방문할 것

해설 | **세부 사항**
두 번째 단락에서 배송 상태를 확인하려면 웹사이트를 방문하라(For
the latest package status information, please go to "My
account" on Worldstore.com)고 안내하고 있으므로, (B)가
정답이다.

어휘 | carrier service 운송 회사

● ETS 실전문제
본책 p. 246

1 (D)	**2** (C)	**3** (D)	**4** (B)	**5** (C)	**6** (D)
7 (D)	**8** (B)	**9** (C)	**10** (C)	**11** (D)	**12** (A)
13 (A)	**14** (D)	**15** (D)	**16** (C)	**17** (A)	**18** (B)
19 (D)	**20** (B)	**21** (A)	**22** (C)		

[1-2] 이메일

발신: 질 켄덜
수신: 나카시마 화장품 직원들
제목: 레야톤 피트니스
날짜: 3월 10일

동료 여러분께,

레야톤 피트니스 센터스(RFC)가 우리 회사 할인 프로그램에
합류했다는 점을 알리게 되어서 기쁩니다. **¹4월 1일부터 RFC 연간
회원권을 구입하는 모든 직원은 정가에서 15퍼센트를 할인받게
됩니다.** 할인을 받으려면 사원 번호, 직책, 근무지 정보를 제공해야
합니다.

회원 양식은 우리 회사 웹사이트의 기업 제휴 페이지에서 다운로드할
수 있으며 RFC 지점에 직접 제출해야 합니다. **²가장 가까운 RFC
시설은 스틸스 가에 있는데 우리 본사에서 불과 2km 떨어져 있으며
두 번째 지점은 윈슬로우 웨스트 가 42번지에 있습니다.**

여러분 모두 이번 기회를 이용하기 바랍니다.

질 켄덜
인사과 직원

---

1 이메일을 쓴 이유는?
(A) 할인되는 운동 장비를 판매하기 위해
(B) 새로운 헬스 클럽의 개장을 알리기 위해
(C) 회사 규정을 소개하기 위해
(D) 직원 혜택을 설명하기 위해

해설 | **주제/목적**
첫 번째 단락에서 4월 1일부터 RFC 연간 회원권을 구입하는 모든
직원은 정가에서 15퍼센트를 할인받게 된다(Beginning on April
1, all staff members ~ will receive 15 percent off the
regular price)며 직원들을 위한 혜택을 안내하고 있으므로, (D)가
정답이다.

2 레야톤 피트니스에 대해 언급된 내용은 무엇인가?
(A) 나카시마 화장품 옆에 있다.
(B) 비용이 최근에 인상되었다.
(C) 지점이 한 군데 이상이다.
(D) 추가 직원을 채용하고 있다.

해설 | **Not/True**
두 번째 단락에서 가장 가까운 RFC 시설은 스틸스 가에 있고, 두
번째 지점은 윈슬로우 웨스트 가 42번지에 있다(The closest RFC
facility is located on Stiles Street ~ a second location
is at 42 West Avenue in Winslow)라고 했으므로, (C)가
정답이다.

[3-4] 편지

3월 1일

줄리엣 스케퍼리 씨
에이커스 로 129번지
린스테드, 세인트 캐서린

스케퍼리 씨께,

**³(B)3월 20일 수요일 오후 6시에 열리는 제33회 몬테고 베이
인베스트먼트(MBI) 사의 연례 주주총회에 귀하를 정중히 초대합니다.**
동봉한 안건과 연례 보고서를 보시기 바랍니다. **³(A)저희 본사 사옥이
공사 중이기 때문에 올해 총회를 기존처럼 그곳에서 개최할 수 없어
타이노 드라이브 135번지에 있는 윈드 차임 호텔에서 개최합니다.**

가장 최근 회계연도의 성공을 고려할 때, 이사회에서는 주당 1달러의
배당금을 제안할 것입니다. 게다가, 이사들이 현 회계연도에 대해
자신하고 있어서, 저가 투자 펀드인 Xchange 21의 개발이 제안되고
있습니다. 이 펀드는 노동인구에 막 편입되는 청년들을 위한 투자
옵션을 제공할 것입니다. **⁴이 두 가지 사안 모두 총회에서 투표에
부쳐질 것입니다.**

**³(C)참석하기로 결정하시면 www.mbi.com.jm/asm/rsvp에서
좌석을 예약하시기 바랍니다.**

에머슨 모틀리
이사회 의장

동봉

어휘 | cordially 정중히 annual 연례의 shareholder 주주
agenda 안건 construction 공사 gathering 모임, 회의 as
is customary 관례대로, 기존에 하던 대로 propose 제안하다
dividend payment 배당금 investment 투자 labor force
노동력, 노동인구 attend 참석하다

3 총회에 대해 명시되지 않은 것은 무엇인가?

(A) 보통은 MBI의 본사에서 열린다.
(B) 30년 넘게 매년 개최되었다.
(C) 사전 등록이 필요하다.
(D) 일반적으로 참석률이 좋다.

해설 | **Not/True**
첫 번째 단락의 '저희 본사 사옥(corporate headquarters)이
공사 중이기 때문에 올해 총회를 기존처럼(as is customary)
그곳에서 개최할 수 없어 타이노 드라이브 135번지에 있는
윈드 차임 호텔에서 개최합니다'에서 (A)를, '제33회 몬테고
베이 인베스트먼트 사의 연례 주주총회(the 33rd annual
shareholders meeting of Montego Bay Investment
Ltd.)'에서 (B)를, 마지막 단락의 '참석하기로 결정하시면, 좌석을
예약하시길 바랍니다(please reserve your seat)'에서 (C)를
확인할 수 있다. 따라서 언급되지 않은 (D)가 정답이다.

4 편지에 의하면, 3월 20일에 어떤 일이 있을 것인가?

(A) 새로운 본사의 공사가 승인될 것이다.
(B) 특정 제안들이 고려될 것이다.
(C) 노동력 내부의 변화를 검토할 것이다.
(D) 새로운 이사들이 선출될 것이다.

해설 | **세부 사항**
3월 20일은 연례 주주총회가 열리는 날인데, 두 번째 단락을 보면
총회에서 제안될 두 가지 사안을 언급한 후, 이 사안들이 투표에
부쳐질 것(Both of these matters will be put to a vote at
the meeting)이라고 했으므로, (B)가 정답이다.

[5-7] 이메일

수신: 메이 잉 <mying@brightstar.com>
발신: 페드로 알바레즈 <palvarez@tbkfoods.com>
제목: 맛있는 음식
날짜: 11월 4일

잉 씨께:

**⁵최근 참여하셨던 아침 식사 설문 조사에서 귀하께 받은 피드백에
대해 감사드립니다.** 귀하의 피드백은 저희가 '맛있는 아침 식사'
신제품을 개발하는 데 아주 요긴했습니다. **⁶감사의 표시로 '맛있는
아침 식사'의 무료 샘플 일부를 보냅니다.** 샘플들은 2주 이내에 도착할
것입니다.

약 3개월 후에 귀하는 '맛있는 아침 식사'에 대한 또 다른 소비자 전화
설문 조사에 참여하라는 요청을 받으실지도 모릅니다. 설문 참여
관련하여 연락을 받고 싶지 않으시면, 제게 이메일을 보내거나 232-
555-0151로 전화하세요.

**⁷'맛있는 아침 식사' 홈페이지 www.tastybreakfastfoods.
com을 방문하셔서 신제품 구입처에 대한 정보를 확인하시기
바랍니다.** 또한 '맛있는 아침 식사' 전 제품에 대한 영양 정보뿐 아니라
할인 쿠폰도 찾아볼 수 있습니다.

페드로 알바레즈
제품 담당 책임자

어휘 | develop 개발하다 as a token of ~의 표시로 appreciation
감사 participate in ~에 참가하다 prefer 선호하다 nutrition 영양

5 잉 씨에게 이메일을 보낸 이유는 무엇인가?

(A) 그녀를 회의에 초대하기 위해
(B) 제품에 대한 그녀의 질문에 답하기 위해
(C) 그녀의 도움에 감사하기 위해
(D) 배송이 지연된 이유를 설명하기 위해

해설 | **주제/목적**
첫 번째 단락에서 잉 씨에게 피드백을 주어 고맙다고(We
appreciate the feedback we received from you) 했으므로,
(C)가 정답이다.

Paraphrasing
지문의 appreciate → 정답의 thank
지문의 feedback → 정답의 help

6 잉 씨에게 보내는 것은 무엇인가?

(A) 설문지   (B) 영양 정보
(C) 소비자 보고서   (D) 제품 샘플

해설 | **세부 사항**
첫 번째 단락에서 무료 샘플을 보내 주겠다(we are sending you
some free samples)고 했으므로, (D)가 정답이다.

7 '맛있는 아침 식사' 홈페이지의 특징으로 언급되는 것은 무엇인가?

(A) 제품을 이용한 조리법 모음
(B) 제품 품질에 대한 소비자들의 의견
(C) 제품의 가격 목록
(D) 제품을 구매할 수 있는 매장 목록

해설 | **Not/True**
세 번째 단락에서 홈페이지를 방문해 신제품 구입처에 대한 정보를
확인할 것(Be sure to check the Tasty Breakfast Foods
Web site ~ for information about where you can
purchase our new products)을 권했으므로, (D)가 정답이다.

[8-10] 편지

이글 록 케이블 컴퍼니
이글 록 웨이 1, 저지 시티, 뉴저지 주 07306

현 거주자
아발론 코트 3382번지
호보켄, 뉴저지 주 07030

**⁸시청하지 않는 채널이 다수 포함된 케이블 TV 패키지 가격을
지불하는 데 지치셨나요? 그렇다면 귀하가 만족할 만한 상품이
있습니다. ⁹(D)이글 록 케이블에서는 월 49.99달러의 낮은
가격에 인터넷 및 TV 약정을 제공하고 있습니다.** 바로 커스터머스
초이스라는 상품입니다. 다른 제공업체의 요금제와 달리, **⁹(A)이글 록
케이블의 커스터머스 초이스는 가입 시 채널을 선택할 수 있습니다.**

뉴스, 스포츠, 영화, 교육, 코미디 등 폭넓은 종합 채널을 최대 12개까지 선택하세요. ^{9(B)}**매월 2.99달러를 더 내면 채널을 추가할 수 있습니다.**

¹⁰**커스터머스 초이스가 더 좋은 점은 연간 약정에 얽매이지 않으셔도 된다는 겁니다.** <u>언제든 서비스를 해지하실 수 있습니다.</u> 본 상품을 이용하시려면 1-201-555-0142로 전화하세요. 이글 록 케이블의 친절한 담당 직원이 상담을 위해 대기하고 있습니다.

로렌 크레이머
고객 서비스 담당자

어휘 | contract 약정, 계약 provider 제공업체 subscription 가입, 구독 represent 나타내다, ~의 예가 되다 assortment 모음, 종합 additional 추가의 be tied to ~에 얽매이다, 묶이다 take advantage of ~를 이용하다 representative 담당 직원, 대표

---

8 편지는 누구를 대상으로 하겠는가?
(A) 지역 업체 소유주
(B) 일반 케이블 방송 약정 고객
(C) 최근 TV를 구입한 사람들
(D) 영화보다 스포츠를 보고 싶어 하는 시청자

해설 | **추론/암시**
첫 번째 단락에서 시청하지 않는 채널이 다수 포함된 케이블 TV 패키지 가격을 지불하는(paying for ~ many channels that you do not watch) 데 지치지 않냐고 반문한 후, 그렇다면 만족할 만한 상품이 있다고 했으므로, 일반 케이블 방송 약정 고객을 대상으로 하는 편지임을 알 수 있다. 따라서 (B)가 정답이다.

9 커스터머스 초이스의 특징으로 언급되지 않은 것은?
(A) 고객이 다수의 TV 채널 중 선택할 수 있다.
(B) 고객이 돈을 더 내고 TV 채널을 추가할 수 있다.
(C) 요금제에 전화 서비스를 추가할 수 있다.
(D) 요금제에 인터넷 서비스가 포함되어 있다.

해설 | **Not/True**
첫 번째 단락의 '커스터머스 초이스는 가입 시 채널을 선택할 수 있습니다(Customer's Choice ~ allows you to choose the channels in your subscription)'에서 (A)를, '매월 2.99달러를 더 내면 채널을 추가할 수 있습니다(you can include additional channels)'에서 (B)를, '이글 록 케이블에서는 월 49.99달러의 낮은 가격에 인터넷 및 TV 약정(an Internet and television contract)을 제공하고 있습니다'에서 (D)를 확인할 수 있다. 따라서 언급되지 않은 (C)가 정답이다.

Paraphrasing
지문의 choose the channels → 보기 (A)의 select from many TV channels
지문의 include additional channels for an extra $2.99 → 보기 (B)의 pay more to add extra TV channels
지문의 offering an Internet and television contract → 보기 (D)의 Internet service is included in the plan

10 [1], [2], [3], [4]로 표시된 곳 중에서 다음 문장이 들어가기에 가장 적합한 곳은?
"언제든 서비스를 해지하실 수 있습니다."
(A) [1]　　　　　　　(B) [2]
(C) [3]　　　　　　　(D) [4]

해설 | **문장 삽입**
주어진 문장에서 언제든 서비스를 해지할 수 있다고 했으므로, 앞에서 서비스 약정과 관련된 내용이 언급되어야 한다. [3] 앞에서 커스터머스 초이스의 장점은 연간 약정에 얽매이지 않아도 된다는 것(Better yet, with Customer's Choice you are not tied to an annual contract)이라고 했으므로, (C)가 정답이다.

[11-14] 이메일

발신: office@chibagrandhotel.com
수신: erik.carlsen@gowmail.com
제목: 최근 귀하의 치바 그랜드 투숙
날짜: 4월 18일

칼슨 씨께,

^{11/12}호텔 경영진 요청으로 귀하의 4월 8일부터 12일까지 치바 그랜드 호텔 투숙과 관련하여 몇 분간 의견을 공유해 주실 수 있는지 여쭤보고자 메일을 드립니다. 저희 호텔에 어떤 인상을 받으셨는지 알고 싶습니다. 편의 시설에 얼마나 만족하셨는지요? 머무시는 동안 즐거우셨습니까? 기대에 미치지 못한 점이 있었는지요? 개선해야 할 여지가 있다면 알려 주십시오. 저희는 고객의 완전한 만족을 위해 오롯이 전념하고 있습니다!

¹³www.chibagrand.com/yourstay에서 '완벽한 만족을 위한 설문조사'를 작성하셔서 직접 의견을 공유해 주십시오. 저희가 귀하의 전체적인 경험을 요약할 수 있도록 목록에 있는 모든 부문에 응답해 주시기 바랍니다. ¹⁴아울러 4월 30일까지 의견을 주시면 치바 그랜드 500달러 추첨 행사에 응모됩니다. 감사합니다.

카나 히로타
치바 그랜드 호텔

어휘 | at the request of ~의 요청에 의해 management 경영진 regarding ~에 관해 impression 인상 amenities 편의 시설 expectation 기대 room for ~의 여지 improvement 개선, 향상 be committed to ~에 전념하다, 헌신하다 satisfaction 만족 complete a survey 설문조사에 기입하다 response 응답 summary 요약 overall 전체적인 sweepstake (상금을 건) 경주, 내기

---

11 이메일을 쓴 이유는?
(A) 좋지 못한 서비스에 대해 사과하려고
(B) 납부 내역 요약서를 전달하려고
(C) 고객에게 변경 사항에 대해 알리려고
(D) 고객 만족도에 대해 알아보려고

해설 | **주제/목적**
첫 번째 단락에서 치바 그랜드 호텔 투숙과 관련하여 의견을 공유해 줄 수 있는지 물어보기 위해 이메일을 보낸다(I am writing to ask if you would ~ share feedback with us regarding your April 8-12 stay)고 했으므로, (D)가 정답이다.

어휘 | apologize for ~에 대해 사과하다 deliver 배달하다, 전달하다 inform 알리다 inquire 알아보다, 묻다

12 칼슨 씨는 호텔에 언제 도착했는가?
(A) 4월 8일　　　　　　(B) 4월 12일
(C) 4월 18일　　　　　　(D) 4월 30일

귀하는 소중한 저희 고객입니다. 저희는 귀하가 회원 자격을 누리시길 바랍니다. ¹⁸**귀하의 편의를 위해 미들린 북스 회원 카드를 동봉하오니 즉시 할인 혜택을 받아보십시오.**

존 휴이트
회원 서비스
미들린 북스
동봉

어휘 | preferred member 우대 회원 valid 유효한 indicate 나타내다, 보여 주다 associate 연계하다 correspondence 서신, 편지 postal mail 우편물 preregister 사전 등록하다 book signing 책 사인회 question-and-answer session 질의응답 시간 notable 유명한 in-store 매장 내의 saving 절약

15 이 편지의 목적은 무엇인가?
 (A) 마감일을 확인하기 위해서
 (B) 기부를 부탁하기 위해서
 (C) 계정을 갱신하기 위해서
 (D) 회원 자격의 세부 사항을 알리기 위해서

해설 | **주제/목적**
첫 번째 단락에서 우대 회원이 되어 주어 감사하다고 한 후, 우대 회원 자격 및 혜택과 관련된 세부 사항을 안내해 주고 있으므로, (D)가 정답이다.

어휘 | donation 기부 renew 갱신하다, 연장하다 detail 세부 사항

16 김 씨에 대해 암시되는 것은 무엇인가?
 (A) 도서전을 준비했다.
 (B) 웹사이트를 디자인했다.
 (C) 온라인으로 책을 구매한다.
 (D) 서점을 운영한다.

해설 | **추론/암시**
세 번째 단락의 첫 번째 문장(You may continue to purchase books from us online)에서 김 씨가 온라인으로 책을 구매하고 있음을 알 수 있으므로, (C)가 정답이다.

어휘 | book fair 도서전

Paraphrasing
지문의 purchase books from us online → 정답의 buys books on the Internet

17 미들린 북스에 대해 알 수 있는 것은 무엇인가?
 (A) 매장에서 홍보 행사를 연다.
 (B) 잡지 할인을 제공한다.
 (C) 여행 도서를 많이 보유하고 있다.
 (D) 지역 신문에 광고한다.

해설 | **Not/True**
세 번째 단락을 보면 우대 회원은 온라인으로 도서 사인회와 기타 서점 내 인기 행사(book signings ~ and other popular in-store events)에 사전 등록할 수 있다고 했으므로, (A)가 정답이다.

Paraphrasing
지문의 book signings, question-and-answer sessions with notable authors, and other popular in-store events
→ 정답의 promotional events in the store

해설 | **세부 사항**
첫 번째 단락에서 4월 8일에서 12일까지의 투숙(your April 8-12 stay)과 관련한 피드백을 요청했으므로, 칼슨 씨가 4월 8일에 호텔에 도착했다는 것을 알 수 있다. 따라서 (A)가 정답이다.

13 이메일에 따르면, 온라인 주소에서 무엇을 찾을 수 있는가?
 (A) 설문지 양식
 (B) 호텔로 찾아가는 길 안내
 (C) 비용 세부 목록
 (D) 호텔 시설 설명

해설 | **세부 사항**
두 번째 단락에서 온라인 주소 링크를 주며 설문조사 양식(Total Satisfaction Survey)을 작성해 달라고 요청했으므로, (A)가 정답이다.

어휘 | questionnaire 설문지 directions 길 안내 detailed 자세한 expense 비용, 경비 description 설명

14 히로타 씨는 칼슨 씨에게 무엇을 제공하는가?
 (A) 전액 환불
 (B) 가이드 투어
 (C) 향후 방문 시 할인
 (D) 당첨 기회

해설 | **세부 사항**
두 번째 단락에서 4월 30일까지 의견을 주면 치바 그랜드 500달러 추첨 행사에 응모된다(you will be entered into the $500 Reward Chiba Grand Sweepstakes)고 했으므로, (D)가 정답이다.

[15-18] 편지

미들린 북스
우드랜드 가 147번지
로어노크, 버지니아 주 24016
전화: (540) 555-0128 · 팩스: (540) 555-0139
www.meadlinbooks.com

김현실
아스펜 드라이브 451번지
리치몬드, 버지니아 주 23219
7월 15일

김 씨께,

¹⁵**미들린 북스의 우대 회원이 되어 주셔서 감사 드립니다. 귀하의 우대 회원 번호는 H2389X이며 회원 자격은 1년간 유효합니다.**

저희 기록에 따르면, 귀하의 계정과 연계된 이메일 주소는 hskim@redkin.net입니다. 요청하신 대로, 모든 서신은 우편물과 이메일로 발송됩니다. 연락처 정보를 변경하려면 월요일부터 금요일까지 오전 9시부터 오후 6시 사이에 (540) 555-0128로 전화하거나 온라인으로 www.meadlinbooks.com을 방문하십시오.

¹⁶**온라인에서 저희 책을 계속 구입할 수도 있고** 아니면 로어노크의 저희 매장에서 회원 카드를 이용하실 수도 있습니다. 회원으로서, 모든 신간 도서를 15퍼센트 할인받고, ¹⁷**도서 사인회, 유명 저자와의 질의응답 시간, 기타 서점 내 인기 행사에 온라인으로 사전 등록하실 수 있습니다.**

18 휴이트 씨가 편지와 함께 보낸 것은 무엇인가?

(A) 영수증   (B) 카드
(C) 주문서   (D) 카탈로그

해설 | **세부 사항**
마지막 단락에서 편의를 위해 회원 카드를 동봉한다(your Meadlin Books membership card is enclosed)고 했으므로, (B)가 정답이다.

[19-22] 편지

오드와이어 목재

5월 12일

모니카 포드
22웰런 퀄리티 리모델링 사무실 관리자
글렌리어 로 146번지
22(B)댄건, 골웨이 NW1

포드 씨께,

오드와이어 목재가 이전한다는 사실을 알려드리려 편지를 씁니다! 5월 26일 월요일부로 더 이상 댄건에서 영업하지 않을 예정입니다. 6월 2일 월요일에 스피들 라스모이 가 54번지에 있는 새 장소에서 문을 엽니다. **19**새로운 시설은 규모가 더 커서 더욱 다양한 건축 자재와 연장을 갖춰둘 수 있습니다.

오드와이어 목재가 이전**20**하는 동안 5월 26일부터 6월 1일까지 문을 닫는다는 사실을 말씀 드립니다. **21**6월 2일 재개장일에는 오전 10시부터 오후 2시까지 개업식을 열어서 신제품 일부를 보여드리고 값비싼 경품 추첨도 있을 예정입니다. **21**아울러 모두 참여하실 수 있는 흥미로운 공구 상식 퀴즈 대회도 개최합니다. 해당일에 이 지역에 계시면 함께해 주십시오.

새로운 시설에 큰 투자를 했기 때문에 저희 제품 일부에 대해 약간의 가격 인상을 시행해야 합니다. 또한 동일한 정책이 배송비에도 적용될 것입니다. **22(A)**귀사와 같이 저희와 5년 이상 거래한 업체들은 1년간 제품 및 배송 가격 인상에서 제외됩니다. 아울러, **22(D)**6월 한 달간 이뤄지는 주문 건에 대해 20퍼센트 할인을 제공해 드립니다.

이전에 관한 질문이나 우려가 있으시면 주저하지 말고 연락 주십시오. 5월 26일자로 저희 전화번호는 020-918-0245가 됩니다. 웰런 퀄리티 리모델링과 계속 거래하기를 바랍니다.

제나 그레인저
오드와이어 목재 마케팅 이사

어휘 | operate 영업하다 location 장소, 지점 effective 시행되는, 발효되는 facility 시설 stock 갖추다 a wide variety of 다양한 material 자재 relocation 이전 demonstrate 보여주다 drawing 추첨, 제비뽑기 valuable 귀중한, 값비싼 trivia 일반상식 competition 경쟁, 대회 significant 커다란 investment 투자 implement 시행하다 modest 소규모의 policy 정책 delivery charge 배송비 be excluded from ~에서 제외되다 additionally 추가로

---

19 오드와이어 목재에 대해 암시된 것은?

(A) 곧 두 개의 지점을 갖게 될 것이다.
(B) 여러 명의 배송 운전기사를 새로 채용했다.
(C) 다른 회사와 합병했다.
(D) 재고품을 늘릴 것이다.

해설 | **추론/암시**
첫 번째 단락에서 새로운 시설은 규모가 더 커서 더욱 다양한 건축 자재와 연장을 갖춰둘 수 있다(allowing us to stock a wider variety of building materials and tools)고 했으므로, 오드와이어 목재가 재고품을 늘릴 것으로 추론할 수 있다. 따라서 (D)가 정답이다.

어휘 | hire 채용하다 merge 합병하다 expand 확대하다, 늘리다 inventory 재고품, 물품 목록

Paraphrasing
지문의 stock a wider variety of building materials and tools → 정답의 expand its inventory

20 두 번째 단락, 두 번째 줄에 쓰인 "carry out"과 의미가 가장 가까운 것은?

(A) 제거하다   (B) 완수하다
(C) 재고하다   (D) 들어올리다

해설 | **동의어 찾기**
carry out을 포함한 부분은 '이전하는 동안(while we carry out our relocation)'이라고 해석되는데, 여기서 carry out은 '수행하다, 완수하다'라는 의미로 쓰였다. 따라서 (B) accomplish가 정답이다.

21 오드와이어 목재 고객은 6월 2일에 무엇을 할 수 있는가?

(A) 대회 참가   (B) 댄건에 있는 창고 방문
(C) 할인 신청   (D) 최고의 신제품 투표

해설 | **세부 사항**
두 번째 단락에서 6월 2일 재개장일(On reopening day, 2 June)에 모두가 참여할 수 있는 흥미로운 공구 상식 퀴즈 대회도 개최한다(We'll also have an exciting tool-trivia competition)고 했으므로, (A)가 정답이다.

어휘 | warehouse 창고 vote 투표하다

Paraphrasing
지문의 an exciting tool-trivia competition → 정답의 a contest

22 웰런 퀄리티 리모델링에 대해 명시되지 않은 것은?

(A) 최소 5년간 영업했다.
(B) 댄건에 있다.
(C) 오드와이어 목재 주문량을 늘릴 계획이다.
(D) 다음 달에 오드와이어 목재에서 구입하는 물품은 비용을 적게 지불할 것이다.

해설 | **Not/True**
세 번째 단락의 '귀사와 같이 5년 이상 거래한 업체(Companies like yours that have been doing business with us for five years or more)'에서 (A)를, 상단에 나와 있는 주소(Dangan)에서 (B)를, 세 번째 단락의 '6월 한 달간 이뤄지는 주문 건에 대해 20퍼센트 할인(a 20% discount on orders placed during the month of June)을 제공합니다'에서 (D)를 확인할 수 있다. 따라서 언급되지 않은 (C)가 정답이다.

어휘 | be in business 영업하다 at least 최소한 purchase 구입, 구입품

Paraphrasing
지문의 for five years or more → 보기 (A)의 for at least five years

지문의 a 20% discount on orders placed during the month of June → 보기 (D)의 pay less for purchases made next month

Unit 18 회람 / 공지 / 광고 / 기사

지문 구성과 독해 전략
본책 p.254

터너 베이 (7월 11일)—리버런 콤플렉스가 올해의 '리본 오브 엑설런스'를 수상했다. 해마다 지역 회사들의 장점을 소개하는 웹사이트 에버트레일에서 리본을 수여한다.

수상 자격이 되기 위해서는, 기업은 별 4개 만점의 평가 척도에서 평균 별 3.5개를 받아야 한다. 평가 지수는 기업의 품질 및 고객 서비스에 대한 헌신도를 나타낸다. 이전 및 현재 수상자들에는 터너 베이 전역의 호텔과 명소, 음식점들이 포함되어 있다. 이번에 리버런은 이 상을 3년 연속으로 수상한 것이다.

"저희 리버런 직원들은 이 영광을 얻게 돼 감격스럽습니다."라고 루시아 베리오스 대변인이 말했다. "6년 전 개장한 이래 저희는 가족들에게 신나는 놀이기구와 건강에 좋은 음식을 제공하기 위해 열심히 일했습니다. 저희는 과학전시장이 특히 자랑스러운데, 모든 연령대의 고객들을 교육시키고 즐거움을 주는 게임 및 쌍방향 체험을 제공하고 있습니다."

어휘 | award 수여하다; 상 showcase (장점 등을) 소개하다 qualify for ~의 자격이 되다 enterprise 기업 average 평균 rating scale 평가 척도 attraction 관광 명소 consecutive 연속의 ride 놀이기구 interactive 양[쌍]방향의, 상호적인

Q1 기사에 의하면, 에버트레일 웹사이트는 어떤 일을 하는가?
(A) 호텔 예약에 할인을 제공한다.
(B) 경치를 즐기는 기차 여행을 설명한다.
(C) 터너 베이에서 제작된 제품을 판매한다.
(D) 지역 회사를 평가한다.

어휘 | describe 설명[묘사]하다 scenic 경치가 좋은 evaluate 평가하다

Q2 [1], [2], [3], [4]로 표시된 곳 중에서 다음 문장이 들어가기에 가장 적합한 곳은?

"평가 지수는 기업의 품질 및 고객 서비스에 대한 헌신도를 나타낸다."

(A) [1]   (B) [2]
(C) [3]   (D) [4]

어휘 | dedication 헌신(도)

● 실전 도움닫기
본책 p.255

1 (A) **2** (B) **3** (A) **4** (B)

[1-2] 광고

신촌에서 여름을

¹서울에서 유행의 첨단을 걷는 지역 중 하나인 신촌에 위치한 방 한 칸

임대!

• 새롭게 단장하였으며, 최신 가전을 포함하여 내부 시설 완비
• 미술관, 식당, 찻집, 쇼핑몰과 인접
• 지하철 2호선 신촌역에서 걸어서 3분 거리
• ¹한국에서 여름 방학을 보내기에 최적기인 8월 1일부터 31일까지만 임대 가능
• 환불 보증금 90만 원에 월세 90만 원

²방 구경을 위해 약속을 잡으시려면 cjgil293@maponet.co.kr로 길찬준에게 연락 주세요.

어휘 | lodging 셋방, 하숙 located in ~에 위치한 trendy 최신 유행의 fully furnished 가구가 완비된, 내부 시설을 전부 갖춘 appliance (가정용) 기구, 전자제품 only steps away from ~에서 불과 몇 걸음 떨어져 있는[근접해 있는] monthly rent 월세 refundable 환불 가능한 security deposit 보증금 viewing 보기, 관람, 구경

1 무엇을 광고하고 있는가?
(A) 단기 임대 매물
(B) 매매를 위해 최근 단장한 주택들

해설 | 주제 / 목적
제목 아래 문구(One-bedroom lodging located in Sinchon, ~ Seoul!)를 통해 임대 광고임을 알 수 있다. 열거된 항목 중 네 번째를 보면, 한 달 동안(Available August 1-31) 임대가 가능하다고 나와 있으므로, (A)가 정답이다.

어휘 | short-term 단기간의 rental 임대의, 임차의 for sale 팔려고 내놓은

Paraphrasing
지문의 August 1-31 → 정답의 short-term

2 광고에 따르면, 집 구경을 하려면 어떻게 해야 하는가?
(A) 전화를 걸어서   (B) 이메일을 보내서

해설 | 세부 사항
광고 하단에 방 구경 약속을 잡으려면 길찬준 씨의 이메일로 연락하라(Contact ~ at cjgil293@maponet.co.kr to schedule an apartment viewing)고 했으므로, (B)가 정답이다.

어휘 | property 부동산, 건물, 건물 내부 place a phone call 전화를 걸다

Paraphrasing
지문의 schedule an apartment viewing
→ 질문의 arrange to look at the property
지문의 Contact Chan Joon Gil at cjgil293@maponet.co.kr
→ 정답의 sending an e-mail

[3-4] 기사

³요하네스버그 (7월 7일)—재킨 출판사는 금요일에 오릴리아 마르티노 씨의 신간 <하늘의 별들>을 9월 8일 출간할 예정이라고 발표했다. 이 책은 마르티노 씨의 두 번째 작품으로 초기 서평들은 이것이 독자들에게 특별한 선물이 될 것이라고 말한다. ⁴마르티노 씨는 요하네스버그 출신의 인정받는 여배우로 2년 전에 첫 아이인 마틸다가 생겼을 때 연기 활동을 중단하고 책을 쓰기 시작하기로 결정했다. 그녀는 <먼로네와 동거하기>라는 남아공의 인기 TV 연속극에서 10년 동안 맡은 엄마 역할로 가장 유명할 것이다.

181

3 기사의 목적은 무엇인가?

(A) 책 출간 날짜를 알리려고 (B) 서평을 하려고

해설 | **주제/목적**

초반부에서 재킨 출판사가 오릴리아 마르티노 씨의 새 책을 출간할 예정(Aurelia Martino's new book ~ will be released on 8 September)이라는 소식을 전한 후 관련 내용을 이어 갔으므로, (A)가 정답이다.

어휘 | opinion 의견

4 마르티노 씨에 대해 암시된 것은 무엇인가?

(A) 10년 넘게 작가 생활을 해 왔다.

(B) 직업을 바꾸었다.

해설 | **추론/암시**

중반부에 마르티노 씨가 인정받는 배우였다가 활동을 중단하고 책을 쓰기 시작했다(Ms. Martino, an acclaimed actress from Johannesburg, decided to give up acting and begin writing books)고 했으므로, 그녀가 직업을 바꾸었음을 알 수 있다. 따라서 (B)가 정답이다.

어휘 | author 작가 career 직업, 경력

Paraphrasing

지문의 give up acting and begin writing books

→ 정답의 change careers

● ETS 실전문제

본책 p. 256

1 (D)	**2** (B)	**3** (A)	**4** (B)	**5** (A)	**6** (D)
7 (B)	**8** (C)	**9** (C)	**10** (B)	**11** (B)	**12** (D)
13 (B)	**14** (A)	**15** (C)	**16** (A)	**17** (C)	**18** (A)
19 (A)	**20** (D)	**21** (D)			

[1-2] 광고

그라운드 디자인

엘스턴 가 43번지

브리즈번, 퀸즐랜드 400

3229 2626

www.grounddesign.com.au

저희는 브리즈번 지역에서 24년이 넘는 주택 실외 건축 및 조경 경력을 보유하고 있습니다.

다음과 같은 건축에 특화되어 있습니다.

- **1(B)**천연석 및 블록 벽
- 테라스
- 진입로 및 보도

1(A)/1(C)정원 디자인, 조명, 나무 등으로 외관을 완성하여 이러한 건축물을 향상시킵니다. **2**저희는 정식 허가 업체로서 이전 고객을 위해 수행한 작업을 담은 완벽한 컬러 포트폴리오를 제공해 드릴 수 있습니다. 무료 상담 일정을 잡으려면 월-금요일에 연락해 주십시오.

1 그라운드 디자인이 광고하는 서비스가 아닌 것은?

(A) 나무 심기 (B) 벽 쌓기

(C) 조명 설치하기 (D) 분수 디자인하기

해설 | **Not/True**

마지막 단락의 '정원 디자인, 조명, 나무 등으로 외관을 완성(garden designs, lighting, and trees to complete your look)'에서 (A)와 (C)를, 두 번째 단락의 '천연석 및 블록 벽(Natural stone and block walls)'에서 (B)를 확인할 수 있다. 따라서 언급되지 않은 (D)가 정답이다.

어휘 | plant 심다 install 설치하다 fountain 분수

2 그라운드 디자인이 잠재 고객에게 제공하는 것은?

(A) 대규모 프로젝트 할인 (B) 과거 작업 사진

(C) 빠른 공사 완료 (D) 무료 페인팅 용품

해설 | **세부 사항**

마지막 단락에서 이전 고객을 위해 수행한 작업을 담은 완벽한 컬러 포트폴리오(a complete colour portfolio of work we have done for previous clients)를 제공할 수 있다고 했으므로, (B)가 정답이다.

어휘 | potential 잠재적인 rapid 빠른 completion 완성 supplies 용품

Paraphrasing

지문의 a complete colour portfolio of work ~ for previous clients → 정답의 Images of past jobs

[3-5] 공지

브리지턴 도보 관광

10월 26일 토요일 오전 10시 30분

지금의 브리지턴 시청 건물이 원래는 1890년에 건축된 브리지턴 국립 은행이었다는 것을 알고 계셨나요? **4**브로드 가와 메인 가의 모퉁이에 있는 피네스코 철물점이 50년 전 개업했고 한때는 최초 공립 도서관이 있던 부지였다는 점을 아시나요? **3**유익한 정보를 제공하는 토요일 오전 산책에 저희와 함께 하셔서 유서 깊은 브리지턴에 대해 배워 보시기 바랍니다.

5베라 로젠스키 사서가 브리지턴의 초창기에 관한 사실과 이야기를 들려주는 이번 관광 프로그램을 진행합니다. 관광은 도서관 정문에서 시작해서 정오쯤 노스사이드 커피숍에서 끝납니다.

5지역 미술가 빌 다카타 씨가 5세에서 12세 사이의 어린이들을 위한 창의적 스케치 수업을 진행하며 그 사이 어른들은 관광에 참여합니다. 참가 인원이 제한되어 있으므로 토요일 전에 도서관에서 신청하시기 바랍니다!

3 공지문의 목적은 무엇인가?

(A) 사람들을 지역 행사에 초대하기 위해
(B) 새로운 서비스에 대한 지지를 얻기 위해
(C) 개보수한 시청을 선보이기 위해
(D) 지역 기념일을 축하하기 위해

해설 | **주제/목적**

첫 번째 단락 후반부에서 브리지턴 시에 대해 배울 수 있는 도보 관광에 참여하라고 초대(Join us for an informative Saturday morning stroll and learn about historic Bridgeton)한 후 관련 내용을 안내했으므로, (A)가 정답이다.

4 브리지턴의 초창기에 무엇이 브로드 가와 메인 가에 있었는가?

(A) 커피숍   (B) 도서관
(C) 은행   (D) 화실

해설 | **세부 사항**

첫 번째 단락에서 브로드 가와 메인 가의 모퉁이에 있는 피네스코 철물점이 50년 전 개업했고 한때는 최초 공립 도서관이던 부지였다(the Finesco Hardware Store, located on the corner of Broad and Main Streets, ~ once was the site of the first public library)고 했으므로, (B)가 정답이다.

5 로젠스키 씨가 진행하는 행사에 대해 암시된 점은 무엇인가?

(A) 어린이들은 행사의 대상이 아니다.
(B) 무료 점심이 포함되어 있다.
(C) 최근에 나온 책을 홍보하고 있다.
(D) 우천 시 취소될 것이다.

해설 | **추론/암시**

두 번째 단락에서 로젠스키 씨가 도보 관광을 진행한다고 했는데, 세 번째 단락을 보면 지역 미술가 빌 다카타 씨가 어린이들을 위한 창의적 스케치 수업을 진행하며 그 사이 어른들이 관광에 참여한다(while adults participate in the tour)고 했다. 이를 통해 어린이들은 도보 관광의 대상이 아니라는 것을 알 수 있으므로, (A)가 정답이다.

Paraphrasing

지문의 children ages 5 to 12 → 정답의 young children

[6-9] 기사

메헬렌의 긍정적 변화

⁶유럽 전역에서 풍력 터빈과 풍력 기술을 생산하는 선두 업체인 윈드 다이나믹스가 벨기에 메헬렌에 생산 공장을 열겠다는 계획을 발표했다. ⁷이 네덜란드 회사는 버려진 캔텍 전화 공장을 매입해서 보수하고 장비를 갖추는 데 1,500만 유로 이상을 쓰고 있다. 이번 사업은 향후 2년간 대략 200개의 생산직과 50개의 사무직 일자리를 새롭게 창출하리라 예상된다. 이것은 최근 공장 폐쇄와 실직으로 큰 타격을 입은 공업 지역인 메헬렌으로서는 기쁜 소식이다. **⁹바텔 빌더스는 이미 공장 전환 작업을 맡는 계약을 체결했다.** 또한 공사 프로젝트를 완료하기 위해 직원을 추가로 더 고용할 예정이다.

공장은 주로 회사의 풍력 터빈에 들어가는 기어 구동장치의 조립 및 테스트 용도로 활용될 것이다. 윈드 다이나믹스는 ⁸**메헬렌 사업 개발 협회(MBDA)와 협력하여** 개발 보조금을 지급해 입사 직원들에게 녹색 기술을 교육시킬 것이다. ⁸**MBDA 제인 아렌스 회장은** "메헬렌이 에너지 절약과 지역 경제 발전에 일조하게 되어 자랑스럽습니다"라고 말한다.

어휘 | leading 선두의 wind turbine 풍력 터빈 production plant 생산 공장 equip 장비를 갖추다 abandoned 버려진 industrial area 공업 지역 be hit hard 큰 타격을 입다 closure 폐쇄 job loss 실직 contract 계약을 맺다 undertake 착수하다, 맡다 transformation 변환, 전환 primarily 주로 assembly 조립 gear drive 기어 구동장치 incorporate 포함시키다 in cooperation with ~와 협력하여 development grant 개발 보조금 incoming workforce 입사 직원 contribute to ~에 기여하다 conservation 보존, 절약 economic growth 경제 성장

6 기사의 주요 내용은 무엇인가?

(A) 신임 회사 CEO 임명
(B) 두 기업의 합병
(C) 풍력 터빈 생산 과정
(D) 시설 개장

해설 | **주제/목적**

초반부에서 '풍력 터빈과 풍력 기술을 생산하는 선두 업체인 윈드 다이나믹스가 벨기에 메헬렌에 생산 공장을 열겠다는 계획을 발표했다(Wind Dynamics ~ has announced plans to open a production plant in Mechelen, Belgium)'고 했으므로, (D)가 정답이다.

Paraphrasing

지문의 open a production plant → 정답의 The opening of a facility

7 캔텍 전화 공장에 무슨 일이 일어날 것인가?

(A) 유적지로 복원될 것이다.
(B) 다른 산업체에 의해 사용될 것이다.
(C) 새 지점으로 옮겨갈 것이다.
(D) 공터를 만들기 위해 철거될 것이다.

해설 | **세부 사항**

초반부에서 윈드 다이나믹스가 버려진 캔텍 전화 공장을 매입해서 보수하고 장비를 갖추는 데(to purchase, renovate, and equip the abandoned Cantek Telephone factory) 1,500만 유로 이상을 쓰고 있다고 했으므로, (B)가 정답이다.

어휘 | restore 복원하다 demolish 철거하다

8 아렌스 씨는 누구인가?

(A) 윈드 다이나믹스 직원
(B) 신문 기자
(C) 협회 회장
(D) 벨기에의 한 도시 시장

해설 | **세부 사항**

후반부에서 'MBDA 제인 아렌스 회장(Jane Arens, MBDA president)'이라고 했는데, MBDA는 앞서 언급된 the Mechelen Business Development Association을 지칭하므로, (C)가 정답이다.

9 [1], [2], [3], [4]로 표시된 곳 중에서 다음 문장이 들어가기에 가장 적합한 곳은?

"또한 공사 프로젝트를 완료하기 위해 직원을 추가로 더 고용할 예정이다."

(A) [1]   (B) [2]
(C) [3]   (D) [4]

해설 | 문장 삽입

공사 프로젝트를 완료하기 위한 세부 계획 중 하나를 언급한 문장이므로, 앞서 이 프로젝트와 관련된 내용이 언급되어야 한다. [3] 앞에서 바텔 빌더스가 이미 공장 전환 작업을 맡는 계약을 체결했다(Battel Builders has already been contracted to undertake the plant's transformations)고 했으므로, (C)가 정답이다. 참고로, 주어진 문장의 It은 Battel Builders를 가리킨다.

어휘 | anticipate 예상하다, 기대하다 additional 추가의 complete 완료하다

[10-13] 회람

회람

날짜: 1월 28일
수신: M 빌딩 커뮤니티
발신: 제니스 팅, 사무 공간 위원회 이사
제목: 제이 분 강당 보수 공사

¹⁰2단계 프로젝트 중 첫 번째 단계인 제이 분 강당 보수 공사가 2월 중순에 시작될 것임을 알려 드리고자 합니다. ¹¹/¹²두 번째 단계인 강당에 인접해 있는 1층 사무실의 재건축은 빠르면 8월에 시작되어 11월 말에 완공될 예정입니다.

¹⁰이번 프로젝트는 중심부를 아우르기 때문에 불가피하게 우리 커뮤니티에 어느 정도 지장을 초래할 것인데, 이를 최소화하기 위해 만전을 기하도록 하겠습니다. 수리 공사 동안 대체할 장소를 제공하도록 이미 계획이 되어 있으며, ¹³대체 장소에서 행사 일정을 잡아야 하는 사람들은 리디아 이브라힘 씨(내선: 3372, librahim@m.galleries.com)에게 가능한 한 빨리 알려 주시기 바랍니다.

작업이 진행되면서 이 일정이 변경될 경우, 저희가 계속해서 여러분께 알려 드리도록 하겠습니다.

시설을 개선하는 동안 양해해 주시면 감사하겠습니다.

어휘 | memorandum 메모, 회람 community 커뮤니티, 공동체 director 국장, 부장, 이사 office space 사무 공간 auditorium 강당, 대강의실 renovation 보수, 개조 alert ~에게 주의를 환기시키다, 경보를 올리다 phase 단계, 시기 reconstruction 재건축 adjacent to ~에 인접한 intended 의도된, 계획된 completion date 완공일 scope 범위 disruption 혼란, 지장 minimize 최소화하다 alternative 선택적인, 대안의 venue 장소 anticipate 기대하다, 예상하다 time line 일정 enhance 늘리다, 강화하다

10 회람을 쓴 이유는 무엇인가?
(A) 대체 장소를 발표하기 위해
(B) 발생 가능한 혼란에 대해 미리 알리고자
(C) 프로젝트 일정을 조정하기 위해
(D) 직원들에게 신입 사원에 대해 알려 주기 위해

해설 | 주제/목적

첫 번째 단락에서 강당 보수 공사가 시작될 예정(the renovation of the Jay Voon Auditorium ~ will begin in mid-February)임을 알렸고, 두 번째 단락에서 이때 초래되는 지장을 최소화하도록 노력하겠다(every effort will be made to minimize this disruption)고 했다. 따라서 보수 공사로 인해 발생 가능한 혼란에 대해 미리 알리고자 작성한 회람이라고 볼 수 있으므로, (B)가 정답이다.

184

어휘 | revise 수정하다

Paraphrasing
지문의 alert → 정답의 warn
지문의 a certain degree of disruption → 정답의 possible disruptions

11 두 번째 단계에 포함되는 것은 무엇인가?
(A) 증축 공사
(B) 사무 공간 재건축
(C) 행사 시설 중앙 배치
(D) 인접 건물 개선

해설 | 세부 사항

첫 번째 단락에서 공사의 두 번째 단계는 강당에 인접해 있는 1층 사무실의 재건축(The second phase, reconstruction of the first-floor offices adjacent to the auditorium)이라고 했으므로, (B)가 정답이다.

어휘 | centralize 중심에 모으다

Paraphrasing
지문의 reconstruction of the first-floor offices
→ 정답의 Reconstructing office space

12 프로젝트는 언제 완성될 것인가?
(A) 1월에   (B) 2월에
(C) 8월에   (D) 11월에

해설 | 세부 사항

첫 번째 단락에서 두 번째 단계가 11월 말에 완공될 예정(with an intended completion date of late November)이라고 했으므로, (D)가 정답이다.

Paraphrasing
지문의 late November → 정답의 in November

13 넓은 공간을 예약하고자 하는 사람들은 어떻게 해야 하는가?
(A) 제니스 팅 씨에게 이메일을 보낼 것
(B) 리디아 이브라힘 씨에게 연락할 것
(C) 새 양식을 작성할 것
(D) 온라인 신청서를 작성할 것

해설 | 세부 사항

두 번째 단락에서 행사를 개최할 대체 장소를 예약해야 할 경우 리디아 이브라힘 씨에게 알리라(for those of you who anticipate needing to schedule events for these alternative venues, inform Lidia Ibrahim)고 하였으므로 (B)가 정답이다.

어휘 | reserve 마련해 두다, 예약하다 complete 빠짐없이 작성하다, 기입하다(= fill out) application 신청서, 지원서

Paraphrasing
지문의 inform → 정답의 contact

[14-17] 구인 광고

리저널 어플라이언시즈 주식회사

리저널 어플라이언시즈 주식회사(RAI)는 민간 제조업체입니다. ¹⁴저희는 국내 및 해외 유통용 에어컨을 제조하고 물류를 관리하는 업무를 하고 있습니다. 새로운 프로젝트가 진행 중이어서 다음 직책들에 맞는 유능한 전문가들을 찾고 있습니다.

인사 관리자 - 토론토 (#4699)

이 흥미로운 직책은 조직 내 직원 채용 및 유지에 중점을 두고 있습니다. 인사 관리자는 운영 요건에 부합하는 충분한 노동 가용성을 확보해야 합니다. 입증된 협상 능력은 필수입니다.

프로젝트 관리자 - 토론토 (#4654)

¹⁶ **프로젝트 관리팀은 리저널 어플라이언시즈 주식회사의 기계 관련 프로젝트를 기획하고 보고하면서 품질 기준과 고객 관계를 관리합니다.** 본 직책은 최소 5년 이상의 프로젝트 관리 경험이 필요합니다.

¹⁵ **수석 견적사 - 캘거리 (#4827)**

본 직책은 재무 및 예산에 관련된 프로젝트 행정 업무를 다루며 프로젝트 관리자 및 회계사들에게 시기적절한 재무보고서를 제공합니다. ¹⁵ **수석 견적사는 하급 견적사들로 이뤄진 팀을 관리하며 연간 실적 평가를 제공합니다.**

회계사 - 캘거리와 토론토 (#4222)

폭넓은 회계 경력을 요구하는 상급 직책입니다. 적합한 지원자는 공인 회계사로서 급성장하는 회사에서 정확한 부기 실적이 입증된 사람입니다.

¹⁷ **이러한 직책 중에서 지원하시려면 이메일 제목에 네 자리 직책 코드를 그대로 넣어서 elevine@raijobs.com으로 이력서를 보내 주십시오.**

> **어휘 |** privately owned 개인이 소유한, 민간의 manufacturing 제조 warehouse 창고; (물류를) 보관하다 domestic 국내의 distribution 유통 under way 진행 중인 position 직위 recruitment 채용 retention 보유, 유지 organization 조직, 단체 sufficient 충분한 availability 가용성 meet an requirement 요건에 부합하다 proven 입증된 negotiation 협상 essential 필수적인, 극히 중요한 mechanical 기계와 관련된 maintain 유지하다 standard 기준 quantity surveyor 견적사 administration 행정, 관리 with regard to ~와 관련하여 finance 재무 accountant 회계사 timely 시기적절한 oversee 감독하다, 관리하다 evaluation 평가 extensive 광범위한, 폭넓은 ideal 이상적인 candidate 지원자, 후보자 licensed 허가를 받은, 공인된 track record 실적 accurate 정확한 bookkeeping 부기, 경리 four-digit 네 자리의

14 리저널 어플라이언시즈 주식회사에 대해 암시된 것은?

(A) 회사의 제품이 다수의 국가에서 판매된다.
(B) 주요 공장이 캘거리에 있다.
(C) 창고를 이전하고 있다.
(D) 최근 기술자 여러 명을 채용했다.

해설 | 추론/암시

첫 번째 단락에서 국내 및 해외 유통용 에어컨을 제조하고 물류를 관리하는 업무를 한다(We manufacture and warehouse air-conditioning units for domestic and international distribution)고 했으므로, 리저널 어플라이언시즈 주식회사의 제품이 다수의 국가에서 판매됨을 추론할 수 있다. 따라서 (A)가 정답이다.

어휘 | multiple 다수의, 많은 relocate 이전시키다

Paraphrasing

지문의 domestic and international → 정답의 multiple countries

---

15 광고에 따르면, 누가 직원으로 이뤄진 팀을 감독하는가?

(A) 인사 관리자
(B) 프로젝트 관리자
(C) 수석 견적사
(D) 회계사

해설 | 세부 사항

수석 견적사(SENIOR QUANTITY SURVEYOR)의 직무 설명을 보면 하급 견적사들로 이뤄진 팀을 관리한다(The senior quantity surveyor will oversee a team of junior quantity surveyors)고 했으므로, (C)가 정답이다.

어휘 | supervise 감독하다

Paraphrasing

지문의 oversee a team of junior quantity surveyors → 질문의 supervising a group of employees

16 프로젝트 관리자에 대해 명시된 것은?

(A) 고객과 교류해야 한다.
(B) 5년 계약을 맺어야 한다.
(C) 캘거리와 토론토를 종종 오간다.
(D) 프로젝트 비용을 종종 협상한다.

해설 | Not/True

프로젝트 관리자(PROJECT MANAGER)의 직무 설명을 보면 품질 기준과 고객 관계를 관리한다(while maintaining quality standards and client relations)고 했으므로, (A)가 정답이다.

어휘 | interact with ~와 상호 작용을 하다 sign a contract 계약을 맺다

Paraphrasing

지문의 maintaining ~ client relations → 정답의 interact with clients

17 지원자들은 이력서와 함께 무엇을 제공하라고 요청받는가?

(A) 희망 연봉
(B) 추천인 목록
(C) 일자리 번호
(D) 전문 면허 증빙

해설 | 세부 사항

마지막 단락에서 지원하려면 이메일 제목에 네 자리 직책 코드를 그대로 넣어서 이력서를 보내 줄 것(e-mail your résumé ~ quoting the four-digit position code)을 요청했으므로, (C)가 정답이다.

Paraphrasing

지문의 the four-digit position code → 정답의 A job number

[18-21] 기사

> **보울랜드, 도매업체들에 위약금 부과**
>
> (10월 5일)—실험 장비 소매업체인 보울랜드는 재고 관리 강화를 위한 노력의 일환으로, ¹⁸상호 합의된 배송 시간을 90퍼센트 이상 충족시키지 못하는 도매업체들에 위약금을 부과하기 시작할 것이라고 오늘 발표했다.

"우리 선반에 최적의 재고 물량을 유지하지 못하면 상당한 금전적 비용이 발생합니다"라고 보울랜드의 수석 입고 관리자인 조카 갈반이 말한다. "그래서 저희 매장들에 상품이 필요하면 즉시 공급업체들이 상품을 배달하는 것이 중요합니다. 우리는 그 업체로 하여금 이 새로운 ¹⁹조건들이 분명히 명시된 최신 서비스 계약에 서명하게 했습니다."

²⁰공급업체들은 보울랜드의 적시 배송 관련 목표를 이해하지만, 일각에서는 공급업체들이 직면한 문제들을 고려하지 않으면 위약금 부과로는 문제를 해결하지 못할 것이라는 말도 나온다.

"정시 배달이 우리 통제에서 벗어나는 상황이 있습니다"라고 보울랜드의 공급업체 중 한 곳의 배송 관리자인 엔리케 자파타가 말한다. "저희 회사는 소매업체에서 재고가 상당히 낮은 수준으로까지 떨어지기 전에 미처 저희에게 알리지 못해 늦어지는 바람에 주문을 맞추려고 고군분투하는 경우가 종종 있습니다. 막판 주문량 수정이 배송 지연의 주요 원인입니다."

²¹자파타 씨는 보울랜드에서 더 좋은 소통 전략을 채택했다면 이 문제는 쉽게 해결될 수 있을 것이라고 주장한다. 하지만 보울랜드에서는 이번 계획을 진행한 후 내년에 재평가할 예정이다.

어휘 | laboratory equipment 실험 장비 retailer 소매업체 inventory control 재고 관리 charge 부과하다 wholesale supplier 도매 (공급)업체 significant 막대한 financial 금전적인, 재정상의 optimal 최적의 critical 중요한 agreement 계약(서), 합의 impose 부과하다 take A into account A를 고려하다[참작하다] struggle 고군분투하다 fulfill 이행하다, 완료하다 adjustment 수정, 조정 strategy 전략 reassess 재평가하다

---

18 기사에 의하면, 공급업체의 어떤 행위가 위약금을 야기할 수 있는가?
(A) 배송 마감 시한을 지키지 못하는 것
(B) 제품을 부적절하게 포장하는 것
(C) 제품 배송 라벨을 잘못 부착하는 것
(D) 재고 갱신을 보고하지 못하는 것

해설 | **세부 사항**
첫 번째 단락에서 상호 합의된 배송 시간을 90퍼센트 이상 충족시키지 못하는 도매업체들에 위약금을 부과하기 시작할 것(it will begin charging its wholesale suppliers penalties if they do not meet agreed-upon delivery windows at least 90 percent of the time)이라고 했으므로, (A)가 정답이다.

어휘 | improperly 적절하지 않게

Paraphrasing
지문의 do not meet agreed-upon delivery windows
→ 정답의 Missing delivery deadlines

19 두 번째 단락, 여덟 번째 줄에 쓰인 "terms"와 의미상 가장 가까운 것은?
(A) 조건   (B) 기간
(C) 보고서   (D) 수치

해설 | **동의어 찾기**
terms를 포함한 부분은 '이 새로운 조건들이 분명히 명시된(with these new terms clearly stated)'이라는 의미로 해석되는데, 여기서 terms는 '조건들'이라는 뜻으로 쓰였다. 따라서 (A) conditions가 정답이다.

20 보울랜드의 계획에 대해 암시된 것은 무엇인가?
(A) 회사의 경영진이 세부 사항을 승인해야 한다.
(B) 홍보가 사업에 좋을 것이다.
(C) 공급업체들이 그 계획의 실행을 간절히 바란다.
(D) 추가 조치들이 필요할 수 있다.

해설 | **추론/암시**
세 번째 단락에서 보울랜드가 공급업체들이 직면한 문제들을 고려하지 않으면 위약금 부과로는 배송 문제를 해결하지 못할 것(imposing charges will not solve the problem unless challenges faced by suppliers are also taken into account)이라고 했으므로, 현 계획에 추가 조치가 필요할 수도 있음을 추론할 수 있다. 따라서 (D)가 정답이다.

어휘 | publicity 홍보(업)

21 자파타 씨가 소통 전략에 대해 언급하는 이유는 무엇인가?
(A) 마케팅 결정에 의문을 제기하려고
(B) 새로운 마케팅 아이디어를 제안하려고
(C) 직업 만족도 향상에 관해 조언을 하려고
(D) 공급 문제에 대한 해결책을 제안하려고

해설 | **세부 사항**
마지막 단락에서 자파타 씨는 보울랜드에서 더 좋은 소통 전략을 채택했다면 문제가 쉽게 해결될 수 있을 것(if Boulland were to adopt better communication strategies, the issue could be readily resolved)이라고 했으므로, 그가 해결책의 일환으로 소통 전략을 언급했음을 알 수 있다. 따라서 (D)가 정답이다.

어휘 | question 의문을 제기하다

Unit 19   기타 양식

지문 구성과 독해 전략 .... 본책 p.262

안나 리치	[오전 9시 2분]

지난달 어디에서 차를 수리하셨어요?

보니 그린	[오전 9시 5분]

린덴 가에 있는 막스 오토모티브에서요. 차에 문제가 있나요?

안나 리치	[오전 9시 6분]

아니요. 직장 동료인 케빈 피터스 씨와 커피숍에서 이야기하는 중이에요. 그가 차를 수리 받아야 한대요.

보니 그린	[오전 9시 8분]

케빈한테 막스가 좋았다고 이야기해 주세요. 거기는 부품 가격도 괜찮은 것으로 구해줬고 인건비도 적당했어요.

안나 리치	[오전 9시 9분]

고마워요. 제가 전해 줄게요.

어휘 | charge 청구하다 reasonable 적당한 pass on 전하다

Q1 리치 씨는 왜 그린 씨에게 연락했겠는가?
(A) 추천을 받고 싶어서
(B) 어떤 장소로 가는 길을 알고 싶어서
(C) 커피를 마시고 싶어서
(D) 차를 수리해야 해서

Q2 오전 9시 9분에 리치 씨가 "제가 전해 줄게요"라고 말한 의도는 무엇인가?

(A) 출근하는 길에 그린 씨를 차를 태울 것이다.

(B) 다른 수리점을 찾을 것이다.

(C) 피터스 씨와 정보를 공유할 것이다.

(D) 피터스 씨에게 돈을 갖다 줄 것이다.

● 실전 도움닫기   본책 p.263

1 (B)   **2** (B)   **3** (B)   **4** (A)

[1-2] 엽서

5월 4일

찰스 서머빌 박사
테일러 가 1785번지
앨런타운, 펜실베이니아 주 18102

[1]귀하의 다음 치아 스케일링이 5월 11일 금요일 오전 8시 30분에 예정되어 있음을 참고로 안내해 드립니다. [2]예약 시간을 지키실 수 없다면 5월 9일 수요일 오후 3시까지 정규 진료 시간에 전화를 주시기 바랍니다. 월요일부터 토요일까지 오전 8시부터 오후 5시까지 555-0119번으로 저희에게 연락하실 수 있습니다.

5월 28일 월요일은 공휴일이라 휴진한다는 점에 유의해 주십시오.

받는 사람: 스티븐 하인즈 씨
그린우드 웨이 15번지
베들레헴, 펜실베이니아 주 18018

어휘 | reminder (약속이나 해야 할 일 등을) 상기시켜 주는 편지[메모] dental cleaning 치아 스케일링 be scheduled for ~로 예정되어 있다 appointment 약속, 예약 reach 연락하다

1 하인즈 씨의 예약 날짜는 언제인가?

(A) 5월 9일   (B) 5월 11일

해설 | 세부 사항

초반부에서 다음 치아 스케일링 날짜가 5월 11일(your next dental cleaning is scheduled for Friday, May 11)이라고 했으므로, (B)가 정답이다.

2 엽서에 따르면, 하인즈 씨는 왜 치과에 전화를 하겠는가?

(A) 예약을 확정하기 위해   (B) 예약을 취소하기 위해

해설 | 세부 사항

중반부에서 예약 시간을 지킬 수 없는 경우 전화를 달라(If you are unable to keep your appointment, please call us)고 했으므로, (B)가 정답이다.

[3-4] 고객용 입장권

1회 무료 방문 체험을 하시려면 본 입장권을 제시하십시오.

블루 리버 피트니스 센터

• 처음 오신 방문객들에게만 유효합니다.

• 손님들은 적어도 18세이거나 아니면 성인을 동반해야만 합니다.

[3]손님들은 시설을 둘러보고 회원권 옵션에 대해 알아 보려면 직원 한 명과 함께하는 설명회에 참석해야만 합니다.

• 한정된 시간에만 유효합니다:

[4]화요일부터 목요일까지 오전 10시-오후 5시, 토요일 오전 10시-오후 3시

블루 리버는 오랫동안 디트로이트 최고의 피트니스 센터로서 연령대와 관심사가 다양한 모든 회원들이 건강을 향상시키는 것을 돕고 있습니다. 귀하가 규칙적인 운동을 시작하려는 초보자이든 새로운 도전을 추구하는 피트니스 전문가이든 블루 리버는 귀하가 목표를 달성하는 데 도움을 드릴 것입니다.

어휘 | pass 출입증, 입장권 valid 유효한 accompany 동반하다, 동행하다 information session 설명회 option 선택(권), 선택 사항 premier 최고의 novice 초보자 challenge 도전 attain 달성하다

3 방문객이 손님용 입장권을 이용하려면 무엇을 해야 하는가?

(A) 신분증을 제시한다.

(B) 직원과 만난다.

해설 | 세부 사항

세 번째 항목에서 시설을 둘러보고 회원권 옵션에 대해 알아 보려면 직원과 함께하는 설명회에 참석해야 한다(Guests must attend an information session with a staff member to ~ learn about membership options)고 했으므로, (B)가 정답이다.

어휘 | identification 신분증

Paraphrasing
지문의 attend an information session with a staff member
→ 보기의 Meet with a representative

4 입장권은 언제 이용할 수 있는가?

(A) 수요일

(B) 금요일

해설 | 세부 사항

네 번째 항목에서 입장권을 사용할 수 있는 요일이 화요일에서 목요일, 그리고 토요일(Tuesday to Thursday, Saturday)이라고 했으므로, (A)가 정답이다.

● ETS 실전문제   본책 p.264

1 (A)   **2** (C)   **3** (A)   **4** (C)   **5** (A)   **6** (C)

7 (C)   **8** (A)   **9** (C)   **10** (B)   **11** (C)   **12** (A)

13 (B)   **14** (A)   **15** (C)   **16** (B)   **17** (A)   **18** (D)

[1-2] 문자 메시지

타니아 하우저   (오전 8시 5분)

오늘 다이아몬드 로드 공사 프로젝트의 최신 설계도를 검토하기 위해 회의하는 것 맞나요? 팀에서 대중 여론 조사를 위해 설계도를 보낼 준비가 된 걸로 알고 있어요.

조애너 레디   (오전 8시 7분)

네, 댄 서번 디자인 부장에게 최신 설계도들을 막 받았어요. 오전 11시 30분에 회의하는 것 여전히 괜찮나요?

타니아 하우저   (오전 8시 9분)

저는 오전 11시 30분까지 아래층에서 또 다른 회의가 있지만, 그 후에 당신 사무실로 바로 갈 수 있어요.

조애너 레디   (오전 8시 12분)

그럼 되겠네요. ²제가 설계도들을 모두 가지고 있으니 여기서 만나기로 하죠.

하우저   (오전 8시 14분)

좋아요. ¹서번 씨도 우리 회의에 참석하나요?

조애너 레디   (오전 8시 15분)

¹아니요, 그는 오늘 스완슨 다리 재건축 현장에서 외근 중이에요.

타니아 하우저   (오전 8시 16분)

알았어요. 이따 오전에 봐요.

어휘 | discuss 논의하다 public comment 대중의 의견, 공개 논평 offsite 부지 밖에서

1 서번 씨에 대해 암시된 것은 무엇인가?

(A) 오늘 회의에 참석할 수 없다.
(B) 새 설계도를 좋아하지 않는다.
(C) 설계도를 받기 위해 기다리고 있다.
(D) 오전 11시 30분에 약속이 있다.

해설 | **추론 / 암시**

하우저 씨가 오전 8시 14분 메시지에서 서번도 회의에 참석하는지(Is Mr. Surban going to join us?) 물었는데, 이에 대해 레디 씨가 오전 8시 15분 메시지에서 그렇지 않다(No)고 한 후, 그가 오늘 외근 중(he's working offsite today)이라고 덧붙였으므로, (A)가 정답이다.

2 오전 8시 14분에 하우저 씨가 "좋아요"라고 쓴 의도는 무엇이겠는가?

(A) 대중 여론 조사를 위해 디자인을 보낼 준비가 되어 있다.
(B) 그 설계도들에 대해 서번 씨에게 연락할 것이다.
(C) 레디 씨의 사무실에서 설계도들을 볼 것이다.
(D) 스완슨 다리에서 만날 예정이다.

해설 | **의도 파악**

레디 씨가 오전 8시 12분 메시지에서 자신이 설계도를 모두 가지고 있으니 자신의 사무실에서 만날 것(We can meet here since I have all the designs)을 제안했는데, 이에 대해 하우저 씨가 '좋아요(Sounds good)'라고 응답한 것이므로, (C)가 정답이다.

[3-4] **주문서**

브릭스턴 앤 크레이
한스데일 로 13번지
오타와, 온타리오 K1V 7W1
(613) 555-0409
주문서

날짜:	3월 6일
고객명:	제니 응우옌 발킨 그래픽 디자인
고객 주소:	모리스 드라이브 185번지, 오타와, 온타리오, K1A OH2
납부 정보:	#281907 계좌로 청구됨
⁴배송 정보:	고객이 늦어도 3월 8일 오후 5시까지 배송해 달라고 요청

상품 번호	³품목 명세	수량	단가	계
1886	³스테이플러	8	9.45달러	75.6달러
1742	³노란색 파일 폴더, 50개들이 상자	3	11.2달러	33.6달러
2480	³검은색 볼펜, 12개들이 상자	2	14달러	28달러
2333	³프린터 용지, A4 크기, 500장 패키지	10	13.25달러	132.5달러
			총계 269.7달러	

주문 처리자: 천 리우

어휘 | payment 지불, 납부 bill 청구서를 보내다 account 계좌, 계정 delivery 배달, 배송 no later than 늦어도 ~까지는 description 설명, 명세

3 브릭스턴 앤 크레이는 어떤 종류의 업체이겠는가?

(A) 사무용품점   (B) 디자인 회사
(C) 도서출판사   (D) 전자제품점

해설 | **추론 / 암시**

품목 명세 내역(Item Description)에 열거된 각 상품(Stapler, file folders, ballpoint pens, Printer paper)을 통해 브릭스턴 앤 크레이가 사무용품점이라는 것을 추론할 수 있으므로, (A)가 정답이다.

4 주문에 대해 명시된 것은?

(A) 천 리우에게 배송될 것이다.
(B) 현금으로 지불해야 한다.
(C) 3월 8일까지 배송되어야 한다.
(D) 다양한 색상의 펜이 포함되어 있다.

해설 | **Not / True**

배송 정보(Delivery Information)에서 고객이 늦어도 3월 8일 오후 5시까지 배송해 달라고 요청한다(Customer requests delivery no later than 5:00 P.M. on March 8)고 했으므로, (C)가 정답이다.

Paraphrasing

지문의 no later than 5:00 P.M. on March 8
→ 정답의 by March 8

[5-7] **일정표**

베이 시티
제19회 연례 지역사회 축제
8월 11일 일요일

오전 9시 - 오후 5시	⁵미술품 전시 및 판매

⁵지역 예술가들이 지역 문화센터 건너편 엘름우드 공원 북쪽을 따라 설치된 부스에서 작품을 전시합니다.

오전 11시 - 오전 11시 30분	가족 인형극

엘름우드 공원 야외무대에서 베이 시티 커뮤니티 극장 단원들이 인기 동화들을 상연합니다.

오전 11시 45분 - 오후 2시	바비큐 시식

베이 시티의 메스키트 그릴이 야외무대 바로 뒤 잔디밭에서 인기 메뉴들의 샘플을 나눠드립니다. 들러서 맛보세요!

---

6 오후 1시 30분 - 오후 2시 30분 블루그라스 음악회
오라일리 사중주단이 야외무대에서 클래식 곡과 옛 인기곡을 연주합니다.

오후 2시 30분 - 오후 3시 30분 **7 탁구 토너먼트 대회**
엘름우드 공원 주 잔디밭에서 개인 및 팀 경기가 열립니다. 대회 참가비는 없습니다. 단, **7 참가자는 축제 안내 부스에서 신청서를 작성해야 합니다.**

더 자세한 정보를 원하시면 **7 사이프레스 가에 있는 엘름우드 공원 입구의 축제 안내 부스를 방문하세요.**

어휘 | annual 연례의 display 전시하다, 진열하다 puppet (인형극에 쓰는) 인형 theater 극장, 극단 food tasting 시식 stop by 들르다 quartet 사중주단 individual 개인의 charge 요금 enter the competition 대회에 참가하다 complete a form 서식에 기입하다 registration 등록 entrance 입구

5 일정표에 따르면, 무엇을 구입할 수 있는가?
(A) 지역 예술가들의 작품
(B) 아동용 도서
(C) 특별 음식
(D) 음반

해설 | **세부 사항**
첫 번째 행사인 '미술품 전시 및 판매(Art Display and Sale)'에서 지역 예술가들이 작품을 전시한다(Local artists will be displaying their work)고 했으므로, (A)가 정답이다.

Paraphrasing
지문의 Sale → 질문의 for purchase

6 음악 행사는 언제 시작하는가?
(A) 오전 9시
(B) 오전 11시
(C) 오후 1시 30분
(D) 오후 2시 30분

해설 | **세부 사항**
일정에서 블루그라스 음악회(Bluegrass Concert)가 오후 1시 30분에 시작한다는 것을 확인할 수 있으므로, (C)가 정답이다.

Paraphrasing
지문의 Bluegrass Concert → 질문의 a musical event

7 운동 경기 신청서는 어디서 얻을 수 있는가?
(A) 지역 문화센터
(B) 주 잔디밭
(C) 공원 입구
(D) 야외무대

해설 | **세부 사항**
운동 경기인 탁구 토너먼트 대회(Table Tennis Tournament)의 참가자는 축제 안내 부스에서 신청서를 작성해야 한다(participants must complete a registration form at the Festival Information Booth)고 했는데, 마지막 단락에서 신청서를 작성해야 하는 축제 안내 부스가 엘름우드 공원 입구에 있다(located at the Elmwood Park entrance)고 했으므로, (C)가 정답이다.

[8-11] 양식

고객님께:
8 귀하의 의견과 생각은 저희에게 중요합니다. 잠깐 시간을 내어 이 설문지를 작성해 주십시오. 감사합니다!
9 경영진
아래 각 항목에 대해 귀하의 호텔 투숙 경험을 가장 잘 묘사하는 항목에 체크(√) 표시를 해 주십시오.

	매우 좋다	좋다	보통	그저 그렇다	좋지 않다
체크인/체크아웃의 용이함		√			
객실 상태		√			
전반적인 서비스 품질	√				
시설 관리과 서비스			√		
전반적인 청결도	√				
11 식음료의 질				√	
가격			√		

기타 의견:
처음에 남편과 저는 이곳에 온 것은 실수였다고 생각했습니다. 몇 달 전에 예약을 했고 예약 확인 번호까지 받았는데도 불구하고 **10 체크인을 할 때 저희 예약 기록이 전혀 없다는 사실을 알고 몹시 화가 났습니다.** 하지만 프런트 직원이 저희가 원래 예약했던 것보다 더 안락하고 널찍한 방을 제공하면서 이 문제를 만족스럽게 해결해 주었습니다. 전반적으로 시설 관리과 직원, 음식점 종업원들, 호텔 셔틀버스 기사를 비롯하여 호텔 직원들의 전문가다운 태도에 만족했습니다. 나중에 이 호텔을 다시 방문하기를 고대하고 있습니다.

리사 브라우닝

어휘 | matter 중요하다; 문제 complete 작성하다, 기입하다 survey 설문 조사 management 경영진, 관리진 category 부문, 범주 fair 그저 그런 ease 쉬움, 용이함 overall 전반적인; 전반적으로 housekeeping (호텔·병원 등의) 시설 관리과 cleanliness 청결 beverage 음료 initially 처음에 book 예약하다(= reserve) in advance 미리 confirmation 확인 clerk 점원, 종업원 resolve 해결하다 satisfactorily 만족스럽게 spacious 널찍한 originally 원래 professional 전문가다운 attitude 태도 personnel 직원들

8 이 양식의 목적은 무엇인가?
(A) 호텔에 관한 의견을 요청하기 위하여
(B) 호텔 방을 예약하기 위하여
(C) 호텔 취업에 관심을 표하기 위하여
(D) 호텔에서 지불 방법을 표시하기 위하여

해설 | **주제 / 목적**
첫 번째 단락에서 고객의 의견과 생각이 중요하다(Your opinions and ideas matter to us)며 호텔 투숙 경험 관련 설문 조사에 참여해 달라고 했으므로, (A)가 정답이다.

9 브라우닝 씨는 누구 앞으로 의견을 보내고 있는가?
(A) 호텔 셔틀버스 기사
(B) 호텔 음식점 종업원들
(C) 호텔 경영진
(D) 호텔 프런트 직원

해설 | **세부 사항**

'Dear Guest'로 시작하는 편지 형식을 띤 짧은 글의 발신인에 The Management라고 적혀 있으므로, 브라우닝 씨가 호텔 경영진에게 의견을 보내는 것임을 알 수 있다. 따라서 (C)가 정답이다.

어휘 | address A to B B에게 A를 보내다

10 브라우닝 씨는 처음에 왜 화가 났는가?
(A) 호텔 요금이 예상했던 것보다 비쌌다.
(B) 호텔에 그녀의 예약 기록이 없었다.
(C) 그녀의 남편이 방을 예약하는 것을 잊었다.
(D) 예약 확인 번호를 분실했었다.

해설 | **세부 사항**

기타 의견(Additional Comments)란을 보면 체크인을 하려는데 예약 기록이 없다고 해서 화가 났다(We were upset when, at check-in, we learned that there was no record of our reservation)고 했으므로, (B)가 정답이다.

11 브라우닝 씨는 호텔의 어떤 점이 가장 마음에 들지 않았는가?
(A) 직원의 태도
(B) 체크아웃 절차
(C) 식사의 질
(D) 객실 상태

해설 | **세부 사항**

표에서 가장 좋지 않은 평가(Fair)를 받은 항목이 식음료의 질(Quality of food and beverages)이므로, (C)가 정답이다.

어휘 | procedure 절차

Paraphrasing

지문의 food and beverages → 정답의 meals

[12-15] 온라인 채팅

헤더 토프 (오전 8시 28분)
¹²회원을 모으는 방법에 대한 아이디어가 있을까요? 현재 강좌들 중 일부는 절반도 차지 않았어요. 등록자 수가 빨리 늘지 않으면 취소해야 할 거예요.

¹³타냐 카탈도 (오전 8시 32분)
¹³제 학생들은 월요일 댄스 강좌가 취소되는 걸 분명 원치 않을 거예요. ¹²/¹⁴현재 회원들이 강좌에 첫 방문 고객을 무료로 데리고 오게 할 것을 제안합니다.

래리 신 (오전 8시 34분)
최근에 제 실내 자전거 수업은 출석률이 낮았어요. ¹²/¹⁴**실내 자전거를 처음 이용하는 사람들을 위해, 그리고 수업에 포함된 운동들에 관해 워크숍을 진행할 수 있죠.** 그러면 그들이 편안하게 시도해 볼 수 있으니까요. 현 회원들은 무료로 참석하고 비회원은 비용을 지불하는 거죠.

타냐 카탈도 (오전 8시 35분)
¹²/¹⁴신규 회원을 위한 특별 프로모션을 하는 건 어때요? 첫 두 달은 한 달 가격으로 한다든지요. 소셜미디어에 광고를 하는 거예요.

헤더 토프 (오전 8시 36분)
모두 진행 가능한 방법들이군요. ¹⁵래리, 제안한 워크숍에 대한 세부 사항을 이메일로 받아 봐야 할 것 같네요.

어휘 | current 현재의 enrollment 등록, 등록자 수 increase 증가하다 definitely 분명히 suggest 제안하다 invite 요청하다, 유도하다 attendance 출석(률) indoor 실내의 lately 최근 stationary bicycle 실내 자전거 newcomer 신참자 involve 포함하다, 수반하다 attend 참석하다 potential 가능성 있는, 잠재적인

12 메시지 작성자들은 무엇에 대해 이야기하는가?
(A) 더 많은 회원을 유치하는 방법
(B) 신규 강좌 일정을 잡는 시기
(C) 워크숍을 하기에 좋은 장소를 찾을 곳
(D) 인상할 회비

해설 | **주제/목적**

토프 씨가 오전 8시 28분 메시지에서 회원을 모으는 방법에 대한 아이디어가 있는지(Do we have any ideas how to build our membership?) 물었는데, 이에 대해 메시지 작성자들이 각자의 의견을 제시하며 온라인 채팅을 이어가고 있으므로, (A)가 정답이다.

어휘 | attract 끌어 모으다 raise 올리다

Paraphrasing

지문의 build our membership → 정답의 attract more members

13 댄스 강좌에 대해 명시된 것은?
(A) 토프 씨가 취소했다.
(B) 카탈도 씨가 가르친다.
(C) 매일 진행된다.
(D) 두 달간 운영 중이다.

해설 | **세부 사항**

카탈도 씨가 오전 8시 32분 메시지에서 자신의 학생들이 월요일 댄스 강좌가 취소되는 걸 분명 원치 않을 거라고(My students would definitely not want their Monday dance class canceled) 했으므로, 카탈도 씨가 댄스 강좌를 진행한다는 것을 알 수 있다. 따라서 (B)가 정답이다.

14 오전 8시 36분에 토프 씨가 '모두 진행 가능한 방법들이군요'라고 말할 때, 그 의도는 무엇인가?
(A) 아이디어들이 고려해 볼 만하다고 생각한다.
(B) 최근 지원자들을 채용하는 것을 고려할 것이다.
(C) 두 직원 모두 승진할 자격이 있다고 생각한다.
(D) 실내 자전거 강좌를 즐겁게 듣고 있다.

해설 | **의도 파악**

메시지 작성자들이 제시한 회원 유치 방법에 대해 토프 씨가 '모두 진행 가능한 방법들이군요(Those are all potential ways to go)'라고 응답한 것이므로, 제시된 아이디어들이 모두 고려해 볼 만하다고 생각하고 있음을 알 수 있다. 따라서 (A)가 정답이다.

어휘 | worth -ing ~할 가치가 있다 consider 고려하다 deserve ~를 받을 만하다 promotion 승진

15 신 씨는 다음으로 무엇을 하겠는가?
(A) 자신의 강좌에 고객 초청
(B) 소셜미디어에 광고
(C) 워크숍에 관한 설명 전송
(D) 전문성 개발 세미나 참가

해설 | **추론/암시**

토프 씨가 오전 8시 36분 메시지에서 신 씨가 제안한 워크숍에 대한 세부 사항을 이메일로 받아 봐야 할 것 같다(Larry, I will need an e-mail with details about the proposed workshop)고 했으므로, 신 씨가 워크숍에 대한 세부 사항을 토프 씨에게 보낼 것으로 추론할 수 있다. 따라서 (C)가 정답이다.

어휘 | description 설명 development 개발

Paraphrasing
지문의 details about the proposed workshop
→ 정답의 a workshop description

[16-18] 웹페이지

하퍼 필즈 비즈니스 뉴스 온라인	검색

홈	회사 소개	무료 자료실	블로그	연락처	나의 계정

18(C)**25년간 <하퍼 필즈 비즈니스 뉴스(HFBN)>는 비즈니스 전문가들에게 주요한 자원이 되어 왔습니다.** 18(B)**인쇄물과 온라인으로 저희는 비즈니스 뉴스를 전문적으로 보도하며, 배경 분석 및 금융계에 관한 논평을 제공합니다.** 18(A)**저희 웹사이트에는 온라인 구독자만 이용할 수 있는 추가 특집 자료들이 있습니다.** 여기에는 직원들이 선정한 자료, 실업계 주요 기업들이 발표한 언론 보도자료, 사용자가 직접 정교한 데이터 차트를 만들 수 있는 다양한 소프트웨어 애플리케이션이 포함됩니다.

16**저희 온라인 서비스 정기 구독에 관심 있는 분들께 30일 무료 체험 기회를 드립니다.** 17**정기 구독을 하시려면 반드시 18세 이상이어야 하며 유효한 신용카드를 제시해야 합니다.** 무료 체험 기간에는 신용카드로 결제 대금이 청구되지 않습니다. 귀하의 신용카드는 무료 체험이 끝나는 시점에 유료 온라인 구독자로 자동 전환하기 위해서만 사용되며, 그때 연간 정기 구독료 45달러가 청구됩니다.

유료 온라인 구독자로 전환을 원하지 않으신다면 반드시 무료 체험 기간이 만료되기 전에 서비스를 취소하셔야만 합니다. 취소를 하시려면 저희 웹사이트에 있는 '나의 계정' 페이지로 들어가서 '업그레이드하지 마세요'를 선택하셔야 합니다. 이렇게 조치하시면 귀하의 신용카드로 결제 대금이 청구되지 않습니다. 하지만 남은 무료 체험 기간 동안 계속 서비스를 이용하실 수 있습니다.

(지금 시작하세요!)

어휘 | resource 자원 coverage 보도, 방송 analysis 분석 commentary 논평 finance 금융, 재정 additional 추가의 feature 특집으로 삼다; 특집 기사, 특집물 available 이용할 수 있는 subscriber 구독자 staff picks 직원들이 선정[추천]해 주는 것 press release 보도자료, 성명 issue 쟁점; 발표하다 application 애플리케이션, 응용 프로그램 sophisticated 정교한 subscription 정기 구독 free trial 무료 체험 valid 유효한 charge 청구하다 status 지위, 상태 annual 연간의 expire 만료되다 prevent 예방하다 remainder 나머지 period 기간

16 웹페이지에는 어떤 내용이 설명되고 있는가?
(A) 소프트웨어 프로그램
(B) 시험 구독
(C) 구독 기한 연장
(D) 고급 비즈니스 과정

해설 | **주제/목적**

첫 번째 단락에서 회사 및 온라인 구독 서비스에 대해 전반적으로 소개한 후, 두 번째 단락부터 30일 무료 체험(a 30-day free trial) 구독에 대해 설명하고 있으므로, (B)가 정답이다.

어휘 | renewal 갱신, 기한 연장 advanced 선진의, 고급의

17 독자들은 무엇을 제시하도록 요청받는가?
(A) 신용카드 정보   (B) 회원 번호
(C) 정기 구독 만료일   (D) 전문 자격

해설 | **세부 사항**

두 번째 단락에서 정기 구독을 신청하고자 하는 사람은 유효한 신용카드를 제시해야 한다(You must ~ provide a valid credit card to subscribe)고 했으므로, (A)가 정답이다.

어휘 | expiration 만료 qualification 자격

18 HFBN에 대해 명시되지 않은 것은?
(A) 온라인 소프트웨어 도구를 제공한다.
(B) 금융 관련 주제를 다룬다.
(C) 25년간 영업을 해 왔다.
(D) 인쇄물 발간을 중단했다.

해설 | **Not/True**

첫 번째 단락의 '온라인 구독자에게 다양한 소프트웨어 애플리케이션(various software applications)을 포함한 추가 특집 자료를 제공한다'에서 (A)를, '인쇄물과 온라인으로 비즈니스 뉴스를 전문적으로 보도하며, 배경 분석 및 금융계(world of finance)에 관한 논평을 제공한다'에서 (B)를, '25년간(For 25 years) 비즈니스 전문가들에게 주요한 자원이 되어 왔다'에서 (C)를 확인할 수 있다. 인쇄물과 온라인으로 뉴스를 보도한다고 했으므로, 인쇄물 발간을 중단했다고 볼 수 없다. 따라서 (D)가 정답이다.

어휘 | related 관련된 publish 출판하다

Paraphrasing
지문의 software applications → 보기 (A)의 online software tools

Unit 20 복수 지문

연계 문제 풀이 전략   본책 p.270

중요 공지:

카터스 팜 프레시가 지난주 자사의 채소 캔 제품(420그램/14.5온스 사이즈) 여러 상자가 잘못된 라벨을 붙인 채 지역 상점에 배송됐다고 알렸습니다. 라벨이 잘못된 캔은 제품 코드가 G7780 또는 G7781로 찍혀 있습니다.

환불을 받으시려면 9월 12일까지 구입이 이뤄진 상점으로 상품을 가져오시기 바랍니다. 제조업체 정책에 따라 반품 상품과 함께 원본 영수증을 제출해야 합니다.

어휘 | announce 알리다, 발표하다 incorrect 부정확한, 맞지 않는 mislabeled 라벨이 잘못 붙여진 purchase 구입 manufacturer 제조자 policy 정책 original 원본의, 원래의 submit 제출하다

델가도 씨께,

귀하의 매장에서 보낸 캔 옥수수 배송을 받았습니다. 2주 후에 우편으로 67.5달러 상당의 수표를 받으실 겁니다. 이는 귀하의 고객들이 라벨이 잘못된 캔을 반품했을 때 환불된 금액을 충당할 수 있을 것입니다. 논의했던 바와 같이, 여기에는 영수증이 없는 고객에게 환불해 주신 7.5달러가 포함되어 있습니다.

귀하와 귀하의 고객에게 불편을 드려 죄송합니다.

카렌 우

카터스 팜 프레시 고객 서비스 담당자

어휘 | shipment 배송품 in the amount of ~의 금액으로 include 포함하다 apologize for ~에 대해 사과하다 inconvenience 불편 patron 고객

Q 우 씨에 대해 암시된 것은?
(A) 캔 제품을 추가로 받기를 기대한다.
(B) 원래 약속했던 것보다 늦게 수표를 보낼 것이다.
(C) 정책에 예외를 뒀다.
(D) 델가도 씨와 회의할 예정이다.

어휘 | additional 추가의 goods 상품 originally 원래 make an exception 예외를 두다, 특별 취급하다

● 실전 **도움닫기**   본책 p. 271

1 (B) **2** (A)

[1-2] 광고+이메일

드라이브 라이트 렌터카
봄 휴가 특별가-3월 30일에서 6월 15일까지 유효

차량 등급	특징	기본 요금
이코노미	2도어, 에어컨 AM/FM 스테레오 4인승	현재 하루에 단돈 39달러
인터미디어트	2도어, 에어컨 CD 플레이어가 장착된 AM/FM 스테레오 4인승	현재 하루에 단돈 45달러
스탠다드	4도어, 에어컨 CD 플레이어가 장착된 AM/FM 스테레오 5인승	현재 하루에 단돈 50달러
[1]프리미엄	4도어, 에어컨 CD 플레이어가 장착된 AM/FM 스테레오 7인승	현재 하루에 단돈 68달러

[2]한시적인 제공입니다. 표에 기재된 기본 요금을 적용 받기 위해서는 렌터카를 6월 15일까지 반납해야 합니다. 기본 요금에는 저희 공항 지점에서 대여한 차량에 부과되는 추가 요금이 포함되지 않습니다. 여러분이 바라는 차량 등급이 모든 드라이브 라이트 지점에서 이용 가능하지는 않은 점 유감스럽게 생각합니다.

어휘 | rent-a-car 임대 자동차, 렌터카(업), 승용차 대여(업) getaway 휴가 valid 유효한 economy 절약 intermediate 중간의, 중급의 standard 일반적인, 표준의 premium 아주 높은, 고급의 limited 제한된, 한정된 qualify 자격을 얻다 list (특정한 순서로) 열거하다, 리스트[목록]에 기재[언급]하다 surcharge 추가 요금 assess (요금 등을) 부과하다, 평가하다

수신: amanda.j.mitchell@raewyncorp.com
발신: ting.c.hwang@raewyncorp.com
날짜: 6월 3일
제목: 새 예약

안녕하세요, 아만다.

곧 있을 켈리스빌 사무소 출장 건으로 다시 한번 당신 도움이 필요합니다. 조던 씨가 저와 켈리스빌 사무소의 우리 팀에게 리카르디 시에서 열리는 회의에 같이 가라고 방금 요청하셨어요. 그러니 일전에 당신이 저를 위해 해준 렌터카 예약을 변경해 주세요. 원래 계획대로 [2]6월 13일 켈리스빌 공항에서 차를 인수할 것이지만, 그 후에는 계획했던 것보다 더 오래 사용할 것입니다. 저는 6월 15일 회의를 위해 켈리스빌 사무소의 사람들을 태우고 리카르디 시까지 갈 것입니다. [1]사람들을 태우기 위해서 6인승 차가 필요할 겁니다. [2]6월 17일 켈리스빌 공항에 차를 반납할 예정입니다. 마지막으로, 6월 17일 저녁에 켈리스빌에서 제가 돌아올 수 있도록 제 비행기 예약을 변경해 주시면 감사하겠습니다.

팅천

어휘 | reservation 예약 pick up 인수하다, 찾아오다 accommodate 공간을 제공하다, 수용하다 seat (특정한 수의) 좌석이 있다 appreciate 감사하다

1 황팅천 씨를 위해 어떤 등급의 차가 예약될 것 같은가?
(A) 스탠다드
(B) 프리미엄

해설 | 연계
이메일 후반부에서 여섯 사람이 탈 차량이 필요하다(I'll need a car that seats six people)고 했는데, 광고를 보면 여섯 명이 탈 수 있는 차량은 7인승인 Premium뿐이므로, (B)가 정답이다.

2 황팅천 씨가 차를 렌트하기 위해 지불할 기본 요금에 대해 암시된 것은 무엇인가?
(A) 광고에 기재된 기본 요금과 다를 것이다.
(B) 그가 공항 지점에서 차를 렌트했기 때문에 비용이 더 저렴할 것이다.

해설 | 연계
이메일에서 황팅천 씨는 13일 공항에서 차를 인수하고 17일에 반납할 예정이라고 했다. 광고를 보면 표에 나와 있는 기본 요금을 적용받기 위해서는(to qualify for base price listed) 15일까지 차를 반납해야 하며, 이 요금에는 공항 지점에서 대여한 차량에 부과되는 추가 요금이 포함되지 않는다(Base prices do not include ~ our airport locations)고 나와 있다. 따라서 황팅천 씨가 지불할 요금이 광고에 나와 있는 기본 요금과 다를 것이라고 추론할 수 있으므로, (A)가 정답이다.

1 (B)	**2** (C)	**3** (C)	**4** (A)	**5** (A)	**6** (C)
7 (A)	**8** (D)	**9** (C)	**10** (D)	**11** (C)	**12** (A)
13 (C)	**14** (B)	**15** (C)	**16** (B)	**17** (C)	**18** (C)
19 (A)	**20** (D)	**21** (D)	**22** (C)	**23** (B)	**24** (C)
25 (A)	**26** (A)	**27** (B)	**28** (C)	**29** (D)	**30** (D)

[1-5] 양식 + 이메일

릴라이어블 패키지 딜리버리
고객 문의

귀하의 문의 사항을 가장 잘 설명한 곳에 체크하세요.

¹X 우편물이 도착하지 않음

_ 취급 시 내용물이 파손됨

_ 우편물이 지나치게 늦게 도착함

_ 도착한 소포의 내용물이 누락되어 있었음

발신인 정보:　　　　　²**수신인 정보:**
트렌트 로렌스　　　　　²라일라 애덤스
소속: 유비크엔 푸드　　　윌슨 코트 101번지
애스펜 로 230번지　　　샐포드 954-372
제임스타운 733-700

우편물 유형: 작은 소포

우편물 발송일자: 7월 12일

문제점 설명:
내용물에 유통기한이 약 4주인 상하기 쉬운 음식 제품이 포함되어
있습니다. 본 문의 사항에 대해 즉시 조치해 주시면 감사하겠습니다.

이름: 트렌트 로렌스　　　**서명:** 트렌트 로렌스

어휘 | inquiry 문의 describe 설명하다 content 내용물 damage
손상시키다 handling 취급 unreasonable 부당한, 지나친 delay
지연 missing 분실된, 없어진 addressee 수신인 perishable 잘
상하는 shelf life 유통기한 prompt attention 즉각적인 조치

발신: jnowak@rpd.com
수신: tlawrence@ubiquenfoods.com
제목: 우편 - 접수 번호 T562-23
발송일자: 7월 22일

로렌스 씨께,

귀하의 소포에 대한 연락을 받았습니다. 10일간의 지연은 용납할
수 없는 수준으로, 저희 사무소에서는 최대한 빨리 소포의 위치를
파악하기 위해 최선을 다하고 있습니다. ²그동안 소포가 목적지에
도착할 수도 있으니 대상 수취인과 계속 확인해 주시기 바랍니다.

³사과의 의미로 저희 우수 고객 서비스 3개월 등록을 추가 비용 없이
해 드리고자 합니다. 여기에는 익일 배송 및 온라인 추적 서비스가
포함됩니다.

⁵이 ⁴사안에 관한 추후 서신에는 본 메시지 제목에 있는 접수 번호를
적어 주십시오.

줄리아 노박
릴라이어블 패키지 딜리버리

어휘 | communication 연락, 의사소통 unacceptable 용납할
수 없는 in the meantime 당분간, 그동안 destination 목적지
intended 대상으로 하는, 의도하는 recipient 수취인 apology
사과 at no charge 무료로 enrollment 등록 tracking 추적
correspondence 서신 concerning ~에 관한 refer to ~을
언급하다, 나타내다

---

1 로렌스 씨에 따르면, 소포는 어떤 상태인가?

(A) 내용물이 잘못 들어간 채 배송됐다.

(B) 목적지에 도착하지 않았다.

(C) 파손된 상태로 도착했다.

(D) 일부 내용물이 누락된 채 도착했다.

해설 | **세부 사항**

고객 문의 양식에서 로렌스 씨가 '우편물이 도착하지 않음(Mail not
received)'에 체크했으므로, (B)가 정답이다.

어휘 | reach 도착하다

Paraphrasing

지문의 not received → 정답의 has not reached its
destination

2 노박 씨는 어떤 조치를 취하라고 권하는가?

(A) 샐포드 우체국 방문하기

(B) 제임스타운 우체국에 전화하기

(C) 애덤스 씨에게 연락하기

(D) 유비크엔 푸드에 편지 쓰기

해설 | **연계**

이메일의 첫 번째 단락에서 노박 씨는 로렌스 씨에게 문제를
파악하는 동안 소포가 목적지에 도착할 수도 있으니 대상 수취인과
계속 확인해 줄 것(I encourage you to continue checking
with the intended recipient)을 권고했는데, 고객 문의 양식을
보면 소포의 수신인(Addressee)이 애덤스 씨임을 확인할 수
있으므로, (C)가 정답이다.

Paraphrasing

지문의 checking with the intended recipient → 정답의
Contacting Ms. Adams

3 로렌스 씨에게 무엇이 제공될 것인가?

(A) 배송용품

(B) 소포 가치에 해당하는 보상

(C) 프리미엄 서비스 약정

(D) 무료 이메일 계정

해설 | **세부 사항**

이메일의 두 번째 단락에서 사과의 의미로 우수 고객 서비스 3개월
등록(three months of enrollment in our Preferred Client
service)을 추가 비용 없이(at no additional charge) 해주고자
한다고 했으므로, (C)가 정답이다.

어휘 | compensation 보상 value 가치 account 계정

Paraphrasing

지문의 our Preferred Client service → 정답의 A premium
service plan

4 이메일의 세 번째 단락, 첫 번째 줄에 쓰인 "matter"와 의미가 가장 가까운 것은?

(A) 상황
(B) 이유
(C) 재료
(D) 요소

해설 | **동의어 찾기**

matter가 포함된 부분은 '이 사안에 관한 추후 서신에서는(In future correspondence concerning this matter)'이라는 의미로 해석되는데, 여기서 matter는 '사안'이라는 뜻으로 쓰였다. 따라서 (A) situation이 정답이다.

5 로렌스 씨는 향후 연락 시 무엇을 하라고 요청받는가?

(A) 식별 번호 포함시키기
(B) 노박 씨의 비서에게 연락하기
(C) 이메일을 한 명의 수신인으로 제한하기
(D) 연락처 업데이트하기

해설 | **세부 사항**

이메일의 세 번째 단락에서 추후 서신에서는 메시지 제목에 있는 접수 번호를 적어 줄 것(refer to the case number listed in the subject line of this message)을 요청했으므로 (A)가 정답이다.

어휘 | identification 식별, 신원 확인 limit 제한하다, 한정시키다

Paraphrasing

지문의 refer to the case number → 정답의 Include an identification number

[6-10] 웹페이지＋이메일

---

http://www.lowrytravel.com/trip_protection_plan

홈	소개	나의 여행	**여행자 보험**	연락처

여행자 보험

⁶여러분은 여행을 예약했고 이를 굉장히 기대하고 있습니다. 하지만 때로 뜻밖의 상황이 발생하기도 합니다. ⁶여러분의 투자를 보호하기 위해, 저희 로리 트래블은 합리적인 가격의 여행자 보험 상품을 제공합니다.

⁸저희 상품은 귀하나 여행 동반자분이 서류로 증명된 질병이나 상해, 또는 큰 태풍 같은 기상 사태로 인해 여행을 취소해야 할 때 전액 환불해 드립니다. ⁷⁽ᶜ⁾/⁸그 밖의 다른 이유로 취소하실 경우, 취소 후 향후 18개월 이내에 여행 예약에 적용될 수 있는 포인트를 받으시게 됩니다. 다른 보험 상품들과 달리, ⁷⁽ᴰ⁾저희 상품은 항공비뿐만 아니라 숙박비도 보장하는데, 로리 트래블에서 항공편을 예약하지 않은 경우도 해당됩니다.

⁷⁽ᴮ⁾이 여행자 보험은 최종 여행비 결제 후 5일 이내에 구매해야 하며, 구매 후 10일 이내에 취소하실 수 있습니다. 보험 상품을 구매하거나 여행을 취소하시려면 800-555-0132로 저희 회사에 전화 주시거나 customerservice@lowrytravel.com으로 이메일을 보내 주십시오.

어휘 | unforeseen 뜻밖의 circumstance 상황 protect 보호하다 reasonably priced 합리적으로 가격이 책정된 documented 서류로 증명된 injury 상해 companion 동반자 credit 포인트, 적립금 cover 충당하다, 보장하다

수신: customerservice@lowrytravel.com
발신: kay.chung@cmail.com
날짜: 7월 5일
제목: 여행 취소

고객 서비스 담당자분께,

저와 제 남편은 현재 7월 9일에 시작하는 '유럽 여행 하이라이트'를 예약한 상태입니다. ⁸하지만 제가 근무하는 회사에 데이터 유출 사고가 발생해서, 이 문제를 처리해야 하기 때문에 전 직원이 다음 주에 출근해야 합니다. 따라서, 유감스럽지만 저희는 취소해야 합니다. 제 여행자 보험 증권 번호는 HE4587입니다.

⁹8월 25일에 출발하는 동일한 여행에 빈자리가 있나요? 아니면, 우리는 9월 7일에 떠나는 '이탈리아 도시와 전원 지역 여행'에도 관심이 있습니다. ¹⁰제가 항공편을 다시 예약할 수 있게 가능한 한 빨리 여행 가능 여부에 대해 알려 주시기 바랍니다.

케이 청

어휘 | suffer 겪다 breach 위반, 침해 report to work 출근하다 attend to ~을 처리하다 availability 이용 가능성, 가능 여부

6 웹페이지는 누구를 대상으로 한 것 같은가?

(A) 여행 가이드
(B) 보험 설계사
(C) 로리 트래블의 고객
(D) 로리 트래블의 직원

해설 | **추론/암시**

웹페이지의 첫 번째 단락에서 여행을 예약한 사람들을 대상으로 로리 트래블이 합리적인 가격의 여행자 보험 상품을 제공한다(To protect your investment, Lowry Travel offers a reasonably priced Trip Protection Plan)고 했으므로, 로리 트래블의 고객을 대상으로 한 웹페이지임을 추론할 수 있다. 따라서 (C)가 정답이다.

7 여행자 보험 상품에 대해 어떤 정보가 언급되지 않았는가?

(A) 보험 상품의 가격
(B) 취소 마감 시한
(C) 포인트를 받는 조건
(D) 상품의 세부적인 보장 범위

해설 | **Not/True**

웹페이지 세 번째 단락의 '여행자 보험은 구매 후 10일 이내에 취소할 수 있습니다(The Trip Protection Plan ~ can be canceled within ten days of purchase)'에서 (B)를, 두 번째 단락의 '그 밖의 다른 이유로 취소할 경우, 포인트를 받게 됩니다(If you need to cancel for any other reason, you will receive a credit)'에서 (C)를, '상품에는 항공비뿐만 아니라 숙박비도 보장하는데, 로리 트래블에서 항공 여행을 예약하지 않은 경우도 해당됩니다(ours covers the cost of your airfare as well as lodging costs, even if you did not book your air travel through Lowry Travel)'에서 (D)를 확인할 수 있다. 따라서 언급되지 않은 (A)가 정답이다.

8 청 씨는 무엇을 받을 자격이 있는가?

(A) 전액 환불   (B) 무료 숙박
(C) 항공비 할인   (D) 향후 여행 시 사용 가능한 포인트

해설 | **연계**

이메일 첫 번째 단락에서 청 씨가 근무하는 회사에 데이터 유출 사고가 발생해서, 전 직원이 다음 주에 출근해야 한다(my employer just suffered a data breach, and all employees are required to report to work next week)고 한 후, 여행을 취소해야 한다고 했다. 웹페이지의 두 번째 단락을 보면, 서류로 증명된 질병이나 상해, 또는 기상 사태로 인해 여행을 취소할 경우 전액 환불이 가능하지만 그 밖의 다른 이유로 취소할 경우에는 향후 여행 예약에 적용될 수 있는 포인트를 받게 된다(If you need to cancel for any other reason, you will receive a credit that can be applied to a future trip booked)고 나와 있다. 이를 통해 청 씨가 향후 여행에 사용 가능한 포인트를 받을 자격이 있음을 알 수 있으므로, (D)가 정답이다.

Paraphrasing

지문의 a credit that can be applied to a future trip
→ 정답의 Credit toward a future trip

9 청 씨가 이메일에서 암시하는 바는?
(A) 항공사에서 일한다.
(B) 막 새로운 일을 시작했다.
(C) 다른 여행을 예약할 의향이 있다.
(D) 유럽을 처음으로 방문하는 것이다.

해설 | **추론/암시**

이메일의 두 번째 단락에서 8월 25일에 출발하는 동일한 여행에 빈자리가 있는지 문의한 후, 9월 7일에 떠나는 '이탈리아 도시와 전원 지역 여행'에도 관심이 있다(we would also be interested in going on the Italian Cities and Countryside tour)고 했으므로, (C)가 정답이다.

Paraphrasing

지문의 interested in going on the Italian Cities and Countryside tour → 정답의 willing to book a different tour

10 청 씨는 로리 트래블에 무엇을 요청하는가?
(A) 자신의 항공편을 재예약하기
(B) 상세한 여행 일정을 보내기
(C) 자신의 여행자 보험 상품을 취소하기
(D) 여행에 빈자리가 있는지 알려 주기

해설 | **세부 사항**

이메일의 두 번째 단락에서 가능한 한 빨리 여행 가능 여부에 대해 알려 줄 것(Please let me know about the availability as soon as possible)을 요청했으므로, (D)가 정답이다.

Paraphrasing

지문의 let me know → 정답의 Inform her

[11-15] 안내문 + 이메일

카마릴로 대학 의료 센터 수요일 강의 시리즈에서
다음 강의를 선보입니다.

<도시권 병원 경영>
¹¹포츠타운 대학의 스티븐 S. 세바스찬 박사
¹⁴11월 12일 수요일 오후 4시
의료 센터 A강당
¹³의과대학장 얀 에릭슨 박사의 소개

세바스찬 박사는 도시 환경에서의 병원 경영 및 의료 서비스에 관해서 국제적으로 유명한 전문가입니다. 그 주제에 관한 최근 저서 <도시 병원: 새로운 경영 도전>이 막 출간되었습니다. ¹¹**그는 포츠타운 의과대학에서 병원 관리와 공중 보건을 가르치고 있습니다.**

그의 강의는 도시 환경으로 인한 병원 경영 및 관리의 어려움을 주로 다룰 것이며, 특히 ¹²**지역사회 관계에 주안점을 둘 것입니다.** 그는 도시 지역사회의 리더십과 조직을 위한 전략을 논의할 것인데, ¹²**그 전략들은 병원 관리자들과 지역 정치인들 및 지역사회 지도자들 간의 더 나은 관계 구축에 도움을 주는 것을 목표로 하고 있습니다.**

카마릴로 대학 의료 센터 수요일 강의 시리즈는 로즈마리 페르난데스 기념 단체의 후한 기부금 지원을 받고 있습니다. 강의 시리즈에 관한 질문이 있으시면 이메일 dgoode@camarillo.edu로 ¹³**의과대학장 조수인 다나 구드 씨에게** 연락하십시오.

어휘 | renowned 유명한, 명성 있는 healthcare 의료 서비스, 건강 관리 (방법) administration 관리, 행정 public health 공중 보건 present 야기하다 emphasis 강조, 주안점 strategy 전략 aim 목표로 하다 administrator 관리자, 행정인 fund 자금[기금]을 대다 generous 후한, 너그러운 trust 위탁 사업체, 자선 단체

수신: sssebastian@pottstown.edu
발신: jzericson@camarillo.edu
날짜: 10월 23일
제목: 최종 세부 사항

스티븐 씨께,

저희 다음 수요일 강의 시리즈에 연설하러 오신다고 하셔서 아주 기쁩니다. 제 여러 동료들처럼, 저는 교수님의 최신 저서를 막 다 읽었고, 저희는 교수님이 그 책에서 제시하는 생각들에 대해 더 자세히 듣기를 바라고 있습니다.

¹³**최근에 전화로 통화할 때 제가 언급한 것처럼, 제 조수가 교수님을 기차역에서 맞이해 의료 센터까지 모시고 올 거라는 점을 확인 드리고 싶습니다.** 또한, 이곳 카마릴로의 새로운 학생처장인 아마드 알-자나비 박사가 교수님의 강의가 오후 5시 30분쯤 끝나면 15분 정도 공중 보건 분야에서 경력을 쌓으려고 하는 우리 학생들 몇몇과 이야기 나누는 것이 가능한지 물어 왔습니다.

¹⁴**마지막으로 강의 후에 이곳 교수진 몇몇과 저녁 식사를 하는 데 같이 가실 의향이 여전히 있으신가요? 제가 카마릴로 인에 오후 6시 30분에 저녁 식사를 예약했습니다. ¹⁵여기서 학창 시절을 보내셨으니 그곳을 기억하실지도 모르겠습니다.** 포츠타운으로 돌아가는 8시 45분 기차에 탑승하실 수 있도록 저희 중 한 명이 기꺼이 차로 교수님을 기차역까지 모셔다 드릴 것입니다.

얀 드림

어휘 | dean of students 학생처장 pursue 추구하다 faculty 교수진 pursue 추구하다, 종사하다

11 강연자는 누구인가?
(A) 병원 관리자
(B) 공중 보건부 공무원
(C) 의과대학 교수
(D) 지역 정치인

해설 | **세부 사항**

안내문 상단을 보면 세바스찬 박사가 강연자임을 알 수 있고, 첫 번째 단락에서 그가 의과 대학에서 가르친다(He teaches ~ at the Pottstown University School of Medicine)고 했으므로, (C)가 정답이다.

어휘 | official 공무원

12 강의에서 무엇을 토론할 것 같은가?

(A) 병원 관리자들과 지역사회 지도자들간의 의사소통
(B) 병원 건축의 최신 경향
(C) 의료 센터의 강의를 위한 기금을 얻는 방법
(D) 도시 지역에 더 많은 의사가 근무하도록 유치하는 전략

해설 | **추론/암시**

안내문의 두 번째 단락에서 세바스찬 박사의 강의는 지역사회 관계(community relations)에 주안점을 둘 것이며, 그가 병원 관리자들과 지역사회 지도자들 간에 더 나은 관계를 구축할 수 있게(build better relationships between hospital administrators ~ and community leaders) 도와줄 전략에 대해 논의할 것이라고 했으므로, (A)가 정답이다.

13 누가 세바스찬 박사를 의료 센터까지 데리고 올 것인가?

(A) 얀 에릭슨
(B) 로즈메리 페르난데스
(C) 다나 구드
(D) 아마드 알-자나비

해설 | **연계**

이메일의 두 번째 단락에서 얀 에릭슨 씨는 자신의 조수가 세바스찬 박사를 의료 센터까지 데리고 올 예정(my assistant will ~ take you to the medical center)이라고 했다. 안내문 상단을 보면 얀 에릭슨 씨가 의과대학장(Dean of Medicine)임을 알 수 있으며, 마지막 단락에 다나 구드 씨가 그의 조수라고 명시되어 있으므로, (C)가 정답이다.

14 11월 12일 오후 6시 30분에 무슨 일이 있을 것 같은가?

(A) 세바스찬 박사의 강의가 끝날 것이다.
(B) 몇몇 교수들이 함께 저녁 식사를 할 것이다.
(C) 공중 보건 분야 직업에 관심 있는 몇몇 학생들이 세바스찬 박사를 만날 것이다.
(D) 세바스찬 박사는 포츠타운으로 돌아가는 기차를 탈 것이다.

해설 | **연계**

안내문 상단을 보면 November 12가 강연일임을 알 수 있는데, 이메일의 세 번째 단락에서 얀 에릭슨 씨가 세바스찬 박사에게 강연 당일 몇몇 교수들과 함께 하는 저녁 식사에 올 의향이 있는지(are you still interested in ~ dinner with some of the faculty here after the lecture?) 물으면서 6시 30분에 예약했다고 하므로, (B)가 정답이다.

15 세바스찬 박사에 대해 암시하고 있는 것은 무엇인가?

(A) 카마릴로 대학 학생처장 자리에 지원했다.
(B) 카마릴로 인에서 하룻밤 묵을 것이다.
(C) 카마릴로 대학 학생이었다.
(D) 카마릴로 대학의 교수들에게 자신의 최신 저서를 몇 부 선물할 것이다.

해설 | **추론/암시**

이메일 세 번째 단락의 '여기서 학창 시절을 보내셨으니 그곳을 기억하실지도 모르겠습니다(you may remember it from your own student days here)'라는 문구에서 세바스찬 박사가 카마릴로 대학의 학생이었다는 것을 알 수 있으므로, (C)가 정답이다.

[16-20] 회람+일정표+이메일

회람

수신: 전 직원
발신: 도나 러더포드, 인사부장
날짜: 5월 2일
제목: ¹⁶가이아나 파이낸셜 서비스 의사소통 지침

1. ¹⁷부서 및 전 직원 회의에 참석해야 합니다. 면제받으려면 관리자의 사전 승인을 받아야 합니다.

2. ¹⁹하루 이상 사무실을 비울 때마다 온라인 일정표에 부재 날짜를 명시하고, 수신 이메일 및 전화 회신용으로 해당 날짜가 포함된 부재중 알림 메시지를 설정하십시오. 긴급한 사안일 경우를 대비해 연락 가능한 동료의 이름을 포함시키는 것이 의무 사항은 아니나 그렇게 하는 것이 바람직합니다.

3. 부재중 알림에 자신의 부서에서 현재 제공하는 상품이나 서비스를 홍보하는 간단한 메시지를 포함시킬 수 있습니다. 이 메시지 유형은 선택 사항입니다.

¹⁶이와 같은 회사 지침에 신경 써주시면 감사하겠습니다.

어휘 | personnel 인사과 attendance 참석 departmental 부서의 prior approval 사전 승인 excuse 면제시키다 indicate 명시하다 absence 부재 notification 알림 appropriate 적절한 mandatory 의무적인 colleague 동료 urgent 긴급한 promote 홍보하다 currently 현재 optional 선택적인 attention 주의, 경청

가이아나 파이낸셜 서비스 (GFS)
인디라 샤르마 5월 일정표

월요일	화요일	수요일	목요일	금요일
1 근로자의 날 휴무	2 CABE 회의 등록 마지막 날	3	4 ¹⁸CABE 발표 개요 완성	5 프로젝트 제안서 작업 시작
8 부서 교육생들과 점심 식사	9	10 프로젝트 제안서 작업	11 이메일로 팀에게 업데이트: 프로젝트 제안서	12 GFS 회사 창립기념일 저녁 식사 오후 6시
15 대출 문의: 힐 씨 부부	¹⁷16 소매금융 부서 회의	17 힐 씨 가족 담보 대출 계약서 작성	18 수리남에서 열리는 CABE 회의 출장	29 CABE
22 CABE	23 CABE 회의 마지막 날	24		

어휘 | register for ~에 등록하다 conference 회의 complete 완료하다 outline 개요 anniversary 기념일 loan 대출 inquiry 문의 retail banking 소매금융 mortgage 담보 대출

수신: hillfamily@viczonicmail.com.gy
발신: isharma@gfs.com.gy
날짜: 5월 22일
제목: 자동 회신 - 담보 대출 요청 업데이트

메시지를 보내 주셔서 감사합니다. ¹⁹저는 5월 18일 목요일부터
5월 23일 화요일까지 캐리비안 은행 근로자 협회(CABE) 연례회의
참석차 자리를 비웁니다. ²⁰주택 또는 상가 대출과 관련하여
즉각적인 답변이 필요하시면 네이든 웨스트포드 씨에게 592-555-
0122로 연락하시거나, nwestford@gfs.com.gy로 메시지를
보내주십시오. 그렇지 않으면 제가 5월 24일에 사무실에 복귀해
답신을 드리겠습니다.

알림: 처음 구매해 보시는 분들을 위한 가이아나 파이낸셜 서비스에서
주택 구매자 교육 워크숍 시리즈를 무료로 제공해 드립니다. 더 자세한
내용은 저희에게 연락 주세요!

인디라 샤르마, 수석 대출 담당자
소매금융

어휘 | automatic 자동의 attend 참가하다 association 협회
require 필요로 하다, 요구하다 immediate 즉각적인 regarding
~에 관해 residential 주택지의 commercial 상업의 property
부동산, 건물 education 교육 free of charge 무료로

16 회람의 목적은?
(A) 다가오는 행사를 알리려고
(B) 회사 정책에 대해 주의를 환기하려고
(C) 일정표를 고치려고
(D) 직원들에게 신규 서비스를 홍보하도록 요청하려고

해설 | 주제/목적
회람 전반에 걸쳐 제목에 있는 가이아나 파이낸셜 서비스 의사소통
지침(Guyana Financial Services Communication
Guidelines)에 대해 설명을 한 후, 마지막에 회사 지침에 신경
써주면 고맙겠다(your attention to these company
guidelines)고 했으므로, 회사 정책에 대해 주의를 환기시키려는
회람임을 알 수 있다. 따라서 (B)가 정답이다.

Paraphrasing
지문의 company guidelines → 정답의 company policies

17 샤르마 씨가 사무실을 비우기 위해 관리자에게 승인을 받아야 할 것
같은 날짜는?
(A) 5월 1일
(B) 5월 12일
(C) 5월 16일
(D) 5월 17일

해설 | 연계
회람의 첫 번째 지침에서 부서 및 전 직원 회의에 참석해야
한다(Attendance at departmental and all-staff meetings
is expected)고 한 후, 면제 받으려면 관리자의 사전 승인을 받아야
한다(You must obtain prior approval from your manager
to be excused)고 했다. 샤르마 씨의 일정표를 보면, 참석이
요구되는 소매금융 부서 회의(Retail banking department
meeting)가 5월 16일로 예정되어 있으므로, (C)가 정답이다.

18 샤르마 씨에 대해 암시된 것은?
(A) 새 집을 구입할 것이다.
(B) 회식에서 연설을 할 것이다.
(C) 전문 회의에서 발표를 할 것이다.
(D) 5월 9일에 행사를 준비할 것이다.

해설 | 추론/암시
샤르마 씨의 일정표를 보면 5월 4일에 'CABE 발표 개요
완성(Complete my presentation outline for CABE)'이라고
적혀 있으므로, 샤르마 씨가 CABE 회의에서 발표할 것임을 추론할
수 있다. 따라서 (C)가 정답이다.

19 이메일에 포함된 어떤 세부 사항이 의사소통 지침에서 요구되는
것인가?
(A) 5월 18일부터 5월 23일까지의 기간
(B) CABE라는 회의명
(C) 동료의 전화번호
(D) 주택 구매자 교육 워크숍

해설 | 연계
회람의 두 번째 지침에서 하루 이상 사무실을 비울 때 수신 이메일
및 전화 회신용으로 해당 기간이 포함된 부재중 알림 메시지를
설정하라(set up an out-of-office notification with those
dates for your incoming e-mails and calls)고 지시했는데,
이메일의 첫 번째 단락에서 샤르마 씨가 5월 18일 목요일부터 5월
23일 화요일까지 자리를 비운다(I am out of the office from
Thursday, 18 May, through Tuesday, 23 May)며 자신의
부재 기간을 명시하고 있다. 따라서 (A)가 정답이다. 다른 보기는
모두 선택 사항이다.

20 샤르마 씨에 따르면 누가 웨스트포드 씨에게 연락하고 싶어
하겠는가?
(A) 부서 교육생들 (B) 워크숍 연사들
(C) CABE 회원들 (D) 대출 신청자들

해설 | 추론/암시
이메일의 첫 번째 단락에서 주택 또는 상가 대출과 관련하여
즉각적인 답변이 필요하면(If you require an immediate
response regarding a residential or commercial
property loan) 웨스트포드 씨에게 연락할 것을 권고했으므로,
대출 신청자들이 그에게 연락할 가능성이 높다는 것을 알 수 있다.
따라서 (D)가 정답이다.

[21-25] 기사 + 이메일 + 평면도

도시권 비즈니스 소식 - 10월

²¹말로우 베이에 있는 오션 크레스트 몰의 개점이 내년 봄으로 예정된
가운데 입점 가능한 공간이 빠르게 채워지고 있다. 일단 쇼핑몰이
개점하면 영업 거래도 그만큼 빠르게 ²²늘어날 것으로 예상된다.
²³오션 크레스트 몰이 말로우 베이에서 유일한 쇼핑몰은 아니지만
해변 산책로 쪽으로 바로 통하는 최초의 쇼핑몰이 될 것이다. 여기에는
양품점, 전문점 및 다양한 음식점들이 들어설 것이다.

쇼핑몰 경영진은 말로우 베이 외부로부터 사업주들을 끌어들이려
한다. 임대 관리자인 바바라 랜서 씨에 따르면 쇼핑 매장을 임차한
많은 사업체들은 처음 이 지역에 들어왔다고 한다. 그녀는 "이건
의도된 것이었어요"라고 말했다. "저희가 새로운 업체를 말로우
베이로 끌어들일 수만 있다면 말로우 베이 시 의회에서 쇼핑몰

소유주들에게 세금 혜택을 주겠다고 했습니다. 아직 쇼핑 매장의 75퍼센트를 외지 업체들에게 대여하려는 목표에는 조금 못 미쳤어요. ²⁴저희는 타지에서 온 업체들에게 신규 임대 계약에 대해 임대료 할인을 해 주고 있어요."

²¹소매 및 식당 매장을 임차하려는 사업주들의 신청서는 마감일인 12월 15일까지 받는다. 관심 있는 사업주들은 랜서 씨에게 이메일 blancer@oceancrestmall.com으로 연락하면 된다.

어휘 | establishment (상점·호텔 등) 시설, 영업점, 기관 boardwalk (널빤지를 깐) 해변 산책로 boutique (유행하는 여성복이나 액세서리를 파는) 양품점 specialty store 전문점 vendor 판매업체 a number of 많은 by design 계획적인, 의도적인 city council 시 의회 tax incentive 세금 혜택 be short of ~에 못 미치다 nonlocal 외지의, 타지의 out-of-town 시외의, 타지의 look to do ~을 고려하다 lease 임대차 계약; 임대[임차]하다

발신: 트레이시 페르난데즈 <tfernandez@kmail.com>
수신: 바바라 랜서 <blancer@oceancrestmall.com>
날짜: 10월 9일
제목: 이용 가능한 공간

랜서 씨께,

²⁴저는 더 슈 혼의 소유주인 에릭 레이 씨의 친구인데요, 그 친구가 오션 크레스트 몰의 임대 공간에 대해 랜서 씨에게 연락해 보라고 권했습니다. 자기가 받은 좋은 혜택이 바로 저 같은 사업주들에게 해당된다고 하더라고요. 저는 엣지 패션을 소유하고 있으며 현대적인 여성복을 판매합니다. ²⁴근처 헤이즐턴 시에서 소매점 두 곳을 운영하고 있으며 말로우 베이로 사업을 확장하려고 합니다. ²⁵가능하다면 제 친구 매장 근처로 가고 싶은데, 식당이나 음식점 옆 자리는 원하지 않습니다. 해변이 내려다보이는 산책로 쪽 매장이면 아주 좋을 것 같습니다.

제 요건에 맞는 임대 공간을 나타낸 쇼핑몰 지도를 보내 주시겠습니까? 그리고 각 공간의 크기와 임대료에 대한 정보도 제공해 주실 수 있을까요?

미리 감사드립니다.

트레이시 페르난데즈

어휘 | rental 임대, 대여 benefit 혜택 contemporary 현대의, 당대의 apparel 의류 retail 소매의 nearby 근처의 overlook 내려다보다 meet 충족시키다, 맞추다

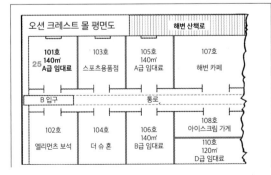

어휘 | rent 임대료 seaside 해변 jewelry 보석류

21 기사의 목적은 무엇인가?
(A) 새 쇼핑몰 개점이 연기된 이유를 설명하기 위해
(B) 새 쇼핑몰 공사 계획을 알리기 위해
(C) 새 쇼핑몰 내의 상점과 식당을 평가하기 위해
(D) 사업주들에게 새 쇼핑몰로의 입점을 권장하기 위해

해설 | **주제 / 목적**
기사의 초반부에서 말로우 베이에 있는 오션 크레스트 몰의 개점(The grand opening of the Ocean Crest Mall in Marlow Bay)을 알린 후 몰에 대해 소개했고, 후반부에서 임차에 관심 있는 사업주들에게 신청 방법(Interested business owners are encouraged to contact Lancer by e-mail)을 안내하고 있으므로, (D)가 정답이다.

22 기사의 첫 번째 단락, 네 번째 줄에 쓰인 "take off"와 의미가 가장 가까운 것은?
(A) 제거하다
(B) 할인하다
(C) 빠르게 증가하다
(D) 갑자기 떠나다

해설 | **동의어 찾기**
take off를 포함한 부분은 '영업 거래도 그만큼 빠르게 늘어날 것으로 예상된다'라고 해석되므로, (C) increase quickly가 정답이다.

23 오션 크레스트 몰에 대해 언급된 내용은 무엇인가?
(A) 말로우 베이의 유일한 쇼핑몰이 될 것이다.
(B) 해변 산책로로 바로 연결될 것이다.
(C) 75개의 임대 공간이 있을 것이다.
(D) 12월 15일에 영업을 시작할 것이다.

해설 | **Not / True**
기사의 첫 번째 단락에서 오션 크레스트 몰이 말로우 베이에서 유일한 쇼핑몰은 아니지만 해변 산책로 쪽으로 바로 통하는 최초의 쇼핑몰이 될 것(it will be the first to open directly onto the boardwalk)이라고 했으므로 (B)가 정답이다.

24 레이 씨에 대해 언급된 것은 무엇인가?
(A) 그는 랜서 씨의 친구이다.
(B) 그의 사업체가 첫 번째로 개업했다.
(C) 그는 할인된 임대료를 지불하고 있다.
(D) 그의 상점은 해변에서 영업한다.

해설 | **연계**
기사의 두 번째 단락을 보면 오션 크레스트 몰이 타지 업체들에게 신규 임대 계약에 대해 임대료를 할인해 주고 있다(We are offering reduced rental prices on new leases for out-of-town businesses)고 했는데, 이메일의 초반부에서 페르난데즈 씨는 자신의 친구인 레이 씨를 언급하며, 그가 자신과 같은 사업주들에게 해당되는 혜택(a great benefit that he received that is available to business owners)을 받았다고 했다. 페르난데즈 씨는 타지(헤이즐턴 시)에서 업체를 운영하고 있으므로, 그녀와 같은 상황인 레이 씨가 타지 업체에게 제공되는 임대료 할인 혜택을 받고 있음을 알 수 있다. 따라서 (C)가 정답이다.

Paraphrasing
지문의 rental prices → 정답의 rental rate

25 페르난데스 씨가 관심을 가질만한 입점 공간은 어디이겠는가?

(A) 101호

(B) 105호

(C) 106호

(D) 110호

해설 | **연계**

이메일의 중반부에서 페르난데스 씨는 친구인 레이 씨의 매장 근처로 가고 싶은데 식당이나 음식점 옆 자리는 원하지 않는다(I do not want a space that is beside a restaurant or food service)고 했다. 평면도에서 이 조건에 해당하는 장소는 101호이므로, (A)가 정답이다.

[26-30] 기사 + 광고 + 이메일

전망 밝은 피부 관리 제품

10월 12일—오늘 캐나다, 프랑스, 한국에 지점을 두고 있는 다국적 기업 리쾨르 제약이 심한 건성 피부용으로 실험 단계에 있는 크림 더마바가 최근 조사 연구에서 매우 효과적인 것으로 입증되었다고 밝혔다. 리쾨르는 크림의 효과가 오래 지속된다는 점을 나타내는 고무적인 결과를 강조했다. 이 크림이 출시되면 지난 5년간 리쾨르가 겪은 제한적 성장을 보상해 줄 수도 있으므로 이 점은 리쾨르에게 좋은 소식이다.

전문 컨설턴트 로라 쉐프너 박사는 "²⁶즉시 나타나는 크림의 효과에 놀라면서도 기뻤습니다. 참가자들은 한 번만 발라 보고도 진정 효과를 느꼈다더군요"라고 말했다. 리쾨르의 선임 연구원 최흥수 박사는 연구 과정에서 약품의 안전성 또한 확인되었다고 덧붙였다.

리쾨르의 대변인은 첫 번째 결과가 긍정적이지만 ²⁷유아와 노인 참가자들을 대상으로 한 후속 연구도 이어 가야 한다고 말했다. ²⁸그런 다음에야 크림이 국제의약협회(IMA)의 승인을 받고 시판될 수 있다. IMA는 연말에 평가를 시작할 것으로 예상된다.

어휘 | show promise 전망이 밝다, 유망하다 pharmaceuticals 제약회사 multinational corporation 다국적 기업 experimental 실험적인 excessively 지나치게 highlight 강조하다 encouraging 고무적인 long-lasting 오래 지속되는 effectiveness 효과(성) bode well for ~에게 좋은 징조이다 release 출시하다 compensate for ~을 보상하다 limited 제한된 expert 전문가 immediate 즉각적인 benefit 이점, 효과 relief 진정, 완화 application (화장품·페인트 등의) 도포, 바르기 medication 약 promising 전망이 밝은, 유망한 follow-up study 후속 연구 participant 참가자 pursue 추구하다, 해 나가다 approve 승인하다 review 평가

캐나다 오타와의 리쾨르 제약 직원 채용

²⁸리쾨르 제약은 새로 나온 건성 피부 치료제 더마바의 출시를 도울 대략 100명의 행정, 고객 서비스, 창고 관리직을 급히 구합니다. ²⁹사전 경력이 필요 없는 시간제 일자리로 12월까지 근무하며, 탁월한 능력을 보여준 직원에게는 업무 연장을 제안할 수도 있습니다. 고객 서비스직 지원자는 불어와 영어에 유창해야 합니다. ³⁰창고 관리직 지원자는 야간과 주말 근무가 가능해야 합니다. 지원자들은 지금

www. ricoeurpharma.ca에 들어가서 지원서를 제출하실 수 있습니다. 관심 있는 분들은 또한 인더스트리얼 웨이 72B번지, 오타와, K2A 3P1에 있는 저희 생산 시설에서 3월 11일 오전 9시에 진행하는 단체 면접에 참석하실 수 있습니다. 이력서와 추천인 명부를 가져오시기 바랍니다.

리쾨르 제약

어휘 | opening 공석 administrative 행정의 warehouse 창고 launch 출시 treatment 치료 previous experience 사전 경력 exceptional 아주 뛰어난, 탁월한 extended 연장된 assignment 업무, 과제 bilingual 2개 국어를 하는 apply for ~에 지원하다 candidate 지원자, 후보자 party 관계자, 당사자 attend 참석하다 facility 시설 reference 추천인, 추천서

수신: 아흐메드 아베디

발신: 시모나 조던

제목: 리쾨르 추천서

날짜: 3월 11일, 오후 1시 43분

아베디 박사님께,

제 추천서를 써 주셔서 감사합니다. 저는 오늘 리쾨르 제약에 고용된 대략 20명의 지원자들 중 한 명이었습니다. 첫 근무는 다가오는 월요일이며 ³⁰박사님의 저녁 수업 직후에 근무할 예정입니다. 시내로 들어가는 오후 7시 15분 버스를 타려면 수업에서 몇 분 일찍 나가야 할지도 모르겠습니다. 이 점이 문제가 되지 않으면 좋겠습니다.

다시 한번 감사드립니다.

시모나 조던

어휘 | applicant 지원자 coming 다가오는 directly after ~ 직후에

26 쉐프너 박사가 더마바에 대해 언급한 점은 무엇인가?

(A) 효과가 매우 빠르게 나타난다.

(B) 하루에 두 번 사용해야 한다.

(C) 놀라울 정도로 저렴하다.

(D) 최대 3일간 사용 가능하다.

해설 | **Not/True**

기사의 두 번째 단락에서 쉐프너 박사가 즉시 나타나는 크림의 효과에 놀라면서도 기뻤다(I was pleasantly surprised by the immediate benefits of the cream)고 했으므로 (A)가 정답이다.

Paraphrasing
지문의 the immediate benefits of the cream → 정답의 It works very quickly

27 기사에 따르면 리쾨르 제약은 무엇을 할 계획인가?

(A) 더욱 안전한 크림 개발

(B) 추가 연구 실시

(C) 연구 참가자들에게 보상

(D) 제품 일정 검토

해설 | **세부 사항**

기사의 세 번째 단락에서 리쾨르의 대변인이 유아와 노인 참가자들을 대상으로 한 후속 연구도 이어 가야 한다(a follow-up study ~ must be pursued)고 했으므로 (B)가 정답이다.

어휘 | conduct (수행)하다

Paraphrasing
지문의 a follow-up study → 정답의 additional research

28 리쾨르 제약에 대해 암시된 점은 무엇인가?
(A) 생산 시설이 프랑스에 있다.
(B) 실험실들이 10월에 점검을 받는다.
(C) 최신 약품이 IMA의 승인을 받았다.
(D) 제품들이 지난 5년간 인기를 얻었다.

해설 | **연계**
기사의 마지막 단락에서 후속 연구가 이루어진 다음에야 더마바 크림이 국제의약협회의 승인을 받고 시판될 수 있다(Only then can the cream ~ become available on the market)고 했는데, 리쾨르 제약에서 게시한 광고의 첫 문장을 보면 더마바의 출시를 지원해 줄(supporting the launch of Dermava, a new medical treatment for dry skin) 행정, 고객 서비스, 창고 관리직을 급히 구한다고 되어 있다. 이를 통해 리쾨르 제약의 크림이 IMA의 승인을 받았다는 점을 알 수 있으므로 (C)가 정답이다.

Paraphrasing
지문의 cream, a new medical treatment → 정답의 medication

29 광고에 언급된 내용은 무엇인가?
(A) 지원자들은 사전 경력이 있어야 한다.
(B) 단체 면접이 며칠에 걸쳐 진행될 것이다.
(C) 지원 과정에 상당히 긴 시간이 소요된다.
(D) 채용 중인 자리들은 임시직이다.

해설 | **Not / True**
광고 초반부에서 채용 중인 자리가 사전 경력이 필요 없는 시간제 근무직이며 12월에 끝난다(Positions do not require previous experience, are part time, and end in December)고 했으므로 (D)가 정답이다.

Paraphrasing
지문의 part time, and end in December → 정답의 temporary

30 조던 씨는 어떤 자리에 채용되었겠는가?
(A) 행정직
(B) 고객 서비스직
(C) 연구직
(D) 창고 관리직

해설 | **연계**
이메일에서 조던 씨는 저녁 수업 직후에 근무할 예정(I'll be working directly after your evening class)이라고 했는데, 광고를 보면 창고 관리직 지원자는 야간과 주말 근무가 가능해야 한다(Those applying for warehouse positions must be able to work nights and weekends)고 나와 있으므로, 그가 창고 관리직에 채용되었음을 추론할 수 있다. 따라서 (D)가 정답이다.